FORMAL METHODS FOR DISTRIBUTED PROCESSING

This book presents the current state of the art in the application of formal methods to object-based distributed systems. A major theme of the book is how to formally handle the new requirements arising from OO distributed systems, such as dynamic reconfiguration, encapsulation, subtyping, inheritance and real-time aspects. These may be supported either by enhancing existing notations, such as UML, LOTOS, SDL and Z, or by defining new notations, such as Actors, Pi-calculus and Ambients. The major specification notations and modelling techniques are introduced and compared by leading researchers, in several cases the inventors of the notations. The book also includes a description of approaches to the specification of nonfunctional requirements, which are typically needed in the specification of multimedia systems, and a discussion of security issues.

Researchers and practitioners in software design, object-oriented computing, distributed systems and telecommunications systems will gain an appreciation of the relationships between the major areas of concern and learn how the use of object-oriented-based formal methods provides workable solutions.

Howard Bowman is a senior lecturer in the Computing Laboratory at the University of Kent at Canterbury. He received his PhD from the University of Lancaster, where he was also a postdoctoral fellow. He is co-author of a book on specifying distributed multimedia systems using real-time temporal logics. His current research interests include the application of formal description techniques in object-oriented distributed systems and the formal specification and validation of multimedia systems (using real-time temporal logics).

John Derrick is a reader in the Computing Laboratory at the University of Kent at Canterbury. He received his DPhil from Oxford University and worked briefly at University College North Wales before joining STC Technology Ltd (now Nortel). In 1990 he joined the Computing Laboratory at the University of Kent. His interests include specification techniques for distributed systems, refinement and testing.

FORMAL METHODS FOR DISTRIBUTED PROCESSING

A Survey of Object-Oriented Approaches

Edited by

HOWARD BOWMAN
University of Kent at Canterbury

JOHN DERRICK
University of Kent at Canterbury

CAMBRIDGE
UNIVERSITY PRESS

CAMBRIDGE
UNIVERSITY PRESS

32 Avenue of the Americas, New York NY 10013-2473, USA

Cambridge University Press is part of the University of Cambridge.

It furthers the University's mission by disseminating knowledge in the pursuit of education, learning and research at the highest international levels of excellence.

www.cambridge.org
Information on this title: www.cambridge.org/9780521771849

First published 2001
First paperback edition 2010

A catalogue record for this publication is available from the British Library

Library of Congress Cataloguing in Publication data

Formal methods for distributed processing: a survey of object-oriented approaches / edited by Howard Bowman, John Derrick.
     p. cm.
ISBN 0-521-77184-6
1. Electronic data processing - Distributed processing. 2. Object-oriented programming (Computer science)   I. Bowman, Howard, 1966-   II. Derrick, John, 1963-

QA76.9.D5 F662 2001
005.1' 17-dc21   2001025501

ISBN 978-0-521-77184-9 Hardback

Contents

Preface

Overview

The aim of this book is to review and reflect on the major recent research developments in the application of formal methods to distributed processing. In doing so the book aims to provide:

- an introduction to modern object-oriented distributed systems;
- an introduction and comparison of the major specification notations and modelling techniques;
- an introduction to the specification of systems involving dynamic reconfiguration;
- a discussion of the role and use of subtyping;
- an introduction to concurrent object-oriented languages and reflection;
- a description of approaches to the specification of nonfunctional requirements, which are needed typically in the specification of multimedia systems;
- a discussion of the role of development architectures in distributed systems modelling.

A strength of the book is that it encapsulates a number of issues in a single text, and this is a feature that we believe readers will find valuable. After providing a background in modern object-oriented distributed systems, a number of themes are developed. Each theme provides a reflective survey of the state of the art of research written by some of the most prominent researchers in the field. We hope that this will enable the reader to gain an appreciation of the relationships between the major areas of concern and how the use of object-based formal methods seeks to provide workable solutions that address these concerns.

Specifying Distributed Systems

This book is about distributed systems, their inherent complexity and how we can specify and analyse such complex systems. In particular, we focus on how to apply formal methods to the design of open object-oriented distributed systems.

Distributed systems have become indispensable in modern society, and the growth of the Internet and the World Wide Web have radically altered how we do business and disseminate information. This has been possible through the realisation of new techniques and technologies, and, in particular, the use of object orientation as an encapsulation mechanism has been vital in building component-based distributed system architectures.

One such architecture is that provided by the Open Distributed Processing (ODP) standard. This has defined a reference model that provides a framework within which distributed applications can be constructed. The CORBA middleware platform can be viewed as an example of realising and using the ODP architecture. In the first part of this book we provide an introduction to some of the important current issues in distributed systems, focusing in Chapter 2 on the ODP model. Although ODP is not the only relevant framework, it does offer a vehicle by which to discuss some of the major issues in distributed systems. In particular, the broad scope of ODP ensures that it provides a framework in which the spectrum of topics and techniques can be studied. These include such topics as multimedia, openness, dynamic reconfiguration, federation, legacy problems and distributed systems management.

The ODP reference model has been important in providing a usable distributed systems architecture. Significant features of ODP include object-based specification and programming, and the use of transparencies to hide aspects of distribution and viewpoints. The latter provides a basic separation of concerns, enabling different participants to observe the system from suitable perspectives and at suitable levels of abstraction. It is a central device for structuring and managing the complexity inherent in describing systems.

ODP uses five predefined viewpoints – the enterprise viewpoint, the information viewpoint, the computational viewpoint, the engineering viewpoint and the technology viewpoint. They each represent a system from one particular perspective, and these perspectives are at potentially different levels of abstraction. For example, the computational viewpoint is concerned with the algorithms and data flow of the distributed system function. It represents the system and its environment in terms of objects that interact by the transfer of information via interfaces. The engineering viewpoint, on the other hand, is concerned more with distribution mechanisms and defines the building blocks that can be combined to provide the system's functionality.

ODP is not prescriptive about the choice of specification language to be adopted with particular viewpoints. However, it does advocate the use of formal techniques to enable the precise description of distributed systems requirements. In one sense, this book is about how to do this.

Furthermore, because of the wide-ranging nature of the ODP standard, the techniques are relevant not just to ODP and its particular viewpoints, but to a whole range of specification approaches where distribution and reliability are important.

A major theme of the book is how to formally handle the new requirements arising from object-oriented distributed systems, for example, dynamic reconfiguration, encapsulation, subtyping, inheritance, real-time aspects, and so on. These may be supported either by enhancing existing notations, like LOTOS, SDL and Z, or by defining new notations, for example, Actors and Pi-calculus. This book describes both approaches in some depth.

Part One provides the context to the technical discussions in later parts. The part begins by discussing current issues in distributed systems, briefly reviewing the available techniques. The second chapter focuses on one such technique, namely, ODP, which it offers as a framework for the construction of modern distributed systems. Finally, an extrapolation is made from the issues highlighted in the first two chapters, and Chapter 3 discusses requirements on the use of formal methods.

Part Two provides a survey of formal description techniques. It considers a collection of related techniques and shows how they support object-oriented concepts. Here finite-state machine techniques such as SDL, process calculi such as E-LOTOS and state-based approaches such as Object-Z are introduced. In addition to these formal notations, semi-formal languages have an important role to play in specification and design, and to this end Part Two also provides an introduction to UML.

Part Three covers dynamic reconfiguration, looking at the different approaches of the Pi-calculus and the Actor model of computation. A discussion of the ambient calculus is also included. This provides an alternative means for describing the movement of processes and devices, including movement through administrative domains.

Part Four considers the issues of subtyping and inheritance. First, the motivation for subtyping and inheritance is considered. In particular, the use of matching in trading, binding, reuse, the role of inheritance vs subtyping and the ideas of incremental development are discussed. Then two important subtyping approaches are considered – state-based behavioural subtyping and subtyping in a process algebra setting.

Part Five provides an introduction to concurrent object-oriented languages. The first chapter in this part discusses reflection as the basis of open implementations, that is, systems that can adapt their implementation behaviour in a disciplined manner. This is followed by a discussion of the role of inheritance in a concurrent object-oriented setting.

Part Six is concerned with the support needed to express nonfunctional requirements of distributed systems using formal notations. Earlier in the book we will have considered the nature of such requirements and introduced key elements of multimedia and quality of service (QoS). This part introduces in more depth what QoS is and discusses QoS management, adaptation, specification, verification, and so on. The issues of real-time specification and validation are particularly focussed on.

Finally, in **Part Seven** the role of development architectures, composition and viewpoints in the construction of distributed systems is considered. In particular, both composition in programming languages as well as specification architectures and viewpoints in distributed systems frameworks are discussed.

Using This Book

This book is intended to be of use to researchers in the field of distributed systems and formal methods. We hope that the book will be accessible to those new to research, for example, PhD students, while providing a standard reference book for those already established in their field. The book aims to be equally relevant to researchers in industry as well as those in the academic sector.

Several chapters in the book are based on material taught in an advanced Masters course in distributed systems, and the different chapters could be used to support MSc courses in a variety of different ways.

Acknowledgements

We would like to acknowledge the efforts of all of the contributors to this book, many of whom provided detailed and accurate texts at very short notice.

The idea for this book was conceived at the IFIP FMOODS (Formal Methods for Open Object-Based Distributed Systems) conference held at the University of Kent at Canterbury in 1997. Thanks are due in particular to Elie Najm, who, along with Jean-Bernard Stefani, initiated the series, and to all those who helped organise the 1997 FMOODS conference at the University of Kent at Canterbury.

The Networks and Distributed Systems group at Kent has over the years provided a conducive environment in which to do research and explore some of the ideas in this book, and we would like to thank in particular Peter Linington, Eerke Boiten and Maarten Steen.

We also wish to thank Lauren Cowles and her team at Cambridge University Press for their support and advice during the production of this book. Janet Bayfield at the University of Kent at Canterbury also provided valuable secretarial assistance during production of the camera-ready copy of the book.

Howard Bowman
John Derrick
Canterbury, England

Part One

Object-Oriented Distributed Systems

1

Issues in Distributed Systems

Peter F. Linington
University of Kent, UK

1.1 A Distributed Systems Perspective

No one can doubt the importance of distributed systems these days, but they do pose a particular challenge to the developers of formal methods: they involve, by their nature, a high degree of independence between components and have dynamically changing structures, the evolution of which needs to be captured in any formal specification. They therefore provide an excellent test of the expressive power and flexibility of the range of modern formalisms available for system specification.

One can imagine specification problems as forming a spectrum from purely local problems, through communication between fixed sets of processes, to dynamically evolving distributed systems. A local problem, such as the description of a file storage system or demonstrating the correctness of a lift scheduling algorithm, is characterized by a single context and a monolithic system state and generally involves a fairly simple view of errors. Specification of a protocol to be used for communication between two systems is more complex, because the systems have independent states and are linked by a medium that is subject to errors. Each system can fail or be restarted independently of the others, and so the behaviour to be described is much more complicated. In short, concurrency and interruption of processes have become the norm rather than the exception. These problems are common to a wide range of protocol specification tasks, from simple data transfer protocols to protocols needed for remote object invocation, transaction management or transmission of streaming media, such as video.

Specification of the behaviour of a distributed system is more complex still. In addition to the protocol problems of physical separation and localized errors, there is a wide variety of other problems associated with the evolution of the system's configuration. The description of a distributed system will generally involve fragments of behaviour in which some components create others, and then publish their availability by passing references to yet further objects that can then exploit the new services being offered. This dynamic behaviour implies that a specification must consider not only the inconsistency of the state of the communicating objects, but it also must deal with inconsistent views of what the set of communicating objects is.

Hand in hand with this increasing emphasis on concurrency and flexible configuration comes an increasing requirement for openness. Once a system is described in terms of a number of distinct, communicating parts the way is open to its realisation using separately implemented components from a variety of sources. The result is an increased emphasis on abstract specification and refinement, because there is more flexibility if the builder of each component is able to choose a style, language and approach without unnecessary systemwide constraints. This is particularly important when considering component reuse and the evolution of legacy systems. It will be easier to incorporate existing components or subsystems if their role in the new system is expressed in high-level terms, without taking account of local details of the implementation of the existing components.

The result of all of these considerations is that thinking about distributed systems leads to a number of shifts in emphasis when compared with centralized systems. In particular there are shifts:

- from central control to autonomy: in a centralized system, there is a single source of control that initiates actions and provides a natural focus for coordination. In a distributed system, each of the components is under independent management and is involved in making independent, unsynchronized decisions. This leads to the potential for much more complicated behaviour, particularly when arbitrary components fail or are reinitialized.
- from global naming to federated local naming: if names are all issued by a single authority, they can be passed to other parts of the system and used anywhere in the system with equal validity and without regard to their origin. If the system contains multiple independent naming authorities, as it must generally do to make the design scalable, there need to be rules for their federation and for ensuring that any name quoted is interpreted correctly in the context in which it was defined, no matter where it is used.
- from shared memory to local encapsulated state: once there is a physical separation between the system components, it becomes impossible for the actions that are to be performed within the system to be specified in terms of arbitrary elements from the system's state. Each component performs actions based on its local state, including actions that communicate with other components, but the behaviour of a component is influenced only by the state of other parts of the system indirectly by receipt of communication events originated by them. Each component maintains a local view of its beliefs about the states of the remaining parts of the system, but this information depends on communication between components for its currency and accuracy.
- from global consistency to weak consistency: since each part of the system is linked to others by communication that may be subject to errors, it becomes likely that the information held by different components will be inconsistent. Invariants and checks on consistency constraints that in a centralized system could be asserted with confidence as true for any correct implementation become ideals that will frequently not be true. The consistency of replicated data, for example, becomes something to strive for, involving a balance with respect to other targets, such as performance and system cost.
- from sequential execution to true concurrency: a single program executing on one proces-

sor will behave in a quite predictable way, with the sequential execution interrupted only at well-defined and controllable points. Thus the language, run-time environment or operating system can provide well-behaved threading and synchronization facilities that can be used to avoid unexpected effects. In a distributed system, the combination of multiple processors progressing independently at different rates and communication with variable delays means that practically any combination of event timings can occur and must be taken into account in describing the behaviour that the system is expected to have. The necessary synchronization of components must be achieved by explicit communication between them.

- from vulnerability to fault tolerance: one of the major benefits of distribution is that errors affect individual components, not the system as a whole. It therefore becomes possible to make the complete system much more robust, because the remaining parts of the system can cooperate to mask the consequences of a failed component. However, this resilience comes at a cost, because the rules and procedures that make the system fault tolerant need to be defined within the system's specification.

- from fixed location to process migration: in a centralized system, location is not an issue. All of the elements of the system are in the same place, and so they can always communicate. Once there is distribution, each part of the system needs to know how to find any other component or service in order to communicate with it. This may be a matter of finding a component when it is first needed, or it may be a matter of tracking a component as it moves, either to another hardware platform or as a result of the supporting hardware itself moving in a wireless or nomadic computing environment.

- from fixed configuration to continuous evolution: once a system is made up of separate components, it becomes possible to upgrade or replace these components while the system is running. Any sufficiently large-scale system is unlikely ever to be initialised as a whole at one time, and the classical waterfall approach to system development ceases to be even a theoretical possibility; there are no more new systems, just incremental changes or extensions to some existing system. Even a new application will generally have dependencies on existing networked services and legacy data.

- from early binding to late binding: in building a monolithic system, it is possible to identify during construction how all of the parts interact, and to perform a considerable number of checks on the consistency of the design, by, for example, applying strong type checking to the linkages made. In a distributed system, the components to be linked may not be identified until after the system has begun operation. There is much more flexibility in configuring the system because of this late binding of components, but it is at the cost of the need to perform some of the necessary checks for correctness while the system is running, and to cope with any failures at that stage. One of the objectives to aim for in providing support for system development is to maximize both the flexibility and the type safety of component binding.

- from a single view of time to multiple clocks: it is a natural consequence of the autonomy of the different hardware components that make up a distributed system that the way in which time is measured by the different components will vary. Clocks will drift, and it will be practically impossible for different parts of the system to initiate actions so that they are guaranteed to be simultaneous. Whatever level of synchronization between clocks is necessary must be constructed by a suitable pattern of communication between the components.

- from homogeneity to heterogeneity: once a system is constructed from independent components, the emphasis shifts from how the components are to be constructed to the external properties that each component must display in order to fulfil its role in the system. This approach makes it possible to construct different components using different languages, platforms or design methodologies. These differences are unimportant as long as the required externally observable behaviour of each component is maintained. The specification of the external interactions becomes paramount.

1.2 Current Issues in Distributed Systems

In addition to these general changes of perspective, there are a number of particular problems or areas of concern that characterize work on distributed systems. These are recurrent issues in research, and solutions to them are likely to be prominent on a list of requirements drawn up by any distributed systems developer.

1.2.1 Federation

Large distributed systems are generally long-lived, and they often span organizational boundaries. They need to evolve to meet changing requirements over a long period of time, and they are typically supported by loosely coordinated management and maintenance teams with divided responsibilities and objectives. Thus any large system is likely to fall into a number of distinct management domains, and any coordinating authority will operate on the basis of a fairly high-level view that is imperfectly communicated to the individual domains. In other words, large distributed systems generally have a federated structure and so their development must pay particular attention to the problems of federation.

What, then, are the characteristics of federated systems? First, there is no single controlling component. Instead, the members of the federation communicate in a number of peer-to-peer dialogues, and, in consequence, federated structures are well-suited to the support of large-scale activities. Second, the constraints placed on members say as little as possible about their internal organization, reducing the cost of federation between systems of different designs and focusing attention on the points at which information crosses system boundaries. This is because incompatibilities often can be solved by translation at these boundaries. Third, the behaviour of a federation is defined in the knowledge that its members will retain a high degree of autonomy and may choose to join or leave the federation at any time, without protracted negotiation processes.

1.2.2 Legacy Systems

One distributed systems problem of great practical importance is the assimilation of legacy systems [BS95]. This can be seen as a special case of federation, since the problem generally arises because there is no practical possibility of making significant changes to the internal structure of the legacy system. The most common approach to solving the legacy problem is to encapsulate the system concerned, identifying the services that it provides and providing a wrapper that offers them to other components via standard interfaces.

The analysis of what a legacy system does, and the formulation of interface definitions that capture only that service, without commitment to a host of obscuring implementation detail, is not an easy task. It needs techniques for abstract specification and for the creation of suitable transforming gateways that provide the translation between the different ways in which the old and new systems refine the overarching description. This is not just a matter of translating message syntax; it also needs to take into account things like the transactional implications of sequences of messages and possible differences between the failure models of the old and new systems.

1.2.3 Distributed Systems Management

Telecommunications networks have always had a need for large-scale distributed management systems. However, these used to be thought of as a largely separate activity, identified architecturally as a separate management plane and supported by special-purpose notations and protocols. As the networks being managed have become less focused on special services, such as voice, and increasingly concerned with the general problem of data transmission, the rationale for separate management facilities has been eroded. There is a move in the newer architectures toward seeing management as just part of a more general distributed systems problem.

However, there is still a tension between the system management and the application builder's view of design. The application builder tries to hide details of infrastructure and internal configuration of components, because exposing such details adds to the constraints under which evolution must be performed, leading to brittle systems. Thus a service is accessed by reference to some interface without exposing the configuration of objects supporting the service or necessarily making visible any other interfaces that those objects support. This leaves sufficient flexibility to reengineer the system as part of an evolution plan, changing the way in which a service is provided and its functions packaged in a particular implementation.

In system management, on the other hand, there is a need for the manager to be able to start from a particular interface, which might, perhaps, have been behaving incorrectly, and to navigate through the configuration of objects supporting the service. This leads to a requirement for a different view of the system, in which one can go from knowledge of an interface to at least knowledge of a management interface responsible for the resources supporting it.

Techniques have recently been introduced that satisfy both requirements, by allowing controlled visibility and manipulation of the properties of the implementation supporting a given service. Component models (see, for example, Chapter 18) provide one approach; another is based on the idea of reflective programming (see

Chapter 14), which allows properties of the implementation to be explored in a uniform and systematic way and makes configuration control much more flexible.

1.2.4 Security

Security is particularly important in distributed systems because physical restrictions on access are no longer an option. Extreme measures, like putting the data processing system inside the bank vault, are of no help if the aim is to support global e-commerce.

There is an immediate apparent conflict between the requirements of security and openness (see Chapter 10, which discusses, for example, security barriers and firewalls). If the aim is to avoid unnecessary barriers to communication between systems by ensuring that there is always a basic level of compatibility, the mechanisms for authentication and privacy become more important, and the specification of security requirements needs to be integrated with other aspects of system design.

Security places some special demands on techniques for system description. In most situations, the objective is to show that the system does something – that it performs some particular behaviour without deadlock, for example. In the security field, however, the requirement is often to show that broad classes of behaviour cannot happen. Thus it is important to show that a design is fully encapsulated, allowing communication only at declared interfaces – that it does not leak. This is a much more difficult problem than showing that it is deadlock-free or refines a given service specification.

1.2.5 Multimedia and Real-Time Systems

Multimedia and real-time requirements (see Chapters 16 and 17) are not inherently related to distribution, since they also occur in localized systems. However, like security, multimedia support is likely to be expected of any general-purpose modern system, and the real-time deadlines that are involved are aggravated by distribution. Continuous media in particular presents new problems both to system implementors and to the designers of description techniques [BS97]. This is because, just as they are continuous, these media require a steady and predictable sequence of media samples, implying a steady succession of cumulative hard timing targets. The resource management at all points along the communications path traversed by the continuous media needs to be coordinated to give the necessary guarantees.

The exact way in which this resource management is carried out will vary from component to component, as a result of different constraints and implementation strategies. This is particularly true where media are multicast to different receivers, which themselves have disparate infrastructure capabilities. An abstract description of a multimedia application should therefore express multimedia traffic in terms of unstructured flows, not of the sequences of samples that represent the medium, to avoid complicating the description with details that are subject to local variation.

1.2.6 The Development Process

To keep the system development costs within reasonable bounds, there need to be development tools and techniques that help to manage the complexity of large systems and which encourage reuse of both previous implementation fragments and services and of their specifications. This implies a need for both the system and its specification to be modular, and for it to be possible to manipulate these modules, combining them in ways not foreseen when they were produced.

The implication for the designer of specification languages is that there need to be good facilities for producing and combining families of specifications, either considering different abstractions or different subdomains within the system. The viewpoints discussed in the next chapter are an example of such a specification framework (see also Chapter 20). Another part of the problem can be solved by concentrating on components that can be composed while retaining interesting aspects of their behaviour in the composition (see Chapter 18).

Support of large teams in which different members may be concentrating on different aspects and using different tools and notations implies a need for mechanisms that support sharing of component specifications and management of their consistency. This is one of the motivations for the creation of integrated development environments, but these often lack flexibility. A more loosely coupled federated approach is attractive, in which emphasis is on shared access to the various specifications via a distributed repository. This leads to tool families centred around shared repositories, such as a type repository or a meta-object facility. This is one of the motivations for subtyping techniques, which are discussed in Part 4.

1.2.7 Potentially Distributed Systems

Although the change of perspective from local to distributed systems is a necessary result of their division into communicating components, many of the approaches taken to support distribution also solve other problems of system structure. Even localized systems benefit from an architecture in which there is a strong encapsulation of processes and protection between different security and management domains. It is no accident that modern operating systems tend to be structured into a minimal kernel and a set of objects providing supporting services. Neither is it surprising that such systems lend themselves well to distribution when the need arises. One of the recognizable diseases of old age in an operating system is the addition of performance-enhancing features that break encapsulation and increase the cost of further evolution. This 'hardening of the linkages' reduces flexibility and adds to maintenance costs.

All systems, then, are potentially distributed. There are significant benefits from architectures and design styles in which there is a well-defined separation into components, with clearly identified points of interaction between them. It is the local systems that are the special case, in which the need for actual distribution has not yet been identified.

1.3 Object-Oriented Design

The key features of an object-oriented system are traditionally taken to be the identification of objects, with classification and inheritance as tools to support their description [Weg86]. For a more recent general review of object orientation, see [BGHS91]. The emphasis on encapsulated objects comes directly from regarding the system as made up of distinct things, which can most simply be considered as objects. This is a natural requirement when considering distributed systems because the elements of a distributed system and the resources that they depend on are individually localized, and the study of a distributed system is, in large part, the study of the interactions of the objects that make it up. It can be argued that viewing things as objects underlies our ability to use language to refer to the real world. Objects emerge from the need to simplify and condense the welter of observations that we make, and we carry this process further by identifying common attributes of the objects perceived [Qui74].

Classification is also fundamental to the way that humans think. Our first step in simplifying or generalizing problems is to identify classes of objects with common characteristics or properties, either in terms of common attributes or common patterns of behaviour. There are long-standing debates as to the relative importance of feature identification or prototype identification (see [Lak86] for one clearly argued view), but there is universal agreement as to the key role of the process of classification in design and specification. Classes as they appear in object-oriented computer languages provide templates for creating objects. They include both the state the object will maintain and the methods that represent its behaviour. The class of an object is thus more prescriptive than the type, which tends to concentrate on the observable properties of the object. This distinction is particularly important in distributed systems, where systems are not constructed as a single comprehensive exercise, but frequently need to incorporate a variety of preexisting components from different sources.

Classifications are rarely flat; making them so involves too much duplication of material, and so something that brings out common features to form a structured classification system is normally adopted. The result is either hierarchical, forming a tree in which classes become more specific when descending from some general root, or based on a more general directed graph, allowing classes to take on the properties of more than one abstract precursor. In either case, the specification of the classification system can be managed by inheritance, so that properties stated once for some node in the structure are implied to hold for all of its descendents. The pure hierarchy relies on single inheritance, and the more general structures exploit multiple inheritance. A discussion of inheritance will appear in Part 4, while a detailed theory of inheritance is documented in Chapter 15.

Inheritance is not just a matter of avoiding duplication; it has positive benefits in making clear where common features are intended rather than accidental. Good use of inheritance avoids most of the need for simultaneous updating and the manual preservation of consistency that would occur if information was duplicated in related definitions, and so the use of inheritance makes specifications easier to maintain.

1.3.1 Inheritance and Distribution

In programming languages, the classification system that is used is an integral part of the language, and there is, increasingly, a tendency to exploit this integration by allowing reflection, so that the running program can take advantage of knowledge of its own structure. Inheritance is therefore seen as fundamental. In specifying a distributed system, which may incorporate existing components in a more open way, as indicated above, things are less clearcut. The specification is not necessarily a template, it may not be in an open form and it may even postdate the component specified. It is for this reason that distributed systems' frameworks are often object-based rather than object-oriented. They depend on the ideas of object and class (often formulated with particular emphasis on the encapsulation boundary by focusing the specification on interfaces), but they are not committed to the strong linkage between system and specification that is needed to exploit inheritance.

This difference might be epitomized by contrasting the Smalltalk programmer with the Java RMI programmer. The first assumes that code written to modify the object representing a class will have an effect that is immediately visible as a change in behaviour of all objects so far created from that class. The second knows that remote invocation can result in a copy of some class being transferred to a remote virtual machine, where it can remain in its original form, even if the original class is updated and replaced locally.

There is still, of course, a need to describe the capabilities of system components and to negotiate a match between requirements and these capabilities. However, a more descriptive approach, based on subtyping and type matching rules (see Chapter 11), is generally used to support open binding mechanisms. Where inheritance is used, it is applied at a specific epoch associated with the binding process.

1.3.2 Problem-Domain Objects and Implementation Objects

Object-oriented specifications come in a wide variety of styles and levels of abstraction. In applying object-oriented techniques to the analysis of system requirements, the objects are generally models that stand for some part of the problem domain and translate into representations of the problem domain that are manipulated by the system that is eventually produced.

When discussing the structure of distribution platforms and the way in which distribution mechanisms are organized, the objects are more directly tied to system components and are often used to encapsulate particular system resources. Object behaviour and object interaction represent the expected behaviour of the system being constructed, and object composition and abstraction provide the invariant properties of the environment in which distribution takes place.

These two approaches can be seen as ends of a spectrum, with actual practice occurring at various points in-between. Some areas, such as system management, overlay the two views, because the components of the system infrastructure themselves become the problem domain to be modelled. We shall see in the following chapter that ODP is structured into a number of viewpoints that fall at different points in this spectrum.

1.3.3 Objects and Interfaces

The distribution architectures typically place more emphasis on interaction via interfaces than the object-oriented programming architectures. In distributed systems, the binding of interfaces represents the creation of necessary local or remote communication paths, and the specification of interfaces captures the constraints on or required properties of these communication paths. Objects can have multiple interfaces of the same or different types, and parts of an object's state can be associated with specific interface instances.

In programming or design languages, such as Java or UML, interfaces are used as a weaker classifier than traditional classes, giving just a signature or collection of operations. They offer more decoupling from implementation and may be used to avoid the problems of multiple inheritance. There is little or no use of multiple interface instances in structuring specifications.

It can be seen from this that the term interface is used with even more variations of meaning than the term object. It is therefore always necessary to check on the way in which any particular author is using it when comparing work from different sources.

1.4 Available Techniques

The aim in supporting distribution is to make the construction of applications as simple as possible, hiding the variety of platforms and networks involved and offering a single unifying paradigm for application development. This leads to emphasis on unifying architecture and on the encapsulation of as much of the variety as possible within a distinct middleware, giving a pervasive distribution environment, and placing as much of the distribution-specific supporting machinery as possible within the middleware, so as to make it portable and reusable. Below the middleware, the local operating system manages local resources and provides convenient abstractions of them. Above the middleware is the application-specific logic, which is built using the shared processing model that it offers.

1.4.1 Open Distributed Processing

Open Distributed Processing, or ODP, is the name of an architecture and an associated set of standards created within the International Organization for Standardization (ISO) in association with the International Telecommunications Union – Telecommunications (ITU–T); it provides a framework and defines a set of interoperable elements to simplify the construction of large distributed systems. It is described in some detail in Chapter 2, but it is introduced here because of its importance in allowing the comparison of a wide range of different distribution mechanisms.

In ODP, the description of systems is structured into a number of distinct areas of concern using different viewpoints, each concentrating on a different part of the design activity. Within the ODP framework defined using these viewpoints, a number of distinct requirements for distribution mechanisms are identified in terms of transparencies that the infrastructure should provide to the application designer. Finally, the ODP reference model catalogues a range of supporting functions that will be needed within a typical distributed system.

1.4.2 The ANSA Consortium and ANSAware

The ANSA consortium had its roots in a cooperative research project that was started in 1985. It was one of the first attempts to harvest early distributed systems research in order to produce a general middleware solution [Her94]. The resultant platform, called ANSAware, was widely used in system integration pilots and as a basis for research into techniques for the construction of distributed applications. Like a number of its research precursors, ANSAware provided language independence by establishing a separate declaration of the properties of the interfaces at which interworking was to take place, using a distinct Interface Definition Language, or IDL, and mapping this onto a variety of implementation languages. As long as an implementation conformed to the IDL declaration for its interfaces, and to a standard invocation protocol, interworking was then assured.

The project also provided an insight into how to manage and configure distributed systems. The ANSAware Trader provided flexible configuration management based on service types, properties and constraints on them, giving much more flexibility than configurations based on simple naming services. Work was also carried out on real-time support and on the incorporation of flexible and dynamically configurable middleware.

Material from the ANSA project made a considerable contribution to the creation of the standard ODP architecture and to the initial work of the OMG.

1.4.3 The OMG and CORBA

In 1989, the Object Management Group was formed to promote open object-based solutions to system development. It defined an object management architecture (the

OMA) and a general-purpose middleware for supporting object interaction called
CORBA (the Common Object Request Broker Architecture) [Sie98]. The interworking between systems was again achieved by reference to an IDL and a well-known
invocation protocol, in this case called the General Inter-ORB Protocol (GIOP).
CORBA has subsequently been developed to provide a powerful set of middleware
facilities, and it is enhanced by a full range of common object services that build on
CORBA to define most of the supporting elements needed for distribution, including a range of specialist repositories, such as naming services, interface (definition)
repositories, implementation repositories and a general meta-object facility. There
are also a basic security architecture and a variety of value-added communication
services such as event notification and transaction support.

Following the development of the initial specifications for CORBA and related
object services, OMG has extended its activities to address the building of CORBA-
based systems. It has developed specifications for modelling distributed object systems (the Unified Modeling Language – UML) and for application-related functions
in such areas as medical informatics, financial services and manufacturing.

There have been regular liaisons between the OMG developers and the standardization group working on ODP. A number of the general ODP ideas have been used
in the OMG, and the OMG adopted the ODP Trader specification. Various of the
key OMG specifications have been processed by ISO, including the definition of
the IDL [ISO99]. Standardization of the GIOP has also recently been completed
[ISO00].

1.4.4 Telecommunications Architectures – TINA and IN

The telecommunications industry probably has a stronger requirement for the generation of robust, large-scale distributed systems than any other market sector. Any
new telecommunication service is a distributed application, and network management is also a distributed system. Both need to be flexible and large-scale. At the
same time, both need to be robust and highly reliable.

Telecommunications has long been an active area for the development and use
of formal methods. The specification of signalling systems, for example, is ideally
suited to the use of a formal approach, and techniques like the Specification and
Description Language (SDL) have been developed to capture the behaviour of such
systems.

The special requirements in this area have lead to the development of specific architectures for telecommunications' use and the concept of intelligent networks that
describes flexible telecommunications systems specifically intended to support and
accommodate new distributed services. The two best-known initiatives in this area
are the Intelligent Networks (IN) architecture and the later Telecommunications Intelligent Networking Architecture (TINA) [ILM99]. TINA, in particular, was based
on ODP and aimed to promote convergence of telecommunications and computing
views of distribution.

1.4.5 DCOM

In addition to the work on open architectures and platforms, there are, of course, vendor-specific proposals. Perhaps the best known of these is DCOM (distributed COM), from Microsoft. While DCOM has much in common with the open platforms, the focus on a single manufacturer's products leads to differences in emphasis. There is a greater level of integration and less concern with openness as a primary objective. This parallels the distinction between emphasis on interworking and emphasis on system management identified previously.

The distinction shows itself in the shift from a descriptive model based primarily on object interactions toward a model based on components. This shift can be seen in greater commitment to a management architecture that is given the same importance as the invocation architecture. The result is that grouping and explicit control of sets of interfaces is more prominent, giving added management functions that are appropriate to the intended style of the operating system and the environment, but at the cost of greater difficulty in integrating systems with significantly different resource models. These differences in scope make interworking between COM and, for example, CORBA quite difficult. Nevertheless, an OMG specification for such interworking has been developed and is being implemented in products.

1.4.6 Java, Java RMI and JINI

The remote system support associated with the Java language illustrates a different approach to the problem of distribution. Instead of using a set of interworking protocols as the basis for openness, this approach depends on the "write-once, run-anywhere" properties of the Java bytecode to transfer the code needed to integrate the system to where it needs to be run. After initial bootstrapping, protocol interworking is no longer an issue, because matching protocol implementations can be downloaded into remote systems. The interworking problem has been exchanged for a portability problem – that of providing uniform support for the Java virtual machine. An open distribution architecture has been replaced by a common language semantics.

Whether this change represents a gain or a loss depends on the system designer's priorities. System evolution is easier in many respects, but federation and legacy management may be harder. Language independence has been lost, but the single language imposed is popular and quite powerful. The overall balance of factors is not clear, and Java is likely to co-exist with middlewares such as CORBA for some considerable time, particularly since Java currently ships with basic CORBA support as a standard feature.

One of the main facilities that code portability allows the Java Remote Method Invocation (RMI) to offer is call by copy. Objects referenced as parameters in a method call can be copied onto the remote system, transferring both their state and their implementation, so that classes not previously present on the remote system can be instantiated and, unless some other action is taken, then remain available for the lifetime of the virtual machine running them.

This mechanism is at the heart of the JINI configuration management facilities [Wal99]. Services are published under JINI in the form of complete proxy objects, rather than object references, as would be the case in CORBA. This means that new services are effectively self-installing, and all that needs to be distributed before a new service can be used is an abstract class defining the new service's methods. JINI also supports a range of typical middleware services providing aspects of security, transactionalization and lease-based resource management. Built above this is a shared-tuple abstraction called Javaspaces, which simplifies the construction of certain kinds of loosely cooperating applications, so long as the performance demands are not too strict. The resulting package of facilities is an attractive alternative to traditional middleware in some application areas.

1.5 Current Developments

There is currently a trend toward the creation of large, more loosely coupled distributed systems. This is being driven by the increasingly widespread access to general networks and the integration of previously distinct market sectors. Some key drivers are

- the increasing emphasis on mobile devices and wireless networks, leading to the need for distributed systems in which intermittent connectivity of platforms is the norm, and so there is more reliance on object mobility, with the need to support a variety of mobility policies.
- the need to incorporate a number of different user interfacing styles that are dynamically selectable as the communication environment changes, allowing components to adapt to communications via the mobile telephone network, local wireless LANs or direct broadband connections, and for users to interact via laptops, PDAs or WAP-phones.
- the expected integration of the distributed systems supporting office tools, interactive televisions, networked consumer products and many others.

All of these factors are increasing the use of distributed systems and thus the demands for powerful and flexible tools for their formal description.

Bibliography

[BGHS91]   G. Blair, J. Gallagher, D. Hutchison, and D. Shepherd, editors. *Object-Oriented Languages, Systems and Applications*. Pitman, 1991.

[BS95]   M. L. Brodie and M. Stonebraker. *Migrating Legacy Systems*. Morgan Kaufmann Publishers, Inc., 1995.

[BS97]   G. Blair and J-B. Stefani. *Open Distributed Processing and Multimedia*. Addison Wesley, 1997.

[Her94]   A. J. Herbert. An ANSA overview. *IEEE Network*, pages 18–23, Jan/Feb 1994.

[ILM99] Y. Inoue, M. Lapierre, and C. Mossotto, editors. *The TINA Book*. Prentice-Hall Europe, 1999.

[ISO99] *ISO/IEC 14750, Open Distributed Processing – Interface Definition Language.* ISO, 1999.

[ISO00] *ISO/IEC DIS 19500-2, Open Distributed Processing – GIOP/IIOP*. ISO, 2000.

[Lak86] G. Lakoff. *Women, Fire and Dangerous Things: What Categories Reveal about the Mind*. University of Chicago Press, 1986.

[Qui74] W. V. Quine. *The Roots of Reference*. The Open Court, 1974.

[Sie98] J. Siegel. CORBA and OMA in enterprise computing. *CACM*, 41(10):37–43, October 1998.

[Wal99] J. Waldo. The JINI architecture for network-centric computing. *CACM*, 42(7):76–82, July 1999.

[Weg86] P. Wegner. Classification in object-oriented systems. *SIGPLAN Notices: Proceedings of the Object-Oriented Workshop*, 21(10):173–182, 1986.

2

Distributed Systems, An ODP Perspective

Peter F. Linington

University of Kent, UK

2.1 Background on ODP

The Reference Model for Open Distributed Processing (RM-ODP) was created within the International Standards Organization during the late 1980s and early 1990s to provide a stable framework for a broad family of standards for middleware and other related technologies [ISO98a, ISO96a, ISO96b, ISO98b]. The main parts of the reference model were published in 1995. More recent work within ISO has concentrated on more detailed elaboration of key parts of the framework and standardization of critical components needed to ease the federation of independently developed systems, such as the ODP Trader [ISO98c] and the Type Repository [ISO00d].

The focus for specification of the basic middleware technologies themselves has shifted into shorter term, industry-based consortia such as the Object Management Group, although there is continuing active liaison to ensure that a coherent technical solution results. A selection of the most important standards is published by both organizations, and others are related by cross-reference.

Although the ODP Reference Model was originally created as a framework for standardization, it has resulted in a very effective tool for analysing and comparing distribution architectures. The ODP model provides specification mechanisms specifically designed to structure descriptions and separate out particular areas of concern. It has therefore been taken up as the basis of a whole school of distributed system analysis and has provided a common language for publication of comparative analysis of architectures.

2.2 Structuring the Reference Model for ODP

The RM-ODP is structured using three key concepts, which are introduced here in general terms before looking at each in more detail. These concepts are viewpoints, transparencies and functions.

2.2.1 The ODP Viewpoints

The RM-ODP recognizes that the design and specification of any significant distributed system is a complex activity, bringing together the work of a wide range of experts. Representing all of the information about a large system in a single specification is just not feasible. However, the design activity can be divided into a number of areas of concern, and a designer considering one part of the problem does not necessarily have to be aware of the full detail being worked out in other areas. The different parts of the design do, however, need to be consistent, and detailed design at the component level must not defeat policies and objectives set out for the system as a whole, such as systemwide security or priority statements. The RM-ODP supports the separation of concerns by introducing the idea of there being a number of viewpoints, each of which is specialized to support one aspect of the design process. The different viewpoints are interrelated by stating a series of correspondences between terms in the specifications for each pair of viewpoints, and by establishing correspondences between the interpretations of the different languages in which the viewpoints are expressed.

The underlying vision behind this model is one of an increasingly mechanized and integrated development environment. System building and system management tools will draw on different parts of the various viewpoints, guaranteeing, for example, that a modification of the system's configuration to extend its function does not conflict with an established systemwide scheduling or accounting policy. The designer would be warned if such a conflict were introduced. A simple example of this kind of division of the system into related parts with differing scopes and lifetimes is already familiar in the division between interface definition languages and object implementation languages. Others can be found in the separation of application design from middleware configuration and feature selection.

Realizing this vision requires the components of the development environment to be designed so as to exploit information from a variety of sources, even if their use falls primarily within a particular viewpoint. Tools need to be able to play their part in validating the complete set of specifications and in giving users meaningful feedback on errors and inconsistencies that may arise from interaction of the various specification elements [Lin99a].

2.2.2 Transparencies

The power of middleware, from the application developer's point of view, is in providing an abstraction of the distributed environment in which many of the common problems are hidden. They are solved by mechanisms within the middleware, and the application developer proceeds on the basis that these problems will not occur. However, a middleware that attempts to solve all possible problems in all circumstances would be catastrophically inefficient. Some guidance is still needed as to which of the distribution problems are important in this particular application, and what are the priorities if resource conflicts exist.

ODP introduces the idea of transparencies to address this problem. A transparency is said to exist if applications can request to operate in an environment where they do not see some specific kind of distribution problem. It is then up to the software providing the application's operating environment, or infrastructure, to provide whatever mechanisms are necessary to make good the guarantees. Different solutions may be available, and the choice of which one to use is of no consequence to the application, so long as the transparency is achieved.

Transparencies are often related to the structuring into viewpoints. The requirements for transparencies are drawn from one or more of the more designer-oriented viewpoints and are expressed in terms of the properties that object interactions are to have in those viewpoints. The templates for the mechanisms that can provide interactions with the right guaranteed properties are defined in other viewpoints. The result is a system in which the application runs within its declared design envelope, supported by the appropriate interaction mechanisms in the infrastructure.

2.2.3 Functions

The final element of the architecture is a library of functions that are of general use in constructing distributed systems. The standard outlines a number of groups of functions that form the building blocks in different areas and indicates how they form basic patterns that can be reused in distributed system specifications.

2.3 Fundamental Concepts
2.3.1 The ODP Object Model

The first normative part of the ODP Reference Model (leaving aside the general tutorial introduction [ISO98a]) is the definition of a set of foundation concepts [ISO96a] that provide a basis for, and are specialized in, the later parts. This starts off with a short section on the relationship between specifications and the things that they specify – their Universe of Discourse – making clear how a specification links to implementations of it. It then goes on to describe a basic object model, starting with the actions that model observable events and hence introducing the objects that perform actions and communicate with other objects via interactions at interfaces.

The definitions given in the foundations are the result of a careful comparison of existing practice in many different languages. It was clear to the authors that these definitions were, in some respects, fundamentally different and could not be completely unified. The standard therefore gives a set of definitions parameterized by detailed choices in particular specification notations; this is particularly important in the area of composition of behaviour. For example, the standard says that behaviour is a collection of actions with a set of constraints on when they may occur, but it goes on to say that different specification languages offer different kinds of primitive constraints, by defining composition operations with different detailed semantics.

Having established a generic object model, the standard defines a set of concepts for structuring specifications and classifying objects, introducing type, class and template. In these definitions, a type is a predicate characterizing some collection, a class focuses on the collection itself and a template is the body of information needed to create new members of the collection; clearly, these are not independent, but have significant overlap. For example, each template has an associated template type guaranteed to apply to the objects instantiated from it.

In the remainder of the foundations standard, a number of further families of concepts for structuring applications are introduced, such as groups, contexts, causal relationships, naming systems and many others.

The foundation concepts are defined in natural language, and there is thus some scope for interpretation of the definitions. Specific interpretations in some of the common formal languages are provided in a separate part of the Reference Model, called the Architectural Semantics [ISO98b] (which is discussed in Chapter 19 of this volume).

2.3.2 Conformance

Conformance is at the heart of any standardization framework, and the RM-ODP is no exception. The final element of the foundations is the definition of a conformance framework. Taken on its own, a specification establishes a formal system that does not itself involve conformance, any more than, say, a programming language grammar involves conformance. However, specific notations derived from the framework will be supported by automated tools and design processes that produce and maintain specifications for systems, and the conformance of these tools and processes can be tested, just as a language compiler can. This testing of tools includes checks of the correct generation of more detailed specifications that conform to the structural or grammatical rules of the architectural description language and the construction of systems that, in operation, perform in a way that is consistent with the semantics of the language.

The ODP model for conformance testing involves three main roles: the specifier, the implementer and the tester. Their responsibilities in the testing process are as follows:

- The specifier defines the expected behaviour, including declaration of a reference configuration identifying the boundaries at which testing should be possible. Since this is part of the specification, it still needs to be interpreted in real-world terms.
- The implementer produces an implementation and makes a claim that it conforms to the specification. In support of the claim, it indicates points in the implementation that correspond to the boundaries in the reference configuration. It also defines an interpretation of observable happenings (such as transfer of a sequence of bits) that allow the identification of events in terms of the vocabulary of the specification.

- The tester inspects the implementation and observes it at the points indicated, applying the interpretation given to identify meaningful events. It then checks that these events satisfy the specified behaviour, and so detects conformance problems. Problems can thus be detected either because the interpretation fails, or because the specification is not adhered to.

In order to facilitate this process, the reference model defines the concepts of reference point and conformance point for identifying the boundaries of interest for testing. It classifies these points, based on the kind of observation that they can support, into four kinds: interworking reference points (on communication media), programmatic reference points (at software boundaries), perceptual reference points (at boundaries between the IT system and the remainder of the physical world) and interchange reference points (where interaction is based on the transfer of recorded media).

2.4 The ODP Architecture

Having established a general conceptual framework in the foundations part, the ODP reference model continues in its third part [ISO96b] by establishing a specific architecture. Whilst the foundation ideas introduced in the previous section can be applied to practically any distributed system, the ODP architecture makes specific choices, which distinguish ODP systems from arbitrary distributed systems. These are, by and large, choices that position the architecture to facilitate efficient middleware support of distribution.

Having identified the technique of using viewpoints in general, the ODP Reference Model then goes on to define a specific architecture, based on the definition of a particular set of viewpoints. The RM-ODP defines five viewpoints. They are the enterprise, information, computational, engineering and technology viewpoints. The different areas of concern that they address have been chosen based on experience in the specification and construction of distributed systems and are intended to reflect the separation of concerns found in a typical design team. Other viewpoints could be defined, but this set was sufficient for the purposes for which the RM-ODP was produced.

These five viewpoints do not relate directly to steps in any design methodology. They will, in general, be developed in parallel, with interaction taking place between the different design groups, and a certain amount of iteration and backtracking must be expected to occur. The relationships between elements of the different viewpoints form a web reflecting the overlap of the different areas of concern that they support.

2.4.1 The Enterprise Viewpoint

The enterprise viewpoint is concerned with establishing the environment in which the system is to operate. It states the relation of the system to the various business processes that it is to support and expresses the requirements of the system in stake-holder terms. It includes both those aspects of the organizational structure and objectives that need to be interpreted or referenced within the remainder of the specification and the systemwide policies that are intended to control the system's design and operation.

The RM-ODP itself gives only rather general information about the form of the enterprise language. This is because the Reference Model is intended to provide a general-purpose framework, applicable to very many different situations and organizational structures, and specific fixed constraints would be likely to restrict its scope. Furthermore, much work has been carried out since the ideas were introduced into the Reference Model, and they are now better understood. Work is now in progress within ISO to create an additional, more detailed enterprise framework that is able to express the constraints applicable to systems used in a wide range of enterprise structures, and this work is making the enterprise language much more specific [ISO00b]. There is also interest in using existing, widely used, design notations such as UML to express enterprise policies [BG99, AM99, Lin99b, SD99, SD00].

In ODP, the primary building blocks of an enterprise specification are communities. A community is a set of interacting objects that have come together into a configuration so that they can interact to achieve some purpose. Communities are typed, and their type determines the broad kinds of behaviour that they can exhibit and the policies that control their formation, interaction and evolution [LMR98].

A community type is parameterized by identifying a set of roles, each of which can be filled by a specific object instance. The community behaviour is expressed in terms of these roles, and so it constrains the actions performed by the objects that fill them. In general, objects can fill multiple roles in the same or different communities, but the assignment of objects to roles may be subject to constraints expressed within the community type definition. Thus, for example, there may be specific requirements that conflicting roles, such as those involved in proposing and authorizing expenditures, are filled by different objects. There may also be requirements that pairs of roles in different cooperating communities be filled by the same object. Thus one community may describe the delegation of authority and another may describe some customer–provider relationship; if they are used in composition to describe a particular enterprise, it may be necessary that, no matter how the roles are filled, the provider role in the second community shall always be filled by an object that also fills the agent role in the first community.

The idea of expressing the enterprise viewpoint as the overlap and interrelationship of a number of communities has some parallels with the patterns movement in software design. Libraries of community specifications can be used to capture well-known organizational patterns and so encourage specification reuse.

Further examples of the use of the enterprise concepts to constrain system design can be found in [TBW97] and [AM98].

2.4.2 *The Information Viewpoint*

The information viewpoint brings together the shared view of the meaning of and constraints on key information elements and, in so doing, gives the basis for system-wide consistency. It is the information viewpoint that provides the common interpretation guaranteeing that a concept identified in, say, a user interface and a concept referenced in a remote invocation of an operation on the interface of a server object are the same concept. In this respect, its aim is to bring the function previously provided by a data dictionary within a consistent architectural framework.

Not surprisingly, the techniques used for specification in the information viewpoint draw on practice in the database world, with emphasis on schema definition and the statements of invariants to express the constraints on the information items being defined.

2.4.3 *The Computational Viewpoint*

The computational viewpoint is the main focus for functional design. The computational language defines an abstract object model – the virtual machine that interprets the computational design and thus has to be realized by any supporting middleware. The computational design identifies interactions between objects at interfaces, and these interactions will need to be supported either by communication between systems or by locally optimized interactions, depending on the way in which the system's functions are to be distributed at any particular moment.

It is here (and in the engineering viewpoint) that the general idea of transparencies is applied. The computational viewpoint identifies the interactions that require specific transparencies from the infrastructure – in terms of the nonfunctional properties of the virtual machine with respect to which the computational specification is interpreted.

The computational specification is expressed in terms of a language whose primitive elements are computational objects, interfaces and interactions, together with the actions that instantiate objects and interfaces and establish bindings between interfaces.

In describing interfaces, the computational language restricts the kinds of interaction patterns allowed to avoid patterns that are difficult or expensive to support if the participants are distributed. For example, client-server interactions are supported, but symmetric rendezvous is not; it requires too much communication to give the necessary synchronization of the behaviours of the objects involved in the rendezvous. The language supports just two kinds of interface: operational interfaces and stream interfaces.

Operational interfaces group together sets of operations that can be either interrogations, of a remote procedure call style, involving a request followed by a response, or unidirectional announcements passed from initiator to responder. These interactions are modelled as indivisible actions. Stream interfaces describe continuous media flows. They are commonly used to describe multimedia systems involving audio or video, but they may also be used to model flows of any kind of repetitive data that the designer does not wish to detail at the granularity of interest, such as streams of sensor readings or system load measures. A stream interface may be structured into a number of distinct unidirectional flows, although a single interface may involve some flows in each direction. A stream is seen as a single, extended action that lasts for as long as the stream binding exists.

In order for an interaction to occur, the interfaces on the objects involved must be associated by the formation of a binding. In simple cases, where detailed properties of the supporting mechanisms are not of interest, this binding may be described as a primitive linkage of objects. But in more complex situations, it may itself be modelled as an object encapsulating the infrastructure resources supporting the communication. Making the binding visible as an object allows it to support control interfaces via which its properties can be manipulated, giving dynamic support of quality of service or change of the binding configuration.

Some of the properties of interactions, such as end to end delay, are only meaningful if the boundaries at which the communication events start and end are made explicit. Transmission delay is only well defined if transmission is from a known point and to a known point. To support this, interactions in either kind of interface can be modelled at a more detailed level as a series of localized signals at the boundary of a binding object to express, for example, quality of service measures in terms of the relative timing of these signals.

Interfaces are typed, and the dynamic construction of systems from existing components that have different histories, and hence different types, results in a need to define what constraints need to be applied for interfaces with different types to be bound together successfully. This generally involves type-matching rules that are related to the causal flow in the interactions, so as to prevent any object from being presented with data that is not consistent with its interface type, either in request or response. The type-matching requirements for streams are more complex and need to be specified by the designer.

2.4.4 *The Engineering Viewpoint*

The engineering viewpoint must define the interpreter for the computational model; it consists of a series of templates for the computational interactions, parameterized so as to support a range of different policies selected either for the enterprise or on a finer scale within the information or computational viewpoints. The RM-ODP supports this parameterization by defining a series of transparencies that represent requirements about which particular common problems (such as a lack of migration transparency) should be solved.

The engineering viewpoint is primarily concerned with two areas – the structuring of responsibilities for objects within a subsystem and the structuring of communication responsibilities between systems.

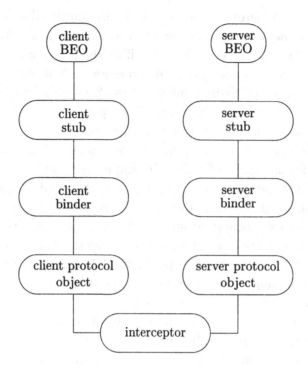

Fig. 2.1. Engineering channel structure – simple client-server interaction.

There are three groupings of objects. The largest is the node, generally corresponding to some hardware platform; it represents the organizational unit within which real resources are managed and allocated, and between which nonlocal communications take place. The next is the capsule, which is a unit for protection purposes, roughly corresponding to an address space. Objects within a capsule share some level of trust that is checked by development tools, such as compilers and linkers, and so lighter weight interaction mechanisms can be used within a capsule. The capsule is therefore the main unit in the software failure model. The smallest unit for grouping objects is the cluster, which identifies objects that have the same lifecycle and so is appropriate for the management of persistence and recovery of state. Clusters may be used to support fine-grain object systems at reasonable cost by allowing groups of objects to be saved or migrated as a whole. For each of these three groupings, there is a corresponding manager object via which it can be configured and controlled.

The main communication structure defined is the channel, which is created when objects are bound together to allow them to interact. The objects that correspond to the computational objects being supported are called basic engineering objects (BEOs). A channel includes three main communication-oriented functions. These are stubs, binders and protocol objects (see Figure 2.1). The stub is concerned with the relation of elements of object state to the payload exchanged in object interaction – the marshalling and unmarshalling processes. Outside the stubs, the infrastructure can consider communications as being in terms of complete messages. The binder manages the configuration of communication paths over which objects interact; it is therefore responsible for managing object location and migration, and the protocol object ensures reliable communication over these paths. Note that these are not, in general, layers. They are interacting functions that may call on one another. For example, the binder may need to access stub functions to add control information to a message. There may also be some recursion to access supporting repositories [ISO98a].

If the path between two systems crosses some boundary where organizational or technical rules change, additional interceptor objects may be introduced into the path to perform control or translation functions. Interceptors may peer with any or all of the stubs, binders or protocol objects supporting the interacting basic engineering objects, depending on the nature of the boundary to be crossed.

The new standard on Interface References and Binding [ISO98d] extends this model by giving a framework for the engineering support of the binding process. It introduces the concept of a binding factory, which is responsible for collecting the necessary resources and constructing the binding object requested. This factory negotiates with the infrastructure components in the systems that are supporting each of the objects to be bound and performs checks to see that the interface types are compatible [Kut99]. It then constructs a suitable channel between the endpoints, taking account of any quality of service constraints on the binding by using the primitive bind operations of the technologies concerned. Constructing this channel involves creating and configuring its supporting stub, binder and protocol objects, and possibly introducing some interceptors. Finally, having checked that the binding object is correctly initialized, the factory returns a reference to the binding's control interface to its client.

The factory is responsible for supporting policies concerned with achieving type compatibility and dealing with federation and the crossing of various kinds of domain boundaries. This process may involve the allocation or creation of suitable interceptors along the communication paths, which can lead to a hierarchical process of channel creation; the establishment of path segments between interceptors is delegated to subsidiary factories, under the control of policies and subgoals established by the top-level binding factory.

2.4.5 The Technology Viewpoint

With the technology viewpoint, emphasis returns to the specification of boundary conditions on the design, this time concentrating on the enumeration of standard technologies on which the design is to be based; it is primarily a catalogue of references to existing standards used by the system's designers, together with a description of the existing configurations of hardware or software components that are to be used, where this is externally constrained.

2.4.6 Viewpoint Correspondences

In general, design tools and processes must manipulate not only one particular viewpoint specification of direct interest, but they must also manage correspondences with other viewpoint specifications, and so wider issues of conformance to complete sets of ODP specifications need to be considered.

Note that there are correspondences between each possible pair of viewpoint specifications, but the issues involved are particularly important in the enterprise language because the policies expressed in the enterprise specification are reflected in all of the other viewpoints.

The underlying rationale in identifying correspondences between different viewpoint specifications of the same ODP system is that there are some entities that are represented in any viewpoint specification which are also represented in other viewpoint specifications. The requirement for consistency between viewpoint specifications is driven by, and only by, the fact that what is specified in one viewpoint specification about an entity needs to be consistent with what is said about the same entity in any other viewpoint specification. This includes the consistency of that entity's properties, structure and behaviour.

The specifications produced in different ODP viewpoints are each complete statements in their respective languages, with their own locally significant names, and so cannot be related without additional information in the form of correspondence statements. What is needed is a set of statements that make clear how constraints from different viewpoints apply to particular elements of a single system to determine its overall behaviour. The correspondence statements are statements that relate the various different viewpoint specifications, but do not form part of any one of the five basic viewpoints. The correspondences can be established in two ways:

- by declaring correspondences between terms in t wo different viewpoint languages, stating how their semantics interact. This implies that the t wo languages are expressed in such a way that they have a common, or at least a related, set of foundation concepts and structuring rules. Such correspondences between languages necessarily imply and entail correspondences relating to all things of interest that the languages are used to model (e.g., things represented by objects or actions).
- by considering the things expressed by terms in each language and asserting that particular entities being modelled in the t wo specifications are in fact the same entity. This relates the specifications by identifying which observations need to be interpretable in both specifications.

2.4.7 The ODP Transparencies

The ODP transparencies are defined by giving a prescription for transforming a set of system specifications in the computational, information and enterprise viewpoints based on an engineering specification that incorporates the various ODP functions needed; the functions are used in a coordinated way so as to provide the necessary transparency. The transformation may result in extensions to a computational object's behaviour and interface signatures, in order to incorporate any control interactions and information needed to guarantee the transparency. Thus, for example, the transaction transparency may require additional commit interactions and the addition of transaction identifiers to the parameters carried by existing computational interactions.

The RM-ODP defines the following transparencies:

- Access and location transparencies: Access transparency is normally provided as part of the basic function of the engineering stub object, and so the transformation to be performed to provide it is a straightforward refinement to introduce the channel structure. In a similar way, location transparency will be provided by some combination of the stubs and protocol objects, cooperating to perform any necessary translation from location-independent to location-dependent naming.

- Failure transparency: Failure transparency is requested by the specification of the kinds of failures that should not be allowed to disrupt the application. It can be provided in a number of ways. First, the objects involved can be placed in an environment that is inherently sufficiently reliable, such as a nonstop system. Second, the checkpointing and recovery mechanisms can be used to overcome faults when they occur. Third, the replication mechanisms can be used to make faults nondamaging to the application. Which of these approaches is to be taken will depend on the relative cost and performance objectives to be met, particularly whether the system has to give real-time guarantees. These choices will be made on the basis of the enterprise policies that have been established to guide the design.

- Migration transparency· The migration transparency is expected to minimize the effect on objects if they are moved. The complexity of this task depends on the set of enterprise policies that constrain object mobility, since if the objects do not move, there is no problem to solve. The decision as to whether objects should be moved will have to take into account issues of resource management, performance targets and security. Once the mobility constraints are established, suitable migration strategies can be determined and the mechanisms needed to support them incorporated. Migration can be managed in a number of ways, depending on the performance requirements that have been set. For example, migration can be based on deactivation and reactivation elsewhere, or on temporary replication.

- Persistence and relocation transparencies: Both the persistence and relocation transparencies will involve the use of the relocator function. This is because they are both involved in changes that may invalidate current interface references, causing subsequent attempts to create a binding to fail and thus to be referred to the relocator. In both cases, the relocation function will need to be used in a way that is coordinated with the resource management and recovery activities, to ensure that sufficient information is provided for the relocator to do its job. If the object has been deactivated, the relocator will need to ask for it to be reactivated. If it has moved, the relocator will need to be aware of its new location.

- Replication transparency: The provision of replication transparency is potentially complex because of the need to consider both the client and server roles of any object being replicated, to ensure that the behaviour of the system as a whole remains consistent. The transformations involved to support replication are therefore potentially less localized than in some of the other transparencies. The cluster managers supporting the replica copies, at least, will need to be involved in the coordination. This implies the need for a realization of the transparency to involve a transformation of the computational specification, introducing additional objects and interactions, before elaboration of individual interfaces into engineering channels can take place.

- Transaction transparency: Transaction transparency is concerned with larger behavioural units rather than simple interactions. Its provision may involve additional coordination of objects and the introduction of new information, such as transaction identification, into the set of information exchanged during interactions. As a result, transaction transparency involves the same sort of complex transformations as replication transparency; the computational description will, in general, need to be extended as part of the transparency provision.

2.4.8 The ODP Functions

The functions identified in the Reference Model are primarily concerned with mechanisms in the engineering viewpoint that provide transparencies, and so would not normally be visible in the computational viewpoint. However, this is actually a designer choice, and certain key functions may be made visible computationally to allow explicit application control if necessary. For example, because of its importance in configuration management and resource discovery, the trading function (one of the repository functions) is generally made visible in the computational viewpoint.

The main groupings of functions are

- Management functions: These include object, cluster, capsule and node management, and allow for the dynamic change of management policies and control of the lifecycle of the corresponding object or group of objects.
- Coordination functions: These provide the ability to express requirements for changes in one object to affect others, and for synchronization between objects. They include event notification functions, checkpointing and recovery functions, group communication and transaction functions and functions for the replication and migration of objects. There is also a reference tracking function intended to support mechanisms for distributed garbage collection.
- Repository functions: These include both general storage and retrieval functions and a number of specialized repositories needed by the infrastructure itself. Under this second category there are relocation functions, which maintain information about changes in configuration; type repository functions, which maintain a shared view of types that need to be interpreted in different parts of the system, and trading functions.
- Security functions: These include the basic mechanisms for implementing security policies, including access control, authentication, audit, integrity control, confidentiality and non-repudiation functions. The whole set is supported by general-purpose key management functions.

The trading function and the type repository function are already the subjects of standards. They are discussed in more detail in the following section.

2.5 Specific ODP Standards

2.5.1 The ODP Trader

The ODP trader provides for the publication and discovery of services [ISO98c]. It aims to allow resource discovery based on service type, and not just on naming. The basic idea behind it is that service providers export services when they become available, and potential clients state their requirements in order to discover if a suitable corresponding service exists. Information about services is published as a number of service offers. A service offer consists of an interface reference via which the service can be accessed and a set of properties (including type information) that describe the service. The properties of the offer are selected by the service provider and can involve technical options, costs, potential performance or whatever else is needed.

The service provider (or its agent) exports the service offer to the trader, which adds it to the set of available offers. This set of offers can be structured to guide retrieval or to help federate the information held by multiple traders. The service offer remains in the trader until it is withdrawn by the provider or found to be invalid following problems notified by its clients.

The potential client interrogates the trader, providing a search expression that gives the client's constraints in terms of combinations of the properties that it is interested in. It may request a best fit or a list of possibilities to investigate. Once the client has received a service offer, it can use the interface reference included in it to make direct access to the service; the trader is no longer involved.

In addition to the properties established at export-time, there can also be properties whose values are requested dynamically by the trader as part of the search process. Dynamic properties allow more flexible search strategies that take note of changing loads or costs.

The trader provides a simple yet effective mechanism for managing configuration. It greatly simplifies the bootstrapping process, because the only piece of configuration information that a new node or application component needs initially is the location of some local trader.

2.5.2 The ODP Type Repository

The sharing of an understanding of types is the basis for any form of communication, and so the ability to organise such information is one of the essential planks for the support of system development. One of the first things to be done when federating systems is to establish correspondences between their views of types.

Types are used in many aspects of system configuration. They are used to express requirements when trading, to check compatibility during binding and to confirm the consistency of implementation during compilation and component integration. The dependencies of system components on types are complex, and there are many different type systems that interrelate and overlap in a wide variety of different ways.

ODP therefore provides a general mechanism for describing the model that represents each type system [ISO00d]; it also allows families of related type definitions to be described by higher level models, or meta-models. In this way, support for a range of different techniques and notations can be provided, and there is a basis for establishing correspondences between the expressions of a single underlying type in a variety of languages.

The type repository provides a link between activities taking part at different stages in the system's lifecycle. It acts as a common store for type information used to express requirements, outline designs, management constraints, policies and implementation details. It can also store the refinement relationships that link types in an abstract system view with more specific types used in a variety of implementations.

The packaging of the repository as a collection of objects accessible using the standard middleware also blurs the distinction between design time and run-time. System components within the infrastructure can access type information deposited when the system was built, facilitating the provision of flexible channel components, such as interceptors that convert from one data representation to another and simplifying interoperation between different implementation domains. Replacing a basic interface repository with a more general type repository simplifies the provision for dynamic invocation and makes possible the selection of marshalling and representation options at binding time. Techniques of this sort can simplify system evolution and the deployment of new services.

2.5.3 The ODP Naming Framework

One of the main practical problems to be faced when federating distributed systems that have been developed by different organizations is the integration of the different naming systems in use. The ODP architecture recognizes that this requirement implies the need for a flexible approach to naming. It defines a suitable naming framework as a separate standard [ISO98e]. This framework asserts that all naming is context-relative, so that every operation that defines or uses names is associated with an appropriate context; operations that attempt to use names in the wrong context will fail.

Most uses of names involve resolving the name to an object that is being named. This will, in general, take place in a series of resolution steps. At each step, the available naming information is analysed in the current context, and the result is either the direct identification of an object or the derivation of a further resolution action, generally in a different naming context. The further action will involve another resolver object and some further naming information that it should be asked to resolve. The process may be a prelude to interaction with the object, or it may form part of the creation of a communication path, or binding, which is extended at each step. This general framework is able to express a wide range of naming structures, including domain hierarchies and name translators.

The naming framework standard describes a number of specific strategies for managing names in federations, by defining special contexts to control and manage the mutual visibility of the naming systems to be linked. These use the general context-relative naming structures to simplify the federated naming problem.

2.5.4 The ODP Quality of Service Framework

Work has recently been going on to provide a clearer definition of the way in which quality of service is expressed and managed in ODP systems [ISO00c]. This framework recognizes that establishing quality of service requirements and constraints creates a form of contract. A component does not offer a defined quality of service in isolation, but it makes guarantees that are conditional on a certain level of cooperation and support from its environment (including its clients). Thus, for example, a server object cannot offer to meet a specific response-time target unconditionally; it needs guarantees that its clients as a whole will not make requests at a rate that is above some design ceiling, and that it will receive at least some stated proportion of the available resources from the nodes that support it.

Thus, each object specification states the quality of service that it can provide, subject to its environment satisfying the quality of service that it requires to operate successfully. The same is true for compositions of objects, and rules can be established for the quality of service compatibility constraints needed for compositions to be successful. Examples of this approach are given in [DTV99].

2.6 Instantiating ODP

There are many examples of the use of ODP in distributed systems' analysis and design, including some very significant influences on the development of open specifications and architectures.

There has been close liaison over many years between the ODP standards group and the work of the OMG; the service envisaged in the CORBA architecture is close in concept to the ODP computational viewpoint. The main difference is that the CORBA architecture does not support objects with multiple interfaces, although the recent work on specifying CORBA components compensates for this. The standard specifying protocol support for ODP computational interaction [ISO00e] is based on the OMG's GIOP, which is itself soon to become an ISO standard [ISO00a].

Other supporting standards have also been developed in collaboration. The OMG Trader is based on the ODP Trader, and the ODP Type Repository draws on the OMG Meta-Object Facility (MOF).

The main market sector to adopt ODP is telecommunications, where a number of network management specifications have been structured using the ODP architecture's viewpoints. See, for example, the PRISM architecture for broadband network management [BB96].

The work of the TINA consortium and its successor projects has been based on the ODP architecture, particularly the computational model, where the interface definition language has been enhanced to support streams and quality of service constraints [BHG00].

These activities, and many others, have shown the power of ODP as an architectural basis for the specification of distributed systems, supporting a broad range of requirements and giving a framework in which to manage system evolution and federation.

Bibliography

[AM98]   J. O. Aagedal and Z. Milosevic. Enterprise modelling and QoS for command and control systems. In *Proc. 2nd International Workshop on Enterprise Distributed Object Computing (EDOC'98)*, November 1998.

[AM99]   J. O. Aagedal and Z. Milosevic. ODP enterprise language: UML perspective. In *Proc. 3rd International Workshop on Enterprise Distributed Object Computing (EDOC'99)*, pages 60–71. IEEE, September 1999.

[BB96]   K. Berquist and A. Berquist. *Managing Information Highways: The PRISM Book*. Number 1164 in Lecture Notes in Computer Science. Springer, 1996.

[BG99]   X. Blanc and M. P. Gervais. Using the UML language to express ODP enterprise concepts. In *Proc. 3rd International Workshop on Enterprise Distributed Object Computing (EDOC'99)*, pages 50–59. IEEE, September 1999.

[BHG00]   H. Berndt, T. Hamada, and P. Graubmann. TINA: Its achievements and its future directions. *IEEE Communications Surveys and Tutorials*, 3(1), 2000.

[DTV99]   J. Daniel, B. Traverson, and S. Vignes. Integration of quality of service in distributed object systems. In *Distributed Applications and Interoperable Systems II*, pages 31–43. Kluwer, 1999.

[ISO96a]   *ISO/IEC IS 10746-2, Open Distributed Processing Reference Model – Part 2: Foundations*. ISO, 1996.

[ISO96b]   *ISO/IEC IS 10746-3, Open Distributed Processing Reference Model – Part 3: Architecture*. ISO, 1996.

[ISO98a]   *ISO/IEC IS 10746-1, Open Distributed Processing Reference Model – Part 1: Overview*. ISO, 1998.

[ISO98b]   *ISO/IEC IS 10746-4, Open Distributed Processing Reference Model – Part 4: Architectural Semantics*. ISO, 1998.

[ISO98c]   *ISO/IEC IS 13235-1, Open Distributed Processing – Trading Function: Specification*. ISO, 1998.

[ISO98d]   *ISO/IEC IS 14753, Open Distributed Processing – Interface References and Binding*. ISO, 1998.

[ISO98e]   *ISO/IEC IS 14771, Open Distributed Processing – Naming Fr amework* ISO, 1998.

[ISO00a]   *ISO/IEC DIS 19500-2, Open Distributed Processing – GIOP/IIOP*. ISO, 2000.

[ISO00b]   *ISO/IEC FCD 15414, Open Distributed Processing – Enterprise Viewpoint*. ISO, 2000.

[ISO00c]   *ISO/IEC FCD 15935, Open Distributed Processing – A framework of QoS in ODP*. ISO, 2000.

[ISO00d]   *ISO/IEC FDIS 14769, Open Distributed Processing – Type Repository Function*. ISO, 2000.

[ISO00e]   *ISO/IEC FDIS 17452, Open Distributed Processing – Protocol Support for Computational Interaction*. ISO, 2000.

[Kut99]　L. Kutvonen. Sovereign systems and dynamic federations. In *Distributed Applications and Interoperable Systems II*, pages 77–90. Kluwer, 1999.

[Lin99a]　P. F. Linington. An ODP approach to the development of large middleware systems. In *Distributed Applications and Interoperable Systems II*, pages 61–74. Kluwer, 1999.

[Lin99b]　P. F. Linington. Options for expressing ODP enterprise communities and their policies by using UML. In *Proc. 3rd International Workshop on Enterprise Distributed Object Computing (EDOC'99)*, pages 72–82. IEEE, September 1999.

[LMR98]　P. F. Linington, Z. Milosevic, and K. Raymond. Policies in communities: Extending the ODP enterprise viewpoint. In *Proc. 2nd International Workshop on Enterprise Distributed Object Computing (EDOC'98)*, November 1998.

[SD99]　M. W. A. Steen and J. Derrick. Formalising ODP enterprise policies. In *Proc. 3rd International Workshop on Enterprise Distributed Object Computing (EDOC'99)*, pages 84–93. IEEE, September 1999.

[SD00]　M. W. A. Steen and J. Derrick. ODP Enterprise Viewpoint Specification. *Computer Standards and Interfaces*, 22:165–189, 2000.

[TBW97]　S. Tyndale-Biscoe and B. M. Wood. Machine responsibility – how to deal with it. In *Proc. 1st International Workshop on Enterprise Distributed Object Computing (EDOC'97)*, October 1997.

3

Issues in Formal Methods

Howard Bowman   John Derrick

University of Kent, UK

The previous two chapters have discussed the construction of distributed systems and highlighted some of the challenges that they pose. The central problem is, of course, how to enhance reliability in the context of distribution. For those interested in a formal approach, this gives rise to a number of requirements on both the theoretical framework and particular engineering approaches. In this chapter we draw on some of the themes introduced in Chapters 1 and 2 to discuss implications on the use of formal methods for the specification of distributed systems.

3.1 A Formal Approach

The term formal methods usually encompasses any specification or design notation that offers precise, unambiguous and abstract definition based around a formal syntax and usually backed up by a well-defined meaning, i.e., a semantics. The requirements of abstraction and unambiguous specification mean that formal methods have become synonymous with a mathematical approach to specification and design. In fact, a more accurate label is formal description techniques, or FDTs for short, which places more emphasis on the descriptive aspect than on the methodological aspect, since some formal methods are concerned with description rather than with the development of a specification.

Formal methods are important. They are important because they provide a medium by which to abstract away from underlying implementation details to specify behaviour in terms of well-defined interactions across well-defined interfaces, that is, they allow precise *specification*. Precision then opens the possibility of *verification* and *validation*, that is, we can check whether a specification meets a set of requirements, or check whether the behaviour of program code meets the behaviour required in a specification. Methodologies such as *refinement* can also be used to help generate programs directly from the specifications themselves. Thus formal methods are important because they seek to enhance the reliability of systems by adding rigour to the specification and design process.

Formal methods are important to distributed systems. This is because, in addition to the general benefits already outlined, distributed systems bring an added level of complexity and a new set of concerns over and above those of a stand-alone system. If a single machine in a travel agent fails, it is inconvenient; if an airline's global on-line booking system fails, the commercial implications are far larger. In addition, over and above aspects of reliability, large distributed systems bring other concerns such as security, which, by the very nature of distribution, are more important and harder to ensure.

Any approach or set of approaches that offer a means to tackle some of these problems is then of interest. Formal methods clearly offer some promise (and indeed a track record) in this respect. Over the years a number of techniques have been developed, some of them general-purpose and others aimed at particular application domains. For example, LOTOS [BB88, ISO87a], Estelle [ISO87b] and SDL [CCI88] are targeted at issues of explicit concurrency and interaction (specifying ordering and synchronization of abstract events). Communication protocols are a typical example of this class of application. In contrast, approaches such as Z [Spi92] and VDM [Jon89] address the specification of software systems in terms of data state changes. Importantly, none of these techniques fully address the specification requirements of modern distributed systems. Such systems are extremely broad, encompassing, for example, both information modelling and the description of engineering infrastructures.

Indeed, the majority of formal methods developed for distributed systems have their origins in the 1980s and were targeted at the early generations of distributed systems. A classic example of the type of problem that they were designed to tackle is the analysis of communication protocols in data networks. For example, a major work item was undertaken in the Open Systems Interconnection (OSI) arena to develop suitable formal notations for specifying and verifying the protocols of the OSI architecture [ISO84]; the two techniques LOTOS [BB88] and Estelle [Tur93] resulted from this activity. In addition, important techniques with related objectives from outside the OSI arena include: CSP [Hoa85], CCS [Mil89], SDL [Tur93] and temporal logics [MP92].

Importantly though, the application of formal techniques to these early generations of systems largely centred on description and verification of event ordering, that is, the allowed order in which events can occur. For example, they would enable the possible orderings of sending, receiving and acknowledging in a data link protocol to be described and then enable deadlock and livelock freeness of the description to be verified. Nearly all of the notations developed abstracted from real-time aspects†; put another way, they allowed the *qualitative* but not the *quantitative* ordering of events to be defined. In addition, the configuration of components and of interactions between components could be defined only statically‡. Thus, mobility (dynamic reconfiguration) could not be expressed.

However, as we have seen previously the current generation of distributed sys-

---

† In fact, Estelle and SDL had some real-time features. However, these features were relatively primitive in nature and have not proved as expressive as required [FL98].

‡ Estelle and SDL had some preliminary (and again expressively limited) features for dynamic configuration.

tems has new features that were not found in the early 1980s. In particular, they are typically *object-oriented*, have *mobile* components and are *time-sensitive*, one reason for which is the advent of *multimedia*. These aspects are to one degree or another central to all of the architectural and programming models being used to build modern distributed systems that were discussed in Chapter 1, for example, CORBA, TINA, Open Distributed Processing, DCOM and Java. In addition, advanced system development architectures are being considered to resolve the significant software engineering problems involved in constructing modern (potentially global) distributed systems, for example, the *viewpoints model* being used in ODP and TINA.

However, despite these new aspects, formal methods are as applicable to modern distributed systems as they were to earlier generations of systems. Indeed, arguments similar to those given for the application of formal methods to the distributed systems of the 1980s are still relevant. For example, as previously suggested, such techniques enable automated and semiautomated verification tools to be used in analysing and debugging system descriptions.

Therefore a major theme of current research is how to enhance the existing formal techniques to support the new features of modern distributed systems. As a reflection of the importance of this topic, the majority of existing formal notations have been through some form of enhancement that has attempted to add features to support the new requirements. Notable examples of such enhancements are those to SDL and to LOTOS, and Part Two of this book covers these two language enhancements in addition to discussing Object-Z [Smi00] and UML [BRJ99].

In addition to these developments in specification languages, a parallel strand of development has taken place in the investigation of underlying concepts. For example, a range of calculi and abstract frameworks have been developed to investigate the issues lying behind mobility, security, subtyping and so on. These include, for example, Actors, mobile ambients and object and process calculi, many of which we shall meet later in this book.

3.2 A Set of Requirements

The typical requirements on a formal technique or method are expressiveness, compositionality, that they be verifiable, have clear semantics and benefit from good tool support. All of these concerns are relevant for distributed systems. However, there are a number of additional requirements that arise from the specific characteristics of distribution, which we discuss in turn now.

3.2.1 Object-Oriented Specification

Modern distributed systems are almost universally object-based [Weg87] and moreover are often object-oriented [Weg87]. At the heart of all of the techniques discussed in Section 1.4 is an object model whereby objects are encapsulated and objects interact only via interfaces. Although the emphasis differs between different approaches and platforms, there is a commonality in the need for object-oriented specification. There is also a need for composition of objects and incremental specification using inheritance. Thus, for use in a distributed systems context formal descriptions must support this paradigm.

3.2.2 Abstraction

By their very nature a specification or architectural model must not be overly prescriptive and must define a framework for building compliant systems that is sufficiently abstract to support all relevant realisations. This is particularly true of frameworks such as ODP, which seeks to embrace a huge spectrum of target systems. Therefore, it is essential that the use of particular formal notations does not compromise this level of abstraction.

3.2.3 Support for Formal Reasoning

Ideally a formal technique should also support formal reasoning. Thus, rigorous and usable semantic definitions must be provided by formal techniques. For example, relations between specifications such as refinement and behavioural subtyping are defined in the ODP Reference Model, and corresponding semantic relations in formal techniques need to be available for the instantiation of these concepts in particular notations.

3.2.4 Dynamic Reconfiguration

As discussed in Section 1.1, the shift of emphasis from fixed location to process migration means that distributed systems can be modified and extended during their lifetime. This is a very important requirement, since the user and system needs may alter dynamically. For example, faulty components may need to be replaced, or it may be desirable to enable components to migrate to enhance performance and availability. In addition, the explosion in availability of mobile techniques (laptops, mobile phones, etc.) has further emphasized the importance of this topic. The majority of semantic models of distribution and concurrency, for example, labelled transition systems [Mil89], event structures [Win88] or Petri nets [Rei82], allow only static configuration. The dynamic reconfiguration requirement is prompting some of the most significant current research in concurrency theory.

3.2.5 Subtyping and Inheritance

As discussed in Section 1.3, object models offer benefits in terms of encapsulation and classification, and this can support reuse as well as maintenance of legacy systems. To do so, the relationships between objects and their classification need to be documented, and thus issues of subtyping and inheritance are important. This requires that formal techniques can explicitly support such notions in addition to offering encapsulation and composition provided by primitive object-based notations.

3.2.6 Continuous and Concurrent Evolution

The shift of emphasis from sequential execution to concurrency and from fixed configuration to continuous evolution has profound effects on specification and programming notations. As commented previously, synchronization between components must be achieved by explicit communication between them. This leads to requirements on notations that can support such communication and that can be mapped to multithreaded programming models, as well as compositional specifications and frameworks.

3.2.7 Nonfunctional Requirements

Broadly speaking, a requirement is nonfunctional if it cannot be represented purely in terms of a sequence of interactions between communicating objects. Examples of nonfunctional requirements arise in the area of quality of service and security. Such requirements are important in supporting multimedia interaction in open distributed systems. The expression of real-time quality of service constraints, such as latency, throughput and jitter, is of particular significance. The provision of support for continuous media, through stream bindings and real-time synchronization, imposes demanding requirements on specification notations for distributed systems.

3.2.8 The Development Process

Section 1.2.6 described the requirements that distributed systems place on the development process and stressed the need for techniques to help manage the complexity of specifications. This gives rise to the use of viewpoints and other specification architectures as a means to cope with complexity, modularisation and compositionality. This in turn places requirements on formal techniques so that they can be used within these frameworks.

For example, it became clear early that a single formal description technique would not have the generality or expressiveness to support the full range of ODP specifications. Even wide spectrum techniques such as RAISE [Lan92] are not able to embrace all needs. Thus, it is now accepted that a multiple language specification paradigm must be employed and that mechanisms must be provided to enable these formal techniques to co-exist.

3.3 A Road Map

The work described in this book in essence describes how formal methods have met the challenges previously outlined, and the material is structured into a series of parts, each one broadly tackling one or more of the themes identified earlier.

3.3.1 Specification Notations

This part constitutes a survey of specification notations, and in particular it considers a collection of related techniques and shows how they support object-oriented concepts. As previously suggested, by the historical nature of their development, early formal methods were limited in their ability to support the requirements identified previously. In particular, techniques such as LOTOS, SDL, Z, and so on, did not offer explicit support for object orientation. This was entirely understandable given when that they were developed and the application areas that they were targeted at. For example, LOTOS, SDL and Estelle grew out of the protocol engineering world, and in particular the needs of OSI, while Z grew out of largely sequential concerns.

However, the rapid growth of object-orientation effected not only programming notations, but also specification notations. Furthermore, the encapsulation offered by object orientation was an opportunity to solve issues of structuring large-scale formal specifications. These concerns led to work on object-oriented extensions of many existing formal notations. The convergence of distributed systems to object-based technologies furthered this trend, as did the increasing use of object-oriented programming languages.

Part Two introduces four techniques that offer object-oriented extensions to underlying notations. SDL is a language that describes systems as asynchronous communicating processes and uses extended finite state machines to do so. It grew out of the need for rigorous specification in telecommunications, and its industrial use has become widespread. There are several reasons for this, but its popularity has certainly been enhanced by its graphical format and industrial-strength tool set. It has also benefited from four yearly revisions, including for example the introduction of object-oriented facilities in SDL 96 and alignment with UML in SDL 2000.

SDL is in many ways a semiformal notation; LOTOS, on the other hand, offers a more formal algebraic approach and, in particular, a process algebraic approach. In addition to the differing levels of formality, the communication model is different since, in contrast to SDL, communication in LOTOS is synchronous. LOTOS has recently undergone revision giving rise to a language called E-LOTOS, which includes quantative time, a new data typing part and greater provision for modularity. The latter, whilst falling short of complete object-orientation, does offer the user certain provisions in that respect.

Z differs from SDL and LOTOS in that it does not offer an explicit model of concurrency or communication; rather, it is based on simple set theory and predicate logic. Furthermore, over the years it has grown to become one of the most popular specification notations available. In particular, it is based on simple mathematical foundations, and it offers a very elegant way of structuring this mathematics using *schemas* to provide a specification of the system under consideration. Z, along with Object-Z, B [Abr96] and VDM, are often called state-based languages because they specify a system by describing the states that it can be in together with a description of how the state evolves over time. In effect, a specification in one of these languages builds a *model* of the system.

Because of the lack of an explicit model of concurrency, Z is a seemingly unlikely candidate for distributed system specification; however, it has gained a certain currency due to its elegant handling of data aspects. In particular, Z is able to specify the format of information and operations to access and manipulate information without prescribing a particular implementation. Therefore Z is recognised as highly appropriate for information modelling and, in particular, the ODP information viewpoint.

The abstract data-typing (ADT) languages incorporated into LOTOS and SDL are also possible vehicles for information specification as found in the information viewpoint. However, the correspondence between such ADT notations and the information language concepts is not as natural as it is for Z. In particular, many of the information viewpoint concepts suggest an interpretation that uses both the process and data parts of LOTOS and SDL. Furthermore, it has been suggested that the ADT definitions are too concrete and force overspecification in information modelling (although the Object-Z approach may be considered as based on ADTs, and this does not force overspecification); for example, see [FPV93] for a comparison of an information model of the ODP Trader in Z and LOTOS.

Object-Z offers the same facilities as Z, but in addition it rectifies the rather flat approach to specification in Z by adding constructs to facilitate specification in an object-oriented style. This also provides an explicit communication mechanism, however, concurrency remains implicit rather than explicit.

The final notation that we consider in this part is UML, which has become the de facto informal design notation amongst many users. However, even though UML is clearly informal in spirit, it builds on many ideas found in formal notations. This is particularly true for the aspects concerned with behavioural specification, such as OCL (drawing heavily on Z) and state diagrams. This is further enhanced by the alignment of SDL and UML, and UML clearly provides a vehicle for introducing notions of formality to many who might otherwise have remained unaware.

3.3.2 Dynamic Reconfiguration

This part discusses approaches to specification where dynamic reconfiguration is explicitly supported. Dynamic reconfiguration, or mobility, concerns the ability to support object identity, explicit creation of objects and the passing of object identities.

Although SDL and Estelle have some facilities for describing mobility, they are limited. It is also possible to develop a specification style for a language like LO-TOS, which mimics mobility. For example, Najm and Stefani [NS91a] describe how mobility can be built into LOTOS by using a particular format of actions within a restricted process style. However, the use of synchronization is not completely natural and neither is the semantic interpretation of the style; in particular, in order to interpret specifications as configurations of objects, a second level of interpretation needs to be built on top of the standard LOTOS semantics.

As suggested by the previous discussion, employing a mobile object-oriented specification style with, for example, LOTOS generates rather artificial specifications. The alternative approach is to use a calculus that explicitly handles mobility. Perhaps the most well known is Milner et al.'s π-calculus [MPW92] and its descendants, the Polyadic π-calculus [Mil93] and PICT [PT94]. Other important approaches include Actors [Agh86], HACL [KY94], OL1 [NS91b] and OC [Nie92]. These calculi contain primitive constructs for sending and receiving channel names along channels, creating channels and running processes in parallel. Many of these calculi have been used to interpret object-oriented programming paradigms, for example, PICT and PICCOLA. Other approaches worthy of mention, since they are ODP oriented, are Mobile LOTOS [NSF94] and the direct semantics for the ODP computational viewpoint [NS97], both due to Najm and Stefani.

In this part we introduce three techniques with explicit support for mobility: Actors, the π-calculus and mobile ambients. The Actor model and π-calculus are aimed at a similar set of concerns, and both offer a model of concurrent computation that supports synchronization and communication of both values and names.

Chapter 8 introduces the Actor model and illustrates its use with the specification and development of a cache coherence protocol. Chapter 9 then discusses in some depth the π-calculus and related work; this includes PICT, a programming language based on the π-calculus, developed mainly by Pierce and Turner.

One aspect that the π-calculus does not cover is that of security, and the ambient calculus described in Chapter 10 addresses this point by explicit consideration of administrative domains. The key idea here is that an ambient is a named, bounded place in which communication takes place. The boundary is important because it represents the administrative domain of interest, and the name is used to control access.

3.3.3 Subtyping

Subtyping and inheritance are key issues in building distributed systems. In particular, subtyping provides support for incremental development, reuse and the use of matching in trading. In this part we consider the issue of subtyping in some depth.

Subtyping is defined in terms of substitutability: type A is a subtype of type B if and only if objects of type A may be used in any situation where an object of type B was expected, without the object's environment being able to tell the difference.

Therefore an object of a type can masquerade as, or stand in for, an object of any of its supertypes.

Subtyping is a central concept in object-oriented development; however, its particular importance in distributed systems arises because it is tied to the important problem of *matching service offers to service requests*. Distributed object-oriented models often contain a repository of services that are currently being offered by objects in the system, for example, the CORBA type repository or the ODP Trader, and clients make requests to this repository for services that they require. Now importantly, in order for a service offer to satisfactorily meet the service request, we need exactly to check that the service offer is a subtype of the service request.

Inheritance plays a central role in obtaining reuse in object-oriented programming models. However, unrestricted approaches to inheritance are problematic in a distributed systems setting. For example, *implementation inheritance*, by which subclasses re-use the implementation code of superclasses, implies that changes to the superclass must be propagated to update all of the subclasses, which is not always feasible in a distributed setting. ODP for example, restricts itself to *incremental inheritance*, whereby *class specifications* can be modified when generating subclasses, but implementations are not reused. However, even incremental inheritance will not guarantee a clean relationship between subclass and superclass (for example, it is well known that subtyping is not preserved by inheritance [CHC90]).

Two forms of subtyping can be identified: signature subtyping and behavioural subtyping, where the term signature refers to the set of operations (with their associated input and output parameters) in the interface of an object. Signature subtyping is a basic interpretation which requires that for all operations in the supertype there exists a corresponding operation in the subtype (corresponding typically meaning 'with the same name') and correctly related parameters, that is, co- and contravariance [ISO98]. Signature subtyping ensures that if a client invokes a supertype operation on a subtype object, a failure will not result because the subtype object does not contain the operation in its interface. Therefore it seeks to ensure that objects are only sent messages that they can interpret.

However, in many circumstances signature-based subtyping is too weak (that is, it identifies subtypes in situations that are inappropriate), and we often need to consider stronger, behavioural, notions of subtyping that do not restrict themselves to the comparison of signatures, but rather ensure that the behaviour of objects is correctly related. One setting in which signature subtyping is not sufficient is when moving to objects with nonuniform service availability.

We begin this part of the book with a discussion of subtyping in distributed systems in general. Chapter 11 motivates the use of subtyping and inheritance in distributed systems, and then looks at signature-based subtyping in some of the techniques and platforms introduced in Chapter 1, comparing their relative strengths. Behavioural subtyping, as a notion stronger than signature-based subtyping, is then introduced and this theme is expanded in the subsequent chapters. In particular, the following two chapters focus first on subtyping in a state-based framework and then subtyping in a process algebraic model.

Liskov and Wing, in Chapter 12, motivate the need for behavioural subtyping with a number of examples before introducing definitions of behavioural subtyping in a simple state-based language. An alternative framework in which to investigate subtyping is a process algebra model. Chapter 13 provides such an investigation, looking at the problem of typing in object and process calculi. The technical discussion takes place in a variant off the π-calculus and thus provides a link to the work described in Part Three.

3.3.4 Concurrent OO Languages

The application of object-oriented principles to the concurrent programming setting has been investigated extensively, with for example a large number of specification and programming language realisations, for example, Actors, Hybrid [Nie87], ABCL [Yon90], POOL [Ame90]. Research on concurrent object-oriented programming is of central relevance to the topic at hand since distributed systems are of course concurrent: components possess their own local thread of control and evolve in parallel. In fact, a lot of the theoretical work on object-oriented distributed systems has its origins in the concurrent object-oriented programming domain, for example, work on process calculus models [Nie95, Nie92, Pap92, PT94].

Reflection is becoming an important tool in the design of distributed systems (e.g., the use of Reflective Java). Reflection is a mechanism that enables programs to modify their own implementation at run-time. This is important in distributed systems because it is highly relevant to the problem of dynamic reconfiguration. Chapter 14 reviews the theoretical basis for reflection, its relationship to concurrent object-oriented languages and its applications in distributed systems.

Inheritance is a key concept in object-oriented specification, design and programming, potentially enabling code reuse. Recently these object-oriented concepts have been applied to the concurrent world, resulting in the development of concurrent object-oriented programming. Chapter 15 discusses inheritance in the context of concurrent object-oriented programming calculi. The introduction of inheritance into the concurrent object-oriented paradigm leads to inheritance anomalies (which make code reuse practically infeasible). The issue of the inheritance anomaly is addressed in some depth in Chapter 15.

3.3.5 Nonfunctional Requirements

This part is concerned with the support needed to express nonfunctional requirements of distributed systems using formal notations. One important source of nonfunctional requirements is multimedia, where three issues are particularly crucial:

- *Continuous Interaction.* Traditional distributed systems' communication paradigms support the interaction of a logically singular character, for example, a remote procedure call. However, the advent of multimedia means that this is not sufficient and interaction of an ongoing nature must be provided, for example, continuous transmission of video frames in a video conferencing application. This, for example, is known as a *flow* in ODP terminology.

- *Quality of Service (QoS).* Timing constraints have to be associated with such continuous interactions. For example, if in a video conferencing application the end-to-end latency delay between the generation of frames and their presentation becomes too great, the sense of simultaneous interaction will be lost. These timing constraints are called quality of service parameters. Typical QoS properties include: *end-to-end latency* between the generation of packets and their presentation, *throughput*, that is, the rate at which packets are presented, and *jitter*, which quantifies the variability of latency. Jitter ensures that there is not an unacceptable variability around the optimum presentation time; for example, if one packet is presented quite early and the next is presented relatively late an unacceptable stutter in the presentation may result.

- *Real-Time Synchronization.* It is also often necessary to synchronize multiple media flows. For example, in order to enforce lip-synchronization, video and audio flows must be synchronized. Application-specific real-time synchronization also arises, for example, if captions need to be presented at particular points in a video presentation.

This part provides both a survey of approaches to multimedia specification using formal techniques as well as focusing on one particular approach, namely, the use of E-LOTOS.

The focus in the first chapter is on the use of a single language, here E-LOTOS, for the specification of QoS requirements and constraints. In particular, an in-depth specification of an ODP multicast binding object is presented. This chapter therefore builds on the introduction to ODP found in Chapter 2, as well as the introduction to the E-LOTOS language given in Chapter 5.

The second chapter widens the scope of the discussion to survey both single-language and dual-language approaches. Single-language approaches, as their name suggests, use one specification notation to describe all aspects of the system behaviour, including the basic functionality, the overall QoS requirements as well as the timings associated with individual events. The use of E-LOTOS, detailed in the previous chapter in this part, is an example of a single-language approach.

Dual-language approaches, on the other hand, apply a basic separation of concerns and specify the system functionality in one language with the required QoS properties being described in another language (for example, a real-time or temporal logic). Going further, multiparadigm approaches use multiple languages to describe the behaviour of different aspects of the system design and requirements.

3.3.6 Development Architectures

The final part of the book looks at the development process and, in particular, the role of development architectures, viewpoints and the associated problems of composition in the construction of distributed systems.

The theme linking the chapters in this part is that the complexity of the development process has a direct impact on which facilities should be provided by programming and specification languages.

The first chapter focuses on components and composition and introduces a language, PICCOLA, that models components and compositional abstractions by means of communicating concurrent agents. The particular approach that is taken is that applications are components plus scripts, the latter describing how the components are plugged together. The language is defined in terms of the π-calculus. Chapter 18 describes this link and then illustrates the language via a number of examples showing how composition of components is achieved.

Chapter 19 then discusses development issues in specification and in particular specification architectures. These are concerned with the structure of specifications and are closely related to architectural semantics in which architectural concepts are represented in particular specification languages.

Interest in architectural semantics arose during the work on a formal description of the protocol layers of the OSI model. Specifically, it was realised that specifications of protocol entities in different techniques could not be combined easily. This was caused by the totally different interpretations of the OSI concepts, such as service access point, in different formal notations. For example, LOTOS uses synchronous communication, while Estelle and SDL use an asynchronous model. The purpose of an architectural semantics is to provide a resolution of this variety of interpretation, by tying the different formal techniques to a single set of architectural concepts. Specifically, interpretations of these architectural concepts are made in each formal technique, thus providing an unambiguous intermediate between the formal notations.

The need for an architectural semantics was recognized from the start of the work on the ODP Reference Model and is reflected in the inclusion of the architectural semantics as Part 4 of the standard. This provides an interpretation of the ODP modelling and specification concepts in LOTOS, Estelle, SDL and Z. A further important objective of the architectural semantics work is to subject the definitions in ODP to a rigorous examination. In this sense the application of formalism forces standards writers to think deeply about the definitions that they are making.

Chapter 19 discusses the origins of architectural semantics and the related issue of specification templates. The purpose of the latter is to code up the architectural semantics in a form that is usable by a specifier by providing templates that will produce specifications that are compatible with the architecture. Commonly occurring components or commonly occurring combinations of components both fall

under the remit of specification templates. The chapter concludes with a discussion
of architectural semantics in the ODP and TINA frameworks.

The final chapter continues the discussion of development by looking at the use
of formal methods in ODP viewpoint modelling. As discussed earlier, there are five
viewpoints defined in the ODP Reference Model: Enterprise, Information, Computational, Engineering and Technology, and they are each partial views of the complete
system specification. However, these viewpoints are not independent. Some items
can, therefore, occur in more than one viewpoint, and there is a set of consistency
constraints arising from the correspondences between terms in two viewpoint languages and the statements relating the various terms within each language. The
checking of such consistency is an important part of demonstrating the correctness
of the full set of specifications.

However, an additional complexity arises because different formal notations are
likely to be used in different viewpoints. This is because the features of the formal
techniques variously support the required abstraction levels and modelling concepts
of each particular viewpoint. This complicates their use in the viewpoints and the
consistency checking process.

Chapter 20 discusses the problem of consistency by developing a case study involving the specification of viewpoints using different formal methods. None of Z,
LOTOS or SDL are seen as suitable candidates for the enterprise viewpoint language
on their own. Enterprise modelling entails statements of policy, of organizational
objectives and obligations that must be discharged. Most current enterprise modelling is performed in 'informal' diagrammatic notations. However, the semantics
of the informal diagrammatic notations is usually not specified precisely, leading to
incomplete, ambiguous and unverifiable specifications. Chapter 20 overcomes this
by using an approach that uses UML together with a tailored policy specification
language based around Object-Z.

This is useful because, as we have already discussed, Z and Object-Z are well
suited in many respects to specification in the information viewpoint, and the case
study in Chapter 20 uses Object-Z for this viewpoint. The need to specify interaction and synchronization, however, prevents Object-Z or Z from being a suitable
choice for computational viewpoint specification. In contrast, LOTOS, SDL and Estelle all offer considerable support for computational viewpoint specification, and in
this chapter E-LOTOS is used as the basis for a brief computational viewpoint specification. Consistency checking between the resultant specifications is then briefly
discussed.

3.4 Conclusions

The subsequent chapters discuss this material in greater depth. Of course the spectrum of techniques and issues that this book covers is necessarily incomplete. In
particular, there are many important techniques that for space considerations we
have been unable to include. For example, we have unfortunately not been able to

devote space to any of the following influential approaches: algebraic specification, such as Goguen's Obj [Gog00] and its object-oriented and concurrency extensions; see for example [Veg97], Estelle [ISO87b], Meseguer's rewriting logic [Mes98], linear logics [KY95], object-based temporal logic [DKR00], the Join Calculus [FLMR97] and Lamport's Temporal Logic of Actions [Lam94]. However, the material included is a representative sample of the spectrum of available techniques that are important in the specification and design of object-based distributed systems.

Bibliography

[Abr96] J. R. Abrial. *The B-Book: Assigning Programs to Meanings.* Cambridge University Press, 1996.

[Agh86] G. Agha. *Actors: A Model of Concurrent Computation in Distributed Systems.* MIT Press, 1986.

[Ame90] P. America. A parallel object-oriented language with inheritance and subtyping. *SIGPLAN Notices*, 25(10):161–168, October 1990.

[BB88] T. Bolognesi and E. Brinksma. Introduction to the ISO Specification Language LOTOS. *Computer Networks and ISDN Systems*, 14(1):25–59, 1988.

[BRJ99] G. Booch, J. Rumbaugh, and I. Jacobson. *The Unified Modeling Language User Guide.* Addison-Wesley, 1999.

[CCI88] CCITT Z.100. *Specification and Description Language SDL*, 1988.

[CHC90] W. R. Cook, W. L. Hill, and P. S. Canning. Inheritance is not subtyping. In *17th ACM Symposium on Principles of Programming Languages*, pages 125–135. ACM, 1990.

[DKR00] D. Distefano, J-P. Katoen, and A. Rensink. On a temporal logic for object-based systems. In S. F. Smith and C. L. Talcott, editors, *Formal Methods for Open Object-Based Distributed Systems IV (FMOODS 2000)*, pages 305–325. Kluwer, 2000.

[FL98] S. Fischer and S. Leue. Formal methods for broadband and multimedia systems. *Computer Networks and ISDN Systems, Special Issue on Trends in Formal Description Techniques and Their Applications*, 1998.

[FLMR97] C. Fournet, C. Laneve, L. Maranget, and D. R´eny. Implicit typing à la ML for the join-calculus. In *CONCUR '97: Proceedings of the 8th International Conference on Concurrency Theory*, volume 1243 of *Lecture Notes in Computer Science*, pages 196–212. Springer-Verlag, 1997.

[FPV93] J. Fischer, A. Prinz, and A. Vogel. Different FDT's confronted with different ODP-viewpoints of the trader. In J. C. P. Woodcock and P. G. Larsen, editors, *FME'93: Industrial Strength Formal Methods*, volume 670 of *Lecture Notes in Computer Science*, pages 332–350. Springer-Verlag, 1993.

[Gog00] J. Goguen. The Obj family, 2000. http://www-cse.ucsd.edu/users/goguen/sys/obj.html.

[Hoa85] C. A. R. Hoare. *Communicating Sequential Processes.* Prentice Hall, 1985.

[ISO84] ISO IS 7498. Information Processing Systems – Open Systems Interconnection – Basic Reference Model, 1984.

[ISO87a] ISO 8807. *LOTOS: A Formal Description Technique based on the Temporal Ordering of Observational Behaviour*, July 1987.

[ISO87b] ISO 9074. *Estelle, a Formal Description Technique Based on an Extended State Transition Model*, June 1987.

[ISO98] ISO/IEC IS 10746. *Open Distributed Processing Reference Model – Parts 1 to 4.* 1998.

[Jon89]   C. B. Jones. *Systematic Software Development using VDM.* Prentice Hall, 1989.

[KY94]   N. Kobayashi and A. Yonezawa. Type-theoretic foundations for concurrent object-oriented prog ramming. In *ACM SIGPLAN Conference on Object-Oriented Programming (OOPSLA' 94)*, 1994.

[KY95]   N. Kobayashi and A. Yonezawa. Asynchronous communication model based on linear logic. *Formal Aspects of Computing*, 7(2):113–149, 1995.

[Lam94]   L. Lamport. The temporal logic of actions. *ACM Transactions on Programming Languages and Systems*, 16(3):872–923, 1994.

[Lan92]   RAISE Language Group. *The RAISE Specification Language.* Prentice Hall, 1992.

[Mes98]   J. Meseguer. A logical framework for distributed systems and communication protocols. In A. Cavalli A. Budkowski and E. Najm, editors, *Formal Description Techniques and Protocol, Specification, Testing and Validation.* Kluwer, November 1998.

[Mil89]   R. Milner. *Communication and Concurrency.* Prentice-Hall, 1989.

[Mil93]   R. Milner. The Polyadic Pi-calculus: a tutorial. In *Logic and Algebra of Specification*, pages 203–246. Springer, 1993.

[MP92]   Z. Manna and A. Pnueli. *The Temporal Logic of Reactive and Concurrent Systems.* Springer, 1992.

[MPW92]   R. Milner, J. Parrow, and D. Walker. A calculus of mobile processes. *Information and Computation*, 100:1–77, 1992.

[Nie87]   O. Nierstrasz. Active objects in hybrid. *ACM SIGPLAN Notices*, 22(12):243–253, 1987. *Proceedings of OOPSLA'87.*

[Nie92]   O. Nierstrasz. Towards an object calculus. In *ECOOP'91 Workshop on Object-Based Concurrent Computing*, volume 612 of *Lecture Notes in Computer Science*, pages 1–20. Springer-Verlag, 1992.

[Nie95]   O. Nierstrasz. Regular t ypes for active objects. In *Object-oriented Software Composition*, pages 99–120. Prentice-Hall, 1995.

[NS91a]   E. Najm and J-B. Stefani. Dynamic configuration in LOTOS. In K. R. Parker and G. A. Rose, editors, *Formal Description Techniques, IV.* North-Holland, 1991.

[NS91b]   E. Najm and J-B. Stefani. Object based concurrency: A process calculus analysis. In *4th International Joint Conference on the Theory and Practice of Software Development, TAPSOFT 91*, 1991.

[NS97]   E. Najm and J-B. Stefani. Computational models for open distributed systems. In H. Bowman and J. Derrick, editors, *Formal Methods for Open Object-Based Distributed Systems II (FMOODS'97)*, pages 157–176. Chapman and Hall, 1997.

[NSF94]   E. Najm, J-B. Stefani, and A. Fevrier. *Introducing Mobility in LOTOS.* ISO/IEC JTC1/SC21/WG1 approved AFNOR contribution, July 1994.

[Pap92]   M. Papathomas. A unifying framework for process calculus semantics of concurrent object-oriented languages. In *ECOOP'91 Workshop on Object-Based Concurrent Computing*, volume 612 of *Lecture Notes in Computer Science*, pages 53–79. Springer-Verlag, 1992.

[PT94]   B. C. Pierce and D. N. Turner. Concurrent objects in a process calculus. In *Theory and Practice of Parallel Programming (TPPP)*, Lecture Notes in Computer Science. Springer-Verlag, 1994.

[Rei82]   W. Reisig. *Petri Nets, An Introduction.* Springer-Verlag, 1982.

[Smi00]   G. Smith. *The Object-Z Specification Language.* Kluwer, 2000.

[Spi92]   J. M. Spivey. *The Z notation: A Reference Manual.* Prentice Hall, second edition, 1992.

[Tur93]   K. J. Turner, editor. *Using Formal Description Techniques, An Introduction to Estelle, LOTOS and SDL.* Wiley, 1993.

[Veg97]   S. Veglioni. Objects as abstract machines. In H. Bowman and J. Derrick, editors, *Formal Methods for Open Object-Based Distributed Systems II (FMOODS'97)*, pages 277–292. Chapman and Hall, 1997.

[Weg87]   P. Wegner. Dimensions of object-based language design. In N. Meyrowitz, editor, *Proceedings of the Conference on Object-Oriented Programming Systems and Applications (OOPSLA'87)*, volume 22 of *ACM-SIGPLAN*, pages 162–182. ACM, 1987.

[Win88]   G. Winskel. An introduction to event structures. In *Linear Time, Branching Time and Partial Order in Logics and Models of Concurrency*, volume 354 of *Lecture Notes in Computer Science*. Springer-Verlag, 1988.

[Yon90]   A. Yonezawa, editor. *ABCL: An Object-Oriented Concurrent System*. MIT, 1990.

Part Two

Specification Notations

4

Finite State Machine Based: SDL

Richard O. Sinnott

GMD-FOKUS Berlin, Germany

Dieter Hogrefe

University of Lübeck, Lübe ck, Germany

4.1 Introduction

SDL [ITU96] is a language for specifying and describing systems. The basic idea of SDL is to describe systems in the form of asynchronously communicating processes represented as extended finite state machines. For this reason SDL is particularly suited to model and develop parallel (e.g., distributed) communicating systems.

In this chapter we do not give a full presentation of all of the features of SDL; rather, we introduce those aspects of the language which will subsequently be used for emphasising the applicability of SDL together with its associated tools for developing specifications of distributed systems. To this end, we develop a specification of a component that is crucial to realising the dynamicity inherent to distributed systems: a trader. Specifically we show how the OMG Trader [OMG97] can be specified by using SDL and its associated tools. Other examples of formal specifications of traders are given in [DD93, FPV93, Sin97, ST97], as well as the other chapters in this part.

For a more detailed description of the SDL language, the reader is referred to the recommendation Z.100 [ITU96], one of the tutorial books, for example, [EHB97, OFMP+94, R. 93], or introductory articles [Bra96]. As an aside we note that SDL has a wide body of literature associated with it. It is likely that this, along with its intuitive syntax and the availability of numerous tools for developing and reasoning about specifications [Hum99, Tel99, Ver99], is the reason that SDL is one of the most popular specification languages around today.

4.1.1 History of SDL

Toward the end of the sixties it was identified that in many areas natural language was inadequate for describing complex behaviours. This was especially the case in telecommunications systems, where increasingly complex functions were required to be described and interpreted exactly. This problem was exacerbated by the international nature of telecommunications, that is, where the description of these functions was not always in the mother tongue of the different manufacturers expecting to implement the functions, yet with the strict requirement that these implementations were expected to interwork with one another.

To address this problem, the International Telephone and Telegraph Consultative Committee (CCITT) – who are now called the International Telecommunications Union (ITU-T) – identified that a standard specification language was needed. This language was to be used to describe precisely complex situations and be intelligible so that readers worldwide could interpret it unambiguously and uniquely. This was only feasible if the syntax as well as the semantics of the language was internationally standardized.

One of the fundamental design criteria in the development of SDL was its ease of use. As an aside we note that ease of use is an issue that is often ignored by developers of formal specification languages, leading to the reputation that formal methods are too often overly mathematical and obscure. SDL, with its intuitive graphical notation, does not suffer from this shortcoming.

All innovations that were incorporated into the initial design of the SDL language originated from groups of people involved in the specification of complex systems. These were primarily employees from telecommunications companies involved in both hardware and software development. Universities and other scientific institutes initially played a subordinate role in the development of SDL. It wasn't until the end of the seventies, with the appearance of scientific institutes largely dedicated to telecommunications, that work on the mathematical underpinnings of SDL was performed. This work was necessary for three main reasons. First, several initial and incompatible versions of the language existed, with each having features incorporated for use in their own particular problem domains. This was primarily caused by the intuitive interpretation model, on which the language was based, which allowed for ad-hoc extensions and modifications. The effect of this was that almost 20 years went by before SDL reached a stable state. This period was especially problematic for users because existing specifications frequently became obsolete or invalid due to language changes.

Second, the development of language-supported tools is very difficult if the language is not clearly defined. In particular, tools for the automatic analysis of specifications cannot be developed under these circumstances. It is also extremely difficult to 'correctly' (whatever this term may mean) specify complex systems when the language used to describe those systems is itself not clearly defined.

Third, the real objective of developing an artificial language for the description of complex systems precisely and unambiguously could not be attained if the language itself was open to interpretation. These three problems gave the impetus for embracing a formal syntax and semantics. The CCITT Study Group 10 published the first formal SDL language version in 1988. In 1992 this version was enhanced by object-oriented features that we discuss in Section 4.1.9. The year 1996 was one of consolidation, with few major changes but mostly error correction. SDL 2000 [ITU00] brings more radical changes to meet the demands of the users. These include a new data model, harmonization with the data-typing language ASN.1 [ISO90a, ISO90b] and alignment with the Unified Modeling Language (UML) [BRJ99]. Other useful features such as remote process creation have also been introduced.

We note that these language updates and improvements that take place every four years are another crucial factor to the success of SDL. The language and hence the associated tools evolve to incorporate current software development approaches. We focus in this chapter on how the language and associated tools address developments in the area of object-oriented distributed systems.

The application range of SDL is broad. Prominent application examples within the standard area are the ISDN protocols [BG96], the signalling system No. 7 [IT96b], intelligent network services [LTT96] and next-generation telecommunication services [SK99a, SK99b]. Almost every major manufacturer of telecommunication systems uses SDL in one form or another.

4.1.2 Basic Concepts of SDL

The basic element in SDL is the process. A process is represented in SDL as an extended finite state machine that can communicate with other processes and the environment of the specification by sending and receiving signals via channels and signal routes. An extended finite state machine differs from a finite state machine in that it can not only store its states, but it also can hold and manipulate data. This data exists in the form of values and variables.

The model on which SDL is based is determined by the characterisation of a process. A process is either undergoing a state transition or is in a state and waiting for an input. There is exactly one input queue for each process. When the process receives an input during a state transition, the input can be stored in the input queue. The input queue and the process operate independently and in parallel. If two inputs reach a process simultaneously, they are buffered, in general, in the input queue in random order.

The dynamic behaviour of an SDL specification is described exclusively by processes that coexist with one another. A process can create another process with the created process immediately becoming equal in ranking to the creating process. A process can disappear from the system only through self-termination.

4.1.3 The Two Syntactic Forms of SDL: SDL/GR and SDL/PR

The SDL language has two syntactic forms, both of which are based on the same semantic model. One is called SDL/GR (SDL Graphical Representation) and the other, SDL/PR (SDL Phrase Representation). Each language element has a representation in SDL/GR and one in SDL/PR. An example of this is given in Figure 4.1, which illustrates a simple alternative that can be used within the specification of a state transition.

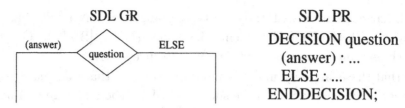

Fig. 4.1. Simple alternative in SDL/GR and SDL/PR.

A specification written in SDL/GR can be transformed into an exactly and semantically fully equivalent SDL/PR representation. SDL is one of the few languages that has a completely defined graphical syntax. Initially only the graphic form of SDL existed, since it was assumed that graphics would be a user-friendly specification method.

With the increasing popularity of SDL, however, there was a growing need for machine-based document processing. Due to the lack of high-quality graphic terminal equipment, the SDL documents had to be processed largely by hand, a very time-consuming effort, particularly when modifying a document. This gave rise to the development of SDL/PR.

Today, SDL/GR can also be machine-processed and SDL/PR appears to be superfluous. However, even if this were the case, the existence of SDL/PR still has a positive side effect. Without a conventional form of the language, similar to programming languages, the development of a formal syntax and semantics would probably not have been feasible. We note that not all language elements are represented differently between SDL/GR and SDL/PR, and in fact a subset of SDL/GR is syntactically equivalent to a subset of SDL/PR; for example, the declaration of variables in both representations is identical. The examples in the following sections are limited to SDL/GR.

4.1.4 States and State Transitions

As stated, a process in SDL is given as an extended finite state machine, that is, states and state transitions are used for describing its behaviour. In the theory of finite state machines, states and state transitions are often represented with the aid of directed graphs, with the nodes representing states and the directed edges representing the state transitions. In the example given in Figure 4.2, which illustrates the state transition behaviour of a protocol entity during the connection setup phase, the finite state machine has the state set {*disconnected, waiting, connected*}.

When an input is received, the finite state machine can leave its current state, attain a new state and, as a result, produce an output. Such a state transition is represented in the graph by a directed edge, starting from the old state to the new state and the pair *Input/Output*.

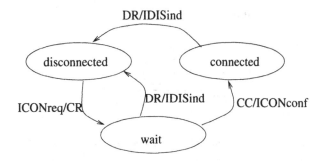

Fig. 4.2. State transition diagram for simple protocol.

In SDL states are graphically described with the state symbol shown in Figure 4.3. Inputs, outputs and starting states also have special symbols defined.

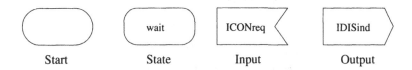

Fig. 4.3. SDL constructs sssociated with state transitions.

With the aid of finite state machines, behaviour can be described. In the graphic desciiption of the finite state machine in Figure 4.2, the viewer can at best implicitly determine that the *disconnected* state should be the first state. Generally, intuition cannot be relied on. For defining the initial state there is a start symbol in SDL that is also shown in Figure 4.3.

Figure 4.4 shows how the behaviour in Figure 4.2 would be described in SDL in the form of a process. The frame around a process diagram is optional, if no further information is located in a document on the same side. If additional text is located on the same page, the frame clearly defines what actually belongs to the process.

In SDL there are various possibilities to prevent the repetition of identical specification sections. For example, when input *DR* is received by the initiator process in states *wait* and *connected*, the same output is given (*IDISind*). To prevent this repetition, multiple states can be defined in a single state symbol as illustrated in Figure 4.5, which shows an alternative but equivalent specification for the initiator.

A second possibility to avoid text repetition is the asterisk (*) notation. An asterisk in a state symbol signifies that the following inputs are possible in any state. In addition there is the dash notation (-). A dash in a state symbol at the end of a transition means that a transition to the same state occurs. These examples illustrate that certain 'syntactic sugar' exists in SDL to help make the life of a specifier easier.

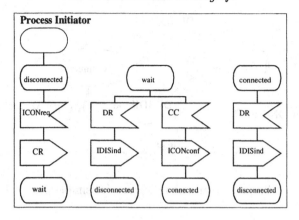

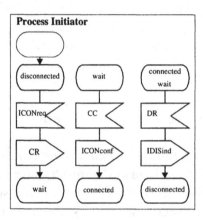

Fig. 4.5. Alternative representation of simple protocol.

4.1.5 Time Definition in SDL

In a specification, time conditions often need to be specified. In SDL this is implemented with the timer mechanism. A timer is similar to a signal. The timer mechanism stimulates a process as a function of the predefined time by placing a timer signal into the input queue of the process. Here we explain the timer mechanism through an example.

In our protocol specification the wait for the connection confirmation *CC* is to be timed. Upon expiry of the waiting period the connection is to be cancelled automatically. Figure 4.6 shows the required extensions to the initiator process given previously.

First a timer must be defined in the process diagram. This is done by using a text symbol. This text symbol also can contain other information, for example, the declaration of variables. Any number of timers can be defined in a process.

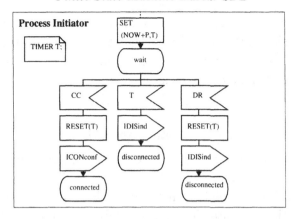

Fig. 4.6. Timed extension to simple protocol.

4.1.6 Declaration and Use of Data

As an extended finite state machine, a process can hold and manage data represented in the form of values and variables. The declaration of data in SDL/GR and SDL/PR is identical and initiated with the keyword DCL. Like the timer definition, a variable declaration is written into a text symbol, which can be positioned anywhere in the diagram.

During a state transition a process can use and manipulate its local data. Data manipulation can be specified with the TASK symbol, which can perform assignments as illustrated in Figure 4.7, where the counter variable is assigned the value 0. Of course the type must be compatible.

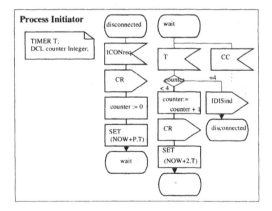

Fig. 4.7. Example of the use of data.

State transitions can be controlled with the aid of variable values. Often it is desirable to specify different state transitions as a function of the content of a variable. In SDL this is implemented with the alternative construct, as shown in Figure 4.7. The question to be resolved through an alternative normally involves an operation on one or more variables. At the time that the question is interpreted, one correct answer must be possible, otherwise the specification is no longer interpretable from this time forward. To ensure that at least one correct answer is possible, the *ELSE* clause is used in SDL if none of the other answers are correct.

4.1.7 Signals and Data

In Section 4.1.4 the concepts of input and output in conjunction with the state transition behaviour of a process were introduced. In SDL, the 'messages' related to an output and the corresponding input are called signals. Signals were used in Section 4.1.4 for initiating state changes. In SDL, inputs and outputs can also be used for transmitting data from one process to another. In this case the output has one or more assigned values. During the corresponding input, variables are specified that store the value of an incoming signal. Of course the types of the transmitted variables must agree with the types of the variables at the receiver. This is illustrated in Figure 4.8.

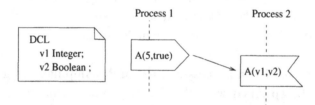

Fig. 4.8. Data transfer in signals.

4.1.8 Specification Structuring and Process Communication

An SDL specification defines an abstract machine that receives inputs from its environment and produces outputs to the environment. This abstract machine is referred to as a system. The system contains everything that should be defined in an SDL specification, but nothing that should not be defined.

The system communicates with the environment via *channels*. From the viewpoint of the system, the objects in the environment have a processlike behaviour, which means that communication with them is possible in the usual manner. The channels through which the system communicates with the environment form the logical interface to the environment.

The system itself consists of one or more blocks that communicate with each other and with the environment through channels. The blocks are the logical system components that provide specification structuring. A block can consist of several other blocks, resulting in a treelike structure. Ultimately, blocks contain processes.

Channels can be unidirectional or bidirectional, and the direction of communication is identified by an arrow. Near the arrows the names of the signals or potentially the name of the list of signals (*signallist*) that can be transmitted in that direction, must be given. An example of a basic SDL system is given in Figure 4.9, where for clarity the signals are omitted from the *channels* and *signalroutes*.

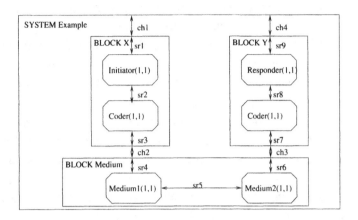

Fig. 4.9. Structuring of basic SDL system.

A channel can optionally delay the transport of a signal. A nondelaying channel has the arrows at the end, for example, touching the blocks, whereas a delaying channel has the arrows somewhere in the middle. For delaying channels, a FIFO delay queue is associated with each channel direction. When a signal is transmitted to a channel, it is inserted into the corresponding delay queue. After an undefined but finite time, the first signal is removed from the delay queue and appears at the end of the corresponding channel.

The structure of the communication between processes is similar, but the connections are called *signalroutes*. Signalroutes do not delay the transportation of signals. They can be created and deleted dynamically with the creation and deletion of a process.

Processes can only communicate with one another using signals if the appropriate signalroutes and channels (if the processes are in different blocks) exist. To overcome this restriction, SDL has introduced the concept of *remote procedures*. These can be *exported* and subsequently *imported* by blocks or processes. The advantage of remote procedures is that they facilitate communication between processes without the need for explicitly denoting the channels, signalroutes and associated signals to be carried. There are some disadvantages in the use of remote procedure calls in SDL, though, for example, the client side is blocked during the remote procedure call and they do not support exceptions.

There is clearly more to say about the semantics of communication, creation and termination of processes than we have space for here. Furthermore, a number of items in the example of Figure 4.9 have not been explained; for example, the (1,1) behind the process name means that one instance of the process exists initially and the maximum number of instances is also one. The reader is referred to [ITU96] for a more detailed explanation.

4.1.9 Object-Orientation in SDL

In 1992, SDL was enhanced by object-oriented features. These included specific language constructs and concepts for supporting object-orientation, and in particular SDL supports interfaces, objects, classes, inheritance and subtyping. It should be noted that SDL uses a different terminology for these concepts for historical reasons. What in object-orientation traditionally is called a class, is called a type in SDL, and objects are called instances in SDL. We discuss the representation of objects and interfaces in SDL in Section 4.2.

SDL defines various kinds of types, including: *system, block, process, service, procedure, signal* and *data*. Instances of these types can be created (instantiated) that will have the same data structure and behaviour. In addition to instantiation, types can be specialized as new types, for example, the definition of subtypes of a type. SDL is unique in comparison with most other object-oriented languages in the sense that SDL offers numerous possibilities for specialized behaviour, whereas in most other languages specializing behaviour is accomplished by redefining (overloading) virtual methods/operations in subtypes. In SDL, specialization of behaviour can be accomplished in numerous ways, for example, by adding new transitions to a process type, or by redefining virtual procedures. SDL also allows for constraints to be given on the specializations, for example, using the **at least** clause.

To allow type specifications to be used across several different specifications, type specifications can be placed in *packages*. These packages can then be referred to in the scope of where the type specification is going to be used. Furthermore, to allow for generic type specifications, a type specification can be parameterized with so-called *formal context parameters*.

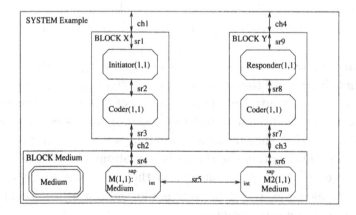

Fig. 4.10. Object-based structuring of SDL system.

Consider the example given in Figure 4.9. Before 1992, when object orientation was not part of SDL, the processes *Medium1* and *Medium2* both had to be specified completely, even if they were really the same and just connected to two different signal routes. With the object-oriented features of SDL 92, the same specification can be rewritten as in Figure 4.10. (Process *Coder* is assumed to exist elsewhere in the specification.)

In the example of Figure 4.10, the process type *Medium* is instantiated twice. In order to specify precisely how such an instance is connected to the infrastructure, that is, through channels and signalroutes, so-called *gates* have to be introduced. In this example these are called *sap* and *int*.

4.2 Applying SDL to Develop a Trader Specification

In this section we show how SDL and its associated tools can be applied to develop a trader specification. We begin with an informal description of trading services.

4.2.1 Introduction to Trading Services

Perhaps the main aim of a distributed system is to provide distribution-transparent utilization of services over heterogeneous environments. In order to use services, users need to be aware of potential service providers and be capable of accessing them. Since sites and applications in distributed systems are likely to change frequently, it is advantageous to allow late binding between service users and providers. If this is to be supported, a component must be able to find appropriate service providers dynamically. The concept of trading has arisen to provide this dynamic selection of service providers at run-time. The interactions that are necessary to achieve this are shown in Figure 4.11.

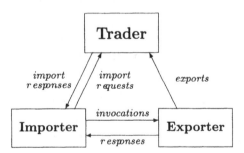

Fig. 4.11. A trader and its users.

Here a trader accepts a *service offer* from an *exporter* wishing to advertise its services. A service offer contains the characteristics of a service that a service provider is willing to provide. We note here that the service provider need not necessarily be the exporter. Similarly, the service user may not be the importer. The trader then stores these service offers for use by importers.

A trader accepts service requests from importers of services. These represent requirements on available services that a trader may or may not have access to. Upon receipt of a request from an importer, the trader searches its store of service offers to see if any offers match the importer's service request. If any matching offers are found, they are returned to the importer, which may then interact directly with the service.

It should be pointed out that a trader might not itself have a service offer that matches an importer's request. In this case, a trader can check whether any other traders that it 'knows' might satisfy the import request. This is known as federated trading. For brevity, we consider only nonfederated trading.

The OMG trading object service specification [OMG97] identifies particular interfaces and associated operations that a trader should support. Here we focus on two of these in particular and the two most basic operations required for trading, namely, export and import†. These operations are offered as part of the *Register* and *Lookup* interfaces, respectively. We also note that, for simplicity, we do not consider the multiple interfaces that are inherited by these interfaces. This simplification avoids the lack of multiple inheritance in SDL. It is possible to manually edit the IDL inheritance hierarchy to overcome this problem, however.

The actual interfaces and operations themselves are defined in [OMG97] by using a combination of CORBA IDL and informal textual description. The *export* operation is given as:

```
module CosTrading {
            interface Register {
                // definition of data types

                OfferId export (in Object reference,
                            in ServiceTypeName type,
                            in PropertySeq properties)
                            raises
                                ( InvalidObjectRef,DuplicatePropertyName,
                                    // ... other exceptions );
                // other operations ...  };
            // other interfaces ...};
```

The parameters associated with this operation include the *reference* that can be used by a client (importer) to interact with that service. We note that the term *Object* is used here. In comparison with other object models, for example, the ODP model, this is really an interface reference. The *type* parameter identifies the service type, which contains the interface type of the reference and a set of named properties that may be used in further describing the offer; that is, it restricts what is acceptable in the *properties* parameter. The *properties* parameter is a list of named values that can be used for describing behavioural aspects, nonfunctional or noncomputational aspects of the service offer. These properties must agree with those described in the *type* parameter.

The *OfferId* returned for a successful export is the handle that can be used by the exporter to identify the exported offer during other operations, that is, to withdraw or modify the offer.

† Or *query*, as it is known in the OMG trader object specification.

Various exceptions can be raised by the trader upon invocation of this operation. For brevity we consider two: the *InvalidObjectRef* exception, which is raised if an invalid reference is supplied, for example, a *nil* reference is supplied, and the *DuplicatePropertyName* exception, which is raised if the exporter submits two or more identical property names in the properties parameter.

The *query* operation of the *Lookup* interface is represented as:

```
module CosTrading {
      interface Lookup {

      // definition of data types

      void query ( in ServiceTypeName type,
                   in Constraint constr,
                   in Preference pref,
                   in PolicySeq policies,
                   in SpecifiedProps desired_props,
                   in unsigned long how_many,
                   out OfferSeq offers,
                   out OfferIterator offer_itr,
                   out PolicyNameSeq limits_applied )
            raises (
                   // ... exceptions );
      // other operations ...   };
```

Here the importer supplies the *type* of the service that they are searching for. This parameter is crucial for future type-safe interactions between importers and exporters. The *constraint* parameter can be used by the importer to capture aspects of the service they are looking for that are not represented in the signature of the service type. The *preference* parameter is used to order offers that satisfy the *constraints*, that is, so that they are presented in the order of greatest interest to the importer. The *policies* parameter allows the importer to influence how the trader performs the search for compatible service offers. The *desired_props* parameter defines the set of properties to be returned with the matching object reference. The *how_many* parameter can be used to state how many offers are to be returned.

The result of the *query* is a sequence of matching *offers* and a reference to an interface *offer_itr*, where other matching offers can be accessed. If the search was subject to any restrictions, for example, policies related to cardinality limits were imposed, then the names of these policies will be returned. There are numerous possible exceptions that can be raised depending on the parameters associated with the *query* operation. For brevity we do not discuss them here, and the reader is referred to [OMG97].

4.2.2 Development of the Trader Specification

Whilst it is quite possible to develop a specification of a trader through interpretation of the IDL and textual description given previously, such an approach is not ideal. A better approach is to use tool support to automatically translate the IDL description to the appropriate target specification language. This is in accordance with the usage of implementation languages such as C++, Java, and so on, for the development of CORBA-based distributed systems. The result of such an automatic translation should be client stubs and server skeletons that capture the syntactic aspects of the communication given by the IDL.

SDL is one of the few specification languages for which such an IDL mapping has been defined. Indeed, more than one mapping has been defined and implemented by different tools and tool vendors [GMD99, Tel99]. We consider the mapping used by the Y.SCE tool [GMD99] because it supports exceptions, a crucial feature present in nearly all IDL descriptions of distributed systems. An outline of the IDL to SDL mapping is presented in Section 19.3.

Before a mapping can be made, however, it is necessary that the syntax of the IDL be compatible with the syntax of the language to be mapped to. In the previous description, various SDL keywords are present that hinder the generation of syntactically correct SDL – this is unsurprising given that there are so many keywords in SDL. Specifically, the variable name *type* and the operation name *export* are reserved words in SDL. It is thus necessary to modify the IDL to overcome this problem, for example, replace the variable named *type* with one named *atype* and the operation *export* with *trader_export*.

The Y.SCE tool [GMD99] generates two SDL packages (*name_interface* and *name_definition*), which provide mappings for the IDL operations and parameters and the client stubs and server skeletons. We note here that tools such as [Tel99] already provide an existing package (*idltypes*) that contains a mapping for many of the basic CORBA types such as short, long, Boolean, and so on. A snapshot of the resultant SDL code generated from this mapping focussing on the signals associated with the export operation as present in the *name_interface* package is shown in Figure 4.12.

```
signal pCALL_CosTrading_Register_export(CORBA_Object, CosTrading_ServiceTypeName,CosTrading_PropertySeq);

signal pREPLY_CosTrading_Register_export(CosTrading_OfferId);

signal pRAISE_CosTrading_Register_InvalidObjectRef(CosTrading_Register_InvalidObjectRef);

signal pRAISE_CosTrading_DuplicatePropertyName(CosTrading_DuplicatePropertyName);

signallist CosTrading_Register_INVOCATIONS = pCALL_CosTrading_Register_export, ....;

signallist CosTrading_Register_TERMINATIONS = pREPLY_CosTrading_Register_export,

                                    pRAISE_CosTrading_Register_InvalidObjectRef,

                                    pRAISE_CosTrading_DuplicatePropertyName, ...;
```

Fig. 4.12. Mapping for trader IDL operations.

The resultant SDL server skeletons as found in the *name_definition* are represented in Figure 4.13. We note that here we show only those aspects of the *Register* interface dealing with the export operation. In reality, virtual procedures for all of the operations would be present along with the appropriate behaviour that enables the local procedures to be called.

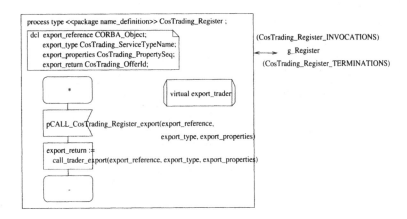

Fig. 4.13. Server skeletons generated through mapping.

Here a process type representing the *Register* interface is generated. This process type has gates (*g_Register*) connecting it that enable the input signals to be delivered, that is, the client invocations, and output signals, that is, server terminations, to be sent. Local variables are also declared in the process type. The values of these variables are set by the client invocation.

The behaviour of the process type itself is such that in all states it accepts the export signal (*pCALL_CosTrading_Register_export*) and calls a virtual local procedure before returning to the same state. The behaviour of this local procedure is minimal and consists of a single output to the *Sender* of the invocation. This is illustrated in Figure 4.14.

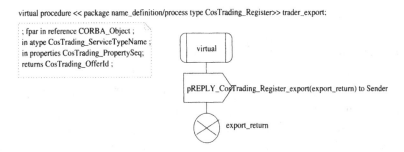

Fig. 4.14. Server side operations to be implemented.

By default this operation returns the successful return result, that is, it returns the *pREPLY_CosTrading_Register_export* signal to the invoking exporter. The operations associated with the trader object are implemented by inheriting and redefining these procedures. It is also possible to modify the trader behaviour so that the operations are not available in all states.

Whilst it is possible to develop clients within the SDL specification itself through specifying the appropriate behaviour in the generated SDL stubs (not shown here), another approach is to treat the clients as being external to the specification itself, as shown in Figure 4.15.

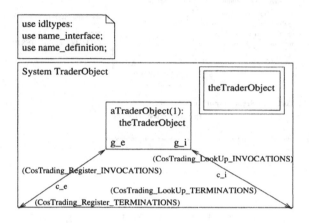

Fig. 4.15. Design of trader specification.

Here, the trader server object interacts with the importers and exporters via channels connected to the environment. Through this approach we overcome one of the limitations of SDL for distributed systems development, namely, that it does not allow for the dynamic communications to be set up between processes existing in different blocks, for example, via the dynamic creation of channels. We note that it is possible to achieve this dynamicity through exported and imported remote procedure calls since the channels are not required to exist, however, as stated remote procedures do not currently support the raising of exceptions.

We note here that the existing package and those that are generated are inherited by the trader system. These will subsequently be used (inherited) in the specification of the trader interfaces.

Having an IDL mapping to SDL is a useful starting point to develop a specification, however, it does not necessarily provide enough information that will lead to a final successful design. Central to this issue is the disparity in the notion of objects having multiple interfaces. For example, it is quite possible to specify independent processes representing the behaviour of the different trader interfaces. The relation between these interfaces is up to the specification designer. Of course, given that the *Register* interface accepts *export* requests that can subsequently be imported by interacting with the *LookUp* interface, there must obviously be some form of interaction between the associated processes – either directly or indirectly. It might be the case that the *Register* process maintains some form of database of exported offers that can be queried by the *LookUp* process. Deciding on such an approach will likely lend itself to a nonscalable design with different interfaces managing their own information that might be needed elsewhere, that is, by other interfaces.

A further vagueness of an IDL-based description is the lifecycle object and the interfaces that it supports. It is often the case that some form of control over different interfaces is required, for example, so that they can be created or deleted as part of the lifecycle of the object itself. One way in which these issues can be overcome is through a process modelling a central object core. This is responsible for the coordination between the separate processes implementing the interfaces to the object, as well as the life-cycle of the object as a whole. One such structure is shown in Figure 4.16.

In Figure 4.16 we note that at system start-up time only a single core object process exists. This process is used to create instances of the interfaces, that is, *Register* and *LookUp* associated with the trader object. We note that we could simply assume that a single core object and single instances of the interfaces exist, however, having creator processes, for example, *theCore* allows for the process identifiers to be obtained both for the creating process (*OffSpring*) and the created processes (*Parent*). Possession of process identifiers is the SDL equivalent of possession of an interface reference in the CORBA domain. This allows, amongst other things, for communications to be checked between core objects and the supported interfaces, for example, to ensure that the signals sent and received are from the expected source.

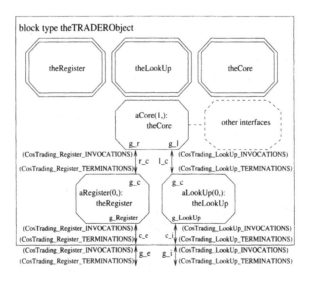

Fig. 4.16. Decomposition of trader object.

As stated earlier, the specification of the server behaviour is achieved by inheriting and redefining the appropriate virtual procedures. Given that a core object has been introduced, it is necessary to extend the process types representing the server interfaces by adding the necessary gates (g_c) to support the interactions with the core object, as shown in Figure 4.17.

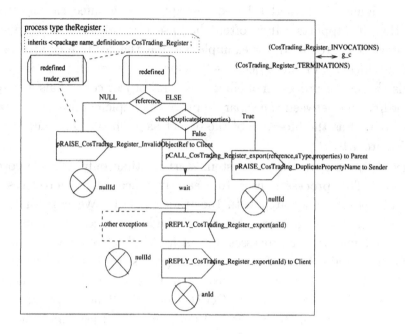

Fig. 4.17. Implementing the trader register interface.

Several things should be noticed in Figure 4.17. First, we note that, for brevity, we have also included the behaviour of the redefined procedure *trader_export*. We also note that the process inherits the appropriate process in the *name_definition* package, that is, *CosTrading_Register*.

The redefined procedure itself checks the details of the client invocation. Specifically, it ensures that a nonnull reference is attached which can subsequently be used by the importers to interact with the service; otherwise it raises the *pRAISE_CosTrading_Register_InvalidObjectRef* exception and returns a null export identifier (*nullId*). If a nonnull reference is passed by the client, the redefined *trader_export* procedure then checks whether any of the properties that have been supplied have identical names. If so, it raises the *pRAISE_CosTrading_DuplicatePropertyName* exception and returns a null export identifier (*nullId*). If no exceptions are raised, then the request is forwarded to the core object (itself represented by the *Parent* process identifier). The core object itself can raise other exceptions (not further specified here) that also result in a *nullId* export identifier being returned to the client. If the export operation was successful, however, then the (*pREPLY_CosTrading_Register_export*) reply is received with an appropriate export identifier (*anId*).

We note that for brevity we omit the task box that is used to assign the *Client* as the *Sender* of the export invocation. We also omit the details of the *checkDuplicates* operation, which checks whether a sequence of properties has two or more properties with identical names.

A simplified example of the structure of the process type representing the core object itself is given in Figure 4.18.

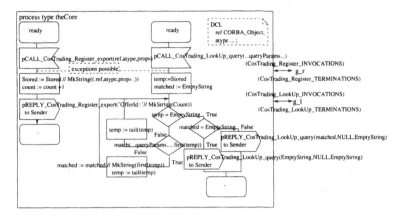

Fig. 4.18. Implementing the trader core object.

Note that to simplify the diagram we have omitted the initial starting behaviour of the core object. This would typically include the creation of the interfaces used by the trader object (*LookUp* and *Register*) and storage of the information associated with them, for example, the process identifiers for the created offspring. In addition, we assume that the variable declarations contain definitions for all of the local variables used.

The process type itself has the gates associated with it that are used for interacting with the *LookUp* and *Register* interfaces, that is, g_l and g_r, respectively, which support the appropriate signal lists.

Upon reception of the export signal from the *Register* process, the core object checks the details of the parameters and that the signal itself is from the correct source, that is, from one of the created and known interfaces of the trader object. If the information associated with the request is not satisfactory, then the appropriate exception is raised; otherwise, the core object stores the information associated with the offer. It might be the case that some process modelling a repository is used to store the service offers. We represent here instead the stored offers as a local variable represented as a sequence of service offers (*Stored*). An export identifier is then returned to the *Register* interface, which then forwards it on to the initial invoker, that is, the invoker.

As with the export invocation, upon reception of a query signal (from the *LookUp* process), the core object checks the details of the invocation and can raise the appropriate exception. For simplicity, the *queryParams* is used to represent the collection of input parameters associated with the *query* operation. If the details of the request are satisfactory, then the core object searches its stored offers. It creates a local copy of the stored offers and traverses this searching for matching offers. If none are found, for example, if no service offers have yet been exported or no match can be found, then an empty sequence (*EmptyString*) is returned; otherwise, the sequence of matching offers is returned. For simplicity we return a *Null* reference to the offer iterator interface and restrict ourselves to the case where no policies have been applied. It might be the case that additional alternatives are included in the core object behaviour, for example, to check if the number of matching offers has reached the maximum limit as defined by the *how_many* parameters of the *query* request. We also assume that the operation *match* is defined, which can be used to judge whether the details of a query request are satisfied by an existing export offer.

4.3 Conclusions

This chapter has provided a brief introduction to the specification language SDL. We have shown its applicability to developing realistic specifications of distributed systems through applying it together with its associated tools to develop a trader specification. We also used current approaches to distributed systems more generally, that is, through the appropriate generation of client stubs and server skeletons whose behaviour is to be implemented.

Such an approach has many direct advantages and certain disadvantages. The main advantage from such an approach is that it allows for a direct relation between a specification and an implementation to be ascertained; for example, tree and tabular combined notation (TTCN) [ISO91] based tests derived from such specifications can be executed against the corresponding implementations [SK99a]. Having an IDL basis for specification and implementation corresponds to having a common level of abstraction – at least at the syntactic interworking level. Through this, specifications can be used as a realistic part of software development. Whilst abstraction is a powerful tool for developing formal specifications, unfortunately it is often the case that too much abstraction results in models of systems that bear little or no relation to the software being developed. On the one hand, this can be seen as a good thing; for example, if requirements capturing is the aim of the specification, however, formal methods will only really be truly accepted if they are seen to help and improve the development of software itself. Starting from a common IDL basis thus represents a unique opportunity for formal methods.

The downside of such a direct relationship between specification and implementation is that, in the development of realistic systems, the specifications themselves can become very large. As a consequence, the models become more difficult to deal with, for example, to check for properties of the specification such as dropped signals via tool support. The problem of state space explosion is an ever-present issue that has to be addressed. From this, many of the misnomers of the application of formal methods into the software development process need to be considered, for example, that they can guarantee perfect systems. Rather, a more pragmatic approach should be adopted. This might include vigorously tested and validated components of some larger system, or the generation of use cases represented as message sequence charts [IT96a] for the system as a whole.

Bibliography

[BG96]   U. Behnke and M. Geipl. Development of broadband ISDN telecommunication services using SDL'92, ASN.1 and automatic code generation. In G. von Bochmann, R. Dssouli, and O. Rafiq, editors, *Formal Description Techniques ,VIII*, pages 237–252. Chapman & Hall, 1996.

[Bra96]   R. Braek. SDL basics. *Computer Networks and ISDN Systems*, 28(12):1585–1602, 1996.

[BRJ99]   G. Booch, J. Rumbaugh, and I. Jacobson. *The Unified Modeling Language User Guide*. Addison-Wesley, 1999.

[DD93]   J. S. Dong and R. Duke. An object-oriented approach to the formal specification of the ODP trader. In *IFIP TC6/WG6.1 International Conference on Open Distributed Processing*, pages 341–352, September 1993.

[EHB97]   J. Ellsberger, D. Hogrefe, and F. Belina, editors. *SDL – Formal Object-Oriented Language for Communicating Systems*. Prentice-Hall, 1997.

[FPV93]   J. Fischer, A. Prinz, and A. Vogel. Different FDT's confronted with different ODP-viewpoints of the trader. In J. C. P. Woodcock and P. G. Larsen, editors, *FME'93: Industrial Strength Formal Methods*, volume 670 of *Lecture Notes in Computer Science*, pages 332–350. Springer-Verlag, 1993.

[GMD99]   GMD Fokus, Berlin, Germany. *Y.SCE Manual*, 1999. More information under http://www.fokus.gmd.de/research.

[Hum99]   Humboldt University, Berlin, Germany. *SDL Integrated Tool Environment*, 1999.

[ISO90a]   ISO/IEC. *Information Processing Systems – Open Systems Interconnection – Specification of Abstract Syntax Notation One (ASN.1)*. ISO/IEC 8824. International Organization for Standardization, Geneva, Switzerland, 1990.

[ISO90b]   ISO/IEC. *Information Processing Systems – Open Systems Interconnection – Specification of Basic Encoding Rules for Abstract Syntax Notation One (ASN.1)*. ISO/IEC 8825. International Organization for Standardization, Geneva, Switzerland, 1990.

[ISO91]   ISO/IEC. *Information Processing Systems – Open Systems Interconnection – Conformance Testing Methodology and Fr amework – Part 3: The Tr æ and Tabular Combined Notation (TTCN)*. ISO/IEC 9646-3. International Organization for Standardization, 1991.

[IT96a]   ITU-T. *Message Sequence Chart (MSC)*. ITU-T Z.120. International Telecommunications Union, 1996.

[IT96b]   ITU-T. *Specification of Signalling System No. 7*. Recommendation Q.701-795. ITU-T, Geneva, Switzerland, 1996.

[ITU96]   ITU. *Specification and Description Language*. ITU-T Z.100. International Telecommunications Union, 1996.

[ITU00]   ITU. *Specification and Description Language*. ITU-T Z.100. International Telecommunications Union, 2000.

[LTT96]   F. Lucidi, A. Tosti, and S. Trigila. Object oriented modelling of advanced IN services with SDL-92. In Z. Brezocnik and T. Kapus, editors, *Applied Formal Methods in System Design*, pages 17–26, Maribor, June 1996. Action COST 247.

[OFMP+94]   A. Olsen, O. Færgemand, B. Mœller-Pedersen, R. Reed, and J. R. W. Smith, editors. *Systems Engineering using SDL-92*. North-Holland, 1994.

[OMG97]   OMG. *Tr ading Object Service: v1.0, OMG Tr ading Function Module*. Object Management Group, Inc., March 1997.

[R. 93]   R. Bræk and O. Haugen, editor. *Engineering Real Time Systems – An Object-Oriented Methodology using SDL*. Prentice-Hall, 1993.

[Sin97]   R. O. Sinnott. *An Architecture Based Approach to Specifying Distributed Systems in LOTOS and Z*. PhD thesis, Department of Computing Science and Mathematics, University of Stirling, UK, May 1997.

[SK99a]   R. O. Sinnott and M. Kolberg. Creating Telecommunication Services based on Object-Oriented Frameworks and SDL. In M. Raynal, T. Kikuno, and R. Soley, editors, *Second IEEE International Symposium on Object-Oriented Real-Time Distributed Computing*, St. Malo, France, May 1999.

[SK99b]   R. O. Sinnott and M. Kolberg. Engineering Telecommunication Services with SDL. In P. Ciancarini, A. Fantechi, and R. Gorrieri, editors, *Formal Methods for Open Object-Based Distributed Systems*, pages 187–203. Kluwer, February 1999.

[ST97]   R. O. Sinnott and K. J. Turner. Applying the Architectural Semantics of ODP to Develop a Trader Specification. *Computer Networks and ISDN Systems: Special Edition on Specification Architecture*, March 1997.

[Tel99]   Telelogic AB, Malmö, Sweden. *Telelogic Manual*, 1999.

[Ver99]   Verilog, Grenoble, France. *ObjectGeode Manual*, 1999.

5

Process Calculi: E-LOTOS

Tomás Robles   Gabriel Huecas   Juan Quemada

Universidad Polit'ecnia de Madrid, Spain

Alberto Verdejo   Luis F. Llana-D'ıaz

Universidad Complutense de Madrid, Spain

In this chapter we discuss a process algebraic approach to specification and introduce the LOTOS language and its extension, E-LOTOS.

5.1 The Process Algebra Approach

Sequential models of computation, though strikingly successful in explaining the working of a single (sequential) computer program and the way in which such programs may be composed of parts, for example, procedures, while maintaining a single locus of control, are seriously deficient in explaining how a heterogeneous assembly of computing agents behave together. In building a model, process algebras are based on some basic principles, which will guide us to a model at the same time as articulating the meaning of these two terms:

- An interaction among processes consists in their participation in a single atomic event. This principle does not require all events to be atomic, but for this short introduction we shall use 'event' to mean 'atomic event', where 'atomic' means 'indivisible in time'. Importantly, the principle does not limit the number of processes that may participate in an interaction; thus, although CSP [Hoa85] and CCS [Mil89] (as they were originally proposed) represent this principle faithfully, they impose a restriction in allowing only two participants.

- Every event is an interaction among processes. This implies, first, that a computational event such as writing a value into a register must be an interaction, and hence that registers and other media must be treated as processes on a par with the active processes that use them; the effect is to impose a strong homogeneity on the model.

- Every n-ary process constructor f must be such that the behaviour of $f(P_1, \ldots, P_n)$ depends only on the behaviour of $P_1, \ldots, P_n$. The conjunction of two processes exhibits exactly that behaviour which is common to both of them; they are required to synchronize on every single action. Moreover, iterated conjunction $P_1 \& P_2 \& \ldots \& P_n$ causes n processes to synchronize.

- (Conjunction) A construct is needed that will force each of n processes to synchronize with all of the others on any of a designated set of actions, but to perform all other actions freely.

- (Encapsulation) A construct is needed that renders a designated set of actions unobservable.

- (Disjunction) A construct is needed that will force each of n processes to synchronize with any one of the others on any of a designated set of actions.

- (Renaming) A construct is needed that changes the action-names of a process.

- Constructs, rich enough to express a wide range of distributed processes, are needed for sequential control. This principle compensates for the emphasis placed on parallel composition by the preceding principles. It turns out that rather simple constructors for sequential composition, alternative action and repetition are sufficient.

- (Simultaneity) The simultaneous occurrence of two actions is also an action.

Based on this mode, process algebras offer a powerful tool for describing systems as black boxes, completely independent of the system implementation. Large systems will be composed of subsystems that are synchronized by external events. Such subsystems will evolve in parallel while no external synchronization is required.

5.2 LOTOS

LOTOS (Language Of Temporal Ordering Specification) was developed within ISO [ISO89] for the formal specification of open distributed systems, and in particular for the OSI (Open Systems Interconnection) computer network architecture. The language is nonetheless applicable to distributed concurrent systems in general. Its behaviour description part is based on process algebraic ideas, predominantly on CCS, but it also borrowed some ideas from CSP. The mechanism to define and to deal with data types is based on ACT ONE [EFH83]. LOTOS was developed from 1981 to 1986 and became an international standard (IS-8807) in 1989.

5.2.1 LOTOS Behaviour

In this section we describe the main elements of the LOTOS behaviour part.

Action The behaviour part of LOTOS (as well as CCS and CSP) is based on the notion of indivisible interaction. An interaction, or simple action, is the primitive concept when modelling concurrent systems. It defines the granularity for modelling. An action might be, for example, the insertion of a coin, the lighting of a lamp or the arrival of a letter. When occurrences that take time are to be modelled, one can use two actions: one for the start of the occurrence and one for its completion. Concurrent systems usually need to interact with other systems and with the environment. These subsystems also could possibly be composed of further subsystems, thus yeilding a hierarchy. The parallel composition of subsystems is as simple as the sequential composition of statements in an imperative programming language. Thus an action can be identified with the interaction point (called *gate* in LOTOS) on which the action takes place. We only need to name gates and can use the same name for the action that takes place on it. Each system has a fixed interface consisting of a number of gates with given names. When two systems agree to interact, that is, synchronize on a gate, they might exchange some values. Communication is possible only through interaction at common gates.

Behaviour Expressions The behaviour of concurrent systems in LOTOS is described by means of behaviour expressions, in the same way as arithmetic expressions describe numeric computations. The simplest system is one that cannot perform any action. It is called **stop**. This is the inaction or deadlock system. There is also another system that does nothing except terminating successfully; this is called **exit**. There are two dimensions to consider: sequentialization and choice. With the prefix operation ';' it is possible to define a system that first is capable of performing an action and then behaves like another system. For example, the behaviour a; P performs action a and then behaves as behaviour P. Selection between alternative behaviours is represented by the choice behaviour operator []. Once an action is chosen from one component, the other component disappears from the resulting expression.

Processes In the same way that an arithmetic expression can be abstracted to a function, a behaviour expression can be abstracted to a process. A process is a behaviour expression parameterized on the names of gates, and it can also depend on additional arguments. The abstraction of a behaviour expression to a process also allows the definition of (directly or mutually) recursive behaviours.

Concurrency It should be noted that all behaviour expressions that can be described in LOTOS can be defined using four operators (**stop**, **exit**, ;, and []) together with recursion. It is nevertheless often useful to describe systems as a composition of subsystems in parallel. LOTOS has several operators for expressing parallel composition:

- Interleaving | | |: concurrent composition without synchronization;
- Total synchronization | |: concurrent composition with synchronization on all gates; and
- Selective synchronization | [. . .] |: concurrent composition with synchronization on the given gates (general case).

Hiding Hierarchy is a very important concept in LOTOS. The **hide** operator allows actions to be made invisible. The actions are internalized so that no behaviour expressions can interact with them.

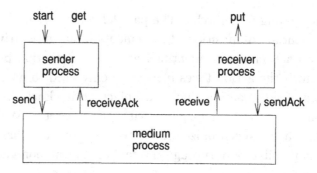

Fig. 5.1. Components in the communication protocol.

Enabling and Disabling The passing of control among processes is described by two operators: enable and disable. Sequential composition is modelled by the enable operator (>>). B_1>>B_2 means that behaviour B_1 is followed by behaviour B_2 if and only if B_1 has terminated successfully (by performing an **exit**). The disable operator ([>) models interruptions and exceptions to the normal behaviour of systems.

5.2.2 Data Types

The definition of a data type is composed of two parts: signature and equations. The signature defines the set of values and the operations to work with these values. This is a point of difference with programming languages where types and operations (functions and procedures) are defined. Equations give the semantics to the operations defined in the signature. They define the properties that the operations have to satisfy. No implementation is needed for the operations. This is the second point of difference with programming languages, where the semantics of the operations is predefined in the language or is given by the implementation of the operation itself. LOTOS has no predefined types, but it allows the use of predefined libraries. These libraries contain the meaningful types for application domains. Nevertheless, new types can be defined in a specification.

5.2.3 Example

As an illustration of LOTOS we present the specification of a small communication protocol, which comprises three components: *a sender process, a receiver process* and *a medium* (or channel). These components are depicted in Figure 5.1. The specification task here is to model the behaviour of the medium (e.g., its ability to lose messages) and to give sender and receiver process specifications that support reliable communication. The specification will use timeouts, sequence numbering and acknowledgement to do this.

The sender process obtains messages to send (also called packets or frames) from outside the protocol system (in terms of a layered protocol model, such as the OSI model, messages to send would be obtained from a previous layer in the protocol stack). The computation steps of the sender are request a message from outside the system, successfully send the message (perhaps with some retransmission) and then request a new message. Thus, the protocol is a *stop and wait* protocol; it waits for the current message to be successfully sent before it requests a new message to send.

Transmission using the protocol is initiated by a request to start from outside the protocol. The sender then obtains a message to send and sends it. Getting a message to send is identified by an interaction *get* between the sender process and the environment outside the system, and sending is identified by an interaction *send* occuring between the sending process and the medium. The medium then relays the message to the receiver. Successful tranmissions cause a *receive* to occur at the receiver process. However, the medium may lose the message, in which case no such event is able to occur. In addition, the receiver sends acknowledgements through the medium (so the medium is a duplex channel). Sending and receiving these acknowledgements are identified by the interactions *sendAck* and *receiveAck*, respectively. Successfully received messages are passed out of the system on the receiver side using the interaction *put*.

In order to keep our presentation as simple as possible, we make two simplifying assumptions. First, we assume that the acknowledgement medium is reliable. Thus, messages sent from the sender to the receiver may be lost, but acknowledgements will always be relayed successfully. Second, we assume an infinite set of sequence numbers, that is, they are modelled as natural numbers. In fact, due to the simplicity of the scenario, the role of sequence numbers is not significant, but we include them to illustrate data passing actions.

The top level behaviour of the communication protocol is as follows:

```
start;
    hide send, receive, sendAck, receiveAck in
        ( (   Sender [get, send, receiveAck] (0)
            | | |
              Receiver [put, receive, sendAck] )
            | [ send, receive, sendAck, receiveAck ] |
              DupMedium [send, receive, sendAck, receiveAck] )
```

The protocol begins when the action *start* is performed. Then the components of the protocol are instantiated, with the parallel composition operators being used to ensure a correct configuration of components. Thus, the *Sender* and *Receiver* evolve independently. However, actions *send*, *receive*, *sendAck* and *receiveAck* are interactions with *DupMedium* (the duplex medium). Notice that the *Sender* process is instantiated with the value of the starting sequence number as an actual parameter. In addition, the actions internal to the protocol are indeed made internal by using hiding.

The behaviour of the sender is specified as follows:

process *Sender* [*get*,*send*,*receiveAck*] (*n*:nat) : **noexit** :=
  get; *send*!*n*; *Sending* [*get*,*send*,*receiveAck*] (*n*)
endproc

process *Sending* [*get*,*send*,*receiveAck*] (*m*:nat) : **noexit** :=
   hide *timeout* **in**
      (*receiveAck*!*m*; *Sender* [*get*,*send*,*receiveAck*] (*m* + 1)
      []
         timeout; *send*!*m*; *Sending* [*get*,*send*,*receiveAck*] (*m*))
endproc

The *Sender* process gets a message, sends it (with a sequence number) and then enters the subprocess *Sending*, which ensures delivery of the message. *Sending* waits for an acknowledgement to be returned; otherwise it times out and retransmits. The behaviour of the receiver is very simple and is specified as follows:

process *Receiver* [*put*,*receive*,*sendAck*] : **noexit** :=
   receive?*n*:nat; *put*; *sendAck*!*n*; *Receiver* [*put*,*receive*,*sendAck*]
endproc

The top level behaviour of the medium is specified as:

process *DupMedium* [*send*,*receive*,*sendAck*,*receiveAck*] : **noexit** :=
   Medium [*send*,*receive*]
   |||
   AckMedium [*sendAck*,*receiveAck*]
endproc

Thus, the 'forward' and 'backward' mediums are independent of each other. The definition of *DupMedium* uses the following two processes:

process *Medium* [*send*,*receive*] : **noexit** :=
   send?*n*:nat;
      (*i*; *Medium* [*send*,*receive*]
      []
         receive!*n*; *Medium* [*send*,*receive*])
endproc

process *AckMedium* [*sendAck*,*receiveAck*] : **noexit** :=
   sendAck?*n*:nat; *receiveAck*!*n*; *AckMedium* [*sendAck*,*receiveAck*]
endproc

The first of these two processes (*Medium*) can lose messages, modelled by the non-deterministic occurrence of an internal action, while the second (*AckMedium*) is reliable.

This protocol will provide reliable delivery if we assume that the medium does not lose messages forever, that is, if it eventually delivers a message (this is a form of fairness property) and also if the timeout action does not occur 'too early', that is, before there has been sufficient time for acknowledgements to be delivered. In fact, the latter of these is an assumption that we cannot ensure in such an untimed setting. This is one of the observations that has motivated the timing extension to LOTOS that has been incorporated in E-LOTOS.

5.3 E-LOTOS

LOTOS has been under revision in ISO [Que98], in the Work Item 'Enhancements to LOTOS', giving rise to a revised language called E-LOTOS (Enhanced LOTOS). Maintaining the strong formal basics of LOTOS, the new language intends to include most of the user's requirements related to expressive power and structuring capabilities, besides user-friendliness [HRLDV99]. User's requirements come from the industrial environment, which wants to use a language that is closer to actual high-level programming languages, reducing the learning curve of new engineers, and the availability of tools that produce effective implementations of the specified products. The scientific community wants to increment the expressive power of the language to deal with classical problems like time analysis, new operators and unification of some language structures. Among the enhancements introduced in E-LOTOS, the most important ones are

- the notion of quantitative time: in E-LOTOS we can define the exact time at which events or behaviours may occur;
- the data part, both the definition of new data types and the construction of values of predefined types, which provides data types similar to those of (functional) programming languages while maintaining a formal approach;
- modularity, which allows the definition of types, functions and processes in separate modules, by controlling their visibility by means of module interfaces, and the definition of generic modules, useful for code reuse;
- several new operators, which increase the expressive power of the language by adding, for example, exception handling and the general composition of parallel processes;
- some instructions from programming languages (loops, if-then-else, case, etc.) that make the language useful for covering the last steps of the software lifecycle, when implementations are developed and make the job of specifying systems easier. Besides these instructions, the use of *write-many* variables, that is, variables that can be assigned several times as in imperative programming language, is another feature introduced in E-LOTOS.

In this section we explain the main implications of the inclusion of these elements and discuss the alternatives considered during the standardization process, remarking on the implications of the use of the language in the software engineering process, systems specifications and standards work. In the following sections we describe each of these points.

5.3.1 Time

The use of time in the specification of protocols is now an important area of research [QMdL94, LL94], but time was not included in the definition of LOTOS because at the time of its definition the research was still in its infancy.

Time can be introduced in the operational semantics of process algebras in two equivalent ways: with time transitions and action transitions [LL94], or with timed action transitions [QMdL94]. In the first, there are two kinds of transitions: timed transitions and action transitions. An *action transition* stands for a communication as in LOTOS, while a *timed transition* indicates the passing of time; that is, $B \xrightarrow{\epsilon(t)} B'$ indicates that behaviour B' is the behaviour B after t units of time have elapsed. The idea of a *timed action transition* is to join an action transition and a time transition in just one transition. So $B \xrightarrow{g\,t} B'$ indicates that behaviour B communicates through gate g at time t. It is also necessary to indicate a function of time passing: $Age(B, t)$ is the behaviour B after t units of time. The first is the approach chosen in E-LOTOS because it is compatible with LOTOS in the sense that it is only necessary to introduce the timed transitions.

5.3.1.1 Time Domain

One of the features that distinguishes timed process algebras is the time domain, which sometimes is discrete [OMdF90, HR95, LdN96] and other times is continuous [RR86, RR88, Sch95, RR99]. The time domain in E-LOTOS can be either discrete or continuous. The standard does not define a type time but instead describes the features that this type has to fulfill in any implementation of E-LOTOS. These properties are

- the time domain is a commutative, cancellative monoid with addition + and unit 0. Thus it satisfies the following properties:
  - $d_1 + d_2 = d_2 + d_1$;
  - if $d_1 + d = d_2 + d$, then $d_1 = d_2$;
  - $d_1 + (d_2 + d_3) = (d_1 + d_2) + d_3$;
  - $d + 0 = 0 + d = d$,

  where d_1, d_2 and d are variables over the time domain.
- the order given by $d_1 \leq d_2$ if and only if $\exists d . d_1 + d = d_2$ is a total order.

At first glance, it seems that it is better to have a continuous time domain. But it has several problems. First, one can specify a Zeno behaviour:

$$B_1 \xrightarrow{\epsilon(1/2)} B_2 \xrightarrow{\epsilon(1/4)} B_3 \xrightarrow{\epsilon(1/8)} \cdots B_k \xrightarrow{\epsilon(1/2^k)} B_{k+1} \cdots$$

This process will not let one unit of time pass; this is an undesirable behaviour. Another problem is more philosophical: can two processes communicate at an exact instant? It seems more realistic to consider a discrete time domain where the unit of time can be as small as one wants, but it is fixed.

5.3.1.2 Urgency

When an action is *urgent* it means that the action must be performed as soon as possible, that is, time cannot be passed if an urgent action is able to be performed. Urgency guarantees the progress of a system: if there were no urgent actions, the systems could idle forever; that is, it would have the possibility of waiting forever before performing any action. In E-LOTOS internal actions are urgent, that is, a process cannot idle if it can execute an internal action. Also, actions carried out on hidden gates are urgent, and, therefore, they happen as soon as possible.

For example, let us imagine that we want to specify a process that produces two values and sends them through gates *p1* and *p2* in that order. We can specify its behaviour by means of another process that produces one value, and by using two different instantiations of this subprocess. These instantiations have to synchronize to produce the values in the desired order, graphically:

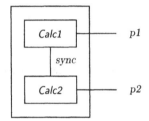

The specification in E-LOTOS of this process is as follows:

process *Producer* [*p1*:data,*p2*:data] **is**
    hide *sync* **in**
        Calculation [*p1*, *sync*] (1)
        | [*sync*] |
        Calculation [*p2*, *sync*] (2)
    endhide
  endproc

where the behaviour

    Calculation [*p1*, *sync*] (1)
  | [*sync*] |
    Calculation [*p2*, *sync*] (2)

can idle forever, even when both instantiations are able to synchronize on gate *sync*. But by using the **hide** operator, actions on gate *sync* become urgent. This ensures the progress of the system; that is, as soon as both *Calculation* process instantiations are able to communicate on gate *sync*, the communication happens, and the second instantiation knows that it can send the second value.

Moreover, it is enough to consider as urgent only internal actions. A complete system can be seen as a black box where all actions are hidden. Without hiding all gates, the whole system could idle forever because nothing could force a communication to occur on a nonhidden gate. When one specifies a behaviour like *a* ; *B*, we might think that we are specifying a process with the possibility of doing nothing because, for any t, we have the transitions

$$a\,;B \xrightarrow{\;\epsilon(t)\;} a\,;B.$$

That is correct, but if there is a user that wants to communicate with that gate and this whole system is under a global **hide** operator, this communication will be executed as soon as possible. So $a\,;B$ will idle only if there is no process that wants to synchronize on gate a. Sometimes we are specifying part of a system that has to synchronize with other parts. In this case, there is no explicit **hide** operator, but we have to suppose it when we specify this concrete part, that is, we can think that every action is urgent. Otherwise, some behaviours make no sense. For example, we can specify a global clock, that is, a clock that measures time since it is started until it is stopped, and to which other processes running in parallel can ask what time it is, as follows:

```
process Clock [stopClock, whatTime:time] (gtime:time) is
  var gt:time:=0, t:time:=0 in
    whatTime(?gt) @?t [gt=gtime+t] ; Clock [...] (gtime+t)
  []
    stopClock
  endvar
endproc
```

where actions are not urgent, but we assume that they will be urgent (because they will be hidden) when this process is used. In Section 5.3.2 we will show how the specification of actions has been changed to deal with time constraints (@ parameter) and the **wait** operator for expressing delays.

5.3.1.3 Time Is Deterministic

Nondeterminism can appear only in a behaviour by *doing something*. It is not possible that a behaviour B evolves to two different behaviours B_1 and B_2 only by time passing. The E-LOTOS static semantics, which checks which behaviours are semantically correct, ensures time determinism, by rejecting behaviours that could be time nondeterministic. For example, let us consider the following behaviour:

$$(?x := 5 \;[]\; ?x := 2)\,;\ \mathbf{wait}(1)\,;P[\ldots](x, \ldots)$$

It is time nondeterministic: intuitively, when one unit of time has passed and process P is executed, variable x may have either the value 5 or the value 2. Time nondeterminism is an undesirable feature, and E-LOTOS forbids it, in this case requiring that when we build a behaviour $B_1\,[]\,B_2$, both behaviours B_1 and B_2 have to be 'guarded', that is, they have to perform an action on a gate (or raise an exception) before they finish; this action decides which branch of the selection operator is selected.

5.3.2 New Operators

The expressive power of LOTOS was one of its stronger points. But several improvements were added in E-LOTOS.

Communication can be made sensitive to time by adding the @ *P* annotation, which pattern-matches the pattern *P* to the time when the action happens, measured from the time when the communication was enabled. We can use this, together with selection predicates, to control the time when actions may be performed. For example, the behaviour†

$inP(?x:int)$ @?*t* [*t*<5]

specifies an action that receives an integer that is bound to the variable *x*, provided that less than five units of time have passed, whereas the action

$inP(?x:int)$ @!5

can occur only five units of time after the action *inP* has been enabled. Thus, if we use the pattern ?*t*, then variable *t* will be bound to the time at which the action happens, and the selection predicate imposes the restriction (*t*<5); but if we use the pattern !5, then the value 5 is compared with the time at which the action happens, and the action will be possible only if this time is also 5.

The delay operator **wait** is another construct related to time. The behaviour

wait(*E*)

is idle while the time indicated by the expression *E* (which must have type time) passes, and then finishes.

From different fields, the need for *exceptions* was clearly established. They were introduced together with the **trap** operator that describes the exception handlers. The instructions **raise** and **signal** are two different ways to throw an exception: **raise** *X* throws exception *X*, and if it is not trapped, the whole behaviour is stopped (it represents an error); **signal** *X* throws exception *X*, and if it is not trapped, the next instruction is executed. If the exception is trapped, the behaviour of both instructions is the same. Exceptions can be thrown outside a system (in JAVA, for example, all exceptions must be captured by a program). There is no default exception manager, and there are no 'finally' clauses (a 'finally' clause is always executed, whether an exception was thrown or not and independently of the exception type).

A more *general parallel operator* was introduced. It is *n*-ary and supports the synchronization of *n* out of *m* processes. The new operator is more readable, as it explicitly identifies the synchronising gates for each composed behaviour. With this new operator we can specify, in an easy way, systems like the one graphically represented by

---

† The pattern ?*v* is used where we want to bind variable *v*, and not just in input attributes of actions as in LOTOS. The pattern !*E* is used to denote a value previously bound.

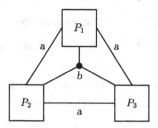

where on gate *a* two processes have to synchronize, and on gate *b* all three processes have to synchronize, in the following way:

> **par** a#2 **in**
>> [a, b] -> P_1
>> || [a, b] -> P_2
>> || [a, b] -> P_3
>
> **endpar**

that is, pairs of processes may synchronize on gate *a*, but all processes synchronize on gate *b*.

Another parallel operator, called *parallel over values*, was also introduced. It represents the interleaving of a series of instantiations of a common (template) behaviour, one for each value in a given list. This allows, for example, to put in parallel a series of nodes of a network, each one with a different identifier, taken from a list of identifiers. For example, if we have a process *Node*[...](*id*:IdType, ...), we can specify a network of five nodes with different identifiers in the following way:

> **par** ?x **in** [1,2,3,4,5] |||
>> *Node*[...](*x*, ...)
>
> **endpar**

The *suspend/resume operator* generalizes the LOTOS disabling. With it, a behaviour may be suspended (as defined in the old disabling operator) and resumed explicitly. That allows the modelling of interruptions, immediate treatment, and so on. With this operator we can specify complex interruption mechanisms, where, for example, a behaviour controls the evolution of others. Let us consider the next process:

> ((B_1 [cont1> stop1; start1; **signal** cont1)
>> |||
>
> (B_2 [cont2> stop2; start2; **signal** cont2))
> | [stop1, stop2, start1, start2] |
>> B_3

The behaviour B_3 controls B_1 and B_2 through gates *stop1*, *start1*, *stop2* and *start2*. B_3 can stop the evolution of B_1 using the gate *stop1* and can restart it using *start1*. Using instead *stop2* and *start2* it can control B_2.

A new, explicit *renaming operator*, applicable to gates and exceptions, was introduced. It allows not just name changing, but also structure modification, such as merging or splitting gates and adding or removing fields from the structure of events. For example, we can also split a gate G into two gates, G_1 and G_2, depending on the values that G carries. Let us suppose that we have defined a process P that sends values (record with two unnamed fields) through a gate *Gout*. It indicates whether they have to go to the right or to the left side, using actions like $Gout(!(left, dat))$ or $Gout(!(right, dat))$ [where *left* and *right* are values of an enumerated type (see Section 5.3.3) and *dat* is a variable with a value of type **data**]. Suppose that we want to use process P in a context where we have two different gates, *LGout* to send values to the left, and *RGout* to send values to the right.

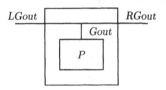

We can use the **rename** operator as follows:

> **rename**
> > **gate** *Gout* $((!left, ?d : \text{data})) : \textbf{any is } LGout(!d)$
> > **gate** *Gout* $((!right, ?d : \text{data})) : \textbf{any is } RGout(!d)$
>
> **in**
> > $P[Gout]()$
>
> **endren**

Process declaration has also been changed. Typed gates, 'in' and 'out' parameters, and abbreviated parameter lists were introduced as helpful shortcuts or useful constructors thanks to the industry feedback to the LOTOS community. 'out' parameters are substituted for the old '**exit**' functionality, improving flexibility and readability.

One of the most powerful characteristics of LOTOS was the modelling of synchronization events: a gate name followed by an expression list. However, there was no way to specify globally which was the communication model for a gate. In other words, each process communicating on a certain gate should know the whole event structure. But there was no way to fix such structures. Two improvements have been included in E-LOTOS to help designers: the first one is that gates can be typed. However, E-LOTOS also allows the old LOTOS style, in which gates were not typed. In fact, that means that a value of *any* type could appear in the event structure. E-LOTOS implicitly types gates with the predefined type **any**, which matches every type in a specification. The second improvement is that partial synchronization is now allowed by means of record subtyping (Section 5.3.3), which is of relevance for using a constraint-oriented approach that can be performed in

E-LOTOS in a much more concise way because each constraint is aware of only the part of the event structure related to it.

A minor difference in E-LOTOS is the removal of precedences. All binary operators (||, |||, |[...]|, [..>) have the same precedence, which is less than ';'. The E-LOTOS grammar forces the user to put parentheses where a behaviour is ambiguous, so that the user cannot mix binary operators without parentheses. Too many parentheses may lead to unreadable specifications, so E-LOTOS also has a *bracketed* syntax for these operators, suggested by Ed Brinksma in his thesis [Bri88] (**sel...endsel, dis...enddis, fullsync...endfullsync**, etc).

5.3.2.1 Imperative Features

In E-LOTOS behaviour sequentialization was given an homogeneous treatment with respect to LOTOS, by merging the action prefix operator (';') and behaviour enabling ('>>') in just one sequential composition operator (';'). Some basic and common imperative constructors were included, such as conditionals (**if − then − else**, **case**) and loops (**for, while**, infinite **loop**). For example, we can define the recursive *Clock* process by using a (possibly) infinite loop:

```
process Clock [stopClock, whatTime:time] (gtime:time) is
  var gt:time:=0, t:time:=0 in
    loop
        whatTime(?gt) @?t [gt=gtime+t] ; ?gtime:=gtime+t
    []
        stopClock; break
    endloop
  endvar
endproc
```

Regarding the use of variables, E-LOTOS was thought of as a functional language, in the sense that there is no state and variables are given a value only once. When a variable is given a value, this value is substituted for the variable in the successive behaviour. However, this idea changed during the design of the language and, finally, E-LOTOS has *write-many* variables, that is, variables that can be assigned several times. The **let** constructor from LOTOS was superseded by a more common, intuitive **var** variable declaration sentence. Besides variable declaration and scope hiding, it allows initialization as well. For example, the behaviour

```
?x := 3;
var x : int := 5 in
  ?y := x
endvar;
inP(!(x,y))
```

offers on the gate *inP* the pair record $(3,5)$.

The key problem was to ensure that some operators were compositional. For example, in the parallel composition $B_1 |[G_1, \ldots, G_n]| B_2$, the branching implies duplication of variable space, as in the UNIX's 'fork(1)', and the behaviours B_1 and B_2 must assign disjoint global variables. There is no *shared memory* that processes running in parallel can use, so communication has to be explicit, that is, B_1 and B_2 can communicate only through gates $G_1, \ldots, G_n$. Besides, if both behaviours were assigned to the same variable, we would not know the last value when the whole behaviour finished.

5.3.3 Data Types

One of the most criticized parts of LOTOS is the data-type definition language, ACT ONE [EFH83], based on algebraic semantics, where equations are used to define the data-type semantics. This language is not user-friendly and suffers from several limitations, such as the semi-decidability of equational specifications (tools cannot implement a procedure that checks equality between two values in a general way), the lack of modularity and the inability to define partial operations.

In E-LOTOS, ACT ONE has been substituted by a new language in which data types are declared in a similar way as they are in functional languages (ML, Haskell), by using more constructive type definitions based on a syntactic and semantic distinction between constructors and functions, which ease the computation of data values, defined in an operational way. In contrast to LOTOS, where there is a separation between processes and functions, E-LOTOS considers functions as kinds of processes. A function in E-LOTOS is any process with the following characteristics: it is deterministic; it cannot communicate (i.e., it has no gates), and so its only capabilities are to return values and raise exceptions; and it has no real-time behaviour (i.e., a function is an immediately exiting process). Therefore, the expression (sub)language is very similar to that of behaviours, once the elements related to these characteristics are removed. This allows that the semantics used to evaluate expressions is the same operational semantics used to describe the execution of a behaviour, that is, there is only one semantics dealing with both expressions and behaviours.

E-LOTOS has a set of predefined, 'built-in' data types (bool, nat, int, rational, float, char and string) with associated operations. These data types are available within any specification. The language allows record types to be easily defined and dealt with: it is possible to declare a record by giving the list of its fields together with their types; for example, we can define the record type

(*name* => string, *address* => string, *age* => nat)

and we can access each field with the '*dot*' notation, for example, *rec*.*name*, provided that variable *rec* has the above type (if variable *rec* is not a record with a field called *name*, then that expression is an error).

There is also a set of *type schemes* that are translated to usual type and function declarations, and which are used to make easier the definition of typical types (as suggested by the 'rich term syntax' of [Pec94]). For example, we can define *enumerated* data types, like

```
type colour is
  enum Blue, Red, Green, Yellow, Pink
endtype
```

In E-LOTOS sets and lists of values of a given type, like sets of naturals or lists of strings, may be defined with (predefined) functions to manipulate their values provided by the language.

Besides the predefined types, the user can define two kinds of types: type synonyms and new data types. A *type synonym* declaration simply declares a new identifier for an existing type, like type Complex to represent complex numbers,†

```
type Complex is
  (real => float, imag => float)
endtype
```

It is also possible to declare a type synonym renaming an existing type. For example, we can define

```
type identifier renames nat endtype
```

and use identifier instead of nat when we declare variables of that type, which can add meaning to the specification.

The declaration of a *new data type* consists of the enumeration of all of the constructors for that type, each one with the types of its arguments (which are optional); for example, the type of messages, data messages or acknowledgement messages may be defined as follows:

```
type pdu is
  send(packet,bit) | ack(bit)
endtype
```

where packet and bit are types defined previously.

These new data types may be recursive, for example, a queue of integers,

```
type intQueue is
  Empty
| Add(intQueue,int)
endtype
```

and functions dealing with this type can be defined in a recursive way, as we show in Section 5.3.4.

Another feature regarding data types is what is called in E-LOTOS 'extensible' record types. The record type

```
(target => address, etc)
```

---

† We have to note that this kind of declaration is mandatory in E-LOTOS since anonymous types such as (*real* => float, *imag* => float) cannot be used to type variables, parameters, gates, etc.

represents a type of records with *at least* one field called *target* of type **address**. This, together with the built-in subtyping relation between record types (a record type is a subtype of another record type that must be extensible, if the former has at least all of the fields that the latter has), means that we have as values of the above type all of the record values that have *at least* a field with that name and type. The following picture illustrates the subtyping relation:

$$(\textit{target} => \text{address}, \text{etc})$$

$(\textit{target} => \text{address}, \textit{id} => \text{identifier}, \text{etc}) \qquad (\textit{target} => \text{address}, \textit{font} => \text{address}, \text{etc})$

$(\textit{target} => \text{address}, \textit{id} => \text{identifier}, \textit{fon t} => \text{address})$

5.3.4 Modularity

LOTOS has a limited form of modularity; modules only encapsulate types and operations but not processes, and they do not support abstraction (every object declared in a module is exported outside).† E-LOTOS has a new modularization system, which allows one to

- define a set of related objects (types, functions and processes) inside a module and to control what objects the module exports (by means of interfaces);
- include within a module the objects declared in other modules (by means of importation clauses);
- hide the implementation of some objects (by means of opaque types, functions and processes); and
- build generic modules.

In order to facilitate this modularization, a separation between the concept of *interface module* and *definition module* is made. An interface declares the visible objects of a module and what the user needs to know about them (the name of a data type or a function profile, for example). A module gives the definition (or implementation) of objects (whether it is visible or not).

E-LOTOS allows one to build *generic modules*, that is, modules with parameters. The features of these parameters are specified by means of interfaces. For example, we can define the data type of queues whose elements are of any type by defining the requirements of these elements in an interface:

> **interface** *Data* **is**
>   **type** elem
> **endint**

and by defining a generic module whose parameter has to fulfill the requirements in the *Data* interface:

---

† A critical evaluation of LOTOS data types from the user point of view can be found in [Mun91].

```
generic GenQueue(D:Data) is
        type queue is
                Empty
              | Add(queue,elem)
        endtype
        function addQueue(q:queue,e:elem):queue is
                Add(q,e)
        endfunc
        function front(q:queue):elem raises [EmptyQueue] is
                case q is
                        Empty -> raise EmptyQueue
                      | Add(Empty,?e) -> e
                      | Add(Add(?q,?e),any:elem) -> front(Add(q,e))
                endcase
        endfunc
        ...
endgen
```

Furthermore, if we want to use queues as abstract data types, that is, only the type queue and the functions could be used but not the constructors (which are internal representations), we can define an interface declaring these objects:

```
interface GenQueueInt is
        type queue
        function addQueue(q:queue,e:elem):queue
        function front(q:queue):elem raises [EmptyQueue]
        ...
endint
```

And we use this interface to restrict the generic module:

```
generic GenQueue(D:Data) : GenQueueInt is
        ...
```

In order to use a generic module we have to instantiate it, by providing actual parameters, which must be modules that match the corresponding interface. A module matches an interface if it implements at least the objects declared in the interface. We can instantiate the above generic queue to make a queue of natural numbers †:

```
module NatQueue is
        GenQueue(D => NaturalNumbers renaming(types nat := elem))
endmod
```

When a module is imported by another module (by means of clause **import**) or is used to instantiate a generic module, the objects it defines can be renamed by means of clause **renaming** followed by the list of renamings. This list can be of different kinds:

- types, **types** $S'_1 := S_1, \ldots, S'_n := S_n$;
- constructors and functions, **opns** $F'_1 := F_1, \ldots, F'_m := F_m$;
- processes; **procs** $\Pi'_1 := \Pi_1, \ldots, \Pi'_p := \Pi_p$; or
- values, **values** $V'_1 := V_1, \ldots, V'_s := V_s$.

† *NaturalNumbers* is one of the predefined modules present in E-LOTOS, which are included in every specification.

The primed identifiers are the old names being renamed, and the unprimed identifiers are the new names.

5.4 A Sender–Receiver Example

In this section, an example based on a sender–receiver specification is used to introduce gently some notions on interfaces and module instantiation, and to show how to produce an E-LOTOS specification from scratch.

The sender–receiver model is presented in Figure 5.2.

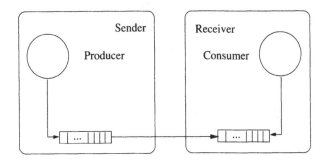

Fig. 5.2. The sender–receiver model.

With this model, an architecture design process starts, establishing the E-LOTOS processes and their relationships, thus specifying the interfaces among processes. A description follows, in Figure 5.3, which represents the design.

The sender communicates with the receiver through a channel of limited bandwidth (bits/second) and a transmission delay (seconds). Each message produced by the sender has a fixed size in bytes. The sender provides a message randomly, which is queued until the channel is available. The channel delivers messages in a receiver queue, in which messages wait for the receiver to pick them up. Both queues can store a limited number of messages. Finally, the channel is a point-to-point, dedicated link.

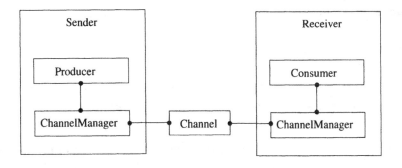

Fig. 5.3. The sender–receiver architecture.

The first step in a top-down design is to establish the communication among the architectural components of the specification. Such interfaces are:

Sender–Receiver Specification

```
specification SenderReceiver imports Messages, SenderMod,
                                     ReceiverMod, ComplexChannel
           is

gates OutIF:msg, InIF:msg

behaviour
    Sender [OutIF] (10.0, 5)  (* sends each 10 time units,
                                 queue length = 5 *)
  |[OutIF]|
    Channel [OutIF, InIF] (0.1, 128*1024) (* delay = 0.1,
                                             bandwidth=10 *)
  |[InIF]|
    Receiver [InIF] (12, 7)   (* consumes each 12 time units,
                                 queue length = 7 *)
endspec
```

A **Sender** process produces an item every 10 time units and delivers it to the channel. The transmission delay is 0.1 time units and there is a bandwidth of 128Kbits/time unit. The **Receiver** consumes a message every 12 time units.

Messages A message is just a piece of data, with no relevant meaning for this specification. Therefore, it is enough to establish that messages accomplish the **Data** interface:

```
interface Data is
    type Elem
endint
```

Queues The **GenQueue** data type was introduced in Section 5.3.4. A generic queue is specified and then instantiated with the **Message** module:

```
module MsgQueue import Messages is
    GenQueue (D => Messages renaming (types msg:=elem))
endmod
```

Sender and Receiver The sender and receiver are processes that each handle a queue to deliver messages to and collect them from the channel. Therefore, a generic **QueueHandler** module will be developed for both processes.

QueueHandler A queue handler process is attached in the outgoing interface of the **Sender** and the coming interface of the **Receiver**. Basically, **QueueHandler** accepts messages and queues them until they can be processed.

```
module QueueHandler import Item, GenQueue is
    process QHandler [in, out] (size:int) is
        var q:Queue := nil in
            loop
                in( ?it:Item ) [length(q) < size];
                q := insert(it, q);
              []
                if (length(q) > 0) then out( !get(q) ) endif
            endloop
        endvar
    endproc
endmod
```

Sender The **Sender** process produces messages with a certain period and submits them to a **QHandler**. Then messages may come out (to the channel). The queue has a limited size, that is, the number of messages is bound, which will stop (back-pressure) the **Producer**. Let us suppose that there is a **Random(N)** function that generates a number with media N and some random distribution. Note how the imported module **QueueHandler** is renamed (Section 5.3.4):

```
module SenderMod
    import Messages,
      QueueHandler renaming (procs QHandler := TransportService)
    is
    process Producer [out] (Period: float) is
        loop
            wait(Random(Period)); out( !msg )
        endloop
    endproc

    process Sender [send] (P : float, N : int) is
        hide deliver in
            Producer [deliver] (P)
          |[ deliver ]|
            TransportService [deliver, send] (N)
        endhide
    endproc
endmod
```

Receiver The **Receiver** process receives messages in a queue (**QueueHandler**). To consume a message takes a certain period of time. In addition, the acceptance queue has a limited storing capability:

```
module ReceiverMod
    import Messages,
      QueueHandler renaming (procs QHandler := TransportService)
    is
    process Consumer [in] is
        loop
            in( ?m:msg )
        endloop
    endproc
```

```
    process Receiver [recv] (N : int) is
        hide give in
            Consumer [give]
        |[ give ]|
            TransportService [recv, give] (N)
        endhide
    endproc
endmod
```

Channel An interface for the channel is provided, so that different implementations may be developed. To simplify, the channel will accept Messages (SDUs) and will deliver them straightforwardly, without packing them in a PDU. A channel is characterized by a propagation delay (in time units) and a bandwidth (in bits per time unit).

```
interface Channel import Messages is
    process Channel [in:msg, out:msg] (delay: float,
                                        bandwidth:float)
endint
```

Hence, we can fulfill a simple channel with a certain delay

```
module SimpleChannel:Channel is
    process Channel [in:msg, out:msg] (delay: float,
                                        bandwidth:float) is
        loop
            in( ?m:msg ); wait(delay); out( !m )
        endloop
    endproc
endmod
```

or we can develop a complete model of a channel (see Figure 5.4):

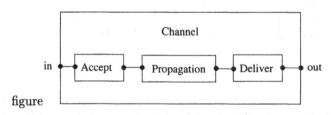

figure

Fig. 5.4. A complex channel architecture.

```
module ComplexChannel:Channel import Messages is
    (* process Accept gets message (i+1) after Pi/B seconds *)
    (* of last messages, being Pi the length of message i *)
    (* and B the bandwidth. Initially, Pi is 0            *)
    process Accept[in:msg, transIn:msg] (bandwidth:float) is
        var Pi:int := 0 in
            loop
                wait(Pi/bandwidth);
                in( ?m: msg);
```

```
                ? Pi := length(m);
                transIn( !m )
          endloop
      endvar
   endproc

   (* process Propagation models the propagation delay
      of the line *)
   process Propagation [transIn:msg, transOut:msg]
                        (delay: float) is
      loop transIn( ?m:msg ); wait(delay); transOut( !m ) endloop
   endproc

(* process Deliver delivers the message in the receiver interface.
   Other messages will be discarded until a message is collected.
   (To be precise, this means that a packet collision occurs, and
   both packet may be dropped, but this simple model will serve
   for our purposes.)                                          *)
   process Deliver [transOut:msg, out:msg] is
     var m:msg, otherM:mgs in
       loop
           transOut( ?m:msg );      (* a message to be delivered *)
           loop
               out( !m ); break          (* delivers the message *)
             []
               transOut( ?otherM:msg ) (* dropped *)
           endloop
       endloop
     endvar
   endproc

   process Channel [in:msg, out:msg] (delay: float,
                                      bandwidth:float) is
       Accept [in, transIn]
     |[ transIn ]|
       Propagation [[transIn, transOut]
     |[ transOut ]|
       Deliver[transOut, out]
   endproc
endmod
```

A `ComplexChannel` is composed by an `Acceptance` process, which models the delay due to the allowed bandwidth and delivered traffic. Then the message goes through a `Propagation` process, which models the transmission delay. Finally, a message arrives at the `in` interface of the receiver, which is modelled by the `Deliver` process. If a message is waiting for delivery, following ones are discarded.

5.5 ODP Trader

In this section we present an overview of the E-LOTOS specification of the ODP Trader computational viewpoint presented in [Que98].

The ODP Trader (see Sections 2.5.1 and 4.2.1) is a good example of how the language can be applied to specify real problems. Our E-LOTOS specification follows the informal computational description of the trading function given in [ISO98].

5.5.1 E-LOTOS Specification of the Trader

This section outlines our E-LOTOS specification of the ODP Trader computational viewpoint. Here we present only the most relevant parts of the specification. In particular, we pay attention to the definition of the trader's behaviour. The reader interested in the complete specification is referred to Annex A of [Que98].

A trader is modelled by a process that can interact with the environment through two ports. In one port, the trader receives operation invocations from clients and management objects. In the other port, it returns the results to the respective invokers. Following the ODP terminology, we will call *termination* the action of returning a result.

A trading community can be described using the new E-LOTOS operator **par** (Section 5.3.2). The following E-LOTOS code shows a scenario where a trader communicates with other client objects. The trader receives invocations on the gate **inv** and sends the respective terminations on the gate **ter**.

```
par inv#2, ter#2, bind#2 in
    [inv,ter]        -> Trader[inv,ter](...)
 || [inv,ter]        -> importer[inv,ter]
 || [bind]           -> importerExporter[bind]
 || [inv,ter,bind] -> bindingObject[inv,ter,bind]
endpar
```

This behaviour expression represents a scenario where the **Trader** and **importer** processes directly interchange data using **inv** and **ter**. The **Trader** and **importer-Exporter** processes are indirectly communicating through the **bindigObject** process, which redirects invocations and terminations of one process to the other.

5.5.1.1 Type Declarations

In the specification, the major part of the type declarations comprise types for the operation parameters. The standard [ISO98] defines these types in CORBA IDL, and their translation to E-LOTOS is very easy. We also translate exception declarations given in CORBA IDL to type declarations in the E-LOTOS notation.

Ports are typed in E-LOTOS; therefore we need to specify types for data exchanged (offered) by E-LOTOS processes. In particular, we need to specify which types are involved in trader interactions.

The signature for operation invocations and terminations is defined as a new data type (Section 5.3.3):

```
type InvocationSig is
   ExportOfferInv ( serviceDescription => ServiceDescription,
                    servicePropValues  => PropertyValueList,
                    offerPropValues    => PropertyValueList,
                    serviceInterfaceId => InterfaceId )
 | ImportOfferInv ( serviceDescription => ServiceDescription,
                    matchingCriteria             => Rule,
                    preferenceCriteria           => Rule,
                    orderingRequirementList      => OrderRequirementList,
                    servicePropertiesOfInterest  => PropertiesOfInterest,
                    offerPropertiesOfInterest    => PropertiesOfInterest )
 | AddLinkInv ( newLinkName     => name,
                linkPropValues   => PropertyValueList,
                targetInterfaceId => InterfaceId )
 | ... (* other invocation signatures *)
endtype

type TerminationSig is
   ExportOfferTer ( offerId => ServiceOfferId )
 | ImportOfferTer ( detailsOfServiceOffers => ServiceOfferDetailList )
 | AddLinkTer ( linkId => LinkId )
 | ... (* other termination signatures *)
endtype
```

Notice that an invocation signature states the input parameters of the respective operation whereas a termination signature states the output parameters.

Every trader or client has an interface identifier that is used in invocations and terminations to distinguish them. Therefore, an invocation (termination) contains the identifier of the invoked trader and the identifier of the originator client. The type of values interchanged in invocations and terminations is defined in E-LOTOS by the following declaration:

```
type Invocation is
   ( interfaceId  => InterfaceIdentifier,
     originatorId => InterfaceIdentifier,
     invocation   => InvocationSig )
endtype

type Termination is
   ( interfaceId  => InterfaceIdentifier,
     originatorId => InterfaceIdentifier,
     termination  => TerminationSig )
endtype
```

5.5.1.2 Computational Behaviour of the Trader

At the most abstract level, the trader object is a parallel composition of three resources (processes). The **ServiceInterface** and **ManagementInterface** processes provide functionality for service operations and management operations, respectively. The process **StateProc** represents the trader state.

```
process Trader [inv: Invocation, ter: Termination]
                ( interfaceId: InterfaceIdentifier,
                  properties : Properties,
                  offerSpace : ServiceOfferSpace,
                  linkSpace :  linkOfferSpace ) is
  hide sa:stateAccess in
      ( ServiceInterface [inv, ter, sa] (interfaceId)
      ||| ManagementInterface [inv, ter, sa] (interfaceId) )
    |[sa]|
      StateProc [sa] ( properties, offerSpace, linkSpace )
  endhide
endproc (* Trader *)
```

Service operations write in only the trader service offer space while management
operations write in the only trader link space and/or change trader properties.
Therefore, service and management operations can be performed in parallel without
destroying the consistency of the trader state.

The process StateProc encapsulates three elements that together comprise the
trader state: a set of trader properties, the service offer space and the link space.
Service and management operations use the trader state through the port sa, which
is hidden within the trader.

In order to illustrate how the operation's behaviour is defined, we give the definition of the ServiceInterface process. In this process, all service operations are
offered to clients in parallel. However, the availability of operations is constrained in
such a way that accessing operations (as import offer) and modifying operations (as
export offer) cannot be overlapped in time. The availability of operations is defined
in a constraint-oriented style by composing the processes representing operations
with the OrderingConstraints process.

```
process ServiceInterface [ inv: Invocation, ter: Termination,
                           sa: stateAccessCh ]
                         ( interfaceId: InterfaceIdentifier ) is
      (     ImportOffer [inv, ter, sa] (interfaceId)
      ||| exportOffer [inv, ter, sa] (interfaceId)
      ||| .... (* other service operations *)     )
  |[inv, ter]|
     OrderingConstraints [inv, ter]
endproc (*ServiceInterface *)
```

The most significant and complex service operation is the importation of an offer.
The behaviour of the operation is given below by the ImportOffer process definition.

Informally, for each invocation the ImportOffer process performs the following activities: receive the invocation; access the state to get the offer database, trader links
and trader properties; match the offers against arguments and propagate the import
invocation to interoperate with 'neighbouring' traders; and, when some trader finds
good matches, they are submitted in the termination.

```
process ImportOffer [ inv: Invocation, ter: Termination,
                      sa: stateAccess ] (id: InterfaceId) is
   inv ( !id, ?origId,
         ImportOfferInv ( ?sd, ?matchingC, ?preferenceC,
                          ?ordering, ?spOfInt, ?opOfInt ) ) ;
   sa ( Read( ?traderProp, ?offers, ?links ) ) ;
   trap
      exception X ( offers: ServiceOfferDetailList ) is
         ter ( !id, !origId, ImportOfferTer(!offers) )
      endexn
      exit is
         ter ( !id, !origId, ImportOfferTer(!emptyOffers) )
      endexit
   in
      ... (* match local offers *)
    |||
      ... (* interoperate with other traders *)
   endtrap
 |||
   ImportOffer [ inv, ter, sa ] ( id )
endproc
```

The above definition illustrates the use of the trap constructor. We use this construct to express that, when several traders are interoperating in an import operation, the matched offers returned to the original importer are those of the 'first' trader that was successful in the matching activity.

5.6 Conclusions

The E-LOTOS language offers key characteristics to succeed in both the industrial and the academic environments. From the industrial point of view, the new language offers a simplified syntax, more friendly data types (similar to high-level programming language data types), imperative-like structures (loops, decisions, exceptions, etc.), write-many variables, and so on. From the academic point of view, it offers formal support for time properties, new parallel operators, typed gates and many other minor modifications that increment the systems description power of the language. Nevertheless, the language does not lose its stronger points: a good and solid formal support for verification, validation and system analysis in general. During the standardization process, inputs have been received and integrated from research and industrial groups in Europe, America and Asia. The new language reflects new trends in formal language definition with influences from other formal languages, and it has borrowed elements from common high-level language paradigms.

Bibliography

[Bri88]   E. Brinksma. *On the Design of Extended LOTOS, a Specification Language for Open Distributed Systems.* PhD thesis, University of Twente, November 1988.

[EFH83]   H. Ehrig, W. Fey, and H. Hansen. ACT ONE: An algebraic specification language with t wo levels of semantics. Technical Report 83–03, Technical University of Berlin, Fachbereich Informatik, 1983.

[Hoa85]   C. A. R. Hoare. *Communicating Sequential Processes*. Prentice-Hall, 1985.

[HR95]   M. Hennessy and T. Regan. A process algebra for timed systems. *Information and Computation*, 117:221–239, 1995.

[HRLDV99]   G. Huecas, T. Robles, L. F. Llana-D´ıaz,and A. Verdejo. E-LOTOS: An Overview. In M. A., J. Quemada, T. Robles, and M. Silva, editors, *Formal Methods and Telecommunications (FM&T99)*, pages 94–102. Universitaria de Zaragoza, 1999.

[ISO89]   ISO. *Information Processing Systems – Open Systems Interconnection – LOTOS - A Formal Description Technique Based on the Temporal Ordering of Observational Behaviour*. IS-8807. International Standards Organization, Geneva, September 1989.

[ISO98]   *ISO/IEC IS 13235-1, Open Distributed Processing - Trading Function: Specification*. ISO, 1998.

[LdN96]   L. F. Llana-Díaz, D. de Frutos, and M. Núñez. Testing semantics for urgent process algebras. In *Third AMAST Workshop in Real Time Programming*, pages 33–46, 1996.

[LL94]   G. Leduc and L. Leonard. An enhanced version of timed LOTOS and its application to a case study. In R. Tenney, P. Amer, and Ü. Uyar, editors, *FORTE '93*. North Holland, 1994.

[Mil89]   R. Milner. *Communication and Concurrency*. Prentice-Hall, 1989.

[Mun91]   H. B. Munster. LOTOS specification of the MAA standard, with an evaluation of LOTOS. NPL Report DITC 191/91, National Physical Laboratory, Teddington, Middlesex, UK, September 1991.

[OMdF90]   Y. Ortega-Mallén and D. de Frutos. Timed observations: a semantic model for real-time concurrency. In M. Broy and C. B. Jones, editors, *TC2-Working Conference on Programming Concepts and Methods*. Noth-Holland, 1990.

[Pec94]   C. Pecheur. A proposal for data t ypesfor E-LOTOS. Technical report, University of Li`ege,October 1994. Annex H of ISO/IEC JTC1/SC21/WG1 N1349 Working Draft on Enhancements to LOTOS.

[QMdL94]   J. Quemada, C. Miguel, D. de Frutos, and L. Llana. A timed LOTOS extension. In T. Rus, editor, *Theories and Experiencies for Real-Time System Development*, volume 2 of *AMAST Series in Computing*, pages 239–263. World Scientific, 1994.

[Que98]   J. Quemada, editor. Final committee draft on Enhancements to LOTOS. ISO/IEC JTC1/SC21/WG7 Project 1.21.20.2.3., May 1998.

[RR86]   G. M. Reed and A. W. Roscoe. A timed model for communicating sequential processes. In *ICALP '86*, volume 226 of *Lecture Notes in Computer Science*, pages 314–323. Springer-Verlag, 1986.

[RR88]   G. M. Reed and A. W. Roscoe. A timed model for communicating sequential processes. *Theoretical Computer Science*, 58:249–261, 1988.

[RR99]   G. M. Reed and A. W. Roscoe. The timed failures-stability model for CSP. *Theoretical Computer Science*, 211:85–127, 1999.

[Sch95]   S. Schneider. An operational semantics for timed CSP. *Information and Computation*, 116(2):193–213, 1995.

6

State-Based Approaches: From Z to Object-Z

Graeme Smith

University of Queensland, Australia

In this chapter we look at state-based specification notations and how they may be extended with concepts from object orientation. In particular, we focus on the Z specification language [ISO00, Spi92] and one of its object-oriented extensions, Object-Z [Smi00, DR00, DRS96]. The state-based paradigm is introduced in Section 6.1 by specifying an ODP Trader object in Z. Section 6.2 provides an overview of other state-based notations, and Section 6.3 discusses how such notations have been extended to support object orientation. In Section 6.4, we present a specification of the ODP Trading function in Object-Z.

6.1 The State-Based Paradigm

The state-based specification paradigm is characterized by the explicit specification of states and the implicit specification of system behaviour: the behaviour must be deduced from initial states and operations modelling possible state transitions. This is in contrast to process algebra approaches, where system behaviour is explicit and states are implicit (see Chapter 5), and it also differs from algebraic techniques, where both states and behaviour are implicitly modelled.

One of the most popular state-based specification notations is Z. Z is based on the mathematics of set theory and first-order predicate logic. It was developed from the work of Abrial et al. [ASM80] by the Programming Research Group at Oxford University [Sør82, MS84, Hay93, Spi92, WD96] and is currently undergoing international standardization [ISO00].

A typical Z specification consists of a number of definitions of data structures used to define the state of the specified system, and a number of schemas that describe the allowable states, initial states and operations of the system. In the remainder of this section, we provide an example of Z specification through the specification of an ODP Trader object. The specification is based loosely on that in the ODP standard [ISO98].

6.1.1 Modelling State

The state space of a system is modelled in Z by a state schema. Such a schema declares a number of typed state variables. The types of the state variables are either basic types, for example, the set of all integers, or constructed from basic types. The kinds of constructed types are set types, Cartesian product types and schema types.

Basic types denoting the set of all integers (denoted $\mathbb{Z}$), the set of all natural numbers (denoted $\mathbb{N}$) and the set of all strictly positive natural numbers (denoted $\mathbb{N}_1$) are implicitly included in all Z specifications. Other basic types can be introduced into a specification as *given sets*. For example, to specify the ODP Trader, we require two given sets: the set of all properties that a service may be associated with, and the set of all identifiers of service offers. The latter is needed to ensure that service offers can be identified unambiguously. These given sets are introduced into our specification by the following notation:

$[ServiceProperty, ServiceOfferIdentifier]$

The set of properties associated with a particular service is a subset of the set *ServiceProperty*. The type of a service is hence defined as a set type as follows. ($\mathbb{P} \, X$ denotes the powerset of set X, that is, the set of all subsets of X including the empty set and the set X itself.)

$Service == \mathbb{P} \, ServiceProperty$

A service offer comprises an identifier and a set of properties corresponding to a service. Hence, its type can be defined as a Cartesian product type, that is, a set of ordered pairs, as follows:

$ServiceOffer == ServiceOfferIdentifier \times Service$

A variable of type *ServiceOffer* will therefore be a single ordered pair. The notation introduced so far can also be used to specify the types of variables whose values are a set of ordered pairs. For example, the type of a set of service offers satisfying some criteria can be specified as follows:

$Criteria == \mathbb{P} \, ServiceOffer$

Sets of ordered pairs can be used to represent commonly occurring constructs such as relations, functions and sequences. For functions, the sets must be constrained so that each domain element (occurring in the first position of an ordered pair) is associated with only a single range element (occurring in the second position of the ordered pair). For sequences, the domain elements must range over a contiguous set of natural numbers starting from 1. These numbers denote the position in the sequence of the range elements.

These additional constraints could be specified in a Z specification by using predicates. However, Z has a number of predefined symbols for such commonly occurring constructs. For example, the notation $X \nrightarrow Y$ denotes the set of all (partial) functions from the set X to the set Y. Similarly, the notation seq X denotes the set of sequences of items from the set X. Hence, we can specify the type of a function that returns the order in which selected service offers are to be returned to an importer as follows:

$$Preference == \mathbb{P}\, ServiceOffer \nrightarrow \text{seq}\, ServiceOffer$$

To constrain this definition further so that the returned sequence comprises exactly those elements of *ServiceOffer* in the set, we add to the specification the following predicate. (ran X and dom X return the set of elements in the domain and range, respectively, of a relation, function or sequence X. $\#X$ returns the number of elements in a set or sequence X.)

$$\forall p : Preference \bullet (\forall q : \text{dom}\, p \bullet \text{ran}(p(q)) = q \wedge \#p(q) = \#q)$$

The conjunct $\text{ran}(p(q)) = q$ assures that the elements in the sequence, that is, $\text{ran}(p(q))$, are the same as those in the set. The conjunct $\#p(q) = \#q$ assures that elements from the set appear only once in the sequence.

The final kind of type is a schema type. Schema types are similar to record types in programming languages. Schemas comprise a number of typed variables and an optional constraint on these variables. They are denoted by a named box in which the variable declarations and constraints are separated by a horizontal line. For example, the type of the trading policy of an ODP Trader object could be specified as follows. (The notation $X \rightarrow Y$ denotes the set of total functions from the set X to the set Y.)

$$
\begin{array}{|l}
\underline{\ \ TradingPolicy} \\
\quad criteria : Criteria \\
\quad modify\_preference : Preference \rightarrow Preference \\
\hline
\quad \forall p_1, p_2 : Preference \bullet \\
\qquad modify\_preference(p_1) = p_2 \Rightarrow \{s : \mathbb{P}\, criteria\} \subseteq \text{dom}(p_2) \\
\end{array}
$$

The variable *criteria* denotes the criteria that service offers must satisfy to be offered to an importer. The variable *modify_preference* denotes the way in which an importer's preference for the ordering of service offers is modified according to the trader's policy. This latter variable is constrained by the schema to ensure that the modified preference orders all sets of service offers satisfying the criteria.

As previously mentioned, schemas are also used in Z specifications to model the state space of the specified system. For example, the state space of an ODP Trader object comprises the trader's policy and a set of service offers that have been exported to the trader. Each service offer in this set must have a unique identifier. The trader's state schema is specified as follows. (The predefined function *first* returns the first element of an ordered pair. The predefined function *second*, not used here, returns the second element.)

```
┌─ Trader ─────────────────────────────────────────────────────
│ policy : TradingPolicy
│ offers : ℙ ServiceOffer
├──────────────────────────
│ ∀ p, q : offers • first(p) = first(q) ⇒ p = q
└──────────────────────────────────────────────────────────────
```

The predicate of a state schema is referred to as a state invariant. In general, more than one state schema can be used to specify a system. The partitioning provided by the schemas in such cases can improve the readability of the specification.

6.1.2 Initialization

The initial state space of a system, that is, those states that the system may be in before any operations have occurred, is specified in Z by placing further constraints on the system's entire state space as defined by the state schemas. It is modelled by schemas that include the declarations and predicates of the state schemas. For example, when a trader is in an initial state, no service offers have been exported. This is specified as follows:

```
┌─ TraderInit ─────────────────────────────────────────────────
│ Trader
├──────────
│ offers = ∅
└──────────────────────────────────────────────────────────────
```

The inclusion of the state schema name *Trader* in the declaration part of this schema denotes that the declarations and predicates of *Trader* are implicitly included. That is, the schema *TraderInit* is equivalent to the following:

```
┌─ TraderInit ─────────────────────────────────────────────────
│ policy : TradingPolicy
│ offers : ℙ ServiceOffer
├──────────────────────────
│ ∀ p, q : offers • first(p) = first(q) ⇒ p = q
│ offers = ∅
└──────────────────────────────────────────────────────────────
```

6.1.3 Operations

The operations of a system model the allowable state changes. They are also modelled by schemas. The operation schemas are required to relate the state before the operation, together with any operation inputs, to the state after the operation, together with any outputs. To do this, Z has a number of conventions for decorating variables associated with operation schemas:

- An undecorated variable denotes the value of that variable before the operation.
- A variable denoted with a prime, for example, *offers'*, denotes the value of a variable after the operation.

- A variable decorated with a query, for example, *new_offer?*, denotes an input to the operation.

- A variable decorated with a shriek, for example, *new_offer_identifier!*, denotes an output to the operation.

Given a state schema S, a schema ΔS is implicitly defined that declares the variables declared in S in both undecorated and primed forms, and constrains both forms of the variables in the same way that they are constrained in S. For example, the following schema is implicitly included in our specification of the ODP Trader object:

```
┌─ Δ Trader ──────────────────────────────────
│ policy, policy' : TradingPolicy
│ offers, offers' : ℙ ServiceOffer
├─────────────────────────────────────────────
│ ∀ p, q : offers • first(p) = first(q) ⇒ p = q
│ ∀ p, q : offers' • first(p) = first(q) ⇒ p = q
└─────────────────────────────────────────────
```

Including such schemas in operation schemas enables access to the variables before and after the operation, and assures that the state invariant is maintained. For example, the operation corresponding to the successful export of a service offer can be specified as follows:

```
┌─ ExportOK ──────────────────────────────────
│ Δ Trader
│ new_offer? : ServiceOffer
│ new_offer_identifier! : ServiceOfferIdentifier
├─────────────────────────────────────────────
│ (∀ p : offers • first(p) ≠ first(new_offer?))
│ offers' = offers ∪ {new_offer?}
│ new_offer_identifier! = first(new_offer?)
│ policy' = policy
└─────────────────────────────────────────────
```

This operation has an input *new_offer?* that, according to the first predicate of the schema, has an identifier that is distinct from those already in the set *offers*. This input is added to the set *offers*. The operation also has an output *new_offer_identifier!* that is equal to the identifier of *new_offer?*. This is required because the source of the service offer identifier is not stated in the standard: it may be generated by the trader. The communication of the identifier in both directions leaves its origin undefined.

The final predicate of *ExportOK* states that the trader's policy is unchanged. This is required because any variable not constrained by the predicates may change to any value consistent with its type. This interpretation is adopted in Z to allow operations in which values are chosen nondeterministically. Support for nondeterminism is desirable in specifications since a purely deterministic specification may unnecessarily constrain the choice of possible system implementations.

To simplify specifying operations that do not change the state of a system, given a state schema S, a schema ΞS is implicitly defined. This schema extends ΔS with the constraint that all primed variables are equal to their undecorated counterparts. For example, the following schema is implicitly included in our specification of the ODP Trader object:

$$
\begin{array}{|l}
\_\Xi\ \textit{Trader}\ \underline{\hspace{8cm}} \\
\Delta\ \textit{Trader} \\
\hline
\textit{policy}' = \textit{policy} \\
\textit{offers}' = \textit{offers} \\
\end{array}
$$

It is included in the definition of the following operation schema, which models a successful search for a particular service offer. (Given a schema S and a variable $s : S$, if x is a variable declared in S, then $s.x$ denotes the value of that variable for the schema instance s.)

$$
\begin{array}{|l}
\_\textit{SearchOK}\ \underline{\hspace{8cm}} \\
\Xi\ \textit{Trader} \\
\textit{criteria?} : \textit{Criteria} \\
\textit{preference?} : \textit{Preference} \\
\textit{search\_result!} : \text{seq}\ \textit{ServiceOffer} \\
\hline
\textbf{let}\ \textit{suitable\_offers} == \textit{offers} \cap \textit{criteria?} \cap \textit{policy.criteria}; \\
\quad \textit{modified\_preference} == \textit{policy.modify\_preference}(\textit{preference?}) \bullet \\
\quad\quad \textit{search\_result!} = \textit{modified\_preference}(\textit{suitable\_offers}) \\
\end{array}
$$

The operation has two inputs denoting the importer's criteria and preference for the ordering of returned service offers. It has a single output denoting the returned service offers whose value is defined in terms of two local variables: *suitable_offers*, denoting previously exported service offers that satisfy both the importer's criteria and the trader's policy, and *modified_preference*, denoting the preference for the ordering returned service offers based on the importer's preference and the trader's policy.

6.1.4 Preconditions

Associated with each operation schema of a Z specification is an implicit precondition. If the operation is applied in a state and with inputs such that its precondition is true, then the state after the operation and the operation's outputs are guaranteed to satisfy the operation's predicate. If the operation is applied in a state or with inputs that do not satisfy its precondition, then the resulting state and outputs are undefined.

The precondition of an operation holds for those inputs and states before the operation for which there exist outputs and states after the operation satisfying the operation's predicate. For example, the precondition of *ExportOK* is given by the following schema:

---
pre *ExportOK*

Trader
new_offer? : *ServiceOffer*

$\exists\, policy'$: *TradingPolicy*; *offers'* : $\mathbb{P}$ *ServiceOffer*;
　　new_offer_identifier! : *ServiceOfferIdentifier* •
　　　　$(\forall\, p : offers \bullet first(p) \neq first(new\_offer?))$
　　　　offers' = *offers* $\cup$ {*new_offer?*}
　　　　new_offer_identifier! = *first*(*new_offer?*)
　　　　policy' = *policy*

The predicate of this schema can be simplified since the existence of primed variables and outputs satisfying the constraints can be implied by the constraints on the undecorated and input variables. That is, the precondition of *ExportOK* is given by the following schema:

---
pre *ExportOK*

Trader
new_offer? : *ServiceOffer*

$\forall\, p : offers \bullet first(p) \neq first(new\_offer?)$

It follows that if *ExportOK* is applied with an input *new_offer?* whose service offer identifier, *first*(*new_offer?*), is equal to that of a service offer already in the set *offers*, then the resulting state and outputs are undefined. The specification therefore could be considered inadequate (since the service offer identifier may be generated by the exporter who has no access to the set *offers* and hence may sometimes generate an identifier that has already been used). A more robust specification can be given by defining another schema modelling this error condition and leaving the trader's state unchanged.

ExportError

Ξ *Trader*
new_offer? : *ServiceOffer*

$\exists\, p : offers \bullet first(p) = first(new\_offer?)$

The export operation can then be defined using the schema disjunction operator of Z as follows:

Export $\mathrel{\widehat=}$ *ExportOK* $\vee$ *ExportError*

The schema disjunction operator produces a new schema by merging the declarations of the argument schemas and disjoining their predicates. The precondition of *Export* holds, therefore, whether or not the identifier of *new_offer?* is in *offers*.

6.1.5 Refinement

Z is a notation, rather than a methodology, and as such it does not include a set of refinement rules. However, a number of approaches to refinement in Z have been proposed [WD96, DB01]. Each of these approaches can be categorized as either procedural or data refinement.

Procedural refinement is concerned with refining operations. This is done in such a way that the possible behaviours of a specification, for a given sequence of operations and inputs, are reduced. This can be achieved by reducing the nondeterminism in the defined outcome of operations. It can also be achieved by weakening operation preconditions, that is, by making preconditions true more often, which makes the resulting states and outputs of the operations defined more often.

The refinement calculus of Morgan [Mor90] introduces a set of rules for the procedural refinement of specification statements. A specification statement is of the form

$$frame : [precondition, postcondition]$$

where *frame* is a list of variables that the operation may change, *precondition* is a predicate denoting the operation's precondition and *postcondition* is a predicate denoting the operation's effect when the precondition holds. As shown by Woodcock and Davies [WD96], among others, Z operation schemas can be easily translated to specification statements.

As well as rules for weakening the preconditions and strengthening the postconditions of specification statements, Morgan's refinement calculus includes rules for decomposing specification statements into sequences of simpler statements, and introducing programming language constructs such as assignments, conditionals and loops.

Data refinement allows, in addition to the refinement of operations, the representation of the state space of a specification to be changed. It requires the existence of a retrieve relation that maps states of the original (abstract) specification to states of the new (concrete) specification. The operations of the concrete specification must be procedural refinements of the abstract operations when this relation is applied to their pre- and poststates. For example, consider changing the representation of the type *TradingPolicy* to include two criteria: a matching criteria and a scope criteria. A service offer is offered to an importer only when it satisfies both criteria.

__ *TradingPolicy*1 _____

matching_criteria, *scope_criteria* : *Criteria*
modify_preference : *Preference* → *Preference*

$\forall\, p_1, p_2 : Preference \bullet$
$\quad modify\_preference(p_1) = p_2 \Rightarrow$
$\qquad \{\, s : \mathbb{P}(matching\_criteria \cap scope\_criteria)\} \subseteq \mathrm{dom}(p_2)$

Let the state schema of the new trader specification be the following:

__ *Trader*1 _____

*policy*1 : *TradingPolicy*1
*offers*1 : $\mathbb{P}$ *ServiceOffer*

$\forall\, p, q : offers1 \bullet first(p) = first(q) \Rightarrow p = q$

The necessary retrieve relation is defined by the schema *Retrieve*:

__ *Retrieve* _____

Trader
*Trader*1

---
policy.criteria = *policy*1.*matching_criteria* ∩ *policy*1.*scope_criteria*
policy.modify_preference = *policy*1.*modify_preference*
offers = *offers*1

The predicate of this schema relates the state variables of *Trader* to those of *Trader*1. In particular, *policy.criteria* is equal to the intersection of *policy*1.*matching-_criteria* and *policy*1.*scope_criteria*. To complete the data refinement, the operations would need to be redefined in terms of *Trader*1, and, in the case of *SearchOK*, the predicate would need to be modified to reflect the use of *matching_criteria* and *scope_criteria* in determining suitable service offers.

6.2 State-Based Techniques

A number of notations exist for writing state-based specifications. Each, like Z, explicitly model a system's state. In this section we provide a brief overview of a few of these and compare them with Z and each other.

6.2.1 VDM

The Vienna Development Method (VDM) [Jon90, JS90] originated at the IBM Laboratory in Vienna [BJ78] and was subsequently developed by Bjørner and Jones [Jon80, BJ82, Jon90]. It is currently undergoing standardization [ISO93]. VDM differs from Z in that it is a development method, including rules for developing

specifications by data refinement and operation decomposition, as well as a notation. Furthermore, it is a wide-spectrum technique having imperative programming
constructs as part of the notation. In this section, however, we will focus on the
specification language used in VDM (referred to as VDM-SL in the VDM standard).

The underlying logic of VDM is 3-valued as opposed to the classical (2-valued)
logic used in Z. This enables undefined values resulting from the application of a
partial function outside its domain to be explicitly treated. Such undefined values
must be avoided in Z, for example, by explicitly ensuring that the domains of partial
functions cover the required values.

Syntactically, the major difference between Z and VDM is that, rather than
schema boxes, VDM uses keywords to delimit different parts of a specification.
These keywords distinguish the different roles of the specification parts. For example, a VDM specification of the state space of a trader object may be specified
as follows. (We assume that the types *TradingPolicy* and *ServiceOffer* have been
suitably defined).

$$Trader :: policy : TradingPolicy$$
$$offers : ServiceOffer\text{-}\mathbf{set}$$
$$\mathbf{inv}\ (mk\text{-}Trader(policy, offers))\ \underline{\Delta}$$
$$(\forall\, p, q \in offers \cdot p.id = q.id \Rightarrow p = q)$$

The keyword **inv** indicates that the predicate following it is an invariant of the
system. The role of the equivalent predicate in the Z specification was indicated
only informally by the accompanying text.

Operations in VDM also have explicit preconditions. While this avoids the need to
derive the precondition, as in Z, it introduces a proof obligation that the operation
is consistent, that is, that the actual precondition of the operation is covered by
the stated one. In addition, VDM has a module structure that encapsulates the
specification of the state space with the specification of operations. Hence, it is not
necessary to include the state in the operations as is done in Z by using schemas of
the form ΔS. Also, VDM operations explicitly list the variables that they change
and hence predicates such as *policy'* = *policy* of *ExportOK* in the Z specification are
not required.

6.2.2 B

The B method [Abr96, SS98] was developed (from early research on Z) by Abrial and
research groups at Oxford University and BP Research, Sunbury, UK. Like VDM
it is a development method, rather than just a notation, and it is a wide-spectrum
technique. It enables refinement down to code in a single semantic framework. In
this section, we will focus on its specification language B AMN (Abstract Machine
Notation).

The underlying logic of B AMN is identical to that of Z. However, syntactically B
AMN is closer to VDM since it uses keywords to delimit parts of specifications and

has explicit preconditions and a module structure. The main difference from both Z and VDM is in the way that B AMN specifies operations. In order to provide a uniform notation from abstract specifications down to procedural code, it defines operations using a notion of generalized substitution. Rather than predicates in terms of before and after values of variables, postconditions are built from basic substitutions, or assignments, of the form **x := e** using a selection of constructs. For example, the operation *ExportOK* could be specified as follows. (We assume that the type **ServiceOffer** has been suitably defined.)

new_offer_identifier ⟵ **export_ok(new_offer)** $\hat{=}$
    PRE **new_offer** ∈ **ServiceOffer** ∧
        (∀ **p.ident**(p) ≠ **ident**(**new_offer**))
    THEN
        offers := offers ∪ **new_offer** ‖
        new_offer_identifier := ident(**new_offer**)
    END

The operation involves two constructs. The first construct, of the form PRE **P** THEN **S** END, denotes that the operation will behave as **S** provided that the precondition **P** holds. As in VDM, the explicit precondition introduces a proof obligation. The second construct, **S1** ‖ **S2**, denotes that the operation results in both **S1** and **S2**.

6.2.3 Liskov and Wing Notation

The notation of Liskov and Wing (see Chapter 12) was developed primarily for investigating notions of behavioural subtyping. It is similar to VDM and B in that it uses keywords to delimit parts of the specification and has explicit preconditions and a module structure. A module in Liskov and Wing's notation, however, corresponds to a type, and its properties are given in terms of instances of that type. It is therefore closer to the notion of a class in object-oriented languages than the modules of VDM or B. A module specification in Liskov and Wing's notation may also have history properties, that is, properties over sequences of states. These are specified using a constraint clause. For example, the fact that the policy of a trader object t never changes is captured as follows:

constraint $t_\rho.policy = t_\psi.policy$

Such explicit constraints make proving the subtype relation between modules simpler. They can also be used to check the correctness of the specification by proving that the operations maintain the history property.

Modules also have a subtype clause for each of their supertypes. Each subtype clause relates the module to one of its supertypes by using an abstraction function similar to the abstraction relation used for data refinement in Z. For example, the fact that a module **trader1** based on the the refined Z specification of Section 6.1.5

is a subtype of a module **trader** based on the original Z specification of Section 6.1
is recorded in the specification of **trader1** as follows:

> **subtype of trader** (*Import* **for** *Search*)
>> $\forall t : trader1 . A(t) = \langle mk\_policy(t.policy), t.offers \rangle$
>>> **where** $mk\_policy : TradingPolicy1 \to TradingPolicy$
>>>> $\forall p : TradingPolicy1$
>>>>> $mk\_policy(p).criteria =$
>>>>>> $p.matching\_criteria \cap p.scope\_criteria$
>>>>> $mk\_policy(p).modify\_preference = p.modify\_preference$

A subtype must have at least all of the operations of its supertypes; however, these
operation may be renamed. The above clause indicates that the *Search* operation
of the type *trader* has been renamed to *Import* in *trader1*. The explicit inclusion of
the abstraction function in a specification enables proofs of subtyping to be carried
out in a relatively straightforward manner.

6.3 Object-Oriented Extensions

State-based specification languages are ideal for modelling in an object-oriented
fashion since states and operations (or methods) are central to both paradigms.
In fact, Z has been used without any extension for object-oriented modelling by
Hall [Hal90, Hal94] and Smith [Smi94b]. These approaches, based on conventions
for writing specifications, do not have explicit notions of encapsulation of state
and operations. They must also model notions such as object identity explicitly.
Furthermore, some conventions, such as that for modelling the effect on a system of
a component object undergoing an operation, are relatively complex.

Therefore, a number of object-oriented extension have been proposed for Z and
VDM [SBC92, LH94]. In this section we provide an overview of how state-based
languages have been extended to incorporate object orientation.

6.3.1 Classes

Syntactically, classes can be incorporated in a state-based language in a similar fashion to modules in VDM and B, that is, by encapsulating the specification of a state
space with all of the operations that can affect its variables. The difference between
classes and modules, however, is that classes define a set of objects. Individual objects may be declared by using the class as a type. In this respect, the modules of
Liskov and Wing's notation can be regarded as classes.

Extensions of VDM and Z incorporating classes include, among others, VDM++
[Lan95], MooZ [MC90], ZEST [ZS96] and Object-Z [Smi00, DR00]. In the former
two languages encapsulation is modelled by using keywords and in the latter two
by extending the schema notation of Z to include a class schema. In addition to
state and operations, classes in VDM++ and earlier versions of Object-Z [DRS96]

include means of specifying behavioural properties of their objects through history properties.

6.3.2 Objects

The notion of objects can be incorporated in a state-based language by using classes as types. An instance of such a type is either an object or an identifier of an object. The former interpretation, used in MooZ and ZEST (and originally in VDM++ and Object-Z), provides a semantics that is closer to that of the notation being extended. The latter interpretation, used in VDM++ and Object-Z, provides a semantics closer to that of object-oriented programming languages, where instances of class types are references, or pointers, to objects. This removes the need to explicitly model object identities as is done in the other languages. Furthermore, it facilitates the refinement of specification to code in an object-oriented programming language and also enables the direct specification of systems in which object sharing and mutual references occur.

Each of the languages has notations for accessing the state of objects and applying operations to them. This notation generally reflects that used in object-oriented programming languages. For example, to apply an operation Op of class A to an object $a : A$, the notation $a.Op$ is used in Object-Z.

6.3.3 Subtyping

As illustrated by Liskov and Wing's approach, behavioural subtyping is based on (data) refinement in the state-based paradigm. That is, a class A is a subtype of a class B precisely when it is a refinement of B. This follows from the observation that both subtyping and refinement require that an object of class B (the refinement or subtype) be substitutable for an object of class A.

The definition of behavioural subtyping (also referred to as *behavioural compatibility* in the literature) inherently depends on this notion of substitutability. Hence, it depends on the allowable interactions between an object and its environment. These are defined by the constructs available in the specification language [Smi95]. In addition, these interactions depend on whether objects are regarded as active entities, which perform operations autonomously, or passive entities, which perform operations only when directed to do so by their environment [BD91, DBS96, Smi94a]. Finally, the interpretation of an operation's precondition must be taken into account. In Object-Z, for example, a precondition corresponds to a guard rather than a precondition in the Z sense. This means that operations are *blocked*, that is, they cannot occur, outside their preconditions rather than having an undefined outcome. Hence, precondition weakening is not appropriate as a means of refinement, and hence subtyping, in Object-Z.

6.3.4 Inheritance

Inheritance is concerned with sharing the structure, that is, state and operations, of classes. Hence, it is easily incorporated into state-based approaches. Syntactically, the notion of inheritance, including multiple inheritance, is easily captured by the inclusion of the names of the superclasses at an appropriate position in a class (usually before the other definitions). This inclusion is analogous to schema inclusion in Z, that is, the definitions from the superclasses are in some way merged with those in the subclass.

Semantically, there are a number of pertinent issues. First, which of the definitions of the superclasses are inherited? VDM++ distinguishes between inheritance of state and inheritance of methods. MooZ enables public definitions to be private in the subclass, that is, not part of its objects' interfaces. Object-Z enables definitions to be effectively removed by excluding them from the subclass's visibility list. Second, how may inherited definitions be redefined in the subclass? The mechanisms described for the selective inheritance of definitions allow cancelled definitions to be redefined in any possible way within the subclass. In addition, MooZ, ZEST and Object-Z utilize Z's notions of schema inclusion or schema conjunction to extend inherited definitions with further constraints in the subclass.

Due to such mechanisms for redefinition, the sharing of structure between classes does not generally lead to their sharing of behaviour. Therefore, inheritance must be suitably constrained to maintain subtyping. Early work on ZEST [Cus91] included, as well as a general form of inheritance, a special form of inheritance that ensured subtyping.

6.3.5 Polymorphism

Polymorphism may be specified based on collections of classes that are related by subtyping or inheritance, or chosen arbitrarily. It may occur either implicitly or by the use of explicit constructs. For example, in ZEST all objects of a class A are implicitly also objects of any class B that is a superclass of A. In Object-Z, an object belongs to only one class but notations exist to declare an object whose class may be any from a particular inheritance hierarchy, that is, a given class and all of its subclasses, or, more generally, from an arbitrary set of classes.

6.4 Object-Z

Object-Z is an extension of Z in which the syntax and semantics of Z are retained and new constructs are added to facilitate specification in an object-oriented style. It was developed over a number of years by a team of researchers at the University of Queensland, Australia [CDD⁺90, DKRS91, DRS96, DR00, Smi00]. In this section, we present a specification of the ODP Trading function by using the most current and complete definition of the language [Smi00].

6.4.1 Classes

The major new construct in Object-Z is the class schema, often referred to simply as a class. A class encapsulates a collection of definitions that together describe the class's objects. These definitions may include type and constant definitions that are local to the class and cannot be used elsewhere, at most one state schema, at most one initial state schema and zero or more operations.

As an example, consider the following class of ODP Trader objects, based on the Z specification of Section 6.1:

```
┌─ Trader ─────────────────────────────────────────────────────────
│  ┌───────────────────────────────────────────────────────────────
│  │ policy : TradingPolicy
│  │ offers : ℙ ServiceOffer
│  ├───────────────────────────────────────────────────────────────
│  │ ∀ p, q : offers • first(p) = first(q) ⇒ p = q
│  └───────────────────────────────────────────────────────────────
│
│  ┌─ INIT ────────────────────────────────────────────────────────
│  │ offers = ∅
│  └───────────────────────────────────────────────────────────────
│
│  ┌─ ExportOK ────────────────────────────────────────────────────
│  │ Δ(offers)
│  │ new_offer? : ServiceOffer
│  │ new_offer_identifier! : ServiceOfferIdentifier
│  ├───────────────────────────────────────────────────────────────
│  │ (∀ p : offers • first(p) ≠ first(new_offer?))
│  │ offers' = offers ∪ {new_offer?}
│  │ new_offer_identifier! = first(new_offer?)
│  └───────────────────────────────────────────────────────────────
│
│  ┌─ SearchOK ────────────────────────────────────────────────────
│  │ criteria? : Criteria
│  │ preference? : Preference
│  │ search_result! : seq ServiceOffer
│  ├───────────────────────────────────────────────────────────────
│  │ let suitable_offers == offers ∩ criteria? ∩ policy.criteria;
│  │     modified_preference == policy.modify_preference(preference?) •
│  │     search_result! = modified_preference(suitable_offers)
│  └───────────────────────────────────────────────────────────────
└──────────────────────────────────────────────────────────────────
```

The role of the schemas in a class is identified by their names. The state schema is nameless; the initial state schema has, as its name, the reserved word *INIT*, and all other schemas are operations.

The initial state schema differs from standard Z schemas in that it has no declaration part. Instead, it is interpreted in an environment that has been enriched with the state schema's declarations and predicates. This is equivalent to implicitly including the state schema in the initial state schema. Similarly, the operations are interpreted in an environment enriched with the declarations and predicates of

the state schema in both undecorated and primed forms. Operations also include a
Δ-list of the state variables that they may change. All other variables are implicitly
unchanged (unless otherwise indicated in the state schema [Smi00]).

Apart from syntactic differences between the Z and Object-Z specifications, there
is also a major semantic difference. An operation, rather than having an undefined
outcome when its precondition is not true, is said to be *blocked*, that is, it cannot
occur. Hence, there is no need to include an error schema for the export operation
as in the Z specification in Section 6.1.4.

Each of the definitions that can occur in a class are optional. For example, the
class *Trader* did not have any type or constant definitions. The state variable *policy*
is not changed by any of the operations and could have been modelled as a constant.
However, modelling it as a state variable allows the class to be refined to include
operations that change the trader's policy if desired.

An exporter class can be modelled as having a single state variable *services* that
models the services which the exporter may make available. The initial values of
services, like the variable *policy* of *Trader*, is undefined. Hence, the exporter class
is specified without an initial state schema as follows:

$$
\begin{array}{l}
\hline
\quad Exporter \\
\hline
\quad services : \mathbb{P}\ Service \\
\hline
\quad\quad Export \\
\quad\quad new\_offer\_identifier? : ServiceOfferIdentifier \\
\quad\quad new\_offer! : ServiceOffer \\
\quad\quad \hline
\quad\quad first(new\_offer!) = new\_offer\_identifier? \\
\quad\quad second(new\_offer!) \in services \\
\hline
\end{array}
$$

The operation *Export* of this class outputs a service offer corresponding to one of
the services in the set *services*. It also inputs the identifier of the service offer to
leave the origin of this identifier undefined.

An importer class can be specified without a state or initial state schema. It simply
comprises an operation *Import* that outputs a request in terms of some criteria and
a preference for the ordering of returned service offers, and inputs the sequence of
returned service offers.

$$
\begin{array}{l}
\hline
\quad Importer \\
\hline
\quad\quad Import \\
\quad\quad criteria! : Criteria \\
\quad\quad preference! : Preference \\
\quad\quad search\_result? : \text{seq}\ ServiceOffer \\
\hline
\end{array}
$$

6.4.2 Inheritance

Inheritance is denoted in Object-Z by including in the subclass the names of the superclass before any other definitions. For example, a trader object that is also an importer can be specified by inheriting both *Trader* and *Importer* as follows:

```
┌─ TraderImporter ──────────────────────────────────
│ Trader
│ Importer
└────────────────────────────────────────────────────
```

The definitions in the superclasses are merged with each other as well as with those in the subclass. Hence the class *TraderImporter* is semantically identical to the class *Trader* with the addition of the *Import* operation of *Importer*.

When two or more superclasses have common-named schemas or a superclass has a schema of the same name as a schema in the subclass, these schemas are implicitly conjoined. For example, in the following class modelling a trader object that is also an exporter, the state schema of *Trader* is conjoined with that of *Exporter*, that is, the state schema of *TraderExporter* includes the declarations and predicates of both schemas.

```
┌─ TraderExporter ──────────────────────────────────
│ Trader
│ Exporter
└────────────────────────────────────────────────────
```

Other types of objects that may occur in a trading system include those that are both importers and exporters, and those that are importers, exporters and traders. The classes of these objects are similarly defined using inheritance, as shown in the following:

```
┌─ ImporterExporter ────────────────────────────────
│ Importer
│ Exporter
└────────────────────────────────────────────────────
```

```
┌─ TraderImporterExporter ──────────────────────────
│ Trader
│ ImporterExporter
└────────────────────────────────────────────────────
```

Object-Z also enables inherited definitions to be renamed, extended and cancelled, that is, removed from the subclass's interface. This is discussed in detail by Smith [Smi00].

6.4.3 Polymorphism

A class in Object-Z may be used as a type, the values of which are identities of objects of the class. The sets of identities, and hence objects, associated with different classes are disjoint. However, polymorphic types, comprising the identities of multiple classes, may be defined in Object-Z in two ways.

First, the set of identities of all classes in a particular inheritance hierarchy may be defined by using the polymorphism operator $\downarrow$. For example, the set of identities of objects of the class *Trader* or any subclass of *Trader* is defined as $\downarrow$ *Trader*. This set contains the identities of objects of *Trader*, *TraderImporter*, *TraderExporter* and *TraderImporterExporter*.

Second, the set of identities of an arbitrary set of classes may be defined by using the class union operator $\cup$. For example, a type *Node* corresponding to the set of identities of all objects that may occur in a trading system can be specified as follows:

$$Node == \downarrow Trader \cup \downarrow Exporter \cup \downarrow Importer$$

6.4.4 Objects

A system of objects is specified in Object-Z by a *system class*. A system class, rather than including the objects directly as state variables or constants, refers to them indirectly via their identities. This is similar to the way in which pointers are used to indirectly refer to objects in object-oriented programming languages. In Object-Z, it allows the types corresponding to the objects' classes to be used to construct the system class's constant definitions and state schema.

To access the constants and state variables of an object or specify the application of an operation to it, a dot notation, also similar to that used in object-oriented programming languages, is employed. That is, if class A has a state variable x and an operation Op, then, given an object identity $a : A$, $a.x$ denotes the value of the x variable of the object identified by a, and $a.Op$ denotes the application of the operation Op of A to the object identified by a. The notation $a.INIT$ can also be employed to indicate that the object identified by a is in an initial state.

To specify interactions between objects, Object-Z has a number of operation operators. In particular, it has a parallel composition operator $\parallel$ that can be used for specifying interobject communication, and a scope enrichment operator $\bullet$ that can be used to access object identities occurring in sets or other aggregates. Both operators are illustrated in the *TradingCommunity* class corresponding to a trading community.

The trading community specified in this class comprises a set of objects, *nodes*, and a distinguished trader object, *trader*. The trader object is not a member of *nodes*. Initially, *nodes* is empty and the trader object is in its initial state, that is, its set of offers is empty, as defined in the class *Trader* of Section 6.4.1.

$$\boxed{\begin{array}{l}
\_\_\textit{TradingCommunity}_____ \\[4pt]
\quad \boxed{\begin{array}{l}
\textit{trader} : \downarrow \textit{Trader} \\
\textit{nodes} : \mathbb{P}\, \textit{Node} \\
\hline
\textit{trader} \notin \textit{nodes}
\end{array}} \\[6pt]
\quad \boxed{\begin{array}{l}
\_\_\textit{INIT}_____ \\
\textit{trader.INIT} \\
\textit{nodes} = \varnothing
\end{array}} \\[6pt]
\quad \boxed{\begin{array}{l}
\_\_\textit{AddNode}_____ \\
\Delta(\textit{nodes}) \\
\textit{node?} : \textit{Node} \\
\hline
\textit{node?} \notin \textit{nodes} \\
\textit{nodes}' = \textit{nodes} \cup \{\textit{node?}\}
\end{array}} \\[6pt]
\quad \textit{Export} \mathrel{\hat=} [\, n : \textit{nodes} \mid n \in \downarrow\textit{Exporter}\,] \bullet \textit{trader.ExportOK} \parallel n.\textit{Export} \\
\quad \textit{Import} \mathrel{\hat=} [\, n : \textit{nodes} \mid n \in \downarrow\textit{Importer}\,] \bullet \textit{trader.SearchOK} \parallel n.\textit{Import}
\end{array}}$$

The operation *AddNode* models a new object joining *nodes*. The operations *Export* and *Import* model an object in *nodes* exporting a service to the trader object, and importing a service from the trader object, respectively. The first part of each operation (on the left-hand side of the scope enrichment operator) declares a variable n that is the identity of an object in *nodes*, which is also an exporter, in the case of the *Export* operation, and an importer, in the case of the *Import* operation. This variable is added to the scope, or environment, in which the second part of the operation (on the right-hand side of the enrichment operator) is interpreted.

The operation *Export* models the object identified by n undergoing an *Export* operation in parallel with the trader object undergoing an *ExportOK* operation. Similarly, the operation *Import* models the object identified by n undergoing an *Import* operation in parallel with the trader object undergoing a *SearchOK* operation. The parallel operator conjoins the respective operations, that is, it merges their declarations and conjoins their predicates and, in addition, identifies and equates input variables in either operation with output variables in the other operation having the same basename, that is, apart from the ? or !. The identified input or output variables are hidden in the resulting operation.

6.4.5 Aliasing

Adopting an approach to system specification based on referring to objects via their identities can lead to aliasing within specifications. Often this is undesirable and must be avoided by explicit invariants such as that distinguishing the trader object from those in *nodes* in the class *TradingCommunity*. In other cases, however, aliasing can be used to model shared references to objects. For example, consider specifying a trading system that integrates a number of trading communities. The objects of one community may also belong to another community, and objects may also have different roles in different communities. Since object identities may be shared between variables, possibly belonging to different objects, this is specified naturally in Object-Z without the need for any additional constraints as follows:

$$
\begin{array}{l}
\hline
\quad TradingSystem \\
\hline
\quad comms : \mathbb{P}\ TradingCommunity \\
\hline
\quad \underline{Init} \\
\quad \forall\, c : comms \bullet c.Init \\
\hline
\quad AddNode \mathrel{\widehat{=}} [\, c : comms\,] \bullet c.AddNode \\
\quad Export \mathrel{\widehat{=}} [\, c : comms\,] \bullet c.Export \\
\quad Import \mathrel{\widehat{=}} [\, c : comms\,] \bullet c.Import \\
\hline
\end{array}
$$

Bibliography

[Abr96]   J. R. Abrial. *The B-Book: Assigning Programs to Meanings.* Cambridge University Press, 1996.

[ASM80]   J.-R. Abrial, S. Schuman, and B Meyer. Specification language. In R. M. McKeag and A. Macnaghten, editors, *On the Construction of Programs: An advanced course.* Cambridge University Press, 1980.

[BD91]   C. Bailes and R. Duke. The ecology of class refinement. In J. Morris and R. Shaw, editors, *4th Refinement Workshop,* Workshops in Computing, pages 185–196. Springer-Verlag, 1991.

[BJ78]   D. Bjørner and C. B. Jones, editors. *The Vienna Development Method: The Meta-Language,* volume 61 of *Lecture Notes in Computer Science.* Springer-Verlag, 1978.

[BJ82]   D. Bjørner and C. B. Jones. *Formal Specification and Software Development.* Prentice Hall, 1982.

[CDD+90]   D. Carrington, D. Duke, R. Duke, P. King, G. A. Rose, and G. Smith. Object-Z: An object-oriented extension of Z. In S. Vuong, editor, *Formal Description Techniques II (FORTE'89),* pages 281–296. North-Holland, 1990.

[Cus91]   E. Cusack. Inheritance in object oriented Z. In P. America, editor, *European Conference on Object-Oriented Programming (ECOOP'91),* volume 512 of *Lecture Notes in Computer Science,* pages 167–179. Springer-Verlag, 1991.

[DB01]   J. Derrick and E. A. Boiten. *Refinement in Z and Object-Z.* Springer-Verlag, 2001.

[DBS96]   R. Duke, C. Bailes, and G. Smith. A blocking model for reactive objects. *Formal Aspects of Computing,* 8(3):347–368, 1996.

[DKRS91]   R. Duke, P. King, G. A. Rose, and G. Smith. The Object-Z specification language. In T. Korson, V. Vaishnavi, and B. Meyer, editors, *Technology of Object-Oriented Languages and Systems (TOOLS 5),* pages 465–483. Prentice Hall, 1991.

[DR00]   R. Duke and G. A. Rose. *Formal Object-Oriented Specification Using Object-Z.* MacMillan, 2000.

[DRS96]   R. Duke, G. A. Rose, and G. Smith. Object-Z: A specification language advocated for the description of standards. *Computer Standards and Interfaces*, 17:511–533, 1996.

[Hal90] J. A. Hall. Using Z as a specification calculus for object-oriented systems. In D. Bjørner, C. A. R. Hoare, and H. Langmaack, editors, *VDM'90: VDM and Z!*, volume 428 of *Lecture Notes in Computer Science*, pages 290–318. Springer-Verlag, 1990.

[Hal94] J. A. Hall. Specifying and interpreting class hierarchies in Z. In J. P. Bowen and J. A. Hall, editors, *Z User Workshop 1994*, Workshops in Computing, pages 120–138. Springer-Verlag, 1994.

[Hay93] I. Hayes, editor. *Specification Case Studies*. Prentice Hall, second edition, 1993.

[ISO93] ISO/IEC JTC1/SC22/WG19 N-20. *VDM-SL. First Committee Draft Standard CD 13817-1*, 1993.

[ISO98] *ISO/IEC IS 13235-1, Open Distributed Processing - Trading Function: Specification*. ISO, 1998.

[ISO00] ISO/IEC JTC1/SC22/WG19. *Formal Specification - Z Notation - Syntax, Type and Semantics. Consensus Working Draft 2.5*, 2000.

[Jon80] C. B. Jones. *Software Development: A Rigourous Approach*. Prentice Hall, 1980.

[Jon90] C. B. Jones. *Systematic Software Development using VDM*. Prentice Hall, second edition, 1990.

[JS90] C. B. Jones and R. C. F. Shaw. *Case Studies in Systematic Software Development*. Prentice Hall, 1990.

[Lan95] K. Lano. *Formal Object-Oriented Development*. Springer-Verlag, 1995.

[LH94] K. Lano and H. Haughton, editors. *Object-Oriented Specification Case Studies*. Prentice Hall, 1994.

[MC90] S. R. L Meira and A. L. C. Cavalcanti. Modular object-oriented Z specifications. In *Z User Meeting 1990*, Workshops in Computing, pages 173–192. Springer-Verlag, 1990.

[Mor90] C. C. Morgan. *Programming from Specifications*. Prentice Hall, 1990.

[MS84] C. C. Morgan and B. Sufrin. Specification of the Unix filing system. *IEEE Transactions on Software Engineering*, SE-10(2):128–142, 1984.

[SBC92] S. Stepney, R. Barden, and D. Cooper, editors. *Object Orientation in Z*. Prentice Hall, 1992.

[Smi94a] G. Smith. Formal definitions of behavioural compatibility for active and passive objects. In *Asia-Pacific Software Engineering Conference (APSEC '94)*, pages 336–344. IEEE Computer Society Press, 1994.

[Smi94b] G. Smith. An object-oriented development framework for Z. In J. P. Bowen and J. A. Hall, editors, *Z User Meeting 1994*, Workshops in Computing, pages 89–107. Springer-Verlag, 1994.

[Smi95] G. Smith. A fully abstract semantics of classes for Object-Z. *Formal Aspects of Computing*, 7(3):289–313, 1995.

[Smi00] G. Smith. *The Object-Z Specification Language*. Kluwer, 2000.

[Sør82] I. H. Sørensen. A specification language. In J. Straunstrap, editor, *Program Specification*, volume 134 of *Lecture Notes in Computer Science*, pages 381–401. Springer-Verlag, 1982.

[Spi92] J. M. Spivey. *The Z Notation: A Reference Manual*. Prentice Hall, second edition, 1992.

[SS98] E. Sekerinski and K Sere. *Case Studies Using the B Method*. Cambridge University Press, 1998.

[WD96] J. C. P. Woodcock and J. Davies. *Using Z: Specification, Refinement, and Proof*. Prentice Hall, 1996.

[ZS96] H. B. Zadeh and S. Stepney. *ZEST – Z Extended with Structuring: A User's Guide, PROST-Objects, BT.7004.0.20.13, Issue 2*, 1996.

7

The Unified Modeling Language

Stuart Kent

University of Kent, UK

The final language that we introduce in this part is UML [GBJ99], and in this chapter we present a subset of the UML that has been found useful for notating what may loosely be called *specification* models. A model of aspects of the ODP Trader case study is developed (a) to provide a vehicle for introducing the notation, and (b) to demonstrate how the notations can be used together in harmony. In the course of the presentation, some issues concerning the precise definition of UML and its possible future status as a formal method are discussed.

7.1 Introduction

Since the UML first emerged in 1997, its popularity has grown beyond all recognition. It has become the de-facto language for informally modelling object-oriented systems. Although its success can be attributed to a number of factors, one of the most important has been the input of the Object Management Group (OMG), which has led a major exercise to provide the UML with a standard definition. Currently, this is at version 1.3, with new versions already in the pipeline. The standard definition also incorporates a semantics document that aims to give a precise description of the language. By providing users with a standard description of the language, the OMG has encouraged the development of a language that can be shared and understood uniformly throughout industry and academia. The benefits that result cannot be overstated – practitioners, teachers, trainers, tool vendors and methodologists now have a single language that they can concentrate their efforts on, with the result that significant advances are likely to be made in all of its aspects. Whilst this is an encouraging start, there are still many problems that need to be addressed before the UML's true potential can be realised. In our view the six most serious issues are

(i) **Size.** UML is a collection of notations that have been found to be of practical use to developers of software-intensive systems. This encompasses a wide range of notations. In addition, the stereotype mechanism has encouraged modellers to add their own, often ad-hoc, extensions to the language. There are also plans to develop various UML profiles that will collect together packages of stereotypes which have been found to be useful. In short, UML is large and growing.

(ii) **Incoherence.** UML has brought together a number of notations from different fields, but it has failed to integrate these notations based on a common set of core concepts. For example, it is not clear how state diagrams relate to class diagrams and sequence diagrams.

(iii) **Different interpretations.** UML is interpreted differently by different people. For example, there has been long standing discussion on the meaning of aggregation and composition, the notions of subsystem/model/package are very unclearly specified, there are at least two very different interpretations of state diagrams, and so on.

(iv) **Frequent subsetting.** Our experience is that organizations tend to define their own UML subset – guidelines on which parts to use; which not to use; own definitions of semantics where the standard is unclear, inconsistent or untenable for the organization concerned; and so on. This mitigates against a goal of UML to increase shared understanding amongst developers.

(v) **Constant evolution and extension.** As indicated in the first point, the stereotype mechanism is being used (some say *abused* [BGJ99]) to continuously extend the language. Combining this with subsetting and multiple interpretations, the language is really still in a state of evolution and change.

(vi) **Limited tools.** Most commercial tools focus on diagramming, perhaps model exchange, and naive code-generation. Some consistency checks are applied, but these are generally restricted to syntactic checks and applied in an ad-hoc fashion. A small number of tools (e.g., Rose Real Time, Project Technology's Bridgepoint tool) work with executable models notated using UML constructs where possible, and their own constructs where UML does not provide what is needed (e.g., an action language). Because of the executable nature of these models, such tools permit some simulation and testing of models, and they usually generate code to a variety of platforms. There are virtually no automated analysis tools that allow nonexecutable models to be simulated/animated, inspected, tested, checked, and so on, although some prototypes are starting to emerge [RG00, Bol00].

Constructing automated analysis tools for a language requires the language to be formally defined. Of course, the language may obtain a formal definition by virtue of tools being constructed to support it. Those tools that do support analysis of models, such as those cited in (vi), will have to have formalized the fragments of UML that they use. Unfortunately, that formalization is usually only implicit in the source code of the tool. Addressing (ii) and (iii) requires a formalization that is explicit and agreed upon.

There are a number of options to consider in trying to address the problem of formalizing the UML. One option is to just treat it as a lost cause, and we reject this out of hand. Another is to provide translations to existing formal languages. This translational approach deals with the semantics of the language – it still requires the syntax to be formalized, which is nontrivial given the diagrammatic nature of the notations. A third option is to define the semantics from the ground up, migrating and adapting ideas and techniques from formal methods as appropriate.

One advantage of the translational approach is that one could make use of tools developed to support the target formal language. However, this is also its weakness. For the practioner, it is important to have analysis tools that give feedback to the engineer in the same language as (s)he is using to construct the model, in this case the UML. A problem with the translational approach to semantics, for example, to an existing formal specification language, is that one is then required to work with that language during the analysis phase. At the very least this requires the engineer to learn two languages rather than one, and, presumably, (s)he is more familiar with and prefers to use the UML.

Furthermore, to address (iii), the definition of any aspect of the UML requires agreement; at the very least, the UML community needs to be able to observe the differences between two definitions. This mitigates against the translational approach: the definition needs to be written in a language that is accessible to those who need to agree to it, that is, people who have the experience to know whether the definition supports the modelling scenarios found in practice. This is probably the reason that the meta-modelling approach to the definition of the UML, where the UML is used to define itself, has proved so popular – anyone with a knowledge of class diagrams can understand the essentials of the definition.

Points (i), (iii), (iv) and (v) pose another challenge to the formalization of the UML: to develop a language definition architecture that not only allows the language to be defined incrementally, but also permits variations and specializations of the language to be constructed, in essence, to find a way of formally defining *families of languages*.

It turns out that this is similar to the problem of defining software (or model) product lines. The extensions required to UML to support product lines (chiefly more powerful model-management mechanisms) can be used in the definition of UML itself as a product line. Combine these with a precise subset of UML for expressing object structures and constraints on those structures (essentially class diagrams and OCL), and the result is a language that seems suitable for defining families of languages, both syntax and semantics. This is a variation of the meta-modelling approach to language definition, and so it has the advantage of being accessible to the OMG. It also seems a very good language within which to define diagrammatic syntaxes. A possible weakness is that the semantics of constructs for expressing dynamic behaviour may be more verbose than if more traditional mathematical syntax was used. A more detailed overview of this approach can be found in [CEF+99, EK99].

An important aspect of this research is that we take UML as it is, making changes to the language only when the formalization process uncovers inconsistencies and errors, or where striking improvements to the language are identified. In particular, the visual flavour that makes it so attractive to engineers should not be lost.

In line with the incremental approach, a first step is to pare down the language to its barest essentials. This chapter describes a subset of UML that, we believe, can be given a precise semantics with little difficulty. Fragments of this semantics have already been developed, together with some tool support [RG98, RG00]. The subset forms the basis of the meta-modelling sublanguage itself, and has also proven to be useful in modelling abstract views of network services and their realisation onto concrete network configurations, such as an IP network. The subset has much in common with the subset used in the Catalysis method [DW98], which has been applied on a number of real projects by its architects. We introduce this subset through a series of sections, with the trader case study used as the running example. The focus of the presentation is on the engineering utility, rather than the formality of the subset, as this, we believe, is the main contribution of the UML.

7.2 Language Versus Method

UML is a language, not a method. It provides a collection of notations that may be used for different sorts of modelling. Its definition gives little advice on what notations are suitable for what kind of modelling, or on what models to build and in what order to achieve a particular goal.

We make use of a general-purpose subset of UML that we hope captures the core concepts of object modelling, can be applied in different modelling circumstances and can be given a precise definition. The essence of the method for building a single model is as follows:

(i) Explore the situation to be modelled by exploring *scenarios*, potential traces through the state of the model. Document these with *filmstrips*. Group the scenarios by *use case*.

(ii) Use *use cases* to separate out the model into overlapping *packages* (one package per use case).

(iii) Use the scenarios as a basis for developing the model. Source class diagrams and invariants from the object diagrams in the filmstrips. Source operations and their pre- and postconditions from the transitions between object diagrams in the filmstrip. Develop state diagrams showing important transitions and changes of state from an object-centred viewpoint.

(iv) Recurse through steps (i) to (iii) until the model is fit for its purpose.

We have built models of software specifications, telecomms networks and services using this method. We are exploring its use in modelling business processes. In the sequel, we build a model of the ODP Trader specification.

We have found that the same modelling techniques can be used to model at different levels of abstraction and to build models that specify how an abstract model is *realized* onto a concrete model, for example, how an abstract model of network services, expressed in terms of end-to-end virtual connections and involving different levels of service, is mapped onto a model of an IP network.

The process of software development can be perceived in a similar way: as mappings from abstract to more concrete models, where, here, a model is more abstract than another if the granularity of the operations in the interfaces specified by the model (the public operations on classes) is coarser than the granularity of the interface operations in the more concrete model, and/or the object structures supported by the abstract model are less detailed than the object structures supported by the concrete model.

Note that realisation is different to *implementation*, where, once one has reached a concrete model that fixes the granularity of the interface for the actual software that is to be constructed, that model can be extended further with implementation information. If the implementation is in an object-oriented programming language, then sequence diagrams can be used to identify new, private operations required to implement the operations on the interface, and these, in turn, may require their own supporting operations, classes and so forth. The translation from such an implementation model to, say, a program in Java would be relatively straightforward.

Within this context, the ODP Trader specification, modelled in the sequel, is a relatively abstract view of the dialogue between service consumers, service providers and service traders, the intermediaries between consumers and providers. It provides the specification of operations that consumers, providers and traders might perform, which, in turn, requires these three concepts to be treated as objects, in addition to concepts such as service, service offer and so on. A more concrete model would begin to detail the actual mechanisms in a particular technology (e.g., CORBA) by which these objects would communicate. There would become a point where the translation of a concrete model to the language(s) of the implementation technology would be relatively systematic, although probably less straightforward than to a single Java program.

Our model is loosely based on [ISO98]. When modelling in an industry setting, we would recommend that the model be constructed *with* the domain experts. Any informal documentation should be regarded as only a starting point and be subject to change as the model is being developed. It should not be regarded as sacrosanct and rigid, otherwise there is little point in developing a more precise model. The end goal is for all descriptions of the system to be consistent with one another.

Finally, we should highlight some deficiencies of our set of modelling techniques:

- UML is weak in its expression of concurrent and real-time behaviour. Some concrete syntax has been inserted into the language, for example, asynchronous message passing on sequence diagrams, but the semantics is poorly specified, unclear and confusing. Therefore, the set of techniques that we use does not include any of these constructs. Some attempts are being made to resolve this problem, in submissions being prepared in response to the OMG's Request for Proposals on an action semantics for UML [Obj98]. We suspect that these submissions will at least bring into focus the detailed problems involved.

- There is, at the time of writing, still no formal definition of the subset used here. However, we are working on providing a formal definition of the subset using the approach proposed in the introduction. Fragments of this subset have been formalized elsewhere and are supported by tools [RG98, RG00].

- To use these techniques successfully on an industrial scale requires much better tools than are currently available. For example, we would like tools that check the consistency of models, assist with the generation of filmstrips from a model and a model from filmstrips, support composition and separation of models, support realization of models, support model templates (patterns), support model refactoring and so on. Building such tools requires a precise definition for the UML.

7.3 Use Cases and Packages

A model is recorded as a UML package. Thus all modelling is done within the context of a package. Packages may be constructed by importing other packages. There may be other relationships between packages (e.g., refinement/realisation). Packages are declared and related through package diagrams. Figure 7.1 is the package diagram for the trader case study. The model is recorded as the `Trader` package, which has been constructed by extending (importing) two smaller, overlapping packages, one concerned with exporting services to a trader and the other focussing on importing services advertised on a trader. The packages correspond to our chosen primary use cases: `Export Service` and `Import Service`.

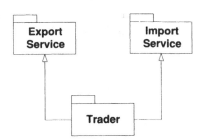

Fig. 7.1. Package diagram for ODP Trader case study.

The semantics of import/extension between packages in UML is still under discussion – recent submissions to the UML 2.0 RFI (see OMG website for details) criticized the model management aspects of UML 1.3. Our working semantics is taken from Catalysis [DW98], which treats imports a little like class inheritance, where things with the same name in two parent packages are merged, unless they are explicitly renamed on import. Of course, this can give rise to an inconsistent child, and there are some remaining research issues concerning how to merge some elements of a package, such as method contracts, sequence diagrams and state diagrams.

Use cases are a useful discovery technique when modelling. A use case focuses on a particular slice of the behaviour, related to a particular process in the system being modelled. For the trader case study we have chosen two use cases, corresponding to the processes of exporting and importing a service, respectively.

There are two styles for characterizing a use case: the goal-oriented style, where the goals of the process that the use case captures are set out; and the scenario-oriented style, where the process is described in terms of particular scenarios or sequences of steps that the process goes through.

There is no prescribed syntax for use cases in UML, although a number of different ways of presenting use cases have been proposed, for example, [Lar97, Coc00]. Common practice is to state both goals and scenarios informally, with scenarios often written out as dialogues or scripts involving the various actors (including computer systems) involved. UML only prescribes the use case diagram syntax. A use case diagram introduces use cases by name, identifies participants (actors) in those use cases and expresses some (not very clearly specified) relationships between uses cases. Use case diagrams can be useful for giving a 30000-foot overview of some kinds of systems, typically those that have external, human actors. However, if packages are organized by use case, then package diagrams can serve a similar purpose.

In order to make use cases more precise, it is necessary to formalize the goals and scripts that accompany them. Goals can be formalized to a certain extent by building a model that treats the use case as a single action with pre- and postconditions written in OCL (the goal is the postcondition), supported by appropriate class diagrams, and so on. However, this tends to lead to a very abstract model, and it is questionable whether the effort is worthwhile. Therefore, we will focus on formalizing use case scripts. This requires identifying the actions involved in the script, the participants of those actions and how those actions affect the state of the system whenever they are performed. This is no more and no less than building a model. Thus our attention returns to focus on the construction of a model as a UML package.

7.4 Scenarios, Filmstrips and Scripts

A model of a use case must stipulate, in general, the admissible scenarios. One way to achieve this is to explore some example scenarios. These can be documented using filmstrips and scripts. A filmstrip is a sequence of object diagrams (*snapshots*) that accompany a script, identifying what happens at each step. UML does not itself support filmstrips, although object diagrams are defined (they are collaboration diagrams without messages). Scripts are commonly used to describe use cases, although, again, UML does not directly support them. Scripts are most often expressed as informal text, although they can be expressed more formally as a list of action invocations that can be visualized via a UML sequence diagram.

7.4.1 Filmstrips

A filmstrip for the import service use case is given in Figure 7.2. Scripts will be discussed in more detail in Section 7.4.2. For the time being we provide just the informal script, which should assist with understanding the filmstrip.

(i) The scene starts with an importer i1 and a trader t1. t1 has already had some service offers registered with it. i1 already has some import policies set up, but not one for use with this trader.

(ii) i1 creates an import policy to be used with t1.

(iii) i1 creates an import request, which carries with it its own import policy.

(iv) t1 handles the import request, sent from i1, and identifies matching service offers.

(v) The selection criteria on the import request are then applied to find the best matching service offer.

Each frame in the filmstrip has been numbered to indicate its position. Due to the formatting limitations, the strip is laid out left to right, top to bottom. Each frame of the filmstrip comprises an object diagram. Objects are rectangles; the class of the object appears after the colon in the label. An optional, arbitrary identity for the object appears before the colon. We have chosen to name only two objects, i1 and t1, so that they can be referred to in the script. Links between objects are shown as lines between rectangles – links are instances of associations. Directed links are instances of one-way associations.

The main points of note concerning this filmstrip are

Frame 1 The service offers for a trader are divided into contexts, where a context is a set of service offers. Contexts may intersect, and so may share service offers. The details of service offers are dealt with in the following section which discusses the details of matching. How service offers get created is part of the Export Services use case.

Frame 2 The new import policy set up by i1 for trader t1 is added to the list of import policies that i1 might use when issuing import requests. It is difficult to imagine an import policy in isolation from a trader, because the policy needs to have some knowledge of the contexts of that trader.

Frame 3 An import request comprises a service request and may come with its own import policy (it does so in this case), which will be one of those identified by the importer to be used with this trader. A service request comes with some selection criteria and a matching constraint. Further details about what a service request comprises will be be dealt with later.

Frame 4 Matches, based on the matching constraint, are created for every service offer in a context belonging to the search scope of the import policy. The import policy used is the one that comes with the import request (this case), or the default policy associated with the trader if no policy comes with the request.

Frame 5 Application of the selection criteria creates a new selection object whose elements are true offer matches that also match the selection criteria. In this case there is only one offer match that matches the selection criteria. The spirit of the text [ISO98] that we are using as the basis for this model suggests that only a single set of selections is applied, and, indeed, this is the situation illustrated in this filmstrip. However, we observe that one could create many selections for an import request, each derived from different selection criteria. This will be reflected in the class diagram introduced in the next section.

[ISO98] mentions two further complications when matching offers to import requests. We sketch how these could be modelled.

Time limits The idea that searches may have a time limit is mooted. This could be modelled by associating an import request with a time limit and every `OfferMatch` object with a time stamp. Then, when a match is performed there will be exactly one `OfferMatch` object with a time stamp that exceeds the time limit. It could also be required that the amount the time limit is exceeded by is also limited. Any efficient implementation of such a specification would stop as soon as it stamps an `OfferMatch` object with a time that exceeds the time limit. An inefficient implementation might find all matches, then discard all but one of those that exceed the time limit. So this specification does presume, to some extent, that only sensible implementations will be built.

Search order The idea that contexts could be searched in order (presumably because there is a time limit) is also mooted. This could be modelled by associating an `ImportPolicy` object with a queue of contexts, representing the order in which contexts must be considered. There is then a constraint on the result of matching that there must be an `OfferMatch` object for every context up to a certain (unspecified) point in the queue and none for contexts thereafter. The last context considered may have some offer matches missing, as it may have been only partially dealt with before the time expired. The offer match with the time stamp exceeding the time limit must be in this last context. Again, any efficient implementation will go through the contexts in the order specified.

The filmstrip in Figure 7.2 indicates the overall structure of the model corresponding to the `Import Service` use case. However, one aspect still needs further clarification, specifically, the conditions that make an offer match true or false. This

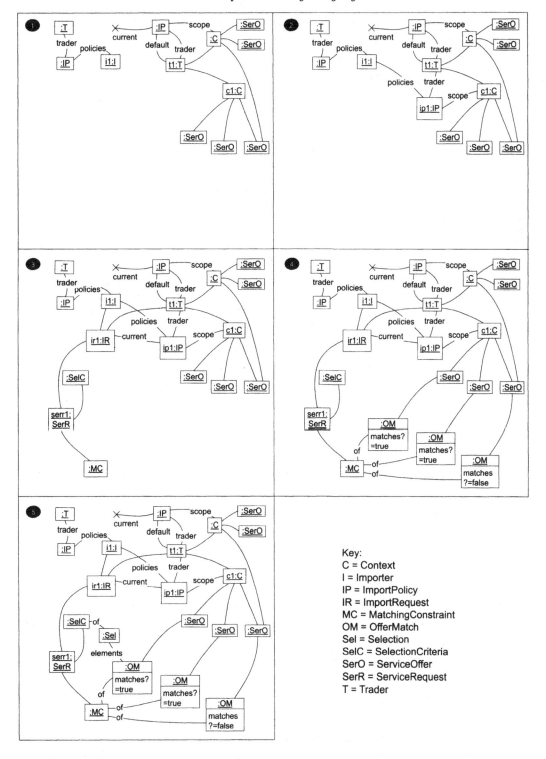

Fig. 7.2. Main filmstrip for import service.

is illustrated by Figure 7.3, which shows one service offer matching an importing request and one that does not.

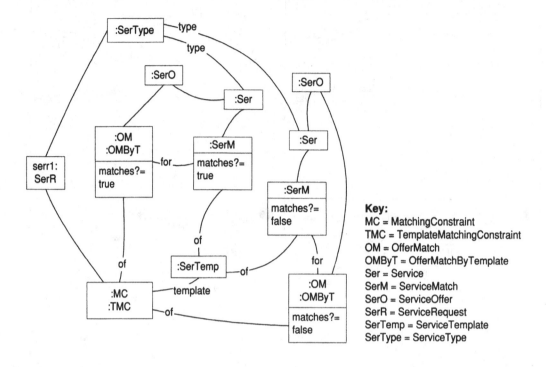

Key:
MC = MatchingConstraint
TMC = TemplateMatchingConstraint
OM = OfferMatch
OMByT = OfferMatchByTemplate
Ser = Service
SerM = ServiceMatch
SerO = ServiceOffer
SerR = ServiceRequest
SerTemp = ServiceTemplate
SerType = ServiceType

Fig. 7.3. Details of matching.

The first condition for a match is that the service type of the service offer must be the same as the service type of the service request. It is for both service offers, in this case. The second condition is dependent on the exact nature of the matching constraint. You will notice that the `MatchingConstraint` object plays a second, more specific role, indicated by it being declared to be of two types. There are likely to be many kinds of matching constraints, expressed in many different ways (the most general probably being an expression in first-order logic). This suggests that objects that play both the general role of being a `MatchingConstraint` (so can be attached to a `ServiceRequest`, for example) and also the more specific role, which governs the specific kind of constraint to be used in the match. The ability of an object to play more than one role is the essence of polymorphism.

In this case, we have identified a `MatchByTemplate` role, where the match is performed by comparing the service of the service offer to the service template associated with the `MatchByTemplate` object. The service template acts as a filter, accepting only those services that match the service template.

You will notice that the results of matches are recorded as objects. There are many ways to model matching. We have chosen this approach because it keeps information about the matches once they have been performed. That then leaves the option of discarding the information, or examining it. For example, if an importer did not get any matches to a request, it may be willing to alter the request to get a match based on information gleaned from the failed matches.

Another approach would be to define a matching function on the matching constraint object, which, when provided with a service offer, would return true or false depending on whether a match was made. This approach could be modelled on a class diagram as a query operation on the class or a qualified association. It has been suggested [DW98] that for specification modelling attributes with arguments should be allowed, but these are not currently part of the UML. There is some discussion to be had as to whether attributes with arguments, qualified associations and query operations are different syntaxes for essentially the same concept (query/function/accessor).

It would be possible to continue to add further detail to how matches are made, and to what goes into making up a service offer. For example, the description of the ODP Trader, from which we have been working, suggests the following:

- A service offer identifies the exporter or provider of the service, its time of registration and its shelf-life, and then the service being offered.
- A service type is comprised of two parts: an interface type and a service property type. Services are comprised of instances of the latter pair of types, that is, an interface and a service property.
- Service properties (and hence their corresponding types) can be composite, in which case they have other properties (which may be composite or atomic) as their parts.

To complete the modelling of this use case we also need to explore a little more about how selections are made.

Filmstrips and further supporting snapshots could be drawn up for the export service use case in a similar way. This would focus on the interaction between exporters and traders, and handle actions such as construct service offer, export service offer to specified trader, withdraw service offer and so on.

As our purpose is not to cover every aspect of the ODP Trader case study, but rather to use this case study to illustrate how UML can be used to specify open distributed systems, we will refrain from considering the Import Service use case in any more detail, and will not pursue the Export Service use case at all in this chapter.

7.4.2 Scripts

The script accompanying the filmstrip can be formalized as a sequence of action invocations, which, in turn, can be visualized using a sequence diagram. In practice, the formalized script and filmstrip evolve together (and indeed did as the model for this case study was developed during the writing of this chapter).

The informal script for the ODP Trader is repeated in the following, now interleaved with formal action invocations. The script is visualized by the *sequence diagram* in Figure 7.4.

(i) The scene starts with an importer i1 and a trader t1. t1 has already had some service offers registered with it. i1 already has some import policies set up, but not one for use with this trader.

    `start`

(ii) i1 creates an import policy to be used with t1.

    `createImportPolicy(i1,t1,c1)`

(iii) i1 creates an import request, which carries with it its own import policy.

    `createImportRequest(i1,serr1,ip1)`

(iv) t1 handles the import request, sent from i1, and identifies matching service offers.

    `t1.handleRequest(ir1)`

(v) The selection criteria on the import request are then applied to find the best matching service offer.

    `ir1.applySelectionCriteria()`

The script is best read in conjunction with the accompanying filmstrip (see Figure 7.2), which provides more information about the objects referred to by name in the script. In the UML, actions are restricted so that they always have a receiver, unless they are creation actions. That is, all actions are assigned to a class, as creation operations – constructors – or as normal operations. UML does not define any textual notation (formal or otherwise) for writing out scripts as we have done. All we have done is write out 'instantiations' of the operations, by instantiating the arguments with objects involved in the particular scenario under consideration, using the ubiquitous 'dot' notation to prefix an action with its particular receiver.

There is no generally accepted textual notation for indicating the sender or invoker of an action. However, this is shown on the sequence diagram whose notation is summarized as follows:

• Arrows represent invocations of actions with sender at the source and receiver at the target. These are sometimes called *messages*.

• As in object diagrams, objects are shown as rectangles. The *lifeline* of an object, representing the life of an object over time, is represented by a vertical line protruding downward from the object.

• An *active object* is shown with a thick border. Active objects can initiate as well as receive messages.

• Creation of objects is shown by targeting the creation message directly on the object that is created (e.g., ip1) as opposed to the lifeline of the object.

One may consider that identifying senders and receivers of actions is a little premature in an analysis/specification model (this probably does not apply for this particular model). Catalysis [DW98] proposes a slight extension to UML, and to

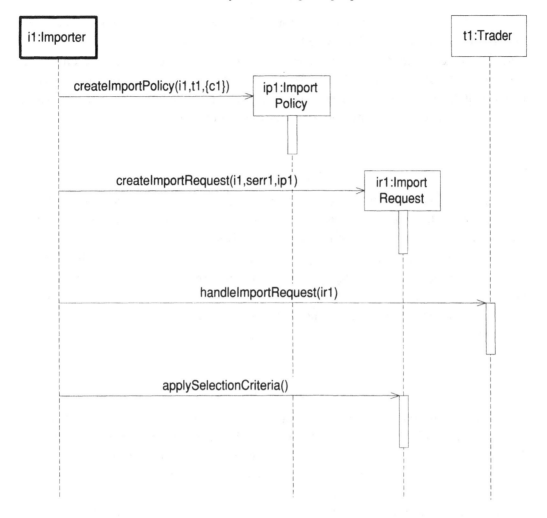

Fig. 7.4. Sequence diagram for Import Service use case.

sequence diagrams in particular, which allows the participants of actions to be identified without necessarily indicating who the sender and receivers are.

If we produced full models of both the Export Service and Import Service use cases, it is likely that we would end up with at least three kinds of active objects: importers, traders and exporters. It is also likely that these objects would work concurrently and the communication between them would not be wholly synchronous. Although UML does provide some syntax for, for example, distinguishing synchronous from asynchronous messages in sequence diagrams, its semantics is far from clear. Its handling of concurrency is weak.

We have also used the sequence diagram to illustrate a specific scenario. Sequence diagrams can be used to specify behaviour in general. Our experience is that they can provided the behaviour that can be expressed purely in terms of a prototypical instance. For sophisticated behaviours this is usually not the case. For more discussion on this topic, see [BGH+98].

An action language for UML is currently under development, in submissions being prepared in response to the OMG's Request for Proposals on an action semantics for UML [Obj98]. This may also cure some of the issues surrounding concurrency, or at the very least bring into focus the detailed problems involved.

7.5 Structure

There are two key concerns when building a model: specifying the structure of and constraints on the state of a system, and specifying the dynamic behaviour of that system. This section deals with the structural aspects.

As indicated in snapshots that make up a filmstrip, the structure of the state of the system is recorded as configurations of objects. In order to specify, in general, what states are and are not admitted by a model, it is necessary to specify what object configurations are and are not admissible. This requires a combination of *class diagrams* and *invariants*.

7.5.1 Class Diagrams

A class diagram sets limits on the kinds of objects and kinds of links that can appear in an admissible object configuration. The class diagram corresponding to the snapshots appearing in the filmstrip of Figure 7.2 is given in Figure 7.5. A class diagram has two main kinds of elements: classes (the boxes) and associations (the lines).

Classes may also have attributes. For example, the class OfferMatch has an attribute isMatch? of type Boolean.

Associations may impose restrictions on the cardinality of links between objects. This is indicated by a numerical range on either or both ends of the association, where * represents a range of zero to infinity (there is no constraint on the number of links). For example, the cardinalities of the association ends of the association between Importer and ImportRequest indicate that an ImportRequest must be associated with exactly one Importer, whereas an Importer may be associated with zero, one or more ImportRequest objects.

A further class diagram can be constructed corresponding to the snapshot in Figure 7.3. This is given in Figure 7.6 and illustrate two aspects of class diagramming:

- Inheritance or generalization, shown by the arrow between, for example, the classes OfferMatchByTemplate and OfferMatch. This means that the child class, at the source of the arrow, has all of the features, for example, attributes (and possibly more) as the parent class, at the target of the arrow. Provided that this previous statement is carefully defined (see, e.g., [LW94]) the upshot is that

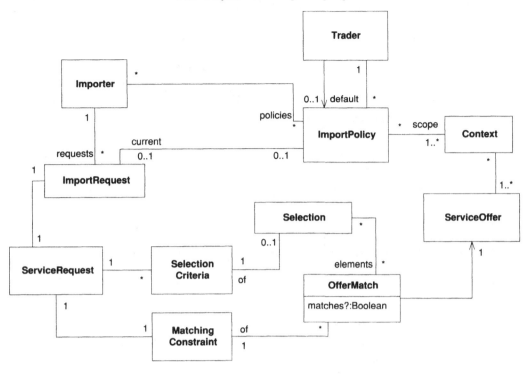

Fig. 7.5. Main class diagram for import service.

objects of the child class may behave as if they are objects of the parent class (polymorphism).

- It is fine for classes and associations to be appear in more than one class diagram. If the class diagrams are in the context of *different* packages, then elements are different. If they are in the context of the same package (for example, we have tacitly assumed that the class diagrams appearing so far are all in the context of the Import Service package), then the elements (classes, etc.) in that package are obtained by *merging* all of the diagrams.

In general, a snapshot is admissible for a particular class diagram, according to the following rules:

- The type of every object appearing in the snapshot is a class in the class diagram.
- Every link in the snapshot corresponds to an association between classes in the class diagram. A link corresponds to an association if its label or labels at each end correspond to the labels at each end of the association and the objects are from classes connected by the association.
- Links do not flout cardinality constraints on associations. (A detailed and precise specification of this can be found in [KH99].)
- Any attribute mentioned in an object on the snapshot must be declared in the

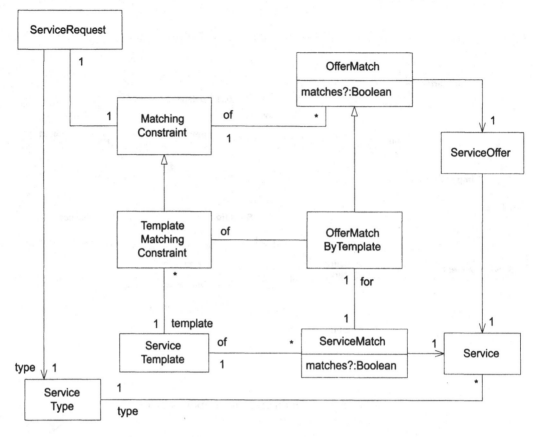

Fig. 7.6. Matching import requests to services: class diagram.

class for that object. The value given to the attribute must be of the type declared
for that attribute in the class diagram.

These rules can be used to guide the construction of a class diagram from a
snapshot. The first rule means that one puts a class in the class diagram for every
type of object in the snapshot. The second rule means that one puts an association
in the class diagram for every different kind of link in the snapshot, where a link x
is of the same kind as another y, if x connects the same types of objects as y and
has the same labels at each end, where ends are matched on the type of object. And
so on for the other rules.

Of course, these rules do not specify completely what must appear in the class
diagram – specifically, they do not stipulate exactly what the cardinality of associations should be. Indeed, what tends to happen is that, as the class diagram is
drawn, new concepts emerge causing new versions of the snapshots to be elaborated,
which in turn might reveal other changes, and so on. Also, an experienced modeller
may well construct snapshots in his or her head, without ever making them explicit.
Nevertheless, they can always be made explicit to anyone challenging the model,

in supporting documentation intended to explain the model, in communicating to domain experts and to help understand subtle behaviours.

There is some debate as to the relationship between attributes and associations. A popular view is that an association can be reduced to a pair of attributes with an additional constraint. For example, the association between the classes `ServiceRequest` and `SelectionCriteria` could be thought of as a pair of attributes `selectionCriteria:SelectionCriteria` and `serviceRequest:ServiceRequest` of `ServiceRequest` and `SelectionCriteria`, respectively, with the additional constraint that each attribute is the inverse of the other (such a constraint could be written as an invariant – see next section – if so desired). Attributes tend to be used instead of associations when the type of the attribute refers to a basic value type, such as `Boolean` or `Integer`, rather than a class.

We have shown only the most basic form of association. There are other kinds of associations, in particular aggregates and qualified associations. Qualified associations are akin to attributes (functions) with arguments, such as is described in [DW98]. We will not enter into a discussion of aggregation here, but suffice it so say that there is still some debate on this topic [HSB99].

In other forms of modelling, such as design/implementation modelling, the situation gets complicated by the introduction of operations on classes, in particular query operations. In this form of modelling one is concerned with distinctions such as: whether a result-returning query is stored or calculated; or whether an operation or attribute/association-end is visible outside a class (public or private). Most modellers at this level tend to treat attributes and associations as (private) storage and define query operations to access the data stored within. One must be slightly careful if adopting this approach. For example, if one is deriving a design from a specification model, one has to be careful to remember that attributes and associations at that level may well correspond to calculated queries (and hence operations) in the design model. This means that a developer must carry around two different interpretations of the same construct (associations and attributes). One must also decide how qualified associations (naturally thought of as functions) should be interpreted in the design model, given that associations are assumed to correspond to stored data: as arrays? as dictionaries?

On balance, our preferred mental model is one where attributes and query operations are treated as the same thing – a query, and an association as a pair of queries. A qualified association can then be thought of as a query with arguments. When design/implementation modelling, a distinction can be made between whether a query is stored or calculated, or whether it is public or private. If one chooses to have the default rule that, unless stated otherwise, all attributes and associations will be treated as stored and private, then that is quite acceptable.

These issues may seem minor, but they can be very confusing to modellers, and what tends to happen is that different organizations, and often different individuals, construct their own interpretations, which only serves to block shared understanding (a goal of the UML). They are the kinds of issues that will only be fully sorted out when the UML has an agreed, precise definition. On the other hand, if a team is prepared to agree on a common interpretation that need only be documented informally, then they are issues that need not get in the way of the modelling activity.

7.5.2 Invariants

The class diagram cannot express all of the constraints that one would wish to impose on the structure of admissible object configurations. Invariants are constraints that all admitted configurations must satisfy. In UML, the Object Constraint Language (OCL) [WK98] has been defined to allow these constraints to be written in a precise syntax.

Some examples of invariants from the trader case study are as follows:

(i) *The trader associated with the default import policy of a trader is the trader itself.*

> **context** t:Trader **inv**:
>   t.default->isEmpty or t.default.trader=t

The preamble **context** t:Trader **inv**: indicates that the constraint which follows applies to all objects t of class Trader. t.default returns the set containing the object(s) found by navigating the default link(s) from t. ->isEmpty indicates that this set is empty. t.default.trader returns the set of object(s) obtained by navigating first the default link(s) from t and then the trader link(s) from all of the objects found through the first step of the navigation. For the clause t.default.trader=t to be true, that set must contain only a single object which is t. Disjunction, as usual, is denoted by or.

(ii) *The service offers matched for the current request being handled by an import policy are within the scope of that policy.*

> **context** ip:ImportPolicy **inv**:
>   ip.scope.serviceOffers->asSet->containsAll(
>   ip.current.serviceRequest.matches.serviceOffer->asSet)

This invariant illustrates navigation expressions that return collections with more than one element. Any navigation expression that spans more than one association returns a bag, by default. Thus ip.scope.serviceOffers returns a bag. This expression is evaluated as follows. Navigating scope from ip returns a set of Context objects. Navigating serviceOffers from each member of this set results in a set of ServiceOffer objects. The bag is created by merging these sets, being careful to keep repeated items. In this case, there are likely to be repeated elements as contexts that may share service offers.

Similarly, `ip.current.serviceRequest.matches.serviceOffer` returns a bag, and `->asSet` coerces a bag into a set.

(iii) *For an offer match to be true, the service type of the service offer must be the same as the service type of the service request.*

> **context** om:OfferMatch **inv**:
>   om.matches?=true implies
>   om.of.serviceRequest.type=om.serviceOffer.service.type

(iv) *For a* `OfferMatchByTemplate` *to be true, the service template must match the service of the service offer.*

> **context** omt:OfferMatchByTemplate **inv**:
>   omt.matches?=true implies
>   omt.serviceMatch.matches?=true

(v) *The service template for a service match must be the service template for the template matching constraint of the* `OfferMatchByTemplate`, *which the service match is for.*

> **context** sm:ServiceMatch **inv**:
>   sm.matches?=true implies
>   sm.template=sm.for.of.template

Combined with the constraint, imposed by the class diagram in Figure 7.6, that the matches of a template matching constraint are always template offer matches, the last three invariants ensure that when the appropriate matches are constructed (see Section 7.6 on dynamic behaviour), they will be designated true or false, as appropriate. Of course we have not stipulated the detailed circumstances under which a service type matches a service; as indicated earlier, that would require further investigation into the detailed structure of services and service templates.

These last two invariants also illustrate how, with inheritance, we are able to push specific behaviour onto the more specific classes. We are at liberty to create a number of other subclasses, with different invariants, capturing different variants of matching constraints. This not only provides a way of separating out the behaviour into appropriate chunks, but it also allows other behaviours to be specified, which is decoupled from the specific variations. So, in Section 7.6 on dynamic behaviour, we are able to specify the result of performing the action `handleRequest`, which results in the creation of the required matches for a request, referring only to the `MatchingConstraint` and `OfferMatch` classes; no mention of their subclasses is made.

The last invariant could have been written in a number of different ways, depending on the class to which the invariant is tied, that is, the class that appears in the **context** part. Other candidate classes are `TemplateMatchingConstraint` and `TemplateOfferMatch`. This illustrates a problem when writing invariants: knowing which class is the best place to put the invariant. A factor that influences this decision is the coupling of classes: if an invariant means unnecessary coupling between classes, then this will mitigate against reuse of the owning class in other models. In this case, the three classes come 'as a package' and are already quite tightly coupled, so it probably does not matter where the invariant is placed. More practical application of writing object-oriented specifications with invariants and the like is required to identify a set of guidelines, or patterns, to support the practising modeller.

Recently there has been considerable work on formalizing and improving OCL. For pointers to some of this work see [ECK+00] and [Ric00].

A visual notation, called *constraint diagrams*, has been defined for expressing constraints, though this is not (yet) part of the UML, but it is compatible with the UML – it may be regarded as a visual alternative to a (sublanguage) of OCL. This language was first introduced in [Ken97] and has been further applied to the expression of action contracts [KG98]. It is currently undergoing revision as it is defined formally [GHK99, HMTK99], and work is continuing on making it a practical technique to be used in harmony, not in conflict, with other approaches to writing constraints [KH99].

7.6 Dynamics

In the modelling context we have chosen (abstract specification), dynamic behaviour is captured in terms of pre- and postconditions on operations. These can be (partially) visualized using state diagrams.

We illustrate the use of OCL to express pre- and postconditions with an example taken from the import service use case. Section 7.4.2 identified a number of actions based on the script for the import service use case. One of these actions was `handleRequest`, which, if we examine the filmstrip in Figure 7.2, has the effect of creating an offer match between the import request and each service offer of the trader handling the request, as governed by the import policy used. In our simplified version, the import policy just identifies a context from which the set of service offers are drawn. The specification of this operation is as follows:

context `Trader::handleRequest(ir:ImportRequest)`:
pre: *The import request has an import policy, or the trader has a default policy. If the import request has a policy, then the trader for the policy is* `self`. *No attempt has been made to handle this request, and any previous attempt has been cleared.*

```
let policy=if ir.importPolicy->notEmpty then
    ir.importPolicy else self.default in
        policy->notEmpty and policy.trader=self
and ir.serviceRequest.matchingConstraint.oclInState(matchCleared)
```

post: *The policy of the request has been set to be the trader's default policy if the* *request has no policy. The import request has been matched against service offers according to the request's policy.*

```
ir.importPolicy@pre->isEmpty implies ir.importPolicy=self.default
and let offers=ir.importPolicy.scope.serviceOffers@pre->asSet in
    let matches=ir.matchingConstraint.offerMatches@pre in
        offers->size=matches->size and matches.serviceOffer=offers
and ir.serviceRequest.matchingConstraint.oclInState(matchCleared)
```

This time the **context** preamble identifies the action concerned together with any arguments. The pre- and postconditions illustrate a number of additional OCL constructs:

- `let` and `if_then_else_` expressions, as found in formal specification languages such as VDM.
- `@pre` in a postcondition, which allows reference to the state when the action is invoked. One could argue that, in this case, `@pre` is not necessary as, for example, `ir.policy` should be the same in both states. However, OCL does not have any notation for expressing frame rules, which is hard in object-oriented models due to the ability to navigate across object structures. One also can make no assumptions about other actions that may occur at the same time as this action, and which may affect objects referred to in the action spec. Our use of `@pre` is therefore a safety measure. The expression of frame rules in OCL is an open issue; we are not sure that a satisfactory solution yet exists for object-oriented specification modelling. Some sources of inspiration might be JML [LB99, LBR99].
- `->size` returns the size of the collection to which it is applied.
- `oclInState(_)` is used to express whether an object is in a particular state, where here we are referring to states in state diagrams.

The use of `oclInState(_)` in the specification of `handleRequest` must be supported by a *state diagram*. This is given in Figure 7.7.

A state diagram applies to a class. It specifies (or visualizes) aspects of the dynamic behaviour of any object of that class. States are shown by rounded rectangles and transitions between states by arrows.

An interpretation for this diagram is as an abstraction of the state space and of dynamic behaviour expressed using pre- and postconditions. That is, when a trader performs the action `handleRequest`, with the request associated with the matching constraint under consideration as argument, and the matching constraint has no matches with service offers, then the result will be that the matching constraint has made a match to service offers. This captures a fragment of the behaviour expressed more completely by the pre- and postconditions above.

The navigation expression to identify the action is nonstandard UML, but is appropriate if state diagrams are to be used for specification purposes.

Under this interpretation state diagrams can be integrated with class diagrams and OCL constraints. One model is to view states as dynamic subclasses of the class

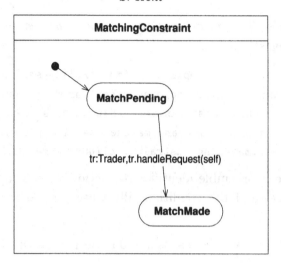

Fig. 7.7. State diagram for the `MatchingConstraint` class.

that they are assigned to in state diagrams: objects belonging to a dynamic class may move to a different (dynamic) class, and vice versa, in which case `oclInState(_)` is just syntactic sugar for `oclIsKindOf(_)`, with a dynamic class as argument, as opposed to a static class.

It is useful to use invariants to tie states to the detailed state space of an object. For example:

Definition of a matching constraint having no matches.

```
context mc:MatchingConstraint inv:
  mc.oclInState(matchPending)=mc.offerMatches->isEmpty
  and mc.oclInState(matchMade)=mc.offerMatches->notEmpty
```

These invariants work, as the cardinality of associations on the class diagram in Figure 7.5 ensures that a context will at least identify one service offer against which to attempt a match. They make the last conjunct of the postcondition of `handleRequest` redundant. Some of the invariants given in Section 7.5.2 could be made more transparent by rewriting parts to involve these states.

The interpretation of state diagrams used here is not the one that is detailed in the UML 1.3 standard, which does not recognize the value of state diagrams for modelling at the specification level. The standard interpretation is one where state diagrams are viewed in an operational rather than declarative way: as a specification of the order in which actions must occur to the point where the state diagram can be executed, rather than a specification of how the actions behave in certain situations. (However, it is recognized that the latter may, as a side effect, constrain the order in which actions occur.) A number of responses to the recent UML 2.0 RFI [OMG99] have argued the case for an interpretation of state diagrams suitable for specification modelling. This interpretation is similar to the one used in Catalysis [DW98].

7.7 Future

This chapter has introduced a subset of UML that potentially can be used to produce precise object-oriented specifications. The subset remains to be formalized, although there are already tool-supported formalizations of parts of it: for example, [RG98, RG00] provides a tool-supported formalization of class diagrams and OCL constraints. There is now even a commercial tool [Bol00] that does much of the same.

The author is currently engaged in work as part of the precise UML (pUML) group [ECK+00] to rearchitect the UML as a family of languages. This work as already influenced the revision of UML within the OMG; the infrastructure RFP for UML 2.0 has the goal of our work at its heart. Our approach to formalization is a variation of the meta-modelling approach to language definition, which has been adopted by the OMG. Essentially we define a family member of UML (a meta-modelling language – MML) that is then used to define itself and other family members. The MML is grounded by an external definition, which in our case is the provision of a tool to support the various features of the language. A key aspect of this approach is that we are able to define, in MML, concrete syntax (both graphical and textual), abstract syntax *and* semantics.

By recognizing UML as a family of languages, the job of defining domain-specific subsets of UML and/or introducing new notations should become more systematic and precise, especially if, as intended, there is a tool-supported framework for defining new family members, by extending and specializing existing language fragments, including a process for signing off, standardizing and evolving language definitions.

This could benefit those working in the distributed systems domain, by providing a platform to support the definition of languages appropriate for modelling in that domain. For example, the Common Information Model (CIM) standard under development under the Distributed Management Task Force of the IETF [DMT99], which is a standard approach to modelling in support of intelligent network management, makes use of a language that is essentially UML class diagrams with its own specializations. Similarly, proposals for using UML as a language for specifying the ODP enterprise viewpoint [AM99, Lin99, SD00] generally make use of a subset of UML specialized with stereotypes. Of course, as is the way with stereotype usage in UML [BGJ99], the intended meaning of the specializations is, at best, informally explained. We would fully expect these languages to be definable as part of the UML family, and there are clear advantages in doing this. In particular, effort put in for one domain can often be reused in other domains. Thus, if one takes the trouble to precisely define a constraint language for use with object models, say, in software specification, that constraint language can be reused in modelling networks, services, policies and the like. If it turns out that the language needs to be extended and/or the concrete syntax is not appropriate for the domain in question, then the appropriate extensions to the base language and/or a new concrete syntax can be provided. On the other hand, it should still be possible to use tools, training materials and so on that support the base language, with the extended/specialized language. Thus if only a different concrete syntax is required, then any semantic checking tools will be unaffected. The purpose of the framework that we are developing is to manage such language development and evolution in a systematic way.

To conclude, we return to one aspect of UML that we identified as a weakness in the subset we have chosen: concurrency and real-time. Part of the problem is that the 1.3 documentation is so ambiguous and contradictory [KER99] that it is hard to know where to start. This might be remedied somewhat in the forthcoming submission to the UML action semantics RFP [Obj98]. The core of this submission is an attempt pin down an 'action semantics' that directly addresses issues of concurrency and real-time. This will identify many of the problems and suggest solutions. However, the submission will still be informal in nature, in the same style as the UML 1.3 standard. One of the goals of the proposed rearchitecting of the UML will be to rework this submission into a more rigorous and organized definition. This will make it much easier to see where existing research results in concurrency and real-time could be used to further improve the UML in this area.

Acknowledgements

Thanks to Andy Evans and John Derrick for feedback on early drafts of this chapter. This work was partly supported by the EPSRC under grant GR/M02606.

Bibliography

[AM99]   J. O. Aagedal and Z. Milosevic. ODP enterprise language: UML perspective. In *Proc. 3rd International Workshop on Enterprise Distributed Object Computing (EDOC'99)*, pages 60–71. IEEE, September 1999.

[BGH+98] R. Breu, R. Grosu, C. Hofmann, F. Huber, I. Krüger, B. Rumpe, M. Schmidt, and W. Schwerin. Exemplary and complete object interaction descriptions. *Computer Standards & Interfaces*, 19(7):335–345, November 1998.

[BGJ99]   S. Berner, M. Glinz, and S. Joos. A classification of stereotypes for object-oriented modeling languages. In R. France and B. Rumpe, editors, *UML'99 - The Unified Modeling Language. Beyond the Standard*, volume 1723 of *Lecture Notes in Computer Science*, pages 249–264. Springer-Verlag, 1999.

[Bol00]   BoldSoft. ModelRun case tool (beta). Available from http://www.boldsoft.com, July 2000.

[CEF+99] A. Clark, A. Evans, R. France, S. Kent, and B. Rumpe. The pUML response to the OMG UML 2.0 RFI. Available from http://www.cs.york.ac.uk/puml, December 1999.

[Coc00]   A. Cockburn. *Writing Effective Use Cases*. Addison-Wesley, 2000.

[DMT99]   DMTF. The common information model (CIM) specification v2.2. Available from http://www.dmtf.org/spec/cims.html, June 1999.

[DW98]   D. D'Souza and A. Wills. *Objects, Components and Frameworks With UML: The Catalysis Approach.* Addison-Wesley, 1998.

[ECK+00]   A. Evans, A. Clark, S. Kent, S. Brodsky, and S. Cook. Feasibility study in rearchitecting UML as a family of languages using a precise OO meta-modeling approach. http://www.puml.org, 2000.

[EK99]   A. Evans and S. Kent. Core meta-modelling semantics of UML: The pUML approach. In R. France and B. Rumpe, editors, *UML'99 - The Unified Modeling Language. Beyond the Standard.*, volume 1723 of *Lecture Notes in Computer Science*, pages 140–155. Springer-Verlag, 1999.

[GBJ99]   J. Rumbaugh G. Booch and I. Jacobson. *The Unified Modelling Language User Guide.* Addison-Wesley, 1999.

[GHK99]   J. Gil, J. Howse, and S. Kent. Formalizing Spider Diagrams. In *IEEE Symposium on Visual Languages (VL99)*. IEEE Computer Society Press, December 1999.

[HMTK99]   J. Howse, F. Molina, J. Taylor, and S. Kent. Reasoning with Spider Diagrams. In *IEEE Symposium on Visual Languages (VL99)*. IEEE Computer Society Press, December 1999.

[HSB99]   B. Henderson-Sellers and F. Barbier. Black and white diamonds. In R. France and B. Rumpe, editors, *UML'99 - The Unified Modeling Language. Beyond the Standard*, volume 1723 of *Lecture Notes in Computer Science*, pages 550–565. Springer-Verlag, 1999.

[ISO98]   *ISO/IEC IS 13235-1, Open Distributed Processing - Trading Function: Specification.* ISO, 1998.

[Ken97]   S. Kent. Constraint Diagrams: Visualizing Invariants in OO Modelling. In *Proceedings of OOPSLA97*, pages 327–341. ACM Press, October 1997.

[KER99]   S. Kent, A. Evans, and B. Rumpe. UML Semantics FAQ. In *ECOOP'99 Workshop Reader*, Lecture Notes in Computer Science. Springer-Verlag, December 1999.

[KG98]   S. Kent and Y. Gil. Visualising Action Contracts in OO Modelling. *IEE Proceedings: Software*, 145(2-3):70–78, April 1998.

[KH99]   S. Kent and J. Howse. Mixing visual and textual constraint languages. In R. France and B. Rumpe, editors, *UML'99 - The Unified Modeling Language. Beyond the Standard*, volume 1723 of *Lecture Notes in Computer Science*, pages 384–398. Springer-Verlag, 1999.

[Lar97]   C. Larman. *Applying UML and Patterns: An Introduction to Object-Oriented Analysis and Design.* Prentice Hall, 1997.

[LB99]   G. Leavens and A. Baker. Enhancing the pre- and postcondition technique for more expressive specifications. In J. M. Wing, J. C. P. Woodock, and J. Davies, editors, *FM'99 World Congress on Formal Methods in the Development of Computing Systems*, volume 1708 of *Lecture Notes in Computer Science*, Berlin, 1999. Springer-Verlag.

[LBR99]   G. Leavens, A. Baker, and C. Ruby. JML: A notation for detailed design. In H. Kilov, B. Rumpe, and I. Simmonds, editors, *Behavioral Specifications for Businesses and Systems*, chapter 9, pages 175–188. Kluwer, September 1999.

[Lin99]   P. F. Linington. Options for expressing ODP enterprise communities and their policies by using UML. In *Proc. 3rd International Workshop on Enterprise Distributed Object Computing (EDOC'99)*, pages 72–82. IEEE, September 1999.

[LW94]   B. Liskov and J. M. Wing. A behavioural notion of subtyping. *ACM Transactions on Programming Languages and Systems*, 16(6):1811–1841, 1994.

[Obj98]   Object Management Group. Action semantics for UML RFP. Available from http://www.omg.org, 1998.

[OMG99]   Analysis and Design Task Force of the OMG. UML 2.0 RFI. Available from http://www.omg.org, 1999.

[RG98]   M. Richters and M. Gogolla. On formalizing the UML Object Constraint

Language OCL. In Tok Wang Ling, Sudha Ram, and Mong Li Lee, editors, *17th Int. Conf. Conceptual Modeling (ER'98)*, volume 1507 of *Lecture Notes in Computer Science*, pages 449–464. Springer-Verlag, 1998.

[RG00]   M. Richters and M. Gogolla. Validating UML models and OCL constraints. In A. Evans, S. Kent, and B. Selic, editors, *The Third International Conference on the Unified Modeling Language (UML'2000)*, volume 1939 of *Lecture Notes in Computer Science*. Springer-Verlag, 2000.

[Ric00]   M. Richters. The University of Bremen UML bibliography. http://www.db.informatik.uni-bremen.de/umlbib/, July 2000.

[SD00]   M. W. A. Steen and J. Derrick. ODP enterprise viewpoint specification. *Computer Standards and Interfaces*, 22:165–189, 2000.

[WK98]   J. Warmer and A. Kleppe. *The Object Constraint Language: Precise Modeling with UML*. Addison-Wesley, 1998.

Part Three
Dynamic Reconfiguration

8

Actors: A Model for Reasoning About Open Distributed Systems

Gul A. Agha   Prasannaa Thati   Reza Ziaei

University of Illinois at Urbana-Champaign, USA

8.1 Introduction

Open distributed systems are often subject to dynamic changes of hardware or software components, for example, in response to changing requirements, hardware faults, software failures or the need to upgrade some component. In other words, open systems are reconfigurable and extensible: they may allow components to be dynamically replaced or connected with new components while they are still executing. The Actor theory that we describe in this chapter abstracts some fundamental aspects of open systems. Actors provide a natural generalization for objects – encapsulating both data and procedures. However, Actors differ from sequential objects in that they are also units of concurrency: each Actor executes asynchronously and its operation may overlap with other Actors. This unification of data abstraction and concurrency is in contrast to language models such as Java, where an explicit and independent notion of thread is used to provide concurrency. By integrating objects and concurrency, Actors free the programmer from having to write explicit synchronization code to prevent harmful concurrent access to data within an object.

There are several fundamental differences between Actors and other formal models of concurrency. First, an Actor has a unique and persistent identity, although its behaviour may change over time. Second, communication between Actors is asynchronous and fair (messages sent are eventually received). Third, an Actor's name may be given out freely – without, for example, enabling other Actors to adopt the same name. Finally, new Actors may be created with their own unique and persistent names. These characteristics provide reasonable abstraction for open distributed systems. In fact, Actors provide a realistic model for a number of practical implementations, including those of software agents [AJ99].

The outline of this chapter is as follows. The next section relates Actors to other models of concurrency. Section 8.3 presents an introduction to Actors. Section 8.4 presents the syntax and semantics of a simple Actor language. Section 8.5 completes the discussion of the language semantics, along with a brief description of a notion of equivalence. Section 8.6 describes an example that shows how Actor theory can be used to reason about open systems. The final section outlines current research directions and provides some perspective. The treatment in this chapter is of necessity rather high-level. Interested readers should refer to the citations for technical details of the work as well as secondary references to the literature.

8.2 Related Work

A number of formal models have been proposed to formalize fundamental concepts of concurrent computation involving interaction and mobility. We relate Actors to the most prominent of these: namely, the π-calculus [Mil93, Mil99] (see also Chapter 9 of this book) and its variants [HT91, Bou92].

The π-calculus evolved out of an earlier formal model of concurrency called the Calculus of Communicating Systems (CCS) [Mil89]. Processes in CCS are interconnected by a static topology. In order to overcome the limitations of CCS that did not model Actor-like systems with their dynamic interconnection topology, the π-calculus was developed. The π-calculus enables dynamic interconnection by allowing channel names to be communicated.

The Actor model and π-calculus are similar in the sense that both model *concurrent* and *asynchronous processes, communication of values* and *synchronization*. However, the two formalisms make different ontological commitments. We examine the most significant of these differences.

- The central difference between the π-calculus and the Actor model is that names in the former identify stateless communication channels, while names in the latter identify persistent agents. Representation of the object paradigm in π-calculus requires imposing a type system [San98, Wal95]. However, the usage of Actor names embodies additional semantic properties that are not captured by these type systems. For instance, an Actor has a unique name, and it may not create new Actors with names received in a message. A typed π-calculus that also enforces these additional constraints is presented in [Tha00].

- Actors provide buffered, asynchronous communication as a primitive while communication in the π-calculus is synchronous. It is possible to simulate one in terms of the other, but such simulations insert a degree of complication in reasoning, while at the same time such simulations only approximate the abstractions. Although synchronous communication can be useful for inferring pairwise group knowledge – a necessary condition for joint action, it should be observed that process actions in both models are asynchronous; thus the synchronous communication in the π-calculus is not useful for any notion of joint action. The Actor model is closer to real distributed systems; one consequence of this proximity of asynchronous communication and distributed systems is that synchronous communication is not as efficient as a default communication mechanism in distributed systems (see [Agh86, Kim97, VA98]).

- Message delivery in the Actor model is fair, which allows greater modularity in reasoning (see Section 8.4.2). It is possible to add different notions of fairness in

π-calculus and its variants, but there is no standard notion of fairness in these models.

Programming languages that have been developed based on π-calculus, such as the Nomadic π-calculus [SWP99], generally adopt key aspects of the Actor model. The Nomadic π-calculus was conceived primarily to study communication primitives for interaction between mobile agents. An agent in a Nomadic π-calculus is essentially a process with a unique name that communicates with other agents via asynchronous messages. The reader may note the similarity with the Actor model.

The Nomadic π-calculus model does have other aspects that are not shared with the Actor model. The model extends the basic ideas in π-calculus with notions of *sites* and *migrating agents*. Every agent is associated with a current host site, and agents may migrate between sites during their execution. The calculus identifies two kinds of communication primitives: location-dependent primitives, which require the knowledge of the current location of the target agent, and location-independent primitives, which do not.

In contrast, Actors are not associated with a host. Moreover, to use the terminology in [Nee89], Actor names are *pure*: they do not contain any information about the creation or location of an Actor. However, variants of the Actor model exist in which Actor names contain both creation and current location information. The agent definition based on Actors explicitly models location [AJ99], and location information has been added to Actor names to provide universal naming for the World Wide Computer model [Var00].

8.3 Actors

The Actor model provides an effective method for representing computation in real-world systems. Actors extend the concept of objects to concurrent computation [Agh86]. Recall that objects encapsulate a state and a set of procedures that manipulate the state; Actors extend this by also encapsulating a thread of control (see Figure 8.1). Each Actor potentially executes in parallel with other Actors. It may know the addresses of other Actors and can send messages to such Actors. Actor addresses may be communicated in messages, allowing dynamic reconfiguration and name mobility. Finally, new Actors may be created; such Actors have their own unique addresses.

A concrete way to think of Actors is that they represent an abstraction over concurrent architectures. An Actor run-time system provides an abstract program interface (API) for services such as global addressing, memory management, fair scheduling and communication. It turns out that the Actor API can be efficiently implemented, thus raising the level of abstraction while reducing the size and complexity of code on concurrent architectures [KA95].

Note that the Actor model is, like the π-calculus, general and inherently parallel. Asynchronous communication in Actors directly preserves the available potential for

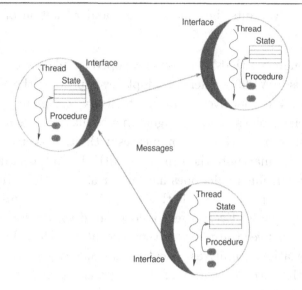

Fig. 8.1. Actors encapsulate a thread and state. The interface is comprised of public methods that operate on the state.

parallel activity: an Actor sending a message does not necessarily have to wait for the recipient to be ready to receive (or process) a message. Of course, it is possible to define Actor-like buffered, asynchronous communication in terms of synchronous communication, provided dynamic Actor (or process) creation is allowed. On the other hand, more complex communication patterns, such as remote procedure calls, can also be expressed as a sequence of asynchronous messages [Agh90]. Higher level Actor languages often provide a number of communication abstractions.

8.4 A Simple Actor Language

It is possible to extend any sequential language with Actor constructs. We use the call-by-value λ-calculus for this purpose. Here we will present a variant of the language presented in [AMST97] together with its formal syntax and semantics.

8.4.1 Syntax

We assume countably infinite sets **X**(variables) and **At** (atoms). **At** contains t and nil for Booleans, as well as constants for natural numbers, **N**. We assume a countably infinite set of Actor addresses. To simplify notation we identify this set with **X** and call the variables used in this way, that is, the free variables in an Actor configuration (see Section 8.4.3) as Actor names. We also assume a set of (possibly empty) sets of n-ary operations, $\mathbf{F}_n$ on **At** for each $n \in \mathbf{N}$ and $\mathbf{F} = \bigcup_{n \in \mathbf{N}} \mathbf{F}_n$. **F** contains arithmetic operations, recognizers isatom for atoms, isnat for numbers, ispair for pairs, branching br, pairing pr, 1st, 2nd and the following Actor primitives: Actor primitives send, newactor and ready.

send(a, v) creates a new message:
- with receiver a, and
- contents v

newactor(b) creates a new Actor:
- with behaviour b, and
- returns its address

ready(b) captures local state change:
- replaces the behaviour of the executing Actor with b
- frees the Actor to accept another message.

The sets of value expressions **V** and expressions **E** are defined inductively as follows:

Definition 1
$$\mathbf{V} = \mathbf{At} \cup \mathbf{X} \cup \lambda\,\mathbf{X}.\mathbf{E} \cup pr(\mathbf{V}, \mathbf{V})$$
$$\mathbf{E} = \mathbf{At} \cup \mathbf{X} \cup \lambda\,\mathbf{X}.\mathbf{E} \cup app(\mathbf{E}, \mathbf{E}) \cup \mathbf{F}_n(\mathbf{E}_n)$$

We let x, y, z range over **X**, v range over **V** and e range over **E**. To simplify the presentation of examples we use several abbreviations. The function br is a strict conditional, and the usual conditional construct if can be defined as the following abbreviation:

if(e_0, e_1, e_2) abbreviates   app$(\text{br}(e_0, \lambda\,z.e_1, \lambda\,z.e_2), \text{nil})$ for z fresh.

Similarly, let, seq and rec are the usual syntactic sugar: let is used for creating local bindings, seq is used as a sequencing primitive and rec is the Y combinator used for recursion in call-by-value λ-calculus. Finally, letactor is a convenient abbreviation used for Actor creations:

letactor$\{x := e\}\,e'$ abbreviates   let$\{x := \text{newactor}(e)\}\,e'$.

Actor behaviours are represented as lambda abstractions. Delivery of a message m is simply the application of Actor's behaviour b to m, denoted by app(b, m). The motivation behind the Actor constructs is to provide the minimal extension that is necessary to lift a sequential language to a concurrent one supporting object-style encapsulation (of state and procedures) and coordination.

In Section 8.4.3 we provide an operational semantics for our language in terms of a transition relation on Actor configurations.

8.4.2 Examples

We provide a few examples to illustrate the Actor model. Since we are not concerned with the structure of messages, we represent messages abstractly by assuming functions to create messages and to test or extract their contents. For example, we assume that $\mathtt{mkget}(c)$ creates a 'get' message with content c and $\mathtt{get?}(m)$ returns true if m is a 'get' message.

Sink. The first example is the behaviour of an Actor that ignores every message that it receives and becomes itself:

$$B_{\mathtt{sink}} = \mathtt{rec}(\lambda\, b.\, \lambda\, m.\mathtt{ready}(b)) \tag{8.1}$$

Cell. The second example is an Actor that models the behaviour of a variable store as used in imperative programming. We call this Actor a *cell*, and it responds to two sorts of messages. A $\mathtt{get}$ message contains the address of an Actor requesting the value of the cell and a $\mathtt{set}$ message that contains a new value to replace the cell's old value. The following code specifies the behaviour of a cell Actor:

$$
\begin{aligned}
B_{\mathrm{cell}} \;=\; &\mathtt{rec}(\lambda\, b.\, \lambda\, c.\, \lambda\, m. \\
&\quad \mathtt{if}(\mathtt{get?}(m), \\
&\qquad \mathtt{seq}(\mathtt{send}(cust(m), c), \mathtt{ready}(b(c))) \\
&\qquad \mathtt{if}(\mathtt{set?}(m), \\
&\qquad\quad \mathtt{ready}(b(\mathtt{contents}(m))), \\
&\qquad\quad \mathtt{ready}(b(c)))))
\end{aligned}
$$

Evaluating

$$
\begin{aligned}
&\mathtt{letactor}\{a := B_{\mathrm{cell}}(0)\} \\
&\quad \mathtt{seq}(\mathtt{send}(a, \mathtt{mkset}(3)), \mathtt{send}(a, \mathtt{mkset}(4)), \mathtt{send}(a, \mathtt{mkget}(b)))
\end{aligned}
$$

will result in the Actor b receiving a message containing either 0, 3 or 4, depending on the arrival order of messages sent to cell a.

Tree Product. Our third example is a divide-and-conquer problem that illustrates how synchronization primitives can be modelled using Actors. Suppose that we want to determine the product of the leaves of a tree. We assume that every internal node of the tree has exactly two children, and that the leaves are integers. A divide-and-conquer strategy is to calculate the product of the leaves of each subtree and then multiply the results. The sequential implementation of this algorithm can be represented by the following recursive function:

$$
\begin{aligned}
\mathtt{treeprod} \;=\; &\mathtt{rec}(\lambda\, f.\, \lambda\, tree. \\
&\quad \mathtt{if}(\mathtt{isnat}(tree), \\
&\qquad tree, \\
&\qquad f(\mathtt{left}(tree)) * f(\mathtt{right}(tree)))
\end{aligned}
$$

However, the same strategy can be used to obtain a parallel algorithm that concurrently evaluates products of subtrees. To synchronize the calculation of subtree products, we use *join continuation* Actors, which guarantee that several concurrent subcomputations are complete before beginning a computation that depends on the results of the subcomputations. The behaviour $B_{\mathtt{treeprod}}$ in the following implements a concurrent evaluation of tree products:

$B_{\texttt{treeprod}} =$

> $\texttt{rec}(\lambda\, b.\, \lambda\, self.\, \lambda\, m.$
>> $\texttt{if}(\texttt{notvalidtree}(\texttt{tree}(m)),$
>>> $\texttt{seq}(\texttt{send}(\texttt{cust}(m), \texttt{error}),$
>>>> $\texttt{ready}(b(self))),$
>>> $\texttt{if}(\texttt{isnat}(\texttt{tree}(m)),$
>>>> $\texttt{seq}(\texttt{send}(\texttt{cust}(m), \texttt{tree}(m)),$
>>>>> $\texttt{ready}(b(self))),$
>>>> $\texttt{letactor}\{jc := B_{\texttt{joincont}}(\texttt{cust}(m), 0, \texttt{nil})\}$
>>>>> $\texttt{seq}(\texttt{send}(self, \texttt{mkprd}(\texttt{left}(\texttt{tree}(m)), jc)),$
>>>>> $\texttt{seq}(\texttt{send}(self, \texttt{mkprd}(\texttt{right}(\texttt{tree}(m)), jc))$
>>>>>> $\texttt{ready}(b(self)))))))))$

The behaviour of the join continuation Actor is specified as:

$B_{\texttt{joincont}} =$

> $\texttt{rec}(\lambda\, b.\, \lambda\, cust.\, \lambda\, nargs.\, \lambda firstnum\, .\, \lambda\, num$
>> $\texttt{if}(\texttt{eq}(nargs, 0),$
>>> $\texttt{ready}(b(cust, 1, num)),$
>>> $\texttt{seq}(\texttt{send}(cust, firstnum * num),$
>>>> $\texttt{ready}(B_{\texttt{sink}}))))$

Note that an Actor with behaviour $B_{\texttt{treeprod}}$ can evaluate multiple tree product requests concurrently. Specifically, the evaluation of a new tree product request can begin even before the evaluation of any previous requests is complete. The structure of many parallel computations, such as parallel search, is very similar.

8.4.3 Reduction Semantics for Actor Configurations

Instantaneous snapshots of Actor systems are called *configurations*. The operational semantics of our language is defined by a transition relation on configurations. The notion of open systems is captured by defining a dynamic interface to a configuration, that is, by explicitly representing a set of *receptionists* that may receive messages from Actors outside the configuration and a set of Actors *external* to the configuration, which may receive messages from the Actors within.

An *Actor configuration* with Actor map α, multiset of messages μ, receptionists ρ and external Actors χ is written

$$\langle\, \alpha \mid \mu \,\rangle^{\rho}_{\chi} \qquad (8.2)$$

where ρ and χ are finite sets of Actor addresses, α maps a finite set of addresses to their behaviour and μ is a finite multiset of (pending) messages. A message m contains the address of the Actor it is targeted to and the message contents, $a \triangleleft v$. We restrict the contents to be any values constructed from atoms and Actor addresses (beta-v) $R[\![\texttt{app}(\lambda\, x.e, v)\,]\!] \overset{\lambda}{\mapsto} R[\![e[x := v]]\!]$

(delta) $R[\![\delta(v_1, \ldots, v_n)\,]\!] \overset{\lambda}{\mapsto} R[\![v']\!]$

   where $\delta \in \mathbf{F}_n$, $v_1, \ldots, v_n \in \mathbf{At}^n$, and $\delta(v_1, \ldots, v_n) = v'$.

(eq) $R[\![\texttt{eq}(v_0, v_1)]\!] \overset{\lambda}{\mapsto} \begin{cases} R[\![\texttt{t}]\!] & \text{if } v_0 = v_1 \in \mathbf{At} \\ R[\![\texttt{nil}]\!] & \text{if } v_0, v_1 \in \mathbf{At} \text{ and } v_0 \neq v_1 \end{cases}$

Fig. 8.2. Reduction rules for the functional case.

using the pairing constructor **pr**. We call these values communicable values and let cv range over them.

Let $\langle \alpha \mid \mu \rangle_\chi^\rho$ be a configuration, and if $A = \mathrm{Dom}(\alpha)$ (domain of α), then the following properties must hold:

(0) $\rho \subseteq A$ and $A \cap \chi = \varnothing$.

(1) If $a \in A$, then $\mathrm{FV}(\alpha(a)) \subseteq A \cup \chi$, where $\mathrm{FV}(\alpha(a))$ represents the free variables of $\alpha(a)$; and if $v_0 \lhd v_1$ is a message with content v_1 to Actor address v_0, then $\mathrm{FV}(v_i) \subseteq A \cup \chi$ for $i < 2$.

To describe local transitions at an Actor, we decompose uniquely a nonvalue expression into a reduction context filled with a redex. A redex identifies the next subexpression that is to be evaluated according to the reduction strategy (which in our case is left-first, call-by-value) [FF86]. Redexes are of two kinds: purely functional and Actor. The Actor redexes are $\texttt{send}(a, v)$, $\texttt{newactor}(b)$ and $\texttt{ready}(b)$. Reduction rules for the functional case are defined by a relation $\overset{\lambda}{\mapsto}$ on $\mathbf{E}$, as shown in Figure 8.2.

The transition relation, that is, $\mapsto$, on Actor configurations is defined by the rules shown in Figure 8.3. The rules are all labelled to indicate the kind of reduction and any additional parameters. The notation $[e]_a$ denotes the (singleton) Actor map that maps the name a to expression e.

The <fun: a> rule simply says that an Actor's internal computation is defined by the semantics of the sequential language that its behaviour is written in. The <new: a, a'> rule says that a new Actor with *fresh* name a' (no external Actor or an Actor already in the configuration can have the same name) is created and ready to receive messages. The new Actor's name, a', is returned to the creating Actor as the result of the **newactor** operation. The <send: a, m> rule defines the asynchronous semantics of message send. The new message is put in the message pool and the sending Actor can continue its execution. The <rcv: a, cv> rule says that an Actor can receive a message only when it is ready. In fact, execution of the **ready** operation blocks the Actor's thread until the delivery of a message. The delivery is performed by applying the new behaviour to the message. The last two rules, <out: m> and

`<fun: a>`

$$e \stackrel{\lambda}{\mapsto} e' \Rightarrow \langle \alpha, [e]_a \mid \mu \rangle^\rho_\chi \mapsto \langle \alpha, [e']_a \mid \mu \rangle^\rho_\chi$$

`<new: a, a'>`

$$\langle \alpha, [R[\![\mathtt{newactor}(v)]\!]]_a \mid \mu \rangle^\rho_\chi \mapsto \langle \alpha, [R[\![a']\!]]_a, [\mathtt{ready}(v)]_{a'} \mid \mu \rangle^\rho_\chi \qquad a' \text{ fresh}$$

`<send: a, m>`

$$\langle \alpha, [R[\![\mathtt{send}(v_0, v_1)]\!]]_a \mid \mu \rangle^\rho_\chi \mapsto \langle \alpha, [R[\![\mathtt{nil}]\!]]_a \mid \mu, m \rangle^\rho_\chi \qquad m = v_0 \lhd v_1$$

`<rcv: a, cv>`

$$\langle \alpha, [R[\![\mathtt{ready}(v)]\!]]_a \mid a \lhd cv, \mu \rangle^\rho_\chi \mapsto \langle \alpha, [\mathtt{app}(v, cv)]_a \mid \mu \rangle^\rho_\chi$$

`<out: m>`

$$\langle \alpha \mid \mu, m \rangle^\rho_\chi \mapsto \langle \alpha \mid \mu \rangle^{\rho'}_\chi$$

  if $m = a \lhd cv$, $a \in \chi$, and $\rho' = \rho \cup (\mathrm{FV}(cv) \cap \mathrm{Dom}(\alpha))$

`<in: m>`

$$\langle \alpha \mid \mu \rangle^\rho_\chi \mapsto \langle \alpha \mid \mu, m \rangle^\rho_{\chi \cup (\mathrm{FV}(cv) - \mathrm{Dom}(\alpha))}$$

  if $m = a \lhd cv$, $a \in \rho$ and $\mathrm{FV}(cv) \cap \mathrm{Dom}(\alpha) \subseteq \rho$

Fig. 8.3. Actor transitions.

`<in: m>`, capture the openness of the configurations by allowing the exchange of messages between the configuration and its environment. Note the dynamic nature of the interface and that the exchange of messages is restricted by the interface.

Because our language is untyped, the creation of Actors with ill-formed behaviours (i.e., behaviours that are not λ abstractions) and the creation of messages with ill-formed contents (i.e., contents that are not communicable values) is possible. But the reduction system will prevent such ill-formed behaviours and messages from being used.

8.4.4 Example

Consider the following Actor behaviour that creates new cell Actors upon request:

$$B_{\text{c-maker}} =$$
$$\mathtt{rec}(\lambda\, b.\, \lambda\, self.\, \lambda\, m.$$
$$\mathtt{letactor}\{newcell := B_{\text{cell}}(0)\}$$
$$\mathtt{seq}(\ \mathtt{send}(\mathtt{cust}(m), newcell)),$$
$$\mathtt{ready}(b(self))))$$

An initial Actor configuration containing a cell-maker Actor is

$$\langle \, [\texttt{ready}(B_{\text{c-maker}}(cm))] \,_{cm} \, \mid \, \rangle_{\varnothing}^{\{cm\}} \qquad (8.3)$$

Let's say that this Actor configuration makes an input transition with the label $\texttt{<in:}\,cm \triangleleft \texttt{mkcell}(a)\texttt{>}$. The resulting configuration will be

$$\langle \, [\texttt{ready}(B_{\text{c-maker}}(cm))] \,_{cm} \, \mid \, cm \triangleleft \texttt{mkcell}(a) \, \rangle_{\{a\}}^{\{cm\}} \qquad (8.4)$$

And after a $\texttt{<rcv:}\,cm,\,cm\triangleleft\texttt{mkcell}(a)\texttt{>}$, a series of $\texttt{fun}$ transitions and a $\texttt{<send:}\,a,\,a\triangleleft$ $a'\texttt{>}$ transition, we reach the following configuration:

$$\langle \, [\texttt{ready}(B_{\text{c-maker}}(cm))] \,_{cm}, [\texttt{ready}(B_{\text{cell}}(0))] \,_{a'} \, \mid \, a \triangleleft a' \, \rangle_{\{a\}}^{\{cm\}} \qquad (8.5)$$

With a final $\texttt{<out:}\,a \triangleleft a'\texttt{>}$, the following configuration will result:

$$\langle \, [\texttt{ready}(B_{\text{c-maker}}(cm))] \,_{cm}, [\texttt{ready}(B_{\text{cell}}(0))] \,_{a'} \, \mid \, \rangle_{\{a\}}^{\{cm,a'\}} \qquad (8.6)$$

Following this transition, the Actor name a' will be known to the outside world and further calls to cm will result in new cells being created.

8.4.5 Local Synchronization Constraints

Different Actors carry out their operations asynchronously. This means that the sender of a message may not know what the state of a recipient is at the time that it sends the message. Moreover, an Actor may not be able to process particular types of messages while in certain states. For example, a lock that is currently owned by a process cannot accept any further requests to acquire the lock until it is released by the current owner. In models relying on synchronous messages, this is handled by guards on ports: different types of messages are received at different ports, and ports may be disabled/enabled depending on the local process state and message contents, thereby blocking a communication.

In Actors, message send is asynchronous and nonblocking. Different approaches to selectively process external communications may be taken to address the problem. One solution is to let an Actor explicitly buffer the incoming communications that it is not ready to process (cf. insensitive Actors [Agh86]). In the Rosette Actor language, Tomlinson and Singh [TKS$^+$89] proposed a mechanism that associates with each potential state of Actor an *enabled set* specifying the particular *methods* that the recipient Actor is willing to invoke. The Actor then processes the earliest received message in its queue, which invokes a method in its current enabled set. The effect is to delay the processing of a message until such time that an Actor is in a state where it is able to process it.

In this chapter, we use a variation of this concept called *local synchronization constraints*. Local synchronization constraints are so called because their scope of

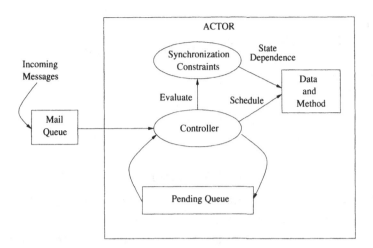

Fig. 8.4. An Actor with local synchronization constraints.

influence is a single Actor [Fro96]. A local synchronization constraint is a predicate that constrains the delivery of messages. Delivery of a message to a constrained Actor is delayed until the message satisfies the constraint (see Figure 8.4). An Actor's synchronization constraint reflects the state of the Actor and therefore is updated every time an Actor moves into its next state by executing a **ready** operation.

To account for synchronization constraints we slightly modify the standard language of Actors as in Figure 8.3. In the new language, the **ready** primitive is modified by adding a second argument: a synchronization constraint that is a predicate over messages. Consequently, the rule **rcv** must be modified to capture the intended semantics of synchronization constraints.

The new semantic rule is shown in Figure 8.5. All of the other rules remain the same. Note that, according to the side condition of the rule, if the computation of $\mathbf{app}(c, a \lhd cv)$ does not terminate, the condition will never hold and therefore the delivery will not take place – which is what we intuitively expect. However, the operational semantics as given is loose – since evaluating the constraint has no side-effects, an implementation could concurrently test the constraint against several messages, but then accept only one of the messages for which the constraint is satisfied (this is similar to the semantics of Dijkstra's guarded command). It should be noted that most Actor languages ensure the termination of testing synchronization constraints by disallowing recursion in constraints.

Finally, note that it is possible to translate the Actors with local synchronization constraints into Actors obeying the primitive semantics ([AKP95]). A proof that this translation is semantics-preserving can be found in [MT99].

$$\texttt{<rcv:}\quad a, cv\texttt{>}$$
$$\langle\, \alpha,\ [R[\![\texttt{ready}(v,c)]\!])\, a \mid a \triangleleft cv, \mu\, \rangle^{\rho}_{\chi} \mapsto \langle\, \alpha,\ [\texttt{app}(v, cv)]\, a \mid \mu\, \rangle^{\rho}_{\chi}$$
$$\text{if } \texttt{app}(c, cv) = \texttt{t}$$

Fig. 8.5. Transitions for Actor configurations with local synchronization constraints.

8.4.6 Example

The example in this section demonstrates how synchronization constraints can modularly control the delivery of messages.

Consider the cell Actor example again. Now, suppose that we want to modify the cell to turn it into a single element buffer. In other words, we want to add the restriction that a `put` message be delivered only when the cell is empty and a `get` message delivered only when the cell is not empty. Assume the following abstract functions on messages: $\texttt{put?}(m)$, $\texttt{get?}(m)$.

The local synchronization constraints over a cell `cell` can be represented as predicate functions over messages as follows:

$$C_{\text{full}} = \lambda\, m.\texttt{get?}(m)$$
$$C_{\text{empty}} = \lambda\, m.\texttt{put?}(m)$$

These constraints must be set by the Actor when a `ready` operation is performed. Now, a single element buffer can be implemented as follows:

$$\begin{aligned}
B_{\text{single-buffer}} = \;& \texttt{rec}(\lambda\, b.\, \lambda(v, sc).\, \lambda\, m.\\
& \quad \texttt{if}(\texttt{get?}(m),\\
& \qquad \texttt{seq}(\ \texttt{send}(cust(m), v),\\
& \qquad\qquad \texttt{ready}(b(v, C_{\text{empty}}), C_{\text{empty}})),\\
& \qquad \texttt{if}(\texttt{set?}(m),\\
& \qquad\quad \texttt{ready}(b(\texttt{contents}(m), C_{\text{full}}), C_{\text{full}})),\\
& \qquad\quad \texttt{ready}(b(c, sc), sc))) \qquad ;\ \text{bad message}
\end{aligned}$$

In the rest of this chapter we assume that $\texttt{ready}(b)$ abbreviates $\texttt{ready}(b, \lambda\, m.\texttt{true})$.

8.5 Theory

In this section we describe a theory of Actor computation. The basis of this theory was introduced in [AMST97]. Here we summarize the main elements of the theory and then introduce a proof technique based on i/o-path correspondence developed in [MT99].

8.5.1 Computation Trees and Paths

The behaviour of an Actor system will be represented by computation trees and paths. We write $\kappa_0 \xrightarrow{l} \kappa_1$ if $\kappa_0 \mapsto \kappa_1$ according to the rule labelled by l in Figure 8.3.

Definition 2 *The* **computation tree** *for a configuration κ, written as $\mathcal{T}(\kappa)$, is defined to be the set of all finite sequences of labelled transitions of the form $[\kappa_i \xrightarrow{l_i} \kappa_{i+1} \mid i < n]$ for some $n \in \mathbf{N}$, with $\kappa = \kappa_0$. We call such sequences* **computation sequences** *and let ν range over them.*

Definition 3 *The sequences of a computation tree are partially ordered by the initial segment relation. A* **computation path** *from a configuration κ is a maximal linearly ordered set of computation sequences in $\mathcal{T}(\kappa)$. Note that a path can also be regarded as a (possibly infinite) sequence of labelled transitions.*

We use $\mathcal{T}^{\infty}(\kappa)$ to denote the set of all paths from κ, and we let π range over computation paths. When thinking of a path as a possibly infinite sequence we write $[\kappa_i \xrightarrow{l_i} \kappa_{i+1} \mid i < \triangleright \triangleleft]$, where $\triangleright \triangleleft \in \mathbf{N} \cup \omega$ is the length of the sequence.

Since the result of a transition is uniquely determined by the starting configuration and the transition label, computation sequences and paths can also be represented by their initial configuration and the sequence of transition labels. The sequence of configurations can be computed by induction on the index of occurrence. We assume this representation of computation paths in the rest of this chapter.

8.5.2 Fairness

The model that we have developed provides fairness, namely, that any enabled transition eventually fires. Under this assumption, not all paths are considered to be admissible. Fairness is an important requirement for reasoning about eventuality properties. It is particularly relevant in supporting modular reasoning.

There are two important consequences of fairness that illustrate its usefulness. The first of these is that each Actor makes progress independent of how busy other Actors are. Therefore, if we compose one configuration with another that has an Actor with a nonterminating computation, computation in the first configuration may nevertheless proceed as before, for example, if Actors in the two configurations do not interact. A second consequence is that messages are eventually delivered. This allows reasoning based on composition with some contexts to be carried forward: thus, if upon composition with a richer context, other requests may be sent to a particular server Actor, previous requests sent to that server will still be received (provided that the server itself does not 'fail').

We now formally define fairness in our model. We say that a label l is *enabled* in configuration κ if there is some κ' such that $\kappa \xrightarrow{l} \kappa'$.

Definition 4 *A path $\pi = [\kappa_i \xrightarrow{l_i} \kappa_{i+1} \mid i < \rhd \dashv$ in $\mathcal{T}^\infty(\kappa)$ is **fair** if each enabled transition eventually happens or becomes permanently disabled. That is, if l is enabled in κ_i and is not of the form $\text{<in:}m\text{>}$, then $\kappa_j \xrightarrow{l} \kappa_{j+1}$ for some $j \geq i$, or l has the form $\text{<rcv:}a,cv\text{>}$ and for some $j \geq i$, a is busy and never again becomes ready to accept a message. For a configuration κ we define $\mathcal{F}(\kappa)$ to be the subset of $\mathcal{T}^\infty(\kappa)$ that contains only fair paths.*

Note that every finite computation path is fair since, by maximality, all of the enabled transitions must have happened.

8.5.3 Interaction Paths and Path Correspondence

In this section we introduce a notion of equivalence based on the idea of interaction paths [Tal96].

Definition 5 *An **interaction path** ip is a subsequence of a computation path π, containing all and only the transitions labels in π that are of the form: $\text{<out:}m\text{>}$ and $\text{<in:}m\text{>}$. We say that ip is the observable projection (or just the projection) of π.*

In other words, an interaction path is a computation path with all internal transitions removed. From now on, we will follow the convention of using π to range over interaction paths and $\tau_0, \tau_1, \ldots$ to range over their transition labels. We also use the list notation $[\tau_0, \tau_1, \ldots]$ to represent (both finite and infinite) interaction paths.

The notion of fairness on computation paths naturally induces a similar notion on interaction paths.

Definition 6 *An interaction path is **observably fair** if it is the projection of a fair computation path.*

Note that an observably fair (just fair from now on) interaction path could be the projection of both fair and unfair computation paths, hence the name *observational fairness*.

A strong motivation for a semantics based on interaction paths is to focus on the observable behaviour of systems as the only criteria for investigating their equivalence and defining their meaning. Any method that makes some part of internal behaviour explicit in the model will undesirably distinguish systems that are otherwise equivalent from an external observer's view.

Now we define our notion of equivalence on configurations based on their set of interaction paths.

Definition 7 *For a configuration κ, its set of **interaction paths** $\mathcal{I}(\kappa)$ is the set of observable projections of each computation path in $\mathcal{F}(\kappa)$.*

Definition 8 *We say that two Actor configurations C_1 and C_2 are equivalent under* **path correspondence** *if they have the same set of recipients and external Actors (same 'interface') and their sets of interaction paths are equal.*

Alternately, we can define the set of all finite prefixes of paths in $\mathcal{I}(\kappa)$ as the meaning of configuration κ. In [AMST97] equivalence relations were introduced based on the notion of testing. An *observable* 0-ary event was added to the transitions, and configurations were tested by composing them with observation contexts (configurations). Two Actor configurations were equivalent if their behaviours were the 'same' in all observation contexts. Three notions of equivalence were defined. Two configurations are *must* equivalent provided that some computation paths in one of them do not exhibit the observable event if and only if some computation paths in the other do not. Two configurations are *may* equivalent provided that some paths in one of them exhibit the observable event iff some paths in the other do. Finally, two configurations are *convex* equivalent if they are both *may* and *must* equivalent. It was shown that under the fairness assumption the three equivalences collapse to just two, with the convex and must equivalences being identical. It is known that the notion of equivalence based on sets of finite prefixes of interaction paths is identical to the *may* equivalence, and the equivalence in Definition 7 is at least as strong as the *must* equivalence.

8.6 An Example Proof of Path Correspondence

In this section we show by an example how the theory of Actors can help us verify, in a rather rigorous way, the correctness of systems modelled as Actor configurations. We will use the tree product example from Section 8.4.2, and we will show the equivalence of two Actor configurations: one based on the sequential implementation and the other based on the concurrent implementation of a tree product.

We first need to define an Actor behaviour based on the sequential definition of `treeprod` given in Section 8.4.2:

$$
\begin{aligned}
B_{\texttt{seqtp}} \; = \\
&\texttt{rec}(\lambda\, b.\, \lambda\, self.\, \lambda\, m. \\
&\quad \texttt{if(}\ \texttt{notvalidtree(tree(}m\texttt{)),} \\
&\qquad \texttt{seq(send(cust(}m\texttt{), error),} \\
&\qquad\quad \texttt{ready(}b(self)\texttt{))),} \\
&\qquad \texttt{seq(send(cust(}m\texttt{), treeprod(tree(}m\texttt{))),} \\
&\qquad\quad \texttt{ready(}b(self)\texttt{))))}
\end{aligned}
$$

The following configuration contains an Actor with behaviour $B_{\texttt{seqtp}}$ and is called $C_{\texttt{seq}}$:

$$ C_{\texttt{seq}} = \langle\, [\texttt{ready}(B_{\texttt{seqtp}})]\,_{tp} \mid\, \rangle_{\varnothing}^{\{tp\}} \tag{8.7} $$

We will verify the correctness of the following configuration by showing its path correspondence to C_{seq}:

$$C_{conc} = \langle\, [\text{ready}(B_{treeprod})]_{tp} \mid\, \rangle_{\varnothing}^{\{tp\}} \tag{8.8}$$

The proof idea is to show that the sets of interaction paths of both configurations are the same. Although we can prove that the two configurations are equivalent in any environment, to simplify matters we assume that all messages targeted to tp are well-formed, that is, they consist of a pair of an Actor name and a finite binary tree with leaves containing integers. Moreover, the external customers always send external Actors as the customer name. In this way we do not have to worry about requests with tp in the customer field.

We also assume that the function `treeprod` is correct in the sense that it terminates and returns the product of the numbers at the leaves of the tree. These can be proved by simple induction.

Definition 9 *Let c be an Actor name and t be a binary tree with integers at its leaves. We say that an input transition label $\tau_{in} = $ `<in:tp ◁ mkprd(c, t)>` has a matching output transition label $\tau_{out} = $ `<out:c ◁ p>` if p is the product of the leaves of t.*

Definition 10 *We say that a (possibly finite) path $\pi = [\tau_1, \tau_2, \ldots]$ is a **tree-product path** if it satisfies the following properties:*

P1 : Every input transition label τ_i has the form `<in:tp ◁ mkprd(cust, tree)>`, where cust is an Actor name different from tp, and tree is a finite binary tree with integers as its leaves. Every output transition label τ_j has the form `<out:cust ◁ p>`, where cust is an Actor name different from tp and p is an integer.

P2 : Let

$$
\begin{aligned}
I &= \{i \mid \tau_i \text{ is an input transition label}\} \\
J &= \{j \mid \tau_j \text{ is an output transition label}\}.
\end{aligned}
$$

There exists a bijection $f_\pi : I \to J$ such that for all $i \in \mathbf{N}$ $f_\pi(i) > i$ and that $\tau_{f_\pi(i)}$ is a matching output for τ_i.

Lemma 1 *Every path π of C_{seq} is a tree-product path.*

PROOF: We need to prove that any path $\pi = [\pi_1, \pi_2, \ldots]$ of C_{seq} has properties P1 and P2.

According to the `<in:_>` rule, only messages targeted to Actors in the reception set can enter a configuration. Therefore, only messages sent to tp can enter C_{seq}. We also assumed that all messages are pairs of a customer Actor and a tree. It is also immediate from the code that the only kind of message sent out of the configuration is of the form $cust \lhd p$ for some Actor name $cust$, which is never tp, and some integer p. Therefore, property P1 holds.

To prove P2, let $\tau_i = $ `<in:`$tp \lhd $`mkprd(`$cust, tree$`)>` be some input transition that will put the message `mkprd(`$cust, tree$`)` in the configuration. The fairness assumption implies that this message will eventually be delivered to tp. From the fairness assumption again we know that tp's computation can always proceed. As the behaviour of tp is terminating, a message of the form $cust \lhd p$, with p being the tree product of $tree$, will finally be sent out. This message in turn triggers a transition of the form $\tau_j = $ `<out:`$cust \lhd p$`>` with $j > i$. We can form a map f by mapping all such i's to their corresponding j's. This map will be a bijection as tp's behaviour cannot generate more than one message per request and there is no pending outgoing messages in the original configuration.

Definition 11 *For configurations C, C' we say that $C \Longrightarrow C'$ if $C = C'$ or for some sequence of configurations $C^1, \ldots, C^n$ and transition labels $l_1, \ldots, l_n$ that are neither input nor output labels, $n > 0$, we have $C_{seq} \xrightarrow{l_1} C^1_{seq} \xrightarrow{l_2} \ldots \xrightarrow{l_n} C'_{seq}$. Further, for an input or output transition label τ we say that $C \stackrel{\tau}{\Longrightarrow} C'$ if for some configurations C_1, C_2 we have $C \Longrightarrow C_1 \xrightarrow{\tau} C_2 \Longrightarrow C'$.*

Thus, if $C \Longrightarrow C'$, then configuration C can evolve into C' without interacting with its environment; and if $C \stackrel{\tau}{\Longrightarrow} C'$, then C can evolve into C' by performing a single (input or output) interaction with its environment.

Lemma 2 *Let $\pi = [\tau_1, \tau_2, \ldots]$ be a (possibly finite) interaction path that satisfies properties P1 and P2. Let's pick f_π to be some bijection as referred to in P2. There exists a sequence of configurations $C^0_{seq}, C^1_{seq}, \ldots$ with $C^0_{seq} = C_{seq}$, such that for every $n > 0$, C^n_{seq} has the following properties:*

S1 The Actor tp is in ready state in C^n_{seq}.

*S2 For every input transition $\tau_i = $ `<in:`$tp \lhd $ *mkprd*$(cust, tree)$`>`, the message instance $tp \lhd $ mkprd$(cust, tree)$ corresponding to transition τ_i is undelivered in C^n_{seq} if and only if $f_\pi(i) > n$.*

S3 $C^{n-1}_{seq} \stackrel{\tau_n}{\Longrightarrow} C^n_{seq}$.

PROOF: We prove this by constructing a recursive function g that maps an interaction path π to a sequence of configurations satisfying the three properties stated in the Lemma.

Since f_π is a bijection, we have $\tau_1 = $ `<in:`$tp \lhd $`mkprd(`$cust, tree$`)>` for some $cust$ and $tree$. Let $g(\tau_1) = C^1_{seq}$, where

$$C^1_{seq} = \langle \, [\texttt{ready}(B_{\texttt{seqtp}})] \, tp \, | \, tp \lhd \texttt{mkprd}(cust, tree) \, \rangle_{\varnothing}^{\{tp\}} \tag{8.9}$$

From the transition rules in Figure 8.3 we can conclude that $C^0_{seq} \stackrel{\tau_1}{\Longrightarrow} C^1_{seq}$. It is easy to verify that C^1_{seq} satisfies properties S1, S2 and S3.

Next we define $g(\tau_n)$ for $n > 1$. We distinguish two cases:

- $\tau_n = \texttt{<in:}\, tp \triangleleft \texttt{mkprd}(cust, tree)\texttt{>}$ (for some $cust$ and $tree$): Let $g(\tau_n) = C_{\texttt{seq}}^n$ be the configuration obtained by adding the message $tp \triangleleft (cust, tree)$ to the messages in $C_{\texttt{seq}}^{n-1}$. Then $C_{\texttt{seq}}^{n-1} \xrightarrow{\tau_n} C_{\texttt{seq}}^n$. It is easy to verify that $C_{\texttt{seq}}^n$ satisfies properties S1, S2 and S3.

- $\tau_n = \texttt{<out:}\, cust \triangleleft p\texttt{>}$ (for some $cust$ and p): Let $i = f_\pi^{-1}(n)$. Therefore, $\tau_i = \texttt{<in:}\, tp \triangleleft \texttt{mkprd}(cust, tree)\texttt{>}$ for some $tree$ with $p = \texttt{treeprod}(tree)$. Assuming that $C_{\texttt{seq}}^{n-1} = g(n-1)$, we can state the rest of the proof in the following steps:

  (i) We know that in $C_{\texttt{seq}}^{n-1}$, the message corresponding to τ_i has not been delivered. This follows from S2 and the fact that $f_\pi(i) > n - 1$.

  (ii) From S1 we know that tp is ready in $C_{\texttt{seq}}^{n-1}$.

  (iii) $C_{\texttt{seq}}^{n-1}$ can perform a $\texttt{<rcv:}\, tp, tp \triangleleft \texttt{mkprd}(cust, tree)\texttt{>}$, followed by a number of $\texttt{<fun:}\, tp\texttt{>}$, and finally a $\texttt{<send:}\, tp, cust \triangleleft p\texttt{>}$. This follows from fairness and the assumption that tp's behaviour terminates and returns the tree product of $tree$.

  (iv) The resulting configuration after the send transition contains an outgoing message of the form $cust \triangleleft p$. So an output transition with the label τ_n can be performed. Hence, $C_{\texttt{seq}}^{n-1} \xRightarrow{\tau_n} C_{\texttt{seq}}^n$.

  (v) It remains to show that $C_{\texttt{seq}}^n$ satisfies S1, S2 and S3. From the code it follows that tp becomes ready to receive the next message after sending the message. So S1 holds. S2 holds as the only message delivered in this step was the one corresponding to τ_i, and $f_\pi(i) = n$. S3 follows from the previous step of the proof. So we can let $g(n) = C_{\texttt{seq}}^n$.

The construction described above forces a certain scheduling order on transitions. This order is fair since no enabled transition remains enabled forever.

Lemma 3 *Every* tree-product *path π can be observed from an execution of C_{seq}.*

PROOF: The lemma follows from Lemma 2 and the observation that the computation path constructed in the proof of Lemma 2 is fair. The interaction path π is just the observable projection of the computation path constructed in Lemma 2.

Lemma 4 (Correctness of $B_{\texttt{treeprod}}$) *Applying $B_{\texttt{treeprod}}$ to a message of the form $tp \triangleleft (cust, tree)$ will eventually result in sending exactly one message of the form $cust \triangleleft p$, where p is the tree product of $tree$.*

PROOF: The proof is by induction on the height of the tree. From $B_{\texttt{treeprod}}$ we can easily see that when the tree is just a leaf, its value is returned to the customer, hence validating the truth of the lemma for trees of height zero.

For $n > 0$, assuming that the lemma is true for trees of height smaller than n, we prove that the Lemma is true for trees of height n. Recall that by our assumption every internal node, and hence the root, of the tree has two children. Following the fairness assumption, the rest of the proof will use the fact that Actors' internal computation can always make progress.

The code creates a join-continuation Actor, initialized with the customer's name. From the code we can infer the following facts:

- Only one join-continuation Actor is created per input message.
- The customer's name is not used by $B_{\mathbf{treeprod}}$ in any other part of the code.
- A continuation Actor sends exactly one message to its customer iff it receives two messages containing integers.

The Actor *tp* sends two messages to itself with two parameters: the join-continuation Actor's name as the customer, and the left (or right) subtree. Both subtrees have a smaller height than the original tree; therefore, according to the induction hypothesis, the product of their leaves will eventually be sent to the join-continuation Actor.

As no one else is aware of the join-continuation Actor's name, these two messages will be the only messages delivered to it. This conclusion plus the three facts above imply that the join-continuation Actor will eventually send exactly one message to the original customer (from the fairness requirement, this message will be delivered). The content of the message is the product of the two numbers sent to the join-continuation Actor, which in turn are the tree products of the left and right subtrees.

Lemma 5 *Every path π of $C_{\mathbf{conc}}$ is a tree-product path.*

PROOF: The proof is the same as that for $C_{\mathbf{seq}}$, except that in the argument for P2 we use Lemma 4 instead of correctness of **treeprod**. Note that in the argument for P1 it is essential to show that *tp* is the only receptionist at any time. This follows from the observation that every message sent by *tp* and its join continuations to anyone other than self contains just an integer. This implies that the names of internal Actors are never sent to external Actors.

Lemma 6 *Every tree-product path π can be observed from an execution of $C_{\mathbf{conc}}$.*

PROOF: The same proof as for $C_{\mathbf{seq}}$, except that Lemma 4 is used instead of correctness of **treeprod**.

Theorem 1 *C_{seq} and $C_{\mathbf{conc}}$ are equivalent under path correspondence.*

PROOF: Immediate from Lemmas 1, 3, 5 and 6 and the definition of equivalence under path correspondence.

8.7 Discussion

We defined an equivalence notion based on interaction paths. Although equivalence based on interaction paths appears to be intuitive, in fact it distinguishes between more configurations than is reasonable. Consider a configuration whose behaviour is represented by a tree consisting of an infinite path and another configuration whose behaviour is represented by a tree consisting of all finite approximations to the path. These two trees cannot be distinguished in any Actor context but do not have the same interaction paths. As was briefly discussed earlier, an equivalence notion based on observations in arbitrary contexts was introduced in [AMST97].

We also described a proof technique for establishing equivalence between configurations based on interaction path correspondence. In earlier work, a proof technique was developed for establishing equivalence in more concrete terms, namely, by establishing the correspondence of the actual paths. A number of results were obtained in that work to show how reasoning could be simplified. These results rely on the ability to exploit asynchrony to shuffle transitions in a way that localizes differences in computations, and to use the concept of *holes* to formalize the aspects of computations that are independent of the local differences.

When compared to many other models of concurrency, the Actor model is very powerful: it supports local procedural and data abstraction, and it provides a simple interface that abstracts the underlying name space management, scheduling, network, and so on. The assumption of asynchrony often allows only canonical message orders to be considered. The concept has been useful in diverse areas such as building animation languages, simulations and enterprise integration systems.

On the other hand, the model is too low-level to allow us to easily reason about complex distributed software systems. For the same reason, such systems also remain very hard to specify, and the software is often error-prone. We have argued that part of the reason for this difficulty is the fact that models of concurrency lack abstractions that represent the interaction patterns in a modular fashion. For example, we described the notion of local synchronization constraints that were used to control the scheduling of messages at an Actor based on the Actor's state. More generally, such scheduling may have to be constrained based on the history of a computation in a number of Actors.

We have developed a number of such abstractions for specifying temporal coordination between Actors [FA93, Fro96], real-time systems [Ren97], distributed interactions [Stu96] and dynamic communication groups [AC93, Cal94]. Such abstractions rely on a meta-architecture that allows the dynamic customization of schedulers, name servers and communication interfaces [AA98]. We believe that such architectures can promote more development of distributed systems as well as simplify the task of reasoning about systems by making both more modular. Some preliminary work in this area uses a two-level semantics [VT95]. However, the development of compositional methods for reasoning, as well as new specification techniques (for example, see [Smi98]), remains an active area of research.

Acknowledgements

The authors would like to thank Carolyn Talcott for her extensive and very useful comments on a previous version of this chapter. Of course, the authors are solely responsible for any remaining errors. The research described here has been supported in part by the National Science Foundation (NSF CCR 96-19522) and the Air Force Office of Scientific Research (AFOSR contract number F49620-97-1-03821).

Bibliography

[AA98]   M. Astley and G. Agha. Customization and composition of distributed objects: Middleware abstractions for policy management. *Sixth International Symposium on the Foundations of Software Engineering ACM SIGSOFT*, 23(6):1–9, November 1998.

[AC93]   G. Agha and C. J. Callsen. ActorSpace: An open distributed programming paradigm. In *Principles and Practice of Parallel Programming '93*, 1993.

[Agh86]   G. Agha. *Actors: A Model of Concurrent Computation in Distributed Systems*. MIT Press, Cambridge, Mass., 1986.

[Agh90]   G. Agha. Concurrent Object-Oriented Programming. *Communications of the ACM*, 33(9):125–141, September 1990.

[AJ99]   G. Agha and N. Jamali. Concurrent programming for distributed artificial intelligence. In G. Weiss, editor, *Multiagent Systems: A Modern Approach to DAI*. MIT Press, 1999.

[AKP95]   G. Agha, W. Kim, and R. Panwar. Actor languages for specification of parallel computations. In *DIMACS Series in Discrete Mathematics and Computer Science*, volume 18, pages 239–258. American Mathematical Society, 1995.

[AMST97]   G. Agha, I. A. Mason, S. F. Smith, and C. L. Talcott. A foundation for actor computation. *Journal of Functional Programming*, 7(1), 1997.

[Bou92]   G. Boudol. Asynchrony and the pi-calculus. Technical Report 1702, Department of Computer Science, Inria Univeristy, May 1992.

[Cal94]   C. J. Callsen. *Open Heterogeneous Distributed Computing*. PhD thesis, Aalborg University, August 1994.

[FA93]   S. Frølund and G. Agha. A language framework for multi-object coordination. In *Proceedings of ECOOP 1993, Volume 707 of Lecture Notes in Computer Science*. Springer-Verlag, 1993.

[FF86]   M. Felleisen and D. Friedman. Control operators, the SECD-machine, and the λ-calculus. In M. Wirsing, editor, *Formal Description of Programming Concepts III*, pages 193–217. North-Holland, 1986.

[Fro96]   S. Frolund. *Coordinating Distributed Objects: An Actor-Based Approach for Synchronization*. MIT Press, November 1996.

[HT91]   K. Honda and M. Tokoro. An object calculus for asynchronous communication. In *Proceedings of ECOOP'91, Volume 512 of Lecture Notes in Computer Science*, pages 133–147. Springer-Verlag, July 1991.

[KA95]   W. Kim and G. Agha. Efficient Support of Location Transparency in Concurrent Object-Oriented Programming Languages. In *Supercomputing '95*. IEEE, 1995.

[Kim97]   W. Kim. *THAL: An Actor System for Efficient and Scalable Concurrent Computing*. PhD thesis, University of Illinois at Urbana-Champaign, May 1997. http://www-osl.cs.uiuc.edu/.

[Mil89]   R. Milner. *Communication and Concurrency*. Prentice Hall, 1989.

[Mil93]   R. Milner. Elements of interaction Turing award lecture. *Communications of the ACM*, 36(1):78–89, January 1993. Turing Award Lecture.

[Mil99]   R. Milner. *Communicating and Mobile Systems: the π-calculus*. Cambridge University Press, 1999.

[MT99]   I. A. Mason and C. L. Talcott. Actor languages: Their syntax, semantics, translation, and equivalence. *Theoretical Computer Science*, 220:409 – 467, 1999.

[Nee89]   R. M. Needham. Names. In S. Mullender, editor, *Distributed Systems*, pages 89–101. Addison-Wesley, 1989.

[Ren97]   Shangping Ren. *An Actor-Based Framework for Real-Time Coordination*. PhD thesis, Department Computer Science, University of Illinois at Urbana-Champaign, 1997.

[San98]   D. Sangiorgi. An interpretation of typed objects into typed pi-calculus. *Information and Computation*, 143(1), 1998.

[Smi98]   S. Smith. On specification diagrams for actor systems. In C. L. Talcott, editor, *Proceedings of the Second Workshop on Higher-Order Techniques in Semantics*, Electronic Notes in Theoretical Computer Science. Elsevier, 1998.

[Stu96]   D. C. Sturman. *Modular Specification of Interaction Policies in Distributed Computing*. PhD thesis, University of Illinois at Urbana-Champaign, May 1996.

[SWP99]   P. Sewell, P. T. Wojciechowski, and B. C. Pierce. Location Independent Communication for Mobile Agents: A Two Level Architecture. Technical Report 462, Computer Laboratory, University of Cambridge, 1999.

[Tal96]   C. L. Talcott. Interaction semantics for components of distributed systems. In E. Najm and J.-B. Stefani, editors, *Formal Methods for Open Object Based Distributed Systems*, pages 154–169. Chapman & Hall, 1996.

[Tha00]   P. Thati. Towards an Algebraic Formulation of Actors. Master's thesis, University of Illinois at Urbana-Champaign, 2000.

[TKS$^+$89]   C. Tomlinson, W. Kim, M. Schevel, V. Singh, B. Will, and G. Agha. Rosette: An Object-Oriented Concurrent System Architecture. *Sigplan Notices*, 24(4):91–93, 1989.

[VA98]   C. Varela and G. Agha. What after Java? *Computer Networks and ISDN Systems: The International Journal of Computer Telecommunications and Networking*, 1998.

[Var00]   C. Varela. *World Wide Computing with Universal Actors: Linguistic Support for Coordination, Naming and Migration*. PhD thesis, University of Illinois at Urbana-Champaign, August 2000.

[VT95]   N. Venkatasubramanian and C. L. Talcott. Reasoning about meta-level activities in open distributed systems. In *Principles of Distributed Computing*, 1995.

[Wal95]   D. Walker. Objects in the Pi-Calculus. *Information and Computation*, 116(2):253–271, 1995.

9

π-Calculi

Peter Sewell

University of Cambridge, UK

Concurrency and communication are fundamental aspects of distributed systems; a great deal of work in process calculi and other areas has developed techniques for programming, specification and reasoning about them. Another basic distributed phenomenon is *name generation* – many computational entities are dynamically created with fresh names; these names can often be communicated within or between machines. The *π-calculus* of Milner, Parrow and Walker [MPW92] generalized earlier process calculi by allowing fresh channel names to be dynamically created and communicated. This gives rise to great expressive power, allowing a very simple π-calculus to be used as the basis for a concurrent programming language. It also involved the development of semantic techniques that can be directly applied to distributed systems. This chapter introduces some of the theory of π-calculi and their applications to concurrent and distributed programming. It provides only a brief and somewhat idiosyncratic introduction – for more detailed texts and pointers into the literature one should refer to Section 9.8.

We begin in Section 9.1 with a core π-calculus, giving some examples and defining the operational semantics in a reduction-semantics style. In Section 9.2 we review the main design choices that give rise to the wide variety of π-calculi in use. Many of these calculi are driven by a particular theoretical result or application, particularly by whether the focus is on modelling or programming. In Section 9.3 we return to the operational semantics, defining a labelled transition semantics and relating it to the earlier reduction semantics. In Section 9.4 we consider the (concurrent, but not distributed) PICT programming language, which is closely based on a π-calculus. In Section 9.5 we return again to semantics, defining operational congruences. A very brief introduction to typing for π-calculi is given in Section 9.6. Finally, in Section 9.7 we consider the application of π-calculus techniques to problems of distributed systems and programming language design. In particular, we discuss the design of grouping and interaction primitives. No proofs are included – they can be found in [Sew00].

9.1 An Introduction to π

The π-calculus is a calculus (an idealised modelling/programming language) in which communication between parallel processes is fundamental. Communication is on named channels: a process that offers an output of value v on the channel named c, written $\bar{c}v$, may synchronise with a parallel process that is attempting to read from c, written $cw.P$. It differs from earlier process calculi in that new channel names can be created dynamically, passed as values along other channels and then used themselves for communication. This gives rise to great expressive power – many computational formalisms, for example, λ-calculi, can be smoothly translated into π-calculus.

Many different π-calculi have been introduced. Some of the differences are essentially minor choices of notation and style; some are important choices that are driven by the application or theory desired. In this section we introduce a core π-calculus that still exhibits the essential phenomenon of new channel creation.

Syntax We take an infinite set $\mathcal{N}$ of *names* of channels, ranged over by a, b and so on. The *process terms* are then those defined by the grammar

$$
\begin{array}{llll}
P, Q & ::= & 0 & \text{nil} \\
 & & P \mid Q & \text{parallel composition of } P \text{ and } Q \\
 & & \bar{c}v & \text{output } v \text{ on channel } c \\
 & & cw.P & \text{input from channel } c \\
 & & \textbf{new } c \textbf{ in } P & \text{new channel name creation}
\end{array}
$$

In $cw.P$ the 'formal parameter' w binds in P; in **new** c **in** P the c binds in P, with scope as far to the right as possible (so **new** c **in** $P \mid Q$ should be read as **new** c **in** $(P \mid Q)$). We will work up to alpha renaming of bound names, so whenever we write a term we actually mean its alpha equivalence class. We write $\mathrm{fn}(P)$ for the set of free names of P, defined by $\mathrm{fn}(0) = \varnothing$, $\mathrm{fn}(P \mid Q) = \mathrm{fn}(P) \cup \mathrm{fn}(Q)$, $\mathrm{fn}(\bar{c}v) = \{c, v\}$, $\mathrm{fn}(cw.P) = \{c\} \cup (\mathrm{fn}(P) - w)$, $\mathrm{fn}(\textbf{new } c \textbf{ in } P) = \mathrm{fn}(P) - c$. We write $\{a/x\}P$ for the process term obtained from P by replacing all free occurrences of x by a, renaming as necessary to avoid capture.

Semantics – Examples The simplest form of semantics for this calculus consists of a *reduction relation* – a binary relation between process terms, written $P \longrightarrow Q$, indicating that P can perform a single step of computation to become Q. The definition of $\longrightarrow$ will be given later; here are some examples.

The calculus allows communication between an output and an input (on the same channel) in parallel. Here the value a is being sent along the channel x:

$$\bar{x}a \mid xu.\bar{y}u \quad \longrightarrow \quad \{a/u\}(\bar{y}u) = \bar{y}a$$

There can be many outputs on the same channel competing for the same input –

only one will succeed, introducing nondeterminism:

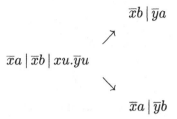

Similarly, there can be many inputs on the same channel competing for an output:

$$\overline{y}a \mid xu.\overline{z}u$$
$$\nearrow$$
$$\overline{x}a \mid xu.\overline{y}u \mid xu.\overline{z}u$$
$$\searrow$$
$$xu.\overline{y}u \mid \overline{z}a$$

A restricted name is different from all other names outside its scope – below the x bound by the **new** x **in** _ is different from the x outside. Note that (using alpha equivalence) the term on the left below is *the same* as $\overline{x}a \mid$ **new** x' **in** $(\overline{x'}b \mid x'u.\overline{y}u)$:

$$\overline{x}a \mid \textbf{new } x \textbf{ in } (\overline{x}b \mid xu.\overline{y}u) \;\longrightarrow\; \overline{x}a \mid \textbf{new } x \textbf{ in } \overline{y}b$$

A name received on a channel can then be used itself as a channel name for output or input – here y is received on x and then used to output c:

$$\overline{x}y \mid xu.\overline{u}c \;\longrightarrow\; \overline{y}c$$

Finally (and most subtlely), a restricted name can be sent outside its original scope. Here y is sent on channel x outside the scope of the **new** y **in** binder, which therefore must be moved (with care, to avoid capture of other instances of y). This is known as *scope extrusion*:

$$(\textbf{new } y \textbf{ in } \overline{x}y \mid yv.P) \mid xu.\overline{u}c \;\longrightarrow\; \textbf{new } y \textbf{ in } yv.P \mid \overline{y}c$$
$$\longrightarrow\; \textbf{new } y \textbf{ in } \{c/v\}P$$

The combination of sending channel names and scope extrusion is the essential difference between the π-calculus and earlier process calculi such as ACP, CCS and CSP.

Semantics – Definition of Reduction The reduction relation can be defined rather simply, in two stages. First we define a *structural congruence*, written $\equiv$. This is an equivalence relation over process terms that allows the two parts of a potential communication to be brought syntactically adjacent. It is the smallest equivalence relation that is a congruence and satisfies the axioms:

$$P \mid 0 \; \equiv \; P$$
$$P \mid Q \; \equiv \; Q \mid P$$
$$P \mid (Q \mid R) \; \equiv \; (P \mid Q) \mid R$$
$$\textbf{new } x \textbf{ in new } y \textbf{ in } P \; \equiv \; \textbf{new } y \textbf{ in new } x \textbf{ in } P$$
$$P \mid \textbf{new } x \textbf{ in } Q \; \equiv \; \textbf{new } x \textbf{ in } (P \mid Q) \qquad x \notin \text{fn}(P)$$

The reduction relation $\longrightarrow$ is then the smallest binary relation over process terms satisfying the following:

Com $\qquad\qquad \dfrac{}{\overline{c}v \mid cw.P \longrightarrow \{v/w\}P}$

Par $\qquad\qquad \dfrac{P \longrightarrow P'}{P \mid Q \longrightarrow P' \mid Q}$

Res $\qquad\qquad \dfrac{P \longrightarrow P'}{\textbf{new } x \textbf{ in } P \longrightarrow \textbf{new } x \textbf{ in } P'}$

Struct $\qquad\qquad \dfrac{P \equiv P' \longrightarrow P'' \equiv P'''}{P \longrightarrow P'''}$

Note that reduction under input prefixes is not allowed – there is no rule

$$\dfrac{P \longrightarrow P'}{cw.P \longrightarrow cw.P'}$$

It is a useful exercise to check that the example reductions can actually be derived.

9.2 Modelling Versus Programming: Choices of Primitives

A good deal of early work on process calculi was focussed around *modelling* protocols (and other systems) and reasoning about those models; this fed into work, for example, on LOTOS and its descendents (see Chapter 5). Some recent developments from the π-calculus, in contrast, have used it as the basis for a *programming* language: a significant shift of emphasis that affects the design of the calculi used. The programming language view is discussed further in Section 9.4; this subsection reviews some of the main calculus-design choices. They are described here rather informally – in some cases precise results have been proved, showing that a particular calculus is encodable in another, but great care must be taken in interpreting such results. There are many possible senses of 'encoding'; the results do not automatically transfer from the precise calculi that they have been proved for to minor variants thereof. In general, we have only the beginnings of a theory of expressiveness for π-based calculi (however, see the recent EXPRESS meetings on this issue, such as [PC98]).

Choice Many process calculi have explicit choice or summation operators for nondeterminism, allowing, for example, $P + Q$, which can behave either as P or as Q (this is imprecise – in fact, several different operators are possible). Explicit choice is useful for modelling and reasoning about systems, especially for writing loose specifications and for developing complete axiomatisations of operational congruences, but seems to be both unnecessary and expensive to implement from the programming language view. In some cases a form of choice is encodable in a choice-free calculus – for example, a purely internal choice can be encoded in the π-calculus given in Section 9.1 by

$$[[P \oplus Q]] \stackrel{def}{=} \textbf{new } c \textbf{ in } (\bar{c}x \,|\, cx.P \,|\, cx.Q) \qquad c, x \text{ not free in } P, Q$$

but in other cases nonencodability results can be proved (see the work of Nestmann and Pierce [NP96] and of Palamidessi [Pal97]).

Asynchrony The calculus of Section 9.1 is *asynchronous* – it has only a bare output $\bar{c}v$, as opposed to an output prefix $\bar{c}v.P$ that starts P when the output has been received. Again, for programming it seems that prefixing (or *synchronous*) output can be uncommon; it can generally be encoded by using explicit acknowledgements (see the work of Honda and Tokoro [HT91] and of Boudol [Bou92]). Moreover, the asynchronous calculi have a closer fit to the asynchronous message delivery of packet-switched networks, and so are used as starting points for distributed calculi. Note that this usage of 'synchronous' is different from that in the work on SCCS (Synchronous CCS) by Milner – there the two sides of a parallel composition were required to execute in lock-step, whereas here it refers only to the synchronization of pairs of an output prefix and an input.

Replication The calculus of Section 9.1 is rather inexpressive – it contains no way to construct infinite computations, and so is clearly not Turing-powerful (to make this precise requires care). One can add either *recursion*, for example, with process variables X and a recursion operator $\textbf{rec}\, X.P$, or *replication* $!P$, which loosely behaves as infinitely many copies of P in parallel. In some sense (again, not made precise here) the two are inter-encodable. Generally theoretical work is simpler with replication; describing actual systems may be simpler with either. A limited form of replication, allowing only replicated input terms such as $!cx.P$, is sometimes used.

Values The calculus of Section 9.1 is further limited in that only single names can be communicated on channels – it is *monadic*. Many variants are *polyadic*, allowing tuples of names to be sent, or allow more general data, for example, arbitrary pairs or tuples. For precise results on encoding a polyadic calculus into a monadic one, see the work of Yoshida [Yos96] and of Quaglia and Walker [QW98]. The addition of basic values such as Booleans and natural numbers is straightforward.

Higher Order Processes A very significant extension is to allow communication not just of basic data, but also of processes themselves, or even higher-order abstractions – see the work of Sangiorgi [San93] and of Thomsen [Tho93]. Many authors have studied encodings of λ-calculi within a π-calculus; see, for example, the work of Milner [Mil92].

Matching For some purposes constructs to test equality (matching) and inequality (mismatching) of names are added, often written $[x = y]P$ and $[x \neq y]P$, or **if** $x = y$ **then** P **else** Q. These can have delicate effects on the theory of operational congruences.

Join Patterns π-calculus channels may have many receivers. It has been argued that for a programming language a better choice of primitive is the *join pattern*, which syntactically gathers together all receivers on a channel (see the work of Fournet, Gonthier and others, e.g. [FG96]). Join patterns combine restriction, replicated input and linearity – **def** $x(w).P$ **in** Q is similar to **new** x **in** $Q \,|\, !xw.P$. For expressiveness one must generalize to multi-inputs such as **def** $(x_1(w_1) \wedge \, .. \, \wedge \, x_n(w_n)).P$ **in** Q, or even to disjunctions of multi-inputs. An example reduction would be

> **def** $(x_1(w_1) \wedge x_2(w_2)).P$ **in** $Q \,|\, \overline{x_1}3 \,|\, \overline{x_2}7$
>
> $\longrightarrow$
>
> **def** $(x_1(w_1) \wedge x_2(w_2)).P$ **in** $Q \,|\, \{3, 7/w_1, w_2\}P$

Concrete Syntax Many minor variations of concrete syntax are used in the literature. Most significantly, if one wishes a syntax with a good representation in plain ASCII, then outputs and inputs can be written as $c!v$ and $c?w.P$ instead of the $\overline{c}v$ and $cw.P$ used in Section 9.1. The exclamation mark would then confusingly be used for both output and replication, so replication (or replicated input) can be written $*P$ (or $*c?w.P$) instead of $!P$ (or $!cw.P$). Restriction has been written either with a greek nu as $(\nu c)P$ or as **new** c **in** P. Some work uses small round brackets to indicate binders and angle brackets to indicate free names, so writing outputs and inputs as $\overline{c}\langle v\rangle$ and $c(w).P$.

9.3 Styles of Operational Semantics

The basic semantic theory for a π-calculus comprises four main parts, which we describe in order of increasing sophistication, usefulness and technical complexity. Most simply, one can define the internal *reduction* relation of processes by means of reduction axioms and a structural congruence, as was done previously. This builds on the Chemical Abstract Machine ideas of Berry and Boudol [BB92] and the π-semantics of Milner [Mil92]. To describe the interactions of processes with their environment one requires more structure: some *labelled transition* relation, specifying the potential inputs and outputs of processes. Several different forms of labelled transition system are discussed later in this subsection. Reduction and labelled transition relations are both very intensional, keeping the algebraic structure of process terms. One can abstract from the internal states of processes by quotienting by some *operational congruence*, such as *bisimulation*, defined using the labelled transition relations or in terms of barbs (a degenerate form of labelled transitions). Bisimulation equivalence classes are still rather intensional, however. They may be appropriate when working with models of concurrent systems and may provide useful proof techniques, but to obtain a clear relationship to the behaviour of programming languages one must abstract further, quotienting by an *observational congruence*. The identification of an appropriate notion of observation for a given programming language may be non-trivial. Operational congruences and observations are discussed further in Section 9.5. We now give a labelled transition semantics for the calculus of Section 9.1.

A Labelled Transition Semantics The labelled transition relation has the form

$$A \vdash P \xrightarrow{\ell} Q$$

where A is a finite set of names, $\mathrm{fn}(P) \subseteq A$ and ℓ is a *label*; it should be read as 'in a state where the names A may be known by process P and by its environment, the process P can do ℓ to become Q'. The labels ℓ are

$$
\begin{array}{llll}
\ell & ::= & \tau & \text{internal action} \\
 & & \overline{x}v & \text{output of } v \text{ on } x \\
 & & xv & \text{input of } v \text{ on } x
\end{array}
$$

The transition relation is defined as the smallest relation satisfying the following rules:

$$\text{Out} \frac{}{A \vdash \overline{x}v \xrightarrow{\overline{x}v} 0} \qquad\qquad \text{In} \frac{}{A \vdash xp.P \xrightarrow{xv} \{v/p\}P}$$

$$\text{Par} \frac{A \vdash P \xrightarrow{\ell} P'}{A \vdash P \mid Q \xrightarrow{\ell} P' \mid Q} \qquad \text{Com} \frac{A \vdash P \xrightarrow{\overline{x}v} P' \quad A \vdash Q \xrightarrow{xv} Q'}{A \vdash P \mid Q \xrightarrow{\tau} \mathbf{new} \; \{v\} - A \; \mathbf{in} \; (P' \mid Q')}$$

$$\text{Res} \frac{A, x \vdash P \xrightarrow{\ell} P' \quad x \notin \mathrm{fn}(\ell)}{A \vdash \mathbf{new} \; x \; \mathbf{in} \; P \xrightarrow{\ell} \mathbf{new} \; x \; \mathbf{in} \; P'} \qquad \text{Open} \frac{A, x \vdash P \xrightarrow{\overline{y}x} P' \quad y \neq x}{A \vdash \mathbf{new} \; x \; \mathbf{in} \; P \xrightarrow{\overline{y}x} P'}$$

$$\text{Struct Right} \frac{A \vdash P \xrightarrow{\ell} P' \quad P' \equiv P''}{A \vdash P \xrightarrow{\ell} P''}$$

In all rules with conclusion of the form $A \vdash P \xrightarrow{\ell} Q$ there is an implicit side condition $\mathrm{fn}(P) \subseteq A$. Symmetric versions of Par and Com are elided. Here the free names of a label are $\mathrm{fn}(\tau) = \{\}$, $\mathrm{fn}(\overline{x}v) = \mathrm{fn}(xv) = \{x, v\}$. We write A, x for $A \cup \{x\}$, where x is assumed not to be in A. If $A = \{a_1, \ldots a_n\}$, then $\mathbf{new} \; A \; \mathbf{in} \; P$ denotes $\mathbf{new} \; a_1 \; \mathbf{in} \; \ldots \mathbf{new} \; a_n \; \mathbf{in} \; P$ (note that if A is not empty or a singleton, then strictly this is only well-defined up to structural congruence).

It is a good exercise to derive τ transitions for the example reductions above – especially for the scope extrusion example. Note that there is a transition

$$\{x\} \vdash \mathbf{new} \; z \; \mathbf{in} \; \overline{x}z \xrightarrow{\overline{x}w} 0$$

for *any* $w \neq x$, as we are working up to alpha equivalence. A more substantial exercise is to extend both this and the reduction semantics with richer values, for example, with arbitrary tupling.

This should now be compared with the reduction semantics. First, one can show that structurally congruent processes have the same labelled transitions (or equivalently, that a STRUCT LEFT rule is admissible).

Theorem 1 *If* $P' \equiv P$, *then* $A \vdash P' \overset{\ell}{\longrightarrow} Q$ *iff* $A \vdash P \overset{\ell}{\longrightarrow} Q$.

One can then show that the reduction and transition semantics give exactly the same internal steps.

Theorem 2 *If* $\mathrm{fn}(P) \subseteq A$, *then* $P \longrightarrow Q$ *iff* $A \vdash P \overset{\tau}{\longrightarrow} Q$.

The reduction semantics is probably easier to understand – it is common when designing a new calculus to first specify its reductions. It does not, however, tell us how an arbitrary subprocess can interact with its environment; for that, and hence for explicit characterizations of operational congruences, we need the LTS. Moreover, the labelled transitions of a process P are defined inductively on its term structure, whereas the reductions are not – broadly, to show that some particular reduction exists, it is easier to use the reduction semantics, but to enumerate *all* of the reductions the LTS is also appropriate.

One can choose to define either the explicitly indexed transitions $A \vdash P \overset{\ell}{\longrightarrow} Q$, as here, or unindexed transitions of the form $P \overset{\mu}{\longrightarrow} Q$. In the former, an output of a free name and an output of a new name can be distinguished by reference to A – we have

$$\{x, y\} \vdash \mathbf{new}\ z\ \mathbf{in}\ \overline{x}y \overset{\overline{x}y}{\longrightarrow} 0 \quad \text{and} \quad \{x, y\} \vdash \mathbf{new}\ z\ \mathbf{in}\ \overline{x}z \overset{\overline{x}w}{\longrightarrow} 0$$

with $y \in \{x, y\}$ and $w \notin \{x, y\}$, respectively. In the latter, the distinction must be carried in the label μ and the rules require more delicate side conditions. The explicitly indexed style seems (to this author) to be conceptually slightly clearer, although at some notational cost; it also leads to simpler notions of trace and generalizes to typed systems with subtyping.

Another semantic choice is that between *early* and *late* transition systems. We have given an early system, with inputs instantiated immediately – see the overview of Quaglia [Qua99] for a discussion of early, late and open semantics.

9.4 Language Implementation: The PICT Experiment

The π-calculus is sufficiently expressive to be used as the basis for a programming language. The literature contains a number of encodings of λ-calculi and data structures into π. For some theoretical work one can therefore combine the benefits of a rather small calculus, having a simple semantics, with the flexibility of high-level constructs, provided by encodings. More practically, the language PICT has been developed since 1992, mostly by Pierce and Turner, to experiment with programming in the π-calculus, with rich type systems for communicating concurrent objects, and with efficient implementation techniques. Loosely, it has the same relationship to the π-calculus as functional languages do to the λ-calculus.

Sequential (functional)	Concurrent
λ-calculus	π-calculus
functions	processes
function application	parallel composition
beta reduction	communication
LISP, ML, Haskell, etc.	PICT

Documentation and an implementation are available electronically [PT98]; descriptions of the design and implementation are in [Tur96, PT00]. See also the implementations and papers on the Join Language [Joi].

A number of programming idioms turn out to be useful – we will now touch on a couple (here we use a polyadic π-calculus, not precisely specified, with tuples $\langle x_1 \mathinner{..} x_n \rangle$, tuple patterns $\langle x_1 \mathinner{..} x_n \rangle$, replicated input $!c\langle x_1 \mathinner{..} x_n \rangle.P$ and basic arithmetic). One can define process abstractions, analogous to local function definitions, as follows:

> **new** *plustwo* **in**
> $\quad !plustwo\langle x\, r \rangle.\overline{r}\langle x + 2 \rangle$
> **| new** *r* **in**
> $\quad \overline{plustwo}\langle 56\, r \rangle \mid r\langle z \rangle.\overline{printi}\langle z \rangle$

Here one can send on the *plustwo* channel a number x and a result channel r; the server will send back $x + 2$ on r. Channels can also be used to implement locking rather directly – here is an approximation to a two-method object implementation, with mutual exclusion between the bodies of the methods:

> **new** *lock* **in**
> $\quad \overline{lock}\langle\rangle$
> **|** $!method_1\langle arg \rangle.$
> $\quad\quad lock\langle\rangle.$
> $\quad\quad\quad \cdots$
> $\quad\quad\quad \overline{lock}\langle\rangle$

> | !method2⟨arg⟩.
>   lock⟨⟩.
>
>   ...
> $\overline{lock}$⟨⟩

Access to the implementation could be passed around as a simple tuple of method (channel) names, for example, as ⟨method1 method2⟩.

The reduction semantics of the π-calculus is highly nondeterministic. There is therefore a basic design decision for any language implementation: how should that nondeterminism be resolved? There are several possible choices:

(i) One could consult a pseudorandom number generator (or a true source of quantum-mechanical randomness) at every choice. This might be desirable for a simulation language, but it is prohibitively expensive for a programming language.

(ii) One could fix an evaluation strategy (as one does in ML, say). This would highly constrain future compiler writers, who would always have to schedule π-processes in the same way. It would prevent optimisations and severely constrain distributed implementations.

(iii) One could allow a compiler to use any 'reasonable' evaluation strategy. This is delicate, as some fairness conditions are required, for example, to ensure that the process **new** x **in** $(\overline{x} \,|\, ! \, x.\overline{x} \,|\, x.\overline{\text{print}}\,\text{"ping"})$ does eventually print the 'ping'.

PICT adopts the third approach. The current implementation has a scheduler as follows: it maintains a *state* consisting of a *run queue* of processes to be scheduled (round robin) together with *channel queues* of processes waiting to communicate. It executes in steps, in each of which the process at the front of the run queue is removed and processed. This internal behaviour of the implementation is described by Turner in Chapter 7 of [Tur96] and incorporated into the abstract machine given in [Sew97]. When an output or input on a library channel reaches the front of the run queue some special processing takes place. For many library channels this consists of a single call to a corresponding Unix IO routine. The implementation is thus entirely deterministic.

Note that a minor syntactic change to a program in such a language, such as swapping two parallel components, may result in completely different behaviour. This can make debugging difficult, but it seems to be inescapable.

9.5 Operational Congruences

A reduction or labelled-transition semantics gives only a rather intensional notion of the behaviour of processes. One often needs a more extensional semantics, abstracting from the syntax of the calculus, for example, to make precise any of the following questions:

- When do two processes have the same behaviour?
- When does a process meet a specification (itself expressed as a process)?
- When is a program transformation-correct?
- When is an abstract machine-correct?
- When are two calculi equally expressive?

An extensional semantics is often defined as a quotient of the syntax by some *operational equivalence* or *operational preorder*, itself defined using reductions or labelled transitions. Much of the π literature involves either a *bisimulation congruence*, defined over labelled transitions, or *barbed bisimulation congruence*, defined using reductions and *barbs* – vestigial-labelled transitions. We will sketch definitions for the π-calculus given earlier.

Take *bisimulation* $\dot\sim$ to be the largest family of relations indexed by finite sets of names such that each $\dot\sim_A$ is a symmetric relation over $\{\, P \mid \mathrm{fn}(P) \subseteq A \,\}$ and for all $P \dot\sim_A Q$,

- if $A \vdash P \overset{\ell}{\longrightarrow} P'$, then $\exists\, Q'\,.\, A \vdash Q \overset{\ell}{\longrightarrow} Q' \wedge P' \dot\sim_{A \cup \mathrm{fn}(\ell)} Q'$

(one must check that $\dot\sim$ exists uniquely, but we omit a rigorous formulation here). Intuitively this says that P is equivalent to Q if any transition of one can be matched by a transition of the other, with the resulting states also equivalent. On occasion a finer relation, obtained by closing up under substitutions, is required. Define $\sim$ by $P \sim_A Q$ iff for all substitutions σ with $\mathrm{dom}(\sigma) \cup \mathrm{ran}(\sigma) \subseteq A$ we have $\sigma P \dot\sim_A \sigma Q$.

On the other hand, to define *barbed bisimulation* we first take barbs as follows: $P\!\downarrow_x$ if P can do an input on channel x and $P\!\downarrow_{\overline{x}}$ if P can do an output on x. Now $\dot\sim^b$ is the largest symmetric relation such that, for all $P \dot\sim^b Q$,

- if $P \longrightarrow P'$, then $\exists\, Q'\,.\, Q \longrightarrow Q' \wedge P' \dot\sim^b Q'$, and moreover
- $P\!\downarrow_\alpha$ implies $Q\!\downarrow_\alpha$.

This requires only the reductions and immediate offers of communication to be matched. Barbed bisimulation congruence is defined by closing under all contexts – say, $P \sim^b Q$ iff for contexts C we have $C[P] \dot\sim^b C[Q]$.

These are rather different styles of definition, yet they sometimes define the same equivalence, giving one confidence that one is dealing with a robust notion [San93, MS92]. Both have advantages. The definition of barbed bisimulation congruence does not depend on an LTS, and so may be readily given for novel calculi in which labelled transitions are not well-understood. On the other hand, the definition involves quantification over all contexts, making it harder to prove instances of the equivalence (but see the techniques in the thesis of Fournet [Fou98]) and to have a clear intuition as to its significance.

For several of the questions at the beginning of this subsection it is important to have an equivalence or preorder that is a *congruence* – that is, it is preserved by the constructors of the calculus. This enables (in)equational reasoning to be used freely. The fact that $\sim^b$ is a congruence is immediate from the definition; the fact that $\dot\sim$

or $\sim$ is may require some delicate proof. Indeed, working with an indexed relation requires a little care even to state the congruence property, to keep the A-indexing straight. Consider a family $\mathcal{S}$ of relations indexed by finite sets of names such that each $\mathcal{S}_A$ is a relation over $\{\, P \mid \mathrm{fn}(P) \subseteq A \,\}$. Say that $\mathcal{S}$ is an indexed congruence if each $\mathcal{S}_A$ is an equivalence relation and the following hold:

$$\text{IN}\ \frac{P\ \mathcal{S}_{A,w}\ P'\quad c \in A}{cw.P\ \mathcal{S}_A\ cw.P'}\qquad \text{RES}\ \frac{P\ \mathcal{S}_{A,c}\ P'}{\textbf{new}\ c\ \textbf{in}\ P\ \mathcal{S}_A\ \textbf{new}\ c\ \textbf{in}\ P'}$$

$$\text{PAR}\ \frac{P\ \mathcal{S}_A\ P'\quad Q\ \mathcal{S}_A\ Q'}{P \mid Q\ \mathcal{S}_A\ P' \mid Q'}$$

Theorem 3 *Bisimulation $\dot{\sim}$ is an indexed congruence.*

This result depends on the exact calculus used; in many variants one must move to $\sim$ to obtain a congruence for input prefixing.

Work on operational congruences for process calculi without scope extrusion showed that there are many more-or-less plausible notions of equivalence, differing, for example, in their treatment of linear/branching time, of internal reductions, of termination and divergence, and so on. Some of the space is illustrated in the surveys of van Glabbeek [vG90, vG93]. Much of this carries over to π-calculi. For example, we can define trace-based equivalences straightforwardly. For partial traces (aka prefix-closed traces) write

$$A_1 \vdash P_1 \xrightarrow{\ell_1} \ldots \xrightarrow{\ell_n} P_{n+1}$$

to mean $\exists\, P_2, \ldots, P_n,\, A_2, \ldots, A_n\,.\, \forall\, i \in 1..n\,.\, A_{i+1} = A_i \cup \mathrm{fn}(\ell_i) \wedge A_i \vdash P_i \xrightarrow{\ell_i} P_{i+1}$. If $\mathrm{fn}(P, Q) \subseteq A$, then the partial A-traces of P and partial trace equivalence are defined by

$$\mathrm{ptr}_A(P) \overset{def}{=} \{\, \ell_1 .. \ell_n \mid \exists\, P'\,.\, A \vdash P \xrightarrow{\ell_1} \ldots \xrightarrow{\ell_n} P' \,\}$$
$$P =^{\mathrm{ptr}}_A Q \overset{def}{\Longleftrightarrow} \mathrm{ptr}_A(P) = \mathrm{ptr}_A(Q)$$

Standard facts such as $P \dot{\sim}_A Q \Rightarrow P =^{\mathrm{ptr}}_A Q$ go through as usual. For π-calculi there are also other choices, for example, between *open*, *late* and *early* bisimulations.

All of this diversity raises a problem: how, in some particular application of a π-calculus, should one choose an *appropriate* equivalence or congruence? This was studied for PICT-like programming languages in [Sew97]. From the discussion of the scheduling behaviour of implementations described in Section 9.4, it is immediate that no realistic implementation will be bisimilar (in any sense) to the labelled-transition semantics; several other choices are arguably determined by more subtle implementation properties.

9.6 Typing

In the Monadic π-calculus of Section 9.1, the value sent on a channel is always of the form expected by a receiver – a single name. In calculi with more interesting values this no longer holds; for example, a polyadic π process might contain an output of a pair in parallel with an input expecting a triple:

$$\bar{c}\langle a\,b \rangle \mid c\langle x\,y\,z \rangle.P$$

Intuitively this should be regarded as an execution error, just as an application to a pair of a function that takes a triple of arguments would be. In both cases such errors can be prevented by imposing a type system. The types for a simple calculus with tuples might be

$$
\begin{array}{llll}
T & ::= & \textbf{chan}\ T & \text{type of channel names carrying } T \\
 & & \langle T_1 .. T_n \rangle & \text{type of tuples of values of types } T_1 .. T_n
\end{array}
$$

with a typing judgement $\Gamma \vdash P\ \textbf{proc}$, where Γ is a finite partial function from names to types, read as 'under the assumptions Γ on names the process P is well-typed'. If Γ takes c to be a channel carrying pairs

$$\Gamma = c : \textbf{chan}\ \langle T\ U \rangle,\ a : T,\ b : U$$

then we would expect $\Gamma \vdash \bar{c}\langle a\,b \rangle\ \textbf{proc}$ to hold but $\Gamma \vdash c\langle x\,y\,z \rangle.P\ \textbf{proc}$ not to hold. Note that types are the types of values, not of processes – in contrast to λ-calculus type systems, a process here does not have a type but is simply well-formed or not.

To make this precise requires the definition of the syntax and semantics (reduction and/or labelled transition) of a π-calculus with polyadic or tuple communication, a definition of execution error and a definition of the typing rules. One should then state and prove that well-typed processes do not have execution errors and that typing is preserved by reductions or (a stronger result) by labelled transitions.

More sophisticated type systems are an active research area, addressing polymorphism, linearity, deadlock freedom, locality and security. We refer the reader to [Pie98] for details and pointers into the literature.

9.7 Distributed π-Calculi

A body of recent research has applied techniques derived from π-calculi to address problems in distributed systems and programming languages. In some ways there is a good match between the asynchronous π-calculus and distributed systems:

- π gives a very clear treatment of concurrency, which is fundamental to distributed systems;
- π asynchronous message passing is close to reliable datagram communication, which lies not far above IP;
- the π treatment of naming is widely applicable: most obviously, there are tight analogies between

  - communication channels (with read/write operations),
  - references (with deref/assign),
  - cryptographic keys (with decrypt/encrypt).

The essential point is that π-*style semantics provide a tractable and compositional way of describing systems that can locally generate fresh names.* Note that π-names are *pure*, in the sense of Needham [Nee89]; they are not assumed to contain any information about their creation.

On the other hand, there are many important issues that standard π-calculi do not address, such as:

- point-to-point and multicast communication;
- failure (of machines and communication links), time and timeouts;
- code and agent migration;
- security (secrecy, integrity, trust, cryptography);
- the distinction between local and nonlocal performance;
- quality of service.

These cannot be abstracted away – there are many interesting language design/semantics problems and, in some cases, delicate protocol design problems. It has proved fruitful to study these problems in the context of particular calculi that are designed for the purpose. In the remainder of this chapter we highlight some of the choices in the (rather large) design space of such calculi, focussing on the possible grouping and interaction primitives. This discussion is only a starting point – we touch on some example calculi but cannot here do justice even to these, let alone to the many other works in the field. Our examples are taken from:

- the π_l-calculus of Amadio and Prasad [AP94], for modelling the failure semantics of Facile [TLK96];
- the distributed join calculus of Fournet et al [FGL$^+$96], intended as the basis for a mobile agent language;
- the Spi-calculus of Abadi and Gordon [AG97], for reasoning about security protocols;
- the Dπ-calculus of Riely and Hennessy [RH99], used to study typing for open systems of mobile agents;
- the dpi-calculus of Sewell [Sew98], used to study locality enforcement of capabilities with a subtyping system;
- the ambient calculus of Cardelli and Gordon [CG98], used for modelling security domains (this is discussed in detail in Chapter 10);
- the Agent and Nomadic π-calculi of Sewell, Wojciechowski and Pierce [SWP98], introduced to study communication infrastructures for mobile agents;
- the Seal calculus of Vitek and Castagna [JC98], focussing on protection mechanisms including revocable capabilities;
- the Box π-calculus of Sewell and Vitek [SV99, SV00], used to study secure encapsulation of untrusted components and causality typing.

In addition, we touch on some aspects of the Actor model described in Chapter 8, although comparisons there are more complex.

Grouping The first point is that standard π-calculi do not have any notion of the identity of processes; the syntax describes only collections of atomic processes (outputs, inputs, etc.) in parallel. For example, suppose that we have two processes P and Q. In π we might have

$$P \mid Q \quad \longrightarrow \ldots \longrightarrow \quad (R_1 \mid .. \mid R_n)$$

for some R_i; the calculus does not have any association between these R_i's and the original P and Q, so the identity of the components is lost. For many purposes, therefore, one must add primitives for grouping process terms into units of:

- failure (e.g., machines or runtime system instances);
- migration (e.g., mobile agents);
- trust (e.g., large administrative domains or small secure critical regions);
- synchronisation (i.e., regions within which an output and an input on the same channel name can interact).

The π-calculus is often referred to as a calculus of mobile processes, but it is perhaps more accurate to view it as a calculus in which the scopes of names are mobile — processes can move only in the sense that their interaction possibilities, represented as the set of channel names that they know, can change.

Hierarchy Grouping primitives can either be given a flat structure, so a whole system is simply a set of groups, or some hierarchy – either two-level or an arbitrary tree. To simply model a flat set of named machines, each of which is running some π-style process code, one might take a new syntactic category of *configuration*, for example, defined by

C, D	$::=$ $m[[P]]$	machine m running process P
	0	nil
	$C \mid D$	parallel composition of C and D
	new c **in** C	new name binder.

This would support a semantics with machine failure or (as in Dπ) systems with code mobility. It is roughly analogous to the Actor configurations of Chapter 8, with $m[[P]]$ representing an Actor with name m and body P – now a single sequential thread. If one wishes to consider the migration of part of the process running at a machine, then a more elaborate hierarchy is required. A two-level hierarchy suffices: a system of named agents, each containing a π-style process and running on a named machine, can be described by the configurations

C, D	$::=$ $a@m[P]$	agent a on machine m running process P
	0	nil
	$C \mid D$	parallel composition of C and D
	new c **in** C	new name binder.

This is roughly the approach of Nomadic π. There are primitives for agent creation and migration:

$$P, Q, R \quad ::= \quad \textbf{agent } b = Q \textbf{ in } R \qquad \text{create a new agent with body } Q$$
$$ \textbf{migrate to } m.P \qquad \text{migrate to machine } m$$
$$ \ldots$$

with b binding in P and Q, and reductions such as

$$a@m[P \,|\, \textbf{agent } b = Q \textbf{ in } R] \quad \longrightarrow \quad \textbf{new } b \textbf{ in } a@m[P \,|\, R] \,|\, b@m[Q]$$
$$a@m[P \,|\, \textbf{migrate to } n.R] \quad \longrightarrow \quad a@n[P \,|\, R]$$

(where $b \notin \text{fn}(P, a, m)$) for creation and migration, respectively. In the first, the new agent b is created on the same machine as the creating agent a; in the second, note that the whole of agent a migrates to machine n. In both reductions the continuation process R can execute only after the creation/migration.

A two-level hierarchy provides a simple setting for considering inter-agent communication (the goal of the Nomadic π work), but for several purposes an arbitrary tree-shaped hierarchy is preferable. One might wish to represent larger units than machines, for example, intranets delimited by firewalls; to model smaller units of software, for example, untrusted components of an application that must be securely encapsulated; or to support a smooth programming style, in which applications automatically take their subcomponents with them on migration. The Distributed Join, dpi, Ambient, Seal and Box π-calculi all take tree-shaped hierarchies. The latter three add a named-group primitive to the syntax of processes

$$P \quad ::= \quad \ldots$$
$$ a[P] \qquad\qquad \text{Ambient/Seal/Box named } a \text{ containing } P$$

– they do not require a separate notion of configuration. The hierarchy is determined by the nesting structure of terms. In the distributed join and dpi calculi groups (there called locations) have unique names and the hierarchy is determined by the binding structure; we omit the details here.

Group Naming Grouped entities can be anonymous or named; if they are named, the names may be unique or nonunique (this, as many other things, might be enforced either by the design of the calculus syntax or by some additional well-formedness or typing condition). Unique naming simplifies some programming and so was adopted in the Distributed Join, dpi and Nomadic π-calculi, and in Actors. One should note, however, that in a network with potentially malicious components a machine (or larger administrative unit) may not have control of the namespace used by incoming entities. In this case nonunique names are appropriate and were adopted in the Ambient, Seal and Box π-calculi.

Interaction There is a vast range of possible primitives for the movement of groups and for interaction between them. We consider the following three aspects.

Interaction across the group hierarchy Calculi differ in the extent to which communication, migration or other interaction is allowed *across* the group hierarchy. There are three main alternatives, which we discuss in the context of π-style communication.

- *Location-independent.* An output $\bar{c}v$ can interact with a corresponding input on c irrespective of their relative position in the hierarchy. This was adopted in the Distributed Join and high-level Nomadic π-calculi, for the ease of programming that it supports, and in Actors (where c is an Actor name). Its implementation requires a complex distributed infrastructure, however, and the high level of abstraction makes failure and attack semantics problematic.
- *Local.* An output can only interact with a 'nearby' input. One might take a subset of the following primitives:

$\bar{c}^{\star}v$	output v on channel c within this group
$\bar{c}^{\uparrow}v$	output v on channel c to parent
$\bar{c}^{\downarrow n}v$	output v on channel c to child n
$\bar{c}^{\rightarrow n}v$	output v on channel c to sibling n
$\bar{c}^{\uparrow n}v$	output v on channel c to parent if a child of n
$\bar{c}^{a@m}v$	output v on channel c to agent a on machine m.

  Local primitives can be implemented more simply (the last was adopted in low-level Nomadic π for this reason). They also support *encapsulation* – constraining the interaction possibilities of untrusted code by containing it within a group. This is important in the Ambient, Seal and Box π-calculi (Box π adopts the first three local output primitives).
- *Path-based.* An intermediate possibility allows nonlocal output but requires the sender to specify an explicit *path* to the receiver.

$\bar{c}^{path}v$	follow path p then output v on channel c

  where paths are sequences of local movements:

$path$	$::=$ $\star$	output within this group
	$\uparrow.path$	go to parent and then follow *path*
	$\downarrow n.path$	go to child n and then follow *path*.

This is a variant of the Ambient calculus mobility primitives, in which an ambient must acquire a path of capabilities in order to migrate; restricting the spread of such capabilities is a basic mechanism for secure programming.

Inputs At the receiver end, one might allow inputs from any source or from a specified source:

$cp.P$	input on channel c from any sender
$c^{\downarrow n}p.P$	input on channel c from child n.

The guarantee of authenticity implied by the latter is used in the Seal and Box π work on encapsulation. Most flexibly, one can input from a set of sources but bind the actual source to a variable, for example, with the following primitive, in which n binds in P and is replaced by the actual source child name in a communication:

$$c^{\downarrow(n)}p.P \qquad \text{input on channel } c \text{ from any child.}$$

Communicated values Finally, we turn to the values that may be involved in a communication or migration. Most simply, one might communicate basic values as in a polyadic π-calculus – names and tuples of names. Generalizing to higher-order communication would allow code – processes and abstractions – to be communicated. A rather different generalization allows an executing process to migrate with all of its state. This is sometimes referred to as *strong* migration, with code mobility as *weak* migration. The two can be unified by introducing a *grab* primitive for capturing the state of a group into a first-class value.

Semantics The detailed design of a syntax and reduction semantics for a distributed π-calculus can be delicate, depending on the choice of primitives (indeed, the desire for a clean reduction semantics may affect that choice). We do not give a full discussion here but refer the reader to the papers introducing particular calculi cited previously. For each, it may be interesting to consider whether the syntax keeps the parts of a group syntactically adjacent (and why!), whether a grouping hierarchy is maintained in the term or binding structure, how uniqueness of naming is enforced, and the locality of the interactions that are permitted.

9.8 Further Reading

The interested reader is referred to the book *Communicating and Mobile Systems: the π-Calculus* by Milner [Mil99] and to the Mobility web page maintained by Uwe Nestmann [Nes], from which much of the literature is accessible electronically. The page includes pointers to the introductory papers by Milner, Parrow and Walker [MPW92]; a tutorial by Parrow; a text on *Foundational Calculi for Programming Languages* by Pierce; an annotated bibliography by Honda and many other useful pointers. An expanded version of this chapter, with proofs of some meta-theoretic results and further discussion of typing, is also available [Sew00].

Acknowledgements

This chapter is partly based on lectures given at the *Instructional Meeting on Recent Advances in Semantics and Types for Concurrency: Theory and Practice* held in July 1998, supported by the MATHFIT initiative of the EPSRC and LMS, and organized by Rajagopal Nagarajan, Bent Thomsen and Lone Leth Thomsen.   I would like to thank the organisers. Some of the technical development is based on joint works with Luca Cattani and Jan Vitek. I acknowledge support from EPSRC grants GR/K 38403, GR/L 62290 and a Royal Society University Research Fellowship.

Bibliography

[AG97]   M. Abadi and A. D. Gordon. A calculus for cryptographic protocols: The spi calculus. In *Proceedings of the Fourth ACM Conference on Computer and Communications Security, Zürich*, pages 36–47. ACM Press, April 1997.

[AP94]   R. M. Amadio and S. Prasad. Localities and failures. In P. S. Thiagarajan, editor, *Proceedings of 14th FSTTCS. Volume 880 of Lecture Notes in Computer Science*, pages 205–216. Springer-Verlag, 1994.

[BB92]   G. Berry and G. Boudol. The chemical abstract machine. *Theoretical Computer Science*, 96:217–248, 1992.

[Bou92]   G. Boudol. Asynchrony and the π-calculus. Technical Report 1702, INRIA Sofia-Antipolis, May 1992.

[CG98]   L. Cardelli and A. D. Gordon. Mobile ambients. In *Proc. of Foundations of Software Science and Computation Structures (FoSSaCS), ETAPS'98, Volume 1378 of Lecture Notes in Computer Science*, pages 140–155. Springer-Verlag, March 1998.

[FG96]   C. Fournet and G. Gonthier. The reflexive CHAM and the join-calculus. In *Proceedings of the 23rd POPL*, pages 372–385. ACM Press, January 1996.

[FGL+96]   C. Fournet, G. Gonthier, J.-J. Lévy L. Maranget, and D. Rémy. A calculus of mobile agents. In *7th International Conference on Concurrency Theory (CONCUR '96). Volume 119 of Lecture Notes in Computer Science*, pages 406–421. Springer-Verlag, August 1996.

[Fou98]   C. Fournet. *The Join-Calculus: A Calculus for Distributed Mobile Programming.* PhD thesis, École Polytechnique, Paris, 1998.

[HT91]   K. Honda and M. Tokoro. An object calculus for asynchronous communication. In *Proceedings of ECOOP '91, Volume 512 of Lecture Notes in Computer Science*, pages 133–147. Springer-Verlag, July 1991.

[JC98]   J.Vitek and G. Castagna. Towards a calculus of mobile computations. In *Workshop on Internet Programming Languages, Chicago, Full version in Volume 1686 of Lecture Notes in Computer Science.* Springer-Verlag, May 1998.

[Joi]   The join-calculus. Papers and implementations available at http://pauillac.inria.fr/join/.

[Mil92]   R. Milner. Functions as processes. *Journal of Mathematical Structures in Computer Science*, 2(2):119–141, 1992.

[Mil99]   R. Milner. *Communicating and Mobile Systems: the π-Calculus.* Cambridge University Press, May 1999.

[MPW92]   R. Milner, J. Parrow, and D. Walker. A calculus of mobile processes, Parts I + II. *Information and Computation*, 100(1):1–77, 1992.

[MS92]   R. Milner and D. Sangiorgi. Barbed bisimulation. In *Proceedings of 19th ICALP. Volume 623 of Lecture Notes in Computer Science*, pages 685–695. Springer-Verlag, 1992.

[Nee89]   R. M. Needham. Names. In S. Mullender, editor, *Distributed Systems*, pages 89–101. Addison-Wesley, 1989.

[Nes]   U. Nestmann. Calculi for mobile processes. Available at http://move.to/mobility and http://www.cs.auc.dk/mobility/.

[NP96]   U. Nestmann and B. C. Pierce. Decoding choice encodings. In *Proceedings of CONCUR '96, Volume 119 of Lecture Notes in Computer Science*, pages 179–194. Springer-Verlag, August 1996.

[Pal97]   C. Palamidessi. Comparing the expressive power of the synchronous and the asynchronous π-calculus. In *Proceedings of POPL 97*, pages 256–265. ACM, 1997.

[PC98]   C. Palamidessi and I. Castellani, editors. *EXPRESS '98: Expressiveness in Concurrency (Nice, France, September 7, 1998)*, volume 16.2 of *entcs*. Elsevier Science Publishers, 1998.

[Pie98]   B. C. Pierce. Type systems for concurrent calculi, September 1998. Invited tutorial at *CONCUR*, Nice, France. Slides available from http://www.cis.upenn.edu/~bcpierce/.

[PT98]   B. C. Pierce and D. N. Turner. Pict: A programming language based on the pi-calculus, March 1998. Version 4.1. Compiler, documentation, demonstration programs, and standard libraries; available from http://www.cis.upenn.edu/~bcpierce/.

[PT00]   B. C. Pierce and D. N. Turner. Pict: A programming language based on the pi-calculus. In *Proof, Language and Interaction: Essays in Honour of Robin Milner*. MIT Press, 2000.

[Qua99]   P. Quaglia. The π-calculus: notes on labelled semantics. *Bulletin of the EATCS*, 68, June 1999. Preliminary version as BRICS Report LS-98-4.

[QW98]   P. Quaglia and D. Walker. On encoding pπ in mπ. In *Proc. 18th FSTTCS, Volume 1530 of Lecture Notes in Computer Science*, pages 42–53. Springer-Verlag, 1998.

[RH99]   J. Riely and M. Hennessy. Trust and partial typing in open systems of mobile agents. In *Proceedings of the 26th POPL*, San Antonio, January 1999. ACM Press.

[San93]   D. Sangiorgi. *Expressing Mobility in Process Algebras: First-Order and Higher-Order Paradigms*. PhD thesis, University of Edinburgh, 1993.

[Sew97]   P. Sewell. On implementations and semantics of a concurrent programming language. In *Proceedings of CONCUR '97. Volume 1243 of Lecture Notes in Computer Science*, pages 391–405. Springer-Verlag, 1997.

[Sew98]   P. Sewell. Global/local subtyping and capability inference for a distributed π-calculus. In *Proceedings of ICALP '98. Volume 1443 of Lecture Notes in Computer Science*, pages 695–706. Springer-Verlag, July 1998. See also Technical Report 435, University of Cambridge, 1997.

[Sew00]   Peter Sewell. Applied π – a brief tutorial. Technical Report 498, Computer Laboratory, University of Cambridge, August 2000.

[SV99]   P. Sewell and J. Vitek. Secure composition of insecure components. In *Proceedings of the 12th IEEE Computer Security Foundations Workshop. Mordano, Italy*, pages 136–150. IEEE Computer Society Press, June 1999.

[SV00]   P. Sewell and J. Vitek. Secure composition of untrusted code: Wrappers and causality types. In *Proceedings of CSFW 00: The 13th IEEE Computer Security Foundations Workshop*, pages 269–284. IEEE Computer Society Press, July 2000.

[SWP98]   P. Sewell, P. T. Wojciechowski, and B. C. Pierce. Location independence for mobile agents. In *Workshop on Internet Programming Languages, Chicago*. Springer-Verlag, May 1998. Full version as Technical Report 462, University of Cambridge, and in Volume 1686 of Lecture Notes in Computer Science, Springer-Verlag.

[Tho93]   B. Thomsen. Plain CHOCS. A second generation calculus for higher order processes. *Acta Informatica*, 30(1):1–59, 1993.

[TLK96]   B. Thomsen, L. Leth, and T.-M. Kuo. A Facile tutorial. In *Proceedings of CONCUR '96. Volume 1119 of Lecture Notes in Computer Science*, pages 278–298. Springer-Verlag, August 1996.

[Tur96]   D. N. Turner. *The Polymorphic Pi-calculus: Theory and Implementation*. PhD thesis, University of Edinburgh, 1996.

[vG90]   R. J. van Glabbeek. The linear time – branching time spectrum. In *Proceedings of CONCUR '90, Volume 458 of Lecture Notes in Computer Science*, pages 278–297. Springer-Verlag, 1990.

[vG93]   R. J. van Glabbeek. The linear time – branching time spectrum II; the semantics of sequential systems with silent moves. In *Proceedings of CONCUR'93, Volume 715 of*

Lecture Notes in Computer Science, pages 66–81. Springer-Verlag, 1993.

[Yos96]   N. Yoshida. Graph types for monadic mobile processes. In *Proceedings of FSTTCS 96*, pages 371–386, 1996.

10

Mobile Ambients†

Luca Cardelli   Andrew D. Gordon

Microsoft Research Cambridge, UK

This chapter introduces a calculus describing the movement of processes and devices, including movement through administrative domains.

10.1 Introduction

There are two distinct areas of work in mobility: *mobile computing*, concerning computation that is carried out in mobile devices (laptops, personal digital assistants, etc.), and *mobile computation*, concerning mobile code that moves between devices (applets, agents, etc.). We aim to describe all of these aspects of mobility within a single framework that encompasses mobile *agents*, the *ambients* where agents interact and the mobility of the ambients themselves.

The inspiration for this work comes from the potential for mobile computation over the World Wide Web. The geographic distribution of the Web naturally calls for mobility of computation, as a way of flexibly managing latency and bandwidth. Because of recent advances in networking and language technology, the basic tenets of mobile computation are now technologically realisable. The high-level software architecture potential, however, is still largely unexplored, although it is being actively investigated in the coordination and agents communities.

The main difficulty with mobile computation on the Web is not in mobility per se, but in the handling of *administrative domains*. In the early days of the Internet one could rely on a flat name space given by IP addresses; knowing the IP address of a computer would very likely allow one to talk to that computer in some way. This is no longer the case: firewalls partition the Internet into administrative domains that are isolated from each other except for rigidly controlled pathways. System administrators enforce policies about what can move through firewalls and how.

Mobility requires more than the traditional notion of authorization to run or to access information in certain domains: it involves the authorization to enter or exit

---

† Work carried out while L. Cardelli was at Digital Equipment Corporation, and A.D. Gordon was at the University of Cambridge. This is an abridged version of the paper 'Mobile Ambients', L. Cardelli and A.D. Gordon, *Theoretical Computer Science*, Vol. 240, No. 1, pp 177–213, July 2000. The paper is reprinted with permission from Elsevier Science.

certain domains. In particular, as far as mobile computation is concerned, it is not realistic to imagine that an agent can migrate from any point A to any point B on the Internet. Rather, an agent must first exit its administrative domain (obtaining permission to do so), enter someone else's domain (again, obtaining permission to do so) and then enter a protected area of some machine where it is allowed to run (after obtaining permission to do so). Access to information is controlled at many levels; thus multiple levels of authorization may be involved. Among these levels we have: local computer, local area network, regional area network, wide-area intranet and internet. Mobile programs must be equipped to navigate this hierarchy of administrative domains, at every step obtaining authorization to move further. Similarly, laptops must be equipped to access resources depending on their location in the administrative hierarchy. Therefore, at the most fundamental level we need to capture notions of locations, of mobility and of authorization to move.

Today, it is very difficult to transport a working environment between two computers, for example, between a laptop and a desktop, or between home and work computers. The working environment might consist of data that has to be copied, and of running programs in various stages of active or suspended communication with the network that have to be shut down and restarted. Why can't we just say 'move this (part of the) environment to that computer' and carry on? When on a trip, why couldn't we transfer a piece of the desktop environment (for example, a forgotten open document along with its editor) to the laptop over a phone line? We would like to discover techniques to achieve all of this easily and reliably.

With these motivations, we adopt a paradigm of mobility where computational ambients are hierarchically structured, where agents are confined to ambients and where ambients move under the control of agents. A novelty of this approach is in allowing the movement of self-contained nested environments that include data and live computation, as opposed to the more common techniques that move single agents or individual objects. Our goal is to make mobile computation scale-up to widely distributed, intermittently connected and well-administered computational environments.

This chapter is organized as follows. In the rest of Section 10.1 we introduce our basic concepts and compare them to previous and current work. In Section 10.2 we describe a calculus based exclusively on mobility primitives, and we use it to represent basic notions such as numerals and Turing machines. In Section 10.3 we extend our calculus with local communication, and we show how we can represent more general communication mechanisms as well as the π-calculus, some λ-calculi and firewall-crossing. Both Section 10.2 and Section 10.3 include an operational semantics.

10.1.1 Ambients

An ambient, in the sense in which we are going to use this word, has the following main characteristics:

- An ambient is a *bounded* place where computation happens. The interesting property here is the existence of a boundary around an ambient. If we want to move computations easily, we must be able to determine what should move; a boundary determines what is inside and what is outside an ambient. Examples of ambients, in this sense, are a Web page (bounded by a file), a virtual address space (bounded by an addressing range), a Unix file system (bounded within a physical volume), a single data object (bounded by 'self') and a laptop (bounded by its case and data ports). Non-examples are threads (where the boundary of what is 'reachable' is difficult to determine) and logically related collections of objects. We can already see that a boundary implies some flexible addressing scheme that can denote entities across the boundary; examples are symbolic links, Uniform Resource Locators and Remote Procedure Call proxies. Flexible addressing is what enables, or at least facilitates, mobility. It is also, of course, a cause of problems when the addressing links are 'broken'.

- An ambient is something that can be nested within other ambients. As we discussed, administrative domains are (often) organized hierarchically. If we want to move a running application from work to home, the application must be removed from an enclosing (work) ambient and inserted into a different enclosing (home) ambient. A laptop may need a removal pass to leave a workplace, and a government pass to leave or enter a country.

- An ambient is something that can be moved as a whole. If we reconnect a laptop to a different network, all of the address spaces and file systems within it move accordingly and automatically. If we move an agent from one computer to another, its local data should move accordingly and automatically.

More precisely, we investigate ambients that have the following structure:

- Each ambient has a name. The name of an ambient is used to control access (entry, exit, communication, etc.). In a realistic situation the true name of an ambient would be guarded very closely, and only specific capabilities would be handed out about how to use the name. In our examples we are usually more liberal in the handling of names, for the sake of simplicity.

- Each ambient has a collection of local agents (also known as threads, processes, etc.). These are the computations that run directly within the ambient and, in a sense, control the ambient. For example, they can instruct the ambient to move.

- Each ambient has a collection of subambients. Each subambient has its own name, agents, subambients, and so on.

In all of this, names are extremely important. A name is

- something that can be created, passed around and used to name new ambients;
- something from which capabilities can be extracted.

10.1.2 Technical Context: Systems

Many software systems have explored and are exploring notions of mobility. Among these are

- Obliq [Car95]. The Obliq project attacked the problems of distribution and mobility for intranet computing. It was carried out largely before the Web became popular. Within its scope, Obliq works quite well, but it is not really suitable for computation and mobility over the Web, just like most other distributed paradigms developed in pre-Web days.
- Telescript [Whi96]. Our ambient model is partially inspired by Telescript but is almost dual to it. In Telescript, agents move while places stay put. Ambients, instead, move while agents are confined to ambients. A Telescript agent, however, is itself a little ambient, since it contains a 'suitcase' of data. Some nesting of places is allowed in Telescript.
- Java [GJS96]. Java provides a working paradigm for mobile computation, as well as a huge amount of available and expected infrastructure on which to base more ambitious mobility efforts.
- Linda [CG89]. Linda is a 'coordination language' where multiple processes interact in a common space (called a tuple space) by dropping and picking up tokens asynchronously. Distributed versions of Linda exist that use multiple tuple spaces and allow remote operations over them. A dialect of Linda [CGZ95] allows nested tuple spaces, but not mobility of the tuple spaces.

10.1.3 Technical Context: Formalisms

Many existing calculi have provided inspiration for our work. In particular:

- The Chemical Abstract Machine [BB92] is a semantic framework, rather than a specific formalism. Its basic notions of reaction in a solution and of membranes that isolate subsolutions closely resemble ambient notions. However, membranes are not meant to provide strong protection, and there is no concern for mobility of subsolutions. Still, we adopt a 'chemical style' in presenting our calculus.
- As discussed in Chapter 9, the π-calculus [MPW92] is a process calculus where channels can 'move' along other channels. The movement of processes is represented as the movement of channels that refer to processes. Therefore, there is no clear indication that processes themselves move. For example, if a channel crosses a firewall (that is, if it is communicated to a process meant to represent a firewall), there is no clear sense in which the process has also crossed the firewall. In fact, the channel may cross several independent firewalls, but a process could not be in all of those places at once. Nonetheless, many fundamental π-calculus concepts and techniques underlie our work.
- As also discussed in Chapter 9, enrichments of the π-calculus with locations have been studied, with the aim of capturing notions of distributed computation. In

the simplest form, a flat space of locations is added, and operations can be indexed by the location where they are executed. Riely and Hennessy [RH98] and Sewell [Sew98] proposed versions of the π-calculus extended with primitives to allow computations to migrate between named locations. The emphasis in this work is on developing type systems for mobile computation based on existing type systems for the π-calculus. Riely and Hennessy's type system regulates the usage of channel names according to permissions represented by types. Sewell's type system differentiates between local and remote channels for the sake of efficient implementation of communication.

- The join-calculus [FG96] is a reformulation of the π-calculus with a more explicit notion of places of interaction; this greatly helps in building distributed implementations of channel mechanisms. The distributed join-calculus [FGL+96] adds a notion of named locations, with essentially the same aims as ours, and a notion of distributed failure. Locations in the distributed join-calculus form a tree, and subtrees can migrate from one part of the tree to another. A significant difference from our ambients is that movement may happen directly from any active location to any other known location.

- LLinda [DNFP97] is a formalization of Linda using process calculi techniques. As in distributed versions of Linda, LLinda has multiple distributed tuple spaces. Multiple tuple spaces are very similar in spirit to multiple ambients, but Linda's tuple spaces do not nest, and there are no restrictions about accessing a tuple space from any other tuple space.

- A growing body of literature is concentrating on the idea of adding discrete locations to a process calculus and considering the failure of those locations [Ama97, FGL+96]. This approach aims to model traditional distributed environments, along with algorithms that tolerate node failures. However, on the Internet, node failure is almost irrelevant compared with the inability to reach nodes. Web servers do not often fail forever, but they frequently disappear from sight because of network or node overload, and then they come back. Sometimes they come back in a different place, for example, when a Web site changes its Internet Service Provider. Moreover, the inability to reach a Web site implies only that a certain path is unavailable; it implies neither failure of that site nor global unreachability. In this sense, an observed node failure cannot simply be associated with the node itself, but instead is a property of the whole network, a property that changes over time. Our notion of locality is induced by a nontrivial and dynamic topology of locations. Failure is represented only, in a weak but realistic sense, as becoming forever unreachable.

- The spi-calculus [AG97] extends the π-calculus with cryptographic primitives. The need for such extensions does not seem to arise immediately within our ambient calculus. Some of the motivations for the spi-calculus extension are already covered by the notion of encapsulation within an ambient. However, we do not know yet how extensively we can use our ambient primitives for cryptographic purposes.

10.1.4 Summary of Our Approach

With respect to previous work on process calculi, we can characterize the main differences in our approach as follows. In each of the following points, our emphasis is on boundaries and their effect on computation.

- The existence of separate locations is represented by a topology of boundaries. This topology induces an abstract notion of distance between locations. Locations are not uniformly accessible and are not identified by globally unique names.
- Process mobility is represented as the crossing of boundaries. In particular, process mobility is not represented as the communication of processes or process names over channels.
- Security is represented as the ability or inability to cross boundaries. In particular, security is not directly represented by cryptographic primitives or access control lists.
- Interaction between processes is by shared location within a common boundary. In particular, interaction cannot happen without proper consideration of boundaries and their topology.

10.2 Mobility

We begin by describing a minimal calculus of ambients that includes only mobility primitives. Still, we shall see that this calculus is quite expressive. In Section 10.3 we then introduce communication primitives that allow us to write more natural examples.

10.2.1 Mobility Primitives

We first introduce a calculus in its entirety, and then we comment on the individual constructions. The syntax of the calculus is defined in Tables 10.1, 10.2 and 10.3. In addition, we write $P\{n \leftarrow m\}$ for the substitution of the name m for each free occurrence of the name n in the process P (and similarly for $M\{n \leftarrow m\}$). The main syntactic categories are processes (including both ambients and agents that execute actions) and capabilities.

The first four process primitives (restriction, inactivity, composition and replication) are commonly found in process calculi. To these we add ambients, $n[P]$, and the exercise of capabilities, $M.P$. Next we discuss these primitives in detail.

Table 10.1. *Mobility Primitives*

n	names
$P, Q ::=$	processes
$\quad (\nu n)P$	restriction
$\quad \mathbf{0}$	inactivity
$\quad P \mid Q$	composition
$\quad !P$	replication
$\quad n[P]$	ambient
$\quad M.P$	action
$M ::=$	capabilities
$\quad in\ n$	can enter n
$\quad out\ n$	can exit n
$\quad open\ n$	can open n

Table 10.2. *Free Names*

$$fn((\nu n)P) \triangleq fn(P) - \{n\} \qquad\qquad fn(in\ n) \triangleq \{n\}$$
$$fn(\mathbf{0}) \triangleq \varnothing \qquad\qquad\qquad\qquad fn(out\ n) \triangleq \{n\}$$
$$fn(P \mid Q) \triangleq fn(P) \cup fn(Q) \qquad fn(open\ n) \triangleq \{n\}$$
$$fn(!P) \triangleq fn(P)$$
$$fn(n[P]) \triangleq \{n\} \cup fn(P)$$
$$fn(M.P) \triangleq fn(M) \cup fn(P)$$

10.2.2 Explanations

We begin by introducing the semantics of ambients informally. A reduction relation $P \to Q$ describes the evolution of a process P into a new process Q.

10.2.2.1 Restriction

The restriction operator:

$$(\nu n)P$$

creates a new (unique) name n within a scope P. The new name can be used to name ambients and to operate on ambients by name. As in the π-calculus [MPW92], the (νn) binder can float outward as necessary to extend the scope of a name and can float inward when possible to restrict the scope. Unlike the π-calculus, the names that are subject to scoping are not channel names, but ambient names. The restriction construct is transparent with respect to reduction; this is expressed by the following rule:

$$P \to Q \Rightarrow (\nu n)P \to (\nu n)Q.$$

Table 10.3. *Syntactic Conventions and Abbreviations*

$(\nu n)P \mid Q$	is read	$((\nu n)P) \mid Q$
$!P \mid Q$	is read	$(!P) \mid Q$
$M.P \mid Q$	is read	$(M.P) \mid Q$

$$(\nu n_1 \dots n_m)P \ \stackrel{\Delta}{=} \ (\nu n_1) \dots (\nu n_m)P$$

$$n[] \ \stackrel{\Delta}{=} \ n[0]$$

$$M \ \stackrel{\Delta}{=} \ M.0$$

10.2.2.2 Inaction

The process:

0

is the process that does nothing. It does not reduce.

10.2.2.3 Parallel

Parallel execution is denoted by a binary operator that is commutative and associative:

$P \mid Q$

It obeys the rule:

$P \to Q \Rightarrow P \mid R \to Q \mid R.$

This rule directly covers reduction on the left branch; reduction on the right branch is obtained by commutativity.

10.2.2.4 Replication

Replication is a technically convenient way of representing iteration and recursion. The process:

$!P$

denotes the unbounded replication of the process P. That is, $!P$ can produce as many parallel replicas of P as needed, and is equivalent to $P \mid !P$. There are no reduction rules for $!P$; in particular, the term P under $!$ cannot begin to reduce until it is expanded out as $P \mid !P$.

10.2.2.5 Ambients

An ambient is written:

$n[P]$

where n is the name of the ambient and P is the process running inside the ambient.

In $n[P]$, it is understood that P is actively running, and that P can be the parallel composition of several processes. We emphasize that P is running even when the surrounding ambient is moving. Running while moving may or may not be realistic, depending on the nature of the ambient and of the communication medium through which the ambient moves, but it is consistent to think in those terms. We express the fact that P is running by a rule that says that any reduction of P becomes a reduction of $n[P]$:

$$P \rightarrow Q \Rightarrow n[P] \rightarrow n[Q]$$

In general, an ambient exhibits a tree structure induced by the nesting of ambient brackets. Each node of this tree structure may contain a collection of (nonambient) processes running in parallel, in addition to subambients. We say that these processes are running in the ambient, in contrast to the ones running in subambients. The general shape of an ambient is, therefore:

$$n[P_1 \mid \ldots \mid P_p \mid m_1[\ldots] \mid \ldots \mid m_q[\ldots]] \qquad (P_i \neq n_i[\ldots]).$$

To emphasize structure we may display ambient brackets as boxes. Then the general shape of an ambient is

Nothing prevents the existence of two or more ambients with the same name, either nested or at the same level. Once a name is created, it can be used to name multiple ambients. Moreover, $!n[P]$ generates multiple ambients with the same name. In this way, for example, one can easily model the replication of services.

10.2.2.6 Actions and Capabilities

Operations that change the hierarchical structure of ambients are sensitive. In particular, such operations can be interpreted as the crossing of firewalls or the decoding of ciphertexts. Hence these operations are restricted by *capabilities*. Thanks to capabilities, an ambient can allow other ambients to perform certain operations without having to reveal its true name. With the communication primitives of Section 10.3, capabilities can be transmitted as values.

The process:

$$M.P$$

executes an action regulated by the capability M and then continues as the process P. The process P does not start running until the action is executed. For each kind of capability M we have a specific rule for reducing $M.P$. These rules are described in the following case by case.

We consider three kinds of capabilities: one for entering an ambient, one for exiting an ambient and one for opening up an ambient. Capabilities are obtained from names; given a name m, the capability *in* m allows entry into m, the capability *out* m allows exit out of m and the capability *open* m allows the opening of m. Implicitly, the possession of one or all of these capabilities is insufficient to reconstruct the original name m from which they were extracted.

10.2.2.7 Entry Capability

An entry capability, *in* m, can be used in the action:

in $m.P$

which instructs the ambient surrounding *in* $m.P$ to enter a sibling ambient named m. If no sibling m can be found, the operation blocks until a time when such a sibling exists. If more than one m sibling exists, any one of them can be chosen. The reduction rule is

$$n[in\ m.P \mid Q] \mid m[R] \quad \to \quad m[n[P \mid Q] \mid R]$$

or, by representing ambient brackets as boxes:

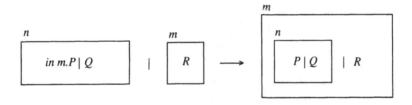

If successful, this reduction transforms a sibling n of an ambient m into a child of m. After the execution, the process *in* $m.P$ continues with P, and both P and Q find themselves at a lower level in the tree of ambients.

10.2.2.8 Exit Capability

An exit capability, *out* m, can be used in the action:

out $m.P$

which instructs the ambient surrounding *out* $m.P$ to exit its parent ambient named m. If the parent is not named m, the operation blocks until a time when such a parent exists. The reduction rule is

$$m[n[out\ m.\ P \mid Q] \mid R] \quad \to \quad n[P \mid Q] \mid m[R]$$

That is

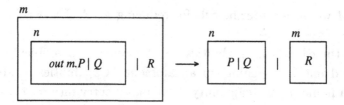

If successful, this reduction transforms a child n of an ambient m into a sibling of m. After the execution, the process *in m.P* continues with P, and both P and Q find themselves at a higher level in the tree of ambients.

10.2.2.9 Open Capability

An opening capability, *open m*, can be used in the action:

open m.P

This action provides a way of dissolving the boundary of an ambient named m located at the same level as open, according to the rule:

open m. P | $m[Q]$ $\rightarrow$ P | Q

That is

$$\text{open } m.P \quad | \quad \boxed{\begin{matrix} m \\ Q \end{matrix}} \quad \longrightarrow \quad P \mid Q$$

If no ambient m can be found, the operation blocks until a time when such an ambient exists. If more than one ambient m exists, any one of them can be chosen.

An *open* operation may be upsetting to both P and Q above. From the point of view of P, there is no telling in general what Q might do when unleashed. From the point of view of Q, its environment is being ripped open. Still, this operation is relatively well-behaved because: (1) the dissolution is initiated by the agent *open m.P*, so that the appearance of Q at the same level as P is not totally unexpected; (2) *open m* is a capability that is given out by m, so $m[Q]$ cannot be dissolved if it does not wish to be (this will become clearer later in the presence of communication primitives).

10.2.3 Operational Semantics

We now give an operational semantics of the calculus of Section 10.1, based on a structural congruence between processes, $\equiv$ and a reduction relation $\rightarrow$. We have already discussed all of the reduction rules, except for one that connects reduction with equivalence. This is a semantics in the style of Milner's reaction relation [Mil92] for the π-calculus, which was itself inspired by the Chemical Abstract Machine of

Table 10.4. *Structural Congruence*

$P \equiv P$	(Struct Refl)
$P \equiv Q \Rightarrow Q \equiv P$	(Struct Symm)
$P \equiv Q, Q \equiv R \Rightarrow P \equiv R$	(Struct Trans)
$P \equiv Q \Rightarrow (\nu n)P \equiv (\nu n)Q$	(Struct Res)
$P \equiv Q \Rightarrow P \mid R \equiv Q \mid R$	(Struct Par)
$P \equiv Q \Rightarrow \,!P \equiv \,!Q$	(Struct Repl)
$P \equiv Q \Rightarrow n[P] \equiv n[Q]$	(Struct Amb)
$P \equiv Q \Rightarrow M.P \equiv M.Q$	(Struct Action)
$P \mid Q \equiv Q \mid P$	(Struct Par Comm)
$(P \mid Q) \mid R \equiv P \mid (Q \mid R)$	(Struct Par Assoc)
$!P \equiv P \mid !P$	(Struct Repl Par)
$(\nu n)(\nu m)P \equiv (\nu m)(\nu n)P$	(Struct Res Res)
$(\nu n)(P \mid Q) \equiv P \mid (\nu n)Q \quad$ if $n \notin fn(P)$	(Struct Res Par)
$(\nu n)(m[P]) \equiv m[(\nu n)P] \quad$ if $n \neq m$	(Struct Res Amb)
$P \mid \mathbf{0} \equiv P$	(Struct Zero Par)
$(\nu n)\mathbf{0} \equiv \mathbf{0}$	(Struct Zero Res)
$!\mathbf{0} \equiv \mathbf{0}$	(Struct Zero Repl)

Berry and Boudol [BB92]. Processes of the calculus are grouped into equivalence classes by the relation, $\equiv$ (defined in table 10.4), which denotes structural congruence (that is, equivalence up to trivial syntactic restructuring).

In addition, we identify processes up to the renaming of bound names:

$$(\nu n)P \;=\; (\nu m)P\{n \leftarrow m\} \quad \text{if } m \notin fn(P)$$

By this we mean that these processes are understood to be identical (for example, by choosing an appropriate representation), as opposed to structurally equivalent.

Note that the following terms are distinct:

$!(\nu n)P \not\equiv (\nu n)!P$	replication creates new names
$n[P] \mid n[Q] \not\equiv n[P \mid Q]$	multiple n ambients have separate identities.

The behaviour of processes is given by the reduction relation defined in Table 10.5. The first three rules are the one-step reductions for *in*, *out* and *open*. The next three rules propagate reductions across scopes, ambient nesting and parallel composition. The final rule allows the use of equivalence during reduction. Finally, $\rightarrow^*$ is the chaining of multiple reduction steps.

Morris-style contextual equivalence [Mor68] is a standard way of saying that two processes have the same behaviour: two processes are contextually equivalent if and only if, whenever they are inserted inside an arbitrary enclosing process, they admit the same elementary observations.

In our setting, we formulate contextual equivalence in terms of observing the

Table 10.5. *Reduction*

$n[in\ m.\ P \mid Q] \mid m[R]\ \rightarrow\ m[n[P \mid Q] \mid R]$	(Red In)
$m[n[out\ m.\ P \mid Q] \mid R]\ \rightarrow\ n[P \mid Q] \mid m[R]$	(Red Out)
$open\ n.P \mid n[Q]\ \rightarrow\ P \mid Q$	(Red Open)
$P \rightarrow Q\ \Rightarrow\ (\nu n)P \rightarrow (\nu n)Q$	(Red Res)
$P \rightarrow Q\ \Rightarrow\ n[P] \rightarrow n[Q]$	(Red Amb)
$P \rightarrow Q\ \Rightarrow\ P \mid R \rightarrow Q \mid R$	(Red Par)
$P' \not\equiv P,\ P \rightarrow Q,\ Q \not\equiv Q'\ \Rightarrow\ P' \rightarrow Q'$	(Red $\equiv$)
$\rightarrow^*$	reflexive and transitive closure of $\rightarrow$

presence of top-level ambients. We say that a process P *exhibits an ambient named* n, and write $P\!\downarrow\!n$, just if P is a process containing a top-level ambient named n. We say that a process P *eventually exhibits an ambient named* n, and write $P\!\Downarrow\!n$, just if after some number of reductions, P exhibits an ambient named n. Formally, we define:

$$P\!\downarrow\!n\ \triangleq\ P \equiv (\nu m_1...m_i)(n[P'] \mid P'') \qquad \text{where } n \notin \{m_1...m_i\}$$
$$P\!\Downarrow\!n\ \triangleq\ P \rightarrow^* Q \text{ and } Q\!\downarrow\!n.$$

Next we define contextual equivalence in terms of the predicate $P\!\Downarrow\!n$. Let a context $\mathbf{C}()$ be a process containing zero or more holes, and for any process P, let $\mathbf{C}(P)$ be the process obtained by filling each hole in $\mathbf{C}$ with a copy of P (names free in P may become bound). Let *contextual equivalence* be the relation $P \simeq Q$ defined by:

$$P \simeq Q\ \triangleq\ \text{for all } n \text{ and } \mathbf{C}(),\ \mathbf{C}(P)\!\Downarrow\!n \Leftrightarrow \mathbf{C}(Q)\!\Downarrow\!n.$$

Finally, we write $P \rightarrow^* \simeq Q$ if there exists an R such that $P \rightarrow^* R$ and $R \simeq Q$.

In [GC99] we present convenient proof techniques for contextual equivalence, and we give a proof of the 'perfect firewall equation': $(\nu n)n[P] \simeq \mathbf{0}$ if $n \notin \mathit{fn}(P)$. This equation allows us to garbage collect some inactive ambients, and is assumed in some of the examples in Section 10.2.4.

10.2.4 Examples

In this section we demonstrate some of the expressive power of the ambient calculus, and we discuss some expressiveness issues.

10.2.4.1 Locks

We can use *open* to encode locks. Let *release* $n.P$ be a nonblocking operation that releases a lock n and continues with P. Let *acquire* $n.P$ be a potentially blocking operation that attempts to acquire a lock n, and that continues with P if and when the lock is released. These operations can be defined as follows:

$$acquire\ n.\ P \quad \triangleq \quad open\ n.\ P$$
$$release\ n.\ P \quad \triangleq \quad n[] \mid P.$$

Given two locks n and m, two processes can 'shake hands' before continuing with their execution:

$$acquire\ n.\ release\ m.\ P \mid release\ n.\ acquire\ m.\ Q$$

10.2.4.2 Mobile Agent Authentication

A process at the top level of an ambient can be said to be privileged because it can directly affect the movement of the surrounding ambient and can open subambients. Suppose that such a privileged process wants to leave its *Home* ambient, and then come back and be reinstated as a privileged process. The *Home* ambient cannot allow just any visitor to become privileged, for security reasons, so the original process must somehow be authenticated.

A solution is given in the following. The top-level process creates a new name, n, to be used as a shared secret between itself and the *Home* ambient; *open n* is left in place to authenticate the process when it comes back. The process then leaves *Home* in the form of an *Agent* ambient. On its return inside *Home*, the *Agent* ambient exposes an n ambient, which is opened by *open n* to reinstate the continuation P of the original process at the top level of *Home*.

$$Home[$$
$$\quad (\nu n)(open\ n\ \mid$$
$$\qquad Agent[out\ home.\ in\ home.\ n[out\ Agent.\ open\ Agent.\ P]])$$
$$\quad]$$

Here is a trace of the computation:

$$Home[(\nu n)(open\ n \mid Agent[out\ home.\ in\ home.\ n[out\ Agent.\ open\ Agent.\ P]])]$$
$$\equiv \quad (\nu n)\ Home[open\ n \mid Agent[out\ home.\ in\ home.\ n[out\ Agent.\ open\ Agent.\ P]]]$$
$$\rightarrow \quad (\nu n)\ (Home[open\ n] \mid Agent[in\ home.\ n[out\ Agent.\ open\ Agent.\ P]])$$
$$\rightarrow \quad (\nu n)\ Home[open\ n \mid Agent[n[out\ Agent.\ open\ Agent.\ P]]]$$
$$\rightarrow \quad (\nu n)\ Home[open\ n \mid n[open\ Agent.\ P] \mid Agent[]]$$
$$\rightarrow \quad (\nu n)\ Home[\mathbf{0} \mid open\ Agent.\ P \mid Agent[]]$$
$$\rightarrow \quad (\nu n)\ Home[\mathbf{0} \mid P \mid \mathbf{0}]$$
$$\equiv \quad Home[P]$$

This example illustrates the creation of a shared secret (n) within a safe location, (*Home*), the distribution of the secret over the network (carried along by *Agent*) and the authentication of incoming processes based on the shared secret.

10.2.4.3 Firewall Access

This is another example of a mobile agent trying to gain access to an ambient. In this case, though, we assume that the ambient, a firewall, keeps its name completely secret, thereby requiring authentication prior to entry.

The agent crosses a firewall by means of previously arranged passwords k, k' and k''. The agent exhibits the password k' by using a wrapper ambient that has k' as its name. The firewall, which has a secret name w, sends out a pilot ambient, $k[out\ w.\ in\ k'.\ in\ w]$, to guide the agent inside. The pilot ambient enters an agent by performing $in\ k'$ (therefore verifying that the agent knows the password) and is given control by being opened. Then, $in\ w$ transports the agent inside the firewall, where the password wrapper is discarded. The third name, k'', is needed to confine the contents Q of the agent and to prevent Q from interfering with the protocol.

The final effect is that the agent physically crosses into the firewall; this can be seen in the following by the fact that Q is finally placed inside w. (For simplicity, this example is written to allow a single agent to enter.) Assume that $(fn(P) \cup fn(Q)) \cap \{k, k', k''\} = \varnothing$ and $w \notin fn(Q)$:

$$Firewall \triangleq (\nu w)\ w[k[out\ w.\ in\ k'.\ in\ w] \mid open\ k'.\ open\ k''.\ P]$$
$$Agent \triangleq k'[open\ k.\ k''[Q]]$$

$Agent \mid Firewall$
$$\equiv (\nu w)\ (k'[open\ k.\ k''[Q]] \mid w[k[out\ w.\ in\ k'.\ in\ w] \mid open\ k'.\ open\ k''.\ P])$$
$$\to^* (\nu w)\ (k'[open\ k.\ k''[Q] \mid k[in\ w]] \mid w[open\ k'.\ open\ k''.\ P])$$
$$\to^* (\nu w)\ (k'[k''[Q] \mid in\ w] \mid w[open\ k'.\ open\ k''.\ P])$$
$$\to^* (\nu w)\ (w[(k'[k''[Q]] \mid open\ k'.\ open\ k''.\ P])$$
$$\to^* (\nu w)\ w[Q \mid P]$$

There is no guarantee here that any particular agent will make it inside the firewall. Rather, the intended guarantee is that, if any agent crosses the firewall, it must be one that knows the passwords.

We use an equation to express the security property of the firewall. If $(fn(P) \cup fn(Q)) \cap \{k, k', k''\} = \varnothing$ and $w \notin fn(Q)$, then we can show that the interaction of the agent with the firewall produces the desired result up to contextual equivalence:

$$(\nu k k' k'')\ (Agent \mid Firewall) \simeq (\nu w)\ w[Q \mid P]$$

Since contextual equivalence takes into account all possible contexts, the equation above states that the firewall crossing protocol works correctly in the presence of any possible attacker that may try to disrupt it. The assumption that an attacker does not already know the password is represented by the restricted scoping of k, k', k''.

This equation is proven using techniques presented in a further paper [GC99].

10.2.4.4 Movement from the Inside or the Outside: Subjective vs. Objective

One may consider alternative primitives to the ones that we have adopted in the ambient calculus. In particular, there are two natural kinds of movement primitives for ambients. The distinction is between 'I make you move' from the outside (*objective move*) or 'I move' from the inside (*subjective move*). Subjective moves, the ones that we have already seen, obey the rules:

$$n[in\ m.\ P \mid Q] \mid m[R] \rightarrow m[n[P \mid Q] \mid R]$$
$$m[n[out\ m.\ P \mid Q] \mid R] \rightarrow n[P \mid Q] \mid m[R].$$

Objective moves (indicated by an *mv* prefix), can be defined by the rules:

$$mv\ in\ m.\ P \mid m[R] \rightarrow m[P \mid R]$$
$$m[mv\ out\ m.\ P \mid R] \rightarrow P \mid m[R].$$

The objective moves have simpler rules. However, they operate only on ambients that are not active; they provide no way of moving an existing running ambient. The subjective moves, in contrast, cause active ambients to move and, together with *open*, can approximate the effect of objective moves (as we discuss later).

Another kind of objective moves that one could consider is

$$mv\ n\ in\ m.\ P \mid n[Q] \mid m[R] \rightarrow P \mid m[n[Q] \mid R]$$
$$m[mv\ n\ out\ m.\ P \mid n[Q] \mid R] \rightarrow P \mid m[P \mid R] \mid n[Q].$$

These are objective moves that work on active ambients. However, they are not as simple as the previous objective moves, and, again, they can be approximated by subjective moves and *open*.

In evaluating these alternative operations, one should consider who has the authority to move whom. In general, the authority to move rests in the top-level agents of an ambient, which naturally act as *control agents*. Control agents cannot be injected purely by subjective moves, since these moves handle whole ambients. Instead, with objective moves, a control agent can be injected into an ambient simply by possessing an entry capability for it. As a consequence, objective moves and entry capabilities together provide the unexpected power of entrapping an ambient into a location that it can never exit:

$$entrap\ m\ \triangleq\ (\nu k)\ (k[]\ \mid\ mv\ in\ m.\ in\ k.\ \mathbf{0})$$
$$entrap\ m\ \mid\ m[P]\ \rightarrow^*\ (\nu k)\ k[m[P]].$$

This is an argument against taking this form of objective moves as primitive.

10.2.4.5 Dissolution

The *open* capability confers the right to dissolve an ambient from the outside and reveal its contents. It is interesting to consider an operation that dissolves an ambient from the inside, called *acid*:

$$m[acid.\ P \mid Q] \rightarrow P \mid Q.$$

Acid gives a simple encoding of objective moves:

$$mv \; in \; n.P \; \triangleq \; (\nu q) \; q[in \; n. \; acid. \; P]$$
$$mv \; out \; n.P \; \triangleq \; (\nu q) \; q[out \; n. \; acid. \; P].$$

Therefore, *acid* is as dangerous as objective moves, providing the power to entrap ambients.

However, *open* can be used to define a capability-restricted version of *acid* that does not lead to entrapment. This is a form of planned dissolution:

$$acid \; n.P \; \triangleq \; acid[out \; n. \; open \; n. \; P]$$

to be used with a helper process, *open acid* (an abbreviation for *open acid.* **0**), as follows:

$$n[acid \; n. \; P \; | \; Q] \; | \; open \; acid \; \rightarrow^* \; P \; | \; Q.$$

This form of *acid* is sufficient for uses in many encodings where it is necessary to dissolve ambients. Encodings are carefully planned, so it is easy to add the necessary *open* instructions. The main difference with the liberal form of *acid* is that *acid n* must name the ambient that it is dissolving. More precisely, the encoding of *acid n* requires an exit and an open capability for *n*.

10.2.4.6 Objective Moves

Objective moves are not directly encodable. However, specific ambients can explicitly allow objective moves. Here we assume that *enter* and *exit* are two distinguished names, chosen by convention:

$$allow \; n \; \triangleq \; !open \; n$$
$$mv \; in \; n.P \; \triangleq \; (\nu k) \; k[in \; n. \; enter[out \; k. \; open \; k. \; P]]$$
$$mv \; out \; n.P \; \triangleq \; (\nu k) \; k[out \; n. \; exit[out \; k. \; open \; k. \; P]]$$
$$n^{\lrcorner}[P] \; \triangleq \; n[P \; | \; allow \; enter] \qquad\qquad (n^{\lrcorner} \; \text{allows} \; mv \; in)$$
$$n^{\ulcorner}[P] \; \triangleq \; n[P] \; | \; allow \; exit \qquad\qquad (n^{\ulcorner} \; \text{allows} \; mv \; out)$$
$$n^{\lrcorner\ulcorner}[P] \; \triangleq \; n[P \; | \; allow \; enter] \; | \; allow \; exit \quad (n^{\lrcorner\ulcorner} \; \text{allows both} \; mv \; in \; \text{and} \; mv \; out).$$

These definitions are to be used, for example, as follows:

$$mv \; in \; n.P \; | \; n^{\lrcorner\ulcorner}[Q] \; \rightarrow^* \; n^{\lrcorner\ulcorner}[P \; | \; Q]$$
$$n^{\lrcorner\ulcorner}[mv \; out \; n.P \; | \; Q] \; \rightarrow^* \; P \; | \; n^{\lrcorner\ulcorner}[Q].$$

Moreover, by picking particular names instead of *enter* and *exit*, ambients can restrict who can do objective moves in and out of them. These names work as keys *k*, to be used together with *allow k*:

$$mv \; in_k \; n.P \; \triangleq \; k[in \; n. \; P]$$
$$mv \; out_k \; n.P \; \triangleq \; k[out \; n. \; P].$$

10.2.4.7 Synchronization on Named Channels

In CCS [Mil80], all communication between processes is reduced to synchronization on named channels. In CCS, channels have no explicit representation other than their name. In the ambient calculus, we represent a CCS channel named n as follows:

$$n^{\lrcorner\lceil}[].$$

A CCS channel n has two complementary ports, which we shall write as $n?$ and $n!$. (We use a slightly nonstandard notation to avoid confusion with the notation of the ambient calculus.) These ports are conventionally thought of as input and output ports, respectively, but in fact during synchronization no value passes in either direction. Synchronization occurs between two processes attempting to synchronize on complementary ports. Process $n?.P$ attempts to synchronize on port $n?$ and then continues as P. Process $n!.P$ attempts to synchronize on port $n!$ and then continues as P. We can encode these CCS processes as follows:

$$n?.P \overset{\Delta}{=} mv\ in\ n.\ acquire\ rd.\ release\ wr.\ mv\ out\ n.P$$
$$n!.P \overset{\Delta}{=} mv\ in\ n.\ release\ rd.\ acquire\ wr.\ mv\ out\ n.P.$$

10.2.4.8 Choice

A major feature of CCS [Mil80] is the presence of a nondeterministic choice operator $(+)$. We do not take $+$ as a primitive, in the spirit of the asynchronous π-calculus, but we can approximate some aspects of it by the following definitions. The intent is that $n \Rightarrow P + m \Rightarrow Q$ reduces to P in the presence of an n ambient and reduces to Q in the presence of an m ambient:

$$n \Rightarrow P\ +\ m \Rightarrow Q \overset{\Delta}{=} (\nu\ p\ q\ r)($$
$$p[in\ n.\ out\ n.\ q[out\ p.\ open\ r.\ P]]\ |$$
$$p[in\ m.\ out\ m.\ q[out\ p.\ open\ r.\ Q]]\ |$$
$$open\ q\ |\ r[]).$$

For example, by assuming that $\{p, q, r\} \cap fn(R) = \varnothing$, we have:

$$(n \Rightarrow P\ +\ m \Rightarrow Q)\ |\ n[R] \rightarrow^* \simeq\ P\ |\ n[R].$$

The use of $\simeq$ in this property, required for removing inert ambients, is justified by the perfect firewall equation discussed in [GC99].

From choice we can derive Boolean conditionals. A Boolean is represented by one of two flags: *flag tt* for true and *flag ff* for false. (We assume that at most one of them is present at any time.) Boolean flags and conditionals are represented as follows:

$$flag\ n \overset{\Delta}{=} n[]$$
$$if\ tt\ P,\ if\ ff\ Q \overset{\Delta}{=} tt \Rightarrow open\ tt.\ P + ff \Rightarrow open\ ff.\ Q.$$

Note that a Boolean flag is consumed every time a branch is taken.

10.2.4.9 Renaming

We can use *open* to encode a subjective ambient-renaming operation called *be*:

$$n \ be \ m. \ P \ \triangleq \ m[out \ n. \ open \ n. \ P] \mid in \ m.$$

For example:

$$n[n \ be \ m. \ P \mid Q] \equiv n[m[out \ n. \ open \ n. \ P] \mid in \ m \mid Q]$$
$$\rightarrow m[open \ n. \ P] \mid n[in \ m \mid Q]$$
$$\rightarrow m[open \ n. \ P \mid n[Q]]$$
$$\rightarrow m[P \mid Q].$$

However, this operation is not atomic: a movement initiated by Q may disrupt it. If it is possible to plan ahead, then one can add a lock within the ambient named n to synchronize renaming with any movement by Q.

10.2.4.10 Seeing

We can use *open* and *be* to encode a *see* operation that detects the presence of a given ambient:

$$see \ n. \ P \ \triangleq \ (\nu \ r \ s) \ (r[in \ n. \ out \ n. \ r \ be \ s. \ P] \mid open \ s).$$

With this definition, P gets activated only if its r capsule can get back to the same place. That is, P is not activated if it is caught in the movement of n and ends up somewhere else.

The previous definition of *see* can detect any ambient. If an ambient wants to be seen (that is, if it contains *allow see*), then there is a simpler definition:

$$see \ n. \ P \ \triangleq \ (\nu \ seen) \ (mv \ in_{see} \ n. \ mv \ out_{seen} \ n. \ P \mid open \ seen).$$

10.2.4.11 Iteration

The following iteration construct has a number of branches $(m_i)P_i$ and a body Q. Each branch can be triggered by exposing an ambient $m_i[]$ in the body, which is then replaced by a copy of P_i:

$$rec \ (m_1)P_1 \ ... \ (m_p)P_p \ in \ Q \ \triangleq$$
$$(\nu \ m_1 \ ... \ m_p) \ (!open \ m_1. \ P_1 \mid ... \mid !open \ m_p. \ P_p \mid Q)$$
$$rec \ (m_1)P_1 \ ... \ (m_p)P_p \ in \ m_i[] \ \rightarrow^* \ rec(m_1)P_1 \ ... \ (m_p)P_p \ in \ P_i.$$

10.2.4.12 Numerals

We represent the number i by a stack of nested ambients of depth i. For any natural number i, let $\underline{i}$ be the numeral for i:

$$\underline{0} \ \triangleq \ zero[] \qquad \underline{i+1} \ \triangleq \ succ[open \ op \mid \underline{i}].$$

The *open op* process is needed to allow ambients named *op* to enter the stack of ambients to operate on it. To show that arithmetic may be programmed on these numerals, we begin with an *ifzero* operation to tell whether a numeral represents 0:

$$ifzero\ P\ Q\ \overset{\triangle}{=}\ zero \Rightarrow P\ +\ succ \Rightarrow Q$$
$$\underline{0}\ |\ ifzero\ P\ Q\ \rightarrow^* \simeq\ \underline{0}\ |\ P$$
$$\underline{i+1}\ |\ ifzero\ P\ Q\ \rightarrow^* \simeq\ \underline{i+1}\ |\ Q.$$

Next, we can encode increment and decrement operations:

$$inc.P\ \overset{\triangle}{=}\ ifzero\ (inczero.P)\ (incsucc.P)$$
$$inczero.P\ \overset{\triangle}{=}\ open\ zero.\ (\underline{1}\ |\ P)$$
$$incsucc.P\ \overset{\triangle}{=}\ (\nu\ p\ q)\ (p[succ[open\ op]]\ |\ open\ q.\ open\ p.\ P\ |$$
$$op[in\ succ.\ in\ p.\ in\ succ.$$
$$(q[out\ succ.\ out\ succ.\ out\ p]\ |\ open\ op)])$$
$$dec.P\ \overset{\triangle}{=}\ (\nu\ p)\ (op[in\ succ.\ p[out\ succ]]\ |\ open\ p.\ open\ succ.\ P).$$

The *incsucc* operation increments a nonzero numeral $\underline{i}$. It does so by inserting an operator at the top level of $\underline{i}$ that moves $\underline{i}$ into a further layer of *succ* ambients, thus producing $\underline{i+1}$. Much of the complexity of the definition is due to activating the continuation P only after the increment.

These definitions satisfy:

$$\underline{i}\ |\ inc.P\ \rightarrow^* \simeq\ \underline{i+1}\ |\ P \qquad\qquad \underline{i+1}\ |\ dec.P\ \rightarrow^* \simeq\ \underline{i}\ |\ P.$$

The use of $\simeq$ in the statement of these properties derives from the use of $\simeq$ in the properties of choice, and was discussed previously.

Given that iterative computations can be programmed with replication, any arithmetic operation can be programmed with *inc*, *dec* and *iszero*.

10.2.4.13 Turing Machines

We emulate Turing machines in a direct 'mechanical' style. A tape consists of a nested sequence of squares, each initially containing the flag $f\!f[]$. The first square has a distinguished name to indicate the end of the tape to the left:

$$end^{\lrcorner\ulcorner}[f\!f[]\ |\ sq^{\lrcorner\ulcorner}[f\!f[]\ |\ sq^{\lrcorner\ulcorner}[f\!f[]\ |\ sq^{\lrcorner\ulcorner}[f\!f[]\ |\ ...\ ]]]].$$

The head of the machine is an ambient that inhabits a square. The head moves right by entering the next nested square and moves left by exiting the current square. The head contains the program of the machine, and it can read and write the flag in the current square. The trickiest part of the definition concerns extending the tape. Two tape-stretchers, *stretchLft* and *stretchRht*, are placed at the beginning and end of the tape and continuously add squares. If the head reaches one end of the tape and attempts to proceed further, it remains blocked until the tape has been stretched:

$$head\ \overset{\triangle}{=}$$

$head[!open\ S_1.$	state #1 (example)
$\quad mv\ out\ head.$	jump out to read flag
$\qquad if\ tt\ (f\!f[]\ |\ mv\ in\ head.\ in\ sq.\ S_2[]),$	head right, state #2

$$if\ \mathit{ff}\ (tt[]\ |\ mv\ in\ head.\ out\ sq.\ S_3[])\ | \qquad\qquad \text{head left, state \#3}$$
$$...\ | \qquad\qquad\qquad\qquad\qquad\qquad\qquad\qquad\qquad\qquad \text{more state transitions}$$
$$S_1[]] \qquad\qquad\qquad\qquad\qquad\qquad\qquad\qquad\qquad\qquad\quad \text{initial state}$$

$stretchRht\ \triangleq$ stretch tape right
    $(\nu r)\ r[!open\ it.\ mv\ out\ r.\ (sq^{\lrcorner\lceil}[\mathit{ff}]]\ |\ mv\ in\ r.\ in\ sq.\ it[])\ |\ it[]]$

$stretchLft\ \triangleq$ stretch tape left
    $!open\ it.\ mv\ in\ end.$
        $(mv\ out\ end.\ end^{\lrcorner\lceil}[sq^{\lrcorner\lceil}[]\ |\mathit{ff}]]\ |$
        $in\ end.\ in\ sq.\ mv\ out\ end.\ open\ end.\ mv\ out\ sq.\ mv\ out\ end.\ it[])$
  $|\ it[]$

$machine\ \triangleq$
    $stretchLft\ |\ end^{\lrcorner\lceil}[\mathit{ff}]]\ |\ head\ |\ stretchRht].$

10.3 Communication

Although the pure mobility calculus is powerful enough to be Turing-complete, it has no communication or variable-binding operators. Such operators seem necessary, for example, to comfortably encode other formalisms such as the λ-calculus and the π-calculus.

Therefore, we now have to choose a communication mechanism to be used to exchange messages between ambients. The choice of a particular mechanism is to some degree orthogonal to the mobility primitives: many such mechanisms can be added to the mobility core. However, we should try not to defeat with communication the restrictions imposed by capabilities. This suggests that a primitive form of communication should be purely local, and that the transmission of nonlocal messages should be restricted by capabilities.

To focus our attention, we pose as a goal the ability to encode the asynchronous π-calculus. For this it is sufficient to introduce a simple asynchronous communication mechanism that works locally within a single ambient.

10.3.1 Communication Primitives

We again start by displaying the syntax of a whole calculus, see Tables 10.6, 10.7, 10.8 and 10.9. The mobility primitives are essentially those of Section 10.2, but the addition of communication variables changes some of the details. More interestingly, we add input $((x).P)$ and output $(\langle M \rangle)$ primitives and we enrich the capabilities to include paths.

We write $P\{x \leftarrow M\}$ for the substitution of the capability M for each free occurrence of the variable x in the process P and similarly for $M\{x \leftarrow M'\}$.

Table 10.6. *Mobility and Communication Primitives*

$P, Q ::=$		processes
	$(\nu n)P$	restriction
	$\mathbf{0}$	inactivity
	$P \mid Q$	composition
	$!P$	replication
	$M[P]$	ambient
	$M.P$	capability action
	$(x).P$	input action
	$\langle M \rangle$	async output action
$M ::=$		capabilities
	x	variable
	n	name
	$in\ M$	can enter into M
	$out\ M$	can exit out of M
	$open\ M$	can open M
	ε	null
	$M.M'$	path

Table 10.7. *Free Names (Revisions and Additions)*

$$fn(M[P]) \triangleq fn(M) \cup fn(P)$$
$$fn((x).P) \triangleq fn(P)$$
$$fn(\langle M \rangle) \triangleq fn(M)$$

$$fn(x) \triangleq \varnothing$$
$$fn(n) \triangleq \{n\}$$
$$fn(\varepsilon) \triangleq \varnothing$$
$$fn(M.M') \triangleq fn(M) \cup fn(M')$$

10.3.2 Explanations

10.3.2.1 Communicable Values

The entities that can be communicated are either names or capabilities. In realistic situations, communication of names should be rather rare, since knowing the name of an ambient gives a lot of control over it. Instead, it should be common to communicate restricted capabilities to allow controlled interactions between ambients.

It now becomes useful to combine multiple capabilities into *paths*, especially when one or more of those capabilities are represented by input variables. To this end we introduce a path-formation operation on capabilities $(M.M')$. For example, $(in\ n.\ in\ m).\ P$ is interpreted as $in\ n.\ in\ m.\ P$.

Note also that, for the purpose of communication, we have added names to the collection of capabilities. A name is a capability to create an ambient of that name.

We distinguish between ν-bound names and input-bound variables. Variables can be instantiated with names or capabilities. In practice, we do not need to distinguish

Table 10.8. *Free Variables*

$$fv((\nu n)P) \triangleq fv(P) \qquad\qquad fv(x) \triangleq \{x\}$$
$$fv(\mathbf{0}) \triangleq \varnothing \qquad\qquad fv(n) \triangleq \varnothing$$
$$fv(P \mid Q) \triangleq fv(P) \cup fv(Q) \qquad\qquad fv(in\ M) \triangleq fv(M)$$
$$fv(!P) \triangleq fv(P) \qquad\qquad fv(out\ M) \triangleq fv(M)$$
$$fv(M[P]) \triangleq fv(M) \cup fv(P) \qquad\qquad fv(open\ M) \triangleq fv(M)$$
$$fv(M.P) \triangleq fv(M) \cup fv(P) \qquad\qquad fv(\varepsilon) \triangleq \varnothing$$
$$fv((x).P) \triangleq fv(P) - \{x\} \qquad\qquad fv(M.M') \triangleq fv(M) \cup fv(M')$$
$$fv(\langle M \rangle) \triangleq fv(M)$$

Table 10.9. *New Syntactic Conventions*

$$(x).P \mid Q \qquad\qquad \text{is read} \qquad\qquad ((x).P) \mid Q$$

between these two sorts lexically, but we often use n, m, p, q for names and w, x, y, z for variables.

10.3.2.2 Ambient I/O

The simplest communication mechanism that we can imagine is local anonymous communication within an ambient (ambient I/O, for short):

$(x).P$	input action
$\langle M \rangle$	async output action.

An output action releases a capability (possibly a name) into the local ether of the surrounding ambient. An input action captures a capability from the local ether and binds it to a variable within a scope. We have the reduction:

$$(x).P \mid \langle M \rangle \ \rightarrow \ P\{x \leftarrow M\}.$$

This local communication mechanism fits well with the ambient intuitions. In particular, long-range communication, like long-range movement, should not happen automatically because messages may have to cross firewalls.

Still, this simple mechanism is sufficient, as we shall see, to emulate communication over named channels, and more generally to provide an encoding of the asynchronous π-calculus.

10.3.2.3 A Syntactic Anomaly

To allow both names and capabilities to be output and input, there is a single syntactic sort that includes both. Hence, a meaningless term of the form $n.P$ can

Table 10.10. *Structural Congruence*

$P \equiv Q \Rightarrow M[P] \equiv M[Q]$	(Struct Amb)
$P \equiv Q \Rightarrow (x).P \equiv (x).Q$	(Struct Input)
$\epsilon.P \equiv P$	(Struct ε)
$(M.M').P \equiv M.M'.P$	(Struct .)

Table 10.11. *Reduction*

$(x).P \mid \langle M \rangle \to P\{x \leftarrow M\}$	(Red Comm)

arise, for instance, from the process $((x).x.P) \mid \langle n \rangle$. This anomaly is caused by the desire to denote movement capabilities by variables, as in $(x).x.P$, and from the desire to denote names by variables, as in $(x).x[P]$. We permit $n.P$ to be formed, syntactically, in order to make substitution always well-defined. A type system distinguishing names from movement capabilities can avoid this anomaly [CG99].

10.3.3 Operational Semantics

For the extended calculus, the structural congruence relation is defined as in Section 10.2.3, with the understanding that P and M now range over larger classes, and with the addition of the equivalences shown in Table 10.10.

We now also identify processes up to the renaming of bound variables:

$$(x).P \ = \ (y).P\{x \leftarrow y\} \quad \text{if } y \notin \mathit{fv}(P).$$

Finally, we have a new reduction rule which is presented in Table 10.11

Now that processes may contain input-bound variables, we need to modify our definition of contextual equivalence as follows: let $P \simeq Q$ if and only if for all n and for all $\mathbf{C}()$ such that $\mathit{fv}(\mathbf{C}(P)) = \mathit{fv}(\mathbf{C}(Q)) = \varnothing$, $\mathbf{C}(P){\Downarrow}n \Leftrightarrow \mathbf{C}(Q){\Downarrow}n$.

10.3.4 Examples

10.3.4.1 Cells

A cell *cell c w* stores a value w at a location c, where a value is a capability. The cell is set to output its current contents destructively, and is set to be 'refreshed' with either the old contents (by *get*) or a new contents (by *set*). Note that *set* is essentially an output operation, but it is a synchronous one: its sequel P runs only after the cell has been set. Parallel *get* and *set* operations do not interfere.

$$\textit{cell } c \ w \ \overset{\Delta}{=} \ c^{\lrcorner\ulcorner}[\langle w \rangle]$$

$$\textit{get } c \ (x). \ P \overset{\Delta}{=} \ \textit{mv in } c. \ (x). \ (\langle x \rangle \mid \textit{mv out } c. \ P)$$

$$\textit{set } c \ \langle w \rangle. \ P \overset{\Delta}{=} \ \textit{mv in } c. \ (x). \ (\langle w \rangle \mid \textit{mv out } c. \ P).$$

It is possible to code an atomic *get-and-set* primitive:

$$get\text{-}and\text{-}set\ c\ (x)\ \langle w \rangle.\ P\ \overset{\triangle}{=}\ mv\ in\ c.\ (x).\ (\langle w \rangle\ |\ mv\ out\ c.\ P).$$

10.3.4.2 Records

A record is a named collection of cells. Since each cell has its own name, those names can be used as field labels:

$$record\ r(l_1 = v_1...l_n = v_n)\ \overset{\triangle}{=}\ r^{\rfloor\lceil}[cell\ l_1 v_1\ |\ ...\ |\ cell\ l_n v_n]$$
$$getr\ r\ l\ (x).\ P\ \overset{\triangle}{=}\ mv\ in\ r.\ get\ l\ (x).\ mv\ out\ r.\ P$$
$$setr\ r\ l\ \langle v \rangle\ P\ \overset{\triangle}{=}\ mv\ in\ r.\ set\ l\ \langle v \rangle.\ mv\ out\ r.\ P.$$

A record can contain the name of another record in one of its fields; therefore, sharing and cycles are possible.

10.3.4.3 Routable Packets

We define *packet pkt* as an empty packet of name *pkt* that can be routed repeatedly to various destinations. We also define *route pkt with P to M* as the act of placing *P* inside the packet *pkt* and sending the packet to *M*; this is to be used in parallel with *packet pkt*. Note that *M* can be a compound capability, representing a path to follow. Finally, *forward pkt to M* is an abbreviation that forwards any packet named *pkt* that passes by to *M*:

$$packet\ pkt\ \overset{\triangle}{=}\ pkt[!(x).\ x\ |\ !open\ route]$$
$$route\ pkt\ with\ P\ to\ M\ \overset{\triangle}{=}\ route[in\ pkt.\ \langle M \rangle\ |\ P]$$
$$forward\ pkt\ to\ M\ \overset{\triangle}{=}\ route\ pkt\ with\ \mathbf{0}\ to\ M$$

Here we assume that *P* does not interfere with routing.

10.3.4.4 Remote I/O

Our basic communication primitives operate only within a given ambient. We now show examples of communication between ambients. In addition, in Section 10.3.5 we treat the specific case of channel-based communication across ambients.

It is not realistic to assume direct long-range communication. Communication, like movement, is subject to access restrictions due to the existence of administrative domains. Therefore, it is convenient to model long-range communication as the movement of 'messenger' agents that must cross administrative boundaries. Assume, for simplicity, that the location *M* allows I/O by providing *!open io*. By M^{-1} we indicate a given return path from *M*:

$$@M\langle a \rangle\ \overset{\triangle}{=}\ io[M.\ \langle a \rangle]\qquad\qquad\qquad\text{remote output at } M$$
$$@M(x)M^{-1}.\ P\ \overset{\triangle}{=}$$
$$(\nu n)\ (io[M.\ (x).\ n[M^{-1}.\ P]]\ |\ open\ n)\qquad\text{remote input at } M.$$

To avoid transmitting P all the way there and back, we can write input as:

$$@M(x)M^{-1}.\ P \triangleq (\nu n)\ (io[M.\ (x).\ n[M^{-1}.\ \langle x \rangle]]\ |\ open\ n)\ |\ (x).\ P.$$

To emulate Remote Procedure Call we write (assuming that *res* contains the result):

$$@M\ arg\langle a \rangle\ res(x)\ M^{-1}.\ P \triangleq$$
$$(\nu n)\ (io[M.\ (\langle a \rangle\ |\ open\ res.\ (x).\ n[M^{-1}.\ \langle x \rangle])]\ |\ open\ n)\ |\ (x).\ P.$$

This is essentially an implementation of a synchronous communication (RPC) by two asynchronous communications ($\langle a \rangle$ and $\langle x \rangle$).

10.3.5 Encoding the π-Calculus

One of our benchmarks of expressiveness is the ability to encode the asynchronous π-calculus. This encoding is moderately easy, given the I/O primitives. We first discuss how to represent named channels: this is the key idea for the full translation.

A channel is simply represented by an ambient: the name of the channel is the name of the ambient. This is very similar in spirit to the join-calculus [FG96], where channels are rooted at a location. Communication on a channel is represented by local communication inside an ambient. The basic technique is a variation on objective moves. A conventional name, *io*, is used to transport input and output requests into the channel. The channel opens all such requests and lets them interact:

$buf\ n$	$\triangleq$	$n[!open\ io]$	a channel buffer
$(ch\ n)P$	$\triangleq$	$(\nu n)\ (buf\ n\ |\ P)$	a new channel
$n(x).P$	$\triangleq$	$(\nu p)\ (io[in\ n.\ (x).\ p[out\ n.\ P]]\ |\ open\ p)$	channel input
$n\langle M \rangle$	$\triangleq$	$io[in\ n.\ \langle M \rangle]$	async channel output.

These definitions satisfy the expected reduction $n(x).P\ |\ n\langle M \rangle\ \to^*\ P\{x \leftarrow M\}$ in the presence of a channel buffer *buf n*:

$$buf\ n\ |\ n(x).\ P\ |\ n\langle M \rangle$$
$$\equiv (\nu p)\ (n[!open\ io]\ |\ io[in\ n.\ (x).\ p[out\ n.\ P]]\ |\ open\ p\ |\ io[in\ n.\ \langle M \rangle])$$
$$\to^* (\nu p)\ (n[!open\ io\ |\ io[(x).\ p[out\ n.\ P]]\ |\ io[\langle M \rangle]]\ |\ open\ p)$$
$$\to^* (\nu p)\ (n[!open\ io\ |\ (x).\ p[out\ n.\ P]\ |\ \langle M \rangle]\ |\ open\ p)$$
$$\to^* (\nu p)\ (n[!open\ io\ |\ p[out\ n.\ P\{x \leftarrow M\}]]\ |\ open\ p)$$
$$\to^* (\nu p)\ (n[!open\ io]\ |\ p[P\{x \leftarrow M\}]\ |\ open\ p)$$
$$\to^* (\nu p)\ (n[!open\ io]\ |\ P\ \{x \leftarrow M\})$$
$$\equiv buf\ n\ |\ P\ \{x \leftarrow M\}.$$

We can fairly conveniently use the above definitions of channels to embed communication on named channels within the ambient calculus (provided that the name *io* is not used for other purposes). Communication on these named channels, though, works only within a single ambient. In other words, from our point of view, a π-calculus process always inhabits a single ambient. Therefore, the notion of mobility

Table 10.12. *The Asynchronous π-Calculus*

$P, Q ::=$	processes
$(\nu n)P$	restriction
$P \mid Q$	composition
$!P$	replication
$M(x).P$	input action
$M\langle M'\rangle$	async output action
$M ::=$	expressions
x	variable
n	name

Table 10.13. *Free Names and Free Variables*

$$fn((\nu n)P) \triangleq fn(P) - \{n\} \qquad\qquad fv((\nu n)P) \triangleq fv(P)$$
$$fn(P \mid Q) \triangleq fn(P) \cup fn(Q) \qquad\qquad fv(P \mid Q) \triangleq fv(P) \cup fv(Q)$$
$$fn(!P) \triangleq fn(P) \qquad\qquad\qquad\qquad fv(!P) \triangleq fv(P)$$
$$fn(M(x).P) \triangleq fn(M) \cup fn(P) \qquad fv(M(x).P) \triangleq fv(M) \cup (fv(P) - \{x\})$$
$$fn(M\langle M'\rangle) \triangleq fn(M) \cup fn(M') \qquad fv(M\langle M'\rangle) \triangleq fv(M) \cup fv(M')$$
$$fn(x) \triangleq \varnothing \qquad\qquad\qquad\qquad\quad fv(x) \triangleq \{x\}$$
$$fn(n) \triangleq \{n\} \qquad\qquad\qquad\qquad\quad fv(n) \triangleq \varnothing$$

in the π-calculus (communication of names over named channels) is different from our notion of mobility.

To make the idea of this translation precise, we fix a formalization of the asynchronous π-calculus given by Tables 10.12, 10.13, 10.14 and 10.15. We consider a formulation where names n bound by restriction are distinct from variables x bound by an input prefix. We have separate functions fn and fv for free names and free variables, respectively.

The encoding of the asynchronous π-calculus into the ambient calculus is given by the translation in Table 10.16. We translate each top-level process in the context of a set of names S that, in particular, can be taken to be the set of free names of the process.

This encoding includes the choice-free synchronous π-calculus, since it can itself be encoded within the asynchronous π-calculus [Bou92, HT91]. Moreover, since the λ-calculus can be encoded in the asynchronous π-calculus [Bou92], we can indirectly encode the λ-calculus.

The encoding respects the semantics of the asynchronous π-calculus, in the sense that a reduction step in the asynchronous π-calculus can be emulated by a number of reduction steps and equivalences in the ambient calculus, as shown by the next proposition. It would be of interest to study questions of whether the translation

Table 10.14. *Structural Congruence*

$P \equiv P$	(Struct Refl)
$P \equiv Q \Rightarrow Q \equiv P$	(Struct Symm)
$P \equiv Q, Q \equiv R \Rightarrow P \equiv R$	(Struct Trans)
$P \equiv Q \Rightarrow (\nu n)P \equiv (\nu n)Q$	(Struct Res)
$P \equiv Q \Rightarrow P \mid R \equiv Q \mid R$	(Struct Par)
$P \equiv Q \Rightarrow !P \equiv !Q$	(Struct Repl)
$P \equiv Q \Rightarrow M(x).P \equiv M(x).Q$	(Struct Input)
$P \mid Q \equiv Q \mid P$	(Struct Par Comm)
$(P \mid Q) \mid R \equiv P \mid (Q \mid R)$	(Struct Par Assoc)
$!P \equiv P \mid !P$	(Struct Repl Par)
$(\nu n)(\nu m)P \equiv (\nu m)(\nu n)P$	(Struct Res Res)
$(\nu n)(P \mid Q) \equiv P \mid (\nu n)Q \;$ if $n \notin fn(P)$	(Struct Res Par)
$(\nu n)P \equiv P \;$ if $n \notin fn(P)$	(Struct Res *fn*)

Table 10.15. *Reduction*

$n\langle m \rangle \mid n(x).P \rightarrow P\{x \leftarrow M\}$	(Red Comm)
$P \rightarrow Q \Rightarrow (\nu n)P \rightarrow (\nu n)Q$	(Red Res)
$P \rightarrow Q \Rightarrow P \mid R \rightarrow Q \mid R$	(Red Par)
$P' \equiv P, \; P \rightarrow Q, \; Q \equiv Q' \Rightarrow P' \rightarrow Q'$	(Red $\equiv$)

preserves or reflects behavioural equivalences, but this would require more semantic machinery than we have developed in this chapter.

We assume that *io* is not a name of the π-calculus.

Lemma 1 *(Substitution)*
$\ll P \gg \{x \leftarrow m\} \; = \; \ll P\{x \leftarrow m\} \gg$.

Proposition 1
(i) If $P \equiv P'$ holds in π and S is a set of names, then $\ll P \gg_S \simeq \ll P' \gg_S$.
(ii) If $P \rightarrow P'$ holds in π and $S \supseteq fn(P)$, then $\ll P \gg_S \simeq \rightarrow^* \simeq \ll P' \gg_S$.

Proof Throughout this proof, we use basic properties of $\simeq$, such as the fact that it is an equivalence, a congruence and that it includes $\equiv$ ([GC99], Proposition 2). The places where $\simeq$ is used critically are the cases for (Struct Res *fn*) and (Red $\equiv$).

(i) We show by induction on the length of the derivation of $P \equiv P'$ that $\ll P \gg \simeq \ll P' \gg$. Then, $\ll P \gg_S \simeq \ll P' \gg_S$ (that is, $\ll S \gg \mid \ll P \gg \simeq \ll S \gg \mid \ll P' \gg$) follows by congruence of $\simeq$.

Table 10.16. *Encoding of the Asynchronous π-Calculus*

$$\ll P \gg_S \triangleq \ll S \gg | \ll P \gg \qquad \qquad \text{where } S \text{ is a set of names}$$
$$\ll \{n_1, ..., n_k\} \gg \triangleq n_1[!open\ io]\ |\ ...\ |\ n_k[!open\ io]$$
$$\ll (\nu n)P \gg \triangleq (\nu n)(n[!open\ io]\ |\ll P \gg)$$
$$\ll P\ |\ Q \gg \triangleq \ll P \gg | \ll Q \gg$$
$$\ll !P \gg \triangleq !\ll P \gg$$
$$\ll M(x).P \gg \triangleq (\nu p)\ (io[in\ M.\ (x).\ p[out\ M.\ \ll P \gg]]\ |\ open\ p)$$
$$\ll M\langle M'\rangle \gg \triangleq io[in\ M.\ \langle M'\rangle]$$

(Struct Refl), **(Struct Symm)**, **(Struct Trans)**, **(Struct Par)**, **(Struct Repl)**, **(Struct Par Comm)**, **(Struct Par Assoc)**, **(Struct Repl Par)**. Directly from the definitions and induction hypotheses.

(Struct Res) $Q \equiv Q' \Rightarrow (\nu n)Q \equiv (\nu n)Q'$.
By the induction hypothesis, $\ll Q \gg \simeq \ll Q' \gg$. Since $\simeq$ is a congruence, we obtain that $(\nu n)(n[!open\ io]\ |\ll Q \gg) \simeq (\nu n)(n[!open\ io]\ |\ll Q' \gg)$. That is, $\ll (\nu n)Q \gg \simeq \ll (\nu n)Q' \gg$.

(Struct Res Res) $(\nu n)(\nu m)Q \equiv (\nu m)(\nu n)Q$.
$\ll (\nu n)(\nu m)Q \gg = (\nu n)(n[!open\ io]\ |\ (\nu m)(m[!open\ io]\ |\ll Q \gg)) \equiv (\nu m)(m[!open\ io]\ |\ (\nu n)(n[!open\ io]\ |\ll Q \gg)) = \ll (\nu m)(\nu n)Q \gg$.

(Struct Input) $Q \equiv Q' \Rightarrow M(x).Q \equiv M(x).Q'$.
By the induction hypothesis, $\ll Q \gg \simeq \ll Q' \gg$. By the congruence property of $\simeq$, we have $(\nu p)(io[in\ M.\ (x).\ p[out\ M.\ \ll Q \gg]]\ |\ open\ p) \simeq (\nu p)(io[in\ M.\ (x).\ p\ [out\ M.\ \ll Q' \gg]]\ |\ open\ p)$. That is, $\ll M(x).Q \gg \simeq \ll M(x).Q' \gg$.

(Struct Res Par) $(\nu n)(Q'\ |\ Q'') \equiv Q'\ |\ (\nu n)Q''$ if $n \notin fn(Q')$.
Note that either $fn(\ll Q' \gg) = fn(Q')$ or $fn(\ll Q' \gg) = fn(Q') \cup \{io\}$, and that $n \neq io$ by global convention. Therefore, $n \notin fn(Q')$ implies that $n \notin fn(\ll Q' \gg)$. Then, $\ll (\nu n)(Q'\ |\ Q'') \gg = (\nu n)(n[!open\ io]\ |\ (\ll Q' \gg |\ \ll Q' \gg)) \equiv \ll Q' \gg |\ (\nu n)(n[!open\ io]\ |\ll Q'' \gg) = \ll Q'\ |\ (\nu n)Q'' \gg$.

(Struct Res fn) $(\nu n)Q \equiv Q$ if $n \notin fn(Q)$.
As in the previous case, $n \notin fn(\ll Q \gg)$. Then, $\ll (\nu n)Q \gg = (\nu n)(n[!open\ io]\ |\ \ll Q \gg) \equiv \ll Q \gg |\ (\nu n)n[!open\ io]$. By the perfect firewall equation [GC99], we have that $(\nu n)n[!open\ io] \simeq \mathbf{0}$. Hence, it follows that $\ll (\nu n)Q \gg \simeq \ll Q \gg$.

(ii) By induction on the length of the derivation of $P \rightarrow P'$.

(Red Comm) $n\langle m\rangle\ |\ n(x).Q \rightarrow Q\{x \leftarrow m\}$.
We need to show that if $S \supseteq fn(n\langle m\ \rangle\ |\ n(x).Q)$, then $\ll n\langle m\rangle\ |\ n(x).Q \gg_S$

$\simeq \rightarrow^* \simeq\ \ll Q\{x \leftarrow m\} \gg_S$. We have $\ll n\langle m\rangle \mid n(x).Q \gg_S\ =\ \ll S \gg \mid io[in\ n.\ \langle m\rangle] \mid (\nu p)\ (io[in\ n.\ (x).\ p[out\ n.\ \ll Q \gg]] \mid open\ p)$.

By assumption, S includes n, and therefore $\ll S \gg$ includes $n[!open\ io]$. Then, by the computation shown at the beginning of this section and by the reflexivity of $\simeq$, we obtain $\ll n\langle m\rangle \mid n(x).Q \gg_S\ \simeq \rightarrow^* \simeq\ \ll S \gg \mid \ll Q \gg \{x \leftarrow m\}$. By the substitution lemma above, the right-hand side is equal to $\ll S \gg \mid \ll Q\{x \leftarrow m\} \gg$, which is equal to $\ll Q\{x \leftarrow m\} \gg_S$.

(Red Res) $Q \rightarrow Q' \Rightarrow (\nu n)Q \rightarrow (\nu n)Q'$.

We need to show that if $S \supseteq fn((\nu n)Q)$, then it follows that $\ll (\nu n)Q \gg_S\ \simeq \rightarrow^* \simeq\ \ll (\nu n)Q' \gg_S$.

If $S \supseteq fn((\nu n)Q)$, then $S \cup \{n\} \supseteq fn(Q)$. Since we identify terms up to the renaming of bound variables, we can assume that $n \notin S$.

By the induction hypothesis, $\ll Q \gg_{S \cup \{n\}}\ \simeq \rightarrow^* \simeq\ \ll Q' \gg_{S \cup \{n\}}$.

By repeated uses of (Red Res) and the congruence of $\simeq$, we derive that $(\nu n)\ \ll Q \gg_{S \cup \{n\}}\ \simeq \rightarrow^* \simeq\ (\nu n)\ \ll Q' \gg_{S \cup \{n\}}$. Since $(\nu n)\ \ll Q \gg_{S \cup \{n\}}\ =$ $(\nu n)(\ll S \cup \{n\} \gg \mid \ll Q \gg)\ \equiv\ (\nu n)(n[!open\ io] \mid \ll S \gg \mid \ll Q \gg)\ \equiv$ $\ll S \gg \mid \ll (\nu n)Q \gg\ =\ \ll (\nu n)Q \gg_S$, and similarly $(\nu n)\ \ll Q' \gg_{S \cup \{n\}}\ \equiv$ $\ll (\nu n)Q' \gg_S$, we obtain that $\ll (\nu n)Q \gg_S\ \simeq \rightarrow^* \simeq\ \ll (\nu n)Q' \gg_S$.

(Red Par) $Q \rightarrow Q' \Rightarrow Q \mid R \rightarrow Q' \mid R$.

By the induction hypothesis, $\ll Q \gg_S\ \simeq \rightarrow^* \simeq\ \ll Q' \gg_S$. By repeated uses of (Red Par) and congruence of $\simeq$, we have that $\ll Q \gg_S \mid \ll R \gg\ \simeq \rightarrow^* \simeq$ $\ll Q' \gg_S \mid \ll R \gg$, that is, $\ll Q \mid R \gg_S\ \simeq \rightarrow^* \simeq\ \ll Q' \mid R \gg_S$.

(Red $\equiv$) $Q' \equiv Q,\ Q \rightarrow R,\ R \equiv R' \Rightarrow Q' \rightarrow R'$.

By the induction hypothesis and *(i)*: $\ll Q' \gg_S\ \simeq\ \ll Q \gg_S$, $\ll Q \gg_S$ $\simeq \rightarrow^* \simeq\ \ll R \gg_S,\ \ll R \gg_S\ \simeq\ \ll R' \gg_S$. By transitivity of $\simeq$ we have $\ll Q' \gg_S\ \simeq \rightarrow^* \simeq\ \ll R' \gg_S$. $\qquad\square$

As a corollary, we obtain that $P \rightarrow P'$ implies $\ll P \gg_{fn(P)}\ \simeq \rightarrow^* \simeq\ \ll P' \gg_{fn(P)}$.

10.4 Conclusions

We have introduced the informal notion of mobile ambients, and we have discussed how this notion captures the structure of complex networks and the behaviour of mobile computation.

We have then investigated an ambient calculus that formalizes this notion simply and powerfully. Our calculus is no more complex than common process calculi, but it supports reasoning about mobility and, at least to some degree, security.

On this foundation, we can now envision new programming methodologies, programming libraries and programming languages for global computation.

Acknowledgements

Thanks to C´edric Fournet, Paul McJones and Jan Vitek for comments on early drafts. Stuart Wray suggested an improved definition of external choice.

Gordon held a Royal Society University Research Fellowship for most of the time that we worked on this chapter.

Bibliography

[AG97]   M. Abadi and A. D. Gordon. A calculus for cryptographic protocols: the spi calculus. In *Proceedings of the Fourth ACM Conference on Computer and Communications Security*, pages 36–47. ACM Press, April 1997.

[Ama97]   R. M. Amadio. An asynchronous model of locality, failure, and process mobility. In *Proc. COORDINATION 97*, number 1282 in Lecture Notes in Computer Science. Springer-Verlag, 1997.

[BB92]   G. Berry and G. Boudol. The chemical abstract machine. *Theoretical Computer Science*, 96(1):217–248, 1992.

[Bou92]   G. Boudol. Asynchrony and the π-calculus. Technical Report 1702, INRIA, Sophia-Antipolis, May 1992.

[Car95]   L. Cardelli. A language with distributed scope. *Computing Systems*, 8(1):27–59, 1995.

[CG89]   N. Carriero and D. Gelernter. Linda in context. *Communications of the ACM*, 32(4):444–458, 1989.

[CG99]   L. Cardelli and A. D. Gordon. Types for mobile ambients. In *26th Annual ACM Symposium on Principles of Programming Languages*, pages 79–92. ACM, 1999.

[CGZ95]   N. Carriero, D. Gelernter, and L. Zuck. Bauhaus Linda. In P. Ciancarini, O. Nierstrasz, and A. Yonezawa, editors, *Object-Based Models and Languages for Concurrent Systems, Volume 924 of Lecture Notes in Computer Science*, pages 66–76. Springer-Verlag, 1995.

[DNFP97]   R. De. Nicola, G.-L. Ferrari, and R. Pugliese. Locality based Linda: programming with explicit localities. In *TAPSOFT'97, Volume 1214 of Lecture Notes in Computer Science*, pages 712–726. Springer-Verlag, 1997.

[FG96]   C. Fournet and G. Gonthier. The reflexive cham and the join-calculus. In *23rd Annual ACM Symposium on Principles of Programming Languages*, pages 372–385. ACM, 1996.

[FGL+96]   C. Fournet, G. Gonthier, J.-J. L´evy L. Maranget, and D. Rémy. A calculus of mobile agents. In *7th International Conference on Concurrency Theory (CONCUR'96), Volume 1119 of Lecture Notes in Computer Science*, pages 406–421. Springer-Verlag, 1996.

[GC99]   A. D. Gordon and L. Cardelli. Equational properties of mobile ambients. In *FOSSACS'99, Volume 1578 of Lecture Notes in Computer Science*, pages 212–226. Springer-Verlag, 1999.

[GJS96]   J. Gosling, B. Joy, and G. Steele. *The Java language specification*. Addison-Wesley, 1996.

[HT91]   K. Honda and M. Tokoro. An object calculus for asynchronous communication. In *Proceedings of ECOOP'91, Volume 521 of Lecture Notes in Computer Science*, pages 133–147. Springer-Verlag, July 1991.

[Mil80]   R. Milner. *A calculus of communicating systems*, volume 92 of *Lecture Notes in Computer Science*. Springer-Verlag, 1980.

[Mil92]   R. Milner. Functions as processes. *Journal of Mathematical Structures in Computer Science*, 2(2):119–141, 1992.

[Mor68]   J. H. Morris. *Lambda-Calculus Models of Programming Languages*. PhD thesis, MIT, December 1968.

[MPW92]   R. Milner, J. Parrow, and D. Walker. A calculus of mobile processes, Parts 1 and 2. *Information and Computation*, 100(1):1–77, 1992.

[RH98]   J. Riely and M. Hennessy. A typed language for distributed mobile processes. In *25th Annual ACM Symposium on Principles of Programming Languages*, pages 378–390. ACM, 1998.

[Sew98]   P. Sewell. Global/local subtyping and capability inference for a distributed π-calculus. In *Proceedings of ICALP'98, Volume 1443 of Lecture Notes in Computer Science*, pages 695–706. Springer-Verlag, July 1998.

[Whi96]   J. E. White. Mobile agents. In J. Bradshaw, editor, *Software Agents*. AAAI Press / The MIT Press, 1996.

Part Four

Subtyping

11

Subtyping in Distributed Systems

Jadwiga Indulska

The University of Queensland, Australia

11.1 Introduction

Distributed computing system models and their existing realisations (CORBA [Gro98b], DCE [SHM94], TINA [Con96], DCOM [Ses97]) (see also Chapter 1) are mostly object-oriented or object-based; therefore, objects in these systems are encapsulated and visible only through their interfaces. The models differ, however, in inconsistencies of the system's overall object model or schema, in the underlying interface type models or languages used to describe object interfaces, and in the expressiveness of the type models. The major areas of discrepancy include [BBB+95, BCI+97, MH93]:

- differences in the notion of an object, for example, visibility or nonvisibility of the object state, attributes, separate model constructs representing object relationships, generic functions and number of interfaces allowed (one or many);
- differences in type systems, including differences in the basic types and type constructors, and in the meanings of inheritance and subtyping relationships;
- differences in modes of interaction between objects (e.g., synchronous or asynchronous communication); and
- differences in the granularity of objects supported by the type model.

Inclusion polymorphism, also known as type compatibility or subtyping, relates types for which instances can be substituted one by another. In this chapter we look more closely into the differences in defining subtyping relationships in various distributed computing systems because this relationship is one of the fundamental properties of any object-oriented or object-based system. There are not only differences in the definition of subtyping relationships in existing approaches, but also the scope of its application differs depending on the overall goal of the system. If a distributed system is built as a closed system (i.e., DCE, DCOM), the compatibility relationship relates objects created based on a common type model. Current trends in distributed computing are, however, toward open systems that extend cooperation of applications beyond the boundary of one system, that is, beyond one homogeneous platform for distributed computing or one distributed operating system. This open cooperation has to deal with the heterogeneity and autonomy of systems present in the environment, including the heterogeneity of their type systems. The RM-ODP framework and distributed systems that are being built based on this framework belong to the latter category (see Chapter 2).

An inherent issue in such open systems is enabling the interoperation of objects whose interfaces have been defined in different type models. Therefore they require a means for representing, storing, retrieving and translating types, and for expressing and evaluating relationships between types in a heterogeneous distributed computing environment, in particular subtyping relationships. If we assume, for simplicity, that the only communication paradigm in these distributed systems is client-server, the requirements for interoperation between objects will translate into:

- The discovery of object types to allow clients to discover available services (the role played in distributed systems by both a type repository, which stores type descriptions, and a trading object, which matches the specification of required services with services available in the system).
- Meaningful and type-safe interactions between clients and discovered services (type safe run-time operations on a client-server binding).
- System evolution, which allows the seamless introduction of new objects with new types, often as replacements for older versions. A variety of interface compatibility problems can arise when these new objects need to interwork with existing objects.
- The discovery and reuse of existing services instead of building new services.

It is the role of the subtyping relationship to support meeting the above requirements because this relationship can be used in:

- dynamic *type matching*, which searches for a set of types that satisfy a type compatibility relationship with a given type, for example, to facilitate discovery, trading and reuse of resources;
- dynamic *type checking*, which compares two types to determine whether they satisfy the compatibility relationship, for example, one that ensures type-safe interaction between dynamically bound objects.

In this chapter the issue of subtyping is discussed, including notions of syntactical (signature-based) subtyping, behavioural subtyping and approaches to subtyping in various existing distributed systems. Section 11.2 discusses the differences between subtyping and inheritance. In Section 11.3, Interface Definition Languages are introduced and various approaches to subtyping are considered. Then Section 11.4 discusses the spectrum of approaches to subtyping in various existing distributed computing frameworks and platforms, including RM-ODP, DCE, CORBA, TINA and DCOM. Section 11.5 reviews approaches to behavioural subtyping.

11.2 Why Subtyping and Inheritance?

Subtyping and inheritance are two fundamental object/type relationships in object-oriented systems and are sometimes confused in spite of their apparent differences.

One of the factors for this confusion is that they both support reuse; however, the subject of reuse differs. The inheritance relationship is commonly used in object-oriented programming, where new classes may be built as extensions to an inherited superclass. The inheritance relationship is therefore used in object implementation and supports code reuse. If the client-server paradigm is used as an example, inheritance supports both code reuse and the incremental development of a server.

Distributed computing systems encapsulate object implementations and make the object visible only through interfaces; therefore the inheritance of code is no longer visible. The subtyping relationship relates interface types. In general, for data types, subtyping relationships are defined by constraining the set of elements, that is, a subset is a subtype. For example, a set of natural numbers ($\mathbb{N}$) is a subtype of integers ($\mathbb{Z}$), a set of *red cars* that is a subset of *cars* is a subtype of type *cars* (a red car behaves like a car). In distributed computing, as objects are visible through interfaces, the subtyping relationship is in general defined by extending the interface (the subtype should have the same operations as the supertype and possibly more). The inheritance relationship can be used in defining the subtyping of interfaces: one interface may inherit some operations from another interface. If, for instance, interface type T_1 represents a stack type, it will comprise two operations T_1 (*push*, *pop*). Let us assume that type T_2 is created by inheriting the operations *push* and *pop*, and by adding a new operation *height* that returns the length of the stack. Type T_2 is a subtype of T_1 (denoted $T_2 \preceq T_1$) as any object of type T_1 can be substituted by an object of type T_2 and a client requesting a service of type T_1 will not notice any difference in service behaviour when invoking the *push* and *pop* operations. It has to be noted, however, that the inheritance relationship applied in this example differs from the inheritance used for code reuse. This inheritance relationship inherits operation signatures from the interface definition but does not imply any relationship between the implementations of the *push* and *pop* operations in T_1 and T_2.

In general, inheritance and subtyping are independent relationships. If two interface types are in a subtype relationship, no conclusion can be made on the inheritance relationship between the objects' implementations. In some of such cases, the inheritance relationship relates signatures of the interface types, but this also depends on the definition of the subtyping relationship, as discussed in the next section. In general, inheritance relationships support code reuse whereas subtyping relationships support object discovery and reuse.

11.3 Basic Principles

Distributed computing systems allow object implementations in various programming languages. Due to this possible heterogeneity of the system, the problem of discovery of services and binding between services becomes very challenging because object interfaces can be specified in various type systems. For this reason, current approaches to interface definition in distributed systems are mainly based on the use of a single Interface Definition Language (IDL). An IDL provides a level of common agreement about the types of system interfaces. Each interface has to be described in IDL, and discovery of services and binding to services is carried out based on this description. As existing distributed systems define their own IDLs (e.g., CORBA IDL, DCE IDL) the cooperation between different distributed computing systems is hindered because the IDL type systems differ. An example CORBA IDL definition of a stack interface type is shown in Figure 11.1. There exist some mappings between IDLs (e.g., CORBA/COM mapping) but very often these mappings incur losses as the differences in type systems cannot be reconciled. The differences in type systems include differences in data types, operation definitions, object reference definitions and also definition of relationships, particularly the subtyping relationship. Therefore a mapping between the subtyping relationships is necessary if cooperation between different distributed computing platforms is required.

```
module Stack {

        exception StackFull{ };
        exception StackEmpty{ };

        interface StackIF {

                void push(in any item) raises(StackFull);

                any pop() raises(StackEmpty);

        };
};
```

Fig. 11.1. An example interface type specification in CORBA IDL.

As already indicated, subtyping relationships can support resource (object) discovery and compatibility (substitutability) of objects. We will first analyse the meaning of the terms involved (type matching, subtyping, compatibility and substitutability) before describing various classes of subtyping relationship that may exist in open distributed systems. Type matching, subtyping, compatibility and substitutability are concepts that are related but not identical. Their meaning in distributed systems can be described in the following way:

Type matching: the act of checking whether two or more types are in a compatibility relationship.

Substitutability: the property that an object of one type may be substituted for an object of another type without displaying any observable differences in behaviour from the original object. Commonly, these two objects are referred to as the subtype and supertype, respectively, as in the principle of substitutability [WZ88]:

An instance of a subtype can always be used in any context in which an instance of a supertype is expected.

This description shows that substitutability is a relationship between instances (objects), while subtyping is a relationship between types.

Subtyping: a relationship between types that is usually defined with reference to the principle of substitutability stated above. As noted previously, there are many different definitions of subtyping relationships, due to differences in interpretation of the principle of substitutability. Subtyping relationships are always reflexive, antisymmetric and transitive.

Compatibility: a generic term for relationships that apply the principle of substitutability. This includes subtyping relationships that result in substitutability of instances, as well as other relationships (e.g., user-defined compatibility).

Many existing models and systems define their own compatibility relationship in terms of interface subtyping, and the differences primarily relate to the level of abstraction used to define subtyping. At the simplest level is a subtyping relationship that relates types by decree. The ANSAware [ANS92] distributed computing platform applied this kind of subtyping relationship. In this system, two interface types are in a subtyping relationship if the creator/owner of the interfaces decrees that there is a subtyping relationship between them. The system uses this information for matching service types with user requests. A different case of subtyping by decree is name- and/or version-based subtyping. In this kind of subtyping, one type is a subtype of another if their 'identifiers' are subtypes. An example is DCE subtyping, where one interface is a subtype of another if they have the same interface name, but the subtype has a later version number [SHM94, RK92]. Syntactical, behavioural and semantic aspects of the interfaces are not considered, because these subtyping relationships assume that all the necessary semantic information for subtyping is captured in the interface name and/or version. Type matching using name/version-based subtyping can be trivially automated.

The next important kind of subtyping relationships are those based on interface syntax only. In these relationships, one type is a subtype of another if one interface signature can be substituted for the other without generating run-time *type errors* (operation invocations are type-safe). This is currently the most common form of subtyping and is used by RM-ODP [ISO95], CORBA [Gro98b], TINA [Con96] and many other distributed computing systems.

There are, however, some subtle differences within this particular kind of subtyping relationship. The simplest syntactical subtyping relationship is subtyping by interface extension (signature-based subtyping). A subtype interface is created by inheriting some operation signatures from supertype interfaces (single or multiple inheritance). The operations that are common for the subtype and supertype have equivalent signatures (the same name of the operation and the same names and types of parameters and results). An example of this kind of subtyping relationship is the previously described stack interface type T_1 (*push, pop*) and its subtype T_2 (*push, pop, height*).

An extension to this kind of subtyping relationship is a relationship that in addition to interface extension also allows the subtyping of operation parameters and operation results for operations common for the super- and subtypes.

> *If* operations $o_i(p_1, r_1) \in Ops(T_1)$, $o_j(p_2, r_2) \in Ops(T_2)$ have one
> argument type and one result type, and:
> o_i and o_j are corresponding operations in T_1 and T_2, and
> p_1, p_2, r_1, r_2 are types of arguments and results, respectively, and
> $p_1 \preceq p_2$ and $r_2 \preceq r_1$,
> *then* $T_2 \preceq T_1$

This subtyping rule is known as the traditional object-oriented notion of contravariance of method arguments and covariance of results [PS92]. The rule is conceptually similar to the weakening of preconditions and the strengthening of postconditions in state-based modelling approaches. This rule guarantees type safety if T_1 is substituted by T_2. To illustrate the rule, let us assume that the two previously mentioned operations o_i and o_j have the following types of arguments and results: $o_i(\mathbb{N}, \mathbb{Z})$ and $o_j(\mathbb{Z}, \mathbb{N})$. If a user requests operation o_i with an argument of type $\mathbb{N}$ and instead operation o_j is invoked, which requires the argument to be of type $\mathbb{Z}$, it will be a type-safe procedure invocation. The user should not detect any type error (nothing bad should happen) as any natural number is also of type integer. On the other hand, to ensure no surprises, the result type $\mathbb{N}$ for procedure o_j is a subtype of the result type for o_i. The reason is that if a user invokes procedure o_i and expects results of type $\mathbb{Z}$, the results for o_j can be of type $\mathbb{N}$ and no run-time type error will be incurred if o_i is replaced by o_j.

In addition, some of these subtyping relationships define the subtyping of parameters identified by parameter name, while others use the parameter position. A side-effect is that when subtyping uses parameter names to identify parameters, the ordering of parameters in the subtype and supertype are irrelevant, which is not the case when parameter position is used. It has to be noted that type matching using signature-based subtyping can be automated. It may, however, require the construction and comparison of type graphs.

Subtyping relationships based on syntax imply type safety (no run-time type errors during operation invocation) but do not imply that the subtype operation will have the same behaviour as its supertype. A simple example could be a stack interface and a queue interface, both of which can have *put* (*push*) and *get* (*pop*) operations and the stack interface has in addition the *height* operation. If the signature-based subtyping relationship is considered, the stack type will be a subtype (by interface extension) of the queue type. This relationship cannot recognize that the semantics of these operations differ.

The next class of subtyping relationships is based on both syntax and visible object behaviour (e.g., ordering of operations, pre- and postconditions of operations).

The addition of behaviour to subtyping relationships improves the likelihood of accurate object substitution compared to signature-based subtyping. The expressiveness of behavioural subtyping relationships depends on the behavioural description technique chosen. For example, POOL-I was one of the first systems to explore behavioural subtyping through pre- and postconditions; however, for implementation purposes all behaviour was captured as user-defined attributes [Ame91]. One type was a subtype of another if it possessed at least those attributes present in the supertype. Following this work was Liskov and Wing's work on behavioural subtyping which used pre- and postconditions as the behavioural formalism [LW93], as will be discussed in the next chapter. This allowed subtyping to be defined in terms of the relationship between the pre- and postconditions of the subtype and the supertype. The level of automation of type matching using behavioural subtyping depends on the behavioural description technique chosen and the scope of permitted behavioural specifications.

The final class of subtyping relationships is based on full, 'real-world' semantics (in addition to syntax and behaviour). This class of relationships is characterized by descriptive techniques such as natural language or structured language, such as conceptual graphs [PMG95]. This class of relationships is suitable only when a human user is available to read the semantic descriptions and make judgements about the existence or absence of subtyping relationships between interface types. In the general case it is impossible to automate matching for type descriptions that include 'real-world' semantics.

11.4 Signature-Based Subtyping – Available Approaches

Existing platforms for distributed computing have adopted their own IDL languages and assumed various definitions for a subtyping relationship. In this section we will characterize the approach to subtyping prescribed by the Reference Model for Open Distributed Processing [ISO95] and relate this approach to several existing platforms for distributed computing: DCE [RK92, SHM94], OMG's CORBA (and OMA) [Gro92, Gro98b], TINA [Con96] and DCOM [Ses97].

The type models for IDL languages in these distributed environments provide different features for type matching [BIBY95]. The distributed environments (DCE, CORBA, TINA, DCOM) all provide a standard set of basic data types and constructors. DCE has a richer set than the other systems, but all provide a set that is satisfactory for describing interface types. All models at least support the concept of operations (methods). All models also support either the concept of interfaces (logical groupings of operations) or objects or both. DCE, CORBA, TINA and DCOM support notifications, and RM-ODP supports signals (one-way typed messages). In addition, RM-ODP and TINA provide stream interfaces. The remaining part of this section will compare subtyping relationships that are part of type models for IDL languages of these distributed environments.

11.4.1 DCE

The Distributed Computing Environment (DCE) utilizes a client-server paradigm for building distributed applications with communication via remote procedure calls. It introduces subtyping as an abstract concept defined on operation signatures. DCE uses interface subtyping by extension, namely, that one interface is a subtype of another if the subtype has at least the same operations as the supertype, and possibly more. Additionally, the operations of the subtype must be in the same order as the supertype. Arguments and results of the operations must be of exactly the same type (subtyping of arguments and results is not allowed).

It has to be emphasized that the concept is abstract and did not find its way into type matching and type checking. DCE has a limited support for interface subtyping through the use of versions. If one interface has the same name and the same major version and a larger minor version number, then it is a subtype. It is up to the owner of the interfaces to appropriately assign names and version numbers based on the interface extension subtyping concept. Figure 11.2 presents an example of a stack interface described in DCE IDL. The interface has two operations, *push* and *pop*. If another interface with operations *push*, *pop* and *height* was created, it could be recognized as a subtype if its version number was defined in the way described above.

```
[
uuid(c985a362-235b-10c8-a50b-07003b0ecbf10  /* Universal unique id */
version(1.0)                                /* Version number */
]
interface stack                             /* interface name is stack */
{

error_status_t    void push([in] any item);

error_status_t    void pop([out] any item);

}
```

Fig. 11.2. An example interface in DCE IDL.

11.4.2 CORBA

The Object Management Architecture (OMA), the OMG distributed computing architecture [Gro92], recognizes the need for a subtyping relationship in order to provide service discovery and service reuse. The OMA also notes that subtyping and inheritance are different concepts, although inheritance often implies subtyping. The OMA defines subtyping based on syntax (interface extension):

Formally, if T_2 is declared to be a subtype of T_1 (and conversely, T_1 is a supertype of T_2), then for each operation $o_i \in Ops(T_1)$ there exists a corresponding operation $o_j \in Ops(T_2)$ such that the following conditions hold:

- the name of the operations match,
- the number and t ypes of the parameters are the same,
- the number and t ypes of the results are the same.

Thus, for every operation in T_1 there must be a corresponding operation in T_2, though there may be more operations in $Ops(T_2)$ than $Ops(T_1)$.

The Common Object Request Broker Architecture (CORBA) [Gro98b] (see also Chapter 1), the distributed computing platform based on the OMA, uses a similar approach. CORBA objects have single interfaces (as opposed to RM-ODP, which allows many interfaces per object). The interface type can be derived from multiple interface types through interface inheritance. CORBA therefore supports subtyping based on a simple form of interface extension.

Figure 11.3 presents an example of subtyping in CORBA IDL. The interface type StackIF has two operations, *push* and *pop*. Its subtype ExtendedStackIF includes these two operations and in addition includes the *height* operation.

```
module Stack {

        exception StackFull{ };
        exception StackEmpty{ };

        interface StackIF {

                void push(in any item) raises(StackFull);

                any pop() raises(StackEmpty);

        };

        interface ExtendedStackIF : StackIF {

                long height();

        };
};
```

Fig. 11.3. Interface inheritance in CORBA IDL.

Type information is used for service selection, and services can be selected dynamically through the use of the CORBA Trader (see Chapter 2 for a description of a trader's functionality). If the specified interface type is not available, the Trader may return a reference to a 'conformant' interface type. The trader can also assist dynamic binding to the server. Type checking of operation invocations is provided if the Dynamic Invocation Interface is used and the type information is provided.

Recent work on a CORBA Component Model extends CORBA's notion of objects into interoperable components [Gro98a]. Components may be assembled from many objects and provide one or more interfaces. The model assumes that subtyping between components will be supported.

11.4.3 RM-ODP

The Basic Reference Model for Open Distributed Processing (RM-ODP) classifies interactions between ODP entities as signals (asynchronous one-way messages), operations (synchronous or asynchronous remote procedure calls) or streams (flows of information), as described in Chapter 2. The Reference Model does not prescribe a particular type model but sets requirements for the type model that would support the interoperability of distributed systems. The RM-ODP defines a type specification as a predicate. The RM-ODP abstract type model includes type constants, functions, cartesian products, records, unions and recursive types. Objects and interfaces are not recognized as first-class types. Interfaces are defined as records consisting of operation (signal, stream) signatures. Objects may provide many interfaces.

The RM-ODP type rules include subtyping rules for signal, stream and operational interfaces (formalized in Annex A of RM-ODP). The RM-ODP does not prescribe any Interface Definition Language but creates a set of subtyping rules that particular IDLs should follow.

The difference between the RM-ODP subtyping definition and that of DCE and CORBA is the addition of subtyping of operation arguments and results to subtyping by interface extension. Parameter subtyping follows the 'contravariant arguments, covariant results' rule.

The subtyping rules for these three interface types are defined as follows:

Signal Interfaces

Signal interface type T_2 is a subtype of signal interface type T_1 if the following conditions are met:

- For every initiating signal signature in T_1 there is a corresponding initiating signal signature in T_2 with the same name, with the same number and names of arguments, and that each argument type in T_2 is a subtype of the corresponding argument type in T_1.
- For every responding signal signature in T_2 there is a corresponding responding signal signature in T_1 with the same name, with the same number and names of arguments, and that each argument type in T_1 is a subtype of the corresponding argument type in T_2.

Stream Interfaces

Stream interface T_2 is a subtype of stream interface T_1 if the following conditions are met:

- At least one corresponding flow is identified in the two interfaces.
- For all flows for which correspondences have been identified, the flow type in T_2 is a subtype of the flow type in T_1.
- For all flows for which correspondences have been identified, the direction of flow in T_2 and T_1 are the same.

Operational Interfaces

Operational interface T_2 is a subtype of interface T_1 if the following conditions are met:

- For every operation signature in T_1, there is an operation signature in T_2 (the corresponding signature in T_2 that defines an operation with the same name).
- For each signature in T_1, the corresponding signature in T_2 has the same number and names of arguments.
- For each signature in T_1, every argument type is a subtype of the corresponding argument type in the corresponding signature in T_2.
- The set of termination names of an operation signature in T_1 contains the set of termination names of the corresponding signature in T_2 (where *termination* denotes both results and exceptions).
- For each operation signature in T_1, a given termination in the corresponding signature in T_2 has the same number and name of result types in the termination of the same name in the signature in T_1.
- For each operation signature in T_1, every result type associated with a given termination in the corresponding signature in T_2 is a subtype of the result type in the termination with the same name in T_1.

RM-ODP introduces a rich infrastructural support for type matching and type checking. A type repository supports the storage and retrieval of type specifications and relationships between types. A trader supports dynamic service selection and dynamic binding of services (see Chapter 2 for a description of the functionality of type repository and trader).

11.4.4 *TINA*

The Telecommunication Information Networking Architecture (TINA) is a software architecture for future telecommunication systems. TINA incorporates distributed computing and purposely adopts CORBA concepts, except for the concepts that are deemed inadequate for telecommunication systems. The main difference from CORBA is the assumption that objects can exhibit many interfaces in which TINA follows the RM-ODP model. Interface type definitions, however, are similar to the CORBA definitions and are described in a superset of the CORBA IDL language called Object Definition Language (ODL) [Con96]. TINA, however, similarly to RM-ODP, assumes three kinds of interfaces (signal, stream, operational) whereas CORBA initially assumed only operational interfaces. TINA adopted CORBA's approach to subtyping, that is, subtyping is achieved by single or multiple interface inheritance. Interface types are created by the addition of operations (or flows for stream interfaces). There is no subtyping of parameters and results. For trading purposes TINA allows the specification of nonfunctional behaviour as attributes. Trading attributes are also inherited and a subtype may have in addition some new attributes.

Due to the differences in the object model (many interfaces versus one interface), TINA applies specification inheritance not only to the specification of interfaces, but also to the specification of objects and groups of objects. This reuse of specification through inheritance assumes that a subtype object can have new interface types added, and the interface types that are not new are subtypes of supertype's interface types.

If $T_1(a_1, b_1)$, and $T_2(a_2, b_2, c_2)$ are object types where a_1, b_1, a_2, b_2, c_2 are
   interface types, and $a_2 \preceq a_1$ and $b_2 \preceq b_1$,
then $T_2 \preceq T_1$.

Figure 11.4 illustrates operational and stream interfaces described in ODL and shows two objects, OB1 and OB2, that provide these interfaces. OB2 is a subtype of OB1.

```
interface OP1{                          /* operational interface */

        typedef datatype1;
        typedef datatype2;

        void operation1 (in datatype1, out datatype2);
};

interface OP2{                          /* operational interface */

        typedef datatype1;

        void operation2 (in datatype1);
};

interface ST1{                          /* stream interface */

        typedef ... VoiceFlowType;      /* flow type */
        typedef ... VoiceQoSType;       /* Quality of Service type */

        source VoiceFlowType voiceDownStream
               with VoiceQoSType voiceDownStreamQoS;

        sink   VoiceFlowType voiceUpStream
               with VoiceQoSType voiceUpStreamQoS
};

object OB1{                             /* object specification */

        behaviour ...
        supports OP1, ST1;
};

object OB2{                             /* object specification */

        behaviour ...
        supports OP1, OP2, ST1;
};
```

Fig. 11.4. Example interface and object definitions in TINA ODL

A similar approach is applied to the inheritance of object group specifications. A group of objects is a subtype of another object group if it has additional objects, and the specifications of objects that are not new are subtypes of object specifications belonging to the supertype object group.

11.4.5 DCOM

The Distributed Component Object Model (DCOM) uses an object remote procedure call (ORPC) for interactions between distributed applications [Ses97]. ORPC is an extension of DCE RPC. The DCOM object model assumes that objects may expose many interfaces and therefore claims no need for interface inheritance. For instance, if a stack interface existed in the CORBA model with two operations *push* and *pop*, then, to create an interface (*push,pop,height*) a new object would be created that inherits two operations from the original stack interface. The fact that in DCOM the object could have two interfaces (*push,pop*) and (*height*) is used as a justification for the lack of interface inheritance. DCOM does not have any support for the recognition of compatible types (subtyping relationship) and system evolution. As far as subtyping relationships are concerned, DCOM is even more constrained than DCE because it does not use DCE versions to show compatibility between types. DCOM does not allow versioning, and each interface type is assigned a globally unique identifier. This implies that if an interface belonged to many types in a lattice of interface inheritance relationship, the interface would need to have a separate unique identifier for each type. DCOM provides a type library that stores interface types but does not describe relationships between these types nor derive such relationships dynamically.

11.4.6 Summary

The existing framework and distributed computing environments differ in their approach to defining subtyping relationships. DCOM does not recognize any need for such relationships. DCE, CORBA and TINA all use the subtyping concept based on interface extension, that is, the addition of operations to a subtype. DCE, however, does not apply this subtyping concept to type matching. DCE matching is done based on version numbers, and the mapping of the relationship between interface types to the version numbers is left to the human user. RM-ODP extends the concept one step further and also supports the subtyping of operation arguments and results (using the contravariance/covariance rule). Figure 11.5 shows an example of parameter subtyping for three interfaces to bank accounts.

The interfaces have two operations, *deposit* and *withdraw*, but the argument type of these operations is defined as either $\mathbb{N}$ or an interval [1,..,1000].

The *bank_account* interface allows any deposits and withdrawals, and *medium_account* and *small_account* have some limitations on the argument that describes how much

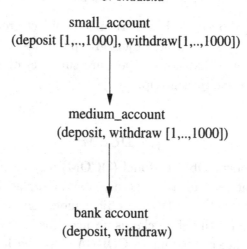

small_account
(deposit [1,..,1000], withdraw[1,..,1000])

medium_account
(deposit, withdraw [1,..,1000])

bank account
(deposit, withdraw)

Fig. 11.5. An example parameter subtyping

can be deposited or withdrawn. The subtyping relationship defined by RM-ODP will recognize compatibility between the interfaces

$$bank\_account \preceq medium\_account \preceq small\_account$$

whereas DCE, CORBA and TINA will not recognize the compatibility.

None of these approaches goes beyond subtyping relationships based on the syntax of interface descriptions. IDL languages do not allow behavioural features to be specified and matched. RM-ODP, however, does acknowledge the benefits of behavioural subtyping and states that the RM-ODP subtyping definition can be extended to include behavioural subtyping. The Reference Model does not provide any prescription for this extension, that is, does not specify what kind of behaviour could be taken into account and how Interface Definition Languages could be extended to allow the specification of behaviour and matching of behaviour descriptions.

When comparing subtyping relationships in existing environments for distributed computing it is interesting not only to compare the relationship definitions but also to compare the purpose for which the relationship is used. Subtyping relationships can ensure type safety and, as discussed earlier, there are three basic points at which type matching and type checking to ensure type safety can occur in a distributed environment: discovery and selection of services, binding between objects (e.g., client-server binding) and invocation of interactions (e.g., remote procedure call invocation). DCE supports matching (based on versions) during service selection; however, type checking during binding and procedure invocation are not provided (type safety of binding and operation invocation is not guaranteed). CORBA and TINA provide type matching during selection and type checking during binding, and invocation is feasible in both systems but not prescribed. RM-ODP recommends the use of subtyping relationships for type matching and type checking at all three points. The described differences in subtyping relationships are summarized in Table 11.1.

Table 11.1. *Differences in Subtyping Relationships*

	subtyping definition		type safety		
	interface extension	parameter subtyping	selection	binding	invocation
DCE	+(versions)	-	+	-	-
OMA/CORBA	+	-	+	possible	possible
RM-ODP	+	+	+	+	+
TINA	+	+	+	possible	possible
DCOM	-	-	-	-	-

It has to be noted that the differences between the subtyping relationships described in this section were shown in isolation from other differences in the IDL-type systems. If interworking between different distributed computing domains were considered, both the type differences in the Interface Definition Languages and the subtyping relationships would have to be analysed.

11.5 Introduction to Behavioural Subtyping

The syntactical subtyping relationships described in the previous sections can support type safety during service selection, binding to services and operation invocation. There are many interfaces that are equivalent or compatible, according to the subtyping relationship based on interface extension, but which expose different behaviour. There are also interfaces that are syntactically different but are behaviourally and semantically equivalent or compatible. For example, Cartesian and polar coordinates are semantically equivalent but not syntactically equivalent. As syntactical subtyping relationships take into account only syntactical features of interface types, they cannot guarantee that the services will have the required behaviour. If a user requests an interface of type T_1 and is instead offered a compatible interface of type T_2, an interaction with the interface will be free from run-time type errors but the service may behave differently than the user expected. Behavioural errors can be limited if Interface Definition Languages are extended to include behaviour specification of object types, and this behaviour description was used in the evaluation of compatibility between objects. In addition, behaviour and semantic descriptions could lead to the recognition of behaviour and semantic compatibility in spite of differences in syntactical interface descriptions and a conversion could be applied to interface descriptions to allow interactions with the compatible interface.

There are, however, some limitations to the suggested extension of subtyping to include behaviour and semantics. The main limitations are

- Techniques used to describe semantics (natural language, conceptual graphs) are not amenable to automation, and a human user has to make judgements about relationships between type semantics. In addition, in the general case, subtyping relationships for semantically described types are undecidable. It has to be noted, however, that many existing models for distributed computing include the natural language description of object semantics and/or behaviour.

- There exist many techniques to specify object behaviour, but each of them captures only some aspects of the behaviour. For instance, state-based modelling approaches can capture information aspects (e.g., operation pre- and postconditions) whereas process algebras can describe the ordering of operations but ignore the information aspect. In addition, various behaviour description techniques are amenable to a different degree to automation. As dynamic selection of services, dynamic binding and dynamic procedure invocation are a prevailing feature of distributed computing systems, the issue of automatic type matching is an important factor in a choice of behaviour description techniques.

- Distributed applications are very diverse, and different kinds of applications may require different behaviour description techniques. For some of these applications both the functional and nonfunctional aspects of behaviour are important. For instance, for real-time multimedia applications, nonfunctional behaviour like timing of interactions is an important feature. In general, many of the services require description and matching of Quality of Service in addition to matching functional behaviour; therefore, a combination of various behaviour description techniques may be necessary.

In this section we present a short overview of behaviour specification techniques. The overview concentrates on aspects of behaviour that are captured by the described technique and definition of subtyping relationships.

11.5.1 State-Based Approaches

State-based formal description techniques describe object behaviour as object state and pre- and postconditions, which describe changes in the state. Examples of state-based approaches are Z, Object-Z, the Liskov and Wing approach, and POOL-I, which are discussed further in Chapters 6 and 12 of this book.

Liskov and Wing's definition of the behavioural interface subtyping relationship includes the subtyping of operations based on syntax and on pre- and postconditions of operations [LW93, LW94]. Syntax-based subtyping is based on contravariant arguments and covariant results in operation signatures. Pre- and postconditions are state predicates and are described in a language based around the Larch specification language [GGH93]; the subtyping is based on the weaker precondition and stronger postcondition rule. To formally relate a subtype to a supertype, Liskov and Wing define an abstraction function to relate values of the subtype to values of the supertype, a renaming function to relate subtype operations to supertype operations and an extension map to explain the effects of any additional operations provided by the subtype. In this approach, type specifications include *invariants* (single-state predicates) and *constraints* (two state-predicates). The subtyping relationship, in addition to applying pre- and postcondition rules to determine subtyping, also checks whether the *invariants* and *constraints* are preserved by the subtype.

The syntactical part of the subtyping relationship in this approach is an extension to the subtyping relationships described in Section 11.4. It allows the renaming of operations, whereas subtyping relationships in existing distributed computing systems require the corresponding operations in the subtype and supertype to have the same names. State-based approaches can capture behaviour and even some semantics of objects but are more suitable for reasoning about subtyping relationships between types rather than automatic type matching.

It has to be noted that the POOL-I language, which also uses a similar, pre- and postcondition-based approach to the behavioural description of types (but does not take history properties into consideration), in the implementation restricts the behaviour description to the use of properties (attributes) [Ame91].

11.5.2 Process Algebras

Process algebras provide an expression of behaviour as ordering of operations. In distributed systems, the most commonly used formalism of this kind is Basic LOTOS (see Chapter 5). In process algebras, behaviour is specified as a set of both allowed traces of actions (interactions), where actions are atomic and deadlock properties. LOTOS has a rich set of relationships, particularly equivalence relationships (weak bisimulation, strong bisimulation, testing equivalence), and also many tools already exist for checking relationships between specifications. There exist approaches to define behavioural subtyping for LOTOS. One of these approaches is based on the extension of functionality by the addition of traces and extends the LOTOS extension relation (**ext**) [Nie95]. Another approach is based on the LOTOS reduction relationship (**red**) [BBSDS97]:

T_2 is a subtype of T_1 if and only if any client using T_2 according to any interface can only observe a trace and then observe a deadlock if the client could observe the same trace and a deadlock if it was using T_1 with the same interface.

There are also extensions of LOTOS to include time constraints (e.g., Timed LOTOS) that define bisimulation relations for comparing timed specifications, but these extensions do not define subtyping relationships. It has to be noted that, if LOTOS specifications are limited to *regular* processes (i.e., the state space is finite), the LOTOS behaviour specification (and any other process algebra specification) can be converted to Finite State Machines and therefore subtyping checking can be automated.

11.5.3 Finite State Machines

Finite State Machines (FSM), which are commonly used for the specification of interacting objects (e.g., communication protocols), are a well-established specification formalism. The FSM formalism describes transitions between states; however, it cannot capture data/information-related behaviour described by state-based approaches. As far as subtyping relationships are concerned, it is possible to automatically verify equivalence and inclusion relationships between two FSM specifications. In addition, an extension of FSM to automata over infinite sequences of words also has a similar feature: equivalence and inclusion relationships can be computed in finite time. There exist extensions of FSM to include time constraints: Timed Muller Automata [AD94] and Event-Clock Automata [AFH94]. For deterministic automata, equivalence and inclusion relationships can be computed in finite time for both of these approaches; however, the expressive power of these formalisms differs.

11.5.4 Temporal Logics

Propositional Linear Temporal Logic (PLTL) is another formalism used in specifying the behaviour of distributed systems. As the specification can be mapped into FSM, the subtyping relationship is computable for this kind of formal specification. One extension to PLTL is Stochastic QoS Temporal Logic (SQTL), which can express real-time Quality of Service requirements [LBC96]. SQTL is defined as a set of temporal logic formulae where each formula is built on system events using logical and temporal operators. The temporal operators describe the temporal ordering of events. In addition, SQTL allows the specification of stochastic distribution of events and the probability of achieving the required Quality of Service. If SQTL is constrained by removing nondeterministic choices, an algorithm exists for the subtyping of such constrained SQTL specifications [Bro99]. The algorithm is based on a mapping from SQTL to Event-Clock Automata and an extension of Niestrasz's algorithm on substitutability of two FSM specifications [Nie95].

11.5.5 Summary

The presented overview is not exhaustive, as there exist other calculi that can be used to specify the behaviour of distributed systems (e.g., the π-calculus based on named channels). The overview was focussed on formal specifications for which research on subtyping between two specifications is most advanced. As can be seen from this overview, complex distributed systems may require a combination of specification formalisms to capture their functional and nonfunctional behaviour as each formalism captures only some aspects of object behaviour. Combined specification formalisms like SQTL have been created to meet this requirement.

11.6 Conclusions

In this chapter, the role of subtyping relationships in distributed systems, both models and existing platforms for distributed computing, has been explored. Subtyping relationships can be used for type matching and type checking in these systems, and RM-ODP recommends using subtyping relationships to support service (object) discovery, service selection, dynamic binding between objects and dynamic invocation of operations. Existing distributed systems like DCE, CORBA and TINA use subtyping relationships for a subset of these activities. In addition, a variety of approaches to define subtyping relationships in distributed systems have been described and compared in this chapter. Distributed systems use subtyping relationships based on the syntax of interface type descriptions (IDL languages) and apply a variety of definitions from the simplest subtyping by decree to the subtyping relationship based on interface extension, which also allows the subtyping of operation arguments and results (assuming contravariance of arguments and covariance of results). Syntactical subtyping relationships guarantee type safety (no run-time type errors) but cannot guarantee that the behaviour of related objects is compatible. RM-ODP recognizes the advantage of extending subtyping relationships to include behaviour; however, behavioural subtyping has not been applied in DCE, CORBA and DCOM, and a very simplified description of nonfunctional object behaviour is used in TINA (matching on trading attributes). An overview of the most advanced research on behavioural subtyping for several formal description techniques has also been presented.

Acknowledgements

This work has been funded in part by the Cooperative Research Centres Program through the Department of the Prime Minister and Cabinet of the Commonwealth Government of Australia.

Bibliography

[AD94]   R. Alur and D. Dill. A theory of timed automata. *Theoretical Computer Science*, 126:183–235, 1994.

[AFH94]   R. Alur, L. Fix, and T. Henzinger. A determinizable class of timed automata. In *Proceedings of the Sixth Annual Conference on Computer-Aided Verification, CAV'94, Volume 818 of Lecture Notes in Computer Science*, pages 1–13. Springer-Verlag, 1994.

[Ame91]   P. America. Designing an object-oriented programming language with behavioural subtyping. In J. W. de Bakker, W. P. de Roever, and G. Rozenberg, editors, *Foundations of Object-Oriented Languages, REX School/Workshop, Noordwijkerhout, The Netherlands, May/June 1990, Volume 489 of Lecture Notes in Computer Science*, pages 60–90. Springer-Verlag, NY, 1991.

[ANS92]   ANSAware. *ANSAware 4.1 Application Programmer's Manual*. APM Ltd, Document RM.102.00, March 1992.

[BBB+95] W. Brookes, A. Berry, A. Bond, J. Indulska, and K. Raymond. A type model
    supporting interoperability in open distributed systems. In *Proceedings of the First
    International Conference on Telecommunications Information Networking Architecture,
    TINA '95*, pages 275–289, February 1995.

[BBSDS97] H. Bowman, C. Briscoe-Smith, J. Derrick, and B. Strulo. On behavioural
    subtyping in LOTOS. In H. Bowman and J. Derrick, editors, *FMOODS'97, Second IFIP
    International Conference on Formal Methods for Open Object-based Distributed Systems*.
    Chapman and Hall, July 1997.

[BCI+97] W. Brookes, S. Crawley, J. Indulska, D. Kosovic, and A. Vogel. Types and
    their management in open distributed systems. *Journal of Distributed Systems
    Engineering*, 4(4):177–190, December 1997.

[BIBY95] W. Brookes, J. Indulska, A. Bond, and Z. Yang. Interoperability of distributed
    platforms: a compatibility perspective. In *Proceedings of the Second International
    Conference on Open Distributed Processing, ICODP'95*, Open Distributed Processing
    III. Brisbane, Australia, 20–24 February, 1995, pages 67–78. Chapman & Hall, 1995.

[Bro99] W. Brookes. A type model and type management supporting interoperability in
    open distributed systems. PhD thesis, The University of Queensland, Australia, 1999.

[Con96] Telecommunications Information Networking Architecture Consortium. Tina
    object definition language manual. version 2.3. TINA-C document, July 1996.

[GGH93] S. Garland, J. Guttag, and J. Horning. An overview of Larch. In *Functional
    Programming, Concurrency, Simulation and Automated Reasoning*, number 693 in
    Lecture Notes in Computer Science, pages 329–348. Springer-Verlag, July 1993.

[Gro92] OMG Object Management Group. *Object Management Architecture Guide*.
    Revision 2.0, OMG TC Document 92.11.1, second edition, September 1992.

[Gro98a] Object Management Group. CORBA components: Joint revised submission
    from BEA systems, DSTC, Expersoft, IONA, Inprise Corporation, IBM, Oracle, Rogue
    Wave Software and Unisys. OMG TC document orbos/99-02-05, December 1998.

[Gro98b] OMG Object Management Group. *The Common Object Request Broker:
    Architecture and Specification, Revision 2.2*, February 1998.

[ISO95] ISO/IEC. International standard 10746-3, ITU-T recommendation X.903: Open
    distributed processing — reference model — part 3: Prescriptive model, January 1995.

[LBC96] A. Lakas, G. S. Blair, and A. Chetwynd. A formal approach to the design of
    QoS parameters in multimedia systems. In J. de Meer and A. Vogel, editors, *Proceedings
    of the Fourth International IFIP Workshop on Quality of Service, IWQoS96*, pages
    139–150, March 1996.

[LW93] B. Liskov and J. Wing. A new definition of the subtype relation. In
    O. Nierstrasz, editor, *Proceedings of the European Conference on Object Oriented
    Programming , ECOOP '93*, number 707 in Lecture Notes in Computer Science, pages
    118–141, Springer-Verlag, July 1993.

[LW94] B. Liskov and J. Wing. A behavioural notion of subtyping. *ACM Transactions
    on Programming Languages and Systems*, 16:1811–1841, 1994.

[MH93] F. Manola and S. Heiler. A 'RISC' object model for object system
    interoperation: Concepts and applications. Technical Report TR-0231-08-93-165, GTE
    Laboratories Incorporated, August 1993.

[Nie95] O. Nierstrasz. Regular types for active objects. In O. Nierstrasz and
    D. Tsichritzis, editors, *Object-Oriented Software Composition*, chapter 4, pages 99–121.
    Prentice Hall, 1995.

[PMG95] A. Puder, S. Markwitz, and F. Gudermann. Service trading using conceptual
    structures. In *Proceedings of the Third International Conference on Conceptual
    Structures, ICCS'95*, 1995.

[PS92] J. Palsberg and M. Schwartzbach. Three discussions on object-oriented typing.
    ACM SIGPLAN OOPS Messenger, 3(2):31–38, 1992.

[RK92] W. Rosenberg and D. Kenney. *Understanding DCE*. Open System Foundation,
    1992.

[Ses97]   R. Sessions. *COM and DCOM: Microsoft's Vision for Distributed Objects.* John Wiley and Sons, 1997.

[SHM94]   J. Shirley, W. Hu, and D. Magid. *Guide to Writing DCE Applications.* O'Reilly & Associates, Inc., second edition, 1994.

[WZ88]   P. Wegner and S. Zdonik. Inheritance as an incremental modification mechanism or what like is and isn't like. In S. Gjessing and K. Nygaard, editors, *Proceedings of the European Conference on Object Oriented Programming, ECOOP'88,* number 322 in Lecture Notes in Computer Science, pages 55–77. Springer-Verlag, 1988.

12

Behavioural Subtyping Using Invariants and Constraints[†]

Barbara H. Liskov

MIT, Cambridge, MA, USA

Jeannette M. Wing

Carnegie Mellon University, Pittsburgh, PA, USA

12.1 Introduction

What does it mean for one type to be a subtype of another? We argue that this is a semantic question having to do with the behaviour of the objects of the two types: the objects of the subtype ought to behave the same as those of the supertype, as far as anyone or any program using supertype objects can tell.

For example, in strongly typed object-oriented languages such as Simula 67 [DMN70], C++ [Str86], Modula-3 [Nel91] and Trellis/Owl [SCB+86], subtypes are used to broaden the assignment statement. An assignment

x: T := E

is legal provided that the type of expression E is a subtype of the declared type T of variable x. Once the assignment has occurred, x will be used according to its 'apparent' type T, with the expectation that if the program performs correctly when the actual type of x's object is T, it will also work correctly if the actual type of the object denoted by x is a subtype of T.

Clearly subtypes must provide the expected methods with compatible signatures. This consideration has led to the formulation of the contra/covariance rules [BHJ+87, SCB+86, Car88] (see Chapter 11). However, these rules are not strong enough to ensure that the program containing the above assignment will work correctly for any subtype of T, since all they do is ensure that no type errors will occur. It is well known that type checking, while very useful, captures only a small part of what it means for a program to be correct; the same is true for the contra/covariance rules. For example, stacks and queues might both have a *put* method to add an element and a *get* method to remove one. According to the contravariance rule, either could be a legal subtype of the other. However, a program written in

---

[†] A version of this chapter was published as 'A Behavioural Notion of Subtyping', by B.H. Liskov and J.M. Wing in the *ACM Transactions on Programming Languages and Systems*, volume 16, number 6, November 1994, pp. 1811–1841. This chapter omits the journal paper's Section 5.3, Section 7, and all related paragraphs throughout Sections 1 through 9 that mention our alternative definition of subtyping. It also omits some related work discussion. Most importantly, the formulation of the key definition is more elegant in this chapter than in the journal paper.

the expectation that x is a stack is unlikely to work correctly if x actually denotes a queue, and vice versa.

What is needed is a stronger requirement that constrains the behaviour of subtypes: properties that can be proved using the specification of an object's presumed type should hold even though the object is actually a member of a subtype of that type:

Subtype Requirement: Let $\phi(x)$ be a property that is provable about objects x of type T. Then $\phi(y)$ should be true for objects y of type S, where S is a subtype of T.

A type's specification determines what properties we can prove about objects.

We are interested only in *safety* properties ('nothing bad happens'). First, properties of an object's behaviour in a particular program must be preserved: to ensure that a program continues to work as expected, calls of methods made in the program which assume that the object belongs to a supertype must have the same behaviour when the object actually belongs to a subtype. In addition, however, properties independent of particular programs must be preserved because these are important when independent programs share objects. We focus on two kinds of such properties: *invariants*, which are properties that are true of all states, and *history properties*, which are properties that are true of all sequences of states. We formulate invariants as predicates over single states and history properties over pairs of states. For example, an invariant property of a bag is that its size is always less than its bound; a history property is that the bag's bound does not change. We do not address other kinds of safety properties of computations, for example, the existence of an object in a state, the number of objects in a state or the relationship between objects in a state, since these do not have to do with the meanings of types. We also do not address *liveness* properties ('something good eventually happens'), for example, the size of a bag will eventually reach the bound.

This chapter provides a general, yet easy to use, definition of the subtype relation that satisfies the Subtype Requirement. Our approach handles mutable types and allows subtypes to have more methods than their supertypes. Dealing with mutable types and subtypes that extend their supertypes has surprising consequences on how to specify and reason about objects. In our approach, we discard the standard data-type induction rule, we prohibit the use of an analogous 'history' rule and we make up for both losses by adding explicit predicates to our type specifications. Our specifications are formal, which means that they have a precise mathematical meaning that serves as a firm foundation for reasoning. Our specifications can also be used informally, as described in [LG85].

Our definition applies in a very general distributed environment in which possibly concurrent users share mutable objects. Our approach is also constructive: one can prove whether a subtype relation holds by proving a small number of simple lemmas based on the specifications of the two types.

The chapter also explores the ramifications of the subtype relation and shows how interesting type families can be defined. For example, arrays are not a subtype of sequences (because the user of a sequence expects it not to change over time) and 32-bit integers are not a subtype of 64-bit integers (because a user of 64-bit integers would expect certain method calls to succeed that will fail when applied to 32-bit integers). However, type families can be defined that group such related types together and thus allow generic routines to be written that work for all family members. Our approach makes it particularly easy to define type families: it emphasizes the properties that all family members must preserve, and it does not require the introduction of unnecessary methods (i.e., methods that the supertype would not naturally have).

The chapter is organized as follows. Section 12.2 discusses in more detail what we require of our subtype relation and provides the motivation for our approach. We describe our model of computation in Section 12.3 and present our specification method in Section 12.4. We give a formal definition of subtyping in Section 12.5, and we discuss its ramifications on designing type hierarchies in Section 12.6. We describe related work in Section 12.7 and summarize our contributions in Section 12.8.

12.2 Motivation

To motivate the basic idea behind our notion of subtyping, let us look at an example. Consider a bounded bag type which provides a *put* method that inserts elements into a bag and a *get* method that removes an arbitrary element from a bag. *Put* has a precondition which checks to see that adding an element will not grow the bag beyond its bound; *get* has a precondition that checks to see that the bag is nonempty.

Consider also a bounded stack type that has, in addition to *push* and *pop* methods, a *swap_top* method that takes an integer, i, and modifies the stack by replacing its top with i. Stack's *push* and *pop* methods have preconditions similar to bag's *put* and *get*, and *swap_top* has a precondition requiring that the stack is non-empty.

Intuitively, stack is a subtype of bag because both kinds of collections behave similarly. The main difference is that the *get* method for bags does not specify precisely what element is removed; the *pop* method for stack is more constrained, but what it does is one of the permitted behaviours for bag's *get* method. Let us ignore *swap_top* for the moment.

Suppose that we want to show that stack is a subtype of bag. We need to relate the values of stacks to those of bags. This can be done by means of an *abstraction function*, like that used for proving the correctness of implementations [Hoa72]. A given stack value maps to a bag value where we abstract from the insertion order on the elements.

We also need to relate stack's methods to bag's. Clearly there is a correspondence between stack's *push* method and bag's *put* and similarly for the *pop* and *get* methods (even though the names of the corresponding methods do not match). The pre- and postconditions of corresponding methods will need to relate in some precise (to be defined) way. In showing this relationship we need to appeal to the abstraction function so that we can reason about stack values in terms of their corresponding bag values.

Finally, what about *swap_top*? Most other definitions of the subtype relation have ignored such 'extra' methods, and it is perfectly adequate do so when programs are considered in isolation and there is no aliasing. In such a constrained situation, a program that uses an object that is apparently a bag but is actually a stack will never call the extra methods, and therefore their behaviour is irrelevant. However, we cannot ignore extra methods in the presence of aliasing, and also in a general computational environment that allows the sharing of mutable objects by multiple users or processes. In particular, we need to pay attention to extra *mutator* methods (like *swap_top*) that modify their object.

Consider first the case of aliasing. The problem here is that within a program an object is accessible by more than one name, so that modifications using one of the names are visible when the object is accessed using the other name. For example, suppose that σ is a subtype of τ and that variables

x: τ
y: σ

both denote the same object (which must, of course, belong to σ or one of its subtypes). When the object is accessed through x, only τ methods can be called. However, when it is used through y, σ methods can be called; and if these methods are mutators, their effects will be visible later when the object is accessed via x. To reason about the use of variable x using the specification of its type τ, we need to impose additional constraints on the subtype relation.

Now consider the case of an environment of shared mutable objects, such as is provided by object-oriented databases (e.g., Thor [Lis92] and Gemstone [MS90]). In such systems, there is a universe containing shared, mutable objects and a way of naming those objects. In general, lifetimes of objects may be longer than the programs that create and access them (i.e., objects might be persistent) and users (or programs) may access objects concurrently and/or aperiodically for varying lengths of time. Of course there is a need for some form of concurrency control in such an environment. We assume that such a mechanism is in place and consider a computation to be made up of atomic units (i.e., transactions) that exclude one another. The transactions of different computations can be interleaved, and thus one computation is able to observe the modifications made by another.

If there were subtyping in such an environment, the following situation might occur. A user installs a directory object that maps string names to bags. Later, a second user enters a stack into the directory under some string name; such a binding is analogous to assigning a subtype object to a variable of the supertype. After this, both users occasionally access the stack object. The second user knows that it is a stack and accesses it using stack methods. The question is, What does the first user need to know for his or her programs to make sense?

We think it ought to be sufficient for a user to know only about the 'apparent' type of the object; the subtype ought to preserve any properties that can be proved about the supertype. In particular, the first user ought to be able to reason about his or her use of the stack object using invariant and history properties of bag.

Our approach achieves this goal by adding information to type specifications. To handle invariants, we add an **invariant** clause; to handle history properties, a **constraint** clause. Showing that σ is a subtype of τ requires showing that (under the abstraction function) σ's invariant implies τ's invariant and σ's constraint implies τ's constraint.

For example, for the bag and stack example, the two invariants are identical: both state that the size of the bag (stack) is less than or equal to its bound. Similarly, the two constraints are identical: both state that the bound of the bag (or stack) does not change. Showing that stack's invariant and constraint, respectively, imply the bag's invariant and constraint is trivial. The extra method *swap_top* is permitted because, even though it changes the stack's contents, it preserves the stack's invariant and constraint.

In Section 12.5 we present and discuss our subtype definition. First, however, we define our model of computation and then discuss specifications, since these define the objects, values and methods that will be related by the subtype relation.

12.3 Model of Computation

We assume a set of all potentially existing objects, *Obj*, partitioned into disjoint typed sets. Each object has a unique identity. A *type* defines a set of *values* for an object and a set of *methods* that provide the only means to manipulate that object. Effectively, *Obj* is a set of unique identifiers for all objects that can contain values.

Objects can be created and manipulated in the course of program execution. A *state* defines a value for each existing object. It is a pair of mappings, an *environment* and a *store*. An environment maps program variables to objects; a store maps objects to values.

$State = Env \times Store$
$Env = Var \to Obj$
$Store = Obj \to Val$

Given a variable, x, and a state, ρ, with an environment, $\rho.e$, and store, $\rho.s$, we use the notation x_ρ to denote the value of x in state ρ; that is, $x_\rho = \rho.s(\rho.e(x))$. When we refer to the domain of a state, $dom(\rho)$, we mean more precisely the domain of the store in that state.

We model a type as a triple, $\langle O, V, M \rangle$, where $O \subseteq Obj$ is a set of objects, $V \subseteq Val$ is a set of values and M is a set of methods. Each method for an object is a *producer*, an *observer* or a *mutator*. Producers of an object of type τ return new objects of type τ; observers return results of other types; mutators modify objects of type τ. An object is *immutable* if its value cannot change and otherwise it is *mutable*;

a type is immutable if its objects are and otherwise it is mutable. Clearly a type can be mutable only if some of its methods are mutators. We allow *mixed methods* where a producer or an observer can also be a mutator. We also allow methods to signal exceptions; we assume termination exceptions, that is, each method call either terminates normally or in one of a number of named exception conditions. To be consistent with object-oriented language notation, we write $x.m(a)$ to denote the call of method m on object x with the sequence of arguments a.

Objects come into existence and get their initial values through *creators*. (These are often called *constructors* in the literature.) Unlike other kinds of methods, creators do not belong to particular objects, but rather are independent operations.

A *computation*, that is, program execution, is a sequence of alternating states and transitions starting in some initial state, ρ_0:

$$\rho_0 \ \ Tr_1 \ \ \rho_1 \ \ \cdots \ \ \rho_{n-1} \ \ Tr_n \ \ \rho_n.$$

Each transition, Tr_i, of a computation sequence is a partial function on states; we assume that the execution of each transition is atomic. A *history* is the subsequence of states of a computation; we use ρ and ψ to range over states in any computation, c, where ρ precedes ψ in c. The value of an object can change only through the invocation of a mutator; in addition, the environment can change through assignment and the domain of the store can change through the invocation of a creator or producer.

Objects are never destroyed:

$$\forall \ 1 \leq i \leq n \ . \ dom(\rho_{i-1}) \subseteq dom(\rho_i).$$

12.4 Specifications

12.4.1 Type Specifications

A type specification includes the following information:

- the type's name;
- a description of the type's value space;
- a definition of the type's invariant and history properties;
- for each of the type's methods:
  - its name;
  - its signature (including signaled exceptions);
  - its behaviour in terms of preconditions and postconditions.

Note that the creators are missing. Omitting creators allows subtypes to provide different creators than their supertypes. In addition, omitting creators makes it easy for a type to have multiple implementations, allows new creators to be added later and reflects common usage: for example, Java interfaces and virtual types provide no way for users to create objects of the type. We show how to specify creators in Section 12.4.2.

In our work we use formal specifications in the two-tiered style of Larch [GHW85]. The first tier defines *sorts*, which are used to define the value spaces of objects. In the second tier, Larch *interfaces* are used to define types.

For example, Figure 12.1 gives a specification for a bag type whose objects have methods *put*, *get*, *card* and *equal*. The **uses** clause defines the value space for the type by identifying a sort. The clause in the figure indicates that values of objects of type bag are denotable by terms of sort B introduced in the BBag specification; a value of this sort is a pair, $\langle elems, bound \rangle$, where *elems* is a mathematical multiset of integers and *bound* is a natural number. The notation $\{\ \}$ stands for the empty multiset, $\cup$ is a commutative operation on multisets that does not discard duplicates, $\in$ is the membership operation and $\mid x \mid$ is a cardinality operation that returns the total number of elements in the multiset x. These operations as well as equality ($=$) and inequality ($\neq$) are all defined in BBag.

The **invariant** clause contains a single-state predicate that defines the type's invariant properties. The **constraint** clause contains a two-state predicate that defines the type's history properties. We will discuss these clauses in more detail in subsequent sections.

---

bag = **type**

uses BBag (bag **for** B)
for all b: bag

invariant $\mid b_\rho.elems \mid \leq b_\rho.bound$
constraint $b_\rho.bound = b_\psi.bound$

put = **proc** (i: int)
      requires $\mid b_{pre}.elems \mid < b_{pre}.bound$
      modifies b
      ensures $b_{post}.elems = b_{pre}.elems \cup \{i\} \;\wedge\; b_{post}.bound = b_{pre}.bound$

get = **proc** ( ) **returns** (int)
      requires $b_{pre}.elems \neq \{\}$
      modifies b
      ensures $b_{post}.elems = b_{pre}.elems - \{result\} \wedge result \in b_{pre}.elems \;\wedge$
               $b_{post}.bound = b_{pre}.bound$

$card$ = **proc** ( ) **returns** (int)
      ensures $result = \mid b_{pre}.elems \mid$

$equal$ = **proc** (a: bag) **returns** (bool)
      ensures $result = (a = b)$

end bag

Fig. 12.1. A type specification for bags.

The body of a type specification provides a specification for each method. Since a method's specification needs to refer to the method's object, we introduce a name for that object in the **for all** line. We use *result* to name a method's result parameter. In the **requires** and **ensures** clauses x stands for an object, x_{pre} for its value in the initial state and x_{post} for its value in the final state.† Distinguishing between initial and final values is necessary only for mutable types, so we suppress the subscripts for parameters of immutable types (like integers). We need to distinguish between an object, x, and its value, x_{pre} or x_{post}, because we sometimes need to refer to the object itself, for example, in the *equal* method, which determines whether two (mutable) bags are the same object.

A method m's *precondition*, denoted $m.pre$, is the predicate that appears in its **requires** clause; for example, *put*'s precondition checks to see that adding an element will not enlarge the bag beyond its bound. If the clause is missing, the precondition is trivially 'true'.

A method m's *postcondition*, denoted $m.post$, is the conjunction of the predicates given by its **modifies** and **ensures** clauses. A **modifies** $x_1, \ldots, x_n$ clause is shorthand for the predicate:

$$\forall \ x \in (dom(pre) - \{x_1, \ldots, x_n\}) \ . \ x_{pre} = x_{post},$$

which says that only objects listed may change in value. A **modifies** clause is a strong statement about all objects not explicitly listed, that is, their values may not change; if there is no **modifies** clause, then nothing may change. For example, *card*'s postcondition says that it returns the size of the bag and no objects (including the bag) change, and *put*'s postcondition says that the bag's value changes by the addition of its integer argument, and no other objects change.

Methods may terminate normally or exceptionally; the exceptions are listed in a **signals** clause in the method's header. For example, instead of the *get* method we might have had:

$get' = $ **proc** ( ) **returns** (int) **signals** (empty)
  modifies b
  ensures if $b_{pre}.elems = \{ \ \}$ **then signal** empty
    else $b_{post}.elems = b_{pre}.elems - \{result\} \ \wedge$
      $result \in b_{pre}.elems \ \wedge \ b_{post}.bound = b_{pre}.bound.$

12.4.2 Specifying Creators

Objects are created and initialized through creators. Figure 12.2 shows specifications for three different creators for bags. The first creator creates a new empty bag whose bound is its integer argument. The second and third creators fix the bag's bound to be 100. The third creator uses its integer argument to create a singleton bag. The assertion **new**(x) stands for the predicate:

† Note that *pre* and *post* are implicitly universally quantified variables over states. Also, more formally, x_{pre} stands for *pre.s(pre.e(x))* and x_{post} stands for *post.s(post.e(x))*.

$x \in dom(post) - dom(pre)$.

Recall that objects are never destroyed, so that $dom(pre) \subseteq dom(post)$.

$bag\_create=$ **proc** (n: int) **returns** (bag)
    requires $n \geq 0$
    ensures **new**(*result*) $\wedge$ *result$_{post}$* $= \langle\{\}, n\rangle$

$bag\_create\_small =$ **proc** ( ) **returns** (bag)
    ensures **new**(*result*) $\wedge$ *result$_{post}$* $= \langle\{\}, 100\rangle$

$bag\_create\_single =$ **proc** (i: int) **returns** (bag)
    ensures **new**(*result*) $\wedge$ *result$_{post}$* $= \langle\{i\}, 100\rangle$

Fig. 12.2. Creator specifications for bags.

12.4.3 Type Specifications Need Explicit Invariants

By not including creators in type specifications, and by allowing subtypes to extend supertypes with mutators, we lose a powerful reasoning tool: data type induction. Data type induction is used to prove type invariants. The base case of the rule requires that each creator of the type establish the invariant; the inductive case requires that each method (in particular, each mutator) preserve the invariant. Without the creators, we have no base case. Without knowing all mutators of type τ (as added by τ's subtypes), we have an incomplete inductive case. With no data type induction rule, we cannot prove type invariants!

To compensate for the lack of a data type induction rule, we state the invariant explicitly in the type specification through an **invariant** clause; if the invariant is trivial (i.e., identical to 'true'), the clause can be omitted. The invariant defines the *legal* values of its type τ. For example, we include

invariant $\mid b_\rho.elems \mid \leq b_\rho.bound$

in the type specification of Figure 12.1 to state that the size of a bounded bag never exceeds its bound. The predicate $\phi(x_\rho)$ appearing in an **invariant** clause for type τ stands for the predicate: for all computations, c, and all states ρ in c,

$\forall x : \tau . x \in dom(\rho) \Rightarrow \phi(x_\rho)$.

Any additional invariant property must follow from the conjunction of the type's invariant and invariants that hold for the entire value space. For example, we could show that the size of a bag is nonnegative because this is true for all mathematical multiset values.

As part of specifying a type and its creators we must show that the invariant holds for all objects of the type. All creators for a type τ must *establish* τ's *invariant*, I_τ:

For each creator for t ype τ, show for all $x : \tau$ that $I_\tau[r \, esul\!t_{\,ost}/x_\rho]$, where $P[a/b]$ stands for predicate P with every occurrence of b replaced by a. Similarly, each producer must establish the invariant on its newly created object. In addition, each mutator of the type must *preserve the invariant*. To prove this, we assume that each mutator is called on an object of type τ with a legal value (one that satisfies the invariant) and show that any value of a τ object that it modifies is legal:

For each mutator m of τ, for all $x : \tau$ assume $I_\tau[x_{pre}/x_\rho]$ and show $I_\tau[x_{post}/x_\rho]$.

For example, we would need to show that the three creators for bag establish the invariant, and that *put* and *get* preserve the invariant for bag. (We can ignore *card* and *equal* because they are observers.) Informally, the invariant holds because each creator guarantees that the size is no larger than the bound; *put*'s precondition checks that there is enough room in the bag for another element; and *get* either decreases the size of the bag or leaves it the same.

The loss of data type induction means that additional invariants cannot be proved. Therefore, the specifier must be careful to define an invariant that is strong enough that all desired invariants follow from it.

12.4.4 Type Specifications Need Explicit Constraints

We are interested in the history properties of objects in addition to their invariant properties. We can formulate history properties as predicates over state pairs and prove them using the *history rule*:

History Rule: For each of the i mutators m of τ, for all $x : \tau$:

$$\frac{m_i.pre \wedge m_i.post \Rightarrow \phi[x_{pre}/x_\rho, x_{post}/x_\psi]}{\phi(x_\rho, x_\psi)}$$

We cannot use this history rule directly, however. It is incomplete since subtypes may define additional mutators. If we use it without considering the extra mutators, it is easy to prove properties that do not hold for subtype objects!

To compensate for the lack of the history rule, we state history properties explicitly in the type specification through a **constraint** clause†; if the constraint is trivial, the clause can be omitted. For example, the constraint

constraint $b_\rho.bound = b_\psi.bound$

in the specification of bag declares that a bag's bound never changes. As another example, consider a fat_set object that has an *insert* but no *delete* method; fat_sets only grow in size. The constraint for fat_set would be

constraint $\forall \ i : int \ . \ i \in s_\rho \Rightarrow i \in s_\psi$.

---

† The use of the term 'constraint' is borrowed from the Ina Jo specification language [SH92], which also includes constraints in specifications.

The predicate $\phi(x_\rho, x_\psi)$ appearing in a **constraint** clause for type τ stands for the predicate: for all computations, c and all states ρ and ψ in c such that ρ precedes ψ,

$$\forall x : \tau \;.\; x \in dom(\rho) \Rightarrow \phi(x_\rho, x_\psi).$$

Note that we do not require that ψ be the immediate successor of ρ in c.

Just as we had to prove that methods preserve the invariant, we must also show that they *satisfy the constraint*. This is done by using the history rule for each mutator.

The loss of the history rule is analogous to the loss of a data type induction rule. A practical consequence of not having a history rule is that the specifier must make the constraint strong enough so that all desired history properties follow from it.

12.5 The Meaning of Subtype

12.5.1 *Specifying Subtypes*

To state that a type is a subtype of some other type, we simply append a **subtype** clause to its specification. We allow multiple supertypes; there would be a separate **subtype** clause for each. An example is given in Figure 12.3.

A subtype's value space may be different from its supertype's. For example, in the figure the sort, S, for bounded stack values is defined in BStack as a pair, $\langle items, limit \rangle$, where *items* is a sequence of integers and *limit* is a natural number. The invariant indicates that the length of the stack's sequence component is less than or equal to its limit. The constraint indicates that the stack's limit does not change. In the pre- and postconditions, [ ] stands for the empty sequence, || is concatenation, *last* picks off the last element of a sequence, and *allButLast* returns a new sequence with all but the last element of its argument.

Under the **subtype** clause we define an *abstraction function*, A, that relates stack values to bag values by relying on the helping function, *mk_elems*, that maps sequences to multisets in the obvious manner. (We will revisit this abstraction function in Section 12.5.3.) The **subtype** clause also lets specifiers relate subtype methods to those of the supertype. The subtype must provide all methods of its supertype; we refer to these as the *inherited* methods†. Inherited methods can be renamed, for example, *push* for *put*; all other methods of the supertype are inherited without renaming, for example, *equal*. In addition to the inherited methods, the subtype may also have some *extra* methods, for example, *swap_top*. (Stack's *equal* method must take a bag as an argument to satisfy the contravariance requirement. We discuss this issue further in Section 12.6.1.)

---

† We do not mean that the subtype inherits the code of these methods, but simply that it provides methods with the same behaviour (as defined below) as the corresponding supertype methods.

stack = **type**

uses BStack (stack **for** S)
for all s: stack

invariant $length(s_\rho.items) \le s_\rho.limit$
constraint $s_\rho.limit = s_\psi.limit$

$push =$ **proc** (i: int)
        requires $length(s_{pre}.items) < s_{pre}.limit$
        modifies s
        ensures $s_{p\,ost}items = s_{pre}.items \; || \; [\,i\,] \; \wedge \; s_{p\,ost}limit = s_{pre}.limit$

$pop =$ **proc** () **returns** (int)
        requires $s_{pre}.items \ne [\,]$
        modifies s
        ensures $result = last(s_{pre}.items) \wedge s_{p\,ost}items = allButLast(s_{pre}.items) \wedge$
                $s_{p\,ost}limit = s_{pre}.limit$

$swap\_top =$ **proc** (i: int)
        requires $s_{pre}.items \ne [\,]$
        modifies s
        ensures $s_{p\,ost}items = allButLast(s_{pre}.items) \; || \; [\,i\,] \; \wedge \; s_{p\,ost}limit = s_{pre}.limit$

$height =$ **proc** ( ) **returns** (int)
        ensures $result = length(s_{pre}.items)$

$equal =$ **proc** (t: bag) **returns** (bool)
        ensures $result = (s = t)$

   subtype of bag (*push* **for** *put*, *pop* **for** *get*, *height* **for** *card*)
        $\forall\, st : S \;.\; A(st) = \langle mk\_elems(st.items), st.limit \rangle$
            where $mk\_elems : Seq \to M$
            $\forall\, i : Int, sq : Seq$
                $mk\_elems([\,]) = \{\,\}$
                $mk\_elems(sq \; || \; [\,i\,]) = mk\_elems(sq) \cup \{i\}$

end stack

Fig. 12.3. Stack t ype.

12.5.2 Definition of Subtype

The formal definition of the subtype relation, $\preceq$, is given in Figure 12.4. It relates
two types, σ and τ, each of whose specifications respectively preserves its invariant,
I_σ and I_τ, and satisfies its constraint, C_σ and C_τ. In the rules, since x is an object
of type σ, its value (x_{pre} or x_{post}) is a member of S and therefore cannot be used
directly in the predicates about τ objects (which are in terms of values in T). The
abstraction function A is used to translate these values so that the predicates about

τ objects make sense. A may be partial, need not be onto, but can be many-to-one. We require that an abstraction function be defined for all legal values of the subtype (although it need not be defined for values that do not satisfy the subtype invariant). Moreover, it must map legal values of the subtype to legal values of the supertype.

DEFINITION OF THE SUBTYPE RELATION, $\preceq$: $\sigma = \langle O_\sigma, S, M \rangle$ is a *subtype* of $\tau = \langle O_\tau, T, N \rangle$ if there exists an abstraction function, $A : S \to T$, and a renaming map, $R : M \to N$, such that:

(i) Subtype methods preserve the supertype methods' behaviour. If m_τ of τ is the corresponding renamed method m_σ of σ, the following rules must hold:

- *Signature rule.*
  - *Contravariance of arguments.* m_τ and m_σ have the same number of arguments. If the list of argument types of m_τ is α_i and that of m_σ is β_i, then $\forall i . \alpha_i \preceq \beta_i$.
  - *Covariance of result.* Either both m_τ and m_σ have a result or neither has. If there is a result, let m_τ's result type be α and m_σ's be β. Then $\beta \preceq \alpha$.
  - *Exception rule.* The exceptions signaled by m_σ are contained in the set of exceptions signaled by m_τ.

- *Methods rule.* For all $x : \sigma$:
  - *Precondition rule.* $m_\tau.pre[A(x_{pre})/x_{pre}] \Rightarrow m_\sigma.pre$.
  - *Postcondition rule.* $m_\sigma.post \Rightarrow m_\tau.post[A(x_{pre})/x_{pre}, A(x_{post})/x_{post}]$

(ii) Subtypes preserve supertype properties. For all computations, c, and all states ρ and ψ in c such that ρ precedes ψ, for all $x : \sigma$:

- *Invariant Rule.* Subtype invariants ensure supertype invariants.
  $$I_\sigma \Rightarrow I_\tau[A(x_\rho)/x_\rho]$$

- *Constraint Rule.* Subtype constraints ensure supertype constraints.
  $$C_\sigma \Rightarrow C_\tau[A(x_\rho)/x_\rho, A(x_\psi)/x_\psi]$$

Fig. 12.4. Definition of the subtype relation.

The first clause addresses the need to relate inherited methods of the subtype. Our formulation is similar to America's [Ame90]. The first two signature rules are the standard contra/covariance rules. The exception rule says that m_σ may not signal more than m_τ, since a caller of a method on a supertype object should not expect to handle an unknown exception. The pre- and postcondition rules are the intuitive counterparts to the contravariant and covariant rules for signatures. The precondition rule ensures that the subtype's method can be called at least in any state required by the supertype. The postcondition rule says that the subtype method's postcondition can be stronger than the supertype method's postcondition; hence, any property that can be proved based on the supertype method's postcondition also follows from the subtype's method's postcondition.

The second clause addresses preserving program-independent properties. The invariant rule and the assumption that the type specification preserves the invariant suffice to argue that invariant properties of a supertype are preserved by the subtype. The argument for the preservation of subtype's history properties is completely analogous, using the constraint rule and the assumption that the type specification satisfies its constraint.

We do not include the invariant in the methods (or constraint) rule directly. For example, the precondition rule could have been

$$(m_\tau.pre[A(x_{pre})/x_{pre}] \wedge I_\tau[A(x_{pre})/x_{pre}]) \Rightarrow m_\sigma.pre.$$

We omit adding the invariant because if it is needed in doing a proof, it can always be assumed, since it is known to be true for all objects of its type.

Note that in the various rules we require $x : \sigma$, yet x appears in predicates concerning τ objects as well. This makes sense because $\sigma \preceq \tau$.

12.5.3 Applying the Definition of Subtyping as a Checklist

Proofs of the subtype relation are usually obvious and can be done by inspection. Typically, the only interesting part is the definition of the abstraction function; the other parts of the proof are usually straightforward. However, this section goes through the steps of an informal proof just to show what kind of reasoning is involved. Formal versions of these informal proofs are given in [LW92].

Let us revisit the stack and bag example using our definition as a checklist. Here

$$\sigma = \langle O_{stack}, S, \{push, pop, swap\_top, height, equal\}\rangle$$
$$\tau = \langle O_{bag}, B, \{put, get, card, equal\}\rangle.$$

Recall that we represent a bounded bag's value as a pair, $\langle elems, bound\rangle$, of a multiset of integers and a fixed bound, and a bounded stack's value as a pair, $\langle items, limit\rangle$, of a sequence of integers and a fixed bound. It can easily be shown that each specification preserves its invariant and satisfies its constraint.

We use the abstraction function and the renaming map given in the specification for stack in Figure 12.3. The abstraction function states that for all $st : S$,

$$A(st) = \langle mk\_elems(st.items), st.limit\rangle,$$

where the helping function, $mk\_elems : Seq \to M$, maps sequences to multisets such that for all $sq : Seq$, $i : Int$:

$$mk\_elems([\,]) = \{\,\}$$
$$mk\_elems(sq \parallel [\,i\,]) = mk\_elems(sq) \cup \{i\}.$$

A is partial; it is defined only for sequence-natural numbers pairs, $\langle items, limit\rangle$, where $limit$ is greater than or equal to the size of $items$.

The renaming map R is

$$R(push) = put$$
$$R(pop) = get$$
$$R(height) = card$$
$$R(equal) = equal.$$

Checking the signature and exception rules is easy and could be done by the compiler.

Next, we show the correspondences between *push* and *put*, between *pop* and *get*, and so on. Let us look at the pre- and postcondition rules for just one method, *push*. Informally, the precondition rule for *put/push* requires that we show†:

$$| \ A(s_{pre}).elems \ |< A(s_{pre}).bound$$
$$\Rightarrow$$
$$length(s_{pre}.items) < s_{pre}.limit.$$

Intuitively, the precondition rule holds because the length of the stack is the same as the size of the corresponding bag, and the limit of the stack is the same as the bound for the bag. Here is an informal proof with slightly more detail:

   (i) *A* maps the stack's sequence component to the bag's multiset by putting all elements of the sequence into the multiset. Therefore the length of the sequence $s_{pre}.items$ is equal to the size of the multiset $A(s_{pre}).elems$.

  (ii) Also, *A* maps the limit of the stack to the bound of the bag, so that $s_{pre}.limit = A(s_{pre}).bound$.

 (iii) From *put*'s precondition we know that $| \ A(s_{pre}).elems \ |< A(s_{pre}).bound$.

 (iv) *push*'s precondition holds by substituting equals for equals.

Note the role of the abstraction function in this proof. It allows us to relate stack and bag values, and therefore we can relate predicates about bag values to those about stack values, and vice versa. Also note how we depend on *A* being a function (in step (iv), where we use the substitutivity property of equality).

The postcondition rule requires that we show that *push*'s postcondition implies *put*'s. We can deal with the **modifies** and **ensures** parts separately. The **modifies** part holds because the same object is mentioned in both specifications. The **ensures** part follows from the definition of the abstraction function.

The invariant rule requires that we show that the invariant on stacks:

$$length(s_\rho.items) \leq s_\rho.limit$$

implies that on bags:

$$| \ A(s_\rho).elems \ |\leq A(s_\rho).bound.$$

We can show this by a simple proof of induction on the length of the sequence of a bounded stack.

The constraint rule requires that we show that the constraint on stacks:

$$s_\rho.limit = s_\psi.limit$$

implies that on bags:

$$A(s_\rho).bound = A(s_\psi).bound.$$

---

† Note that we are reasoning in terms of the *values* of the object, *s*, and that *b* and *s* refer to the same object (*b* appears in the bag specification).

This is true because the length of the sequence component of a stack is the same as the size of the multiset component of its bag counterpart.

Note that we do not have to say anything specific for *swap_top*; it is taken care of just like all the other methods when we show that the specification of stack satisfies its invariant and constraint.

12.6 Type Hierarchies

The requirement that we impose on subtypes is very strong and raises a concern that it might rule out many useful subtype relations. To address this concern we looked at a number of examples. We found that our technique captures what people want from a hierarchy mechanism, but we also discovered some surprises.

The examples led us to classify subtype relationships into two broad categories. In the first category, the subtype extends the supertype by providing additional methods and possibly an additional 'state'. In the second, the subtype is more constrained than the supertype. We discuss these relationships in the following. In practice, many type families will exhibit both kinds of relationships.

12.6.1 Extension Subtypes

A subtype extends its supertype if its objects have extra methods in addition to those of the supertype. Abstraction functions for extension subtypes are onto, that is, the range of the abstraction function is the set of all legal values of the supertype. The subtype might simply have more methods; in this case the abstraction function is one-to-one. Or its objects might also have more 'state', that is, they might record information that is not present in objects of the supertype; in this case the abstraction function is many-to-one.

As an example of the one-to-one case, consider a type intset (for set of integers) with methods to *insert* and *delete* elements, to *select* elements and to provide the *size* of the set. A subtype, intset2, might have more methods, for example, *union*, *is_empty*. Here there is no extra state, just extra methods. Suppose that intset's invariant and constraints are both trivial; intset2's would be as well. Thus, proving that intset2 preserves intset's invariant and constraint is trivial.

It is easy to discover when a proposed subtype really is not one. For example, the fat_set type discussed earlier has an *insert* method but no *delete* method. Intset is not a subtype of fat_set, because fat_sets only grow while intsets grow and shrink; intset does not preserve various history properties of fat_set, in particular, the constraint that once some integer is in the fat_set, it remains in the fat_set. The attempt to show that the intset constraint (which is trivial) implies that of fat_set would fail.

As a simple example of a many-to-one case, consider immutable pairs and triples (Figure 12.5). Pairs have methods that fetch the first and second elements; triples have these methods plus an additional one to fetch the third element. Triple is a subtype of pair and so is semimutable triple with methods to fetch the first, second

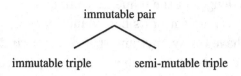

Fig. 12.5. Pairs and triples.

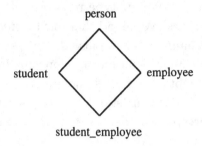

Fig. 12.6. Person, student and employee.

and third elements and to replace the third element, because replacing the third element does not affect the first or second element. This example shows that it is possible to have a mutable subtype of an immutable supertype, provided that the mutations are invisible to the users of the supertype.

Mutations of a subtype that would be visible through the methods of an immutable supertype are ruled out. For example, an immutable sequence whose elements can be fetched but not stored is not a supertype of a mutable array, which provides a *store* method in addition to the sequence methods. For sequences we can prove that elements do not change; this is not true for arrays. The attempt to construct the subtype relation will fail because the constraint for sequences does not follow from that for arrays.

Many examples of extension subtypes are found in the literature. One common example concerns persons, employees and students (Figure 12.6). A person object has methods that report its properties, such as its name, age and possibly its relationship to other persons (e.g., its parents or children). Student and employee are subtypes of person; in each case they have additional properties, for example, a student id number, an employee employer and salary. In addition, type student_employee is a subtype of both student and employee (and also person, since the subtype relation is transitive). In this example, the subtype objects have more state than those of the supertype, as well as more methods.

Another example from the database literature concerns different kinds of ships

[HM81]. The supertype is generic ships with methods to determine such things as who is the captain and where the ship is registered. Subtypes contain more specialized ships such as tankers and freighters. There can be quite an elaborate hierarchy (e.g., tankers are a special kind of freighter). Windows are another well-known example [HO87]; subtypes include bordered windows, colored windows and scrollable windows.

Common examples of subtype relationships are allowed by our definition provided that the *equal* method (and other similar methods) are defined properly in the subtype. Suppose that supertype τ provides an *equal* method and consider a particular call *x.equal(y)*. The difficulty arises when x and y actually belong to σ, a subtype of τ. If objects of the subtype have additional state, x and y may differ when considered as subtype objects but ought to be considered equal when considered as supertype objects.

For example, consider immutable triples $x = \langle 0, 0, 0 \rangle$ and $y = \langle 0, 0, 1 \rangle$. Suppose that the specification of the *equal* method for pairs says that

equal = **proc** (*q:* pair) **returns** (bool)
      ensures $result = (p.first = q.first \wedge p.second = q.second)$.

(We are using p to refer to the method's object.) However, we would expect two triples to be equal only if their first, second and third components were equal. If a program using triples had just observed that x and y differ in their third element, we would expect *x.equal(y)* to return 'false'; but if the program were using them as pairs and had just observed that their first and second elements were equal, it would be wrong for the *equal* method to return false.

The way to resolve this dilemma is to have two equal methods in triple:

pair_equal = **proc** (*p:* pair) **returns** (bool)
      ensures $result = (p.first = q.first \wedge p.second = q.second)$

triple_equal = **proc** (*p:* triple) **returns** (bool)
      ensures $result = (p.first = q.first \wedge p.second = q.second$
              $\wedge\ p.third = q.third)$.

One of them (*pair_equal*) simulates the *equal* method for pair; the other (*triple_equal*) is a method just on triples. (In some object-oriented languages, such as Java, the additional equal methods are obtained by overloading.)

The problem is not limited to equality methods, or even, more generally, binary methods [B+95]. It also affects methods that 'expose' the abstract state of objects, for example, an *unparse* method that returns a string representation of the abstract state of its object. *x.unparse()* ought to return a representation of a pair if called in a context in which x is considered to be a pair, but it ought to return a representation of a triple in a context in which x is known to be a triple (or some subtype of a triple).

The need for several equality methods seems natural for realistic examples. For example, asking whether *e1* and *e2* are the same person is different from asking if they are the same employee. In the case of a person holding two jobs, the answer might be true for the question about person but false for the question about employee.

12.6.2 Constrained Subtypes

The second kind of subtype relation occurs when the subtype is more constrained than the supertype. In this case, the supertype specification is written in a way that allows variation in behaviour among its subtypes. Subtypes constrain the supertype by reducing the variability. The abstraction function is usually into rather than onto. The subtype may extend those supertype objects that it simulates by providing additional methods and/or a state.

Since constrained subtypes reduce variation, it is crucial when defining this kind of type hierarchy to think carefully about what variability is permitted for the subtypes. The variability will show up in the supertype specifications in two ways: in the invariant and constraint, and also in the specifications of the individual methods. In both cases the supertype definitions will be nondeterministic in those places where different subtypes are expected to provide different behaviour.

A very simple example concerns elephants. Elephants come in many colors (realistically grey and white, but we will also allow blue ones). However, all albino elephants are white and all royal elephants are blue. Figure 12.7 shows the elephant hierarchy. The set of legal values for regular elephants includes all elephants whose color is grey or blue or white:

invariant $e_\rho.color = white \lor e_\rho.color = grey \lor e_\rho.color = blue$.

The set of legal values for royal elephants is a subset of those for regular elephants:

invariant $e_\rho.color = blue$

and hence the abstraction function is into. The situation for albino elephants is similar. Furthermore, the elephant method that returns the color (if there is such a method) can return grey or blue or white, that is, it is nondeterministic; the subtypes restrict the nondeterminism for this method by defining it to return a specifc color.

This simple example has led others to define a subtyping relation that requires nonmonotonic reasoning [Lip92], but we believe that it is better to use variability in the supertype specification and straightforward reasoning methods. However, the example shows that a specifier of a type family has to anticipate subtypes and capture the variation among them in the specification of the supertype.

The bag type discussed in Section 12.4.1 has two kinds of variability. First, as discussed earlier, the specification of *get* is nondeterministic because it does not constrain which element of the bag is removed. This nondeterminism allows stack to be a subtype of bag: the specification of *pop* constrains the nondeterminism. We

Fig. 12.7. Elephant hierarchy.

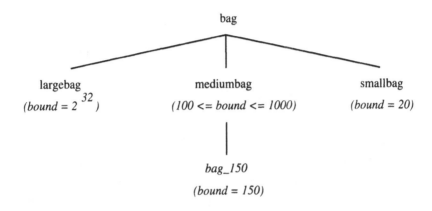

Fig. 12.8. A type family for bags.

could also define a queue that is a subtype of bag; its *dequeue* method would also constrain the nondeterminism of *get*, but in a way different from *pop*.

In addition, the actual value of the bound for bags is not defined; it can be any natural number, thus allowing subtypes to have different bounds. This variability shows up in the specification of *put*, where we do not say what specific bound value causes the call to fail. Therefore, a user of *put* must be prepared for a failure. (Of course the user could deduce that a particular call will succeed, based on a previous sequence of method calls and the constraint that the bound of a bag does not change.) A subtype of bag might limit the bound to a fixed value, or to a smaller range. Several subtypes of bag are shown in Figure 12.8; mediumbags have various bounds, so that this type might have its own subtypes, for example, bag_150.

The bag hierarchy may seem counterintuitive, since we might expect that bags with smaller bounds should be subtypes of bags with larger bounds. For example, we might expect smallbag to be a subtype of largebag. However, the specifications for the two types are incompatible: the bound of every largebag is 2^{32}, which is clearly not true for smallbags. Furthermore, this difference is observable via the methods: it is legal to call the *put* method on a largebag whose size is greater than or equal to 20, but the call is not legal for a smallbag. Therefore the precondition rule is not satisfied.

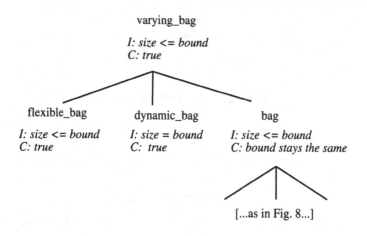

Fig. 12.9. Another type family for bags.

Although the bag type can have subtypes with different bounds, it cannot have subtypes where the bounds of the bags can change dynamically. If we wanted a type family that included both bag and such dynamic bags, we would need to define a supertype in which the bound is allowed, but not required, to vary. Figure 12.9 shows the new type hierarchy. Dynamic_bags have a bound that tracks the size: each time an element is added or removed from a dynamic_bag, the bound changes to match the new size. Flexible_bags have an additional mutator, *change_bound*:

$change_bound = $ **proc** $(n: \text{int})$
　　　 requires $n \geq \mid b_{pre}.elems \mid$
　　　 modifies b
　　　 ensures $b_{post}.elems = b_{pre}.elems \wedge b_{post}.bound = n.$

Notice that other types in the family need not have a *change_bound* method.

This example illustrates the different ways that subtypes reduce variability. All varying_bag subtypes reduce variability in the specification for the *put* method; varying_bag's *put* method is nondeterministic, since it might add the element (and change the bound) if the size is the same as the bound, or it might not. Bag and flexible_bag reduce this variability by not adding the element, whereas dynamic_bag does add the element. In addition, bag reduces variability by restricting the constraint: the trivial constraint for varying_bag can be thought of as stating 'either a bag's bound may change or it stays the same'; the constraint for bag reduces this variability by making a choice ('the bag's bound stays the same'), and users can then rely on this property for bags and its subtypes. Dynamic_bag reduces variability by restricting varying_bag's invariant, so that it no longer allows the size to be less than the bound. Finally, flexible_bag reduces variability because of the extra mutator, *change_bound*; all of its subtypes must allow explicit resetting of the bound.

Another example is a family of integer counters shown in Figure 12.10. When a

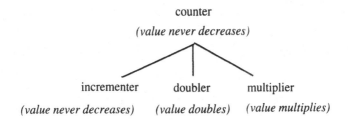

Fig. 12.10. Type family for counters.

counter is advanced, we only know that its value gets bigger, so that the constraint is simply

constraint $c_\rho \leq c_\psi$.

The doubler and multiplier subtypes have stronger constraints. For example, a multiplier's value always increases by a multiple, so that its constraint is

constraint $\exists\ n : int\ .\ [\ n > 0 \land c_\rho = n * c_\psi\ ]$.

For a family like this, we might choose to have an *advance* method for counter (so that each of its subtypes is constrained to have this method), or we might not. If we do provide an advance method, its specification will have to be nondeterministic (i.e., it merely states that the size of the counter grows) to allow the subtypes to provide the definitions that are appropriate for them.

In the case of the bag family illustrated in Figure 12.8, all types in the hierarchy might be 'real' in the sense that they have objects. However, sometimes supertypes are *virtual*; they define the properties that all subtypes have in common but have no objects of their own. Varying_bag of Figure 12.9 might be such a type.

Virtual types are useful in many type hierarchies. For example, we would use them to construct a hierarchy for integers. Smaller integers cannot be a subtype of larger integers because of observable differences in behaviour; for example, an overflow exception that would occur when adding two 32-bit integers would not occur if they were 64-bit integers. Also, larger integers cannot be a subtype of smaller ones, because exceptions do not occur when expected. However, we clearly would like integers of different sizes to be related. This is accomplished by designing a virtual supertype that includes them. Such a hierarchy is shown in Figure 12.11, where integer is a virtual type whose invariant simply says that the size of an integer is greater than zero. Integer types with different sizes are subtypes of integer. In addition, small integer types are subtypes of regular_int, another virtual type; the invariant in the specification for regular_int states that the size of an integer is either 16 bits or 32 bits. An integer family might have a structure like this, or it might be flatter by having all integer types be direct subtypes of integer.

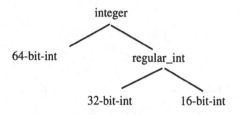

Fig. 12.11. Integer family.

12.7 Related Work

Some research on defining subtype relations is concerned with capturing constraints on method signatures via the contra/covariance rules, such as those used in languages like Trellis/Owl [SCB+86], Emerald [BHJ+87], Quest [Car88], Eiffel [Mey88], POOL [Ame90] and to a limited extent Modula-3 [Nel91]. Our rules place constraints not just on the signatures of an object's methods, but also on their behaviour.

Our work is most similar to that of America [Ame91], who has proposed rules for determining based on type specifications whether one type is a subtype of another. Meyer [Mey88] also uses pre- and postcondition rules similar to America's and ours. Cusack's [Cus91] approach of relating type specifications defines subtyping in terms of strengthening state invariants. However, none of these authors considers neither the problems introduced by extra mutators nor the preservation of history properties. Therefore, they allow certain subtype relations that we forbid (e.g., intset could be a subtype of fat_set in these approaches).

Our use of constraints in place of the history rule is one of two techniques discussed in [LW94]. That paper proposes a second technique in which there is no constraint; instead, extra methods are not allowed to introduce new behaviour. It requires that the behaviour of each extra mutator be 'explained' in terms of existing behaviour, through existing methods. We believe that the use of constraints is simpler and easier to reason about than this 'explanation' approach.

The emphasis on semantics of abstract types is a prominent feature of the work by Leavens. In his Ph.D. thesis, Leavens [Lea89] defines types in terms of algebras and subtyping in terms of a *simulation relation* between them. His simulation relations are a more general form of our abstraction functions. Leavens considered only immutable types. Dhara [Dha92, DL92, LD92] extends Leavens' thesis work to deal with mutable types, but he rules out the cases where extra methods cause problems, for example, aliasing. Because of their restrictions, they allow some subtype relations to hold where we do not. For example, they allow mutable pairs to be a subtype of immutable pairs, whereas we do not.

Others have worked on the specification of types and subtypes. For example, many have proposed Z as the basis of specifications of object types [CL91, DD90, CDD+89]; Goguen and Meseguer [GM87] use FOOPS; Leavens and his colleagues use Larch [Lea91, LW90, DL92]. Although several of these researchers separate the specification of an object's creators from its other methods, none has identified the problem posed by the missing creators, and thus none has provided an explicit solution to this problem.

12.8 Summary

We defined a new notion of the subtype relation based on the semantic properties of the subtype and supertype. An object's type determines both a set of legal values and an interface with its environment (through calls on its methods). Thus, we are interested in preserving properties about supertype values and methods when designing a subtype. We require that a subtype preserve the behaviour of the supertype methods and also all invariant and history properties of its supertype. We are particularly interested in an object's observable behaviour (state changes), thus motivating our focus on history properties and on mutable types and mutators.

We also presented a way to specify the semantic properties of types formally. One reason we chose to base our approach on Larch is that it allows formal proofs to be done entirely in terms of specifications. In fact, once the theorems corresponding to our subtyping rules are formally stated in Larch, their proofs are almost completely mechanical – a matter of symbol manipulation – and could be done with the assistance of the Larch Prover [GG89, ZW97].

In developing our definition, we were motivated primarily by pragmatics. Our intention is to capture the intuition that programmers apply when designing type hierarchies in object-oriented languages. However, intuition in the absence of precision can often go astray or lead to confusion. This is why it has been unclear how to organize certain type hierarchies, such as integers. Our definition sheds light on such hierarchies and helps in uncovering new designs. It also supports the kind of reasoning that is needed to ensure that programs that work correctly using the supertype continue to work correctly with the subtype.

Programmers have found our approach relatively easy to apply and use it primarily in an informal way. The essence of a subtype relationship is expressed in the mappings. These mappings can be defined informally, in much the same way that abstraction functions and representation invariants are given as comments in a program that implements an abstract type. The proofs can also be done informally, in the style given in Section 12.5.3; they are usually straightforward and can be done by inspection.

We also showed that our approach is useful by looking at a number of examples. This led us to identify two kinds of subtypes: ones that extend the supertype, and ones that constrain it. In the former case, the supertype can be defined without a great deal of thought about the subtypes, but in the latter case this is not possible; instead, the supertype specification must be done carefully so that it allows all of the intended subtypes. In particular, the specification of the supertype must contain sufficient nondeterminism in the invariant, constraint and method specifications.

Our analysis raises two issues about type hierarchy that have been ignored previously by both the formal methods and object-oriented communities. First, subtypes can have more methods, specifically more mutators, than their supertypes. Second, subtypes need to have different creators than supertypes. These issues forced us to revisit proof rules normally associated with type specifications: the data type induction rule and the history rule. We decided to preclude the use of these rules, and to have explicit invariants and constraints to replace them. Although it is possible to define a subtype relation that avoids explicit invariants and constraints, doing so is awkward and often requires the invention of superfluous supertype methods and creators. We prefer to use explicit invariants and constraints because this allows a more direct way of capturing the designer's intent.

Acknowledgements

B. Liskov is supported in part by the Advanced Research Projects Agency of the Department of Defense, monitored by the Office of Naval Research under contract N00014-91-J-4136, and in part by the National Science Foundation under Grant CCR-8822158. J. Wing is supported in part by the Defense Advanced Research Projects Agency and the Wright Laboratory, Aeronautical Systems Center, Air Force Materiel Command, USAF, F33615-93-1-1330, and Rome Laboratory, Air Force Materiel Command, USAF, under agreement number F30602-97-2-0031; and in part by the National Science Foundation under Grant No. CCR-9523972.

Views and conclusions contained in this document are those of the authors and should not be interpreted as necessarily representing official policies or endorsements, either expressed or implied, by the U.S. Government.

Bibliography

[Ame90] P. America. A parallel object-oriented language with inheritance and subtyping. *SIGPLAN*, 25(10):161–168, October 1990.

[Ame91] P. America. Designing an object-oriented programming language with behavioural subtyping. In J. W. de Bakker, W. P. de Roever, and G. Rozenberg, editors, *Foundations of Object-Oriented Languages, REX School/Workshop, Noordwijkerhout, The Netherlands, May/June 1990*, volume 489 of *Lecture Notes in Computer Science*, pages 60–90. Springer-Verlag, 1991.

[B+95] K. Bruce et al. On binary methods. *Theory and Practice of Object Systems*, 1(3):221–242, 1995.

[BHJ+87] A. P. Black, N. Hutchinson, E. Jul, H. M. Levy, and L. Carter. Distribution and abstract types in Emerald. *IEEE TSE*, 13(1):65–76, January 1987.

[Car88] L. Cardelli. A semantics of multiple inheritance. *Information and Computation*, 76:138–164, 1988.

[CDD+89] D. Carrington, D. Duke, R. Duke, P. King, G. Rose, and P. Smith. Object-Z:

An object oriented extension to Z. In *FORTE89, International Conference on Formal Description Techniques*. North-Holland, December 1989.

[CL91]   E. Cusack and M. Lai. Object-oriented specification in LOTOS and Z, or my cat really is object-oriented! In J. W. de Bakker, W. P de Roever, and G. Rozenberg, editors, *Foundations of Object Oriented Languages, Volume 489 of Lecture Notes in Computer Science*, pages 179–202. Springer-Verlag, June 1991.

[Cus91]   E. Cusack. Inheritance in object oriented Z. In *Proceedings of ECOOP '91*. Springer-Verlag, 1991.

[DD90]   D. Duke and R. Duke. A history model for classes in object-Z. In *Proceedings of VDM '90: VDM and Z*. Springer-Verlag, 1990.

[Dha92]   K. K. Dhara. Subtyping among mutable types in object-oriented programming languages. Master's thesis, Iowa State University, Ames, Iowa, 1992. Master's Thesis.

[DL92]   K. K. Dhara and G. T. Leavens. Subtyping for mutable types in object-oriented programming languages. Technical Report 92-36, Department of Computer Science, Iowa State University, Ames, Iowa, November 1992.

[DMN70]   O-J. Dahl, B. Myrhaug, and K. Nygaard. SIMULA common base language. Technical Report 22, Norwegian Computing Center, Oslo, Norway, 1970.

[GG89]   S. J. Garland and J. V. Guttag. An overview of LP, the Larch Prover. In *Proceedings of the Third International Conference on Rewriting Techniques and Applications, Volume 355 of Lecture Notes in Computer Science*, pages 137–151, April 1989.

[GHW85]   J. V. Guttag, J. J. Horning, and J. M. Wing. The Larch family of specification languages. *IEEE Software*, 2(5):24–36, September 1985.

[GM87]   J. A. Goguen and J. Meseguer. Unifying functional, object-oriented and relational programming with logical semantics. In Bruce Shriver and Peter Wegner, editors, *Research Directions in Object Oriented Programming*. MIT Press, 1987.

[HM81]   M. Hammer and D. McLeod. A semantic database model. *ACM Trans. Database Systems*, 6(3):351–386, 1981.

[HO87]   D. C. Halbert and P. D. O'Brien. Using types and inheritance in object-oriented programming. *IEEE Software*, 4(5):71–79, September 1987.

[Hoa72]   C. A. R. Hoare. Proof of correctness of data representations. *Acta Informatica*, 1(1):271–281, 1972.

[LD92]   G. T. Leavens and K. K. Dhara. A foundation for the model theory of abstract data types with mutation and aliasing (preliminary version). Technical Report 92-35, Department of Computer Science, Iowa State University, Ames, Iowa, November 1992.

[Lea89]   G. Leavens. Verifying object-oriented programs that use subtypes. Technical Report 439, MIT Laboratory for Computer Science, February 1989.

[Lea91]   G. T. Leavens. Modular specification and verification of object-oriented programs. *IEEE Software*, 8(4):72–80, July 1991.

[LG85]   B. H. Liskov and J. V. Guttag. *Abstraction and Specification in Program Design*. MIT Press, 1985.

[Lip92]   U. Lipeck. Semantics and usage of defaults in specifications. In *Foundations of Information Systems Specification and Design*, March 1992. Dagstuhl Seminar 9212 Report 35.

[Lis92]   B. H. Liskov. Preliminary design of the Thor object-oriented database system. In *Proceedings of the Software Technology Conference*. DARPA, April 1992. Also Programming Methodology Group Memo 74, MIT Laboratory for Computer Science, Cambridge, MA, March 1992.

[LW90]   G. T. Leavens and W. E. Weihl. Reasoning about object-oriented programs that use subtypes. In *ECOOP/OOPSLA '90 Proceedings*, 1990.

[LW92]   B. H. Liskov and J. M. Wing. Family values: A semantic notion of subtyping. Technical Report 562, MIT Laboratory for Computer Science, 1992. Also available as CMU-CS-92-220.

[LW94] B. H. Liskov and J. Wing. A behavioural notion of subtyping. *ACM Tr ansactions on Programming Languages and Systems*, 16:1811–1841, 1994.

[Mey88] B. Meyer. *Object-oriented Software Construction*. Prentice Hall, 1988.

[MS90] D. Maier and J. Stein. Development and implementation of an object-oriented DBMS. In S. B. Zdonik and D. Maier, editors, *Readings in Object-Oriented Database Systems*, pages 167–185. Morgan Kaufmann, 1990.

[Nel91] G. Nelson. *Systems Programming with Modula-3*. Prentice Hall, 1991.

[SCB⁺86] C. Schaffert, T. Cooper, B. Bullis, M. Kilian, and C. Wilpolt. An introduction to Trellis/Owl. In *Proceedings of OOPSLA '86*, pages 9–16, September 1986.

[SH92] J. Scheid and S. Holtsberg. Ina Jo specification language reference manual. Technical Report TM-6021/001/06, Paramax Systems Corporation, A Unisys Company, June 1992.

[Str86] B. Stroustrup. *The C++ Programming Language*. Addison-Wesley, 1986.

[ZW97] A. M. Zaremski and J. M. Wing. Specification matching of software components. *ACM Trans. on Software Engineering and Methodology*, 6(4):333–369, October 1997.

13

Behavioural Typing for Objects and Process Calculi

Elie Najm   Abdelkrim Nimour

ENST – Ecole Nationale Supérieure des T´eléommunications, France

Jean-Bernard Stefani

France Telecom R&D

In this chapter we discuss issues regarding behavioural typing in concurrent processes and object calculi. In contrast to the functionnal paradigm, processes and objects do exhibit state, interaction and behaviour. The actions that may be engaged by a process (we can similarly talk about the methods that may be invoked on an object) depend on its state. Using object terminology, objects are said to manifest non uniform service offers. Behavioural typing is then highly relevant. It allows one to reason about types in this dynamic setting. For instance, behavioural type systems may be used to statically check properties such as 'no service denial'. First, we introduce and motivate behavioural typing and briefly present its main characteristics and issues. Then we discuss one of the approaches based on explicit, interface-based behavioural typing.

13.1 Introduction

Let us start with a motivating example. Consider the typical case of an object representing a one-place buffer. As only one element at a time can be stored in this buffer, it offers alternatively the **put** and the **get** methods. An implementation of this buffer in Java would be as shown in Figure 13.1.

In this example, the **Buffer** class has a Boolean member named **empty**. Initially, **empty** is **true**. The service **put** is available only if **empty** is **true**, and, conversely, the service **get** can be performed only if **empty** is **false**.

The inspection of the code of the buffer reveals that, to be used correctly, only the **put** method can be called initially, henceforth allowing the **get** method. Note that it is not possible to know this just by examining the type of the buffer as seen by Java. This information is hidden in the 'synchronization constraints' of the object code. Invoking a method when it is not available yields a 'service not available' error. Statically checking for this kind of errors is very difficult if the synchronisation constraints do not relate to the type of the object.

In addition, let us consider this same buffer in a distributed environment, and let us imagine that two clients of this buffer, a producer and a consumer, have

```
public class Buffer{
  private Boolean empty;
      ...
  public Buffer(){
    empty := true;
    ...
  }
  public void put(Object o) throws ServiceNotAvailable {
    if(!empty) throw new ServiceNotAvailable();
    else{
      empty := false;
      ...
    }
  }
  public Object get() throws ServiceNotAvailable {
    if(empty) throw new ServiceNotAvailable();
    else{
      empty := true;
      ...
    }
  }
}
```

Fig. 13.1. The one-place buffer in Java.

concurrent access to its services. In this case, the producer and the consumer have to coordinate their actions to avoid a service call when it is not available.

One approach to solve this problem consists in defining a type language that embraces (an abstraction of) the behaviour of the objects. Many authors have taken this approach, which has now become an active field of research. We present a discussion of some of these contributions in the last section of this chapter.

13.2 Dimensions of Behavioural Typing

Behavioural typing is being investigated along a variety of dimensions: expressiveness of the typed language, expressiveness of the type language, the involved semantical relations (equivalences and preoreders), the communication medium, the failure model and the properties enforced by the type system. We discuss these dimensions briefly in the following:

- The languages studied are generally based on mobile process algebras [MPW92] (see also Chapter 9 of this book) or on an Actors model [AMST92] (see also Chapter 8 of this book). They may involve higher order constructs, like, for example, polymorphism and code mobility. Some approaches also involve security, real-time and quality of service. In general, a compromise is sought between the expressive power of the language (and its associated type language) and the complexity and decidability of the type system.

- A diversity of abstractions can be retained from the code for inclusion in the type language. In the earliest proposals, types reflected the capacity of the communication ports (input or output) or their sorts (their signature). An important dividing line is drawn between state-based (see Chapter 12) and interface-based (see Chapter 11) typing. In the former a part of the internal object state is included in the type, whereas in the latter only elements of information from the interfaces are included in the type. Both approaches have their pros and cons. State-based typing is more powerful and can discriminate between, for example, a two-place FIFO buffer and a two-place stack. Interface-based typing is less intrusive in the object code and thus can be applied more generally. As with typing in general, behavioural typing can be either implicit or explicit. The usual pros and cons apply: implicit typing makes code more concise, whereas explicit typing clarifies the contract between an object and its environment. Explicit typing also allows the constitution of shared type repositories. This falicitates the safe extension of distributed applications. An interesting hybrid approach is synthesized types, whereby the type is synthesized from the code and then exported to the type repository.

- The definition of the type system is based on notions of type equality and subtyping. These make use of well-known equivalence and preorder relations defined on behaviours and transition systems [BD99, BBSDS97].

- In some approches, the typing system addresses the issues related to distribution: asynchrony, concurrency, resource sharing, failures, communication. Some proposals involve the concept of locality, which then represents the unit of failure. Various semantics are being considered for communication media: reliable or lossy, order-preserving or not, with or without bounded latencies. The complexity of the type system is dependent on the assumed properties of the communication and execution environments.

- The properties guaranteed by the type system span from simple usage properties, like, for example, linear types (ports are used once), unique receptionists (ports have unique receptors), port capabilities (input, output, client, server, etc); to more involved properties, like, for example, deadlock avoidance and the absence of service denial. Of particular importance are the substitution properties (strong, weak) between subtypes. Some proposals deal with the issue of smooth and safe extension of existing configurations.

13.3 An Explicit Behavioural Interface-Based Typing Example

In the sequel, we present an approach for behavioural typing based on an explicit type language for interfaces. This is an integration of previous work of the authors [NN97, NNS99a, NNS99b] and also an extension to that work. A type of an interface is a labelled transition system that specifies the temporal ordering of the available methods (services) at the interface. Each transition label is a method signature. In addition, each interface has to be declared to be public or private. A private object interface has only one client at a time and may offer nonuniform services, depending on the 'protocol' that the client and the server have agreed on. On the other hand, a public interface can have multiple clients at the same time and is required to perform the same services for all of its potential clients: the services on a public interface are uniform.

To enforce coordination between objects, the type system does not allow duplication of private interface references; hence, only one client at a time can invoke the services of a private interface. Thus, holding the client role of a private interface is similar to holding a token allowing access to the server interface. Multiple clients of a given private server interface must 'cooperate' by passing the client role. The matching between the sending and receiving of client roles can be statically checked to enforce the coordination of clients.

An interface type specifies:

- the **behaviour type** of the interface, that is, the succession of available services;
- the **mode** of the interface: public or private;
- the **role** of the interface: client or server. An object that has the client role (noted !) of an interface can invoke the services offered at this interface. An object that has the server role (noted ?) can offer services on the interface.

Remark: Usually, the client role of an interface is called a reference to this interface, whereas the server role of an interface is simply called the interface.

13.4 Behaviour Types

A behaviour type is a triplet (E, x, r), noted $E \triangleright rx$, where x is the behaviour type identifier, r is a set of role (also called capabilities) capabilities ($r \subset \{!, ?\}$) and E a finite set of equations of the form $x_k = e_k$, where each x_k is a behaviour type identifier that appears once and only once on the left-hand side of an equation and e_k is an expression of the form:

$$e ::= \sum_{i=1}^{n} m_i(\tilde{\rho}_i \tilde{x}_i); \ x_i' \quad \text{with } l \neq l' \Rightarrow m_l \neq m_{l'}.$$

where:

- each m_i is a method name. We call $\mathcal{M}$ the set of method names.
- each $\tilde{\rho}_i \tilde{x}_i$ is a list of the form: $\rho_i^1 x_i^1, \cdots, \rho_i^k x_i^k$, describing the behaviour types of the arguments of method m_i. Each x_i^j is a behaviour type identifier and ρ_i^j a role, that is, client (!), server (?) or both (!?).
- each x_i' is a behaviour type identifier.

There exists a predefined behaviour type, **nil**, that does not appear in the left-hand side of any equation.

In our model we consider only deterministic types, that is, if there is a choice between two messages of a behaviour type expression, the names of the messages must be different.

Note: In the following we will consider, without loss of generality†, that all of our behaviour types are defined in the same environment, E. We will then omit this environment when writing a behaviour type, that is, $E \triangleright rx$ will be written rx. We let X, Y, Z range over behaviour types.

13.4.1 Type Behaviour

In this section we define the dynamic aspects of behaviour types. A behaviour type X that performs action a and then evolves to a new behaviour type X' is denoted by the transition:

$$X \xrightarrow{\ a\ } X'.$$

An action is a method signature annotated with a role: $\rho m(X_1, \ldots, X_n)$.

Behaviour type transitions are defined by the following rule:

$$
\boxed{
\begin{array}{c}
x = \displaystyle\sum_{i=1}^{n} m_i(\rho_i^1 x_i^1, \cdots, \rho_i^k x_i^k);\ x_i' \qquad \text{where} \quad \rho \in \{!, ?\} \text{ and} \\[4pt]
\hline
\\[-6pt]
r\ x \xrightarrow{\ \rho m_j(\rho_j^1 x_j^1, \cdots \rho_j^k x_j^k)\ } r\ x_j'
\end{array}
\quad
\begin{array}{l}
\rho \sqsubset r \text{ and} \\
1 \le j \le n
\end{array}
\quad (\text{Type} - \text{Act})
}
$$

Note: The behaviour type, $r\ \mathbf{nil}$, where r is any (valid) set of capabilities, cannot evolve.

We define now the function $possible(X)$, which is the set of method names that can be handled by the behaviour type X.

Definition 1 *(Possible)*

$$possible(X) = \{m \in \mathcal{M}, \exists\, X'\ \exists\, \tilde{Y} \mid X \xrightarrow{\ \rho m(\tilde{Y})\ } X'\}$$

13.4.2 Behaviour Type Equivalence

Bisimulation is a behavioural equality relation over behaviour types. This definition is very close to the definition of process bisimulation in CCS (see [Mil89]). The main difference is that in our case the actions need to be bisimilar, too.

---

† Two behaviour types defined in two distinct environments can be simply redefined in the union of these environments with an appropriate renaming of type variables.

Definition 2 *(Bisimulation)*

A binary relation β over behaviour types is a bisimulation if $(X_1, X_2) \in \beta$ implies :

    i) $X_1 \xrightarrow{pm(\tilde{Y}_1)} X_1' \Rightarrow X_2 \xrightarrow{pm(\tilde{Y}_2)} X_2'$ *and* $(X_1', X_2') \in \beta, (\tilde{Y}_1, \tilde{Y}_2) \in \beta$

    ii) $X_2 \xrightarrow{pm(\tilde{Y}_2)} X_2' \Rightarrow X_1 \xrightarrow{pm(\tilde{Y}_1)} X_1'$ *and* $(X_2', X_1') \in \beta, (\tilde{Y}_2, \tilde{Y}_1) \in \beta.$

Definition 3 *(Behaviour type equivalence)*

Two behaviour types X_1 and X_2 are equivalent, noted $X_1 \sim X_2$, if and only if there exists a bisimulation β such that $(X_1, X_2) \in \beta$.

We define a predicate $uniform(X)$ formalizing the notion of uniform behaviour type.

Definition 4 *(Uniform)*

$uniform(X)$ *holds if* $X \xrightarrow{pm(\tilde{Y})} X'$ *implies* $X \sim X'$

13.4.3 Behaviour Subtypes

Our subtyping relation is based on a simulation relation ([Mil89]).

Definition 5 *(Simulation)*

A binary relation S over behaviour types is a simulation relation if $(X_1, X_2) \in S$ implies :

    i) $X_1 \xrightarrow{?m(\tilde{Y}_1)} X_1' \Rightarrow X_2 \xrightarrow{?m(\tilde{Y}_2)} X_2'$ *and* $(X_1', X_2') \in S, (\tilde{Y}_1, \tilde{Y}_2) \in S$

    ii) $X_2 \xrightarrow{!m(\tilde{Y}_2)} X_2' \Rightarrow X_1 \xrightarrow{!m(\tilde{Y}_1)} X_1'$ *and* $(X_2', X_1') \in S, (\tilde{Y}_2, \tilde{Y}_1) \in S$

Informally, an interface type X_1 is a subtype of a type X_2 iff:

client case: the processable messages of X_2 are a subset of the processable messages of X_1.

server case: the processable messages of X_1 are a superset of the processable messages of X_2.

This guarantees the safe substitution of a supertype by its subtype.

Definition 6 *(Subtypes)*

A behaviour type X_1 is a subtype of a behaviour type X_2, noted $X_1 \preceq X_2$, if there exists a simulation $\mathcal{S}$ such that $(X_1, X_2) \in \mathcal{S}$.

13.5 The Object Calculus

Our object calculus, OL, contains ingredients from both the π-calculus (see Chapter 9 of this book) and the Actors model (see Chapter 8 of this book). Among its distinguishing features are the use of syntactic sugar for method definition and the restriction of the choice operator to receiving actions only. Communication is asynchronous for public interfaces and by rendez-vous for private interfaces (Note: the rendez-vous can be replaced by ordered reliable communication). Our calculus is in fact asynchronous. We have chosen rendez-vous communication for private interfaces for technical reasons and for simplifying the presentation. The formal syntax of the calculus is given in Figure 13.2.

$$
\begin{array}{rcl}
I & ::= & u : T \text{ (interface typing)} \\
Dcl & ::= & A[\tilde{I}] = B \text{ (behaviour definition)} \\
Rcp & ::= & u[m_1(\tilde{I}_1) = B_1, \cdots, m_n(\tilde{I}_n) = B_n] \text{ (reception action)} \\
B & ::= & \mathbf{0} \text{ (inactive behaviour)} \\
& | & u.m(\tilde{\rho}\tilde{v}) > B \text{ (emitting action)} \\
& | & \sum_{i=1}^{n} Rcp_i \text{ (multi} - \text{interface choice)} \\
& | & \mathbf{new}\ u : T\ \mathbf{in}\ B \text{ (interface definition)} \\
& | & A[\tilde{\rho}\tilde{v}] \text{ (behaviour instantiation)} \\
& | & \mathbf{create}\ A[\tilde{\rho}\tilde{v}] > B \text{ (behaviour creation)} \\
C & ::= & B \text{ (simple behaviour)} \\
& | & [u.m(\tilde{v})] \text{ (message)} \\
& | & \mathbf{new}\ u : T\ \mathbf{in}\ C \text{ (interface scope)} \\
& | & C \mid C \text{ (parallel composition)}
\end{array}
$$

Symbol	Signification
T	interface type
A	behaviour name
u, v	interface name
$m, m_1, \cdots, m_n$	method name
ρ	role
B	behaviour
C	configuration

Fig. 13.2. Syntax of OL.

13.5.1 Operational Semantics

We present the operational semantics of object configurations in two steps. We first define a structural congruence relation, and then we give a reduction relation that specifies how object configurations evolve.

13.5.1.1 Structural Congruence

Bound and free variable occurrences are defined as usual.

Definition 7 *(Bound and free variables)*

---

*Interface name occurrences appearing in the scope of a behaviour definition ($A[\tilde{I}] = B$), a reception action ($u[m_1(\tilde{I}_1) = B_1, \cdots, m_n(\tilde{I}_n) = B_n]$) or an interface creation (**new** $u : T$ **in** B) are bound; otherwise they are free.*

Definition 8 *(Substitution)*

The substitution $B[v/u]$ denotes the simultaneous replacement of all of the free occurrences of u by v in B.

We can define the congruence relation, denoted $\equiv$. The first structural rules state that the choice operator between receptions is commutative and associative:

$$Rcp_1 + Rcp_2 \equiv Rcp_2 + Rcp_1$$

$$(Rcp_1 + Rcp_2) + Rcp_3 \equiv Rcp_1 + (Rcp_2 + Rcp_3)$$

The parallel operator is also commutative and associative, and 0 is its neutral element:

$$C_1 \mid C_2 \equiv C_2 \mid C_1$$

$$(C_1 \mid C_2) \mid C_3 \equiv C_1 \mid (C_2 \mid C_3)$$

$$C \mid 0 \equiv C$$

The order of the introduction of the interfaces is meaningless:

new $u_1 : T_1$ **in** (**new** $u_2 : T_2$ **in** C) $\equiv$ **new** $u_2 : T_2$ **in** (**new** $u_1 : T_1$ **in** C)
$$\text{for } u_1 \neq u_2.$$

The last two rules are the π-calculus scope extrusion and alpha-conversion:

(**new** $u : T$ **in** C_1) $\mid C_2 \equiv$ **new** $u : T$ **in** ($C_1 \mid C_2$)   if u is not free C_2

new $u : T$ **in** $C \equiv$ **new** $v : T$ **in** $C[v/u]$ if v is not free C

13.5.1.2 Reduction Rules

The evolution of object configurations is given using reduction rules (see Figure 13.3). A reduction rule specifies how a configuration can evolve by making a single and atomic step. The evolution of configurations involves message creation and absorption. The syntax of a message is similar to the syntax of the method invocation, except that the message has no continuation. To avoid any ambiguity, messages are written between brackets: $[u.m(\tilde{v})]$.

In some cases, the reductions will be annotated by a 'label': $C_1 \xrightarrow{l} C_2$. The labels are of the form $u.m$, where u is an interface name and m a method name. These labels will be used to keep track of the evolution of private interface types.

To distinguish between the interactions on public and private interfaces, the emitting actions on public interfaces will be denoted '$*$', whereas the emitting actions on private interfaces will remain denoted '.' (dot).

In OL, interactions on private interfaces are by *rendez-vous*. The emitter and the receiver must synchronize (see rule R1).

An interaction on a public interface is performed in two steps. First, the emitter generates an asynchronous message (see rule R2); then this message is absorbed by its destination interface (see rule R3).

An object instantiation is performed simply by the syntactic replacement of the formal parameters by the actual ones (see rule R4), whereas an object creation instantiates a new object that runs in parallel with its creating object (see rule R5).

The type of a private interface is updated each time an interaction occurs on this interface (see rule R7). The rule label (set by rule R1) is used to determine the interface on which the interaction took place. The type of a private interface remains unchanged (see rule R9).

13.5.2 Static Semantics

13.5.2.1 Introduction

An interface type is a pair (μ, X), noted $\mu\, X$, where μ is the mode of the interface (public or private) and X its behaviour type. Interface types will be ranged over by the meta-variable T.

We extend type transitions and subtyping to interface types.

Definition 9 *(Interface's type behaviour)*

An interface type can perform the same actions as its behaviour type:
$\mu\, X \xrightarrow{\rho m(\mu_1\, Y_1, \cdots, \mu_n\, Y_n)} \mu\, X'$ *if* $X \xrightarrow{\rho m(Y_1, \cdots, Y_n)} X'$.

$$\left(\begin{array}{l} u[\cdots, m(\tilde{v}:\tilde{T}) > B, \cdots] + \Sigma Rcp_j \\ \\ | \\ \\ u.m(\tilde{w}) > B' \end{array}\right) \xrightarrow{\;u.m\;} B[\tilde{w}/\tilde{v}] \mid B' \quad \text{(R1)}$$

$$u_* m(\tilde{v}) > B \longrightarrow B \mid [u.m(\tilde{v})] \quad \text{(R2)}$$

$$\left(\begin{array}{l} u[\cdots, m(\tilde{v}:\tilde{T}) > B, \cdots] + \Sigma Rcp_j \\ \\ | \\ \\ [u.m(\tilde{w})] \end{array}\right) \longrightarrow B[\tilde{w}/\tilde{v}] \quad \text{(R3)}$$

$$\frac{A[\tilde{u}:\tilde{T}] \overset{Dcl}{=} B}{A[\tilde{v}] \longrightarrow B[\tilde{v}/\tilde{u}]} \quad \text{(R4)}$$

$$\frac{A[\tilde{u}:\tilde{T}] \overset{Dcl}{=} B}{\text{create } A[\tilde{v}] > B' \longrightarrow B[\tilde{v}/\tilde{u}] \mid B'} \quad \text{(R5)}$$

$$\frac{B_1 \xrightarrow{\;a\;} B_1'}{B \mid B_1 \xrightarrow{\;a\;} B \mid B_1'} \quad \text{(R6)}$$

$$\frac{C \xrightarrow{\;u.m\;} C' \quad T \xrightarrow{\;\rho\, m(\tilde{T})\;} T'}{\text{new } u:T \text{ in } C \longrightarrow \text{new } u:T' \text{ in } C'} \;\text{with } \rho \in \{!,?\} \quad \text{(R7)}$$

$$\frac{C \xrightarrow{\;v.m\;} C'}{\text{new } u:T \text{ in } C \xrightarrow{\;v.m\;} \text{new } u:T \text{ in } C'} \;\text{with } v \neq u \quad \text{(R8)}$$

$$\frac{C \longrightarrow C'}{\text{new } u:T \text{ in } C \longrightarrow \text{new } u:T \text{ in } C'} \quad \text{(R9)}$$

$$\frac{C_1' \xrightarrow{\;l\;} C_2' \quad C_1 \equiv C_1' \quad C_2 \equiv C_2'}{C_1 \xrightarrow{\;l\;} C_2} \quad \text{(R10)}$$

Fig. 13.3. Reduction rules.

Definition 10 *(Interface subtyping)*

An interface type T_1 is a subtype of an interface type T_2 if they have the same mode μ and if the behaviour type of T_1 is a subtype of the behaviour type of T_2:
$$\mu X_1 \preceq \mu X_2 \text{ if } X_1 \preceq X_2.$$

Our typing system must be careful about the capabilities of interfaces. We need to formalize the mechanism by which behaviours acquire new roles. To this end, we define a role addition operation as follows.

Definition 11 *(Role addition)*

Role addition is defined by the following equations and is undefined otherwise:

$$
\begin{aligned}
(\mu\, r\, x) \oplus ? &= \mu(r \cup \{?\})\, x && \text{if } ? \notin r \\
(\text{private } r\, x) \oplus ! &= \text{private } (r \cup \{!\})\, x && \text{if } ! \notin r \\
(\text{public } r\, x) \oplus ! &= \text{public } (r \cup \{!\})\, x.
\end{aligned}
$$

The client role of public interfaces can be 'added' without restriction. In the other cases, the role addition is permitted only if the role is not present yet in the interface type. To understand this operation, one may consider its inverse: role subtraction. Each time an interface role is passed (as an argument of a method invocation), this role is subtracted from the interface type. If an object passes the server role of one of its interfaces, then this object loses the capability to offer services on this interface. Similarly, if an object passes the client role of one of its private interfaces, this object will no longer have the capability to invoke services on this interface. This mechanism ensures that server roles (both public and private) and private client roles are not duplicated. Conversely, public client roles can be shared by many objects. Thus a public interface type remains unchanged after the subtraction of a client role.

Notation: The expression $T \oplus !?$ denotes the successive additions of the client and server roles: $(T \oplus !) \oplus ?$.

Definition 12 *(Interface type addition)*

Interface type addition is defined by the following equations and is undefined otherwise:

$$
\begin{aligned}
(\mu\, r_1\, x) \oplus (\mu\, r_2\, x) &= \mu((r_1\, x) \oplus r_2) && \text{if } r_2 \neq \varnothing \\
(\mu\, r_1\, x) \oplus (\mu\, r_2\, x) &= \mu\, r_1\, x && \text{if } r_2 = \varnothing.
\end{aligned}
$$

The second equation is necessary because role addition is not defined for an empty capability.

A typing context Γ is a set of bindings of the form: $u : T$ or $A : (T_1, \ldots, T_n)$. The set of interface names appearing in a context Γ is called the context domain:

$Dom(\Gamma)$. The static semantics is given using the following judgments:

Judgment	Signification
$\Gamma \vdash u : T$	In the context Γ the interface u has type T.
$\Gamma \vdash A : (\tilde{T})$	In the context Γ the object A has type $(\tilde{T})$.
$\Gamma \vdash B$	In the context Γ the behaviour B is well $-$ typed.
$\Gamma \vdash C$	In the context Γ the configuration C is well $-$ typed.

The context extension, denoted $\Gamma, u : T$ or $\Gamma, A : (\tilde{T})$, is defined such that $\Gamma, u : T \vdash u : T$ and $\Gamma, A : (\tilde{T}) \vdash A : (\tilde{T})$.

We extend $\oplus$ to typing contexts as follows:

Definition 13 *(Context addition)*

The addition of two contexts is defined by the following equation and is undefined otherwise:

$$(\Gamma_1, u : T_1) \oplus \Gamma_2, u : T_2 = (\Gamma_1 \oplus \Gamma_2), u : (T_1 \oplus T_2), \text{ if } Dom(\Gamma_1) = Dom(\Gamma_2) \text{ and } T_1 \oplus T_2$$
and $\Gamma_1 \oplus \Gamma_2$ are defined.

Definition 14 *(Addition of interface roles)*

The addition of an interface role to a context, denoted $\Gamma \oplus \rho u$, is defined if $u \in Dom(\Gamma)$ by the following equations and is undefined otherwise:

$$(\Gamma, u : T) \oplus \rho u = \Gamma, u : (T \oplus \rho)$$
$$(\Gamma, u : T) \oplus \rho v = (\Gamma \oplus \rho v), u : T \quad \text{if } u \neq v.$$

13.5.3 Typing Rules

The basic idea underlying our typing system is to guarantee that each object uses the interfaces in a way that is compatible with the declared behaviour type. These rules also ensure that there is no undesired duplication of interface roles:

$$\frac{\Gamma \vdash u : \mu \ r \ x \ \Rightarrow \ ((? \in r) \Rightarrow x = \mathbf{nil})}{\Gamma \vdash \mathbf{0}} \quad (T1)$$

This rule introduces the notion of receiving obligation. If the behaviour type of a server can perform an action (different from **nil**), then this server cannot stop:

$$\frac{\begin{array}{c} \Gamma, u: T_2 \vdash B \\ T_1 \xrightarrow{!m(X_1,\cdots,X_n)} T_2 \\ \Gamma \vdash v_1 : \mu_1 \, r_1 \, x_1 \cdots \Gamma \vdash v_n : \mu_2 \, r_n \, x_n \\ \rho_1 \, x_1 \preceq X_1 \cdots \rho_n \, x_n \preceq X_n \\ \Gamma \oplus \tilde{\rho}\tilde{v} \text{ \textbf{defined}} \end{array}}{\Gamma \oplus \tilde{\rho}\tilde{v}, u: T_1 \vdash u.m(\rho_1 v_1, \cdots, \rho_1 v_1) > B} \quad (T2)$$

This rule checks that the actual arguments of method m, v_1 of type $\mu_1 \, r_1 \, x_1$, ..., v_n of type $\mu_n \, r_n \, x_n$, are subtypes of the expected argument types X_1, ..., X_n. The behaviour type of u and the capabilities of the arguments $\tilde{v}$ are updated in the new context:

$$\frac{\begin{array}{c} I \subset [1..n] \\ \Gamma, u: T_i', \tilde{v}_i : \tilde{T}_i \vdash B_i \text{ for } i \in I \\ T \xrightarrow{?m_i(\tilde{T}_i)} T_i' \text{ for } i \in I \\ possible(T) = \{m_i \mid i \in I\} \end{array}}{\Gamma, u: T \vdash u[m_1(\tilde{v}_1 : \tilde{T}_1) = B_1 \cdots, m_n(\tilde{v}_n : \tilde{T}_n) = B_n]} \quad (T3)$$

This rule checks that each behaviour is well-typed in a context where the method parameters have their declared type. Servers must offer all of the services that are defined by their behaviour type, but are free to offer additional services:

$$\frac{\Gamma \vdash Rcp_1 \ldots \Gamma \vdash Rcp_n}{\Gamma \vdash \sum_{i=1}^{n} Rcp_i} \quad (T4)$$

The context is simply propagated as it is in all of the branches of a choice:

$$\frac{\begin{array}{c} \Gamma, u: \text{private } X \vdash B \\ Capabilities(X) = \{!, ?\} \end{array}}{\Gamma \vdash \textbf{new } u: \text{private } X \textbf{ in } B} \quad (T5.1)$$

A newly created interface has both roles†: client and server:

$$\frac{\begin{array}{c} \Gamma, u: \text{public } X \vdash B \\ Capabilities(X) = \{!, ?\} \\ uniform(X) \end{array}}{\Gamma \vdash \textbf{new } u: \text{public } X \textbf{ in } B} \quad (T5.2)$$

In the case of a public interface, its behaviour type must be uniform:

$$\frac{\Gamma, A:(\tilde{T}), \tilde{u}:\tilde{T} \vdash B}{\Gamma, A:(\tilde{T}) \vdash A[\tilde{u}:\tilde{T}] = B} \quad (T6)$$

† The function *Capabilities* is simply defined as follows: $Capabilities(r\,x) = r$.

This rule enforces that, in the case of an object declaration, the behaviour of the object is well-typed in a context where the declaration formal arguments have their declared types:

$$\Gamma \vdash B$$

$$\Gamma \vdash A : (\mu_1 \, X_1, \cdots, \mu_n \, X_n)$$

$$\Gamma \vdash u_1 : \mu_1 \, r_1 \, x_1 \cdots \Gamma \vdash u_n : \mu_n \, r_n \, x_n$$

$$\rho_1 \, x_1 \preceq X_1 \cdots \rho_n \, x_n \preceq X_n$$

$$\frac{}{\Gamma \vdash A[\tilde{\rho}\tilde{u}]} \quad (T7)$$

An interface having a subtype of another can replace it in an object instantiation:

$$\Gamma \vdash B$$

$$\Gamma \vdash A : (\mu_1 \, X_1, \cdots, \mu_n \, X_n)$$

$$\Gamma \vdash u_1 : \mu_1 \, r_1 \, x_1 \cdots \Gamma \vdash u_n : \mu_n \, r_n \, x_n$$

$$\rho_1 \, x_1 \preceq X_1 \cdots \rho_n \, x_n \preceq X_n$$

$$\frac{\Gamma \oplus \tilde{\rho}\tilde{u} \text{ defined}}{\Gamma \oplus \tilde{\rho}\tilde{u} \vdash A[\tilde{\rho}\tilde{u}] > B} \quad (T8)$$

This is the same case as the last, except that here we must update the capabilities of the interfaces $\tilde{u}$:

$$\Gamma_1 \vdash B_1$$

$$\Gamma_2 \vdash B_2$$

$$\frac{\Gamma_1 \oplus \Gamma_2 \text{ defined}}{\Gamma_1 \oplus \Gamma_2 \vdash B_1 \mid B_2} \quad (T9)$$

Finally, this last rule states that there is no duplication of the roles of a client interface when composing configurations.

Note: Similar rules can also be given for configurations involving messages. We omitted them here for the sake of brevity.

13.6 An Example

We present a small buffer example intended to show how interface types can be defined and used in a configuration of objects. We also demonstrate how coordination can be modelled using private interfaces.

Our initial step is to declare the interface type for a one-place buffer that stores elements (interfaces) of type elem:

```
Buff = put(!elem) ; Full
Full = get(!r_elem) ; Buff.
```

These two equations simply state that a buffer is initially waiting for the message put carrying an element of type !elem (a reference on elem) and then behaves according to the behaviour type Full. When full, the buffer waits for the message get with an argument of type !r_elem, which corresponds to the return address.

Interfaces of type r_elem return elements of type elem:

```
r_elem = ret(!elem) ; 0
```

The behaviour type 0 is a predefined behaviour type that cannot evolve.

13.6.1 A Buffer and a Client

An object that encapsulates a one-place buffer can now be written:

```
Buffer[self: private ?Buff] =

  self[put(e: private !elem) =
          Full-Buffer[?self, !e]
      ]
```

This object starts with an initial server interface self, which is ready to accept a put method. Method put takes an argument e, which is the client role (the reference of the object to be stored) of an interface of type elem. After accepting method put, the object becomes a Full-Buffer, which has the continuation of the server role for self and a client role for interface e. Full-Buffer is ready for method get, which takes an interface r that is used as a target for returning the value e:

```
Full-Buffer[self: private ?Full,
                e: private !elem ] =
  self[get(r: private !r_elem) =
          r.ret(!e) > Buffer[?self]
      ]
```

Note how, at the initial state of Full-Buffer, the behaviour type of interface self is ?Full. We can now define a client that uses our buffer:

```
Buffer-Client[ buf: private !Buff,
                e: private  !elem ]=
  buf.put(!e) >
  new r: private !?r_elem in
    buf.get(!r) >
    r[ret(e: private !elem) =
          Buffer-Client[!buf, !e]
      ]
```

Object Buffer-Client is parameterized with the (client) interface of the buffer and the (client) interface of the element that is to be stored in the buffer. It starts by invoking method **put**, and then it creates a new interface (a newly created interface always has both roles, client and server) that is used in the argument of the invocation of method **get**.

13.6.2 A Buffer and Two Clients

We turn now to modeling two coordinated clients for our buffer: a producer and a consumer. We will take advantage of the private interface **buf** to synchronize these two objects: the client role for **buf** is passed between the two objects – the producer after storing an element in the buffer, and the consumer after getting this element. The **Producer** object is as follows:

```
Producer[buf: private !Buff,
            e: private   !elem,
         prod: private   ?s_empty,
         cons: private   !s_full]=
  buf.put(!e) >
  cons.token(!buf) >
  prod[token(buf: private   !Buff) =
          Producer[!buf,!e,?prod,!cons]
      ]
```

and the **Consumer** object is given hereafter:

```
Consumer[cons: private ?s_full,
         prod: private   !s_empty ]=
  cons[token(buf:private !Full) =
            new r: private   !? r_elem in
              buf.get(!r) >
              r[ret(e: private !elem) =
                  prod.token(!buf) >
                  Consumer[?cons, !prod]
              ]
      ]
```

The previous objects make use of interface behaviour types **s_full** and **s_empty**, which are simply defined by the following equations:

```
s_full = token(!Full) ; s_full
s_empty = token(!Buff) ; s_empty
```

13.7 Run-Time Safety

We first define run-time failures using the following rules:

$$\frac{m \neq m_i \ , \ \forall \, i \in [1..n]}{\left(\begin{array}{l} u[m_1(\cdots) > B_1, \cdots, m_n(\cdots) > B_n] + \Sigma Rcp_j \\ \ \ | \\ u.m(\tilde{v}) > B' \end{array} \right) \longrightarrow error} \quad (E1)$$

A configuration where the server on a private interface is not ready to accept a message m while the client of this interface is trying to invoke this service reduces to *error*:

$$\frac{k \neq l}{\left(\begin{array}{l} u[\cdots, m(u_1, \ldots, u_k) > B, \cdots] + \Sigma Rcp_j \\ \ \ | \\ u.m(v_1, \ldots, v_l) > B' \end{array} \right) \longrightarrow error} \quad (E2)$$

Similarly, a configuration where the server is ready to process the message m, but where there is a parameter arity mismatch, reduces to *error*:

$$\frac{m \neq m_i \ , \ \forall \, i \in [1..n]}{\left(\begin{array}{l} u[m_1(\cdots) > B_1, \cdots, m_n(\cdots) > B_n] + \Sigma Rcp_j \\ \ \ | \\ [u.m(\tilde{v})] \end{array} \right) \longrightarrow error} \quad (E3)$$

A configuration where a message is addressed to a public interface that cannot process it reduces to *error*:

$$\frac{k \neq l}{\left(\begin{array}{l} u[\cdots, m(u_1, \ldots, u_k) > B, \cdots] + \Sigma Rcp_j \\ \ \ | \\ [u.m(v_1, \ldots, v_l)] \end{array} \right) \longrightarrow error} \quad (E4)$$

As for the private interface case, a configuration where there is a parameter arity mismatch reduces to *error*:

$$\frac{B \longrightarrow error}{\mathbf{new} \ u\!:\!T \ \mathbf{in} \ B \longrightarrow error} \quad (E5)$$

$$\frac{B_1 \longrightarrow error}{B_1 \mid B_2 \longrightarrow error} \quad (E6)$$

If a subconfiguration reduces to *error*, then so does the entire configuration.

Theorem 1 *(Subject reduction)*

If a configuration C_1 is well-typed in the context Γ_1, and if $C_1 \overset{l}{\longrightarrow} C_2$ or $C_1 \longrightarrow C_2$, then there exists a context Γ_2 where C_2 is well-typed.

Justification of the theorem: This result is mainly due to the following properties of our calculus. These properties are enforced by the typing discipline defined and by the synchronization mechanisms of the calculus (see [Nim99] for the proof).

- Behaviour types of public interfaces are uniform.
- Client roles of private interfaces cannot be duplicated.
- Synchronization on private interfaces is by *rendez-vous*.
- Objects use their interfaces according to their declared type.

Theorem 2 *(Run-time safety)*

A well-typed configuration C cannot reduce to error: $\Gamma \vdash C \Rightarrow C \xrightarrow{\;\;/\;\;} error$.

Justification of the theorem: This theorem follows (almost) immediately from the subject reduction property.

13.8 Conclusions

The object calculus that we have presented combines features of the asynchronous π-calculus [MPW92] (see Chapter 9) and the Actors model [AMST92] (see Chapter 8). This calculus is endowed with typing rules that guarantee a safety result, which is that there are no 'message not understood' errors at run-time. We extended this result to infinite types in [NNS99a] and to guarantee a liveness property in [NNS99b] with proofs in [Nim99].

Type systems for concurrent object-oriented languages is an active research topic. Many authors have tackled this issue in the realm of the π-calculus [MPW92] and the Actors [AMST92] paradigms. Concerning the former, a wide variety of typing systems have been proposed that deal with the problem of channel typing. The simplest one [Mil93] just checks the arity of the channels. This type system has been extended such that it can handle polymorphism and type inference [Gay93, VH93, Tur95] and subtyping [PS93, PT00]. None of these typing systems handles dynamic service behaviour.

The importance of distinguishing public from private interfaces has been identified by [Nie95], but, without giving it a formal treatment. [Nie95] has also introduced the concept of nonuniform service availability and has used traces to specify the constraints on the ordering of the messages that can be handled by a channel (an interface). Our work extends [Nie95] in two ways: by formally introducing the concept of privacy of interfaces, and by allowing message types to include parameter types.

Takeuchi et al. [THK94] define a typed process calculus called ϖ with the notion of *session*: 'a semantically atomic chain of communication actions' between two processes. In *OL*, a session is represented by a communication between two objects using a private interface. But unlike *OL*, the session channels are static and the roles of the partners of a session cannot be passed. In *OL*, an object can pass its client or the server role of a private interface and so delegate to another object the continuation of a 'session'.

In [Pun96] the author provides a typing system that handles the dynamic behaviour of Actors. [Pun96] features the concept of type spliting, allowing the introduction of a form of parallelism in the types. The type language is based on traces, but the possibility of having recursion and nonterminating behaviour are not explicitly treated.

The work that is the closest to ours is perhaps [Kob98]. It is based on the asynchronous π-calculus and has a typing system that ensures a certain form of deadlock freeness. The main difference between [Kob98] and our approach is that only a restricted form of behaviour, without loops, is allowed in the liveness fragment of the calculus proposed in [Kob98].

TYCO [Vas94, RV97] is another interesting endeavor that is worth mentionning. TYCO is a calculus that is built for the purpose of experimenting with behavioural type issues. In [RRV98] a type discipline is exhibited on TYCO that is less restrictive than the one presented here, but which guarantees weaker properties.

A recent interesting deadlock freeness result was achieved in [Bou97] on a process calculus that is more expressive than *OL* and which unifies the π- and λ-calculi. This result, in fact, is more about verifying complex configurations using typing techniques. Our aim is different, and we are more concerned with open configurations and issues of extending applications at run-time.

The technical treatment of the contexts in the static semantics of *OL* has been inspired by [KPT96]. In this version of the π-calculus the authors use the linear capabilities of some special channel to ensure that they are used (at most) once. We use a similar mechanism to ensure that there is no duplication of the roles of private interfaces.

As seen in our two small examples, a well-known problem with object calculi based on process calculi is the intensive use of intermediate channels for returning results. In our case this leads to an increase of interface type declarations, since types have to be declared explicitly.

Thus it is worth exploring the possibility of using functional behaviour types. For example, the behaviour type of a one-place buffer would be something like:

```
Buff = put(elem) ; Full
Full = get() -> elem ; Buff
```

The buffer itself could be written in pseudocode as follows:

```
Buffer[store: elem]: Buff
begin
void put(e: elem){
        store := e;
```

```
}

elem get(){
    return store;
}
end
```

The buffer encapsulates a state that is the store in this case and possesses two methods: put and get. The declaration of Buffer of type Buff specifies the synchronization constraints on its methods. This way, we can separate the functional aspects of the objects from the synchronization aspects. In addition, the synchronization aspect are 'visible' from the outside world of the object. In such a language, one should be careful about the semantics of a private reference and about the meaning of reference passing in a method call.

Bibliography

[AMST92]   G. Agha, I. A. Mason, S. F. Smith, and C. L. Talcott. Towards a theory of actor computation. In *The Third International Conference on Concurrency Theory (CONCUR '92), Volume 630 of Lecture Notes in Computer Science*, pages 565–579. Springer-Verlag, August 1992.

[BBSDS97]   H. Bowman, C. Briscoe-Smith, J. Derrick, and B. Strulo. On behavioural subtyping in LOTOS. In H. Bowman and J. Derrick, editors, *FMOODS'97, Second IFIP International Conference on Formal Methods for Open Object-based Distributed Systems*, pages 335–351. Chapman and Hall, July 1997.

[BD99]   H. Bowman and J. Derrick. A junction between state based and behavioural specification. In A. Fantechi P. Ciancarini and R. Gorrieri, editors, *International Conference on Formal Methods for Open Object-based Distributed Systems (FMOODS'99)*. Kluwer, 1999.

[Bou97]   G. Boudol. Typing the use of resources in a concurrent calculus. In *The Asian Computing Science Conference (ASIAN'97), Volume 1345 of Lecture Notes in Computer Science*, pages 239–253. Springer-Verlag, 1997.

[Gay93]   S.J. Gay. A sort inference algorithm for the polyadic π-calculus. In *Proceedings of the Twentieth ACM Symposium on Principles of Programming Languages*. ACM, January 1993.

[Kob98]   N. Kobayashi. A partially deadlock-free typed process calculus. *ACM Transactions on Programming Languages*, 20(2):436–482, 1998.

[KPT96]   N. Kobayashi, B.C. Pierce, and D.N. Turner. Linearity and the pi-calculus. In *Principles of Programming Languages*, 1996. Full version to appear in *ACM Transactions on Programming Languages and Systems (TOPLAS)*, 1999.

[Mil89]   R. Milner. *Communication and Concurrency*. Prentice Hall, 1989.

[Mil93]   R. Milner. The polyadic pi-calculus: a tutorial. In *Logic and Algebra of Specification*, pages 203–246. Springer-Verlag, 1993.

[MPW92]   R. Milner, J. Parrow, and D. Walker. A calculus of mobile processes (Parts I and II). *Information and Computation*, 100:1–77, 1992.

[Nie95]   O. Nierstrasz. Regular types for active objects. In O. Nierstrasz and D. Tsichritzis, editors, *Object-Oriented Software Composition*, pages 99–121. Prentice Hall, 1995. Earlier version in proceedings of *OOPSLA '93*, published in *ACM Sigplan Notices*, 28(10), October 1993, pp. 1–15.

[Nim99]   A. Nimour. *Types non-uniformes pour les objets repartis*. PhD thesis, École Nationale Sup´erieuredes T´el´ecommunications, 1999.

[NN97]   E. Najm and A. Nimour. A calculus of object bindings. In H. Bowman and J. Derrick, editors, *International Conference on Formal Methods for Open Object-based Distributed Systems (FMOODS'97)*, pages 5–20. Chapman and Hall, 1997.

[NNS99a]   E. Najm, A. Nimour, and J-B. Stefani. Infinite t ypesfor distributed objects interfaces. In A. Fantechi P. Ciancarini and R. Gorrieri, editors, *International Conference on Formal Methods for Open Object-based Distributed Systems (FMOODS'99)*, pages 351–370. Kluwer, 1999.

[NNS99b]   E. Najm, A. Nimour, and J-B. Stefani. Liveness properties through behavioral t yping of objects. In *Joint International Conference Formal Description Techniques For Distributed Systems and Communication Protocols and Protocol Specification, Testing, and Verification (FORTE/PSTV'99)*. Kluwer, 1999.

[PS93]   B.C. Pierce and D. Sangiorgi. Typing and subtyping for mobile processes. In *Logic in Computer Science*, 1993. Full version in *Mathematical Structures in Computer Science*, Vol. 6, No. 5, 1996.

[PT00]   B.C. Pierce and D.N. Turner. Pict: A programming language based on the pi-calculus. In *Proof, Language and Interaction: Essays in Honour of Robin Milner*. MIT Press, 2000.

[Pun96]   F. Puntigam. Types for active objects based on trace semantics. In E. Najm and J-B. Stefani, editors, *International Conference on Formal Methods for Open Object-based Distributed Systems (FMOODS'97)*, pages 4–19. Chapman and Hall, 1996.

[RRV98]   A. Ravara, P. Resende, and V.T. Vasconcelos. Towards an algebra of dynamic object types. In *Workshop on Semantics of Objects as Processes*, volume NS–98–5 of *BRICS Notes Series*, June 1998.

[RV97]   A. Ravara and V.T. Vasconcelos. Behavioural t ypesfor a calculus of concurrent objects. In *Euro-Par'97, Volume 1300 of Lecture Notes in Computer Science*, pages 554–561. Springer-Verlag, 1997.

[THK94]   K. Takeuchi, K. Honda, and M. Kubo. An interaction-based language and its t yping system. In *Proceedings of PARLE'94, Volume 817 of Lecture Notes in Computer Science*, pages 398–413. Springer-Verlag, 1994.

[Tur95]   D.N. Turner. *The Polymorphic Pi-calulus: Theory and Implementation*. PhD thesis, University of Edinburgh, 1995.

[Vas94]   V.T. Vasconcelos. Typed concurrent objects. In *Proceedings of the Eighth European Conference on Object-Oriented Programming (ECOOP), Volume 821 of Lecture Notes in Computer Science*, pages 100–117. Springer-Verlag, July 1994.

[VH93]   V.T. Vasconcelos and K. Honda. Principal typing schemes in a polyadic pi-calculus. In *Proceedings of CONCUR '93*, July 1993. Also available as Keio University Report CS-92-004.

Part Five
Concurrent OO Languages

14

Reflection in Concurrent Object-Oriented Languages

Hidehiko Masuhara   Akinori Yonezawa

University of Tokyo, Japan

14.1 Concurrent Object-Oriented Languages

In recent developments in network intensive applications and parallel high-performance applications, concurrent object-oriented programming languages [Agh86, YBS86, Yon90, AWY93] are becoming widely used.

In concurrent object-oriented languages, objects have their own activities (threads of control), and exchange messages between each other. This language model can be viewed as the sequential object-oriented language model augmented with multithreading and serialization (mutual exclusion) facilities, which are integrated in method invocations.

```
class Tree {
    Tree left, right;                    // sub-nodes
    boolean empty = true;                // true if it has no value
    int value;
    void insert(int v) {                 // insert a new value in a tree
        if (empty) {
            empty = false; value = v;    // set the value to the node
            left = new Tree(); right = new Tree();
        } else if (v < value) left←insert(v); // delegate to one of the sub-nodes
        else right←insert(v);            // by an asynchronous message
    }
    int sum() {                          // accumulate the values in a tree
        if (empty) return 0;
        else {
            Future⟨int⟩ leftSum, rightSum;  // reply-boxes for receiving results
            leftSum = left←sum();           // invoke methods on both sub-nodes
            rightSum = right←sum();
            // receive results, and return the sum
            return leftSum.touch() + rightSum.touch() + value;
        }
    }
}
```

Fig. 14.1. A tree structure in a concurrent object-oriented language.

Figure 14.1 shows a binary tree program in a pseudoconcurrent object-oriented language that has Java-like syntax. The method insert creates a new node at an appropriate position in a tree. By using an asynchronous method invocation, multiple insertion requests can be handled in a tree. The method sum accumulates the values in a tree by concurrently executing the method sum of its subtrees. The language is extended from Java in the following respects:

- A form '$o \leftarrow m(arg, \ldots)$' *asynchronously* invokes the method m of object o. The caller continues its execution without waiting for the completion of m.
- An asynchronous method invocation may create and return a *reply box*, which stores the return value from the method. The type of a reply box is Future$\langle t \rangle$, where t is the return type of the invoked method.
- The evaluation of a return form stores its return value into a reply box that is created for the invocation. The value can be extracted by calling the method touch of the reply box. When touch is called before the evaluation of return (i.e., the reply box is empty), the caller of the touch is blocked until any value is returned to the reply box.
- Method invocations on an object are *serialized* (or *synchronized*, in Java's terminology); at most one thread can run a method on an object at a time.

From a different point of view, concurrent object-oriented languages can be understood as object-oriented languages with multithreading and mutual exclusion mechanisms that are integrated with objects. In parallel and distributed applications, programmers need to manage the distribution of data and computation explicitly. In order to exploit distributed processes while keeping consistency among them, those object-integrated multithreading and mutual exclusion mechanisms are useful, as well as a number of benefits in traditional object-oriented programming such as data encapsulation and inheritance.

14.2 Motivation for Reflection

Parallel and distributed applications often require complicated structures in order to achieve practical efficiency and robustness. If we wrote such an application in a language solely equipped with primitive parallel/distributed constructs, the program would be difficult to understand because the code for the original algorithm and the code for the optimization of efficiency or robustness would be intertwined. As a result, the program would be less portable since the optimizations tend to be machine-dependent.

Such optimizations might be easily realized if we could modify the implementation of the language system. In fact, many language systems offer APIs to alter their implementations. However, the solution is less modular because the APIs are unstructured. In addition, it is difficult to implement optimizations that need runtime information from the program and the execution environments by using those APIs.

Assume a parallel program that can be optimized by introducing application-specific scheduling. If the language provides no ways to control the scheduling of threads in application programs, the program should be restructured so that the threads in the program are to be explicitly controlled by a user-level scheduler. The modification may not be trivial; it would be difficult to separate the code for scheduling and the code for the original application in the modified program. Even if the language system provided the ways to control thread scheduling, for example, an API for setting a priority number of a thread, the solution might have portability and modularity problems. This is because (1) the API may not be common to all of the implementations, and (2) it is difficult to give priority numbers that are consistent with the ones used in the other program modules.

In summary, we need

- ways to access an implementation of the language system under high-level language abstraction so that the modifications to the implementation can be portable and modular, and
- ways to introduce new linguistic constructs and to modify the behaviour of existing constructs in order to describe complicated modifications separately from original algorithms.

14.3 Introduction to Reflection

Computational reflection was first proposed as a computational model for self-extensible programming languages [Smi84, Mae87], and then was recognized as a theoretical basis of *open implementations* – systems that allow the extension of their internal implementations in a disciplined manner [Kic92]. As stated in the previous section, concurrent object-oriented languages need the abilities to modify/extend their implementations in portable and modular ways. A number of reflective concurrent object-oriented languages have thus been developed in the preceding decade. This section introduces the basic concepts of reflection and then reviews two major approaches: run-time and compile-time reflection.

14.3.1 Basic Concepts of Reflection

14.3.1.1 Tower of Meta-Levels

A model of a computational system consists of a problem domain (P) and a system (S) that manipulates the entities in the problem domain (Figure 14.2(a)). We call the levels of P and S *base-level* and *meta-level*, respectively. A reflective system can manipulate not only the entities of P, but also the entities of S; the system can operate on its implementations (Figure 14.2(b)). Such operations, however, are difficult to be realized safely. When an operation on S changes the behaviour of S, the behaviour of the operation itself might be changed.

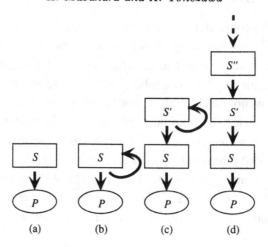

Fig. 14.2. Tower of meta-levels.

To distinguish the system that performs operations and the system that is operated on, we consider another system S' that executes S (Figure 14.2(c)). The operations on S can be clearly understood by regarding S' as the system that performs those operations. The level of S' is called the *meta-meta-level*. Consequently, we also consider that a system S'' executes S', and S''' executes S'', and so forth, making the system at each level reflective. As a result, we obtain an infinite tower of meta-levels, or a *reflective tower* (Figure 14.2(d)).

14.3.1.2 *Level-Shifting Operations and Causally Connected Self-Representation*

In order to access the meta-level, reflective systems provide *level-shifting operations*, which change the current execution level to the next level above. For example, assume that a program is running at the base-level; the program is a list of instructions of how the system (S) operates on the entities (objects) in a problem domain (P). When a level-shifting operation is executed in the program, the meta-meta-system (S') starts operations on the entities of meta-system S.

Those entities of S are called *causally connected self-representations* (CCSR) of the system if each of them satisfies the following conditions:

- Changes in the system's state are observable through values in CCSR.
- When a CCSR is modified, the behaviour of the system reflects the modification.

In other words, a CCSR of a system is an implementation of the system that can be accessed as 'objects' in the programming language.

The process that obtains a CCSR from the current execution state is called *reification*. The inverse process is called *reflection*. When a system evaluates a level-shifting operation at level n, it reifies the current execution state of the process at level $(n + 1)$ and continues its computation with the reified data (i.e., CCSR) at level $(n + 1)$.

Simple reflective languages usually have a monolithic CCSR. For example, the CCSR in 3-Lisp [Smi84] is the state of a meta-interpreter, namely, the expression to be interpreted, the environment and continuation, which are extracted from the actual implementation of the system.

14.3.1.3 Meta-Objects

The design of CCSR, which is usually called the *meta-level architecture*, in reflective languages is crucial to its expressiveness. The scope of a CCSR – a group of base-level objects represented by the CCSR – is especially important in concurrent object-oriented languages. In these languages, a monolithic CCSR, whose scope is all of the objects in the base-level program, is inappropriate because it is difficult to take a snapshot of concurrent and distributed activities. In addition, the scope should have a grain that suits users' customizations.

Many object-oriented reflective languages provide a CCSR called a *meta-object*, whose scope is an individual base-level object. In this chapter, $\uparrow x$ denotes a meta-object of object x. Since an object is a fundamental unit of manipulation, encapsulation, reuse, and so on, in object-oriented languages, a meta-object is an appropriate unit of customization in most cases.

In addition to meta-objects, various CCSRs are provided for representing concepts that are specific to a base language. For example, class-based object-oriented languages usually have a meta-level object – called a *class object* – that represents the notion of a class in a base-level program. The scope of a class object is all of the base-level objects that belong to the class. This naturally reflects the fact that objects that belong to the same class share the same behaviour.

14.3.2 Run-Time Reflection

When a CCSR includes a run-time state of a language system, the language is *run-time reflective*. In run-time reflective languages, a level-shifting operation has two aspects: (1) dynamically obtaining meta-level objects (i.e., CCSRs), and (2) executing user-defined programs at the meta-level.

A simple operation offers only the former aspect. For example, the $\uparrow$ operator gives a reified meta-object of a given object. A base-level program can inspect and modify the meta-level information of an object by invoking methods of the obtained meta-object.

Another type of level-shifting operations is *annotations*, which associate user-defined meta-objects to specific base-level objects. Reification is implicit in this type of operation. When a base-level object that has a user-defined meta-object is accessed (e.g., a method of the object is invoked), the system automatically reifies relevant run-time states and executes a method (program) of the meta-object. In other words, the meta-object defines customized behaviour of the associated base-level object. Operations that can be customized by user-defined meta-objects typically include:

- invoking a method (method lookup and execution of the body),
- reading/writing an instance variable,
- obtaining information about the object (class name, list of methods, list of instance variable names, etc.),
- installing/replacing a method and
- changing the class.

14.3.3 Compile-Time Reflection

In *compile-time reflective* languages, CCSRs embody the internals of the compilers, such as a parse tree, a symbol table and a code generator. A user-defined program at the meta-level is executed when the system compiles (i.e., before executing) a base-level program. Customization of behaviour of the base-level program is achieved by generating compiled code that realises meta-level programmers' intention. Since compilation is performed before the execution of the target program by nature, there are no ways to access the run-time states of the system.

Compile-time reflective languages usually provide annotations that associate user-defined meta-level programs to specific base-level programs. In class-based object-oriented languages, the association may be established on a per-class basis. When the system compiles a base-level program module, the system reifies the compiler's internal states into CCSRs and executes the associated meta-level program as a part of the compiler.

In some compile-time reflective languages, the meta-level represents merely the preprocessor of the language. In such a language, the user-defined meta-level programs perform source-to-source transformation.

Since the meta-level and the base-level are not executed at the same time, different languages can be used at each level [LKRR92, Rod92]. When the meta- and base-level languages are the same, the meta-level program can also be compiled under the user-defined meta-meta-level programs; the language has a tower of compilers [Chi95].

14.4 Reflection in Concurrent Object-Oriented Languages

14.4.1 Run-Time Reflection in Concurrent Object-Oriented Languages

14.4.1.1 What is 'Meta-Level' in a Concurrent System?

In concurrent object-oriented languages, an object is a unit of concurrency control, reuse, encapsulation, and so on. As discussed in the previous section, a *meta-object* is a standard CCSR in concurrent object-oriented languages. Figure 14.3 and Figure 14.4 show a structure of a meta-object in ABCL/R [WY88]. Its components include a message queue, a method table†, a list of instance variables, and an evaluator.

---

† Since ABCL/R is based on a prototype-based concurrent object-oriented language ABCL/1 [YBS86, Yon90], its meta-object has its own method table.

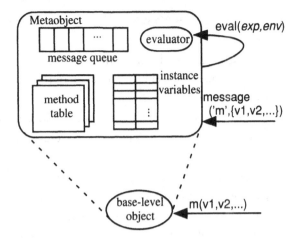

Fig. 14.3. A meta-object in ABCL/R.

```
class Metaobject {
  Dictionary instanceVars, methodTable;
  Queue messageQueue;              // queue for pending requests
  Eval evaluator;                  // interpreter for evaluation of method body
  void message(String name, Object args[]) { // method invocation request
    if (the object is executing another method) {
      suspend the request until the object becomes idle.
    } else {
      Method m = this.lookupMethod(name);
      Environment env = new Environment(instanceVars, m.formals(), args);
      evaluator←eval(m.body(),env);   // evaluate the body of the method.
    }
  }
  // methods for introspecting object's state
  Method lookupMethod(String name) { return methodTable.get(name); }
  Object lookupInstVar(String name) { return instanceVars.get(name); }
    ⋮
  // methods for altering object's state
  void addMethod(String name, Method m) { methodTable.put(name,m); }
  void addInstVar(String name, Object value) { instanceVars.put(name,value); }
    ⋮
}
```

Fig. 14.4. A meta-object of ABCL/R in pseudocode.

The methods of the meta-object define the behaviour of the respective base-level object. When a base-level program evaluates '$o.m(v_1, v_2, \ldots)$', where o, m and v_i are a receiver object, a method and the ith argument of m, respectively, the following operations are performed at the meta-level:

(i) The system invokes a method **message** of the meta-object of o with 'm' and a list of $v_1, v_2, \ldots$ as its arguments.

(ii) The method **message** first checks if the object is executing another method. If it is, the meta-object suspends the invocation request by inserting it into the message queue†.

(iii) If it is not (i.e., the object is idle), the meta-object looks for a method that matches to m in its method table. When no matching method is found, it reports an error.

(iv) The meta-object then evaluates the body of the matched method by asynchronously invoking method **eval** of the **evaluator** subobject. Since the meta-object does not wait for the termination of the evaluation, it can receive other requests while the base-level object is executing a method.

(v) The subobject **evaluator** interprets the body of a method, like meta-circular interpreters of Lisp.

The customization of an object's behaviour is typically achieved by defining an extended meta-object that overrides some of its methods and instance variables. For example, a new inheritance mechanism can be implemented by overriding the method **lookupMethod**. A meta-object also has several methods for reasoning about the structure of the object, such as adding a new method. Those methods can be invoked from base-level programs.

14.4.1.2 Varieties of Meta-Level Designs

The reflective architecture of ABCL/R, which is presented in the previous subsection, is called an *individual-based architecture* (IBA), in the sense that each base-level object has its own meta-object (Figure 14.5(a)). Parallel and distributed applications, on the other hand, often require global control, such as scheduling and load balancing. In order to easily describe meta-level programs for controlling global behaviour, varieties of reflective architectures are proposed.

Group-Wide Architecture (GWA) Watanabe and Yonezawa proposed the notion of a *group-wide reflective architecture (GWA)* in their language, ACT/R [WY91]. In ACT/R, a CCSR is a collection of meta-level objects that form a transition system of concurrent objects. The scope of a CCSR is a *group* of base-level objects; the behaviour of objects in a group can be globally controlled by modifying the CCSR of the group, the *meta-group*. Since a meta-group is also an object-group, there is a meta-group of the group, a meta-meta-group at the meta-meta-level. Consequently, the architecture has towers of meta-groups, as illustrated in Figure 14.5(b). A meta-group of a GWA has no explicit object that individually corresponds to a base-level

---

† The actual meta-object definition is more complicated, as it is designed as a state-transition machine in order to suspend method invocation requests. See [WY88] for details and [MY98] for an alternative design.

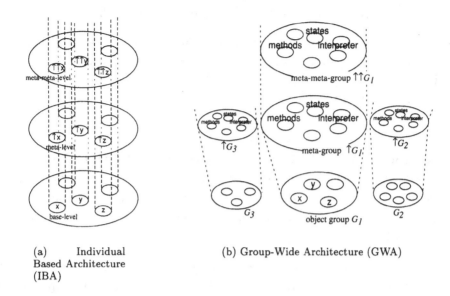

(a)   Individual
Based Architecture
(IBA)

(b) Group-Wide Architecture (GWA)

Fig. 14.5. Individual-based architecture and group-wide architecture.

object. As a result, it is difficult to customize the behaviour of individual base-level objects.

Hybrid Group Architecture (HGA) The meta-level architecture of ABCL/R2, is basically similar to IBA, but meta-objects in a group share some resources, like a GWA [MWY91, MMWY92]. The architecture called *hybrid group architecture (HGA)* enables global control of objects, as well as customization of individual objects' behaviour. In ABCL/R2, a meta-interpreter and a meta-object creator (a meta-level object that is used for creating new base-level objects) are shared by group members.

Multimodel Reflection Framework (MMRF) Okamura et al., in their study on AL-1/D [OIT93, OI91], proposed a *multimodel reflection framework (MMRF)*, in which several types of CCSRs (which are called *models* in their study) are available for supporting different kinds of customizations at the meta-level. For example, a CCSR has meta-objects that correspond to individual base-level objects, like an IBA. Another CCSR provides a meta-level object that represents a group of base-level objects, like a GWA. The programmer can access an appropriate CCSR for his/her customization. Implementing an MMRF is not an easy task because it should preserve the consistency of multiple models when a modification is performed on a single model. Their implementation [OIT93] provides the multiple models by creating projection from an actual implementation.

14.4.1.3 Mechanisms for Dynamic Modification

User-defined meta-level algorithms are often dynamic in nature; it is desirable to select a control policy that is suitable to the run-time state of the system and application program. Several mechanisms that support dynamic modification of meta-levels have been studied:

Dynamic Modification of Meta-Level Through Meta-Meta-Level In reflective languages with an infinite tower of meta-levels, a meta-level object also has its meta-object at the meta-meta-level. Therefore, the behaviour of a meta-level object can be dynamically modified by sending requests to its meta-object.

Decomposition of Meta-Object Functionalities of a meta-object, which are usually implemented by the methods of the meta-object in simple reflective architectures, can be defined by several subobjects. This 'decomposition' makes it possible to dynamically alter the behaviour of a meta-object by replacing its subobject. In the CodA [McA95] reflective Smalltalk language, a meta-object has several sub-objects, each of which implements specific functionality of the base-level object's behaviour, such as sending a method invocation request. In MAUD (Meta-level Architecture for UltraDependability) [AFPS93], a message queue and a dispatcher, which handles incoming and outgoing method invocation requests, respectively, can be replaced dynamically for implementing fault-tolerant mechanisms.

Object Migration Between Meta-Spaces In the Apertos reflective operating system [Yok92], a *meta-space,* which is a similar notion to a meta-group in GWA, is a collection of meta-level programs that provides a set of OS services. When a base-level object requires an OS service, the request is handled by a meta-level object in the meta-space to which the base-object belongs. A base-level object can dynamically *migrate* to another meta-space. From the viewpoint of base-level programs, they can switch the implementation of OS services by migrating to another meta-space.

Dynamic Adaptation Amano and Watanabe proposed the dynamically adaptable software system (DAS) in their work on LEAD++ [AW99]. When a generic function of LEAD++ is invoked, the system selects a method that matches not only the types of arguments, but also the states of the run-time environment. The selection mechanism itself is implemented as DAS methods at the meta-level. Therefore, the programmer can install his or her own method-selection mechanisms. Furthermore, a method-selection mechanism that is most suitable to the current state of the run-time environment can be dynamically selected by the DAS mechanism.

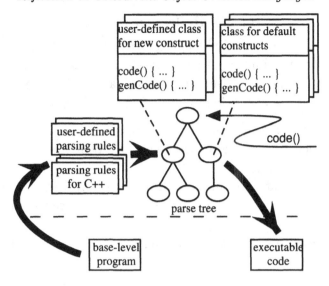

Fig. 14.6. Meta-level architecture of MPC++.

14.4.2 Compile-Time Reflection for Concurrent Objects

One of the major applications of concurrent object-oriented programming is parallel high-performance computing. Concurrent objects are especially attractive because they could easily describe irregular parallelism while retaining reusability. MPC++ is a parallel extension of C++ with a compile-time reflective architecture [IHS$^+$96, IHT$^+$96].

The major purposes of the reflective architecture of MPC++ are the:

- introduction of new parallel syntactic constructs,
- customization of behaviour of existing programming constructs and
- implementation of hardware specific optimisations.

The meta-level of MPC++ is a compiler that consists of an extensible parser and classes that implement a code generator, as shown in Figure 14.6. A new parallel syntactic construct can be introduced in the following ways:

- define a class for the construct at the meta-level;
- define a new parsing rule for the construct and associate the above class with the rule;
- define a code-generation rule (or a program-transformation rule) as a method of the above class.

When the system parses an expression that matches the user-defined parsing rule, it creates an object that belongs to the associated class as a node of the parse tree. At the code-generation phase, a method **code** of each node in the parse tree is recursively invoked. Consequently, the user-defined code generation rule is applied to the newly defined constructs.

14.4.3 Reflection in Java

Java is a sequential object-oriented language with support for distributed programming: a thread library, a built-in object-marshaling mechanism, high availability to multiple platforms, secure execution mechanisms, and so on. A number of reflective mechanisms for Java are also being studied. Some of them are

- run-time reflection based on fully fledged interpreters [DS99];
- run-time reflection that can alter the behaviour of method invocations [Gui98, WS99];
- run-time reflection that only supports introspective operations [Jav97];
- compile-time reflection whose meta-level serves as a source-to-source preprocessor [TC98];
- compile-time reflection whose meta-level serves as a just-in-time compiler [MOS+98].

Most reflective architectures are similar to those studied in languages other than Java, but these pay special attention to the characteristics of Java, such as secure execution and bytecode level compatibility.

14.5 Applications

There are several studies that demonstrated how reflection can be used in parallel and distributed applications. In the following subsections, we will see (1) a simple language extension that is implemented on run-time and compile-time reflective architectures, (2) an implementation of a new language mechanism, and (3) an implementation of performance optimisations described separately from applications.

14.5.1 Object Migration

As a simple example, we first demonstrate the implementations of an object migration mechanism in run-time and compile-time reflective languages. For simplicity, the object migration mechanism merely (1) creates a 'clone' of a specified object at a remote site, and (2) forwards subsequent method invocations on the original object to the clone object. We also assume that the languages already have basic functions for distributed programming, such as remote object creation and remote method invocation.

14.5.1.1 Object Migration with Run-Time Reflection

In a run-time reflective language, we define a customized meta-object that has:

- an additional method migrate that creates a clone of the object at the specified remote site. Since the state of the base-level object is represented as the values of instance variables in the meta-object, the meta-object merely copies the values of those variables to the newly created meta-object. (Our current example omits the migration of a running object, because it generates complicated issues.)

```
class MigratoryMeta extends Metaobject { // inherits the default meta-object
    MigratoryMeta migrated = null;      // reference to the clone
    void migrate(Site destination) {
        if (migrated == null) {          // create a meta-object at remote site
            migrated = new MigratoryMeta() @ destination;
            migrated←setState(instanceVars, methodTable, messageQueue);
        } else migrated←migrate(destination); // forward the migration request
    }
    void setState(Dictionary v, Dictionary m, Queue q) {
        instanceVars = v; methodTable = m; messageQueue = q;
    }
    void message(String name, Object args[]) {
        if (migrated == null)            // let the superclass handle the invocation
            super.message(name, args);   // request if it is not yet migrated
        else migrated←message(name,args); // forward the invocation request
    }                                    // to the migrated meta-object
}
```

Fig. 14.7. Object migration in a run-time reflective language.

- an additional instance variable **migrated** that keeps the reference to the clone object.

- a method **message** that overrides the one in the original meta-object definition so that it will forward method invocation requests to the clone object if it is already created.

Figure 14.7 shows an outline of the meta-object. Evaluation of the expression new MigratoryMeta() @ destination in method migrate creates a new object at the site specified by destination. In addition to the above modifications, the meta-object has an auxiliary method setState for setting instance variables after object creation.

14.5.1.2 Object Migration with Compile-Time Reflection

In a compile-time reflective language, object migration can be implemented by translating an original class into the new one. The translated class has an additional method that creates a clone of an object at a remote site. Each method of the class is modified so that it will delegate an invocation request to the clone, if it has been created.

Figure 14.8 shows an outline of the meta-class in OpenC++ [Chi95]. (For brevity, we omit several complications due to the syntax of C++.) When a base-level class that is associated with the meta-class, like the one shown in Figure 14.9(a), is compiled, an object of MigratoryClass is created, and its method TranslateClass is called during compilation. A call to member.SetFunctionBody in the method inserts a conditional branch for delegating method invocations. (The function Ptree::Make generates a parse tree from a string. The pattern '%p' in the string argument is replaced with a parse tree given as a subsequent argument.) Also, calls to Append-

```
class MigratoryClass : Class { // inherits the standard meta-class
  void TranslateClass(Environment* env) {
    Member member;
    int i = 0;
    Ptree *iVars = NIL, *args = NIL, *assignments = NIL;
    while (NthMember(i++, member)) // for each method & inst. var. in a class
      if (member.IsFunction() && !member.IsConstructor()) {
        // insert a conditional branch at the beginning of each method
        member.SetFunctionBody
          (Ptree::Make
            ("{ if (migrated==0) %p else migrated->%p(%p); }",
              member.FunctionBody(), member.Name(), member.Arguments()));
        ChangeMember(member);
      } else if (!member.IsFunction()) {
        given a list of instance variables (v₁ : t₁, v₂ : t₂,...) in the target class,
        it generates a list of variable names [v₁, v₂, ...] into iVars, a list of
        temporary variables with types [t₁ x₁, t₂ x₂, ...] into args, and a list
        assignment statements [v₁ = x₁;  v₂ = x₂; ...] into assignments.
      }
    // add a new instance variable for referencing the migrated object
    AppendMember(Ptree::Make("%p *migrated = 0;", Name()));
    // add a migration method
    AppendMember(Ptree::Make("%p *migrate(int dest) { \
                              migrated = new %p() @ dest;\
                              migrated->setState(%p);\
                              return migrated; }",
                            Name(), Name(), iVars));
    // add an auxiliary method for setting instance variables
    AppendMember(Ptree::Make("void setState(%p) { %p }",
                            args, assignments));
  }
};
```

Fig. 14.8. Object migration in a compile-time reflective language

Member insert a new instance variable migrated, and methods migrate and setState for creating a clone object.

The result of the translation is shown in Figure 14.9(b). In the example, we assume that the language has built-in distributed facilities, although OpenC++ itself does not. The expression new Point(...) @ dest creates an object of the class Point at a remote site and returns a remote reference to the object.

14.5.2 Time Warp: Discrete Event Simulation Algorithm

Meta-level objects can be used to implement an extended language. The second example is an implementation of a *Time Warp* mechanism, which supports discrete event simulations in a distributed environment [Jef85]. The mechanism requires that each object manages its local clock (called *virtual time*) and optimistically processes incoming events for maximizing parallelism. Since there is no global synchronization,

```
metaclass MigratoryClass Point; // annotation for using user-defined meta-class
class Point {
    int x,y;
    Point() { x = 0; y = 0; }
    void move(int dx, int dy) { x += dx; y += dy; }
};
```

(a) before translation

```
class Point {
    int x,y;
    Point() { x = 0; y = 0; }
    void move(int dx, int dy) {
        if (migrated==0) {              // check if it is already migrated
        x += dx; y += dy;
        } else migrated→move( dx , dy );   // forward the invocation r quest
    }
    Point *migrated = 0;
    Point *migrate(int dest) {
        migrated = new Point() @ dest;    // create a new object at r emote site
        migrated→setState( y ,x );        // copy instance variables
        return migrated;
    }
    void setState( int temp2 , int temp1 )  // r einitialize instance variables
        { y = temp2; x = temp1; }
};
```

(b) after translation

Fig. 14.9. Base-level programs in a compile-time reflective language (underlined are inserted by the user-defined meta-class).

an object sometimes receives conflicting events, which should be processed before some events that are already processed by the object. The mechanism solves it by performing rollback.

Watanabe and Yonezawa showed that the Time Warp mechanism can be implemented elegantly by using meta-objects in ABCL/R [WY88]. The meta-object has:

- an instance variable that represents its local clock time,
- a customized message queue and a table of instance variables that can restore their states to the ones at the specified time,
- an instance variable for recording outgoing method invocation requests,
- a customized evaluator that attaches a time stamp for each outgoing method invocation request and records those outgoing requests,
- a customized method that processes method invocation requests, so that the

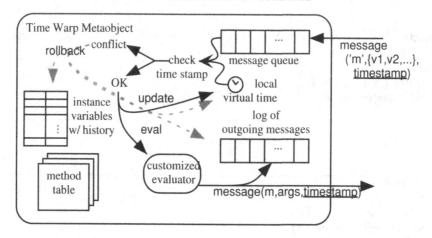

Fig. 14.10. A meta-object that implements the Time Warp mechanism.

method compares the time stamp in the incoming request with the local clock
of the object, and then either (1) advances the clock to the time stamp or (2)
performs a rollback to the time stamp.

Of course, such a mechanism can be implemented in nonreflective languages. The
benefit of the reflective implementation is the separation of the Time Warp mechanism from the code for simulation, which are otherwise written in an intertwined
way. From the viewpoint of the simulation code programmer, the meta-object implements a new simulation language that assures global consistency. Moreover, the
separation enables the further optimization of the Time Warp mechanism, such as
priority-based scheduling [MMWY92], without modifying the simulation code.

14.5.3 Dynamic Selection of Object Migration Policies

Meta-level programming in reflective languages is useful to implement complex optimization strategies separately from application programs. Okamura et al. demonstrated that object migration strategies for reducing network overheads of distributed applications can be implemented at the AL-1/D's meta-level [OI91].

In distributed applications, when an object frequently accesses to objects at a
remote site, the migration of the object to the remote site could reduce the network
overheads. However, there is no general rule that correctly determines when and
which object should migrate for all types of applications.

Using the 'distributed environment' model of AL-1/D, which exposes a method
send that sends a method invocation request, they demonstrated several customized
versions of send that trigger object migration. A version counts a number of remote
method invocations and makes the sender object migrate to the receiver's site when
the number exceeds a threshold (Figure 14.11). Another version moves not only

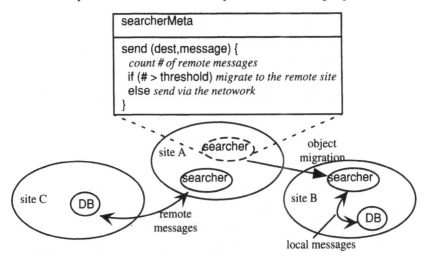

Fig. 14.11. A meta-object that implements an object migration strategy.

the sender object, but also the objects that appear in the parameter of the method invocation, like the *call-on-move* mechanism of Emerald [JLHB88].

14.6 Efficient Implementation Techniques for Run-Time Reflection

Although reflection is a powerful mechanism for customizing/extending languages, its model – tower of meta-levels – prevents efficient execution. A naïve implementation that actually runs meta-interpreters has orders of magnitude of overheads. In order to execute practical applications in reflective languages, efficient implementation techniques are essential.

14.6.1 Compiling Away the Meta-Level by Using Partial Evaluation

The primary source of overheads in reflective languages is interpretive execution; the meta-level program computes how an expression in a base-level program should behave at run-time. This means that the behaviour of a base-level program cannot be determined without executing meta-level programs. A compiler for such a language is not trivial to build.

When there are definitions of an interpreter and an interpreted program, a program specialization technique called *partial evaluation* [JGS93] can generate a *compiled* program. The scheme is also known as *the first Futamura projection* [Fut71]. When both base- and meta-level programs are available at compile-time, we could apply the scheme to reflective languages.

Unfortunately, most practical partial evaluators target sequential languages; application of the first Futamura projection to concurrent object-oriented reflective languages is not trivially achieved. Masuhara et al. showed a compilation framework of concurrent object-oriented reflective languages by using partial evaluation in their study on ABCL/R3 [MMAY95, MY98]. Their framework first translates the sequential part of the meta-level program (i.e., the method dispatching in meta-objects and evaluation of the method body in meta-interpreters) into a sequential language and then applies partial evaluation. The specialized (compiled) program is translated back into concurrent objects for further compilation. Since the overheads of meta-level execution are mostly written in the sequential part, compiled programs run faster than the interpretive ones by orders of magnitude.

14.6.2 Memoization of Functional Behaviour

When functional behaviour is dominant in meta-level execution in terms of execution time, *memoization* would be a useful optimization technique.

For example, consider a process of a meta-object that realizes method dispatching for a base-level method invocation. In the process, the meta-object searches the method definition that has the specified name and is defined in the most specific class to the receiver object. When the base-level program later requests another method invocation that has the same method name and the same receiver class, the meta-object can reuse the result of the previous search. This is because the search process has a functional behaviour. In such a case, we can remember a tuple of the method name, the receiver class name and the searched method body. Later, when a method invocation is requested and there is a tuple that has the same method name and receiver class name, the remembered method body can be used without traversing the class hierarchy. The optimization, called *memoization*, is known to be especially effective if the process is heavy (e.g., when we employ complicated inheritance rules).

The problem of the memoization technique is that it is only applicable to the procedures that have functional behaviour. Kiczales et al. designed the meta-object protocols of CLOS, in which the memoization technique can effectively optimize the overheads of meta-level execution (Chaper 4.4 in [KdRB91]). In their design, meta-level procedures are explicitly separated into *functional* and *procedural* ones, which would be defined in an intertwined way in naïve meta-level design.

Compared to compilation by using partial evaluation, the memoization technique is simpler to implement and easier to cope with dynamic modifications. On the other hand, when functional and procedural behaviours are intertwined in meta-level programs, the effectiveness of the memoization technique is very limited.

14.7 Summary

This chapter briefly introduced the notion of reflection and reviewed several reflective architectures of concurrent object-oriented languages. Reflection is useful for parallel and distributed applications in describing various meta-level controls (performance optimization, fault-tolerance, etc.) separately from application programs. It is also useful in implementing extended languages for specific purposes, such as distributed simulation. Although several studies have shown the usefulness of reflection, sophisticated meta-level design and efficient execution mechanisms need to be investigated further to make it more practical. As for efficient execution, two major approaches are being studied: compile-time reflection and compilation using partial evaluation.

Bibliography

[AFPS93]   G. Agha, S. Frølund, R. Panwar, and D. Sturman. A linguistic framework for dynamic composition of dependability protocols. In C.E. Landwehr, B. Randell, and L. Simoncini, editors, *IFIP Third Working Conference on Dependeble Computing for Critical Applications*, IFIP Transactions, pages 345–363, 1993.

[Agh86]   G. Agha. *ACTORS: A Model of Concurrent Computation in Distributed Systems*. MIT Press, 1986.

[AW99]   N. Amano and T. Watanabe. Reflection for dynamic adaptability: A linguistic approach using LEAD++. In Cointe [Coi99], pages 138–140.

[AWY93]   G. Agha, P. Wegner, and A. Yonezawa, editors. *Research Directions in Concurrent Object-Oriented Programming*. MIT Press, 1993.

[Chi95]   S. Chiba. A metaobject protocol for C++. In Loomis [Loo95], pages 285–299.

[Coi99]   P. Cointe, editor. *Second International Conference Reflection'99*. Springer-Verlag, July 1999.

[DS99]   R. Douence and M. Südholt. The next 700 reflective object-oriented languages. Technical Report 99-1-INFO, École des mines de Nantes, Dept. Informatique, 1999.

[FC98]   J.-C. Fabre and S. Chiba, editors. *OOPSLA'98 Workshop on Reflective Programming in C++ and Java*, volume 98-4 of *Technical Report of Center for Computational Physics, University of Tsukuba*, October 1998.

[Fut71]   Y. Futamura. Partial evaluation of computation process – an approach to a compiler-compiler. *Systems, Computers, Controls*, 2(5):45–50, 1971.

[Gui98]   J. O. Guimarães. Reflection for statically t ype languages. In Jul [Jul98], pages 440–461.

[IHS+96]   Y. Ishikawa, A. Hori, M. Sato, M. Matsuda, J. Nolte, H. Tezuka, H. Konaka, M. Maeda, and K. Kubota. Design and implementation of metalevel architecture in C++: MPC++ approach. In G. Kiczales, editor, *Reflection'96*, pages 153–166, April 1996. See http://jerry.cs.uiuc.edu/reflection/reflection96/index.html.

[IHT+96]   Y Ishikawa, A. Hori, H. Tezuka, M. Matsuda, H. Konaka, M. M., T. Tomokyo, J. Nolte, and M. Sato. MPC++. In G V. Wilson and P. Lu, editors, *Parallel Programming using C++*, chapter 11, pages 429–464. MIT Press, 1996.

[Jav97]   JavaSoft, Mountain View, CA. *Java Core Reflection: API and Specification*, January 1997.

[Jef85]   D. R. Jefferson. Virtual time. *ACM Transactions on Programming Languages and Systems*, 7(3):404–425, July 1985.

[JGS93]   N. D. Jones, C. K. Gomard, and P. Sestoft. *Partial Evaluation and Automatic Program Generation*. Prentice Hall, 1993.

[JLHB88]   E. Jul, H. Levy, N. Hutchinson, and A. Black. Fine-grained mobility in the Emerald system. *ACM Transactions on Computer Systems*, 6(1):109–133, February 1988.

[Jul98]   E. Jul, editor. *European Conference on Object-Orienetd Programming (ECOOP'98), Volume 1445 of Lecture Notes in Computer Science*. Springer-Verlag, July 1998.

[KdRB91]   G. Kiczales, J. des Rivi`eres,and D. G. Bobrow. *The Art of the Metaobject Protocol.* MIT Press, Cambridge, MA, 1991.

[Kic92]   G. Kiczales. Towards a new model of abstraction in software engineering. In Yonezawa and Smith [YS92], pages 1–11.

[LKRR92]   J. Lamping, G. Kiczales, L. Rodriguez, and E. Ruf. An architecture for an open compiler. In Yonezawa and Smith [YS92], pages 95–106.

[Loo95]   M. E. S. Loomis, editor. *Proceedings of Object-Oriented Programming Systems, Languages and Applications (OOPSLA'95),* volume 30(10) of *ACM SIGPLAN Notices.* ACM, October 1995.

[Mae87]   P. Maes. Concepts and experiments in computational reflection. In N. Meyrowitz, editor, *Proceedings of Object-Oriented Programming Systems, Languages, and Applications (OOPSLA'87),* volume 22(12) of *ACM SIGPLAN Notices,* pages 147–155. ACM, October 1987.

[McA95]   J. McAffer. Meta-level programming with CodA. In W. Olthoff, editor, *European Conference on Object-Orienetd Programming (ECOOP'95),* pages 190–214. Springer-Verlag, August 1995.

[MMAY95]   H. Masuhara, S. Matsuoka, K. Asai, and A. Yonezawa. Compiling away the meta-level in object-oriented concurrent reflective languages using partial evaluation. In Loomis [Loo95], pages 300–315.

[MMWY92]   H. Masuhara, S. Matsuoka, T. Watanabe, and A. Yonezawa. Object-oriented concurrent reflective languages can be implemented efficiently. In Paepcke [Pae92], pages 127–145.

[MOS+98]   S. Matsuoka, H. Ogawa, K. Shimura, Y. Kimura, and K. Hotta. OpenJIT – a reflective Java JIT compiler. In Fabre and Chiba [FC98], pages 16–20.

[MWY91]   S. Matsuoka, T. Watanabe, and A. Yonezawa. Hybrid group reflective architecture for object-oriented concurrent reflective programming. In P. America, editor, *European Conference on Object-Orienetd Programming (ECOOP'91),* pages 231–250. Springer-Verlag, July 1991.

[MY98]   H. Masuhara and A. Yonezawa. Design and partial evaluation of meta-objects for a concurrent reflective language. In Jul [Jul98], pages 418–439.

[OI91]   H. Okamura and Y. Ishikawa. Object location control using meta-level programming. In M. Tokoro and R. Pareschi, editors, *European Conference on Object-Orienetd Programming (ECOOP'94),* pages 299–319. Springer-Verlag, July 1991.

[OIT93]   H. Okamura, Y. Ishikawa, and M. Tokoro. Metalevel decomposition in AL-1/D. In Nishio and Yonezawa, editors, *Proceedings of the International Symposium on Object Technologies for Advanced Software (ISOTAS'93), Volume 742 of Lecture Notes in Computer Science,* pages 110–127. Springer-Verlag, 1993.

[Pae92]   A. Paepcke, editor. *Proceedings of Object-Oriented Programming Systems, Languages and Applications (OOPSLA'92),* volume 27(10) of *ACM SIGPLAN Notices.* ACM, October 1992.

[Rod92]   L. Rodriguez, Jr. A study on the viability of a production-quality metaobject protocol-based statically parallelizing compiler. In Yonezawa and Smith [YS92], pages 107–112.

[Smi84]   B. C. Smith. Reflection and semantics in Lisp. In *Conference Record of Symposium on Principles of Programming Languages (POPL'84),* pages 23–35, 1984.

[TC98]   M. Tatsubori and S. Chiba. Programming support of design patterns with compile-time reflection. In Fabre and Chiba [FC98], pages 56–60.

[WS99]   I. Welch and R. Stroud. From Dalang to Kava - the evolution of a reflective jana extension. In Cointe [Coi99], pages 2–21.

[WY88]   T. Watanabe and A. Yonezawa. Reflection in an object-oriented concurrent language. In *Proceedings of Object-Oriented Programming Systems, Languages, and Applications (OOPSLA'88),* volume 23(11) of *ACM SIGPLAN Notices,* pages 306–315. ACM, November 1988.

[WY91]   T. Watanabe and A. Yonezawa. An actor-based metalevel architecture for group-wide reflection. In *REX School/Workshop on Foundations of Object-Oriented Languages 1990, Volume 489 of Lecture Notes in Computer Science*, pages 405–425. Springer-Verlag, 1991.

[YBS86] A. Yonezawa, J.-P. Briot, and E. Shibayama. Object-oriented concurrent programming in ABCL/1. In N. Meyrowitz, editor, *Proceedings of Object-Oriented Programming Systems, Languages, and Applications (OOPSLA'86)*, volume 21(11) of *ACM SIGPLAN Notices*, pages 258–268. ACM, October 1986.

[Yok92] Y. Yokote. The Apertos reflective operating system: The concept and its implementation. In Paepcke [Pae92], pages 414–434.

[Yon90] A. Yonezawa, editor. *ABCL: An Object-Oriented Concurrent System*. MIT Press, 1990.

[YS92] A. Yonezawa and B. C. Smith, editors. *Proceedings of International Workshop on New Models for Software Architecture (IMSA92): Reflection and Meta-Level Architecture*, November 1992.

15

Inheritance in Concurrent Objects

Cosimo Laneve

University of Bologna, Italy

15.1 Introduction

Inheritance is the basic mechanism of object-oriented programming for supporting abstraction, incremental development and code reuse. In the object-oriented programming style, the code is usually structured in object patterns, called *classes*, that are defined out of basic definitions or preexisting classes.

When object-oriented languages are integrated with concurrency primitives, the emphasis is usually laid on the modelling of parallelism and of mutual exclusion (see, for instance, POOL [Ame89], ABCL [YBS86], Obliq [Car94] or Java [GJS96]). No special care is given to inheritance, which is mostly handled as in the sequential setting. As a result, one often stumbles into subtle typing flaws [Sar97] or into anomalies that compel one to redefine the inherited code [MY93].

Some progress in devising a rigorous model bringing objects and concurrency together has recently been made. Several researchers have in fact defined basic languages for the concurrent object-oriented paradigm, equipping them with precise and clear semantics, simple type systems and equational theories. To date two approaches have emerged. One consists of recasting some well-established object calculus and enriching it with concurrent primitives (parallel composition and the operation of scope restriction) [BF96, GH98]. The second attempts the other way around, trying to extend process calculi with objects by introducing record types [Vas94, DZ98].

However, there is an apparent distance among these calculi and concurrent object-oriented languages that jeopardizes their utility. The focus in the latter is on classes and the inheritance of class definitions while the former, being object-based, largely overlook these issues. Regrettably, forgetting about classes prevents any treatment of inheritance, which is even more crucial when concurrency is added.

In this chapter we define a concurrent object-based calculus, in the same style as [BF96, GH98], but it is simpler because it uses a name passing discipline. Then, on top of it, we introduce classes and inheritance. The full calculus is used to review and systematize the main developments in the design of concurrent object-oriented languages; viz, concurrency primitives, inheritance and synchronization operations for inheritance.

Synchronization operations for inheritance allow concurrent objects to be assembled and, at the same time, modify the internal synchronization between the methods. For instance, consider a two-cell buffer defined by inheriting the code of a one-cell buffer. In this case, reads and writes must be desynchronized to admit a further method for emptying the cell and storing the value in another field. This amounts to redefining the whole code, if standard inheritance is used.

Two basic inheritance mechanisms to refine an object's internal synchronizations are *enabled sets* (developed for Rosette [TS89]) and *method guards* (proposed for Guide [DKM$^+$89]). The former specify the set of methods that can be invoked through the life of an object: objects always accept invocations of methods in the active enabled set and refuse the others. Enabled sets may be suitably refined during inheritance, thus implicitly changing the object's behaviour. Method guards are Boolean expressions attached to each method that must be satisfied in order that the method can execute. Also, method guards may be refined during inheritance, therefore altering the overall behaviour. We prove that two class-based languages, respectively, with enabled sets and with method guards, can be encoded in a compositional way into our basic language when extended with an operation testing for object name equality. In particular we demonstrate that name disequality is not necessary to encode enabled sets.

Therefore, we may conclude that enabled sets and method guards do not seem to solve any anomaly about inheritance (of the synchronization code) that cannot be solved in a simple calculus without any synchronization mechanism. Perhaps a rigorous analysis of the inheritance of the synchronization code could shed some light and suggest some new models. In this respect, the work [FLMR00] should contribute to this aim.

The rest of the chapter is organised as follows. In Section 15.2 we present the sequential object calculus, including the underlying model, the observational semantics and the class extension. In Section 15.3 we extend the basic calculus with primitives for concurrency and discuss other proposals in the literature. In Section 15.4 we introduce the problem of the inheritance anomaly and discuss an example. In Section 15.5 we describe two languages, one with enabled sets and the other with method guards, and determine their expressive powers. Proofs are omitted, but may be retrieved from http://www.cs.unibo.it/~laneve/papers/UBCLSinhco.ps, where the full paper can be found. We conclude in Section 15.6.

15.2 The Object Calculus

In this section we introduce the core, sequential object calculus, detailing the underlying model and the observational semantics.

15.2.1 Syntax

We consider three countable disjoint sets of names: *object names* – ranged over by $x, y, u, \cdots$; *method names* – ranged over by $m, n, \cdots$; and *field names* – ranged over by $a, b, \cdots$. Tuples of names are written $u_i^{i\in 1..n}$, or abbreviated as $\widetilde{u}$.

The syntax of the *object calculus* consists of *terms* p and *expressions* e that are defined by:

$$
\begin{array}{llll}
p & ::= & 0 & \qquad\qquad e \quad ::= \quad x \\
  & | & x.m(\widetilde{e}) & \qquad\qquad\qquad\qquad | \quad x.a \\
  & | & x.a := e ; \ p & \\
  & | & \mathbf{obj}\ x = \varsigma(z)\,[a_i = u_i^{\,i\in 1..h}, m_i(\widetilde{x}_i) = p_i^{\,i\in 1..k}]\ \mathbf{in}\ p.
\end{array}
$$

Sequences of fields and methods $a_i = z_i^{\,i\in 1..h}, m_i(\widetilde{x}_i) = p_i^{\,i\in 1..k}$ are ranged over by σ. In a term $\mathbf{obj}\ x = \varsigma(z)\,[\sigma]$ in p, the *object names* x and z are bound and their scopes are p and $[\sigma]$, respectively. In a record $[a_i = u_i^{\,i\in 1..h}, m_i(\widetilde{x}_i) = p_i^{\,i\in 1..k}]$, the object names $\widetilde{x}_i$ are bound and their scope is p_i. As usual, a name that is not bound is called *free*, and we write $p\{e/x\}$ for the substitution of e for each free occurrence of x in p. Terms will be identified when equal up-to renaming of bound names. Finally, a trailing 0 in a term p will often be omitted. Also, the binder $\varsigma(z)$ is omitted when z is not free in σ.

A term may be the inert program 0 or $x.m(\widetilde{e})$, the asynchronous invocation of the method m in the object x with arguments $\widetilde{e}$; or $x.a := e ; \ p$, the updating of the field a in the object x with the (value of the) expression e and with continuation p; or the object definition $\mathbf{obj}\ x = \varsigma(z)\,[\sigma]$ in p, where z is the *internal name* of the object x. As usual, we assume that two record values are equal if they are different for the order of fields and methods. Expressions have two shapes: they may be object names x or field selectors $x.a$.

As a simple example of an object, consider the cell with the field *val* and methods *read* and *write*:

$$
\begin{array}{ll}
\mathbf{obj}\ cell = \varsigma(x) & [val = 0, \\
& read(z) = z.reply(x.val), \\
& write(z, u) = x.val := u ; \ z.reply() \\
&]\ \mathbf{in}\ \cdots
\end{array}
$$

The object *cell* has a field *val* that is initialized to 0, and two methods *read* and *write*, to retrieve and update the cell. The *cell* reacts to a *read*-invocation by passing the value to the continuation parameter z; it reacts to a *write*-invocation by updating the value of the cell to the argument u and replying to the parameter z with an empty message.

Another, more difficult example is the encoding of λ-calculus in our object calculus. The λ-expressions consist of variables, λ-abstractions and function applications. The translation $[\![\cdot]\!]$ takes a λ-expression and a continuation object u, and gives a term in the object calculus. The style is the same as [Mil92].

$$
\begin{aligned}
[\![x]\!]_u &= x.val(u) \\
[\![\lambda x.\,M]\!]_u &= \text{obj } v = [lambda(x, w) = [\![M]\!]_w] \text{ in } u.apply(v) \\
[\![M\ N]\!]_u &= \text{obj } v = [apply(v') = \text{ obj } x = [val(w) = [\![N]\!]_w] \\
&\qquad\qquad\qquad\qquad \text{in } v'.lambda(x, u) \\
&\quad] \text{ in } [\![M]\!]_v
\end{aligned}
$$

The translation of $M\ N$ first evaluates M until an abstraction value is reached. This results in a message, $u.apply(v)$, requesting the argument. The encoding of the application replies to this message by sending back a message, $v.lambda(x, u)$, giving a pointer x to N and to the continuation u for evaluating the body of the function. Every occurrence of the bound variable into the body of a function is therefore translated as an invocation of the argument with a suitable continuation (message $x.val(u)$). In the next section, once the formal semantics of the object calculus has been introduced, we illustrate the evaluation of the encoding of a sample λ-expression.

In this chapter we shall also use an extension of the object calculus with a *name comparison operator* $[x = y]\,p,\,p'$, which has the intended meaning that p or p' is performed, according to whether $x = y$ holds. A weaker operator is *name matching*, which has no continuation in the case of disequality. We write name matching as a derived operator: $[x = y]\,p,\,0$. Name comparisons will make easy the encoding of inheritance mechanisms in our basic calculus. See [NP96] for an analysis of the expressiveness of name comparison in process algebras.

15.2.2 Semantics

The operational semantics is defined as a *reflexive chemical abstract machine* – RCHAM, for short – in the style of [FG96]. The chemical rules are given in Table 15.1. They define disjoint sets of transitions $\rightharpoonup$ (*heatings*), $\leftharpoonup$ (*coolings*), $\longrightarrow$ (*reductions*) between solutions $\mathcal{O} \Vdash p$, where $\mathcal{O}$ is a set of *named definitions* $x = [\sigma]$ and p is the term to evaluate. In a named definition $x = [\sigma]$, x is called the *name*.

As is usual in chemical semantics, each rule mentions only the components that participate in the rewriting, and the rewriting applies to every chemical solution that contains them. Solutions will be ranged over by $\mathcal{S}, \mathcal{T}, \cdots$. In Table 15.1, the rules for name comparison have been given.

The meaning of the rules is as follows. Rules (NIL) and (OBJ) describe structural, reversible rearrangements in a solution. They serve to prepare terms for (proper) reductions. The rule (OBJ) describes the introduction of objects in a solution; the side condition of the rule enforces a static scoping discipline by substituting a fresh name for the local variable when the object is introduced, and checking that the object name does not appear elsewhere in the solution when folding it back as a local object definition. Moves $\rightleftharpoons$ are called *structural moves* and the reflexive and transitive closure of $\rightleftharpoons$, denoted $\equiv$, is called *structural equivalence*.

Rule (MET) models method invocation: it happens when all of the arguments have been evaluated into object names and the effect is to trigger the method body where the formal arguments have been replaced by the actual ones. The rule (ASG) defines field updating. Observe that the continuation p is evaluated with the updated object. Rules (ARG) and (EXP) model expression evaluation; according to (ARG), arguments of method invocations may be evaluated in any order.

The last two rules describe name comparison: (NMY) and (NMN) define the behaviour of the process $[o = o']\, p,\, p'$ when the Boolean guard is true and false, respectively.

We write $\equiv\!\longrightarrow\!\equiv$ for reductions up-to structural equivalence, and we let $\Longrightarrow$ be the reflexive and transitive closure of $\equiv\!\longrightarrow\!\equiv\; \cup \equiv$. To illustrate the semantics, we compute the transitions of $[\![(\lambda\, x.\, x)N]\!]_u$, where $[\![\cdot]\!]$ is the translation of λ-expressions in the previous subsection. Let $p = \mathsf{obj}\; x = [val(u') = [\![N]\!]_{u'}]$ in $v'.lambda(x, u)$:

$$
\begin{aligned}
&\Vdash\; [\![(\lambda\, x.\, x)N]\!]_u\\
\equiv\;\; & v = [apply(v') = p],\; w = [lambda(z, w') = z.val(w')]\\
& \Vdash\; v.apply(w)\\
\longrightarrow\;\; & v = [apply(v') = p],\; w = [lambda(z, w') = z.val(w')]\\
& \Vdash\; \mathsf{obj}\; x = [val(u') = [\![N]\!]_{u'}]\; \text{in}\; w.lambda(x, u)\\
\equiv\;\; & v = [apply(v') = p],\; w = [lambda(z, w') = z.val(w')],\\
& x = [val(u') = [\![N]\!]_{u'}]\; \Vdash\; w.lambda(x, u)\\
\longrightarrow\;\; & v = [apply(v') = p],\; w = [lambda(z, w') = z.val(w')],\\
& x = [val(u') = [\![N]\!]_{u'}]\; \Vdash\; x.val(u)\\
\longrightarrow\;\; & v = [apply(v') = p],\; w = [lambda(z, w') = z.val(w')],\\
& x = [val(u') = [\![N]\!]_{u'}]\; \Vdash\; [\![N]\!]_u\\
\approx\;\; & \Vdash\; [\![N]\!]_u.
\end{aligned}
$$

The $\equiv$ steps introduce fresh object names in the solution. Note that the scope of these names is the term on the right-hand side of $\Vdash$. The reduction steps are straightforward. The last step is a case of barbed congruence, to be discussed in the next subsection. It represents the garbage collection of object definitions that can no longer be used.

Our object calculus is different from most of the calculi in the literature. Both the calculus in [FHM93] and the ς-calculus in Chapter 6 of [AC96] are functional; the former is also higher-order (expressions may be complex objects) and has 'extensible' objects, meaning that attributes may be lengthened as wished. The closest relative of the object calculus in this section is the untyped imperative calculus **imp**ς in Chapter 10 of [AC96]. However, **imp**ς is somehow more involved: the updating operation may not terminate and the (big-step) semantics is also not so simple. Still we have defined an encoding of **imp**ς into our object calculus, although we omit it here. It relies on defining suitable objects for every method body and storing the names of these objects in suitable fields of the original object. Then method calls reduce to dereferentiations and method update just relies on updating the field

(NIL)		$\Vdash 0$	$\rightleftharpoons$ $\Vdash$
(OBJ)		$\Vdash \mathbf{obj}\ x = \varsigma(z)\,[\sigma]\ \mathbf{in}\ p$	$\rightleftharpoons$ $x' = [\sigma]\{x'/z\} \Vdash p\{x'/x\}$
(MET)	$x = [m(\tilde{z}) = p, \sigma] \Vdash x.m(\tilde{u})$	$\longrightarrow$	$x = [m(\tilde{z}) = p, \sigma] \Vdash p\{\tilde{u}/\tilde{z}\}$
(ASG)	$x = [a = y, \sigma] \Vdash x.a := z;\ p$	$\longrightarrow$	$x = [a = z, \sigma] \Vdash p$
(ARG)	$x = [a = y, \sigma] \Vdash z.m(\tilde{e_1}, x.a, \tilde{e_2})$	$\longrightarrow$	$x = [a = y, \sigma] \Vdash z.m(\tilde{e_1}, y, \tilde{e_2})$
(EXP)	$x = [b = y, \sigma'] \Vdash z.a := x.b;\ p$	$\longrightarrow$	$x = [b = y, \sigma'] \Vdash z.a := y;\ p$
(NMY)		$\Vdash [x = x]\,p, p'$	$\longrightarrow$ $\Vdash p$
(NMN)		$\Vdash [x = y]\,p, p'$	$\longrightarrow$ $\Vdash p'$

With side condition:

(OBJ) x' is a fresh name.

(NMN) x and y are two different names.

Table 15.1. *The Reflexive Cham of the Object Calculus*

related to the method. We conjecture that this encoding is adequate with respect to the barbed congruence defined in the following subsection.

15.2.3 Barbed Congruence

The extensional semantics of the object calculus is *barbed congruence*. We recall its definition below, and refer to [MS92, GR96] for discussion.

Some notation is required. A *context* $C[\cdot]$ is a term with a placeholder $[\cdot]$; $C[p]$ denotes the term obtained by inserting p in the placeholder.

The *barb* $\downarrow_x$ is a predicate over terms that tests for the potential access to a free object name x. It is inductively defined by the following rules:

- $x.a := z;\ p \downarrow_x$, $z.a := x.b;\ p \downarrow_x$, $x.m(\tilde{e}) \downarrow_x$, $x.m(\tilde{e}, x, \tilde{e'}) \downarrow_x$, $x.m(\tilde{e}, x.a, \tilde{e'}) \downarrow_x$,
- $\mathbf{obj}\ z = \varsigma(z')[\sigma]\ \mathbf{in}\ p \downarrow_x$, if $p \downarrow_x$ and $x \neq z$.

The definition of $\downarrow_x$ lifts to solutions as follows: $(\mathcal{O} \Vdash p) \downarrow_x$ if $p \downarrow_x$ and $\mathcal{O}$ does not contain any named definition with name x. Finally, let *weak-barb* $\Downarrow_x$ be the predicate over solutions defined as follows:

$$\mathcal{S} \Downarrow_x \stackrel{\triangle}{=} \mathcal{S} \Longrightarrow \mathcal{T} \text{ and } \mathcal{T} \downarrow_x$$

Definition 15.2.1 *A relation ϕ on solutions is a* barbed simulation *if, whenever $\mathcal{S}\,\phi\,\mathcal{T}$, we have*

- *if $\mathcal{S} \Downarrow_x$ then $\mathcal{T} \Downarrow_x$;*

- *if $S \equiv \longrightarrow \equiv S'$ then $T \Longrightarrow T'$ and $S' \phi T'$.*

A relation ϕ is a barbed bisimulation *if both ϕ and ϕ^{-1} are barbed simulations.*

A barbed congruence *is a barbed bisimulation ϕ such that, if $(\Vdash p) \phi (\Vdash q)$, then $(\Vdash C[p]) \phi (\Vdash C[q])$, for every context $C[\cdot]$ (context closure). We let $\approx$ be the largest barbed congruence.*

Barbed bisimulation is not a congruence. For instance, $x.m()$ and $x.n()$ are barbed bisimilar, but $x.m() \not\approx x.n()$ because the context obj $x = [m() = y.a(), \ n() = z.b()]$ in $[\cdot]$ separates them. Also, barbed congruence is insensitive to divergence, that is, $0 \approx$ obj $x = [m() = x.m()]$ in $x.m()$.

Barbed congruence coincides with (may) testing congruence because the RCHAM of the object calculus is deterministic (there is always at most one successor solution). These two semantics differ when the model is nondeterministic, which will be the case when concurrency comes onto the scene. We commit to barbed congruence because it is easier to check than testing semantics.

15.2.4 *Classes and Inheritance*

The object calculus misses a crucial feature of object-oriented programming: the *possibility of reusing the code*. For instance, to specify two objects with the same definitions, the entire code has to be copied. This problem is usually solved by promoting object templates, called *classes*, and adding class instantiations to object definitions.

It is often the case that, in reusing a definition, one needs to perform some smooth adaptations. To deal with these situations, languages also offer mechanisms for expanding, modifying or combining class definitions. In this context, a class that is defined out of another one is called a *subclass* of the latter, or, alternatively, it *inherits* the code of the latter. For instance, in Smalltalk a subclass can add additional methods to a class or replace existing methods [GR83]; and in general there is no relation between methods in a class and those in a subclass (attributes of the parent class may be accessed from the subclass with the directive **super**). To avoid this anomaly, **Beta** forces inherited definitions to have precedence over extensions [KMMPN87]. See [BC90] for a detailed comparison between the two forms of single inheritance.

We illustrate classes and inheritance by extending our basic calculus to cover the new features. Two new countable sets of names are introduced: *class names*, ranged over by $c, c', \cdots$, and *super names*, ranged over by $s, s', \cdots$; and a new syntactic category is added: *definitions d*. The grammar for terms and definitions is the following (expressions are unchanged):

$$
\begin{aligned}
p \quad ::=& \quad \ldots \text{(as before)} \qquad d \quad ::= \quad [a_i = u_i{}^{i \in 1..h}, m_i(\widetilde{x}_i) = p_i{}^{i \in 1..k}] \\
& \mid \ \textsf{obj } x = c \textsf{ in } p \qquad\qquad\quad \mid \quad c \\
& \mid \ \textsf{class } c = \varsigma(x)\, d \textsf{ in } p \qquad\ \mid \quad \varsigma(x)\, d \\
& \qquad\qquad\qquad\qquad\qquad\qquad\quad \mid \quad [a_i = u_i{}^{i \in 1..h}, m_i(\widetilde{x}_i) = p_i{}^{i \in 1..k}] \textsf{ extends } d \\
& \qquad\qquad\qquad\qquad\qquad\qquad\quad \mid \quad d \textsf{ rename } m \textsf{ as } s.
\end{aligned}
$$

The class constructor $\textsf{class } c = \varsigma(x)\, d \textsf{ in } p$ defines a class name c whose scope is the term p; d is out of the scope of c – recursive class definitions are not allowed. The scope of the self-object name x is the definition d. Definitions now have a broad range of alternatives. They may be simple definitions, as before, or they may inherit definitions of another class c. The operation $\varsigma(x)\, d$ abstracts the self-name of the class. The extension and the possible replacement of the attributes of a definition d are managed by $[a_i = u_i{}^{i \in 1..h}, m_i(\widetilde{x}_i) = p_i{}^{i \in 1..k}]$ extends d; the intended meaning of this operation is the one of $\textsf{Smalltalk}$; however, $\textsf{Beta}$ enthusiasts may recover the other form of inheritance by changing the replacement operation σ'/σ, which will be discussed soon. The last operation, d rename m as s, is similar to the rename operation of $\textsf{Eiffel}$. This operation replaces the method definition $m(\widetilde{x}) = p$ occurring in d by $s(x) = p$ and gives to subclasses a way in which to invoke methods of the superclass.

The semantics of classes and inheritance is given by compiling class expressions into terms of the basic object calculus. This definitely strengthens the fact that these features are just syntactic sugar for organizing and combining code; no expressivity is added to the core calculus. To formalize this compilation, we introduce the notation σ/σ'. Let σ be $a_i = u_i{}^{i \in 1..h}, m_i(\widetilde{x}_i) = p_i{}^{i \in 1..k}$ and σ' be $a_i = v_i{}^{i \in h'..h}, a_i = u_i{}^{i \in h+1..h''}, m_i(\widetilde{x}_i) = q_i{}^{i \in k'..k}, m_i(\widetilde{x}_i) = p_i{}^{i \in k+1..k''}$; then σ/σ' abbreviates the tuple $a_i = u_i{}^{i \in 1..h''}, m_i(\widetilde{x}_i) = p_i{}^{i \in 1..k''}$.

Table 15.2 defines the compilation step. There are two reductions: $\stackrel{x}{\leadsto}$ for definitions and $\leadsto$ for terms; and context rules for the latter are omitted. We discuss the rule $[a_i = u_i{}^{i \in 1..h}, m_i(\widetilde{x}_i) = p_i{}^{i \in 1..k}]$ rename m as $s \stackrel{x}{\leadsto} [a_i = u_i{}^{i \in 1..h}, m_i\{s/m\}(\widetilde{x}_i) = p_i{}^{i \in 1..k}]$, since the others are fairly straightforward. This rule implements the so-called *late binding* mechanism because renaming applies to the method heading only: every invocation to m in the body will refer to the last definition of m in the inheritance hierarchy. Therefore it implicitly assumes that the renamed method is also redefined in the subclass. The untyped calculus has no mechanism to force this redefinition; rather, a typing system in the style of [FLMR00] could solve this flaw.

Example 15.2.2 Let us put our compiler to work with a standard example of class

For definitions: $\overset{x}{\leadsto}$

$$\varsigma(z)\, d \quad \overset{x}{\leadsto} \quad d\{x/z\}$$

$$[\sigma]\ \text{extends}\ [\sigma'] \quad \overset{x}{\leadsto} \quad [\sigma/\sigma']$$

$$[a_i = u_i{}^{i \in 1..h}, m_i(\widetilde{x}_i) = p_i{}^{i \in 1..k}]\ \text{rename}\ m\ \text{as}\ s \quad \overset{x}{\leadsto} \quad [a_i = u_i{}^{i \in 1..h}, m_i\{s/m\}(\widetilde{x}_i) = p_i{}^{i \in 1..k}]$$

$$\frac{d \overset{x}{\leadsto} d'}{[\sigma]\ \text{extends}\ d \overset{x}{\leadsto} [\sigma]\ \text{extends}\ d'} \qquad\qquad \frac{d \overset{x}{\leadsto} d'}{d\ \text{rename}\ m\ \text{as}\ s \overset{x}{\leadsto} d'\ \text{rename}\ m\ \text{as}\ s}$$

For terms: $\leadsto$

$$\text{class}\ c = \varsigma(x)\,[\sigma]\ \text{in}\ p \leadsto p\{\varsigma(x)\,[\sigma]/c\} \qquad \frac{d \overset{x}{\leadsto} d'}{\text{class}\ c = \varsigma(x)\,d\ \text{in}\ p \leadsto \text{class}\ c = \varsigma(x)\,d'\ \text{in}\ p}$$

$+$ context closure

Table 15.2. *The Compilation of Class Expressions into Object Terms*

and subclass: cells and logged cells:

$$
\begin{aligned}
\text{class}\ cell = \varsigma(z) \quad & [val = 0, \\
& read(x) = x.reply(z.val), \\
& write(x,u) = z.val := u;\ x.reply(), \\
&] \\
\text{in class}\ logcell = \quad \varsigma(z) & [write(x,u) = \\
& \quad \text{obj}\ y = [reply() = z.log(x,u)]\ \text{in}\ z.Write(y,u), \\
& \quad log(x,u) = \text{print}(x, \text{``writes''}, u);\ x.reply() \\
&]\ \text{extends}\ (cell\ \text{rename}\ write\ \text{as}\ Write)
\end{aligned}
$$

where **print** is a directive (system call) added to the basic calculus. A logged cell improves (i.e., overrides) the *write* operation to keep track of updates. In particular, for each update, the new *write* also calls the method *log* that prints who is updating and the new value. According to Table 15.2, this definition of *logcell* expands as follows:

$$
\begin{aligned}
\text{class}\ logcell = \quad & \\
\varsigma(z) \quad & [val = 0, \\
& read(x) = x.reply(z.val), \\
& Write(x,u) = z.val := u;\ x.reply() \\
& write(x,u) = \text{obj}\ y = [reply() = z.log(x,u)]\ \text{in}\ x.Write(y,u), \\
& log(x,u) = \text{print}(x, \text{``writes''}, u);\ x.reply() \\
&]
\end{aligned}
$$

The compilation steps in Table 15.2 do terminate and give a unique result (they are determinate). The crucial statements entailing these properties are collected in the following lemma.

Lemma 15.2.3

(i) *Reductions $\overset{x}{\leadsto}$ and $\leadsto$ are confluent.*

(ii) *Both $\overset{x}{\leadsto}$ and $\leadsto$ do terminate.*

Multiple Inheritance Several programming languages, such as C++, Eiffel, CLOS and Self, allow the definition of classes with more than one ancestor, called *multiple inheritance*. In these cases, the problematic issue becomes the resolution of the ambiguities of attributes conjointly defined by several classes. In C++ these ambiguities are ruled out by overriding in the subclass the methods with multiple definitions. The mechanism of multiple inheritance is still richer in CLOS. In this language ambiguities are solved by *linearizing* the ancestor graph of a class to produce an inheritance list (see [Sny87] for a criticism of this process). In Self linearization is further weakened, yielding *partial orders* of ancestors and solving ambiguities with error messages [CUCH91].

To introduce multiple inheritance in our framework we extend definitions with

$$d \quad ::= \quad \text{... (as before)}$$
$$| \quad \tilde{d},$$

meaning that s inherits all of the attributes in every class in $\tilde{d}$. Ambiguities may be solved by suitable rewriting rules for definitions. For instance, a rule solving multiple inheritance as in CLOS could be the following:

$$[\sigma_1], [\sigma_2], \cdots, [\sigma_n] \overset{x}{\leadsto} ([\sigma_1] \text{ extends } ([\sigma_2] \text{ extends } \cdots [\sigma_n]) \cdots),$$

where classes to the left override those to the right. It is beyond the scope of this chapter to detail further this topic; the reader is referred to the literature. Multiple inheritance plays a prominent rule in concurrency; a thorough discussion can be found in [FLMR00].

15.2.5 Typing Issues

There is a broad literature about types for object-oriented languages, mainly covering the relationships between subtyping polymorphism and other features, such as recursive definitions, width and depth subtyping, binary methods, existential types, and so on (see [AC96] and the references therein).

The extended object calculus of Section 15.2.4 may be equipped with a polymorphic type system à la ML that can ban *message-not-understood errors* as well as some encapsulation violations (fields and supermethods can be accessed by methods in the same object). We overlook this issue in the present chapter; the reader can find in [FLMR97] an analogous typing system.

15.3 Adding Concurrency: Threads and Locks

In this section our basic object calculus is extended with concurrency primitives. To this end, we commit to choices that have a simple formal foundation; the other proposals are discussed briefly later.

The presence of concurrent computations may compromise the encapsulation property of objects because they may invalidate the consistency of object's internal state. To avoid this flaw, most of the proposals in the literature rely on locks and primitives for acquiring and releasing locks (*mutexes*). We give a slightly more general solution than [GH98], by introducing *lock fields* and primitives for acquiring and releasing locks (in [GH98], every object has exactly one lock; here this constraint is relaxed). Actually, since the concurrent object calculus can express atomic reads and writes on a shared memory, the mutexes are not strictly needed because we could use a standard mutual exclusion algorithm for synchronizations. However, this would lead to complex programs that would be difficult to read. It is better to have mutexes as primitive operations and study the internal encoding of the calculus with mutexes into the one without them.

Let *locks* be a new countable set of names, ranged over by ℓ, ℓ'. Locks get two primitive object values: *tt* and *ff*. We use the notation '-' to mean one of the two values *tt* or *ff*. The syntax of terms p, from now on called *processes*, is extended as follows:

$$
\begin{aligned}
p \quad ::= \quad & \cdots \text{ (as before)} \\
& | \quad p \mid p \\
& | \quad acquire(x.\ell) \, ; \;\, p \\
& | \quad release(x.\ell).
\end{aligned}
$$

This extension encompasses the parallel composition of processes and two new directives, $acquire(x.\ell)$ and $release(x.\ell)$, respectively, for setting and releasing the locks. The intended meaning of $p \mid q$ is that the operations of p and q may be performed in any order, $acquire(x.\ell) \, ; \; p$, may be performed provided the lock ℓ of the object x is *tt* (so it is blocking); then it sets this lock to *ff* and triggers the continuation p. $release(x.\ell)$ sets the lock ℓ of the object x to *tt*, regardless of its value, it is not blocking. We write $\times_{i \in 1..n} p_i$ for the parallel composition $p_1 \mid \cdots \mid p_n$.

Table 15.3 defines the RCHAM for the object calculus with threads and locks. Note that now solutions are $\mathcal{O} \Vdash \mathcal{P}$, where $\mathcal{P}$ is a *multiset* of processes. Notice also that the test and set operations in (ACQ) are atomic.

Example 15.3.1 A standard example of a concurrent class is the *asynchronous channel*. It consists of a value field and two methods for reading and writing. In order to sequentialize reads and writes, two locks are added, ℓ_w and ℓ_r, that respectively enable read and write when set to *tt*. At the beginning ℓ_w is set to *tt*

Rules of Table 15.1 +

$$(\text{PAR}) \qquad \Vdash p \mid q \quad \rightleftharpoons \quad \Vdash p, q$$

$$(\text{ACQ}) \qquad x = [\ell = tt, \sigma] \Vdash acquire(x.\ell) \,;\ p \quad \longrightarrow \quad x = [\ell = f\!f, \sigma] \Vdash p$$

$$(\text{REL}) \qquad x = [\ell = \text{-}, \sigma] \Vdash release(x.\ell) \quad \longrightarrow \quad x = [\ell = tt, \sigma] \Vdash$$

Table 15.3. *The Reflexive Cham of the Object Calculus with Threads and Locks*

and ℓ_r is set to $f\!f$

class *channel* =
$$\varsigma(z)\ [val = 0,\ \ell_w = tt,\ \ell_r = f\!f,$$
$$read(x) = acquire(z.\ell_r)\,;\ \ \text{obj } y = [val = 0] \text{ in}$$
$$y.val := z.val\,;\ (x.reply(y.val) \mid release(z.\ell_w)),$$
$$write(x, u) = acquire(z.\ell_w)\,;\ z.val := u\,;\ (x.reply() \mid release(z.\ell_r))$$
$$]\text{ in } \cdots$$

Note that *read* sends back to the caller the field of a local object, rather than the value of the channel. Indeed, a body such as $acquire(z.\ell_r)\,;\ (x.reply(z.val) \mid release(z.\ell_w))$ would be wrong because the value returned by $x.reply(z.val)$ would in general be different from the value of the channel when $release(z.\ell_w)$ was performed.

Given the definition of asynchronous channels, it is straightforward to translate process calculi – like the asynchronous π-calculus [ACS98] – into our concurrent object calculus. This highlights the expressiveness of the concurrent object calculus as far as concurrency is concerned. We shall return to this issue in Section 15.5.

15.3.1 Reentrant Mutexes and Self-Serializations

Cardelli [Car94] separates *external* and *self-inflicted* operations. The former are those operations that a method performs on objects other than the method host object; the latter are operations that a method performs on its own object (*self*). In our calculus self-inflicted calls may deadlock when the caller does not reset the state before the call.

Several object-oriented programming languages avoid these misbehaviours by giving rights to threads instead of methods (see Java [GJS96], for example). In this refined variant of mutexes, called *reentrant mutexes*, a thread does not deadlock if it acquires a lock that is already locked by itself. To model correctly reentrant mutexes, one should keep track of the acquired locks and, when a thread forks, of the lock ownerships of the parent thread. This clearly makes the semantics more difficult. Still, the solution is also questionable because it is somehow too liberal and too restrictive at the same time. It is liberal because external calls calling back methods of the original object do deadlock. It is restrictive because the notion of thread is local to an address space, whilst weaker notions are needed when features such as process migration are added to the language.

An intermediate proposal between mutexes and reentrant mutexes is the so-called *self-serialization* (see [Car94] and [BF96]). With self-serialization a method can invoke an external operation, provided that the target object is 'idle' (no other thread is performing operations on that object). On the other hand, self-inflicted operations can be invoked without deadlocking. Therefore, the property of whether an operation is self-inflicted is crucial. This property cannot be set at compile-time; hence it is necessary to keep track at run-time of the current host object. This proposal is also subject to criticism because deadlocks can occur when an external method invokes back a method of the original object.

Instead of discussing a tricky solution, we have committed ourselves to simplicity in this chapter (i.e., simple mutexes), leaving to programmers the complete responsability of avoiding deadlocks in the design of complex algorithms. A detailed analysis of self-serialization can be found in [BF96]. On the contrary, formal studies on reentrant mutexes are missing.

15.4 The Inheritance Anomaly

In the last two decades several people have stumbled on oddities when inheriting concurrent code. America was the first to observe that there is no practical advantage in inheriting concurrent code because large redefinitions were usually needed to avoid synchronization flaws [Ame89]. Since then, a number of proposals to reduce this problem have appeared in the literature; in [MY93] the reader can find a survey and a comparison of most of the techniques, together with a name for this phenomenon: *the inheritance anomaly*.

We introduce the problem with an example; the inheritance anomaly is discussed soon after.

Example 15.4.1 Let us define a two-place buffer out of the asynchronous channel in Subsection 15.3. Therefore, we extend the asynchronous channel with a new field, called *valr*, that will store the second message. We then add a new method, named *daemon*, that will fill the field *valr* when *val* is full and, at the same time, empty *valr*. The method *daemon* also allows reads and writes to be parallelized. So, as a first approximation, the class *channel* could be extended by the definition:

$$\varsigma(z) \; [valr = 0, \; daemon() = z.valr := z.val] \; \text{extends } channel$$

The body of *daemon* is clearly broken because it must synchronize with *read* and *write*. This amounts to introducing two new locks, ℓ_W and ℓ_R, and changing *read* and *write*:

```
class two-channel =
    ς(z) [valr = 0, ℓ_W = tt, ℓ_R = ff
        read(x) = acquire(z.ℓ_r);  obj y = [val = 0] in
                            y.val := z.valr;  (x.reply(y.val) | release(z.ℓ_W)),
        write(x, u) = acquire(z.ℓ_w);  z.val := u;  (x.reply() | release(z.ℓ_R))
        daemon() = acquire(z.ℓ_W);  acquire(z.ℓ_R);  z.valr := z.val;
                            (release(z.ℓ_w) | release(z.ℓ_r) | z.daemon())
    ] extends channel in · · ·
```

(We assume that 'daemon' is invoked when the class is instantiated.) There is a slightly more conservative solution where only the method *read* is redefined and the field ℓ_r plays the same role as ℓ_R.

The inheritance anomaly is now evident because only fields val, ℓ_w and ℓ_r are inherited from *channel*, thus causing the benefits of inheritance to vanish in this case.

Actually this is a controversial issue. One can argue that there may be some basic concepts in common between 'channels' and 'two-place channels' such that, once these concepts have been turned into a class, it is possible to inherit without redefining the methods therein. Or, perhaps there are better reuses of the 'channel' in Section 15.3.

It is difficult to reply to these remarks. Nevertheless, notice that the naive solution seems impractical in this case and many others. This has to be considered as a noisy alarm bell, justifying a serious analysis of the problem.

What hinders code reuse in the above example is that we must weaken the synchronization between the methods *read* and *write*. This requires us to understand deeply the code of these two methods and to completely rewrite them to match the new requirements. Actually, even a smooth change of a method may have effects on every method interacting with it, and so on with the methods interacting with these latter ones. It is not surprising that such a propagation of changes may usually concern all of the methods of the class. For this reason, *inheritance of the control*, or of the *synchronization code*, of a class is a critical issue in concurrent object-oriented languages. On the contrary, the inheritance anomaly is harmless in sequential languages because methods have no competing behaviour there (i.e., no need for synchronizing code).

It is beyond the scope of this chapter to do a detailed analysis of the inheritance anomaly; rather, we point to references [MY93, Ber94, McH94]. In the next section we focus on two basic mechanisms for inheriting the control and compare their expressive power.

15.5 Proposals for Inheriting the Control

Several proposals to alleviate the inheritance anomaly have been studied in the literature. A thorough description of every mechanism would require too much space and would even be boring because many of them are somehow naive, without a rigorous motivation for the design choices. In this section we focus on two mechanisms that underlie most of the proposals:

(i) *enabled sets* by Tomlinson and Singh [TS89],

(ii) *method guards* by Decouchant et al. [DKM$^+$89].

In particular, *path expressions* refine enabled sets by adding regular expressions [CH73]; the Maude system [Mes93] or the *negative method guards* [Frø92] propose more elaborate method guards; the *synchronization schemas* [MY93] combine different synchronization mechanisms based on enabled sets and method guards.

We formally define the two models supporting enabled sets and method guards; then we systematize the expressive power of these mechanisms by proving the existence of a translation into our concurrent object calculus when it is extended with *name comparison*. Remarkably, we provide two compositional encodings of the class-based languages with the operations for enabled sets and method guards into our language with classes. As a consequence, every solution to the problem of the inheritance anomaly in the former two models may be immediately rephrased in our simple class language at the cost of using name comparison operators. This confirms, at least for enabled sets and method guards, what emerges from McHale's PhD thesis (see Chapter 13 of [McH94]), namely, that all of the proposals for inheriting the control vary in the expressive power that they possess.

15.5.1 Enabled Sets

An *enabled set* $\rho : \tilde{m}$ is a labelled set of method names of an object; it specifies the set of methods $\tilde{m}$ that can be invoked during the life of an object when ρ is 'active'. Enabled sets are activated by the special operation $\mathsf{become}(x.\rho)$, where x is the object to whom the enabled set belongs. Locks and the corresponding directives for acquiring and releasing them are now removed: all of the synchronizations are delegated to enabled sets. The methods of an object are performed in a mutually exclusive way.

Enabled sets have been developed in the concurrent object-oriented language Rosette [TS89]. To illustrate programming practice with them, we rewrite the channel in Section 15.3 into a Rosette-like language. We are informal at this stage:

The Syntax:

$$p ::= \ 0$$
$$| \ x.m(\widetilde{e})$$
$$| \ x.a := e \ ; \ p$$
$$| \ \mathsf{obj} \ x = \varsigma(z) \, [a_i = u_i{}^{i\in 1..h}, m_i(\widetilde{x}_i) = p_i{}^{i\in 1..k}], r \ \mathsf{in} \ p$$
$$| \ p \ | \ p$$
$$| \ \mathsf{become}(x.\rho)$$

$$e ::= \ x$$
$$| \ x.a$$

$$r ::= \ \rho : \widetilde{m}$$
$$| \ r, r$$

The Semantics: Rules (NIL), (ASG), (ARG), (EXP) of Table 15.1 + (PAR) of Table 15.3 +

(OBJ) $\qquad \Vdash \mathsf{obj} \ x = \varsigma(z) \, [\sigma], r \ \mathsf{in} \ p \quad \rightleftharpoons \quad x' = [\sigma\{x'/z\}], r \Vdash p\{x'/x\}$

(MET) $\quad x =_{m',\widetilde{m}} [m'(\widetilde{z}) = p, \sigma], r \Vdash x.m'(\widetilde{u}) \quad \longrightarrow \quad x = [m'(\widetilde{z}) = p, \sigma], r \Vdash p\{\widetilde{u}/\widetilde{z}\}$

(BEC) $\quad x = [\sigma], (\rho : \widetilde{m}, r) \Vdash \mathsf{become}(x.\rho) \quad \longrightarrow \quad x =_{\widetilde{m}} [\sigma], (\rho : \widetilde{m}, r) \Vdash$

With side condition:

(OBJ) $\quad x'$ is a fresh name.

Table 15.4. *The Concurrent Object Calculus with Enabled Sets*

any doubt will be clarified later.

```
class channel =
    ς(z)   [val = 0,
           read(x) = obj y = [val = 0] in
                     y.val := z.val ; (x.reply(y.val) | become(z.empty)),
           write(x, u) = z.val := u ; (x.reply() | become(z.full))
           ], (empty = {write}, full = {read})
```

When an object of class *channel* begins in a state where 'empty' is enabled, then the method *write* can execute. The termination of *write* activates the enabled set 'full', thus allowing the execution of a *read* operation. With respect to '*channel*' in Section 15.3, there is no lock and no primitive operation *acquire* and *release*. On the other hand, now, when a class is instantiated, one has to specify the active enabled set.

We split the analysis of the expressivity of enabled sets into two parts: we first focus on a basic object calculus of enabled sets and present the encoding into the calculus of Section 15.3. Then we consider classes and inheritance operations over enabled sets.

Table 15.4 collects the syntax and the semantics of the object calculus with enabled sets. Objects on the left-hand side of solutions have two shapes, $x =_{\widetilde{m}} [\sigma], r$ and $x = [\sigma], r$. The former relates an object name to a definition and a collection of enabled sets, and also specifies the set of methods $\widetilde{m}$ that can be invoked. The latter describes the state of the object where no method can be invoked. When a method invocation does succeed – see rule (MET) – the state of the object is turned into $x = [\sigma], r$, thus guaranteeing mutual exclusion. A method may be called again when the directive **become** is performed.

The Encoding of Objects To translate the object calculus with enabled sets into the concurrent object calculus of Section 15.3, we systematically add a method ctr to every object. The method ctr forces method sequentialization and constrains method executions to fit with what is defined by the directive **become** and by the enabled sets. In this setting, every method call is turned into an invocation of ctr to check whether the object can accept such a call. This is possible provided that the method name belongs to the current enabled set.

In more detail, let $\{m_1, \cdots, m_k\}$ be the set of method names of the object and let $\rho_i : S_i^{i \in 1..j}$ be its collection of enabled sets. To check whether a given method name m belongs to the current enabled set $\rho : S$, the method ctr invokes the following process $P_{S,j}$:

$$P_{S,j}(z, x) \;\triangleq\; \begin{cases} [z = z_{m_j}](x.\alpha := x \,;\; release(x.\ell_{m_j})), 0 & \text{if } m_j \in S \\[2mm] [z = z_{m_j}](x.ctr(z, x.\alpha) \mid release(x.\ell)), 0 & \text{otherwise.} \end{cases}$$

The process $P_{S,j}$ requires two sets $\{z_{m_1}, \cdots, z_{m_k}\}$ and $\{z_{\rho_1}, \cdots, z_{\rho_j}\}$ of pairwise different object names, which respectively encode method names and enabled set names. The names z_{m_i} and z_{ρ_i} are dummy object names that are added beforehand – see the translation of **obj** in the sequel. The process P_S also assumes that every object has a field α that stores (the encoding of) the name of the current enabled set. Then, $P_{S,j}$ checks whether the argument z is an object name encoding a method in S. In the first case, P_S locks the object x, by storing in α a value that is different from any enabled set name (we have chosen the self-object name x) and then releases the lock of the corresponding method. In the second case P_S returns, by again invoking ctr. (The translation introduces divergence.)

The translation of the object calculus with enabled sets is defined by $[[\cdot]]$, which in turn relies on the auxiliary function $[[\cdot]]_x$. This latter function takes a sequence of fields, method definitions, enabled sets and a fresh object name x, the self-object; its result is the following sequence of fields and method definitions:

$$[[a_i = u_i^{i \in 1..h}, \; m_i(\widetilde{x}_i) = p_i^{i \in 1..k}, \; \rho_i : S_i^{i \in 1..j}]]_x \;\triangleq\;$$

$$\alpha = x, \; \ell_{m_i} = f\!f^{i \in 1..k}, \; \ell = t\!t,$$
$$ctr(z, z') = \times_{i \in 1..j}[z' = z_{\rho_i}](\times_{i' \in 1..k} P_{S_i, i'}(z, x)), \, 0 \,,$$
$$a_i = u_i^{i \in 1..h},$$
$$m_i(\widetilde{x}_i) = \Big((acquire(x.\ell_{m_i}) \,;\; [[p_i]]) \mid (acquire(x.\ell) \,;\; x.ctr(z_{m_i}, x.\alpha)) \Big)^{i \in 1..k}.$$

The above encoding introduces a mutex ℓ_m for every method m of the object, as well as a mutex ℓ for the ctr method. A method calls ctr to check whether it has the right to continue. This invocation takes two arguments: a dummy object name related to the method and the current state of the object, stored in the field α. The method body is blocked on its own lock.

The method *ctr* verifies whether a method name belongs to an enabled set through a sequence of two name matchings: in case the method name belongs to the current enabled set, *ctr* releases the lock of the method, thus triggering its execution; otherwise, *ctr* again emits the same call to itself – see the definition of $\mathsf{P}_{S,j}$.

The definition of $[\![p]\!]$ is by structural induction (we omit those cases where $[\![\cdot]\!]$ is homomorphic with respect to the syntactic operator):

$$[\![\mathsf{obj}\ x = \varsigma(z)\,[\sigma],\ r\ \mathsf{in}\ p]\!] \overset{\triangle}{=} \mathsf{obj}\ z_\rho = [\,]^{\rho=\widetilde{m}\in r},\ z_m = [\,]^{m(\widetilde{x})=p\in\sigma}\ \mathsf{in}$$

$$\mathsf{obj}\ x = \varsigma(z)\,[\,[\![\sigma,\ r]\!]_z\,]\ \mathsf{in}\ [\![p]\!]$$

$$[\![\mathsf{become}(x.\rho)]\!] \overset{\triangle}{=} x.\alpha := z_\rho\,;\ release(x.\ell)$$

$$[\![x.m(\widetilde{e})]\!] \overset{\triangle}{=} x.m(\widetilde{e})\ |\ x.ctr(z_m, x.\alpha).$$

To formalize the correspondence between a term and its translation, we have to lift the encoding $[\![\cdot]\!]$ to solutions. Let $(x = [\sigma])_{x.a:=u}$ be the object $x = [\![(a = u)/\sigma]\!]$:

$$[\![\mathcal{O} \Vdash \mathcal{P}]\!] \overset{\triangle}{=} \bigcup_{x=[\sigma],r\in\mathcal{O}}\left(\begin{array}{l}(x = [\![\sigma,r]\!]_x)_{x.\ell=\mathit{ff}}\\x_\rho = [\,]^{\rho=\widetilde{m}\in r},\ x_m = [\,]^{m(\widetilde{x})=p\in\sigma}\end{array}\right)$$

$$\bigcup_{x=\widetilde{m}'[\sigma],r\in\mathcal{O}}\left(\begin{array}{l}(x = [\![\sigma,r]\!]_x)_{x.\alpha=z_{\rho'}},\\x_\rho = [\,]^{\rho=\widetilde{m}\in r},\ x_m = [\,]^{m(\widetilde{x})=p\in\sigma}\end{array}\right)$$

$$\Vdash\ \biguplus_{p\in\mathcal{P}} [\![p]\!].$$

where $\rho : \widetilde{m}'$ is an enabled set in r. Observe that we provide a translation of the two types of object state: $x = [\sigma], r$ and $x =_{\widetilde{m}} [\sigma], r$. In the state $x = [\sigma], r$ the object x is locked and no method can be scheduled. This is enforced in the encoding by setting the lock ℓ to ff. In the state $x =_{\widetilde{m}} [\sigma], r$ the object x is unlocked for methods in $\widetilde{m}$. By default, the encoding $[\![\cdot]\!]_{x,s}$ sets ℓ to tt. Therefore, for modelling the above state, it suffices to update α to z_ρ (ρ is the label of $\widetilde{m}$). For simplicity we assume that, if $\rho : \widetilde{m}, \rho' : \widetilde{m}' \in r$ and $\rho \neq \rho'$, then $\widetilde{m} \neq \widetilde{m}'$. (The general case can be reduced to this one, up-to barbed congruence).

Lemma 15.5.1 *Let $\mathcal{S}$ and $\mathcal{T}$ be solutions of the* RCHAM *defined in Table 15.4. Then*

(i) *If $\mathcal{S} \equiv\longrightarrow\equiv \mathcal{T}$, then $[\![\mathcal{S}]\!] \Longrightarrow [\![\mathcal{T}]\!]$.*

(ii) *If $\mathcal{S} \Downarrow_x$, then $[\![\mathcal{S}]\!] \Downarrow_x$.*

The adequacy of our encoding is a straightforward consequence of this lemma. (Barbed congruence may be easily transposed to the object calculus with enabled sets.)

Theorem 15.5.2 *For p, q, two processes in Table 15.4, $[[p]] \approx [[q]]$ implies $p \approx q$.*

The Encoding of Classes and Inheritance In this paragraph we demonstrate that the full class-based calculus of Table 15.5, with the operations over enabled sets, may be encoded into the calculus without enabled sets. This definitely fixes the expressive power of enabled sets.

Table 15.5 also collects the syntax and the compilation step of the language with enabled sets. Note that a class definition now carries a non-empty sequence of enabled sets, and enabled sets are first-class entities since it is possible to modify them when the class is inherited. These changes are done by $c \,\&\, \tilde{m}$, meaning that every enabled set of the class c is inherited provided that it contains the methods $\tilde{m}$ and $c + \tilde{m}$, which means that every enabled set of c is augmented with the methods $\tilde{m}$.

Note that, according to the syntax of Table 15.5, objects may be created as instances of classes. The object definition of Table 15.4 has been removed. Moreover, we assume that class definitions do not occur inside definitions d (classes are at the top level). Both of these restrictions simplify the foregoing encoding while keeping the expressivity of the language.

We define two translation functions $[[\cdot]]_E$ and $([\cdot])_{E,x}$ taking processes and definitions, respectively. The index E is a function that returns the set of method names of the class that it takes as argument. This set may be statically determined by a type system or by an abstract interpretation. The name x is the self-object name.

Let $S = \{m_1, \cdots, m_k\}$ be the set of method names of the class c. Also let $meth[\sigma]$ be the set of method names in the sequence σ. In the following translations we always take fresh supernames s, s'. We detail the cases where $[[\cdot]]_E$ and $([\cdot])_{CTR}^{o,E}$ are not homomorphic:

$$[[\text{class } c = \varsigma(z)\, d, r \text{ in } p]]_E \;\triangleq\; \text{obj } z_m = [\,]^{m \in M},\; z_\rho = [\,]^{\rho = \tilde{m} \in r} \text{ in}$$
$$\text{class } c = \varsigma(z)\, (d, r)_{E,z} \text{ in } [[p]]_{E+(c \mapsto M)}$$

$$[[\text{obj } x = c \text{ in } p]]_E \;\triangleq\; \text{obj } x = c \text{ in } [[p]]_E$$

$$([\sigma], r)_{E,x} \;\triangleq\; [[\sigma, r]]_x$$

$$(d)_{E,x} \;\triangleq\; c$$

$$([\sigma] \text{ extends } d, r)_{E,x} \;\triangleq\; [ctr(z, z') = \times_{m \in meth[\sigma]}[z = z_m]x.s'(z, z')$$
$$| \times_{m \in E(c) \backslash meth[\sigma]}[z = z_m]x.s(z, z')$$
$$]((([\sigma], r)_{E,x} \text{ extends } ((d, r)_{E,x} \text{ rename } ctr \text{ as } s)$$
$$\text{rename } ctr \text{ as } s')$$

$$(c \,\&\, \tilde{m})_{E,x} \;\triangleq\; [\, ctr(z, z') = \times_{m' \in \tilde{m}}[z = z_{m'}]x.s(z, z'), 0$$
$$| \times_{m' \in E(c) \backslash \tilde{m}}[z = z_{m'}](x.ctr(z, z') \mid release(z.\ell)), 0$$
$$] \text{ extends } (c \text{ rename } ctr \text{ as } s)$$

The Syntax:

$$p ::= \quad 0 \qquad\qquad\qquad d ::= \quad [\sigma]$$

$\mid \quad x.m(\widetilde{e})$	$\mid \quad c$
$\mid \quad x.a := e\,;\ p$	$\mid \quad \varsigma(x)\, d$
$\mid \quad \mathsf{obj}\ x = c\ \mathsf{in}\ p$	$\mid \quad [\sigma]\ \mathsf{extends}\ d$
$\mid \quad \mathsf{class}\ c = \varsigma(x)\, d, r\ \mathsf{in}\ p$	$\mid \quad d\ \mathsf{rename}\ m\ \mathsf{as}\ s$
$\mid \quad p \mid p$	$\mid \quad c\ \&\ \widetilde{m}$
$\mid \quad \mathsf{become}(x.\rho)$	$\mid \quad c + \widetilde{m}$

The Compilation: (d is a shortening for $d, \varnothing$ and $[\sigma]\ \&\ \widetilde{m} = [\sigma] + \widetilde{m} = [\sigma]$)

For definitions: $\overset{x}{\leadsto}$

$$\varsigma(z)\, d, r \quad \overset{x}{\leadsto} \quad d\{x/z\}, r$$

$$[\sigma]\ \mathsf{extends}\ [\sigma'], r \quad \overset{x}{\leadsto} \quad [\sigma/\sigma'], r$$

$$[a_i = u_i{}^{i\in 1..h}, m_i(\widetilde{x}_i) = p_i{}^{i\in 1..k}], r \quad \overset{x}{\leadsto} \quad [a_i = u_i{}^{i\in 1..h}, m_i\{s/m\}(\widetilde{x}_i) = p_i{}^{i\in 1..k}],$$
$$\mathsf{rename}\ m\ \mathsf{as}\ s \qquad\qquad\qquad\qquad\qquad\qquad r$$

$$d, r\ \&\ \widetilde{m} \quad \overset{x}{\leadsto} \quad d\ \&\ \widetilde{m}, \bigcup_{\rho:\widetilde{m}\cup\widetilde{n}\in r} \rho : \widetilde{m}\cup\widetilde{n}$$

$$d, r + \widetilde{m} \quad \overset{x}{\leadsto} \quad d + \widetilde{m}, \bigcup_{\rho:\widetilde{n}\in r} \rho : (\widetilde{m}\cup\widetilde{n})$$

+ closure under contexts $D[\,\cdot\,] ::= [\,\cdot\,] \mid [\sigma]\ \mathsf{extends}\ D[\,\cdot\,] \mid D[\,\cdot\,]\chi$
(χ ranges over " $\mathsf{rename}\ m\ \mathsf{as}\ s$", "$\&\ \widetilde{m}$", "$+\widetilde{m}$", "$,r$")

For processes: $\leadsto$

$$\mathsf{class}\ c = \varsigma(x)\, [\sigma], r\ \mathsf{in}\ p \quad \leadsto \quad p\{\varsigma(x)\, [\sigma], r/c\}$$

$$\frac{D[d, r] \overset{x}{\leadsto} D'[d', r']}{\mathsf{class}\ c = \varsigma(x)\, D[d, r] \leadsto \mathsf{class}\ c = \varsigma(x)\, D'[d', r']\ \mathsf{in}\ p}$$

+ context closure

Table 15.5. *Classes and Inheritance in Enabled Sets*

$$(\![\mathsf{c} + \widetilde{m}]\!)_{E,x} \quad \overset{\triangle}{=} \quad [\ ctr(z, z') = \times_{m'\in E(c)\backslash\widetilde{m}}[z = z_{m'}]x.s(z, z'), 0$$
$$\mid \times_{m'\in\widetilde{m}}[z = z_{m'}](x.\alpha := x\,;\ release(x.\ell_{m'})), 0$$
$$] \mathsf{extends}\ (c\ \mathsf{rename}\ ctr\ \mathsf{as}\ s)$$

Note that the dummy names z_m and z_ρ are now introduced once, for all of the instances of a class. The translation of '$[\sigma]$ extends d, r' is done in two steps: first d, r is translated, by renaming the control method with a fresh name s. The resulting expression is extended with the translation of $[\sigma], r$, where the control method is now renamed into s'. A new control method is defined, dispatching the ctr invocations to s or s' accordingly. Observe that the overall expression encoding '$[\sigma]$ extends d, r'

has unique locks ℓ and ℓ_m, for every m, because of the definition of the updating operation.

The translations of '$c \,\&\, \tilde{m}$' and '$c + \tilde{m}$' refine only the control method of the inherited class. The new behaviour performs additional checks (according to the primitives $\&\, \tilde{m}$ and $+\tilde{m}$) and then forwards the invocation to the old behaviour of ctr.

The next theorem states the correctness of the encoding. Its proof consists in providing a barbed congruence for every pair of terms p, p' such that $p \rightsquigarrow p'$.

Theorem 15.5.3 *Let p be a process of the language in Table 15.5 without free class names. If $p \rightsquigarrow p'$, then $[\![p]\!]_\varnothing \approx [\![p']\!]_\varnothing$.*

15.5.2 Method Guards

A *method guard* is a Boolean expression attached to each method that must be satisfied before the execution of the method may start. Method guards take terms that are constants, variables, object fields and synchronization counters. A *synchronization counter* is a value that specifies the number of started method executions, completed executions, pending invocations, and so on. These counters are updated by the run-time system through atomic operations.

Method guards have been proposed as the synchronization mechanism of the notation Guide [DKM+89]. We illustrate this mechanism by rewriting the asynchronous channel in Example 15.3.1 into a Guide-like notation. The notation should be self-explanatory, nevertheless we will clarify it afterwards:

$$
\begin{aligned}
&\text{class } channel = \\
&\quad \varsigma(z) \;\; [val = 0, \\
&\qquad\qquad read(x) = \text{obj } y = [val = 0] \text{ in } y.val := z.val \,;\; x.reply(y.val) \,: \\
&\qquad\qquad [\text{completed}(write) = \text{completed}(read) + 1][\text{current}(write) = 0], \\
&\qquad\qquad write(x, u) = z.val := u \,;\; x.reply() \,: \\
&\qquad\qquad\qquad [\text{completed}(write) = \text{completed}(read)][\text{current}(read) = 0] \\
&\qquad\qquad]
\end{aligned}
$$

Observe that, for a *read* to be executed, it requires a *write* to have already been performed – the number of previous *writes* must be greater – and no other *read* can currently be executing – because *reads* consume the message. On the contrary, a message can be written provided that the previous message has been read – the number of completed *writes* and *reads* is the same.

We use the same pattern as in the previous section to translate method guards into our language: we first translate objects, and then classes.

Table 15.6 collects the syntax and semantics of the object calculus with method guards. We only consider the '*started*' synchronization counter because its encoding in our calculus is rather simple. Other synchronization counters, such as the

The Syntax: p, without the operation **become**, and e are as in Table 15.4;
the process **obj** is redefined as follows (n are integer numbers):

$$p ::= \quad \cdots \quad | \quad \textbf{obj } x = \varsigma(z)[a_i = u_i{}^{i \in 1..h}, m_i(\widetilde{x}_i) = p_i \ : \ g_i{}^{i \in 1..k}] \textbf{ in } p$$

$$g ::= \quad [\varepsilon = \varepsilon] \qquad\qquad\qquad \varepsilon ::= \quad e$$
$$ \quad | \quad g\, g \qquad\qquad\qquad\qquad\quad | \quad n$$
$$ | \quad \text{started}(x.m)$$

The judgment $\mathcal{O} \models g$:

$$\mathcal{O} \models [x = x] \qquad\qquad \frac{\mathcal{O} \models [\varepsilon = \varepsilon'] \quad \mathcal{O} \models g}{\mathcal{O} \models [\varepsilon = \varepsilon']\, g}$$

$$\frac{\mathcal{O} \models [z = \varepsilon] \quad x = [a = z, \sigma] \in \mathcal{O}}{\mathcal{O} \models [x.a = \varepsilon]} \qquad \frac{\mathcal{O} \models [\varepsilon = z] \quad x = [a = z, \sigma] \in \mathcal{O}}{\mathcal{O} \models [\varepsilon = x.a]}$$

$$\frac{\mathcal{O} \models [\text{started}(x.m) = \varepsilon] \quad x = [\alpha_m = n, \sigma] \in \mathcal{O}}{\mathcal{O} \models [n = \varepsilon]}$$

$$\frac{\mathcal{O} \models [\varepsilon = \text{started}(x.m)] \quad x = [\alpha_m = n, \sigma] \in \mathcal{O}}{\mathcal{O} \models [\varepsilon = n]}$$

The Semantics: Rules (NIL), (ASG), (ARG), (EXP) of Table 15.1 +
(PAR) of Table 15.3 +

(OBJ) $\quad \Vdash \textbf{obj } x = \varsigma(z)[\sigma] \textbf{ in } p \ \rightleftharpoons \ x' - [\alpha_m - 0^{m \in meth[\sigma]}, \upsilon]\{x'/z\} \Vdash p\{x'/x\}$

(MET) $\quad \mathcal{O}, x = [\alpha_m = h, m(\widetilde{z}) = p \ : \ g, \sigma] \Vdash x.m(\widetilde{u}) \ \longrightarrow$
$$\qquad\qquad\qquad\qquad \mathcal{O}, x = [\alpha_m = h + 1, m(\widetilde{z}) = p \ : \ g, \sigma] \Vdash p\{\widetilde{u}/\widetilde{z}\}$$

With side condition:

(OBJ) $\quad x'$ is a fresh name.
(MET) $\quad$ provided $\mathcal{O}, x = [\alpha_m = h, m(\widetilde{z}) = p \ : \ g, \sigma] \models g$.

Table 15.6. *The Concurrent Object Calculus with Method Guards*

'*completed*' one, could be considered as well. However, they require a continuation passing style to check method terminations.

Expressions that occur in method guards may be standard expressions (hence, accesses to object fields), integer numbers or *started*$(x.m)$, which returns the number of times the method m of the object x has started. The case of expressions with arithmetic operations can be handled at the cost of adding rules to the judgment $\mathcal{O} \models g$.

The semantics of the calculus with method guards differs from the others in two rules: (OBJ) and (MET). Rule (OBJ) also allocates special fields α_m, one for each method, when an object definition is heated. These fields store the counters required by the *started* expression and cannot be updated by the program. It is rule (MET) that performs such updates, once the method body can be evaluated. Method bodies are evaluated when the test of the guard succeeds. This check is performed by the judgments $\mathcal{O} \models g$ (see the side condition of (MET)).

The Encoding of Objects To implement method guards in our basic calculus we use the full expressive power of name comparison. We also augment the calculus with integers and summations, with the expected semantics.

We model synchronization counters through special object fields. To encode atomic updates of synchronization counters, we associate a lock to every one of them. Since we only consider the *started* synchronization counter, we use the field α_m for the counter of the method m and ℓ_m for the lock associated to that counter. We also use a lock ℓ to verify method guards in an atomic way.

The following translation $[[\cdot]]$ takes a process p or an expression e and returns a process or an expression in the calculus in Sections 15.2.4 and 15.3. Similarly, $[[\cdot]]_x$ takes a sequence σ and gives a sequence of fields and methods in our basic calculus. We focus on the unique cases where $[[\cdot]]$ and $[[\cdot]]_x$ are not homomorphic:

$$[[a_i = u_i{}^{i \in 1..h}, m_i(\widetilde{x}_i) = p_i : [e_1 = e_2] \cdots [e_{j-1} = e_j]^{i \in 1..k}]]_x \triangleq$$

$$\ell = tt, \; \ell_{m_i} = tt^{i \in 1..k} ,$$
$$a_i = u_i{}^{i \in 1..h} ,$$
$$m_i(\widetilde{x}_i) = \mathsf{obj} \; y = [cont() = acquire(x.\ell_{m_i}) ; \; x.\alpha_{m_i} := x.\alpha_{m_i} + 1 ;$$
$$\hspace{5cm} (release(x.\ell) \mid release(x.\ell_{m_i}) \mid [[p_i]]),$$
$$\hspace{2.5cm} retry() = release(x.\ell) ; \; x.m_i(\widetilde{x}_i)]$$
$$\hspace{1.5cm} \mathsf{in} \; acquire(x.\ell) ; \; x.do_{m_i}(y) \; {}^{i \in 1..k}$$
$$do_{m_i}(y) =$$
$$\hspace{0.8cm} \mathsf{obj} \; z = [eval(z_1, \cdots, z_j) = [z_1 = z_2] \cdots [z_{j-1} = z_j] \; y.cont() , \; y.retry()$$
$$\hspace{1cm}] \; \mathsf{in} \; z.eval([[e_1]], \cdots, [[e_j]])$$

$$[[\mathsf{obj} \; x = \varsigma(z) \, [\sigma] \; \mathsf{in} \; p]] \; \triangleq \; \mathsf{obj} \; x = \varsigma(z) \, [\alpha_m = 0^{m \in meth[\sigma]}, \; [[\sigma]]_z] \; \mathsf{in} \; [[p]]$$

$$[[started(x.m)]] \; \triangleq \; x.\alpha_m$$

The translation $[[\cdot]]$ introduces an auxiliary method do_m that checks the method guard of m. When m is invoked, it acquires the lock ℓ to verify its guard (method guards are tested in a mutually exclusive way) and invokes do_m. If the test is positive, then the counter α_m is increased and both of the locks ℓ and ℓ_m are released. If the test of the method guard is negative, then ℓ is released and the method invocation is emitted again. Note that the special fields α_m are added by $[[\cdot]]$ rather than $[[\cdot]]_x$. The reason for this is to be consistent with the following encoding of solutions $\mathcal{O} \Vdash P$, since, according to the semantics of Table 15.6, fields α_m occur in named definitions of $\mathcal{O}$.

As for enabled sets, to formalize the correspondence between a term and its translation, we lift the encoding $[[\,\cdot\,]]$ to solutions:

$$[[\mathcal{O} \Vdash \mathcal{P}]] \;\stackrel{\triangle}{=}\; \biguplus_{x=[\sigma]\in\mathcal{O}} \big(x = [[\sigma]]_x \big) \;\Vdash\; \biguplus_{p\in\mathcal{P}} [[p]].$$

Lemma 15.5.4 *Let $\mathcal{S}$ and $\mathcal{T}$ be solutions of the RCHAM defined in Table 15.6. Then:*

   (i) *If $\mathcal{S} \equiv\!\longrightarrow\!\equiv \mathcal{T}$, then $[[\mathcal{S}]] \Longrightarrow [[\mathcal{T}]]$.*

   (ii) *If $\mathcal{S} \Downarrow_x$, then $[[\mathcal{S}]] \Downarrow_x$.*

It is an exercise to equip the calculus with method guards with barbed congruence. Then, the adequacy of our encoding is a straightforward consequence of the above lemma.

Theorem 15.5.5 *For p, q, two processes in Table 15.6, $[[p]] \approx [[q]]$ implies $p \approx q$.*

The Encoding of Classes and Inheritance Table 15.7 defines the class extension of the calculus with method guards. The new primitives, with respect to the previous class calculi, are those refining the method guards during the inheritance. There are two basic ones: '$c : m + g$' and '$c : m\#g$'. The former adds g to the method guards of m in c (it acts as a conjunction), while the latter removes the method guards of m in c and promotes g as a new method guard for m. The compilation step $\stackrel{x}{\rightsquigarrow}$ formalizes this behaviour.

The language in Table 15.7 can be encoded into our class language of Sections 15.2.4 and 15.3 with the name comparison operator. We use the function $[[\,\cdot\,]]$ to encode processes and $[[\cdot]]_x$ to encode definitions. These two functions are almost homomorphisms, except for the following cases (s_m is always a fresh name):

$$[[\text{class } c = \varsigma(x)\, d \text{ in } p]] \;\stackrel{\triangle}{=}\; \text{class } c = \varsigma(x)\, [[d]]_x \text{ in } [[p]]$$

$$[[c : w : (m + [e_1 = e_2] \cdots [e_{j-1} = e_j])]]_x \;\stackrel{\triangle}{=}$$

$$\begin{aligned}
[\, &do_m(y) = \\
&\quad \text{obj } z = [eval(z_1, \cdots, z_j) = [z_1 = z_2] \cdots [z_{k-1} = z_j]\, x.s_m(y), \\
&\qquad\qquad\qquad\qquad\qquad\qquad\qquad\qquad\qquad\qquad y.retry() \\
&\quad \,]\text{ in } z.eval(e_1, \cdots, e_j) \\
]\, &\text{extends } ((c : w) \text{ rename } do_m \text{ as } s_m)
\end{aligned}$$

$$[[c : w : (m\#[e_1 = e_2] \cdots [e_{k-1} = e_k])]]_x \;\stackrel{\triangle}{=}$$

$$\begin{aligned}
[\, &do_m(y) = \\
&\quad \text{obj } z = [eval(z_1, \cdots, z_j) = [z_1 = z_2] \cdots [z_{k-1} = z_j]\, y.cont(), \\
&\qquad\qquad\qquad\qquad\qquad\qquad\qquad\qquad\qquad\qquad y.retry() \\
&\quad \,]\text{ in } z.eval(e_1, \cdots, e_j) \\
]\, &\text{extends } (c : w)
\end{aligned}$$

The Syntax:

$$
p ::= \quad 0
$$
$$
\mid \quad x.m(\tilde{e})
$$
$$
\mid \quad x.a := e\,; \ p
$$
$$
\mid \quad \text{obj } x = c \text{ in } p
$$
$$
\mid \quad \text{class } c = \varsigma(x)\, d \text{ in } p
$$
$$
\mid \quad p \mid p
$$

$$
d ::= \quad [a_i = u_i{}^{i \in 1..h}, \, m_i(\tilde{x}_i) = p_i \, : \, g_i{}^{i \in 1..k}]
$$
$$
\mid \quad c
$$
$$
\mid \quad \varsigma(x)\, d
$$
$$
\mid \quad [\sigma] \text{ extends } d
$$
$$
\mid \quad d \text{ rename } m \text{ as } s
$$
$$
\mid \quad c : w
$$

$$
w ::= \quad m + g
$$
$$
\mid \quad m \# g
$$
$$
\mid \quad w : w
$$

The Compilation: (d is a shortening for $d : \varnothing$ and $[\sigma] : m + g = [\sigma] : m \# g = [\sigma]$
if m is not a method occurring in σ)

For definitions: $\overset{x}{\leadsto}$

$$
\varsigma(z)\, d \quad \overset{x}{\leadsto} \quad d\{x/z\}
$$

$$
[\sigma] \text{ extends } [\sigma'] \quad \overset{x}{\leadsto} \quad [\sigma/\sigma']
$$

$$
\begin{array}{c} [a_i = u_i{}^{i \in 1..h}, \, m_i(\tilde{x}_i) = p_i \, : \, g_i{}^{i \in 1..k}] \\ \text{rename } m \text{ as } s \end{array} \quad \overset{x}{\leadsto} \quad [a_i = u_i{}^{i \in 1..h}, \, m_i\{s/m\}(\tilde{x}_i) = p_i \, : \, g_i{}^{i \in 1..k}]
$$

$$
[m(\tilde{x}) = p \, : \, g, \, \sigma] : m + g' \quad \overset{x}{\leadsto} \quad [m(\tilde{x}) = p \, : \, gg', \, \sigma]
$$

$$
[m(\tilde{x}) = p \, : \, g, \, \sigma] : m \# g' \quad \overset{x}{\leadsto} \quad [m(\tilde{x}) = p \, : \, g', \, \sigma]
$$

+ closure under contexts $D[\cdot] ::= [\cdot] \mid [\sigma] \text{ extends } D[\cdot] \mid D[\cdot]\chi$
(χ ranges over "rename m as s", ": $m + g$", ": $m \# g$")

For processes: $\leadsto$

$$
\text{class } c = \varsigma(x)\, [\sigma] \text{ in } p \leadsto p\{\varsigma(x)\,[\sigma]/c\}
$$

$$
\frac{d \overset{x}{\leadsto} d'}{\text{class } c = \varsigma(x)\, d \text{ in } p \leadsto \text{class } c = \varsigma(x)\, d' \text{ in } p}
$$

+ context closure

Table 15.7. *Classes and Inheritance in Method Guards*

As expected, the inheritance of a class where method guards are refined only concerns the control methods *do*. In particular, when the definition is '$m + g$', do_m is refined first by checking g and then, when the answer is positive, checking the rest of the guard (forwarding the invocation to the super do_m). In case the test of g fails, the call of m must be delayed and the lock ℓ is released. The encoding of '$m \# g$' is similar, except that no forward to the super do_m is done because the method guard of m in c has been overridden.

The next theorem gives the correctness of the encoding. The proof is similar to the corresponding theorem for enabled sets.

Theorem 15.5.6 *Let p be a process of the language in Table 15.7 without free class names. If $p \rightsquigarrow p'$, then $[\![p]\!]_\varnothing \approx [\![p']\!]_\varnothing$.*

15.6 Conclusions

We have reviewed inheritance in both the sequential and concurrent settings. To this end we have defined a concurrent object-oriented language and used it to systematize the proposals in the literature.

We strongly believe that inheritance is much more important for concurrent objects, due to the variety of forms that it takes. However, to benefit from this programming concept one should define a small set of expressive operators, with a formal semantics and for which it is possible to develop proof techniques. Some progress in this direction is made in [FLMR00], where a class-based calculus has been developed out of a well-known process calculus, and a small set of algebraic operators for inheriting concurrent code is defined.

Whether the operators proposed in [FLMR00] are the right ones is open to debate. Future research could bring strong motivation for positive or negative answers and therefore devise a rigorous *algebraic theory for the inheritance of control*.

Bibliography

[AC96]   M. Abadi and L. Cardelli. *A Theory of Objects*. Monographs in Computer Science. Springer-Verlag, 1996.

[ACS98]   R. M. Amadio, I. Castellani, and D. Sangiorgi. On bisimulations for the asynchronous π-calculus. *Theoretical Computer Science*, 195(2):291–324, 1998.

[Ame89]   P. America. Issues in the design of a parallel object-oriented language. *Formal Aspects of Computing*, 1(4):366–411, 1989.

[BC90]   G. Bracha and W. Cook. Mixin-based inheritance. *ACM SIGPLAN Notices*, 25(10):303–311, October 1990.

[Ber94]   L. Bergmans. *Composing Concurrent Objects*. Ph.D. thesis, University of Twente, 1994.

[BF96]   P. Di Blasio and K. Fisher. A calculus for concurrent objects. In *CONCUR '96: Concurrency Theory, 7th International Conference, Volume 1119 of Lecture Notes in Computer Science*, pages 406–421. Springer-Verlag, 1996.

[Car94]   L. Cardelli. Obliq A language with distributed scope. SRC Research Report 122, Digital Equipment, June 1994.

[CH73]   R. H. Campbell and A. N. Habermann. The specification of process synchronisation by path expressions. In *Volume 16 of Lecture Notes in Computer Science*, pages 89–102. Springer-Verlag, 1973.

[CUCH91]   C. Chambers, D. Ungar, B. Chang, and U. Hölzle. Parents are shared parts of objects: Inheritance and encapsulation in SELF. *Lisp and Symbolic Computation*, 4(3):207–222, July 1991.

[DKM+89]   D. Decouchant, S. Krakowiak, M. Meysembourg, M. Riveill, and X. Rousset de Pina. A synchronization mechanism for typed objects in a distributed system. *ACM SIGPLAN Notices*, 24(4):105–107, April 1989.

[DZ98]   S. Dal-Zilio. Quiet and bouncing objects: Two migration abstractions in a simple distributed blue calculus. In H. Hüttel and U. Nestmann, editors, *SOAP '98: Semantics of Objects as Processes*, volume NS-98-5 of *BRICS Notes Series*, pages 35–42, 1998.

[FG96]   C. Fournet and G. Gonthier. The reflexive chemical abstract machine and the join-calculus. In *Conference r&ord of the 23th ACM SIGPLAN-SIGACT Symposium on Principles of Programming Languages (POPL '96)*, pages 372–385. ACM, 1996.

[FHM93]   K. Fisher, F. Honsell, and J. C. Mitchell. A lambda calculus of objects and method specialization. In *Proceedings, Eighth Annual IEEE Symposium on Logic in Computer Science*, pages 26–38. IEEE Computer Society Press, June 1993.

[FLMR97]   C. Fournet, C. Laneve, L. Maranget, and D. R'eny. Implicit typing à la ML for the join-calculus. In *CONCUR '97: Proceedings of the 8th International Conference on Concurrency Theory, Volume 1243 of Lecture Notes in Computer Science*, pages 196–212. Springer-Verlag, 1997.

[FLMR00]   C. Fournet, C. Laneve, L. Maranget, and D. Remy. Inheritance in the join calculus. Available at `http://www.cs.unibo.it/~laneve/papers/UBCLSinhjoin.ps`, July 2000.

[Frø92]   S. Frølund. Inheritance of synchronization constraints in concurrent object-oriented programming languages. In *Proceedings ECOOP'92, Volume 615 of Lecture Notes in Computer Science*, pages 185–196. Springer-Verlag, June 1992.

[GH98]   A. D. Gordon and P. D. Hankin. A concurrent object calculus: reduction and typing. In *HLCL '98: High-Level Concurrent Languages*, volume 16(3) of *Electronic Notes in Theoretical Computer Science*. Elsevier, 1998.

[GJS96]   J. Gosling, B. Joy, and G. Steele. *The Java Language Specification*. Addison Wesley, 1996.

[GR83]   A. Goldberg and D. Robson. *Smalltalk-80: The Language and its Implementation*, pages 674–681. Addison-Wesley, 1983.

[GR96]   A. D. Gordon and G. D. Rees. Bisimilarity for a first-order calculus of objects with subtyping. In *23rd ACM Symposium on Principles of Programming Languages (POPL '96)*, pages 386–395. ACM Press, 1996.

[KMMPN87]   B. B. Kristensen, O. L. Madsen, B. Moller-Pedersen, and K. Nygaard. The BETA programming language. In B. Shriver and P. Wegner, editors, *Research Directions in Object-Oriented Programming*, pages 7–48. MIT Press, 1987.

[McH94]   C. McHale. *Synchronisation in Concurrent, Object-oriented Languages: Expressive Power, Genericity and Inheritance*. PhD thesis, Department of Computer Science, Trinity College, 1994.

[Mes93]   J. Meseguer. Solving the Inheritance Anomaly in Concurrent Object-Oriented Programming. In O. Nierstrasz, editor, *Proceedings of the ECOOP '93 European Conference on Object-oriented Programming, Volume 707 of Lecture Notes in Computer Science*, pages 220–246. Springer-Verlag, 1993.

[Mil92]   R. Milner. Functions as processes. *Mathematical Structures in Computer Science*, 2:119 – 141, 1992.

[MS92]   R. Milner and D. Sangiorgi. Barbed bisimulation. In *Automata, Languages and Programming, 19th International Colloquium*, volume 623 of *Lecture Notes in Computer Science*, pages 685–695. Springer-Verlag, 1992.

[MY93]   S. Matsuoka and A. Yonezawa. Analysis of inheritance anomaly in object-oriented concurrent programming languages. In G. Agha, P. Wegner, and A. Yonezawa, editors, *Research Directions in Concurrent Object-Oriented Programming*, chapter 4, pages 107–150. MIT Press, 1993.

[NP96]   U. Nestmann and B. C. Pierce. Decoding choice encodings. In *CONCUR '96: Proceedings of the 7th International Conference on Concurrency Theory, Volume 1119 of Lecture Notes in Computer Science*, pages 179–194. Springer-Verlag, 1996.

[Sar97]   V. Saraswat. Java is not Type Safe. Technical report, AT&T research, 1997. http://www.att.research.com/ vi.

[Sny87]   A. Snyder. Inheritance and the development of encapsulated software components. In B. Shriver and P. Wegner, editors, *Research Directions in*

Object-Oriented Programming, pages 165–188. MIT Press, 1987.

[TS89]   C. Tomlinson and V. Singh. Inheritance and Synchronization with Enabled Sets. In *Proceedings of the OOPSLA '89 Conference on Object-Oriented Programming Systems, Languages and Applications*, pages 103–112. ACM, 1989.

[Vas94]   V. T. Vasconcelos. Typed concurrent objects. *Volume 821 of Lecture Notes in Computer Science*, pages 100–117, 1994.

[YBS86]   A. Yonezawa, J.-P. Briot, and E. Shibayama. Object-oriented concurrent programming in ABCL/1. In N. Meyrowitz, editor, *Proceedings of Object-Oriented Programming Systems, Languages, and Applications (OOPSLA '86)*, volume 21(11) of *ACM SIGPLAN Notices*, pages 258–268. ACM, October 1986.

Part Six

Nonfunctional Requirements

16

Multimedia in the E-LOTOS Process Algebra

Guy Leduc

Research Unit in Networking, University of Liège, Belgium

16.1 Introduction

The description and analysis of multimedia distributed systems is a challenge for formal techniques. Traditionally these techniques have focussed on the description of functional aspects of distributed systems and their mathematical analysis. However, until recently, almost all formal techniques were still unable to tackle real-size problems, which require more expressivity or flexibility to describe complex data types, to define generic components, to support their easy combination and/or reuse in several contexts and to describe sophisticated architectures where many processes are involved.

In addition to these more classical functional aspects, multimedia systems are basically real-time systems, whose main behaviour is so intrinsically related to timing requirements that their specifications with traditional techniques would lack the essence of the behaviour. For an in-depth introduction to the nature of distributed multimedia systems and the requirements that arise from such systems, the reader is referred to the next chapter of this part (Chapter 17).

In response to the requirements arising from multimedia (and other time-dependent) systems, in recent years much research effort has been dedicated to the problem of real-time specification. This is the case in particular for process algebras, which we will consider in the present chapter.

The first process algebras that were able to express time quantitatively are called synchronous process algebras. Examples are SCCS [Mil83], Meije [AB84] or CIRCAL [Mil85]. These languages are called synchronous because actions can occur only at precise regular times, like in synchronous circuits for which they where mainly targeted.

A more flexible, also called asynchronous, approach was needed to describe software systems that are not so closely driven by a clock. In fact, a better model of real-time systems is a model in which actions (i.e., processing) and time passing (i.e., idling) alternate more freely. At a certain level of abstraction, one can even consider that actions are atomic and instantaneous. This leads to an elegant, simple model where systems alternate between two phases: an execution phase, where actions are executed instantaneously, and an idle phase, where the system ages [NS92]. For actions whose duration is such that they cannot be abstracted as instantaneous, it suffices to split them into a beginning and an ending action.

This principle has lead to many extensions of well-known process algebras, such as Timed CSP [RR88, DS94], Timed CCS [MT90, Wan91, Han91], Timed ACP [BB91, BB96, Gro90] and Timed LOTOS [MFV94, CdO94, BLT94b, BLT94a, LL97, LL98, QMdFL94]. New timed process algebras have also been proposed, such as TPL [HR95] and ATP [NS94].

Even though these languages propose interesting facilities to specify real-time behaviours, very few of them were designed as complete languages suitable for tackling real-size systems. Basically, they are not very well equipped for software engineering in general:

- Most of them, except some LOTOS extensions, are basic algebras with little support to define more complex data structures.
- They have no module system, or a limited one.
- They do not support exception handling, subtyping, and so on.

For these reasons, ISO has decided to improve LOTOS more substantially than by merely adding real-time. This initiative has lead to E-LOTOS [ISO98], which has been presented in Chapter 5.

In the present chapter we will illustrate how E-LOTOS can be used to describe an ODP multicast multimedia binding object of some complexity. The timing features of the language will be recalled briefly, and will play a major role in the description of the example, but many other features of E-LOTOS are also very useful to obtain a more modular and more readable specification. Users familiar with LOTOS will also learn how some E-LOTOS features can advantageously replace the traditional LOTOS ones.

Our approach is based on a single language. In the next chapter, the same binding object will be described using a multiparadigm approach.

16.2 Timing Facilities in E-LOTOS

The expression of real-time behaviours in E-LOTOS is based on three simple language constructions:

- A type time with associated operations. Usually specifiers simply define this type as a renaming of either the natural numbers to get a discrete time domain, or the positive rational numbers to get a dense time domain, for example,

  `type time renames nat endtype`

- A wait operator, which introduces a delay. For example:

  `input; wait(1); output`

More interestingly, we can also specify nondeterministic delays. For example, the next specification describes a process that will choose internally some delay (within some bounds) and introduce it between input and output:

```
input;
?t := any time [(min <= t) and (t <= max)];
        (* The question mark always indicates a variable binding
           It is used consistently both for classical assigments and
           for variable binding resulting from synchronisations *)
wait (t);
output
```

The timed value can also be received from the environment of the process, such as in

```
get ?t;   (* we suppose that this gate is typed
              in such a way that t should be a time value *)
input ?data; wait (t); output !data
```

- An extended communication operator, which is sensitive to delay:

```
input ?data @?t;  (* ?data is the classical variable binding,
                     @?t is the time capture, see below *)
wait (10-t);
ouput !data
```

In the former example, t is bound to the time at which the communication along input happens (measured from when the communication was enabled).

When the variable binding is replaced by a value expression, the same language construction can be used as a compact way to specify a unique possible occurrence time. For example, in input ?data @!3, the input action is only enabled at time 3, which is the only timed value allowed by the value expression. This behaviour is in fact equivalent to input ?data @ ?t [t = 3].

Besides these three constructions, E-LOTOS is based on the following basic principles:

- The internal action i cannot be delayed. It should occur immediately, or another competing action has to occur immediately instead.
- Observable actions are delayed until synchronization is made possible by the environment. They cannot be forced to occur before that.
- Exceptions cannot be delayed. The exception handler is started instantaneously.
- When a process terminates successfully, the following process starts immediately (no delay). Note, however, that when a process is composed of several processes in parallel, termination can occur only when all subprocesses have finished.
- Two successive actions can occur at the same time. There is no minimum delay between them. Infinitely many actions can thus potentially occur in a finite time.
- A function is merely an immediately exiting process: it does not communicate and executes instantaneously.

16.3 A Multicast Multimedia Binding Object

In this section we first present informally the ODP Binding Object and then its formal description in E-LOTOS. This object was first used in [FNLL96].

Part One of this book discusses ODP concepts in detail. Therefore, we will recall only a few of them here. In the ODP Computational Model the binding objects are used to convey interactions between interfaces of other objects. In fact, in the Computational Model, the programmer can choose one of two ways for describing the interactions between interfaces: (i) either explicitly through a binding object, or (ii) implicitly without exhibiting a binding object. When specifying a binding object, the programmer may incorporate the Quality of Service (QoS) requirements (order, timeliness, throughput, etc.) on the transport of interactions supported by that binding object. In contrast, in an implicit binding between two interfaces, no specific requirements are made on the transport of interactions: interfaces interact by message passing with no explicit ordering or delay required on the transport of these messages.

There are three kinds of interfaces in computational objects: signal, operational and stream. Signal interfaces are the most primitive: operational and stream interfaces can be modelled as special types of signal interfaces. A signal is an operation name and a vector of values. A signal interface is an interface that emits and receives signals. An operational interface is an interface that can receive invocations and possibly react with result messages. Invocations and result messages are signals. An operational interface has a type that is roughly defined to be the type of the operations that it can handle. A subtyping system allows for the safe substitution of an interface of a given type by another interface having a subtype of this type. A stream interface is an abstraction of a signal interface: the type of a stream interface is simply a name and a role (sender or receiver).

Binding objects are important for both application and system designers and developers, and they can be used in many different ways. For instance, application designers may specify their transport requirements and let system designers develop new networks and protocols that match these requirements. On the other hand, application programmers may use the abstraction provided by existing binding objects to develop and analyse their applications. A specification of a binding object should cover the functional and QoS requirements. Functional requirements include: connection establishment, dynamic reconfiguration, orderly transport of information, and so on. QoS requirements involve: connection establishment delay, jitter, throughput, error rate, inter- and intraflow synchronization, and so on. Thus the specification language should be expressive and able to address real-time constraints.

The binding object that we consider in this chapter executes the following operations:

- It listens to a source emitting t wo synchronized flows, an audio and a video, and multicasts the t wo flows to a dynamically changing set of clients.

- At any time a client can request to join the audio, or the video or both the audio and video streams by providing the reference of one (or t wo) receiving interface(s).
- At any time a client may request to leave the audio, or the video or both the audio and video flows.
- It tries to enforce the intra- and intersynchronization of flows and notifies failures to do so.

The source flows are 25 images per second, that is, the video stream is composed of packets delivered every 40 ms, and the sound is sampled every 30 ms, that is, a sound packet is delivered every 30 ms.

We suppose that the two sources do not deviate from the above figures and that both flows are fully synchronized. The binding object accepts these flows and delivers them to any requesting customer. Since the binding object will encapsulate the behaviour of a concrete network, it will have to deal the with usual networking problems, such as jitter, packet loss, end to end delay, and so on. Nevertheless, the customers expect a minimal QoS, which is twofold:

- Each flow must respect a QoS: sound should have no jitter, and video can have a jitter of 5 ms, that is, consecutive images may be separated by 35 to 45 ms.
- Both must be reasonably synchronous, as defined below. This is known as lip-synchronization.

Lip-synchronization is considered correct if the sound is not too late from, or ahead of, the corresponding lip movement. The actual figures are:

- The sound must not come more than 15 ms ahead of the lip movement.
- The sound must not come later than 150 ms after of the lip movement.

16.4 E-LOTOS Specification of the Multimedia Multicast ODP Binding Object

The binding object will be defined as a generic process handling generic data. It will be composed of several other processes and will use some basic data types. Therefore, the best way to specify the system is by way of a generic module as follows:

```
interface data is
   type data
endint


generic binding-object (D:data) imports NaturalNumbers is

type stream is a | v endtype      (* audio and video streams *)
type client renames Nat endtype
                        (* client ids are just numbers *)
type time renames Nat endtype       (* time is discrete *)
type clients is set of client endtype
```

```
type fifo is list of client endtype
type req_code  is Creq_a | Creq_v | Creq_av | Dreq endtype
                 (* enumeration of possible request primitives *)
type er_code is e_delay | e_jitter | e_sync | released endtype
                    (* enumeration of possible error codes *)
type id_data is (client,data) endtype
          (* a record composed of a client id and some data *)
type ctrl is (req_code,client) endtype
        (* a record composed of a request code and a client id *)
type er_tuple is (er_code,client) endtype
        (* a record composed of an error code and a client id *)
type release is (req_code,stream,client) endtype
          (* a record composed of a request code, a stream type
              and a client id *)
function empty := {} endfunc
value epsilon:time is 1 endval
value mindelay:time is 0 endval     (* Minimum transit delay *)
value maxdelay:time is 100 endval   (* Maximum transit delay *)
value arate:time is 30 endval
                  (* Interval between two audio data packets *)
value vrate:time is 40 endval
                  (* Interval between two video data packets *)
value ajitter:time is 0 endval
                       (* Maximum jitter on audio packets *)
value vjitter:time is 5 endval
                       (* Maximum jitter on video packets *)
value abv:time is 15 endval
  (* Maximum lead of the audio stream over the video stream *)
value vba:time is 150 endval
  (* Maximum lead of the video stream over the audio stream *)

(* And we would insert here all the processes defined below *)
endgen
```

We first identify a collection of generic components that are suitable for the specification of functional and QoS requirements of a multimedia binding object. We present them in the following, together with their E-LOTOS specification. In these specifications, dt represents a generic data packet, which can contain audio or video data.

The first component is called Medium. This component describes a point-to-point transmission medium. Packets are received on gate ist (input stream) and are delivered on gate ost (output stream). Medium is very general. The only constraint it expresses is that no packet is lost. On the other hand, the transmission delay of each packet is totally unconstrained and the ordering of the packets is not preserved. After the reception of a packet on ist, an unbounded nondeterministic delay is introduced before the delivery on ost. In parallel, a new occurrence of Medium handles the subsequent packets.

```
Process Medium [ist:data,ost:id_data] (id: client) is
   ist ?dt;
   (?t := any time; wait (t); ost(!id,!dt); stop
    |||
    Medium [ist,ost] (id))
endproc (* Medium *)
```

Next we add the FIFO_Const component. It ensures that the packets are delivered in the same order as they are received. This component also considers gates ist, where packets are received, and ost, where these packets are delivered. In process FIFO_Const, the ordering is handled with an appropriate data structure, q, which describes a FIFO queue. At any time, FIFO_Const can accept (ist?dt) a new packet that is appended at the end of q, or deliver ((ost!id!head(q))) the first packet in q.

```
process FIFO_Const [ist:data,ost:id_data](id:client,q:fifo) is
   ist ?dt; FIFO_Const [ist,ost] (id,tcons(dt,q))
                                  (* tcons = tail cons *)
   []
   if not(IsEmpty(q)) then
           ost (!id,!head(q));
           FIFO_Const [ist,ost] (id,tail(q))
   endif
endproc (* FIFO_Const *)
```

The third component, Delay_Const, ensures that at least a minimal delay delmin elapses between the reception of a packet on ist and its delivery on ost. Here again, the same two gates are considered.

```
process Delay_Const [ist:data,ost:id_data]
                    (id:client,delmin:time) is
   ist ?dt ;
   (Wait (delmin); ost (!id,!dt); stop
    |||
    Delay_Const [ist, ost] (id, delmin))
endproc (* Delay_Const *)
```

The fourth component, Delay_Obs, expresses a requirement on the service provided by a transmission medium. It verifies that the delay between the reception and the delivery never exceeds a maximal value. If the packet is not delivered before this maximal delay, an exception is raised. After the reception of a packet,

`Delay_Obs` proposes `ost` (`!id,!dt`) during a time `delmax`. On the other hand, the exception `error` (`e_delay`) is delayed by `delmax+epsilon`. In other words, it is raised when the delivery can no longer occur.

```
process Delay_Obs [ist:data,ost:id_data]
                  (id:client,delmax:time)
                  raises [error:er_code] is
   ist ?dt ;
     (ost (!id,!dt)@?t [t <= delmax]; stop
     []
     wait(delmax+epsilon); raise error (e_delay))
   |||
   Delay_Obs [ist,ost](id,delmax)
endproc (* Delay_Obs *)
```

The fifth component, `Jitter_Const`, has an effect similar to `Delay_Const`, but on just one gate. It enforces that at least a minimal delay, `jmin`, elapses between any two successive deliveries of packets at gate `ost`.

```
process Jitter_Const [ost:id_client] (id:client,jmin:time) is
   loop
     ost (!id,?dt);
     wait (jmin)
   endloop
endproc (* Jitter_Const *)
```

The sixth component, `Jitter_Obs`, has an effect similar to `Delay_Obs`, but on just one gate. It verifies that the delays between successive deliveries of packets on gate `ost` do not exceed `jmax`. Like `Delay_Const`, it raises an exception if this happens.

```
process Jitter_Obs [ost:id_data] (id:client,jmax:time)
                        raises [error:er_code] is
   ost (!id,?dt);
   loop
     ost (!id,?dt)@?t [t <= jmax]
     []
     wait (jmax+epsilon); raise error (e_jitter)
   endloop
endproc (* Jitter_Obs *)
```

The next process, called `One_Ind_Flow`, gives a first example of the modularity allowed by E-LOTOS. It describes a flow that combines the effects of the previous components. Therefore, this flow loses no packet and preserves their order; the transmission delay of each packet is undetermined, but it is at least of `delmin`, and it cannot exceed `delmax`; otherwise, an exception is raised and the transmission is stopped. The delay between successive deliveries of packets (the jitter) is at least of jmin and at most of jmax. If this maximal value is exceeded, an exception is also raised and the transmission is stopped.

One_Ind_Flow is obtained simply by putting in parallel the various constraints (or processes) and by enforcing their synchronisation on the gates ist and ost. In this case, One_Ind_Flow integrates all of the constraints, but any other combination of them would have been possible too (e.g., with no lower bound on the transmission delay or with no preservation of the order), resulting in a less constrained flow.

```
process One_Ind_Flow [ist:data,ost:id_data]
        (id:client-id,q:fifo,delmin,delmax,jmin,jmax:time)
        raises [error:er_code] is
    (Medium [ist,ost] (id)
     ||
     FIFO_Const [ist,ost] (id,q)
     ||
     Delay_Const [ist,ost] (id,delmin)
     ||
     Delay_Obs [ist,ost] (id,delmax)
    )
    |[ost]|
    Jitter_Const [ost](id,jmin)
    |[ost]|
    Jitter_Obs [ost](id,jmax)
endproc (* One_Ind_Flow *)
```

We continue with process Two_Sync_Flows. This component gives a new example of the modularity allowed by E-LOTOS. One_Ind_Flow was already the composition of several features. Two_Sync_Flows combines two flows and enhances the result with Inter_Sync_Const, a synchronization mechanism between the flows. Again, the addition of a constraint is obtained simply by putting a new process in parallel. Furthermore, each flow can be stopped independently by way of a disrupt message on gates ma or mv, and in that case the interflow constraint will also be removed, that is, the constraint is replaced by the neutral process Sink.

```
Process Two_Sync_Flows [isa,isv:data, osa,osv:id_data,
                        ma,mv:ctrl] (id:client)
                        raises [error:er_code] is
  (* gates isa and isv are the audio and video source gates
     respectively
     gates osa and osv are the audio and video output gates
     respectively
  *)
((One_Ind_Flow [isa,osa] (id,empty,mindelay,maxdelay,
```

```
                          arate- ajitter,arate + ajitter)
               [> ma (!Dreq,!id); Sink[isa])
   |||
  (One_Ind_Flow [isv,osv] (id,empty,mindelay,maxdelay,
                            vrate - vjitter,vrate + vjitter)
               [> mv (!Dreq,!id); Sink[isv])
)
|[osa,osv,ma,mv]|
((Inter_Sync_Const [osa,osv] (id,0,0)
               [> (ma (!Dreq,!id) []  mv (!Dreq,!id))
endproc (* Two_Sync_Flows *)
```

The Sink process enforces no constraint on the actions occurring on a gate. It is specified as a process with a single gate st, and no predicate or time constraint restricts the acceptance of packets on st.

```
process Sink [st:data] is
   st ?dt; Sink [st]
endproc (* Sink *)
```

The Inter_Sync_Const process controls the synchronisation between the packets delivered by two flows. The way in which Inter_Sync_Const is combined with the flows is illustrated in the previous component: Two_Sync_Flows. The effect of Inter_Sync_Const is to ensure that the packets on one flow are not delivered too late or too early with respect to the packets on the other flow. If these constraints cannot be met, an exception is raised and the two flows are interrupted. The meanings of the parameters used in this process are as follows:

- last_a is the time elapsed since the last audio packet delivery.
- last_v is the time elapsed since the last video packet delivery.

```
process Inter_Sync_Const [osa,osv:id_data]
                         (id:client, last_a,last_v:time)
                         raises [error:er_code] is
  osa (!id,?dt)@?t [t >= vrate - last_v - abv];
     Inter_Sync_Const [osa,osv] (id,0,last_v + t)
  []
  osv (!id,?dt)@?t [t >= arate - last_a - vba];
     Inter_Sync_Const [osa,osv] (id,last_a + t, 0)
  []
  wait (vrate - last_v + vba + epsilon); raise error (e_sync)
  []
  wait (arate - last_a + abv + epsilon); raise error (e_sync)
endproc (* Inter_Sync_Const  *)
```

The next process, MGR, is the main one. It realizes the multicasting by creating as many channels as necessary. A new flow manager, One_client_MGR, is created on receipt of a c!Creq... request. When a client requests a channel, it has to provide its id. This id will allow the MGR to connect the channel to gates r!id, mgt!id and osa!id (and/or osv!id). The MGR also ensures that a client can request at most one channel.

```
process MGR [c:ctrl, isa,isv:data, osa,osv:id_data,
             mgt:release, r:er_tuple] (Ids:Clients) is
(* gate c is the controlling gate of the binding object
   gate r is used to report errors to clients
   gate mgt allows clients to manage their flow(s)
*)


c (?cmd,?id) [(id notin Ids) and
             (cmd = Creq_a or cmd = Creq_v or cmd = Creq_av)];
   (One_client_MGR [c,isa,isv,osa,osv,mgt,r] (id,cmd)
    |[isa,isv]|
    MGR [c,isa,isv,osa,osv,mgt,r] (insert(id,Ids))
   )
[]
isa ?dt; MGR [c,isa,isv,osa,osv,mgt,r] (Ids)
[]
isv ?dt; MGR [c,isa,isv,osa,osv,mgt,r] (Ids)
endproc (* MGR *)
```

The next process, One_Client_MGR, describes the behaviour of a client's manager. There are three distinct cases, according to the nature of the client's request, which can be for:

- an audio stream: One_Ind_Flow [isa,osa];
- a video stream: One_Ind_Flow [isv,osv];
- an audio stream and a video stream synchronized together:
  Two_Sync_Flows [isa,isv,osa,osv,ma,mv]

```
process One_Client_MGR [c:crtl,isa,isv:data,osa,osv:id_data,
                        mgt:release,r:er_tuple]
                        (Id:Client,cmd:req_code) is


trap exception error:(?er:er_code)
    is r (!er,!id);       (* notify user *)
       c (?cmd,!id) [(cmd = Creq_a or cmd = Creq_v
                     or cmd = Creq_av)];
              (* ready to recreate the flow(s) *)
       One_Client_MGR [c,isa,isv,osa,osv,mgt,r] (id,cmd)
```

```
      endexn
in
case cmd is
  Creq_a ->
      (One_Ind_Flow [isa,osa] (id,empty,mindelay,maxdelay,
                              arate,ajitter)
        |||
        One_Flow_MGR [mgt] (id,a))
| Creq_v ->
      (One_Ind_Flow [isv,osv] (id,empty,mindelay,maxdelay,
                              vrate,vjitter)
        |||
        One_Flow_MGR [mgt] (id,v))
| Creq_av ->
    hide ma,mv:ctrl in
      (Two_Sync_Flows [isa,isv,osa,osv,ma,mv] (id)
       |[ma,mv]|
        Two_Flows_MGR [mgt,ma,mv] (id))
    endhide
endcase
endtrap
endproc (* One_client_MGR *)
```

The final components are the processes that control the flows. We first define the
process managing a single flow, and then another one managing two synchronized
flows.

```
process One_Flow_MGR [mgt:release] (id:client,s:stream)
                    raises [error:er-code] is
  mgt (!Dreq,!s,!id) ; raise error (released)
endproc (* One_Flow_MGR *)

process Two_Flows_MGR [mgt:release,ma,mv:ctrl] (id:client)
                    raises [error:er-code] is
  mgt (!Dreq,!a,!id) ;
  ma (!Dreq,!id);
  Client_One_Flow_MGR [mgt] (id,v)
 []
  mgt (!Dreq,!v,!id) ;
  mv (!Dreq,!id);
  Client_One_Flow_MGR [mgt] (id,a)
endproc (* Two_Flows_MGR *)
```

16.5 Analysis of E-LOTOS Specifications

We have illustrated that E-LOTOS allows us to produce elegant formal descriptions of complicated objects. However, the main interest of using the language lies in the automatic computations that we could perform on such specifications. This requires of course the development of appropriate tools.

Prototype tools exist for LOTOS NT [Sig99], which is a slight variant of E-LOTOS. The TRAIAN tool performs the following operations:

- lexical and syntactic analysis;
- static semantic analysis, including modules;
- flattening of nongeneric modules;
- C code generation for the data t ype.

A translation from E-LOTOS to timed automata would also open very interesting perspectives. The idea is of course to define a mapping between E-LOTOS and a timed automaton, allowing the former to benefit from the model checking theory and tools developed for the latter. Then, the KRONOS tool [DOTY96] can be used. It takes a timed automaton and a TCTL formula as input and checks whether the formula is verified on the automaton. In [DOY95] a similar method is proposed for a subset of ET-LOTOS [LL97, LL98], which is roughly the timed subset of E-LOTOS.

More recently, this work has been extended to cope with a larger subset of ET-LOTOS. In [Her98] a hybrid automaton model, called ETL-automaton, is proposed, which is especially designed to support ET-LOTOS. Informally, it can be seen as a timed automaton extended with memory cells and ASAP (as soon as possible) transitions. The values of the memory cells and clocks can be used in guards to constrain the occurrence of transitions. Each state has an invariant condition, which must be verified for the automaton to stay in it. A transition can reset clocks and change the memory cells. In particular, it is possible to capture the clock values in memory cells, which makes it possible to capture the occurrence time of a transition in a variable, that is, to model the @?t operator. The transitions are labelled either with a LOTOS action (i.e., an i or an observable gate with a list of attributes) or with a third special action marking the expiry of a delay. Each transition is also associated with a predicate on the clocks and the variables, which constrains its occurrence and determines the possible values of the attributes when the label is an observable action. This ETL-automaton model covers nearly all of the features of ET-LOTOS. The restrictions merely ensure the finiteness of the resulting automaton (e.g., no recursion through the parallel and the left part of the enabling and disabling operators) or ease the translation process (e.g., no recursion through the hiding operator, nor unguarded recursions through the delay or the guard operators). A simulator of ETL-automata has been developed, which thus supports a very large subset of the language. In [Her98] the author also studies how ETL-automata can be mapped onto underlying models of existing model checkers, such as HyTech [HHWT95], KRONOS [DOTY96] and UPPAAL [LPW97]. Although the hybrid automata accepted by HyTech are the most general ones among these three, they are less expressive than ETL-automata, so that further restrictions should be considered. Basically, the ET-LOTOS expressions used in delays, life-reducers, selection predicates, offers, and so on must be linear, and the hide operator can only be used on non-time-restricted actions. This still covers a large subset of the language, and the semidecidable algorithm of HyTech can be used for reachability analysis. As regards KRONOS, its more restricted timed automaton model, motivated by decidability purposes, requires further restrictions. Basically, at first glance it seemed difficult to model the time capture operator of ET-LOTOS because there are no memory cells. However, [Her97] shows that an extension of timed automata with semitimers remains decidable and can support this operator. A timer is a clock that can be stopped and restarted, and a semitimer is always reset before being restarted. The interesting feature is that a semitimer can be modelled by two auxiliary ordinary clocks, in fact by their difference, so that, at the price of a larger number of clocks, the time capture operator of ET-LOTOS can be supported by the KRONOS timed automata. Anyway, other restrictions exist: for example, expressions in delays should be constants, and expressions in selection predicates and guards are restricted. The same conclusion applies to UPPAAL, but the supported subset of ET-LOTOS is slightly larger, especially as regards the expressions in selection predicates and guards.

16.6 Conclusion

We have illustrated how E-LOTOS can be used to describe complex objects, such as an ODP multicast multimedia binding object. The structuring capabilities of E-LOTOS, together with its real-time features, were particularly relevant to achieve concise and readable specifications.

In contrast to our approach, which is based on a single specification language, the next chapter will describe the same binding object using a multiparadigm approach.

Bibliography

[AB84]   D. Austry and G. Boudol. Algèbre de processus et synchronisation. *Theoretical Computer Science*, 30:91–131, 1984.

[BB91]   J. C. M. Baeten and J. A. Bergstra. Real Time Process Algebra. *Formal Aspects of Computing*, 3(2):142–188, 1991.

[BB96]   J. C. M. Baeten and J. A. Bergstra. Discrete Time Process Algebra. *Formal Aspects of Computing*, 8(2):188–208, 1996.

[BLT94a]   T. Bolognesi, F. Lucidi, and S. Trigila. A Timed Full LOTOS with Time/Action Tree Semantics. In T. Rus and C. Rattray, editors, *Theories and Experiences for Real-Time System Development*, Amast Series in Computing, pages 205–237. Word Scientific, 1994.

[BLT94b]   T. Bolognesi, F. Lucidi, and S. Trigila. Converging Towards a Timed LOTOS Standard. *Computer Standards and Interfaces*, pages 87–118, 1994.

[CdO94]   J-P. Courtiat and R. de Oliveira. About time nondeterminism and exception handling in a temporal extension of lotos. In S. Vuong and S. Chanson, editors, *Protocol Specification, Testing and Verification, XIV*, pages 37–52. Chapman & Hall, 1994.

[DOTY96] C. Daws, A. Olivero, S. Tripakis, and S. Yovine. The tool KRONOS. In *Hybrid Systems III, Verification and Control, Volume 1066 of Lecture Notes in Computer Science*. Springer-Verlag, 1996.

[DOY95] C. Daws, A. Olivero, and S. Yovine. Verifying ET-LOTOS programs with KRONOS. In D. Hogrefe and S. Leue, editors, *Formal Description Techniques, VII*, pages 227–242. North-Holland, 1995.

[DS94] J. Davies and S. Schneider. Real-time CSP. In T. Rus and C. Rattray, editors, *Theories and Experiences for Real-Time System Development*, Amast Series in Computing. Word Scientific, 1994.

[FNLL96] A. F´evrier,E. Najm, G. Leduc, and L. L´eonard. Compositional Specification of ODP Binding Objects. In F. Aagesen, editor, *Information Network and Data Communication*. Chapman & Hall, 1996.

[Gro90] J. F. Groote. Specification and Verification of Real Time Systems in ACP. In L. Logrippo, R. Probert, and H. Ural, editors, *Protocol Specification, Testing and Verification, X*, pages 261–274. North-Holland, 1990.

[Han91] H. Hansson. *Time and Probability in Formal Design of Distributed Systems*. PhD thesis, Uppsala University, Dept. of Computer Science, P.O. Box 520, S-75120 Uppsala, Sweden, 1991. DoCS 91/27.

[Her97] C. Hernalsteen. A timed automaton model for ET-LOTOS verification. In T. Mizuno, N. Shiratori, T. Higashino, and A. Togashi, editors, *Formal Description Techniques X and Protocol Specification, Testing and Verification XVII*, pages 193–204. Chapman & Hall, 1997.

[Her98] C. Hernalsteen. *Specification, Validation and Verification of Real-Time Systems in ET-LOTOS*. Doctoral thesis, Free University of Brussels, Belgium, 1998.

[HHWT95] T. Henzinger, P.-H. Ho, and H. Wong-Toi. A user guide to HyTech. In K. Larsen, T. Margaria, E. Brinksma, W. Cleaveland, and B. Stoffen, editors, *TACAS'95: Tools ans Algorithms for the Construction and Analysis of Systems, Volume 1019 of Lecture Notes in Computer Science*, pages 41–71. Springer-Verlag, 1995.

[HR95] M. Hennessy and T. Regan. A Process Algebra for Timed Systems. *Information and Computation*, 117:221–239, 1995.

[ISO98] ISO/IEC FCD 15437 - Enhancements to LOTOS (E-LOTOS), May 1998. ISO/IEC JTC1/SC33 N0188, 209 p.

[LL97] L. Léonard and G. Leduc. An Introduction to ET-LOTOS for the Description of Time-Sensitive Systems. *Computer Networks and ISDN Systems*, 29(3):271–292, 1997.

[LL98] L. Léonard and G. Leduc. A formal definition of time in LOTOS. *Formal Aspects of Computing*, 10:248–266, 1998.

[LPW97] K. Larsen, P. Pettersson, and Y. Wang. Uppaal in a nutshell. *International Journal of Software Tools for Technology Transfer*, 1, 1997.

[MFV94] C. Miguel, A. Fernández, and L. Vidaller. Extended LOTOS. In A. Danthine, editor, *The OSI95 Transport Service with Multimedia Support*, pages 312–337. Springer-Verlag, 1994.

[Mil83] R. Milner. Calculi for Synchrony and Asynchrony. *Theoretical Computer Science*, 25(3):267–310, 1983.

[Mil85] G. Milne. CIRCAL and the Representation of Communication, Concurrency and Time. *ACM Transactions on Programming Languages and Systems*, 7(2):270–298, 1985.

[MT90] F. Moller and C. Tofts. A temporal calculus of communicating systems. In J. C. M. Baeten and J. W. Klop, editors, *CONCUR'90, Theories of Concurrency: Unification and Extension, Volume 458 of Lecture Notes in Computer Science*, pages 401–415. Springer-Verlag, 1990.

[NS92] X. Nicollin and J. Sifakis. An Overview and Synthesis on Timed Process Algebras. In K. G. Larsen and A. Skou, editors, *Computer-Aided Verification, III*, volume 575 of *LNCS*, pages 376–398. Springer, Berlin, 1992.

[NS94]   X. Nicollin and J. Sifakis. ATP: Theory and Application. *Information and Computation*, 114:131–178, 1994.

[QMdFL94]   J. Quemada, C. Miguel, D. de Frutos, and L. Llana. A Timed LOTOS extension. In T. Rus and C. Rattray, editors, *Theories and Experiences for Real-Time System Development*, Amast Series in Computing, pages 239–263. Word Scientific, 1994.

[RR88]   G. M. Reed and A. W. Roscoe. A Timed Model for Communicating Sequential Processes. *Theoretical Computer Science*, 58:249–261, 1988.

[Sig99]   M. Sighireanu. *Contribution à la définition et à l'impl´ementationdu langage Extended LOTOS*. Doctoral thesis, Universit´eJoseph Fourier, Grenoble, France, 1999.

[Wan91]   Y. Wang. CCS + Time = an Interleaving Model for Real Time System. In J. Leach Albert, B. Mounier, and M. Rodríguez Artalego, editors, *Automata, Languages and Programming, 18*, volume 510 of *Lecture Notes in Computer Science*, pages 217–228. Springer-Verlag, 1991.

17

Specifying and Analysing Multimedia Systems

Lynne Blair   Gordon Blair

Lancaster University, UK

17.1 Introduction

Formal methods have been successfully deployed in the field of telecommunications. A range of languages have emerged for this purpose, including the standardized formal description techniques (FDTs) LOTOS (see Chapter 5), Estelle and SDL (see Chapter 4). Furthermore, there has been significant interest in applying such techniques in the more general area of distributed systems, as reported in the first three chapters of this book. Whilst considerable progress has been made towards this goal, it is crucial that such techniques evolve to meet the new challenges of distributed systems such as multimedia, mobile computing and the emergence of object-oriented or component-based approaches. This chapter focusses exclusively on the impact of *multimedia* on the formal specification of distributed systems. More specifically, the aims of this chapter are

- to consider the implications of (distributed) multimedia for the field of formal specification and verification;
- to survey the existing body of work in this area (including single-language, dual-language and multiparadigm approaches);
- to discuss the potential advantages of the multiparadigm approach over the alternatives.

The chapter is structured as follows. Section 17.2 presents some background information on multimedia computing, with particular emphasis on quality of service management. This section also considers the resulting challenges for formal specification, including the need to specify and verify quality of service properties and, crucially, the requirement to represent and reason about key quality of service management functions. Section 17.3 then surveys the existing literature in this field, considering in turn single-language approaches, dual-language approaches and multiparadigm approaches. Emphasis is also given to the key issue of separation of concerns in the different approaches. Following this, Section 17.4 focusses on a multiparadigm approach developed by the authors. In particular, a specification is presented of a QoS-managed audio stream featuring functional, nonfunctional and management aspects of the system. Note that this is an extension of part of the multimedia binding object example from the previous chapter. The topic of verification is considered in Section 17.5, including consideration of model checking, reachability analysis and testing techniques. This section also considers the availability of tool support in this area. Finally, Section 17.6 presents some concluding remarks.

17.2 What is Multimedia?

17.2.1 Background on Multimedia

Multimedia is now a pervasive feature of modern computer systems. Consequently, software engineering methodologies must provide support for the development of such systems. More specifically, it is essential that formal methods support the specification and analysis of multimedia systems, particularly their real-time and management aspects.

Because of the breadth of work on multimedia, it is notoriously difficult to provide an all-encompassing definition of the term. For the purposes of this chapter, though, we define multimedia to mean 'the handling of a *variety* of (digital) media types in an *integrated* manner' [BS98]. Expanding on this, the essence of multimedia is not just supporting audio or video; rather, it is handling the breadth of media types that can be accommodated in modern computer systems. Furthermore, to achieve integration, all media types must be given first class status in terms of support for storage, transmission, interchange, presentation, and so on. In other words, you should be able to carry out similar functions of video and audio as are currently provided for text and graphics. It should also be stressed that, for the purposes of this chapter, we focus exclusively on *distributed* multimedia systems; we are not concerned with multimedia systems that are restricted to, say, one PC. We are hence concerned with formal support for applications and services such as desktop conferencing, Internet telephony, video-on-demand, and so on.

In general, media types can be classified as either *continuous* or *discrete*. Continuous media types are those with an implied temporal dimension; items of data must be presented according to particular real-time constraints for a particular length of time (examples include audio, video and animation). In contrast, discrete media types are self-contained entities with no temporal dimension (e.g., text and graphics).

One of the major challenges of multimedia is to be able to support continuous media. In terms of formal specification, this equates to being able to represent continuous media types and, more importantly, continuous media interactions. We will refer to these from now on as *stream interactions* or, more simply, *streams* (also referred to as *flows* in the previous chapter). In general, formal specification techniques are designed to model or reason about discrete interaction; for example, many offer facilities such as synchronous or asynchronous message passing between processes. To support streams, it is generally sufficient to provide a library (set) of abstractions, for example, as with the generic components of Section 16.4.

The second major challenge is to provide appropriate support for *quality of service.* In more traditional computer systems, it is sufficient to provide a given service. With multimedia, however, the quality of this service is as important as the service itself. For example, it is not sufficient just to offer audio and video streams from a video-on-demand service. It is also crucial to provide certain qualities in terms of the throughput, jitter and latency of the individual streams, and also the required real-time synchronization between the streams. In many ways, this presents a bigger challenge for formal specification techniques. Hence we examine this area in more depth in the following.

17.2.2 Focus on Quality of Service

A service in a distributed system is normally defined by its interface, which describes the set of operations that can be carried out on this service. For example, a camera might have an interface offering operations such as pan, tilt and zoom. These are often referred to as the functional aspects of the service, that is, what it offers to the outside world. In contrast, *quality of service* (QoS) is concerned with the nonfunctional aspects of the service, that is, how well it offers this service. This applies to both continuous media and discrete media. In addition, quality of service can relate to an individual media item (*intramedia*) or to constraints across multiple media items (*intermedia*). A good example of the latter is the requirement for *lip-synchronization* between an audio and a related video stream. *Quality of service management* is then defined as the necessary support functions, for example, in terms of supervision and control, to try to ensure that the required qualities are maintained.

There is a considerable body of work on quality of service management in distributed systems; good overviews can be found in [VKvBG95] and also [BS98]. For the purposes of this chapter, we focus on the (ongoing) ISO work on introducing QoS into the Open Distributed Processing Reference Model [ISO00], known as *QoS in RM-ODP* (see also Chapters 1 and 2 of this book). This aims to provide a general framework for the provision of QoS in (open) distributed systems (cf. the OSI 7-layer model). In addition, the work is based on an object-oriented model of computation (through its roots in RM-ODP). This is important given the prevalence of this approach in modern distributed systems.

In the work on QoS in RM-ODP, the nonfunctional properties of the system are subdivided into a number of different *QoS characteristics* (aspects of the QoS of an object that can be identified and quantified), including:

- time-related characteristics [date, time, time delay, latency (end-to-end delay), jitter (delay variance), synchronization skew, and so on];
- capacity-related characteristics (throughput, processor load, and so on);

- security-related characteristics (protection, access control, authentication, confidentiality, and so on);
- and so on.

Crucially, a contractual approach is used for the *specification* of particular QoS properties. With this approach, a QoS contract for an object is specified in terms of a set of QoS relations. A given relation then defines (i) the *expectations* of an object from its environment (i.e., what the object requires to provide a given level of QoS), and (ii) the obligation of QoS to the environment (i.e., what the object will provide in terms of QoS, assuming that its expectations are met from the environment). The environment is given by the set of all other objects. More precisely, a relation is denoted as:

$$Exp(A) \to Obl(A).$$

This can informally be read as 'constraint $Obl(A)$ will hold as long as constraint $Exp(A)$ is met'. Given this approach, there are clearly some advantages of using formal specification techniques to express expectations and obligations, for example, to prove if contracts can indeed be met.

The draft standard also highlights a distinction between *static* and *dynamic* approaches to QoS management. The former is more applicable to traditional (*hard*) real-time systems, and considers QoS only at the design and configuration stages. In other words, QoS is engineered or hard-wired into the system, for example, by overprovision of resources. In dynamic approaches, it is recognised that QoS must also be considered during the lifetime of the system. With this approach, QoS violations may occur, but emphasis is placed on the *recovery* from such violations, for example, through adaptive behaviour (cf. *soft* real-time). Clearly, this approach is more applicable to distributed multimedia systems given the unpredictability of, for example, the underlying networks. The standard defines a QoS management architecture that spans the spectrum between the two approaches. This includes the identification of key QoS management functions for *QoS provision* (at installation time) and *QoS maintenance* (at run-time). These functions are negotiation, contract refinement, admission testing and resource reservation (for QoS provision), and monitoring and control (for QoS maintenance).

Interestingly, the standards document uses Lamport's Temporal Logic of Actions (TLA) [Lam94] to provide a formal semantics to key aspects of the approach. For example, the relation '$\to$' introduced above is given a formal interpretation in terms of TLA constructs.

17.2.3 Implications for Formal Methods

As stated in the previous section, given the pervasive nature of multimedia, it is increasingly important for formal specification techniques to be able to specify and analyse such systems. This, however, places certain demands on the field of formal specification.

Before addressing this, we first consider the requirements imposed by distributed systems. As stated previously, most modern distributed systems adopt an object-oriented or indeed component-based computational model. Hence, it is crucial that formal specification techniques can capture the elements of data abstraction and polymorphism inherent in such approaches. It is also necessary to be able to provide a model of concurrency/ reactivity and interaction that is compatible with such approaches. Other important requirements include the ability to describe dynamic systems (in terms of, for example, system reconfiguration) and the need to express locality of objects (e.g., which machine, which address space, and so on). Many of these concerns are addressed however in other chapters of this book and hence will not be considered further. Note that there are a large number of languages that (at least partially) meet the above requirements, including various process algebras, temporal logics, Actor-based notations, timed automata, synchronous languages, and so on. For further discussion, please refer to the literature [BBBC98, Sin97].

Multimedia, more specifically QoS, adds a number of important requirements to this list:

- First, it is crucial to support the specification of *quality of service constraints* (or contracts), and to be able to reason about such constraints. In general, this requires the ability to specify *real-time* properties and behaviours. Given the nature of multimedia, it is also arguable that it is necessary to be able to specify *probabilistic* and/or *stochastic* properties, for example, to reason about the effects of cell or packet loss, or to represent the interarrival times of video frames.

- Second, it is necessary to be able to represent and reason about *dynamic QoS management functions*, in particular the functions of monitoring and control. While it is reasonable to abstract over some aspects of QoS management in system specification (e.g., those related to QoS provision), we believe that it is crucial to be able to reason about the impact of different adaptive control strategies on the behaviour of the overall system.

In the following section, we consider some research in this area. As will be seen, a large number of projects have addressed the first of these requirements, using a variety of notations. In contrast, the second area has often been overlooked. However, it is this aspect that distinguishes multimedia systems from other work, for example, the real-time community. As will also be seen, this is an interesting area where theory meets practice. It is often the case that there is a gulf between work on formal specification and on system development. In this area, however, there are a number of interesting examples where theoretical models also map directly to aspects of the system development.

17.3 Formal Specification Techniques

17.3.1 Overview

There is now a considerable body of research on the use of formal specification techniques to support the development of distributed multimedia systems. From this literature, a number of different approaches can be identified. In particular, it is possible to provide a strong classification on such techniques depending on the range of (formal) languages adopted. In the first approach, a *single-language* is used for all aspects of the system behaviour, including the basic model of the system, the overall QoS requirements and the underlying real-time assumptions on the occurrence patterns of events. This approach has the advantages that (i) it is necessary to master only one language to develop or comprehend the specification, and (ii) verification is relatively straightforward in a single-language environment. Other researchers have adopted a *dual-language* approach, whereby the system behaviour is specified in one language and the required QoS properties are given in another language (typically a real-time logic or temporal logic). Well-established model checking techniques can then be used to verify the required system properties (see Section 17.3.4). This approach is particularly prevalent in the real-time community and has the advantages that (i) more appropriate languages can be used for the specification of behaviour and properties, and (ii) a range of verification techniques and tools are available to support model checking. Finally, more general *multiparadigm* approaches have also been investigated, whereby a range of different languages can be used for different aspects of the system specification. This has the obvious advantage that the most appropriate language can now be adopted for each part of the specification, but, clearly, verification is now a more complicated issue (we return to this point in Section 17.5).

Another important, and closely related, issue is the degree to which there is a *separation of concerns* in the resultant specifications. There is a demonstrable requirement in multimedia systems to have such an element of separation in the architecture of specifications. For example, it is necessary to be able to easily identify key real-time assumptions and requirements, and to be able to isolate and reason about important QoS functions. As will be seen, the various approaches differ in the degree to which they support such a separation or make it explicit. It is fair to say though that many approaches exhibit some degree of separation, even when using a single-language (e.g., through a constraint-oriented specification style). Examples of more complete separation include aspect-oriented specifications (as adopted by the authors), viewpoints [ISO95, BBDS96] and perspectives [FS96]. Further details on aspects can be found later in this chapter (Section 17.3.4), and viewpoints modelling is addressed in detail in Chapter 20.

We now consider the three different approaches in more detail.

17.3.2 Single-Language Approaches

An Actor-Based Approach Researchers at the Open System Laboratory at the University of Illinois at Urbana-Champaign have specified multimedia systems using an Actor-based approach [RVA97] (see also Chapter 8) and have focussed mainly on real-time-based QoS constraints such as latency, jitter and synchronization skew.

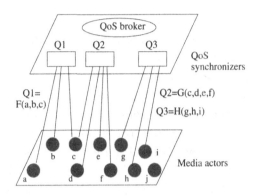

Fig. 17.1. An Actor-based specification architecture.

Their approach is to adopt a specification architecture that makes explicit the distinction between service specification and QoS requirements (see Figure 17.1, reproduced from [RVA97]). With this approach, a multimedia application is a collection of autonomous, concurrent and interacting entities referred to as *media-Actors*. Coordination constraints are then provided by special Actors, referred to as *QoS synchronizers*, the semantics of which are based on a real-time extension to the Actor model. Note that in their approach each QoS synchronizer handles one active session, with a QoS broker acting as an overall coordinator for all ongoing sessions. A given session is a distinct multimedia interaction, such as a video-on-demand session.

Whilst both media-Actors and QoS synchronizers share an Actor-based semantics, RTsynchronizers differ in that they may not send or receive messages; their functionality is to simply impose timing constraints on message invocations.

The specification of a QoS synchronizer consists of (i) the declaration of state variables, which may be changes by observing the underlying media-Actors; (ii) the constraints that should be enforced; and (iii) the rules for state changes. As an example, consider imposing a maximum end-to-end delay (`maxEED`), that is, latency, on a single stream:

```
RTSynchronizer ... {
  Declare
    int  i;               /* array index */
    real arrtime = sendtime = EED = 0;
  Constrain
    true:( (*,*),(msg),(EED >= maxEED) )(inf,inf);
```

```
Update
  streamptrn: arrtime[i]  = currentTime;
              sendtime[i] = sendTime;
              EED[i] = sendtime[i] - arrtime[i];
              ...

}
```

In the above, having declared the appropriate variables, a constraint is given of the form condition:action. Since the condition is true, *all* messages fitting the given pattern such that EED ≥ maxEED are infinitely delayed. This is stated by the timing condition (inf,inf) and is logically equivalent to dropping the packet. The final part states how the synchonizer should change its state on observing certain events. When a packet arrives at the appropriate media-Actor, the local variable arrtime is updated to the current time. Having set the sendtime, the end-to-end delay is calculated. An extended version of this example can be found in [RVA97].

Note that this work builds on previous research, looking more generally at synchronizers in real-time systems [Frø96].

Timed Extensions to LOTOS We have already seen one example of such an approach in the previous chapter, where E-LOTOS is used to specify a multiparty stream binding. As with the work on Actors, Leduc maintains a separation of concerns in the specification between the functional behaviour and (most of) the timing constraints. However, this time the separation is achieved through adopting a constraint-oriented specification style [Tur88]. We illustrate this with a small example, repeated from the previous chapter. We again consider the specification of a maximal delay on packet transmission times across the medium (i.e., latency). This time, however, if the packet is not delivered before this maximum, an exception (error) is raised:

```
process Delay_Obs [ist:data, ost:id_data](id:client,
                   delmax:time) raises [error:er_code] is
  ist ?dt;
    ( ost (!id,!dt)@?t [t<=delmax]; stop
      []
      wait(delmax+epsilon); raise error (e_delay) )
  |||
  DelayObs [ist,ost](id,delmax)
endproc (* Delay_Obs *)
```

Note that in this example the medium has an input stream of data (ist) and an output stream of data (ost). A timer is started after each ist event. If the corresponding ost event occurs at a time t ≤ delmax, all is well and the process can continue through the recursive call after the interleaving operator. If, however, the process waits for longer than delmax, an error (e_delay) is raised and transmission is stopped. Further details of this example can be found in the previous chapter.

Similar work has also been carried out by Regan [Reg93], in which he has formally specified a lip-synchronization algorithm using Temporal LOTOS. This specification consists of two data sources, each of which is connected to a presentation device by an associated stream. A controller process monitors all incoming data and determines when this data should be presented to maintain lip-synchronization. Since this example is concerned with lip-synchronization at the presentation device, it does not address end-to-end delay (as we have considered for the two examples above). Consequently, we illustrate the approach with a process that checks the overall synchronization of the presentation. If it drifts out of the acceptable bounds, it reports a synchronization error:

```
process VIDEO_SYNC[v_avail, v_present, sound_query]
                (v_time:nat) : noexit :=
  v_avail; VIDEO_CHECK[...](v_time+40)
where
  process VIDEO_CHECK[v_avail, v_present, sound_query]
                (v_time:nat) : noexit :=
  sound_query ?s_time:nat; (* check sound stream's clock *)
  ( [s_time-v_time>150] -> synch_error; exit
    []
    [v_timo-o_timo>15]  ->
      σ (* delay *); VIDEO_CHECK[...](v_time)
    []
    [not(s_time-v_time>150) and not(v_time-s_time>15)] ->
      v_present; (* now wait for next available frame *)
      VIDEO_SYNC[...](v_time)
  endproc (* VIDEO_CHECK *)   endproc (* VIDEO_CHECK *)
```

This process enforces the synchonization constraint that the video presentation may precede the sound presentation by at most 15 ms and lag the sound presentation by at most 150 ms.

Note that, in general, it is more difficult to carry out verification with temporal extensions to LOTOS due to the lack of industrial-strength tools. However, some prototype tools are starting to appear for E-LOTOS (as discussed in the previous chapter).

Other Approaches A number of other interesting studies have been carried out using single-languages. For example, the lip-synchronization example given above has also been specified using Esterel [BS98] and Timed CSP [FABSS96]. Interestingly, the Esterel version has also been used to drive an actual audio-visual presentation. In addition, Fischer and Leue have carried out a number of studies on the formal specification of multimedia systems using Real-Time Estelle [Fis96, FL98]. The

Temporal Logic of Actions (TLA) has also been used to specify the Joint Viewing and Tele-Operating Service (JVTOS) and its associated quality of service parameters [DT94].

At the University of Kent at Canterbury, researchers have investigated the use of stochastic specification techniques to specify multimedia applications. In particular, they have used both PEPA and Spades (both stochastic process algebras) to specify a multimedia stream [BBD98, BD99]. Ongoing research is investigating the provision of verification techniques, in particular stochastic model checking, to support the formal analysis of quality of service properties.

Finally, a number of researchers have used formal languages for the specification of particular aspects of a system (i.e., they do not attempt to model the whole system formally). One very active area of research is the use of formal specification techniques to specify and potentially verify the structure and real-time constraints in a multimedia document. For example, Santos et al. [SCdSS98] translate a high-level hypermedia document structure into RT-LOTOS for subsequent analysis. Diaz et al. have also used a timed extension to Petri Nets, HTSPN (Hierarchical Time Stream Petri Net), for the specification and analysis of logical and temporal synchronization constraints in hypermedia documents [DS97, OD99]. Bowman et al. and Sampaio et al. have used Interval Temporal Logic and E-LOTOS, respectively, for a similar purpose [BCKT97, SSdS97]. Rajan et al. have used the Prototype Verification System (PVS) from SRI International to model the temporal relationships between multimedia sessions in structure multimedia collaborations [RRV95]. They also adopt a transformational approach to automatically synthesize low-level network-specific constraints for managing communication in such multimedia collaborations. Finally, Li and Nahrstedt use an approach based on fuzzy logic to implement algorithms for dynamic reconfiguration in complex multimedia applications, such as a distributed visual tracking application [LN99]. As can be seen, many of these projects successfully bridge the gap between theory and practice (as discussed above).

17.3.3 Dual-Language Approaches

Use of the Real-Time Logic QL Researchers at CNET have developed a logic called QL for the specification of quality of service properties in an RM-ODP based environment. The language can be used with any appropriate notation that is able to express the RM-ODP computational model [BS98]. QL is a first-order real-time logic based closely on RTL [JM86], and with an underlying event model based on the work of Caspi and Halbwachs [CH86]. Events in this model equate to signals in RM-ODP and are denoted by an interface name, a signal name and a causality. For example, the event *producer.frameOut.SE* indicates that a producer interface has emitted a signal called *frameOut*.

QoS contracts (annotations) are then constructed by defining a set of provided clauses and associated required clauses (cf. expectations and obligations in the QoS in RM-ODP work). For example, a simple contract expressed in QL might be

Provided clause
$$\forall\, n, \tau(type1.s2.SE, n) \leq \tau(type1.s1.SR, n) + 10$$
Required clause
$$\forall\, n, \tau(type2.s4.SE, n) \leq \tau(type2.s3.SR, n) + 5$$

where τ is a dating function associating a time with a particular event.

This says that the interface *type1* should bound the delay (latency) between receiving a signal ($s1$) and emitting a response to that signal ($s2$) to 10 units of time. This assumes, however, that a delay bound of 5 can be guaranteed for signals on an interface of type *type2*.

As a second example, the following QL formula provides an expression of throughput for incoming video frames:

Provided clause
$$\forall\, n, \tau(videoWin.videoIn.SR, n + \underline{k}) \leq \tau(videoWin.videoIn.SR, n) + \underline{\delta}$$
Required clause
    True

This states that $\underline{k}$ instances of the *videoIn* signal should be received within $\underline{\delta}$ units of time. In this case, this is unconditional (i.e., there are no requirements placed on the environment). Note that these and further examples can be found in [BS98].

Some work has been carried out on formal analysis with QL. For example, *weaker* and *stronger* rules are defined over QL contracts to be used with subtyping rules to determine *substitutability*. In addition, it is possible to check the *consistency* of a set of QoS annotations on an interface or indeed of an interface and its environment. Finally, some work has been carried out on the synthesis of QoS monitors in Esterel from QL formulae.

Using the Real-Time Temporal Logic QTL Researchers at Lancaster have developed an approach based on LOTOS with the real-time temporal logic QTL. This work is different from most research on dual-languages in that the temporal logic is used to express both real-time requirements and real-time assumptions, with LOTOS being used to describe the abstract, untimed behaviour. Effectively, the real-time assumptions are used to ground the LOTOS specification in real-time. For example, whereas LOTOS would express the relative ordering of events relating to a video presentation, the real-time assumptions would state when precisely they would happen. This has the advantage of maintaining a clean separation of concerns between timed and untimed behaviour (as well as between QoS requirements and the system model).

QTL is based closely on the bounded operator, linear-time temporal logic MTL [Koy90]. However, the logic is modified to permit the use of LOTOS-like actions in place of propositions. For example, the formula $\diamond(receive?x : id)$ means that eventually we will get a receive event with identifier x. Similarly, the notation !x on a particular gate can be used to specify the output of data.

A number of examples have been developed, including analyses of QoS in RPC protocols and continuous media streams, and consideration of lip-synchronization between audio and video streams. To illustrate the approach, we provide a simple example of bounding the end-to-end transmission delays, that is, latency (adapted from [BBBC98]). We begin by describing the transmission channel using LOTOS. The internal action, i, is used to denote the loss of a frame during transmission.

```
process Channel[transmit, receive] : noexit :=
  transmit ?id:frame_id;
  ( ( receive !id; stop (* received successfully *)
      []
      i; stop ) (* frame is lost *)
    ||| Channel[transmit, receive] )
endproc (* Channel *)
```

The logic QTL can now be used over the above LOTOS events to specify QoS constraints such as end-to-end delay:

$$\Box(receive?id : frame\_id \rightarrow \bigvee\nolimits_{delmin \leq t \leq delmax}(\Diamond_{=t} \ transmit!id))$$

This means that, whenever a receive event occurs, then, at some state in the past (between *delmin* and *delmax* time units ago) the given frame was transmitted. Note that in the example this constraint is not specified the other way around (e.g., after a transmit a receive will occur) because the channel is assumed to be unreliable and messages may be lost during transmission.

It is important to understand that the logic formula above is intended as a statement of the *behaviour* of the system, and not a *requirement* that must later be checked (cf. provided and required clauses mentioned above). However, the logic can also be used to express QoS requirements that can then be verified. Because of the three-way split between abstract behaviour, real-time assumptions and requirements, verification is more complex than for standard dual-language techniques. In particular, extra steps are required to deal with the real-time assumptions. First, it is necessary to compose the real-time assumptions with the untimed LOTOS specification to produce a model of the timed behaviour (in practice, a timed automaton). Second, the real-time assumptions together with the real-time requirements must be checked for consistency. Following this, a standard model checking procedure can be used to check the requirements against the timed behaviour. The verification procedure is described in detail in [BBBC98].

In [LBC96b] and [LBC96a] this work was extended to include a probabilistic and stochastic logic. Derivation rules were also presented to allow formulae written in a subset of the logic to be (automatically) translated into Büchi automata (cf. the automata-theoretic work of Vardi [Var96]). These automata can then be used as *schedulers* in a running system to ensure that the real-time assumptions are realised.

Other Approaches Bowman et al. have used timed automata to specify and anal-yse different multimedia behaviours. In particular, they used the UPPAAL toolkit to carry out the analysis of, first, a multimedia stream [BFM98] and, second, a lip-synchronization algorithm [BFK+98]. The stream is described using the timed automata notation defined by UPPAAL with the required QoS properties checked using a combination of testers (written as automata) and the temporal logic CTL. The testers represent monitoring objects in the specification, which enter an error state should the QoS condition be violated. It is then a simple matter to verify this using reachability analysis (as provided by the UPPAAL toolkit). The second example revisits the lip-synchronization problem of Regan [Reg93] and Blair et al. [BBBC98] as described above. Using similar techniques, they revealed some flaws in the algorithm (in particular, the potential for timelocks).

In related work, researchers at Cornell have used HyTech, a symbolic model checker for linear hybrid systems, to analyse an audio control protocol [HWT95] (a previous manual analysis had been carried out by Bosscher et al. [BPV94]). In addition, Fischer and Leue have developed an approach based on SDL and Met-ric Temporal Logic (MTL) [Leu94, FL98]. In their words, 'when conjoining both specifications ... the temporal logic specifications can be thought of as filters on the admissable sequences specified by the SDL specification'. Their work includes examples of a range of QoS properties including latency, jitter, interstream syn-chronization, as well as lower level ATM-related properties. Interestingly, they also briefly consider the specification of QoS monitorinng and re-negotiation functions (cf. the work of the authors presented in Section 17.3.4 later). The paper [FL98] also contrasts this dual-language approach with their work on Real-Time Estelle mentioned previously.

There is also a large body of work on using dual-language techniques in the more general field of real-time systems. For example, Ostroff uses a combination of the extended state machine notation, TTM, with the real-time temporal logic, RTTL, to specify and verify a range of real-time systems [Ost89]. An excellent survey of other techniques for real-time systems can be found in [Ost92]. Finally, amongst others, Alur et al. [ACHH93] have studied the specification and verification of *hybrid* systems, for example, systems with a discrete-time controller working in a continuous-time environment.

17.3.4 Multiparadigm Approaches

Zave and Jackson Pioneering work in this area was carried out by Zave and Jackson [ZJ93, ZJ96]. In their work, case studies are presented using a wide variety of languages such as logic (including ordinary predicate logic, first-order logic, higher order logic and Horn clauses), automata, Statecharts, regular grammars (including Jackson diagrams) and Z specifications. In order to prove properties about the overall system behaviour, 'necessary' parts of the different paradigms are translated into assertions in first-order predicate logic. The *composition* of the set of partial specifications is then equivalent to the conjunction of their associated assertions. They also discuss problems associated with checking *consistency* across language boundaries. Note that the issues of composition and consistency are closely related, since they define a set of partial specifications to be consistent 'if and only if its composition is satisfiable' [ZJ93]. Issues of consistency checking are discussed further in Chapter 20 of this book.

In [ZJ96], a simplified version of a specification of a real AT&T switching system is presented. In this example, the states of individual telephones, including their indicator lights and sounds, are specified using finite automata, digit analysis is represented by parse trees associated with a grammar and voice connections among an arbitrary number of telephones are specified in Z. Their specification is compared to four other single-paradigm specifications of switching systems from the literature, written in Z, LOTOS and Timed CSP. They argue that their specification is an order-of-magnitude more complex and that none of the single-paradigm specifications could be extended to a switching system of realistic complexity. In particular, they point out the need to rigorously address 'user-interface' issues and the parsing of digits to extract commands controlling a wide variety of features. The latter point is most obviously specified using a grammar. They conclude by stating that 'a realistic switching specification must be multiparadigm, and must be built on a foundation for multiparadigm specification that has grammars on the list of allowable specification languages'. Unfortunately, their examples do not contain any reasoning about real-time issues, although [ZJ93] states that real-time can be introduced through the use of a predicate *timestamp(e,t)*, meaning that event *e* occurs at real-time *t*. Furthermore, there are inevitably certain features of the specification that cannot be translated into first-order logic (e.g., infinite sets, liveness properties, etc.).

Our Approach The authors also now adopt a multiparadigm approach to the specification of multimedia systems, as a generalisation of the LOTOS/ QTL work described above. In this work, we effectively extend the research on *aspect-oriented programming* [LK98] into the field of formal specification (i.e., aspect-oriented specification). In our examples of QoS management systems, we identify three key aspects: functional, nonfunctional and management aspects. The latter is subdivided further into aspects of monitoring and controlling. Typically, functional and nonfunctional aspects are specified using LOTOS and QTL, respectively (as in our previous work). However, we choose to describe management aspects using timed automata. Using this approach, we can easily express dynamic QoS management functions and analyse their behaviour both in isolation and in composition with the rest of the system. The overall approach is summarised in Figure 17.2.

The global model is derived using a *composition algorithm*, which relies on a common underlying semantic model based on *timed labelled transition systems* [BB99]. We have also developed a *tool suite* to support this process. Currently, this tool suite supports the composition of specifications written in LOTOS, timed automata and

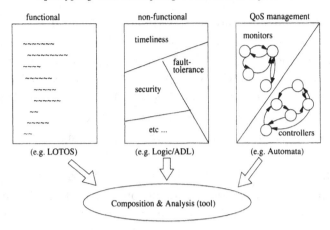

Fig. 17.2. Our multiparadigm specification approach.

a real-time temporal logic, QTL [BJB99]. The output of the composition process is a single timed automaton. The behaviour of this timed automaton can then be investigated using a simulator (to interactively step through behaviour) or a model checker (to verify the desired properties as expressed using temporal logic). An example of this approach will be given in Section 17.4. Note that our tool supports the use of the Fc2 automaton format [MdS93] to allow inter-operability with other formal tools such as Eucalyptus [Gar96], FcTools [BRRdS96] and UPPAAL [BLL$^+$98] (through the use of Autograph, as discussed in [BRRdS96]).

Importantly, timed automata, once verified by the tool, can be used directly to generate actual QoS management components. More specifically, we inject these components into an experimental middleware platform, where they act as interpreters for a given timed automaton script. Note that ongoing work is extending the tool to allow the specification and verification of stochastic behaviour (see also Section 17.4).

17.3.5 Analysis

As can be seen, a wide range of languages have been used for the specification of distributed multimedia systems, including various process algebras and timed process algebras, temporal and real-time logics, Petri Nets, timed automata and Actor-based approaches. One major distinction is whether a single-language is used throughout the specification, or whether dual-language or indeed multiparadigm approaches are preferred.

The authors, in previous research, carried out a detailed comparison of single- vs dual-language approaches [BBBC98]. In particular, we compared Regan's lip-synchronization specification in Temporal LOTOS with an equivalent specification using our dual-language approach (as reported in Section 17.3.3). This comparison highlighted some important benefits of the dual-language approach. In particular, logic provides a more natural and declarative statement of nonfunctional (QoS) requirements than the equivalent in Temporal LOTOS. In addition, there is a clear separation between nonfunctional and functional aspects (and indeed timed and untimed behaviour). The resulting specification is also more maintainable, in that changes can be made easily to the specification. For example, a different synchronization strategy was introduced with ease in the dual-language approach. In the Temporal LOTOS specification, however, this required significant restructuring of the specification.

Multiparadigm approaches can be viewed as a generalisation of dual-language approaches, encouraging further separation of concerns and the choice of appropriate languages for each system aspect. This can be particularly useful when modelling and reasoning about (dynamic) QoS management and its impact on the behaviour of the system. In distributed systems, there is increasing interest in the role of *adaptive* techniques in the construction of services and applications. Consequently, it is important to represent such concerns in the specification of such systems. From our experience, multiparadigm approaches give the specifier the freedom to choose appropriate languages for different aspects of the system. More specifically, we believe that they provide a natural way of accommodating (adaptive) management components in a specification, for example, as timed automata.

17.4 An Example of Dynamic QoS Management in a Multimedia System

17.4.1 Overview

We have stressed the importance of the ongoing *management* of multimedia systems, and yet it is this aspect that is so often overlooked in the specifications found in the literature. In this section we revisit parts of the multicast binding object example from the previous chapter. Due to space restrictions, and in the interest of simplicity, we restrict our attention to the process `One_Ind_Flow` and its subprocesses, that is, a simple point-to-point stream. In other words, we avoid the complex issues that need to be addressed with the management of (multimedia) multicast communications [MJV96, YMGH96].

To summarise the behaviour, process `One_Ind_Flow` describes an independent stream of data that is subject to no packet loss, it preserves the ordering of packets, the end-to-end transmission delay of each packet (latency) is at least `delmin` but no more than `delmax` and the variance of the delay (jitter) is bounded by `jmin` and `jmax`. Importantly, if one of the real-time constraints cannot be met (e.g., the transmission delay or jitter exceeds its upper limit), an exception is raised and the transmission is stopped. This is more analogous to *hard* real-time systems, where falling outside some bounds is completely unacceptable and perhaps even life-threatening. However, this is rarely the case in multimedia systems, which are more typically *soft* real-time. In such systems, trade-offs with the quality of service are acceptable. For example, if the transmission delay has a tendency to be too large, then the quality of the audio and video could be slightly reduced, thus reducing the amount of data to be transferred and hence resulting in lower delays. Alternatively, if the transmission delay was generally acceptable, and only occasionally exceeded the limit, the presentation of the data could be interrupted temporarily, allowing time for more data to be buffered, thus smoothing out such problems.

Incorporating such policies into the specification of multimedia systems requires that the systems be *monitored* and *controlled*. For example, in the previous chapter, the system specification raises errors that can be monitored easily by another process or object. If the monitor decides that corrective action should be taken (e.g., to reduce the quality of the audio), it needs to be able to give appropriate *feedback* to the system specification. For example, it may need to alter the values of parameters in the specification (such as the transmission rate) or possibly send *control* messages back to be intercepted by processes in the original specification. Clearly, the example in the previous chapter was not designed with our monitors and controllers in mind. Hence, to provide examples of typical multimedia monitoring and control, a few changes will be required to the example. These will be explained as appropriate in the following.

We take our example of monitors and controllers from a real system that has been built for audio presentations across a network [San99]. The underlying system has a number of possible frequencies (sampling rates) that can be used; these range from 8000Hz through to 44100Hz. Data can also be sampled using either 8 or 16 bits to give different quality sound. For the sake of simplicity in the example, we do not consider differences between mono and stereo presentations; all transmission rates quoted are assumed to be for mono presentations. Note that 11025kHz at 8 bits corresponds to *telephone quality*, 22050kHz at 8 bits corresponds to *radio quality* whilst 44100Hz at 16 bits corresponds to *CD quality*. Similar wide-ranging standards also exist for the quality of video presentations.

Initially, we consider monitoring for delayed packets across the stream (process One_Ind_Flow). The figures that we use assume that this is an audio stream. Our monitor watches for delay errors from the underlying specification (process Delay_Obs). For ease of reading, we assume that these errors are signaled by the occurrence of the event ERROR_RAISED !e_delay !audio. Importantly, in the E-LOTOS specification transmission should *not* be stopped once an error has occurred. The number of such errors within a given period of time (constant mon_period_delay) is counted (variable num_delays). If this exceeds a maximum (constant max_delays), then an event DELAYS_TOO_OFTEN !audio is raised by the monitor. This event will synchronize with a corresponding event in the controller (see below), and the controller will take any appropriate action. For reasons that will become clearer below, we also monitor for periods of no delay. If the number of such periods (variable num_no_delays) exceeds a maximum (constant max_no_delays), then an event NO_DELAYS is raised by the monitor (again, this event will synchronize with a corresponding event in the controller). Once the time period is completed, variables are reset and the algorithm repeats. This delay monitor is shown in Figure 17.3.

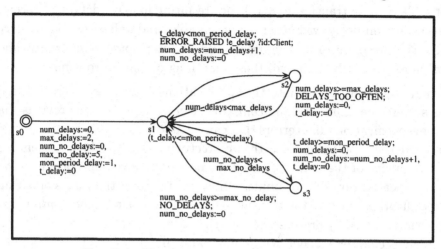

Fig. 17.3. The delay monitor (timed) automaton.

Note that in our real system we also have a monitor for packet loss, the structure of which is very similar to our delay monitor. However, in the example of the previous chapter, it is assumed that the medium is reliable and hence no packet loss can occur. In order to incorporate a packet loss monitor, process Medium should to be rewritten to allow packet loss, and such a loss should be signalled by an event such as ERROR_RAISED !e_loss !audio.

Now consider the job of the *controller*. On receiving a DELAYS_TOO_ OFTEN !audio signal, the controller can reduce either the sampling rate or the number of bits per sample to reduce the quality of the presentation (these parameters are denoted sr and bits in Figure 17.4). This reduces the amount of network traffic, which, in turn, corrects the excessive number of delays. However, note that this only allows presentations to be *reduced* in quality. We also need to specify some mechanism by which the quality can be *increased*. To do this, on receiving a NO_DELAYS signal, the controller can increase either the sampling rate (sr) or the number of bits per sample (bits) to increase the quality of the presentation. Our strategy for how the parameters are altered is shown in Table 17.1. In this table, the arrows show the next throughput rate to try from a given point when increasing or decreasing the quality of the presentation. The controller automaton is shown in Figure 17.4.

Note that this controller requires that we be able to access and change the values of some of the *parameters* set in the E-LOTOS specification (such as the rate of audio transmission, arate). The controller also sends a *control* message back to the system specification through the event ERROR !failed_to_ adjust. This is a new event that needs to synchronize with a corresponding event in the E-LOTOS specification and be processed in an appropriate way.

We have now considered the specification of different aspects of our system, and have used E-LOTOS for the combined functional behaviour and timeliness properties

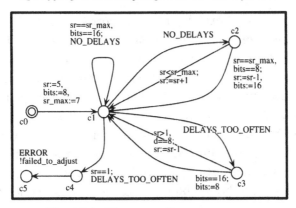

Fig. 17.4. The controller automaton.

kHz	8000	11025	16000	18900	22050	32000	44100
kb/sec @ 8 bit	7 ↔	10 ↔	15 ↔	18 ↔	21 ↔	30 ↔	43
	↑	↑	↑	↑	↑	↑ ↙	↑
kb/sec @ 16 bit	15 →	21 →	32 →	37 →	43 →	64 →	86

Table 17.1. *Different Sample Rates (kHz), Number of Bits (8 or 16) and the Required Throughput (kb/sec)*

(nonfunctional) and timed automata for the QoS management components. We are now likely to want to reason about the overall behaviour, and achieve this by considering the parallel composition of the different aspects, that is, the E-LOTOS and timed automata specifications. One way to do this composition would be to translate the E-LOTOS specification into a timed automaton and then compose all automata together (cf. the discussion in Section 16.5 that addresses the mapping of E-LOTOS to timed automata). However, since the tool that we have developed for our approach (mentioned in Section 17.3.4) does not support E-LOTOS (only LOTOS), we cannot illustrate this process further.

Finally, to complete the specification, we need to consider our *requirements* for the overall system. Our aim is that, when our algorithm is subject to real network delays, it will continually be able to adapt the quality of service provided (to the best possible with the given resources). The algorithm will only fail to adapt if it is at the lowest possible sampling rate and still suffering excessive delays. In this case, the controller automaton (Figure 17.4) emits an error signal having visited state $c4$ and then stops in state $c5$. Reachability analysis can be used to detect if state $c4$ (or $c5$) is ever reached. For example, by using a tool such as UPPAAL we could check this property by specifying our requirement in CTL as follows:

$$E <> Controller.c4$$

Note that the use of UPPAAL would require either *all* aspects of our specification to be written as timed automata or, alternatively, just their composition to be written as a timed automaton. Note also that the correctness of this property depends (amongst other things) on the range of values chosen for the transmission delay. Ideally, these should be sampled from an appropriate distribution that models the real pattern of network delays. To accommodate this, ongoing work is developing a stochastic extension to our tool based on our recently developed model of stochastically enhanced timed automata (SETAs) [BB00]. This will allow our algorithms to be analysed under more realistic conditions, for example, by allowing the inter-arrival times of packets to be sampled from an exponential distribution. By varying the parameters of the distribution, we will then be able to perform 'worst-case' analysis and deduce a lower bound on the conditions under which the algorithm will continue to adapt.

17.5 Verification Techniques and Tools

17.5.1 Overview

We now consider in more detail different verification techniques that can be applied to multimedia systems (and more generally real-time systems). In the literature such analysis comes in a variety of forms, including simulation (exhaustive and random-walks), testing (with partial and complete state coverage), consistency checking (e.g., seeing if different contradictory requirements exist), reachability analysis (proving if a given state is, or is not, reachable) and model checking (checking whether all possible paths through the system satisfy a given temporal logic formula). In this section we focus mainly on the last of these categories, namely, model checking, and the tools that are currently available to support this style of analysis.

17.5.2 Model Checking

Model checking has become an important technique by which a system can be checked for correctness, typically against a temporal logic formula. One method is based on an automata-theoretic approach (or ω-automaton approach) developed by Vardi and Wolper (e.g., [Var96]). In this method, assume that a formula f is to be checked against a system S (often described in terms of a labelled transition system). Using established techniques, an automaton A_f can be derived from f such that it accepts exactly the same 'words' as the original formula. It is then necessary to take the cross-product of S and A_f. Commonly, the formula actually represents the *negated* requirement to be checked. In this case, the existence of a particular type of path in $S \times A_f$ indicates that certain behaviour satisfies both the system *and* the negated formula. This indicates that the requirement does *not* hold over the system (since *no* behaviour should satify S and the negated formula). An alternative, but similar, technique is that of the tableau method (e.g., [Wol85]).

Model checking becomes more complex once the real-time behaviour of systems is considered, primarily because of the increased state-space (and consequently time) required for verification. As a result, several more-advanced techniques have been developed such as symbolic model checking [BCM⁺90, HNSY94, LPY95] (including on-the-fly techniques [BTY97]), partial-order methods [GW91] and techniques based on abstractions [DT97] and symmetries [EJ93].

Symbolic model checking is perhaps the most popular of these techniques and is often achieved through the use of *binary decision diagrams* (BDDs) [BCM⁺90]. Such diagrams are symbolic representations of Boolean functions and provide efficient encodings of very large state-spaces.

Note that, more recently, model checking techniques have also been developed for probabilistic and stochastic systems. Several examples of these can be found in [Kat99].

17.5.3 Tool Support for Formal Verification

There are now several mature formal tools to support the verification process. In this section we concentrate on HyTech [HHWT97], Kronos [Yov97], Spin [Hol97] and UPPAAL [LPY97]. Note that all of these tools incorporate one or more of the advanced model checking techniques mentioned in the previous section. A more extensive list of tools can be found on the website at [WWW00]. Furthermore, a comparison of five model checkers (including Spin) can be found in [DDR⁺99].

HyTech is a symbolic model checker for linear hybrid automata and can thus verify properties over systems exhibiting both discrete-time and continuous-time behaviour. The automata are input textually whilst the properties to be checked are specified in a simple programming language. In this language assertions are provided as a primitive data type, and various macros are also defined to aid the user with analysis such as testing reachability. Importantly, HyTech can be used to compute necessary and sufficient constraints on the parameter values that guarantee correctness. For example, [HHWT97] specifies a rail-road crossing and computes the exact cut-off point from the crossing at which the train has to signal its approach in order for the gate to be closed in time.

In Kronos, processes are modelled through the use of timed automata. Verification can be achieved either by specifying formulae in a timed temporal logic (TCTL) and then using model checking techniques or by specifying the correctness criteria as timed automata and then using bisimulation algorithms to check whether the two automata are *equivalent*. In [Yov97] this latter technique makes use of algorithms developed for the CADP toolbox [GJM⁺97] to test for bisimilarity.

In the Spin model checker, processes are modelled as nondeterministic finite-state machines using the language Promela (Process Meta Language). Properties to be verified are expressed in a linear temporal logic and are made available to the model checker via *never claims* (which embody the negation of the formula). These never claims describe the undesirable behaviour of the system and can be generated from the original property; they can be checked using automata-theoretic techniques (see above). Various other algorithms for validating behaviour, including partial-coverage techniques, can be found in the original text on Spin [Hol91].

Finally, UPPAAL is a graphical toolbox in which processes are modelled using timed automata. Analysis is possible through simulation (interactive and graphical) and model checking techniques. For reasons of efficiency, model checking is restricted to checking for invariant and reachability properties. However, in practice, this is not a major drawback since various techniques have been developed to check other properties such as bounded liveness. These techniques use a combination of testing automata (that can be derived from a timed modal logic, STL [LPY97]) and various different *annotations* that can be added to the automata, for example, as in [HLS99]. Note that a new graphical user-interface has recently been developed for UPPAAL, providing a more consistent look-and-feel to the tool [BLL+98].

17.6 Conclusions

This chapter has addressed the implications of multimedia on the formal specification and verification of distributed multimedia systems. Key requirements identified include the ability to specify (and verify) quality of service properties and, crucially, the ability to reason about the impact of dynamic QoS management functions such as monitoring and control. A considerable body of research has addressed the first of these requirements. There is, as yet, no clear consensus as to the best approach for multimedia systems (single-language, dual-language, etc.). It is clear however that whatever technique is adopted, it is important to maintain a clear separation of concerns in the specification, particularly between functional and nonfunctional aspects. There has been much less research on the second of the requirements and yet the authors feel that explicit modelling of (dynamic) QoS management functions is crucial to the understanding of multimedia behaviours. The authors also argue that, to accommodate this extra aspect, it is important to adopt a multiparadigm approach (i.e., it is undesirable to use a single notation to express functional, nonfunctional and management aspects). The challenge is then to provide techniques and tools to support verification and validation in such a multiparadigm environment. This can be provided, for example, by mapping each language on to a common underlying semantic model such as that provided by timed labelled transition systems.

One of the most fascinating features of the work in this area is the strong bridge between theory and practice. In particular, formal specifications are used not only at design time; they are also used to synthesize components in the final system. This is an important trend that can only enhance the uptake of formal specification techniques in next generation of computer systems.

Acknowledgements

This work was carried out under the V-QoS project with the financial support of EPSRC (GR/L28890). We would like to acknowledge the contribution of our collaborators on this project, namely, Howard Bowman, John Derrick and Jeremy Bryans (University of Kent at Canterbury). We would also like to thank Trevor

Jones (Lancaster University) for his work on the development of our tool suite, and Mandy Chetwynd and Abderrahmane Lakas for their work on earlier EPSRC projects in this area.

Bibliography

[ACHH93]   R. Alur, C. Courcoubetis, T. A. Henzinger, and P.-H. Ho. Hybrid automata: An algorithmic approach to the specification and verification of hybrid systems. In *Hybrid Systems, Volume 736 of Lecture Notes in Computer Science*, pages 209–229. Springer-Verlag, 1993.

[BB99]   L. Blair and G. Blair. Composition in multi-paradigm specification techniques. In P. Ciancarini, A. Fantechi, and R. Gorrieri, editors, *Proceedings of the 3rd International Workshop on Formal Methods for Open Object-based Distributed Systems (FMOODS'99)*, pages 401–417, Florence, Italy, February 1999. Kluwer.

[BB00]   L. Blair and G. Blair. Stochastically enhanced timed automata. In S. F. Smith and C. L. Talcott, editors, *Proceedings of the 4th International Workshop on Formal Methods for Open Object-based Distributed Systems (FMOODS'00)*, pages 327–347, Stanford, California, September 2000. Kluwer.

[BBBC98]   G. Blair, L. Blair, H. Bowman, and A. Chetwynd. *Formal Specification of Distributed Multimedia Systems*. UCL Press, 1998.

[BBD98]   H. Bowman, J. Bryans, and J. Derrick. Analysis of a multimedia stream using stochastic process algebra. In C. Priami, editor, *Proceedings of the Sixth International Workshop on Process Algebras and Performance Modelling (PAPM98)*, pages 51–69, 1998.

[BBDS96]   E. Boiten, H. Bowman, J. Derrick, and M. Steen. Issues in multi-paradigm viewpoint specification. In *Proceedings of the SIGSOFT '96 International Workshop on Multiple Perspectives in Software Development (Viewponts'96)*. ACM Press, 1996.

[BCKT97]   H. Bowman, H. Cameron, P. King, and S. Thompson. Specification and prototyping of structured multimedia documents using Interval Temporal Logic. In *Proceedings of the International Conference on Temporal Logic*. Kluwer, 1997.

[BCM+90]   J. R. Burch, E. M. Clarke, K. L. McMillan, D. L. Dill, and L. J. Hwang. Symbolic model checking: 10^{20} states and beyond. In *Proceedings of the 5th IEEE Symposium on Logic in Computer Science*, Philadelphia, June 1990. IEEE.

[BD99]   J. Bryans and J. Derrick. Stochastic specification and verification. In *Proceedings of the Third Irish Workshop in Formal Methods*, Electronic Workshops in Computing. Springer-Verlag, 1999.

[BFK+98]   H. Bowman, G. Faconti, J-P. Katoen, D. Latella, and M. Massink. Automatic verification of a lip synchronisation algorithm using UPPAAL. In B. Luttick, J. F. Groote, and J. van Wamel, editors, *Proceedings of the Third International on Formal Methods for Industrial Critical Systems (FMICS'98)*, 1998.

[BFM98]   H. Bowman, G. Faconti, and M. Massink. Specification and verification of media constraints using UPPAAL. In *Proceedings of the 5th Eurographics Workshop on the Design, Specification and Verification of Interactive Systems (DSV-IS98)*. Springer-Verlag, 1998.

[BJB99]   L. Blair, T. Jones, and G. Blair. A tool suite for multi-paradigm specification. In J.-P. Finance, editor, *Proceedings of 2nd International Conference on Fundamental Approaches to Software Engineering (FASE'99), Volume 1577 of Lecture Notes in Computer Science*, pages 234–238, Amsterdam, The Netherlands, March 1999. Springer-Verlag.

[BLL+98]   J. Bengtsson, K. Larsen, F. Larsson, P. Pettersson, W. Yi, and C. Weise. New generation of UPPAAL. In *Proceedings of the International Workshop on Software Tools for Technology Transfer*, Aalborg, Denmark, July 1998.

[BPV94]   D. Bosscher, I. Polak, and F. Vaandrager. Verification of an audio-control protocol. In *Proceedings of Formal Techniques in Real-time and Fault-tolerant Systems (FTRTFT'94), Volume 863 of Lecture Notes in Computer Science*, pages 170–192. Springer-Verlag, 1994.

[BRRdS96]   A. Bouali, A. Ressouche, V. Roy, and R. de Simone. FcTools user manual (version 1.0). Technical Report Technical Report 191, INRIA, 1996. See http://www.inria.fr/meije/verification/doc.html.

[BS98]   G. Blair and J.-B. Stefani. *Open Distributed Processing and Multimedia*. Addison-Wesley, 1998.

[BTY97]   A. Bouajjani, S. Tripakis, and S. Yovine. On-the-fly symbolic model checking for real-time systems. In *Proceedings of the 18th IEEE Real-Time Systems Symposium*. IEEE, 1997.

[CH86]   P. Caspi and N. Halbwachs. A functional model for describing and reasoning about time behaviour of computing systems. *Acta Informatica*, 22:595–627, 1986.

[DDR+99]   Y. Dong, X. Du, Y. S. Ramakrishna, C. R. Ramakrishnan, I. V. Ramakrishnan, S. A. Smolka, O. Sokolsky, E. W. Stark, and D. S. Warren. Fighting livelock in the i-Protocol: a comparative study of verification tools. In W. R. Cleaveland, editor, *Proceedings of Tools and Algorithms for the Construction and Analysis of Systems (TACAS'99), Volume 1579 of Lecture Notes in Computer Science*, pages 74–88, Amsterdam, The Netherlands, 1999. Springer-Verlag.

[DS97]   M. Diaz and P. Senac. The HSTPN model and its applications. In *Proceedings of the 1st Workshop on Multimedia and Concurrency, International Conference on the Theory and Applications of Petri Nets*, Toulouse, France, June 1997.

[DT94]   A. J. M. Donaldson and K. J. Turner. Formal specification of QoS properties. In J. de Meer, G. von Bochmann, and A. Vogel, editors, *Proceedings of the Workshop on Distributed Multimedia Applications and QoS Verification*, pages 1–14, Montreal, Canada, May 1994.

[DT97]   C. Daws and S. Tripakis. Model checking of real-time reachability properties using abstractions (full version). Technical Report Technical Report 97-08, Verimag, October 1997. See http://www.imag.fr/VERIMAG/PEOPLE/Conrado.Daws.

[EJ93]   E. A. Emerson and C. S. Jutla. Symmetry and model checking. In *Proceedings of Computer-Aided Verfication (CAV'93), Volume 697 of Lecture Notes in Computer Science*. Springer-Verlag, 1993.

[FABSS96]   A. Feyzi Ates, M. Bilgic, S. Saito, and B. Sarikaya. Using Timed CSP for specification, verification and simulation of multimedia synchronisation. *IEEE Journal on Selected Ar as in Communications*, 14:126–137, 1996.

[Fis96]   S. Fischer. Implementation of multimedia systems based on a real-time extension of estelle. In R. Gotzhein and J. Bredereke, editors, *Proceedings of Formal Description Techniques IX – Theory, Applications and Tools*, pages 310–326, Kaiserslautern, Germany, 1996. Chapman and Hall.

[FL98]   S. Fischer and S. Leue. Formal methods for broadband and multimedia systems. *Computer Networks and ISDN Systems*, 30:865–899, 1998.

[Frø96]   S. Frølund. *Coordinating Distributed Objects*. MIT Press, 1996.

[FS96]   A. Finkelstein and G. Spanoudakis, editors. *Proceedings of the SIGSOFT '96 International Workshop on Multiple Perspectives in Software Development (Viewponts'96)*. ACM Press, 1996.

[Gar96]   H. Garavel. An overview of the Eucalyptus Toolbox. In *Proceedings of the International Workshop on Applied Formal Methods in System Design*, pages 76–88, Maribor, Slovenia, June 1996. See also http://www.inrialpes.fr/vasy/Publications/Garavel-96.html.

[GJM+97]   H. Garavel, M. Jorgensen, R. Mateescu, C. Pecheur, M. Sighireanu, and B. Vivien. CADP'97 – status, application and perspectives. In *Proceedings of the 2nd*

COST 247 International Workshop on Applied Formal Methods in System Design, Zagreb, Croatia, June 1997.

[GW91]   P. Godefroid and P. Wolper. A partial approach to model checking. In *Proceedngs of Logic in Computer Science*, 1991.

[HHWT97]   T. A. Henzinger, P.-H. Ho, and H. Wong-Toi. HyTech: a model checker for hybrid systems. In *Proceedings of the 9th International Conference on Computer-aided Verification (CAV'97), Volume 1254 of Lecture Notes in Computer Science*, pages 460–483. Springer-Verlag, 1997.

[HLS99]   K. Havelund, K. Larsen, and A. Skou. Formal verification of a power controller using the real-time model checker UPPAAL. In J.-P. Katoen, editor, *Proceedings of the 5th International AMAST Workshop on Formal Methods for Real-Time and Probabilistic Systems, Volume 1601 of Lecture Notes in Computer Science*, Bamberg, Germany, May 1999. Springer.

[HNSY94]   T. A. Henzinger, X. Nicollin, J. Sifakis, and S. Yovine. Symbolic model checking for real-time systems. *Information and Computation*, 1994.

[Hol91]   G. J. Holzmann. *Design and Validation of Computer Protocols*. Prentice-Hall, New York, 1991.

[Hol97]   G. J. Holzmann. The model checker SPIN. *IEEE Transactions on Software Engineering*, 23(5), May 1997.

[HWT95]   P.-H. Ho and H. Wong-Toi. Automated analysis of an audio-control protocol. In *Proceedings of the 7th International Conference on Computer-Aided Verification (CAV'95), Volume 939 of Lecture Notes in Computer Science*, pages 381–394. Springer-Verlag, 1995.

[ISO95]   ISO/IEC. Open Distributed Processing - Reference Model: Parts 1-4. Technical report, ITU Recommendation X.901-904, ISO/IEC 10746 1-4, July 1995.

[ISO00]   ISO/IEC. ISO/IEC FCD 15935, Open Distributed Processing – a framework of QoS in ODP. Technical report, ISO, 2000.

[JM86]   F. Jahanian and A.K. Mok. Safety analysis of timing properties in real-time systems. *IEEE Transactions on Software Engineering*, 12(9), 1986.

[Kat99]   J.-P. Katoen, editor. *The 5th International AMAST Workshop on Formal Methods for Real-Time and Probabilistic Systems, Volume 1601 of Lecture Notes in Computer Science*, Bamberg, Germany, May 1999. Springer-Verlag.

[Koy90]   R. Koymans. Specifying real-time properties with Metric Temporal Logic. *Real-time Systems*, 2:255–299, 1990.

[Lam94]   L. Lamport. The temporal logic of actions. *ACM Transactions on Programming Languages and Systems*, 16(2):872–923, May 1994.

[LBC96a]   A. Lakas, G. Blair, and A. Chetwynd. Specification and verification of real-time safety and liveness properties. In *Proceedings of the Eighth International Workshop on Software Specification and Design*, pages 75–84, 1996.

[LBC96b]   A. Lakas, G. Blair, and A. Chetwynd. Specification of stochastic properties in real-time systems. In M. Merabti, M. Carew, and F. Ball, editors, *Proceedings of the Eleventh UK Performance Engineering Workshop for Computer and Telecommunication Systems*. Springer-Verlag, 1996.

[Leu94]   S. Leue. QoS specification based on SDL/MSC and temporal logic. In J. de Meer, G. von Bochmann, and A. Vogel, editors, *Proceedings of the Workshop on Distributed Multimedia Applications and Quality of Service Verification*, Montreal, Quebec, Canada, May 1994.

[LK98]   C.V. Lopes and G. Kiczales. Recent developments in AspectJ. In S. Demeyer and J. Bosch, editors, *Proceedings of the Aspect-Oriented Programming Workshop, In Object-Oriented Technology: ECOOP'98 Workshop Reader, Volume 1543 of Lecture Notes in Computer Science*, pages 398–401. Springer, 1998.

[LN99]   B. Li and K. Nahrstedt. Dynamic reconfiguration for complex multimedia applications. In *Proceedings of the IEEE International Conference on Multimedia Computing and Systems*. IEEE, 1999.

[LPY95]   K. G. Larsen, P. Petterson, and W. Yi. Model checking for real-time systems.
In *Proceedings of the Fundamentals of Computation Theory*, Dresden, Germany, August
1995.

[LPY97]   K. Larsen, P. Pettersson, and W. Yi. UPPAAL in a nutshell. *Springer
International Journal of Software Tools for Technology Tr ansfer*, 1(1/2), October 1997.

[MdS93]   E. Madelaine and R. de Simone. Fc2: Reference manual version 1.1. Technical
report, INRIA Sophia-Antipolis, 1993. See
http://www.inria.fr/meije/verification/doc.html.

[MJV96]   S. McCanne, V. Jacobson, and M. Vetterli. Receiver-driven layered multicast.
In *Proceedings of ACM SIGCOMM'96*, pages 117–130, Stanford, California, August
1996. ACM.

[OD99]   P. Owezarski and M. Diaz. A new architecture for enforcing multimedia
synchronization in videoconferencing applications. *Telecommunication Systems*,
11(1-2):161–185, 1999.

[Ost89]   J. S. Ostroff. *Temporal Logic for Real-Time Systems*. Research Studies Press
Limited (distributed by John Wiley and Sons), 1989.

[Ost92]   J. S. Ostroff. Formal methods for the specification and design of real-time safety
critical systems. *Journal of Systems and Software*, 18(1), April 1992. See also
http://www.cs.yorku.ca/ jonathan/ttm.rttl.htm.

[Reg93]   T. Regan. Multimedia in Temporal LOTOS: A lip synchronisation algorithm. In
A. Danthine, G. Leduc, and P. Wolper, editors, *Proceedings of the Thirteenth
International IFIP Symposium on Protocol Specification, Testing and Verification*, pages
127–142. Elsevier, 1993.

[RRV95]   S. Rajan, P. V. Rangan, and H. M. Vin. A formal basis for structured
multimedia collaborations. In *Proceedings of the 2nd IEEE International Conference on
Multimedia Computing and Systems*. IEEE, 1995.

[RVA97]   S. Ren, N. Venkatasubramanian, and G. Agha. Formalising multimedia QoS
constraints using actors. In H. Bowman and J. Derrick, editors, *Proceedings of the IFIP
International Workshop on Formal Methods for Open Object-based Distributed Systems
(FMOODS'97)*, pages 139–153. Kluwer, 1997.

[San99]   D. Sanchez. QoSMonAuTA - QoS monitoring and adaptation using timed
automata. Master's thesis, Dept. of Computing, Lancaster University, Bailrigg,
Lancaster, LA1 4YR, UK, October 1999.

[SCdSS98]   C. A. S. Santos, J.-P. Courtiat, and P. de Saqui Sannes. A design
methodology for the formal specification and verification of hypermedia documents. In
S. Budkowski, A. Cavalli, and E. Najm, editors, *Formal Description Techniques and
Protocol Specification, Testing and Verification (FORTE/PSTV'98)*, pages 163–178,
Paris, France, November 1998. Kluwer.

[Sin97]   R. O. Sinnott. *An Architecture Based Approach to Specifying Distributed Systems
in LOTOS and Z*. PhD thesis, Department of Computer Science, Stirling University,
1997.

[SSdS97]   P. N. M. Sampaio, C. Y. Shiga, and W. L. de Souza. Enabling temporal
synchronization in E-LOTOS specifications and MHEG-5 applications. In *Proceedings of
the IEEE Conference on Protocols for Multimedia Systems – Multimedia Networking
(PROMS-MnNet'97)*, pages 92–100, Santiago, Chile, November 1997. IEEE Press.

[Tur88]   K. Turner. Constraint-oriented style in LOTOS. In *Proceedings of the British
Computer Society Workshop on Formal Methods in Standards*, pages 1–13. British
Computer Society, 1988.

[Var96]   M. Y. Vardi. An automata-theoretic approach to linear temporal logic. In
*Proceedings of the 8th Banff Higher-Order Workshop on Logic for Concurrency:
Structure vs Automata, Volume 1043 of Lecture Notes in Computer Science*, pages
238–266, Banff, Alberta, 1996. Springer-Verlag.

[VKvBG95]   A. Vogel, B. Kerherve, G. v. Bochmann, and J. Gecsei. Distributed
multimedia applications and quality of service: A survey. *IEEE Multimedia*, 2(2):10–19,

1995.

[Wol85]   P. Wolper. The tableau method for temporal logic: an overview. *Logique et Analyse*, 28:119–136, 1985.

[WWW00]   Formal methods web site, 2000. See hhttp://www.comlab.ox.ac.uk/archive/formal-methods.html.

[YMGH96]   N. Yeadon, A. Mauthe, F. Garcia, and D. Hutchison. QoS filters: Addressing the heterogeneity gap. In *Proceedings of the European Workshop on Interactive Distributed Multimedia Systems and Services (IDMS'96)*, Berlin, Germany, March 1996.

[Yov97]   S. Yovine. Kronos: A verification tool for real-time systems. *Springer International Journal of Software Tools for Technology Tr ansfer*, 1(1/2), October 1997.

[ZJ93]   P. Zave and M. A. Jackson. Conjunction as composition. *ACM Transactions on Software Engineering and Methodology*, 2(4):379–411, October 1993.

[ZJ96]   P. Zave and M. A. Jackson. Where do operations come from? A multiparadigm specification technique. *IEEE Transactions on Software Engineering*, XXII(7):508–528, July 1996.

Part Seven

Development Architectures

18

PICCOLA – A Small Composition Language

Franz Achermann   Markus Lumpe   Jean-Guy Schneider   Oscar Nierstrasz

University of Berne, Switzerland

Although object-oriented languages are well-suited to implement software components, they fail to shine in the construction of component-based applications, largely because object-oriented design tends to obscure a component-based architecture. We propose to tackle this problem by clearly separating component implementation and composition. In particular, we claim that application development is best supported by consciously applying the paradigm 'Applications = Components + Scripts'. In this chapter we introduce PICCOLA, a small 'composition language' that embodies this paradigm. PICCOLA models components and compositional abstractions by means of communicating concurrent agents. Flexibility, extensibility and robustness are obtained by modelling both interfaces of components and the contexts in which they live by 'forms', a special notion of extensible records. Using a concrete example, we illustrate how PICCOLA offers explicit support for viewing applications as compositions of components and show that separating components from their composition improves maintainability.

18.1 Introduction

Component-based software development offers a plausible solution to one of the toughest and most persistent problems in software engineering: how to effectively maintain software systems in the face of changing and evolving requirements. Software systems, instead of being programmed in the conventional sense, are constructed and configured using libraries of components. Applications can be adapted to changing requirements by reconfiguring components, adapting existing components or introducing new ones.

We argue that the flexibility and adaptability needed for component-based applications to cope with changing requirements can be enhanced substantially if we think not only in terms of *components*, but also in terms of *architectures*, *scripts*, *coordination* and *glue*. In particular, we claim that application development is best supported by consciously applying the paradigm

$$\text{Applications} = \text{Components} + \text{Scripts}.$$

Components are black-box entities that encapsulate services behind well-defined interfaces, whereas scripts encapsulate how the components are composed. This paradigm helps to make a clear separation of computational elements and their relationships.

However, currently there exists no general-purpose composition language that (i) offers explicit support for the paradigm introduced above and (ii) fulfils the requirements for a composition language (see [NM95a, NM95b, NSL96]). Object-oriented programming languages and design techniques, for example, go a long way towards supporting component-based development, and the languages are nearly ideal for *implementing* components, but current practice actually hinders component-based development in a number of significant ways:

- **Reuse comes too late:** Object-oriented analysis and design methods are largely domain-driven, which usually leads to designs based on domain objects and non-standard architectures. Most of these methods make the assumption that applications are being built from scratch, and they incorporate reuse of the existing architectures and components in the development process too late (if at all).
- **Overly rich interfaces:** Being domain-driven, OOA and OOD lead to rich object interfaces and interaction protocols, but component composition depends on adherence to *restricted, plug-compatible interfaces* and *standard interaction protocols*.
- **Lack of explicit architecture:** Object-oriented source code exposes *class hierarchies*, but not *object interactions*. How the objects are plugged together is typically distributed amongst the objects themselves. As a result, adapting an application to new requirements typically requires *detailed study*, even if the actual needed changes are minimal.

In order to solve these problems, we argue that it is necessary to define a language specially designed to compose software components and to base this language on an appropriate semantic foundation. Although to some extent the concepts that we identified can be applied in traditional object-oriented languages, we believe that a specially designed language is better for explaining, highlighting and exploring compositional issues as opposed to general-purpose programming issues. Furthermore, if we can understand all of the aspects of software components and their composition in terms of a small set of primitives, then we have a better hope of being able to cleanly integrate all required features for software composition in one unifying concept.

We are developing PICCOLA, a small composition language. PICCOLA version 1 is based on PICT [PT00] (described in [Lum99, Sch99]). Version 2 simplifies the usage of the core primitives of the underlying calculus so that programs can be written in a more declarative style. It also introduces user-defined operators and explicit namespaces [AN00]. Currently we are in the process of integrating our experience into version 3 of PICCOLA. These language versions are implemented in Java, Delphi or Squeak. The version described in this paper is PICCOLA2, implemented in Java. For simplicity, we refer here to this version as PICCOLA.

The language features of PICCOLA are defined by transformation to a core language that implements the $\pi\mathcal{L}$-calculus [Lum99], an inherently polymorphic variant of the π-calculus [Mil90, HT91] (see also Chapter 9) in which agents communicate by passing *forms* (a special notion of extensible records) rather than tuples. By this approach, we address the problem that reusability and extensibility of software components are limited due to position-dependent parameters.

Besides forms, which have their analogues in many existing programming languages and systems (e.g., HTML, Visual Basic, Python), the $\pi\mathcal{L}$-calculus also incorporates *polymorphic form extension*, a concept that technically speaking corresponds to asymmetric record concatenation [CM94], as a basic composition operation for forms. As we will show in Sections 18.4 and 18.5, both forms and polymorphic extension are the key mechanisms for extensibility, flexibility and robustness as (i) clients and servers are freed from fixed, positional tuple-based interfaces; (ii) abstractions are more naturally polymorphic as interfaces can be easily extended; and (iii) environmental arguments (such as communication policies or default I/O services) can be passed implicitly.

This chapter is organized as follows: in Section 18.2 we summarize our requirements for PICCOLA in terms of a conceptual framework for software composition. In Section 18.3 we illustrate the ideas behind the $\pi\mathcal{L}$-calculus, the formal foundation of PICCOLA. We introduce PICCOLA in Section 18.4 and present an extended example that illustrates how PICCOLA supports the conceptual framework for composition in Section 18.5. We conclude with a comparison of related work and present some perspectives on future work in Sections 18.6 and 18.7, respectively.

18.2 Components, Scripts and Glue

Component-based applications, we argue, provide added value over conventionally developed applications, since they are easier to adapt to new and changing requirements. This is the case since we can (i) configure and adapt individual components, (ii) unplug some components and plug in others, (iii) reconfigure the connections between sets of components at a high level of abstraction, (iv) define new, plug-compatible components from either existing components or from scratch, (v) take legacy components and adapt them to make them plug-compatible and (vi) treat a composition of components as a component itself. In the rest of this section we introduce a few important terms and illustrate that a composition language has to provide support for the following key concepts.

Components A *component* is a 'black-box' entity that both *provides* and *requires* services. These services can be seen as 'plugs' (or, more prosaically, interfaces). The added value of components comes from the fact that the plugs must be standardized (i.e., a component must be designed to be composed [ND95]). A 'component' that is not plug-compatible with anything can hardly be called a component. The plugs of a component take many different shapes, depending on whether the component is a function, a template, a class, a data-flow filter, a widget, an application or a server. It is important to note that components also require services, as this makes them individually configurable (consider a sorting component that behaves differently given different containers or comparison operators [MS96]).

Architectures Components are elements of a *component framework*: they adhere to a particular *compositional style* that defines the plugs, the connectors and the corresponding composition rules. A *connector* is the wiring mechanism used to plug components together [SG96]. Again, depending on the kind of components that we are dealing with, connectors may or may not be present at run-time: contrast C++ template composition to Unix pipes and filters. The composition rules tell us which compositions of components are valid (e.g., we cannot make circular pipes and filters chains). A so-called *architectural description language* (ADL) allows us to specify and reason about architectural styles [SG96]. Note that we adopt here a very restricted view of component architecture, ignoring such issues as module architecture or configuration management [Kru95]. We use the term compositional style in favour of architectural style. In a compositional style, the connection of two or more components with a connector is again a component, which must not necessarily be the case for an architectural style.

Scripts A *script* specifies how components are plugged together [NTMS91]. Think of the script that tells actors how to play various roles in a theatrical piece. The essence of a scripting language is to configure components, possibly defined *outside the language*. A 'real' scripting language will also let you treat a script as a component: a Unix shell script, for example, can be used as a Unix command within other scripts. At the minimum, a scripting language must provide (i) an encapsulation mechanism to define scripts, (ii) basic composition mechanisms to connect components and (iii) abstractions to integrate components written outside the language (i.e., a *foreign code concept* [Sch99]). Note that a script makes architectures explicit by exposing exactly (and only) how the components are connected.

Coordination If the components are agents in a distributed (or at least concurrent) environment, then we speak of *coordination* rather than scripting. A coordination language is concerned with managing dependencies between concurrent or distributed components. Classical coordination languages include Linda [CG89], Darwin [MDK92] and Manifold [Arb96].

Glue Although we claimed that components must be designed to be composed, the simple fact is that we are often constrained to use (legacy) components that are not plug-compatible with the components that we want to work with. These situations are referred to as *compositional mismatches* [Sam97], and *glue code* overcomes these

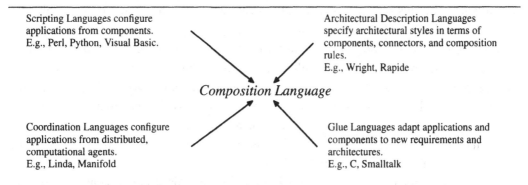

Fig. 18.1. Conceptual framework for software composition.

mismatches by adapting components to the new environment that they are used in. Glue adapts not only interfaces, but may also adapt client/server contracts or bridge platform dependencies. Glue code may be *ad hoc*, written to adapt a single component, or it may consist of generic *glue abstractions* to bridge different component platforms.

From our point of view, a *composition language* is a combination of the aspects of (i) ADLs, allowing us to specify and reason about compositional styles; (ii) scripting languages, allowing us to specify applications as configurations of components according to a given compositional style; (iii) glue languages, allowing us to specify component adaptation, and (iv) coordination languages, allowing us to specify coordination mechanisms and policies for concurrent and distributed components. Figure 18.1 illustrates this point.

A particular challenge for a composition language is the ability to define new, higher level composition and coordination abstractions in terms of the built-in ones [Nie93a]. Consider, for example, the difficulty of defining in a conventional object-oriented language a generic synchronization policy, such as a readers-writers policy, that can be applied to existing, unsynchronized objects. Typically, this would either not be possible, or it would require a language extension or a programming language with a meta-reflective architecture. A composition language not only lets us instantiate and compose components, but also provides the means to define higher level abstractions to compose and coordinate components.

18.3 Foundations for Software Composition

In order for a composition language to meet our requirements, it must be based on a semantic foundation that is suitable for modelling different kinds of components and compositional abstractions. A precise semantics is essential if we are to deal with multiple compositional styles and component models within a common, unifying framework.

The simplest foundation that seems appropriate is that of communicating, concurrent agents. For this reason we have extensively explored the asynchronous polyadic π-calculus [Mil90, HT91] as a tool for modelling objects, components and software composition [LSN96, SL97]. The tuple-based communication of the π-calculus, however, turns out to restrict extensibility and reuse. These observations have led us to explore the communication of *forms* – a special notion of extensible records – instead of tuples. In the rest of this section we illustrate briefly the nature of problems that the $\pi\mathcal{L}$-calculus solves and show how forms are the key concept to extensibility, flexibility and robustness; a detailed discussion of π and $\pi\mathcal{L}$ is beyond the scope of this chapter (refer to [Mil90, Lum99] for details).

Let us consider the following expression in the polyadic π-calculus as an example to highlight the difference between π and $\pi\mathcal{L}$:

$$!w(a,b,r).(\nu\ r')(\ \overline{f}\langle a,b,r'\rangle\ \mid\ r'(x,y).\overline{r}\langle x,y\rangle\ ).$$

This models a process providing a service at a channel w and acts as a wrapper for another process providing a service at channel f. The process listens repeatedly at channel w for a triple (a,b,r), where, by convention, a and b are service parameters and r is a channel to which the reply will be sent. After receiving a message, the process creates a new private channel r' and forwards the message to f, substituting the new reply channel. In parallel, it starts a new process that listens at channel r', picks up the response and forwards it to the original client along channel r. This particular wrapper does nothing exciting, but the same pattern can be used for more interesting wrappers. The important point is that the wrapper code *hard-wires* the protocol, so it will not work if the service at f extends its interface to accept more (or less) parameters or to return a result with a different arity.

In the $\pi\mathcal{L}$-calculus, the same example can be encoded as follows:

$$!w(X).(\nu\ r')(\ \overline{f}(X\langle reply = r'\rangle)\ \mid\ r'(Y).\overline{X_{reply}}(Y)\ ).$$

Instead of expecting a tuple as input, the wrapper receives a single form X. The original service is requested by overriding the binding of the reply channel to r'. Finally, when the result (Y) is obtained, it is forwarded to the original client by looking up the reply binding in the original form X. The interesting point to note is that the wrapper in the $\pi\mathcal{L}$-calculus is completely generic, assuming only that the message received contains a reply channel.

As a second example, consider the specification of invariants (e.g., default arguments) using polymorphic form extension. Let us assume that a service located at channel g provides a query interface for a simple database. This service requires a binding for *output* to display a query result. To facilitate the usage of this service, we define a wrapper located at channel u guaranteeing the invariant that the query result is passed to a default output service located at channel p:

$$!u(X).\overline{g}(\langle output = \mathrm{p}\rangle X).$$

The term $\langle output = \mathrm{p}\rangle X$ defines a form with the binding $\langle output = \mathrm{p}\rangle$ extended by all of the bindings in X. The effect is to define a default binding for output that may be overridden by X. Using this scheme, we guarantee that (i) by default, query results are passed to channel p (as desired) and (ii) the default output behaviour can be overridden by providing an additional binding for label *output*. Note that the same behaviour cannot be expressed without polymorphic form extension.

Similar schemes can be used to simplify the modelling of numerous object-oriented and component-based abstractions [Sch99]. For example, it is much easier to model generic synchronization policies (such as a readers-writers mutual exclusion policy) in the $\pi\mathcal{L}$-calculus than in the polyadic π-calculus [SL97].

Although the $\pi\mathcal{L}$-calculus makes a fundamental modification to the π-calculus, it is possible to translate $\pi\mathcal{L}$-agents to π-processes and back, *preserving behavioural equivalence both ways* [Lum99]. Furthermore, the concept of expressing computation by means of exchanging messages is computationally complete [Mil90], and, therefore, any programming scheme and model can be encoded in the $\pi\mathcal{L}$-calculus. This is of major importance in the context of adapting and composing components defined in different programming environments.

18.4 Piccola in a Nutshell

Although the $\pi\mathcal{L}$-calculus has been designed for reasoning about concurrency and communication, it turns out to be extremely low-level as a programming language. The natural style of interaction described by the $\pi\mathcal{L}$-calculus is that of directed channel communication. Other types of interactions such as event-based communication or failures, can be encoded, but they often turn out to be awkward.

PICCOLA addresses this shortcoming by defining language constructs to simplify these encodings. These constructs are services, infix and prefix operators to support an algebraic notion of compositional style, and the explicit notion of both the static and dynamic context for agents. We use the term 'services' instead of functions to stress that components provide and require services.

Higher level abstractions can then be defined as library functions on top of this core language much in the same way that CLOS is defined on top of Common Lisp [KdRB91]. In both systems, we can define an abstraction `Class` that allows the programmer to build classes for object-oriented programming [Sch99]. However, the fundamental difference with respect to CLOS is that PICCOLA's abstractions are defined in terms of a formal foundation of agents, forms and channels, instead of functions and lists.

18.4.1 Core Elements

In this section we give a brief overview of the PICCOLA language elements. The driving principle of PICCOLA is *everything is a form*. A form expression unifies both $\pi\mathcal{L}$-agents and $\pi\mathcal{L}$-forms. Form expressions are sequences of form terms (e.g., function calls or binding extensions). An agent evaluating a form expression builds up a form value by extending the empty form with the bindings specified by the terms.

PICCOLA has a syntax similar to that of Python and Haskell (i.e., newlines and indentation, rather than braces or **end** statements, are used to delimit forms or blocks). Forms, however, may also be specified on a single line by using commas and brackets as separators.

The following are the core elements of PICCOLA:

- `label = e` – defines a binding of the label to the form expression.
- `label(ident`$_1$`)...(ident`$_n$`):   e` – defines a parameterised abstraction over the form expression `e` and binds that service to the given label. This notation is syntactic sugar for the binding `label = \(ident`$_1$`)...(ident`$_n$`):   e`. Services are first class values; thus they get curried when $n > 1$. They are translated to $\pi\mathcal{L}$-agents that wait for requests at a service channel bound in the form representing the service.
- `return e` – returns the expression `e`. The return statement is used to enforce encapsulation for preceding bindings.
- `e.label` – this term denotes the projection of the label in the form expression `e`.
- `label(e)` – invokes the service `label` with the actual form argument `e`.
- *Infix operators* – Operators like +, -, |, > are syntactic sugar to denote designated services; they are encoded as label bindings `_+`, `_-`, `_|`, and `_>` that map the corresponding operations. For example, the expression $e_1 | e_2$, denotes the call of the pipe service within the context e_1 using e_2 as its argument.
- `def` *binding* – a binding prefixed with **def** takes a fixed point. This is used for recursive functions.
- `root` – denotes the static context where labels are looked up as identifiers. For instance, the identifier `x` denotes the binding of label `x` in the root context, that is, it is the projection `root.x`.
- `dynamic` – denotes the dynamic context passed on function invocations. Agents explicitly extend their dynamic context.

Using form expressions, PICCOLA scripts are programmed without using the low-level primitives of the underlying $\pi\mathcal{L}$-calculus. The parallel composition operator is made available as a service `run(Block)` that evaluates the passed block in an asynchronous agent. The service `newChannel` creates a fresh $\pi\mathcal{L}$-channel and returns a form with the bindings `send` and `receive`. To send or to receive a value to/from the $\pi\mathcal{L}$-channel, one has to use the corresponding bindings of the returned form.

Finally, constants like numbers or strings can be represented in the pure $\pi\mathcal{L}$-calculus using the scheme presented by Milner [Mil93] or Turner [Tur96] for the π-calculus. Therefore, adding *constant values* to the PICCOLA language does not change the underlying semantics. However, if constant values are available, then calculations involving such values are more efficient.

External components are accessed from PICCOLA by means of a corresponding gateway interface and can be transparently integrated into the PICCOLA system. Such components are represented by a PICCOLA form expression that defines the bindings for the provided and required services of the external component. In PIC-COLA2 implemented in Java, we use the reflection package of Java. With this approach it is possible to embed arbitrary Java objects into PICCOLA scripts.

18.4.2 Example: A Compositional Abstraction

The following example illustrates several key concepts of PICCOLA and shows how higher level abstractions can be defined. Suppose that we have a Multiselector and a GUIList component. The GUIList component provides two services, paint and close, whereas the Multiselector provides the services select, deselect and close. A composition of these two components offers the union of both sets of services, and, in order to close the composite component correctly, an invocation of close must be forwarded to both components. The following service specifies the close dispatch:

```
dispatchClose(L)(R)():  (L.close(), R.close())
```

The (curried) service dispatchClose expects two arguments L and R and yields a new service that invokes the close service on both arguments L and R.

Now, to compose the components GUIList and Multiselector, we can define the following service (note that the result of the service is in indented form):

```
fixCompose(L)(R):
    paint = L.paint
    select = R.select
    deselect = R.deselect
    close = dispatchClose(L)(R)
```

The service fixCompose can be used to compose two components. For example, the form c = fixCompose(GUIList)(Multiselector) would provide the required four services and correctly dispatch close calls to both subcomponents.

Unfortunately, this function explicitly refers to the services of the composite component. Therefore, this function cannot be used in a context where the composition should also provide possible extensions of the involved components. For example, the GUIList component may be extended with a resize service and the Multiselector component may define a new service selectAll. In such a case, the above abstraction would not reflect these extensions and the extra services would not be available. This problem, however, can be solved if we use polymorphic extension to define the composition:

```
compose(L)(R):
    L                               # all the bindings in L
    R                               # extended with all bindings in R
    close = dispatchClose(L)(R)     # extended with close
```

Given the original `GUIList` and `selector` components, the new abstraction returns a composite component with the same behaviour as the old version. However, due to the usage of polymorphic form extension, the resulting composite component also reflects extensions of the argument components like `resize` or `selectAll`. The `compose` abstraction is more generic than `fixCompose` because it assumes only that both arguments offer a `close` service. Note that if both arguments offer other services with the same name, only that of the second argument will be available in the composite component.

Our experiences have shown that polymorphic form extension is a fundamental concept for defining adaptable, extensible and more robust abstractions. It is also used in several PICCOLA library abstractions for object-oriented programming (e.g., in the `Class` abstraction that we use in following section).

18.5 Applications = Components + Scripts

In this section we illustrate how PICCOLA supports our conceptual framework for composition using an example of a Wiki Wiki Web Server (Wiki for short). A Wiki is a simple hypertext system that lets users both navigate and modify pages through the World Wide Web. The original Wiki was implemented by Ward Cunningham as a set of Perl scripts (available at c2.com). Wiki pages are plain ASCII text augmented with a few simple formatting conventions for defining, for example, internal links, bulleted lists and emphasized text. Wiki pages are dynamically translated to HTML by the Wiki server. A Wiki allows its users to collaborate on documents and information webs.

In the available Perl implementation, it is not easy to understand the flow of control since, as is typical in Perl, the procedural paradigm is mixed with the stream-based processing of the web pages. Execution is sensitive to the sequence in which the declarations are evaluated. To make a long story short, the architecture of the scripts is not evident, and that makes it hard to extend the functionality. Typical extensions that users ask for are reversing the order of new entries to the `RecentChanges` log (so that the latest changes appear at the top instead of at the bottom), extending the formatting rules to use embedded HTML, support for version control or an additional concurrency control mechanism (optimistic transaction control, access control, etc.).

We do not argue that the available Perl implementation is weak. (On the contrary, it is a good example of disciplined Perl programming.) The Perl scripts simply make use of the style provided by Perl (i.e., sequentially modifying buffers using regular expressions), which, however, generally does not make the underlying architecture explicit. In the following we will present the implementation of a component framework supporting a pipe-and-filter compositional style that allows us to make the architecture of the Wiki application explicit. This framework essentially gives the user a specialized scripting language for composing filters and streams.

The PICCOLA Wiki illustrates how the architecture of a scripted application can be made explicit. In particular, it shows that there is a clear separation between the computational elements and their relationships. Furthermore, glue and coordination abstractions are used which adapt and coordinate components that are not part of the component framework. The Wiki application is presented as follows:

- We define the top-level PICCOLA script that implements the Wiki by composing components that conform to a pull-flow stream-based compositional style [BCK98].
- We illustrate the implementation of an object-oriented (white-box) framework incorporating *streams*, *transformers* and *files* corresponding to the compositional style mentioned above. Java streams are integrated into the framework by means of gateway agents. We extend the framework with black-box abstractions that allow us to create transformers and streams without subclassing.
- We integrate components of a push-flow compositional style (i.e., components that *push* data downstream instead of *pulling* it from upstream). A coordination layer is used to adapt push-flow components so that they can work within a pull-flow architecture.

18.5.1 Scripting the Wiki in a Pipes-and-Filters Style

The PICCOLA Wiki script is embedded into a Java servlet [Hun98] that delegates its HTTP requests to the corresponding agents. The script defines the following services:

- A `repository` service that manages files. The contents of a file can be read or written. Each file must be protected against concurrent write access.
- A `doGet` service that handles HTTP GET requests. Depending on whether the request is to view a Wiki file or to edit it, the service returns the appropriate HTML document.
- A `doPost` service that handles HTTP POST requests to update a Wiki page. After modifying the file, it forwards the request to `doGet` so that a user sees the updated page. Finally, a log entry is appended to a recent changes file.
- Several *transformers* that translate the stream of stored ASCII text into HTML documents.

In general, stream composition is done using transformers. Furthermore, we use files and the HTTP connections as sources and sinks for streams. Using this approach makes it easier to add, remove or substitute transformers (thus changing the formatting rules) since their interconnections are made explicit in the source code.

Figure 18.2 shows the definition of the two services `getRequest` and `editRequest`. These services convert ASCII files into streams of HTML text. The service `doGet` (not shown in Figure 18.2) uses these functions to serve the HTTP requests. Note the pipes-and-filter composition with the intentional syntactic resemblance to Unix shell scripts. The main differences with shell scripts are that transformers (i) work

```
getRequest(F):
    file = repository.getFile(F)
    body = byParagraphs < file | mkStrong | mkEmphasis |
          mkLinks | mkList
    return mkHead(F) + body + mkTail(F)          # stream concatenation

editRequest(F):
    file = repository.getFile(F)
    return mkEditHead(F) + file.getStream() + mkEditTail(F)
```

Fig. 18.2. Scripting streams.

$S \mid T \to S$	A stream may be piped into a transformer, yielding a new stream.
$T \mid T \to T$	A transformer may be piped into another transformer, yielding a new transformer.
$T < F \to S$	A file may be piped into a transformer, yielding a stream.
$S > F \to F$	A stream may be dumped into a file, yielding the file.
$S >> F \to F$	A contents of a stream may be appended to a file, yielding the appended file.
$S + S \to S$	Two streams may be concatenated, yielding a stream.

Table 18.1. *Composition Rules for the Stream Style.*

record-at-a-time rather than byte-at-a-time and (ii) are purely pull-flow components, using the **next** method of the previous component, whereas Unix filters read and write simultaneously. The component framework adopted here also supports stream concatenation using the + operator.

18.5.2 *Stream Composition in* Piccola

A compositional style defines a set of components and rules governing their composition. We define a pull-flow stream compositional style whose components are streams (S), Transformers (T) and Files (F). The components can be composed (or 'connected') using the operators |, +, <, > and >>. The corresponding compositions rules are given in Table 18.1.

Compositions like $F + S$ are not permitted. Furthermore, we require that the operators | and + be associative, making it possible to consider compositions of streams and transformers as first class values. The *algebraic* notation employed by the framework provides a compact formalism for describing the compositional style that the component framework conforms to.

In order to ensure the correct behaviour of composite components, each component of the framework offers an interface that enables low-level interaction. The interface of a stream component, for example, provides three services to access the

```
AbstractInputStream = Class
    super = Object
    delta(X):
        next():  raise("subclass responsibility")
        isEOF():  raise("subclass responsibility")
        close():  ()
        # infix operators: Stream 'op' Other
        # NB: double dispatch for |
        __|(Right):  Right.prefixStream(X.self)
        __+(Right):  ConcatStreams(first = X.self, second = Right)
        __>(File):
            File.write(X.self)
            return File
        __>>(File):
            File.append(X.self)
            return File
```

Fig. 18.3. The class `AbstractInputStream`.

elements of the stream: `next`, `isEOF` and `close`. Note that these services must not be used by the application programmer; they are used only in the 'internal' protocol of composed stream and transformer components. The connectors ensure that these internal services get wired correctly.

In order to illustrate the framework implementation, we show the implementation of the abstract superclass for streams `AbstractInputStream` in Figure 18.3.

The abstraction `Class` used in Figure 18.3 denotes an abstraction to create class meta-objects with a Smalltalk-like inheritance and method dispatch semantics. We will not show the corresponding code here (refer to [Sch99] for details), but it is important to note that `Class` takes a parent-class meta-object (`Object` in the case of `AbstractInputStream`) and a `delta` function as parameters to create a class meta-object. The formal parameter `X` in `delta` provides access to `self`.

The composition interface of a transformer component is similar to that of a stream, but since (unconnected) transformers do not contain any elements, there are no services to access them. Transformers implement a service `prefixStream`, which is used to compose a transformer with an input stream (or a file) and yields a new (transformed) stream of elements. This ensures the correct wiring that the pipe connector relies on.

Files and streams of the operating system are made available as instances of the Java class `java.io.Reader`. We embed such objects as external components. The embedding requires only a small amount of glue code to rename the provided services and to set the end-of-file flag when the Java `read` method returns null.

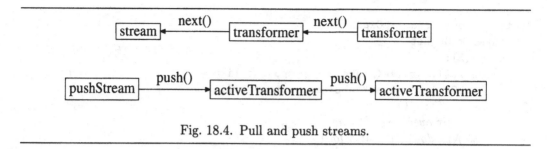

Fig. 18.4. Pull and push streams.

18.5.3 From White-Box to Black-Box Composition

In order to use the stream framework without subclassing abstract framework classes, we have implemented various factory services that, appropriately parameterized, yield components with the required behaviour. As an example, the service `newTransformer` requires a parameter `transformElement`, denoting a function that transforms each element of the stream. This parameter is a *required* service of the component. The following example uses this service to instantiate the transformer that is responsible for translating the intentional links of a Wiki page into an HTML link. In this case, all words starting with a question mark are substituted by the appropriate HTML fragment to make it a hyperlink.

```
mkLinks =
    newTransformer
        transformElement(Elem):
            substituteAll
                regexp = "\\?(\\w+)"
                text = Elem
                by = "<A HREF='$1'>$1</A>"
```

18.5.4 Overcoming Compositional Mismatch

In its current form, the Wiki components strictly adhere to the pull-flow compositional style illustrated in Section 18.5.2. As we extend the functionality of the Wiki, however, we may need functionality offered by external components that do not conform to this style. In many cases, it will not be possible to simply adapt methods by renaming or adding parameters, and some components are more naturally specified in terms of push rather than pull operations (i.e., rather than having upstream components 'passively' waiting for downstream components to ask for the next element, upstream components push elements to downstream components; see Figure 18.4).

In the Wiki application, we use wrapped Java output streams for writing HTML. However, these output streams are push-flow and not pull-flow streams, and components conforming to these two styles cannot be freely mixed. Consider the following function that emits an HTML header in our Wiki server:

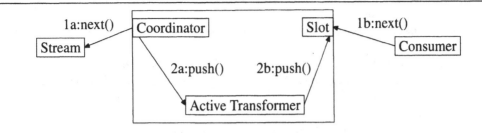

Fig. 18.5. Coordinating push and pull streams.

```
printHeader(File):
    push("<HEAD>")
    push("<TITLE>" + File + "</TITLE>")
    ...
```

It is not immediately obvious how to define this functionality as a pull stream. The occurring compositional mismatch can be solved, however, by (i) adapting **printHeader** as a push stream and by (ii) applying a generic glue abstraction (i.e., a *mediator*) that bridges the gap between push and pull streams. The corresponding glue abstraction illustrated in Figures 18.5 and 18.6 consists of a coordinator and a one-slot buffer. The coordinator pulls elements from the upstream component and pushes them into the downstream active transformer, which in turn pushes elements into the slot. The downstream consumer can then pull elements from the slot.

The push stream requires a **push** service in its context. This operation is provided by the adapter. The adapter injects the push service into the dynamic environment visible by the stream. That way, we can decouple the definition of the push stream and the adapter. For that purpose, the stream style contains a definition:

```
push(X): dynamic.push(X)
```

which forwards push operations to the push service stored in the dynamic context of the caller. This approach makes use of the fact that the dynamic environment is accessible as a form in PICCOLA[AN00].

The glue abstraction is defined as an abstract class that instantiates and binds the coordinator and the slot. The coordinator runs a loop that pulls elements and processes them with the required **processElement** service. The class **ActiveWrapper** creates the slot, adapts it to the stream interface and starts the coordinator. The coordination agent is defined in a loop: while the element read is not empty, the active transformer can process it in its own context. When the loop terminates, the slot and the stream are closed, and the hook service **done** of the client is called.

Note that the coordinator is open for future adaptations and extensions in the sense that it makes only a few assumptions about the context. We use form extension to map **push** onto the slot's **push** method and do not change any other external services for the service **processElement**.

```
ActiveWrapper = Class
   super = AbstractInputStream
   delta(X):
      slot = newSlot()                        # create Buffer
      atEOF = newRefcell(false)               # terminate coordinator
      read():  X.init.IS.next()               # pull next element
      run(do:                                 # start coordinator
            # inject read and push into the dynamic context
            dynamic = (dynamic, read = read, push = slot.push)
            def loop():
               elem = read()                  # get next element and process it
               if (isEmpty(elem))             # unless it is the empty form: i.e. eof
                     else:
                           X.init.processElement(elem)
                           loop()
            loop()                            # process all pushed elements
            slot.close()
            X.init.done()                     # hook for client
            atEOF.set(true)
            X.init.IS.close())                # close stream when done
         return                               # return adapted Stream Interface
            next = slot.pull
            isEOF = atEOF.get
            close = X.init.IS.close
```

Fig. 18.6. Generic glue abstraction.

Instead of having to subclass **ActiveWrapper**, we prefer to use black-box composition. In our case, the abstraction **asStream** requires a **start** service. Now, we can apply our glue abstraction to the given **printHeader** service.

```
   mkHead(File):
      asStream (start():  printHeader(File))
```

18.5.5 Lessons Learned

The Wiki example illustrates a number of principles that we claim can also be applied to other contexts. We started by selecting a compositional style that was appropriate for our problem. The fact that PICCOLA offers user-defined operators allows us to use a syntax that highlights the chosen style. External components like Java streams can be integrated by means of ad hoc wrappers. In PICCOLA, adapting interfaces is done simply by composing forms since the interface of a service is represented as a label in a form.

Components that do not correspond to the required compositional style of a framework may be integrated by means of glue abstractions. We have shown a generic coordinator that mediated the compositional mismatch between push-flow and pull-flow streams. This is possible because there is a simple, unifying foundation of agents and forms in which we can model both styles.

The Wiki application also embodies natural guidelines for maintenance. Changing requirements may be addressed by reconfiguring individual components (i.e., replacing their required services), reconfiguring interconnections between components (i.e., adapting the scripts), introducing new external components (i.e., possibly using glue or coordination abstractions) and deriving new components from old ones.

The PICCOLA Wiki can be easily extended in a number of interesting ways. For example, we can make file streams thread-safe by applying a generic readers-writers synchronization policy to them [Lea99]. Writing and appending files requires exclusive access, whereas several readers may be active concurrently. Another possible extension is to replace the repository with one using a version control system like RCS.

We do not pretend that all possible changes in requirements can be addressed while maintaining a single compositional style. A style itself may have to evolve with time, or eventually have to be replaced if it no longer provides a suitable metaphor for the problem domain.

We have shown using the Wiki example that a pipes-and-filters compositional style can be made explicit in PICCOLA. At the very end, this means that we have modelled streams in the $\pi\mathcal{L}$-calculus. This is not surprising per se since the $\pi\mathcal{L}$-calculus is Turing-complete. However, encodings of higher level interaction types, like event-based notification, often turn out to be quite awkward in the $\pi\mathcal{L}$-calculus itself. When we enrich the calculus to a language that defines forms, functional applications and contexts as primitives, these encodings turn out to be more compact, understandable and composable.

18.6 Related Work

In the past 20 years, there has been considerable research into the foundations of concurrency, and much of this research has focussed on process algebras (i.e., equational theories of communicating processes) and process calculi (i.e., operational theories of evolving systems of communicating processes). The π-calculus has proven to be successful for modelling object-oriented concepts [HT91, Jon93, Vas94, BS95, Wal95], and Sangiorgi has demonstrated that Abadi and Cardelli's first-order functional *Object Calculus* [AC96] can be faithfully translated to the π-calculus [San96].

The design of PICCOLA owes a great deal to the experimental programming language PICT [PT00]. PICT's programming constructs are provided as syntactic sugar and as library abstractions on top of a core language that implements the asynchronous π-calculus. We have used PICT extensively to experiment with different ways of modelling compositional abstractions in the π-calculus [LSN96, SL97]. These experiments led us to conclude that form-based communication is a better basis for modelling composition than tuple-based communication, which resulted in the development of the $\pi\mathcal{L}$-calculus.

PICCOLA differs from PICT in significant ways. First, PICT was developed primarily to experiment with type systems, whereas PICCOLA was developed to experiment with abstractions for software composition. As a consequence, PICCOLA is an untyped language and provides different abstractions than PICT (although an experimental, typed version of PICCOLA has also been implemented [Lum99]). Second, record-like structures (i.e., forms) in PICCOLA are part of the underlying calculus whereas they are defined as syntactic sugar on top of the core of PICT. Furthermore, PICCOLA supports asymmetric record concatenation, which is not available in PICT.

The class abstractions implemented in PICCOLA are based on object encodings defined in PICT [PT95, LSN96]: an object is viewed as an agent containing a set of local agents and channels representing methods and instance variables, respectively, whereas the interface of an object is a form containing bindings for all exported features. Classes are reified as first class entities (i.e., class meta-objects), which allow us to integrate features such as controlled object instantiation, class variables and methods, inheritance, reusable synchronization policies and different method dispatch strategies into the model. In contrast to the object model defined in PICT and other object-oriented programming languages, PICCOLA's object model makes a stronger separation between functional elements (i.e., methods) and their compositions (i.e., inheritance), which allows us to define multiple object models supporting different kinds of inheritance and method dispatch strategies [Sch99]. Other compositional styles implemented in PICCOLA include an event-based style, a style for doing visual layout and a style for coordinating Actors [AKN00].

The syntax of PICCOLA2 presented in this chapter deliberately resembles that of *Python*, an object-oriented scripting language that supports both scripting and programming in the large [vR96, WvRA96]. It supports objects, classes as first class values, single and multiple inheritance, modules as well as a run-time (meta-)object protocol. In fact, Python has a unifying concept: everything is an object, including functions and classes. By analogy, PICCOLA adopts the maxim that everything is a form. Functions in Python (and methods) can be defined in such a way that they support positional parameters (i.e., tuples) or keyword arguments (i.e., à la forms). Python provides operator overloading based on features of the (meta-)object protocol, which can be used to make the architecture of an application explicit in the source code [Sch99], similar to the approach that we have described in Section 18.5. Furthermore, the (meta-)object protocol offers limited support to change the underlying object model, although it does not have a meta-reflective architecture like Smalltalk [GR89]. Finally, Python is not inherently concurrent, although there is a POSIX-dependent threads library, and some researchers have experimented with active object models for Python [PHMS97].

Odersky is using the join-calculus [FG96] as a semantic basis for programming functional nets [Ode00]. The join-calculus is semantically richer than the π-calculus because it allows more than two agents to be synchronized at a single location. Thus some coordination abstractions can be encoded in functional nets more compactly than in PICCOLA. On the other hand, Odersky uses static records for primitive objects and can thus not have the flexibility given by forms, used, for instance, in the implementation of mixins.

PICCOLA can also be compared to numerous coordination languages. *Linda* is generally considered to be the prototypical coordination language, although it is not a language on its own, but a *coordination medium*, consisting of a tuple space (i.e., a blackboard) to which agents may 'put' and 'get' tuples by using primitives added to a host language [CG89]. The main problem with Linda is that computational and coordination code are typically intertwined, making it difficult or impossible to define separate coordination abstractions. *Darwin* is a 'configuration language' for distributed agents that models composition in terms of data flow [MDK92]. The composition primitives of Darwin have a formal semantics specified in terms of the π-calculus [EP93]. *Manifold* is a 'pure coordination language' that models external components as processes [Arb96]. A manifold is a process that can dynamically connect input and output ports depending on its current state. Therefore, it is particularly suitable for specifying reusable higher level coordination abstractions and protocols as well as for implementing dynamically evolving architectures. Manifold has some interesting successes in parallelizing sequential legacy code by splitting monolithic applications into parallel components that are coordinated by a Manifold layer [Arb95].

Forms have appeared in countless shapes and guises in programming languages over many years: as dictionaries, records, keyword arguments, environments and URLs. Although forms are clearly not a new idea, we believe that PICCOLA is the first language that adopts forms as a basic mechanism for concurrent programming, and in particular as the key concept for modelling extensible and composable systems.

Aspect-Oriented Programming is an approach for separating certain aspects of programs that cannot be easily specified as software abstractions, and there exists a Java implementation of an *aspect language* called ASPECTJ that allows us to specify aspects to be tangled into Java source code [KLM+97]. Initial experiments have shown that certain aspects can be expressed nicely in PICCOLA. For example, readers and writers synchronization policies cannot be factored out as software abstractions in Java [Lea99], but it is relatively straightforward to achieve this in both ASPECTJ and in PICCOLA. Whether aspects in general can be addressed by PICCOLA's compositional paradigm of agents and forms, however, is still an open question.

18.7 Concluding Remarks

In this chapter we have argued that the flexibility and adaptability needed for component-based applications to cope with changing requirements can be substantially enhanced if we think not only in terms of *components*, but also in terms of *architectures, scripts, coordination* and *glue*. Furthermore, we have presented PIC-COLA, a small language for specifying applications as compositions of components, that embodies the paradigm of 'Applications = Components + Scripts' and fulfils the requirements for a general-purpose composition language.

PICCOLA's language constructs are defined in terms of the πL-calculus, an inherently polymorphic variant of the π-calculus. A component is viewed as a set of interconnected agents. The interface of a component is represented as a form, a special notion of extensible records. PICCOLA models composition in terms of agents that exchange forms along private channels, whereas higher level compositional abstractions are introduced as sets of operators over sorts of components. Using such an approach, we intend to cleanly integrate all required features for software composition in one unifying concept (i.e., the concept of agents and forms) and to reason about components, compositions, architectures and compositional styles.

The PICCOLA prototype that we have presented demonstrates the following:

- The architecture of a component-based application can be made explicit by separately specifying components, the compositional styles they conform to and the script that composes them.
- Separating an application into components and scripts enhances its configurability, extensibility and maintainability.
- A composition language generalizes scripting languages by providing additional support for specifying compositional styles, compositional abstractions, coordination abstractions as well as glue abstractions.
- A composition language can be built directly on top of a unifying foundation of agents and forms.
- This foundation provides a good basis for specifying higher level components and connectors; forms are needed to model extensible interfaces and contexts, and agents are needed to model coordination abstractions.
- Multiple object models can be represented, which makes it possible to bridge compositional mismatches in heterogeneous applications.

Ultimately we are targeting the development of a general-purpose composition language as well as a formal model for component-based application development. In order to achieve this goal, future work in the following areas is needed:

Language The πL-calculus underlying PICCOLA does not have a notion of locality. But locality is needed to reason about distributed systems. Can the language be easily extended to explicitly model the location of distributed agents, as in the ambient calculus [CG98]? Open systems allow the administrator to plug in components at at run-time – what reflective features are needed in PICCOLA to compose components dynamically? We are currently experimenting with a lightweight approach to reflection so that we can iterate over the labels of a form and use the visited labels, but not create new labels dynamically. As the language design stabilises, we will attempt to improve the tools and composition environment, with a particular focus on visualisation [Cri99].

Applications Although we claim that PICCOLA can be used to compose applications according to different compositional styles, we have only demonstrated a single, well-understood style, namely, that of pipes-and-filters. We plan to experiment with specifying other compositional styles, in particular domain-specific composition (e.g., for workflows).

Object Models PICCOLA does not have a built-in object model but can support multiple models as library abstractions. We further plan to investigate how PICCOLA can be used to mediate between different external object and component models (such as those of different programming languages and middleware platforms). We are particularly interested in identifying necessary glue and coordination abstractions for bridging compositional mismatches.

Reasoning The original motivation for developing PICCOLA 'bottom-up' from a process calculus foundation was to ensure that the interaction of high-level compositional abstractions has a precise semantics in terms of a simple computational model. This goal has been reached. In addition, however, we wish to exploit the established theory and techniques for reasoning about software composition. The next steps are to express formally the contracts that are often implicit in an compositional style, in order to reason about valid compositions and about compositional mismatches (e.g., protocol mismatches [Nie93b]).

PICCOLA is an attempt to design a language that supports a particular paradigm for software composition in terms of components, compositional styles, scripts, coordination and glue. In this chapter we have focussed mainly on technical issues. This work, however, should be understood in a broader context of component-based software development [ND95, NM95b]. There are just as many, and arguable equally important, *methodological issues*: component frameworks focus on software solutions, not problems, so *how can we drive analysis and design* so that we will arrive at the available solutions? Frameworks are notoriously hard to develop, so *how can we iteratively evolve existing object-oriented applications* in order to arrive at a flexible component-based design? Given a problem domain and a body of experience from several applications, how do we reengineer the software into a component framework? As we develop a component framework, how do we select a suitable compositional style to support black-box composition? Finally, and perhaps most important, software projects are invariably focussed toward the bottom line, so *how can we convince management* to invest in component technology?

Although we do not pretend to have the answers to all of these questions, we believe that separating applications into components and scripts (i.e., making a clear separation between computational elements and their relationships) is a necessary step toward a methodology for component-based software development.

Acknowledgements

We thank all members of the Software Composition Group for their support of this work, especially Juan Carlos Cruz, Serge Demeyer, Robb Nebbe and Tamar Richner for helpful comments. We also express our gratitude to the anonymous reviewers of an earlier draft of this chapter.

This work has been funded by the Swiss National Science Foundation under Project No. 20-53711.98, 'A framework approach to composing heterogeneous applications'.

Bibliography

[AC96]   M. Abadi and L. Cardelli. *A Theory of Objects.* Springer-Verlag, 1996.

[AKN00]   F. Achermann, S. Kneubuehl, and O. Nierstrasz. Scripting coordination styles. In A. Porto and G.-C. Roman, editors, *Coordination Languages and Models*, volume 1906 of *Lecture Notes in Computer Science*, pages 19–35, 2000.

[AN00]   F. Achermann and O. Nierstrasz. Explicit Namespaces. In J. Gutknecht and W. Weck, editors, *Modular Programming Languages*, volume 1897 of *Lecture Notes in Computer Science*, pages 77–89, 2000.

[Arb95]   F. Arbab. Coordination of massively concurrent activities. Technical report, Centrum voor Wiskunde en Informatica (CWI), 1995.

[Arb96]   F. Arbab. The IWIM Model for Coordination of Concurrent Activities. In P. Ciancarini and C. Hankin, editors, *Coordination '96 - Coordination Languages and Models*, volume 1061 of *Lecture Notes in Computer Science*, pages 34–56, April 1996.

[BCK98]   L. Bass, P. Clements, and R. Kazman. *Software Architecture in Practice.* Addison-Wesley, 1998.

[BS95]   M. Barrio Solorzano. *Estudio de Aspectos Dinamicos en Sistemas Orientados al Objecto.* PhD thesis, Universidad de Valladolid, September 1995.

[CG89]   N. Carriero and D. Gelernter. How to write parallel programs: A guide to the perplexed. *ACM Computing Surveys*, 21(3):323–357, September 1989.

[CG98]   L. Cardelli and A. D. Gordon. Mobile ambients. In M. Nivat, editor, *Foundations of Software Science and Computational Structures*, volume 1378 of *Lecture Notes in Computer Science*, pages 140–155. Springer-Verlag, 1998.

[CM94]   L. Cardelli and J. C. Mitchell. Operations on records. In *Theoretical Aspects of Object-Oriented Programming.* MIT Press, 1994.

[Cri99]   C. Gheorghiu Cris. Visualisierung von π-programmen. Informatikprojekt, January 1999. University of Bern.

[EP93]   S. Eisenbach and R. Paterson. Pi-Calculus Semantics of the Concurrent Configuration Language Darwin. In *26th Annual Hawaii International Conference on System Sciences*, volume 2. IEEE Computer Society Press, 1993.

[FG96]   C. Fournet and G. Gonthier. The reflexive chemical abstract machine and the join-calculus. In *Proceedings of the 23rd ACM Symposium on Principles of Programming Languages*, pages 372–385. ACM, 1996.

[GR89]   A. Goldberg and D. Robson. *Smalltalk-80: The Language.* Addison-Wesley, September 1989.

[HT91]   K. Honda and M. Tokoro. An Object Calculus for Asynchronous Communication. In P. America, editor, *Proceedings of ECOOP '91*, volume 512 of *Lecture Notes in Computer Science*, pages 133–147. Springer-Verlag, July 1991.

[Hun98]   J. Hunter. *Java Servlet Programming.* O'Reilly & Associates, 1998.

[Jon93]   C. B. Jones. A pi-calculus semantics for an object-based design notation. In

E. Best, editor, *Proceedings of CONCUR '93*, volume 715 of *Lecture Notes in Computer Science*, pages 158–172. Springer-Verlag, 1993.

[KdRB91]   G. Kiczales, J. des Rivi`eres,and D. G. Bobrow. *The Art of the Metaobject Protocol.* MIT Press, 1991.

[KLM+97]   G. Kiczales, J. Lamping, A. Mendhekar, C. Maeda, C. Lopes, J.-M. Loingtier, and J. Irwin. Aspect-oriented programming. In M. Aksit and S. Matsuoka, editors, *Proceedings of ECOOP '97*, volume 1241 of *Lecture Notes in Computer Science*, pages 220–242. Springer-Verlag, June 1997.

[Kru95]   P. B. Kruchten. The 4+1 View Model of Architecture. *IEEE Software*, 12(6):42–50, November 1995.

[Lea99]   D. Lea. *Concurrent Programming in Java[tm]: Design principles and Patterns.* The Java Series. Addison-Wesley, 2nd edition, 1999.

[LSN96]   M. Lumpe, J.-G. Schneider, and O. Nierstrasz. Using metaobjects to model concurrent objects with PICT. In *Proceedings of Langages et Modèles à Objets '96*, pages 1–12, Leysin, October 1996.

[Lum99]   M. Lumpe. *A π-Calculus Based Approach to Software Composition.* PhD thesis, University of Bern, Institute of Computer Science and Applied Mathematics, January 1999.

[MDK92]   J. Magee, N. Dulay, and J. Kramer. Structuring parallel and distributed programs. In *International Workshop on Configurable Distributed Systems*, March 1992.

[Mil90]   R. Milner. Functions as Processes. In *Proceedings of ICALP '90*, volume 443 of *Lecture Notes in Computer Science*, pages 167–180. Springer-Verlag, July 1990.

[Mil93]   R. Milner. The polyadic pi-calculus: a tutorial. In *Logic and Algebra of Specification*, pages 203–246. Springer-Verlag, 1993.

[MS96]   D. R. Musser and A. Saini. *STL Tutorial and Reference Guide.* Addison-Wesley, 1996.

[ND95]   O. Nierstrasz and L. Dami. Component-oriented software technology. In O. Nicrstrasz and D. Tsichritzis, editors, *Object-Oriented Software Composition*, pages 3–28. Prentice Hall, 1995.

[Nie93a]   O. Nierstrasz. Composing active objects. In G. Agha, P. Wegner, and A. Yonezawa, editors, *Research Directions in Concurrent Object-Oriented Programming*, pages 151–171. MIT Press, 1993.

[Nie93b]   O. Nierstrasz. Regular t ypes for active objects. In *Proceedings OOPSLA '93*, volume 28 of *ACM SIGPLAN Notices*, pages 1–15, September 1993.

[NM95a]   O. Nierstrasz and T. D. Meijler. Requirements for a composition language. In P. Ciancarini, O. Nierstrasz, and A. Yonezawa, editors, *Object-Based Models and Languages for Concurrent Systems*, volume 924 of *Lecture Notes in Computer Science*, pages 147–161. Springer-Verlag, 1995.

[NM95b]   O. Nierstrasz and T. D. Meijler. Research directions in software composition. *ACM Computing Surveys*, 27(2):262–264, June 1995.

[NSL96]   O. Nierstrasz, J.-G. Schneider, and M. Lumpe. Formalizing composable oftware ystems – A research genda. In E. Najm and J.-B. Stefani, editors, *Formal Methods for Open Object-based Distributed Systems (FMOODS'96)*, pages 271–282. Chapman & Hall, 1996.

[NTMS91]   O. Nierstrasz, D. Tsichritzis, V. de Mey, and M. Stadelman. Objects + Scripts = Applications. In *Proceedings of Esprit 1991 Conference*, pages 534–552. Kluwer, 1991.

[Ode00]   M. Odersky. Functional nets. In *Procceedings of European Symposium on Programming*, volume 1782 of *Lecture Notes in Computer Science*, pages 1–25. Springer-Verlag, March 2000.

[PHMS97]   M. Papathomas, J. Hernandez, J. M. Murillo, and F. Sanchez. Inheritance and expressive power in concurrent object-oriented programming. In R. Ducournau and S. Garlatti, editors, *Proceedings of Langages et Modèles à Objets '97*, pages 45–60, Roscoff, October 1997. Hermes.

[PT95]   B. C. Pierce and D. N. Turner. Concurrent objects in a process calculus. In

T. Ito and A. Yonezawa, editors, *Theory and Practice of Parallel Programming (TPPP)*, volume 907 of *Lecture Notes in Computer Science*, pages 187–215. Springer-Verlag, April 1995.

[PT00]   B. C. Pierce and D. N. Turner. Pict: A programming language based on the pi-calculus. In *Proof, Language and Interaction: Essays in Honour of Robin Milner*. MIT Press, 2000.

[Sam97]   J. Sametinger. *Software Engineering with Reusable Components*. Springer-Verlag, 1997.

[San96]   D. Sangiorgi. An interpretation of t yped objects into t yped pi-calculus. Technical Report RR-3000, INRIA Sophia-Antipolis, September 1996.

[Sch99]   J.-G. Schneider. *Components, Scripts, and Glue: A conceptual framework for software composition*. Ph.D. thesis, University of Bern, Institute of Computer Science and Applied Mathematics, October 1999.

[SG96]   M. Shaw and D. Garlan. *Software Ar chitecture: Perspectives on an Emerging Discipline*. Prentice Hall, April 1996.

[SL97]   J.-G. Schneider and M. Lumpe. Synchronizing concurrent objects in the pi-calculus. In R. Ducournau and S. Garlatti, editors, *Proceedings of Langages et Mod`elesà Objets '97*, pages 61–76, Roscoff, October 1997. Hermes.

[Tur96]   D. N. Turner. *The Polymorphic Pi-Calculus: Theory and Implementation*. PhD thesis, Department of Computer Science, University of Edinburgh, UK, 1996.

[Vas94]   V. T. Vasconcelos. Typed concurrent objects. In M. Tokoro and R. Pareschi, editors, *Proceedings of ECOOP '94*, volume 821 of *Lecture Notes in Computer Science*, pages 100–117. Springer-Verlag, July 1994.

[vR96]   G. van Rossum. Python Reference Manual. Technical report, Corporation for National Research Initiatives (CNRI), October 1996.

[Wal95]   D. J. Walker. Objects in the pi-calculus. *Information and Computation*, 116(2):253–271, 1995.

[WvRA96]   A. Watters, G. van Rossum, and J. Ahlstrom. *Internet Programming with Python*. MIS Press, October 1996.

19

Specification Architectures

Kenneth J. Turner

University of Stirling, UK

Richard O. Sinnott

GMD-FOKUS Berlin, Germany

In this chapter we turn our attention from programming languages, as discussed in the last chapter, to issues of specification and structuring. In particular we discuss the role of specification architectures and architectural semantics.

19.1 Architecture and Specification

19.1.1 Basic Concepts

The term 'architecture' is widely used (and perhaps abused) in computer science. For the purposes of this chapter, the following definitions are used. *Architecture* means a structure, whether for specification or for design. An architecture thus deals with the overall organization of a system in terms of its components and how they are combined. *Architectural style* is the manner in which a class of related architectures is structured. The style may be embodied in a set of rules or constraints, and may be reflected in the way that an architecture is specified in some language. An architectural style determines the nature of a particular architecture. *Specification style* is the manner in which specifications in some language are written. The style may restrict the set of language constructs or may stipulate how they are used. The style determines how a particular specification is structured. *Specification architecture* deals with the structuring of a specification, and thus also reflects the style in which it is written. *Architectural specification* is an approach to specification that reflects the underlying architecture of a system. *Architectural semantics* defines how architectural concepts are represented in a specification language. Architectural concepts are thus given a formal interpretation, bridging the gap between architecture and specification.

Many different architectures may be defined for the same system. For example, various architectures may be defined at different stages during development and thus may have differing levels of abstraction (e.g., for requirements or implementation). The relationship between such architectures is one of refinement. Another possibility is that the architectures reflect different viewpoints and so may not be strictly comparable. This occurs in ODP (see Chapter 2), for example, where various viewpoints may be specified. Consistency among such architectures is still an open area of research and is discussed in Chapter 20.

A specification architecture may be purely syntactic and reflect textual or graphical layout. More importantly, the structure may have semantic significance: reflecting how components interact, hierarchical dependencies among components, and so on. In general, the architecture of a specification is concerned with its components and the way in which they are combined.

The relationship between an architecture and a specification language defines an architectural semantics. This will reflect the concepts of both domains. The specifier should ideally be able to work at the level of architectural components and their combinations. A certain architectural feature should immediately suggest a particular way of specifying it. Conversely, it should be obvious from a specification that certain parts of it correspond to well-known architectural features. This approach is termed architectural specification. Specification architecture is used to mean the structuring of specifications [TS97].

Architecture Description Languages (ADLs) are used to describe the high-level structure of a (software) system. A collection of papers on software architecture is found in [GP95]. ADLs support the concepts of component, connector and configuration as the means of expressing system structure. Although ADLs emphasize architectural aspects, they are often supported by formal specification languages. ADLs thus have strong similarities to the idea of architectural semantics discussed in this chapter, although the approaches are rather different. The notion of architectural style is central to much of the work on software architecture. In this context it refers to the way in which a family of related systems is structured. Architectural styles may be embodied in a reference architecture or in an idiom, such as the hierarchical decomposition or pipe-and-filter connection of components.

In the object-oriented world, architectural issues have been considered in the context of patterns and frameworks for design (e.g., [GHJV95]). Design patterns reflect the importance of components (objects) as well as combinators (their interconnections), as required by the view of architecture adopted in this chapter. Although design patterns were initially investigated in the context of GUIs (Graphical User Interfaces), they have been extended to a number of other domains. The emphasis in design patterns is on object-oriented software reuse. Formal specification therefore plays a lesser part, although formal object-oriented languages certainly exist (e.g., see [NS96]).

19.1.2 Specifying Architecture

Perhaps surprisingly, specification architecture appears to have attracted only limited attention in the literature. [Par72] is a classical discussion of important structuring issues. Specification architecture seems to have manifested itself mainly in the discussion of specification style. In standardization bodies, work on architectural semantics [ISO90] began with OSI (Open Systems Interconnection [ISO94]).

Similar work [ISO98b] has also been undertaken for ODP. Interestingly, much of the work on specification architecture has been stimulated by the use of just one formal approach: LOTOS (see Chapters 5 and 16). Various projects [BvV95] have included work on the architecture of LOTOS specifications. [Tur88] contributed to this by defining an architectural semantics for OSI using LOTOS. [VSv91] introduced the idea of specification style and its relationship to structuring.

Except for completely trivial specifications, a specification necessarily has a significant structure – its specification architecture. An architecture is implied even for nonconstructive specifications (those that state properties of a system rather than give an explicit model of it). An effective specification architecture is important and hard to achieve, but there are general principles that can guide the specifier. Neglecting the architecture of a specification can cause difficulty in understanding, expense in modification and extension, problems in analysis, and so on. When a formal specification is required, a good architecture is all but essential. Specification architecture becomes particularly significant when the problem under study is ill-defined. In fact, defining a good architecture without actually formalizing it is a major step forward. Architectural matters are essentially conceptual and thus not formal in themselves. It is therefore not possible to give an entirely rigorous way of formalizing architectural concepts. It is, however, possible to adopt a systematic approach to formalizing architectural concepts.

Architectural semantics involves two kinds of activity: conceptual analysis based on the informal description of an architecture, and specification based on a formal language. The conceptual analysis provides a framework within which consistent formalization is possible. Of course, the architectural semantics is unlikely to be unique; there may be a number of reasonable ways of analysing the concepts of an architecture and formalizing them. The combined experience of architects and specifiers is necessary in order to choose a good approach. The existence of an architectural semantics, even if it is not unique, is a powerful aid in ensuring consistent specification style.

Specification languages are often developed for a particular class of systems, such as communications software, hardware or distributed systems. However, it is rarely possible to use a language on a new class of system without considerable investigation of how best to specify the concepts of such systems. In other words, it is necessary to establish a relationship between the concepts of the new systems and those of the specification language. It would be time-consuming to develop this relationship afresh for every new system architecture and for every language that might be applied to it. In general, it could be necessary to consider a full mapping between all architectures and specification languages of interest – a costly approach. A practical strategy is therefore required to reduce the work involved. As will be seen, an architectural semantics can be developed in a way that efficiently allows for multiple architectures and multiple languages. An effective architectural semantics can be supported by specification templates based on the analysis of some class of systems.

A specifier who worked purely at the level of the specification language would be constantly making decisions about how best to model architectural concepts in the language. This would be like an electronics engineer always having to design circuits from first principles. Complex circuits are usually designed in a hierarchical fashion, building from lower level components. Many components are available off-the-shelf to the circuit designer. And even if not, the designer can often rely on existing designs for such components. Awareness of higher level structures allows an engineer to look at components in a circuit diagram and recognize the blocks and their relationships. Understanding as well as design are thus enhanced by attention to architecture.

Templates are the practical goal of architectural semantics work, since they considerably increase the efficiency and consistency of specification. A template library can be supported by tools that help to automate the process of specification, although of course it remains a highly creative task. In order to reach the goal of specification templates, several intermediate stages are required. A consistent hierarchy of architectural concepts is of considerable benefit. Many architectural concepts can be mapped onto more fundamental concepts, which may also be developed as a consistent hierarchy. An understanding of fundamental concepts is useful because they are common to a number of architectures. Formal representations can then be defined for the chosen specification language. A taxonomy of architectural concepts is helpful at this point to achieve a consistent formalization. Finally, the formal representations can be embedded in specification templates that can be called up from a library.

Alternative ways of organizing a specification may yield different benefits, such as clarity, conciseness, comprehensibility, extensibility and analysability. Such structuring may differ only in essentially syntactic ways. However, much deeper variations may arise from substantial differences in the language constructs used, even if the resulting specifications are formally equivalent. Differences among such specification architectures are termed 'horizontal' since they do not concern changes in the level of abstraction or nondeterminism (implementation freedom).

Specification architecture may alternatively reflect some inherent or intended structure in the system being considered. The structure might be in the formulation of requirements, that is, defining a framework for thinking about the system. The structure might be in the formulation of how the system should be built, that is, defining a framework for constructing it. Specifications of the same thing may be written at many levels of abstraction, from fully abstract to fully concrete. The more abstract (nonconstructive) levels of specification may be considered as requirements and the more concrete (constructive) levels as implementations. Differences among such specification architectures are termed 'vertical' since they stem from differing levels of abstraction or nondeterminism.

Despite the dependency of specification architecture on problem domain and specification language, there is general guidance that is relevant in most contexts. Behind an architectural approach are principles that provide overall guidance. Such principles are put to work by using architectural techniques that realize them. There is only a matter of degree between principles and techniques; it would be possible to regard techniques as subsidiary principles. At best, principles can only guide the architect. However, they can serve as a useful checklist of ideas to try. Architectural principles can be drawn from many disciplines. For example, software engineering draws inspiration from systems theory, software design and formal methods. Communications system engineering builds on software engineering principles but also on information theory, distributed system design and hardware engineering.

Enunciating principles will not guarantee their effective use. How can it be recognized that some principle has been properly applied? A complementary approach is therefore the use of architectural criteria to assess whether principles have been adhered to. Together, the principles (prescriptive) and the criteria (evaluative) provide a framework for the architect. There are many principles that can be adopted, for example, [Tur97b]. The important point is that the architect should employ *some* systematic approach.

19.1.3 Architectural Semantics

When formal specifications of OSI standards were first written, it soon became clear that there were many possibilities for representing architectural concepts in a formal way. To some extent this reflected the intention to keep the architecture at a broad, implementation-independent level. The varieties of interpretation also stemmed from the use of natural language in the defining documents. Having to specify broadly defined concepts in an FDT forced attention onto how these concepts should be interpreted. It was clear from the experience of trying to formalize OSI standards that much more guidance was needed on understanding architectural concepts. An architecture subgroup in ISO was therefore charged with developing a proper relationship between OSI and the FDTs. [Tur88] reports early work on an architectural semantics for OSI using LOTOS. With three standardized FDTs available, ISO and CCITT (International Consultative Committee on Telegraphy and Telephony), now ITU-T (International Telecommunications Union – Telephony), considered it important to offer guidance to specifiers using these techniques [ISO90].

Although the architecture subgroup was focussed on OSI, it turned out that much of the work was directly relevant to the emerging definition of ODP. The architectural semantics project was transferred to the ODP group and expanded to cover its requirements. Apart from ESTELLE, LOTOS and SDL, the project [ST95] also studied the use of RAISE (Rigorous Approach to Industrial Software Engineering [RL92]) and variants of Z.

An architectural semantics is intended to support specifications of particular architectures. The aim is to interpret the concepts of that architecture in a particular specification language. Ideally, such a semantics should prescribe how each archi-

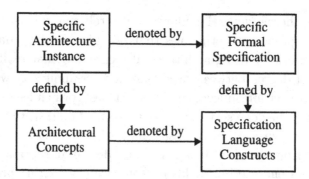

Fig. 19.1. Relationship between architecture and specification.

tectural concept is represented in the language. However, to be prescriptive requires agreement on the 'best' approach to specification. Often there are several reasonable specification styles for a concept, and it takes time and experience to evolve a recommended practice. Even then, it may be easier to give a sample specification than to give rules for modelling a concept. Architectural semantics has therefore tended to be a mixture of the prescriptive and the descriptive.

In considering the concepts of an architecture or the constructs of a language, it is often useful to distinguish between components and combinators. The components are the building blocks, and may be elementary or composite. The combinators are the means of creating more complex components from simpler ones. For an architecture, there may not be explicit recognition of combinators as such. For a language, the combinators are often called its operators.

A specific instance of some architecture (e.g., a protocol standard) conforms to that architecture, making reference to and being built from its components and combinators. An actual formal specification (e.g., in LOTOS) conforms to the constructs of the language and is defined by its semantics. The relationships among these elements are shown in Figure 19.1. If the architectural concepts have a defined representation in terms of the language constructs, this induces a relation between the architecture instance and its formal specification. Alternatively, if the architecture instance has a defined denotation directly in terms of the formal specification, this induces a relation between the architectural concepts and the basic language constructs. Figure 19.1 thus shows a kind of homomorphism (relationship between structures).

There is a choice of whether an architectural semantics is developed primarily at the level of specific architecture instances or at a more basic level. A direct mapping between all A architectures of interest and all S specification languages would require $A \times S$ mappings, which would be costly to define. However, there is a solution if the architectures can be restricted to some very general class such as information processing systems (of which OSI and ODP are examples). Such systems share many components out of which more complex components are built.

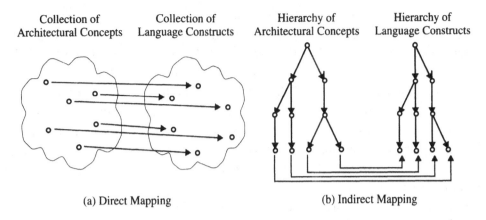

Fig. 19.2. Relationship between architectural concepts and language constructs.

The systems may also share combinators for building these higher level components. If these fundamental components and combinators can be established for a class of architectures and can be denoted in each specification language, then the number of mappings to be considered falls to $A+S$.

A separate issue is whether architectural concepts should be directly mapped to specification constructs or via some intermediate hierarchy that exploits the dependencies between concepts in the architecture and constructs in the language. The two approaches are depicted in Figure 19.2. The direct mapping in (a) gives each architectural concept a specific denotation in some language. As a result, the mapping could be complex to define, would not show a clear hierarchical relationship and could risk inconsistent specification of concepts at different levels in the architecture. A direct mapping would also be required for each architecture-language pair. An indirect mapping is shown in (b). Here there is a clear hierarchy, and the extent of the mapping is reduced because it can be restricted to the fundamental concepts.

With many architectures and many languages, an indirect mapping between each architecture and language would be required at the fundamental level. However, an indirect mapping would result in a less obvious relationship between composite architectural concepts and their denotations. A mapping like this might offer little practical guidance to the specifier; thus compromise is desirable. A hierarchy of architectural concepts and language constructs should be established along with a mapping at various levels. The mapping should exploit the hierarchy and thus define the denotation of a composite architectural concept using the denotations of its constituent parts. Such a mapping would be intermediate in size and complexity between the extremes of $A \times S$ and $A+S$.

Developing an architectural semantics begins with the consideration of a new architecture. A core set of fundamental information processing components and combinators should already exist, but may have to be extended for the new architecture. Fundamental components are things like activity, information and object. Sample fundamental combinators are hiding and partial ordering. The concepts of the architecture will usually, but not necessarily, have been defined in a hierarchical fashion. When there is no hierarchy, part of defining the architectural semantics includes establishing this. Even if there is an existing hierarchy, it may not be sufficiently precise to allow immediate formalization. It is unlikely that the architecture will have been expressed in terms of fundamental components and combinators; doing this will be another part of the architectural semantics. Even without considering issues of formalization, the development of a consistent concept hierarchy can be a valuable exercise.

The architectural semantics can now deal with the specification languages of interest. For a new specification language it is necessary to define a denotation for each fundamental component and combinator. If the language is insufficiently expressive, this may prove to be awkward or even impossible, thus limiting the use of the language for some architectures. The final step is to provide a denotation for each composite architectural concept, building on the denotations already defined. The development of an architectural semantics is relatively intricate. However, analysing an architecture is necessary to achieve a systematic formal representation of concepts.

19.1.4 Specification Templates

Defining an architectural semantics establishes a sound relationship between an architecture and the language used to formalize it. However, an architectural semantics may not be of immediate practical use to the specifier. What is required is a codification of the architectural semantics to assist in producing compatible specifications of an architecture more directly. The concept of a specification template is therefore introduced. Component reuse is possible when a frequently occurring element of a system can be specified in isolation. Structural reuse is possible when a context or configuration of components is identified as a common pattern. This is the idea behind design patterns.

At a basic level, a specification template is simply a syntactic device like a macro. It is merely a fragment of specification text that can be conveniently recalled and inserted in a specification. To enhance the value of such templates they can be parameterized to increase their generality. Parameterization might be at the level of the specification language (e.g., value or type parameters), however, parameters could in principle take any syntactic form, such as pieces of behaviour, declarations or expressions. Indeed the power of templates comes as much from specifying combinations as from specifying components. The emphasis on combinations reflects the fact that it is easier to fill in parts of a defined framework than to specify such a framework from scratch.

From another viewpoint, specification templates embody component reuse. Of course, the components used in a specification are likely to be very different from software components. Specification components will usually reflect abstract statements of requirements. They may simply be common data types, such as addresses or data units in a communications system. A specification component may describe an abstract computation, such as routing or multiplexing in a communications system. Specification components may also be logical statements defining constraints, assertions or invariants.

Specification templates should ideally have an architectural meaning. The concepts of an architecture should correspond to templates that the specifier can instantiate. This allows specification at a higher, architectural level. Consistency, productivity and comprehensibility are thus improved. Templates should therefore be based on architectural semantics, making architectural specification relatively direct. However, it is not always useful to define a template for each architectural concept. In some cases the concept may be intermediate or auxiliary, serving to define a more specific concept. In other cases, the concept may be so general that a template would say little. In these circumstances it may be better to define templates for only more definite instances of the concept.

It may be convenient to focus verification on specification templates, emphasizing their semantics rather than their syntactic form. As [Tur93] contends, success in engineering depends on combining known components in known ways to produce predictable results. In a specification context, templates should have known properties that have been verified in advance. The difficulties of verifying the overall specification may then be reduced by a hierarchical approach: known combinations of verified specification components leading to trusted components at a higher level.

Specification templates suggest the use of tools. A translator is required that will replace references to templates with the corresponding specification text. Such a translator might act as a property-oriented compiler – one that generates 'code' according to the required properties rather than according to a specified algorithm. The use of templates can support a declarative style of specification, facilitating the translation of architectural properties into the specification language.

Ideally, templates would be expressed directly in the specification language itself. To some extent this is possible, but unfortunately the flexibility needed in parameterization and textual substitution is beyond convenient reach in most languages. The preferred approach is therefore to express templates in a form that is preprocessed into the specification language (e.g., [Tur93, Tur98]). For the architectural semantics of ODP, [Vog93b] advocates the use of LOTOS templates, although the expansion of templates was not the main point of this work.

A template library must exist for each architecture-language pair. Fortunately, a basis in architectural semantics reduces the work involved in building such libraries. Indeed, definition of an architectural semantics and a template library can usefully proceed together. By focusing attention on architectural issues, the specifier can think in problem-oriented rather than language-oriented terms.

19.1.5 Architectural Semantics for Open Systems Interconnection

As an illustrative example, a small part of the architectural semantics for OSI will be presented using ESTELLE, LOTOS and SDL. Some OSI architectural concepts will be formulated in terms of fundamental ones so that a simpler mapping can be defined. A more fully worked-out exposition of OSI architectural semantics is given in [ISO90], and in [Tur97a] that forms the basis of the discussion here.

address: an *identifier* for a *service access point*

function: a self-contained *activity* of a *protocol entity*

protocol entity: a *service user* capable of supporting associations with other *service users* of the same underlying *service provider*

service access point: an *interaction point* between a *service user* and a *service provider*

service data unit: *information* that may be conveyed in a *service primitive parameter* without interpretation by the *service provider*

service primitive: an *interaction* between a *service user* and a *service provider*

service provider: a *provider*

service user: a *user*

The architectural combinators for OSI include:

association: a partition of *service user interactions* requiring *communication* via the *service provider* of *interactions* with other *service users*

blocking: a one-to-many relation among *service data units* of a *service user* and its supporting *protocol entity*

multiplexing: a many-to-one relation among associations of *service users* and their supporting *protocol entity*

protocol: a supply composition of *protocol entities* considered as *users* and an underlying service considered as *provider*

service: the hiding of *interactions* between the *protocol entities* and the underlying service of a protocol

The relationships among the architectural concepts are summarized in Figure 19.3. Notice the recursive interdependency between service and protocol – a consequence of building a layered architecture. For clarity, the use of fundamental concepts is shown separately in Figure 19.4; *protocol entity* is shown floating here because it does not rely on any fundamental concepts. For brevity, the formalization of fundamental and architectural concepts is not given here, but can be found in [Tur97a].

For concreteness, specification templates for OSI have to be defined for a particular language – LOTOS, in what follows. The templates allow services to be described compactly but be translated automatically to LOTOS. For example, a typical connection-oriented service can be described in about 10 lines with the library; its translation to LOTOS results in about 500 lines of specification.

A service provider sees a *service data unit* (user data) as an unstructured sequence of octets. The template defining it is therefore a straightforward renaming of the library type for an octet string:

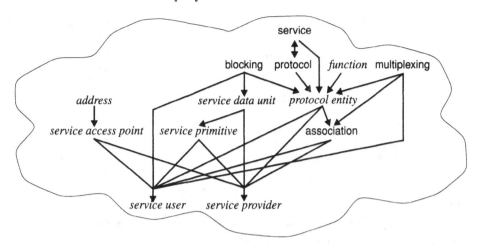

Fig. 19.3. Relationships among architectural concepts.

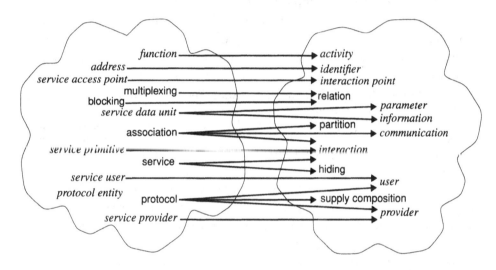

Fig. 19.4. Relationships among architectural and fundamental concepts.

type Data **is** OctetString **renamedby**	(* rename library t ype *)
sortnames Data **for** OctetString	(* new name for values *)
endtype	

A *service data unit* may be blocked (combined) with others into a *protocol data unit*; the inverse operation at the receiver is deblocking. The LOTOS template for (de)blocking defines operations on *service data units*. Deblocking in fact requires two operations: one to extract an SDU (*service data unit*) embedded in the whole PDU (*protocol data unit*), and one to extract the remainder of the PDU. In the following definition, $<>$ is an empty string.

type Block **is** Data	(* import Data t ype *)
opns	(* define operations *)
deblock_sdu: Data $\twoheadrightarrow$ Data	(* get SDU *)
deblock_pdu: Data $\twoheadrightarrow$ Data	(* get rest of PDU *)

```
        block_pdu: Data, Data -> Data                        (* add SDU to PDU *)
    eqns                                                     (* rules for operations *)
      forall pdu: Data, sdu, sdu1, sdu2: Data         (* declare equation variables *)
        ofsort Data                                       (* rules returning Data *)
          deblock_sdu (<>) = <>;                        (* no SDU in empty PDU *)
          deblock_sdu (block_pdu (<>, sdu)) = sdu;        (* get the only SDU *)
          deblock_sdu (block_pdu (block_pdu (pdu, sdu1), sdu2)) = (* get earlier *)
            deblock_sdu (block_pdu (pdu, sdu1));
          deblock_pdu (<>) = <>;                           (* no PDU if empty *)
          deblock_pdu (block_pdu (<>, sdu)) = <>;        (* no PDU if one SDU *)
          deblock_pdu (block_pdu (block_pdu (pdu, sdu1), sdu2)) = (* go earlier *)
            block_pdu (deblock_pdu (block_pdu (pdu, sdu1)), sdu2);
    endtype
```

Architectural combinators usually appear in process definitions. According to the architectural semantics, a protocol consists of a set of interleaved *protocol entities* synchronized with an underlying service. The template for this might include the following process definition. Template parameters are numbered $1, $2, and so on. Parameter $1 names the upper protocol gate (for communication with the user), while parameter $2 names the lower protocol gate (for communication with the underlying service). These parameters also qualify the address types. The protocol template uses subsidiary templates for protocol entities and the underlying service.

```
    process Protocol [$1, $2] ($1_Addrs: $1_Addr_Set) : noexit :=
      choice $2_Addrs: $2_Addr_Set []                  (* choose lower addresses *)
        protocoL entities($1, $2, $1_Addrs, $2_Addrs)   (* protocol entities template *)
      | [$2] |                                            (* use shared channel *)
        underlying_service($2, $2_Addrs)               (* underlying service template *)
    endproc
```

The final example of a specification template is for a service. This is obtained by hiding the lower *service access points* (and hence gate) of a protocol. Parameter $1 corresponds to that of the protocol (its upper interface), while 'Lower' corresponds to parameter $2 of the protocol (its lower interface).

```
    process Service [$1] ($1_Addrs : $1_Addr_Set) : noexit :=
      hide Lower in
        protocol($1,Lower)                               (* hide shared channel *)
                                                         (* protocol template *)
    endproc
```

19.2 Developing an Architectural Semantics for ODP

19.2.1 Introduction

The term 'open' in ODP is crucial in understanding its goals, and hence the goals of the architectural semantics work. Numerous interpretations of this term exist in the context of distributed systems. [LCFA+93] identifies several definitions that can be considered as correctly interpreting the term open as found in distributed systems literature. While all of these definitions are adequate in some contexts, the openness of a distributed system should ideally be based around extensibility. This concerns how new resource-sharing can be added to a system without disrupting existing services. Typically this is achieved by making available the descriptions of specific entry points (interfaces) into the system. From these, it should be possible to add new (possibly heterogeneous) hardware and software to the system.

In the context of ODP, this implies that the specifications (or standards) developed from the architecture should be precise, extensible and able to interwork. This last point in particular is essential. Interworking should be based on successful interactions between specifications (or implementations or systems/enterprises) to achieve some predetermined goal. Unfortunately, current distributed technologies (e.g., [Obj98]) tend to deal solely with the syntactic aspects of systems, using IDLs (Interface Definition Languages). While this overcomes heterogeneity in implementation languages and systems, the approach does not lend itself to building fully interworking systems. Rather, the approach supports a 'message is understood' paradigm at the syntactic level only. To build truly open interworking systems requires the semantics of messages, that is, the behaviour of the interacting systems [Sin97, Sin98].

There are many different ways that behaviour can be expressed. The main advantage of formal techniques in this regard is their precision and conciseness. However, depending on the problem under consideration and the formal language used, a specification may not always be concise. As such, a formal approach to representing an architecture – the development of an *architectural semantics* – offers many potential benefits, many of which were discussed in the previous section. One of the main benefits is the potential to structure specifications using templates. This section illustrates the ODP architectural semantics [ISO98a, ISO96c]. It will be seen that the ODP architectural semantics did not succeed in producing templates, but did succeed in other ways.

There follows an overview of the ODP architectural semantics, highlighting its scope and the approaches that were put forward. It will be shown why the architectural development of ODP specifications was not fully achieved, but how it could be achieved with other, more prescriptive, architectures.

19.2.2 *Approaches to Developing an Architectural Semantics*

The architectural semantics of ODP was initially focussed on the formalization of the core set of concepts that underpin the rest of the architecture. Specifically, the architectural semantics work was focussed on the formalization of the Basic Modelling and Specification concepts contained in the Foundations standard [ISO96a]. The scope of the architectural semantics work was then later extended to cover the viewpoint languages contained in the Architecture standard [ISO96b].

Three main approaches were put forward to represent the ODP architecture and architectural concepts: interpretation, specification templates and a mapping from a direct (mathematical) interpretation. Each approach has its own advantages and disadvantages.

The interpretation-based approach suggests how a given architectural concept might be represented in a given formal language. The result of this is a precise natural language statement of how that concept might best be represented in the formal language. There may well be choices of how concepts can be represented in a given language. The approach therefore documents these choices and, where possible, gives advice on the advantages and disadvantages of modelling concepts a given way. The advantage of this approach is that it enables an in-depth comparison of *all* concepts in *all* formal languages. Through this approach the semantics of all of the concepts may be checked against the semantic models of the formal languages. In doing so, more understanding of the concepts is developed. The approach also gives specifiers guidance without being prescriptive as to how they should specify certain concepts. This last point is also perhaps the greatest weakness of the interpretation-based approach. For instance, since the approach is not prescriptive, it is not possible to immediately identify whether some specification complies with the architecture. Similarly, the lack of prescriptivity prohibits specifications from being built directly. Instead, explanations as to how the concepts and structuring rules are to be represented provide the only information for specifiers. While useful in itself, a more directly accessible approach is to provide specification templates.

The template-based approach provides specification templates for concepts and structuring rules. Through this approach a structuring of specifications can be achieved. [Vog93a] presents a template-based architectural semantics for ODP using LOTOS. There are certain limitations of this approach, however, which are discussed in [Sin97]. Although the most appealing of the three approaches to developing an architectural semantics, a template-based approach has some drawbacks. For example, certain concepts may be so generic that developing specification fragments for them is impossible, or possible only in some specification languages. Another limitation is that arbitrary specifications cannot be checked for compliance with the architecture under consideration. Despite these limitations, the approach is attractive and arguably the most useful.

As a third alternative, a direct mathematical interpretation may be given of the concepts and structuring rules of the architecture. [Got95] gives an approach based on a direct interpretation of architectural concepts. This work focussed predominantly on a direct mathematical formalization of the more fundamental concepts – specifically the concepts of objects, actions and interaction points. More complex structures can be built from these basic concepts and some functions that relate them. This abstract approach can then be mapped into a temporal logic specification. A basis for specification language comparison can thus be achieved in a formal manner. Unfortunately, the work on comparing other formal languages based on this direct mapping has not progressed.

In a similar vein, [NS95] also provides a direct mathematical formalization of concepts and structuring rules. This work focussed on the computational viewpoint of ODP, providing transition rules that characterize valid behaviours of interacting computational objects. From this mathematical interpretation it was argued that mappings to different formal languages could be defined, resulting in a formal basis for language comparison.

Unfortunately, mapping the direct formalizations to different specification languages has not proven practicable for two main reasons. First, specification languages have fundamentally different semantic bases. In general it is unlikely that there is a common base for comparing all formal languages, although it is possible in particular cases (e.g., [BBDS96, DBBS99, WC89]). One of the main issues is that specification languages are often developed for entirely different purposes. There is a span of applications from low-level, intricate behaviours (e.g., in communications protocols) to broad statements about entire systems and enterprises. Second, and perhaps more problematically, mappings have not proven possible due to the lack of prescription given in the ODP reference model. Note that this is a natural consequence of the role of ODP. It is a standard for developing numerous distributed systems that may have completely different properties. Hence there is a limit to how prescriptive the architecture can be.

19.2.3 Example of the ODP Architectural Semantics

As an example of the ODP architectural semantics and the issues involved in producing reusable specification templates, consider an *action* as an architectural concept and its representation in LOTOS. An *action* is defined as follows [ISO96a]:

Something which happens. Every action of interest for modelling purposes is associated with at least one object. The set of actions associated with an object is partitioned into internal actions and interactions. An internal action always takes place without the participation of the environment of the object. An interaction takes place with the participation of the environment of the object. The granularity of actions is a design choice. An action need not be instantaneous. Actions may overlap in time. Interactions may be labelled in terms of cause-and-effect relationships between the participating objects.

The LOTOS representation of this concept may be given as follows. Actions in the process algebra part of LOTOS are modelled as either internal or observable events; all such events are atomic. An internal action may be given explicitly by the internal event symbol, **i**, or by an event occurrence whose associated gate is hidden from the environment. An interaction is represented by a synchronization between two or more behaviour expressions associated with objects at a common interaction point (gate). Interactions may support pure synchronization, value passing or value establishment. If a nonatomic granularity of actions is required, event refinement may be used. This allows noninstantaneous and overlapping actions to be modelled. It should be noted that event refinement is a nontrivial problem, especially when behavioural compatibility is to be maintained. The issues surrounding event refinement in process algebras are considered in detail in [CS93].

There exists no construct in the process algebra part of LOTOS to express cause-and-effect relationships, although it might sometimes be possible to represent this by convention. Value passing may be regarded as sending a value from one process to another. This has aspects of client/server behaviour, that is, one process sends a message to another process to obtain some service. Semantically, causality is not explicit in LOTOS. Processes synchronize instantaneously or not at all. There is no real notion of sending a message between objects. This is exemplified further by synchronizations involving multiway value passing, for example, event offers with action denotations such as *g ?x:Nat !true*.

The LOTOS representation of an action is useful and informative for specifiers of ODP standards, and for readers of the Foundations and Architecture standards themselves. However, the formalization given above is in itself not directly usable in the sense of a specification template. This is a consequence of the ODP concept being rather general. It is reasonably precisely defined, but in a manner that does not lend itself to direct formalization.

ODP is more prescriptive in its Architecture standard [ISO96b] and in the viewpoint languages. The most prescriptive viewpoint that was considered in the architectural semantics work was the computational viewpoint. Unfortunately, the prescription is given in such a way that it is not directly usable or, as with the Foundation concepts, can be used only for guidance. For example, many of the concepts and rules are based on syntactic aspects of interfaces, for example, operational interfaces should have uniquely named operations in the context of the interface in which they exist. These rules are used to determine the legality of binding (composing) the interfaces and hence the objects that they are associated with. While useful and important for writing specifications, such information is not in itself usable in terms of specification fragments directly applicable during specification. Rather, such rules act as a guide, as opposed to something that a specifier can immediately write down. Put another way, the ODP reference model provides well-defined concepts and constructs for creating and composing specification fragments, rather than being directly useful for specification. The ODP reference model does not explicitly describe the behaviour of particular objects, or even the syntactic aspects of object interfaces, as might be represented in an IDL. As a result, the development of useful specification templates is especially difficult. At best, the specification templates can provide some simplistic structuring of concepts. However, these structures are largely void of behavioural information for specifiers.

From these discussions it is apparent that the possibilities for developing ODP specifications through an architectural approach were somewhat limited. However, there were numerous other indirect advantages that stemmed from the ODP architectural semantics work. Since the work was developed in parallel with the Foundations and Architecture standards, the 'fine tooth comb' required to develop an architectural semantics identified numerous discrepancies in the standards that were subsequently rectified.

The architectural semantics work also identified the strengths and weaknesses of various formal languages for modelling ODP concepts, and hence for modelling open distributed systems more generally. Of course, given the object-based approach of

ODP, languages that support objects and related concepts are naturally more suitable. It was often the case, however, that a language limitation for modelling a particular concept resulted in a new approach being put forward to show how the language could be used for a work-around solution. For example, it was shown how Z, which is essentially a flat notation, could be used in an abstract manner to model object-based systems [Sin97, ST96b, ST97]. Another example is modelling interface references in the computational viewpoint. These should contain enough information so that an object (or interface) in possession of such a reference can decide whether to interact with this interface, and hence to bind subsequently to the interface. While LOTOS can model interfaces directly, references to an interface cannot be passed around and used for subsequent interaction with the interface. Object identifiers (e.g., as in [Mor94]) permit structured interactions between objects (processes). However, a process cannot obtain an object reference and then determine its associated behaviour. That is, object identities support references to objects, but these references do not contain sufficient information to restrict potentially unwanted behaviours between objects. Nevertheless, it was shown in [Sin97] just how this could be achieved using a particular specification style in LOTOS.

Other work-around solutions developed in the architectural semantics work included showing how nonfunctional aspects of systems could be modelled and reasoned about in notations not specifically designed for that purpose. For example, it was shown how constraints related to temporal aspects, resource limitations and cost issues could be modelled in LOTOS and Z [Sin97, Sin99a, Sin99b, ST96a]. These constraints were then used as a basis for checking the legality of compositions and substitutions, for example, that a client's demands can be met by a server (and vice versa) or that an environment cannot distinguish a client or server replacement.

Despite the lack of prescriptiveness in ODP, the goal of architectural specification is still a desirable one. As will now be explained, there *is* a more prescriptive architecture based on the concepts and structuring rules of ODP.

19.3 Architectural Development of Telecommunications Services

TINA (Telecommunications Information Networking Architecture [DNI95]) is an architecture based on the principles of ODP, for example, it considers viewpoint languages and objects having potentially more than one interface. TINA is more prescriptive than ODP, however, in that it gives explicit ODL (Object Definition Language [Par96]), IDL [Obj98] and textual descriptions of the expected behaviour of many of the architectural components. ODL is an extension of IDL that allows, amongst other things, the specification of multiple-interface objects and groups. It also makes a distinction between interfaces required by objects from their environment and those supported by objects, that is, offered to their environment.

TINA is decomposed into four main architectures dealing with *Service, Network, Management* and *Computing*. The Service Architecture [Kri97] introduces the underlying concepts and provides information on the behaviour of telecommunications applications and the components that they are built from. Central to the Service Architecture is the concept of a *session*. This is defined as the temporary relationship between a group of resources assigned to fulfill collectively a task or objective for a time period. Three kinds of sessions are identified. The *access session* provides mechanisms to support access to services (service sessions) that have been subscribed to. The *service session* includes functionality to execute, control and manage the services themselves. The *communication session* controls communication and network resources required to establish end-to-end connections for the services.

Although TINA is more prescriptive than ODP, it is not *overly* prescriptive in giving explicit ODL/IDL and textual descriptions of session components and their interactions. That is, the architecture can be used to support a multitude of different services with different functionalities. However, note that the architecture has been designed specifically with the intention of supporting distributed multimedia services such as chat-line, videophone, news on demand, tele-learning and multimedia conferencing. Recent work has considered how such services can be engineered and validated in a rapid manner through object-oriented design frameworks [SK98, SK99a, SK99b].

19.3.1 Service Frameworks Based on Tina

Frameworks are almost complete software (or specifications) that have been engineered for maximum possible reuse of code *and* design. In relation to specification architecture, frameworks represent not simply a collection of specification fragments that can be combined in some way, but an almost complete specification with certain parts deliberately left unspecified – so-called flexibility points. The key issue here is that the bulk of the specification architecture is given, that is, the majority of its behaviour.

The question immediately arises as to where frameworks themselves come from. TINA offers some guidance in terms of the possible decomposition of the services that it supports. Loosely speaking, TINA proposes that service sessions consist of an SSM (Service Session Manager, to control the global service behaviour) and a collection of USMs (User Service Session Managers, to control a user's participation in a service). Both types of components are instantiated by an SF (Service Factory) when requested to do so by components (user agents) in the access session. The ssUAP (Service Session related User Application) is typically a graphical user interface that permits the user to interact with the service. The exact functionality allowing the user to interact with a service depends on the service itself, for example, the buttons and windows available on the ssUAP and how these are handled by the USM and SSM.

Like ODP, TINA is not too prescriptive. That is, it does not describe in detail the precise behaviour of all of the services that it can support. Nevertheless, through a knowledge of the kinds of services supported by TINA and the suggested decomposition of these services, it is possible to identify a common service functionality as the basis for the core framework behaviour and structure. Although the following summarizes some of the core behaviour for suspending or terminating a user's participation in a service, there are numerous other core behaviour scenarios.

TINA services allow users to suspend or terminate their participation. This impacts directly on the behaviour of the associated service session components. For example, the ssUAP should be designed in the framework to allow user suspension or termination, perhaps via a user interface button. The USM should be designed so that it can suspend or terminate itself and all of the objects or interfaces that it might consist of. The SSM should be designed so that it can make appropriate requests on the communication session to suspend or terminate a user's connections. Thus a large part of the core behaviour is given directly.

Identifying a core behaviour is the starting point in developing a framework. The hard part comes in identifying how the core behaviour can have flexibility added [SK98]. There are numerous flexibility points that one might arguably associate with a TINA-based framework. We can roughly split these into two main groups: those based on user sessions (i.e., the ssUAP and USM functionalities) and those based on service sessions (i.e., the SF and SSM functionalities). Note that these sets are likely to be disjoint. Examples of service session flexibility points might be whether the service session terminates when the number of user sessions falls below a certain amount or if the cost of running the service exceeds certain bounds.

The majority of the flexibility points stem from the functionality that a user is offered to interact with a service, and hence what the service must support. This derives from the windows, menus and buttons provided by the ssUAP, and hence what functionality the USM or SSM might need to support the interfaces. For example, some services might support certain users terminating or suspending other user sessions. This might be the case in telelearning, say, where a teacher can suspend or terminate a disruptive student's session. Similarly, services might allow certain users to suspend or terminate the service session itself (e.g., so a teacher can terminate a telelearning service). Some services might allow particular users to invite others (e.g., multimedia conferencing services), while some may not (e.g., chat-line services). Services might also permit user voting, different usage charges, different policies on suspension or resumption of user sessions, and so on. As can be seen, there is a whole range of behaviours that certain services might support. The success of a TINA-based service framework may be judged from the number of useful services that can be created from the framework, that is, the extent of the flexibility that it offers [Sin98].

19.3.2 Formal Development of Service Frameworks

Once a core behaviour and associated flexibility points have been identified for a particular framework, the next phase is of course to build the framework itself. Given the ODL/IDL basis of TINA, a tool-supported mapping to a formal language

ODL/IDL Structure	SDL Structure
group type	block type
object type	block type
interface type	process type
object reference	process identifier
one-way operation	signal prefixed with *pCALL_*
operation	signal pair: first prefixed with *pCALL_*, second prefixed with *pREPLY_* or *pRAISE_*
exception	signal prefixed with *pRAISE_*
basic IDL types	syntype
any	not supported
enum	newtype with corresponding literals
typedef	syntype
struct	newtype with corresponding structure
constant	synonym

Table 19.1. *Sample ODL/IDL to SDL Mapping*

is highly desirable to reduce specification development time, among other things.

Currently very few formal languages support an IDL mapping. One language that does is SDL (see Chapter 4). As well as supporting ODL/IDL mapping, SDL has other advantages, such as an appealing graphical notation and commercial tools for specification development, analysis, test derivation and code generation. Several mappings have been proposed from IDL to SDL. [Bjo97] is based on remote procedure calls, while [BHW+97] uses sequences of signals. Both of these have advantages and disadvantages [SKL+99], an important issue being the lack of exceptions in [Bjo97]. Table 19.1 summarizes the mapping in [BHW+97].

The mapping creates two SDL **packages** that include the client stubs and server skeletons as the basis for behaviour, as well as data-type mappings. Since SDL supports inheritance, these packages can be inherited and the associated framework behaviour then added. Once specified, the framework itself can be saved as a package and subsequently used to create services. More information on the issues involved in the development of SDL frameworks for TINA-based services can be found in [SK98, SK99b, SK99a, SKL+99].

19.4 Conclusion

The importance and role of specification architectures have been explained. It has been argued that specification architecture, not specification writing, is difficult. The use of multiple specification languages with multiple architectures can lead to inconsistency and duplicated effort. An approach to defining architectural semantics via fundamental information processing concepts has been described. It has been shown how architectural semantics can be embodied in a library of specification templates as a practical tool for the specifier. An architectural semantics for OSI was presented briefly.

An overview of the ODP architectural semantics was given along with the different approaches that were taken. The issues associated with the development of specification templates for ODP were discussed. The primary problem with ODP for structuring specifications is a lack of prescription. As an alternative, it was shown how TINA could be used as the basis for developing specification architectures. Specifically, an approach based on object-oriented frameworks was presented. To realize such frameworks, it is essential that formal methods embrace current developments in distributed systems and object technology. In particular, given the widespread acceptance of distributed system approaches like CORBA, support for IDL mapping to formal languages is essential. This improves the potential for directly comparing formal models and their implementations, for example, tests derived from formal models can be executed against the associated implementations. Through a link to IDL, formal methods can gain more widespread acceptance and be made more practical and useful in distributed software development.

Acknowledgements

The authors gratefully acknowledge permission from Elsevier Science BV to reproduce material from [Tur97a, Tur97b].

Bibliography

[BBDS96]   H. Bowman, E. A. Boiten, J. Derrick, and M. W. A. Steen. Supporting ODP: translating LOTOS to Z. In E. Najm and J.-B. Stefani, editors, *Formal Methods for Open Object-based Distributed Systems (FMOODS'96)*, pages 399–406. Chapman & Hall, 1996.

[BHW+97]   M. Born, A. Hoffmann, M. Winkler, J. Fischer, and N. Fischbeck. Towards a behavioural description of ODL. In *Proceedings of TINA'97*, Santiago, Chile, November 1997. IEEE Computer Society.

[Bjo97]   M. Bjorkander. Using SDL to develop CORBA object implementations. In H. Bowman and J. Derrick, editors, *Formal Methods for Open Object-based Distributed Systems (FMOODS'97)*, pages 177–192. Chapman & Hall, 1997.

[BvV95]   T. Bolognesi, J. van de Lagemaat, and C. A. Vissers, editors. *The LOTOSPHERE Project*. Kluwer, 1995.

[CS93]   J.-P. Courtiat and D. E. Saïdouni. Action refinement in LOTOS. In A. A. S. Danthine, G. Leduc, and P. Wolper, editors, *Protocol Specification, Testing and Verification XIII*, pages 341–354. North-Holland, May 1993.

[DBBS99]   J. Derrick, E. A. Boiten, H. Bowman, and M. W. A. Steen. Viewpoints and consistency - translating LOTOS to Object-Z. *Computer Standards and Interfaces*, pages 251–272, December 1999.

[DNI95]   F. Dupuy, G. Nilsson, and Y. Inoue. The TINA consortium: Towards networking telecommunications information services. *IEEE Communications Magazine*, pages 78–83, November 1995.

[GHJV95]   E. Gamma, R. Helm, R. Johnson, and J. Vlissides. *Design Patterns Elements of Reusable Object-Oriented Software*. Addison-Wesley, September 1995.

[Got95]   R. Gotzhein. Towards a basic reference model of Open Distributed Processing. *Computer Networks and ISDN Systems*, 27:1263–1304, 1995.

[GP95]   D. Garlan and D. Perry. Introduction to the special issue on software architecture. *IEEE Transactions on Software Engineering*, 21(4), April 1995.

[ISO90]   ISO/IEC. *Information Processing Systems – Open Systems Interconnection – Guidelines for the Application of ESTELLE, LOTOS and SDL*. ISO/IEC TR 10167. International Organization for Standardization, 1990.

[ISO94]   ISO/IEC. *Information Processing Systems – Open Systems Interconnection – Basic Reference Model*. ISO/IEC 7498. International Organization for Standardization, 1994.

[ISO96a]   *ISO/IEC IS 10746-2, Open Distributed Processing Reference Model - Part 2: Foundations*. International Organization for Standardization, 1996.

[ISO96b]   *ISO/IEC IS 10746-3, Open Distributed Processing Reference Model - Part 3: Architecture*. International Organization for Standardization, 1996.

[ISO96c]   ISO/IEC. *Basic Reference Model of ODP – Part 4.1: Architectural Semantics Amendment*. ISO/IEC JTC1/SC21/WG7 FDAM ballot text N2122. ISO/IEC ITU-T, 1996.

[ISO98a]   *ISO/IEC IS 10746-4, Open Distributed Processing Reference Model - Part 4: Architectural Semantics*. International Organization for Standardization, 1998.

[ISO98b]   ISO/IEC IS 10746. Open Distributed Processing Reference Model, 1998. Parts 1 to 4.

[Kri97]   L. Kristiansen. *Service Architecture*. version 5.0. TINA-C, July 1997.

[LCFA+93]   H. Leopold, G. Coulson, K. Frimpong-Ansah, D. Hutchison, and N. Singer. The evolving relationship between OSI and ODP in the new communications environment. Technical Report MPG-93-16, University of Lancaster, England, 1993.

[Mor94]   A. M. D. Moreira. *Rigorous Object-Oriented Analysis*. PhD thesis, Department of Computing Science and Mathematics, University of Stirling, 1994.

[NS95]   E. Najm and J.-B. Stefani. A formal semantics for the ODP computational model. *Computer Networks and ISDN Systems*, 27:1305–1329, 1995.

[NS96]   E. Najm and J.-B. Stefani, editors. *Formal Methods for Open Object-based Distributed Systems (FMOODS'96)*. Chapman & Hall, 1996.

[Obj98]   Object Management Group. Common Object Request Broker: Architecture and Specification. Technical Report Revision 2.3, Object Management Group, Framingham, USA, July 1998.

[Par72]   D. L. Parnas. On the criteria to be used in decomposing systems into modules. *Communications of the ACM*, 5(12):1053–1058, December 1972.

[Par96]   A. Parhar. *TINA Object Definition Language Manual*. version 2.3. TINA-C, July 1996.

[RL92]   RAISE Language Group. *The RAISE Specification Language*. Prentice-Hall, 1992.

[Sin97]   R. O. Sinnott. *An Architecture Based Approach to Specifying Distributed Systems in LOTOS and Z*. PhD thesis, Department of Computing Science and Mathematics, University of Stirling, 1997.

[Sin98]   R. O. Sinnott. Frameworks: The future of formal software development.

Computer Standards and Interfaces: Special Edition on Semantics of Specifications, August 1998.

[Sin99a] R. O. Sinnott. Specifying aspects of multimedia in LOTOS. In B. Verma, editor, *Computational Intelligence and Multimedia Applications*, New Delhi, India, 1999. IEEE Computer Society.

[Sin99b] R. O. Sinnott. Specifying multimedia configurations in Z. In B. Verma, editor, *Computational Intelligence and Multimedia Applications*, New Delhi, India, 1999. IEEE Computer Society.

[SK98] R. O. Sinnott and M. Kolberg. Business-oriented development of telecommunication services. In H. Kilov, B. Rumpe, and I. Simmonds, editors, *Seventh OOPSLA Workshop on Behavioural Semantics and OO Business and System Specifications*, Vancouver, Canada, August 1998.

[SK99a] R. O. Sinnott and M. Kolberg. Creating telecommunication services based on object-oriented frameworks and SDL. In M. Raynal, T. Kikuno, and R. Soley, editors, *Second IEEE International Symposium on Object-Oriented Real-Time Distributed Computing*, St. Malo, France, May 1999. IEEE Press.

[SK99b] R. O. Sinnott and M. Kolberg. Engineering telecommunication services with SDL. In P. Ciancarini, A. Fantechi, and R. Gorrieri, editors, *Formal Methods for Open Object-Based Distributed Systems (FMOODS IV)*, pages 187–203, February 1999.

[SKL+99] R. O. Sinnott, M. Kolberg, F. Lodge, M. Björkander, A. Olsen, D. Demany, and E. Cardoso. The pros and cons of using SDL for creation of distributed services. In H. Zuidweg, M. Campolargo, J. Delgado, and A. Mullery, editors, *6th. International Conference on Intelligence and Services in Networks*, Barcelona, Spain, April 1999.

[ST95] R. O. Sinnott and K. J. Turner. Applying formal methods to standard development: The Open Distributed Processing experience. *Computer Standards & Interfaces*, 17:615–630, 1995.

[ST96a] R. O. Sinnott and K. J. Turner. Specifying multimedia binding objects in Z. In O. Spaniol, C. Popien, and B. Meyer, editors, *Trends in Distributed Systems: CORBA and Beyond*, Lecture Notes in Computer Science. Springer-Verlag, October 1996.

[ST96b] R. O. Sinnott and K. J. Turner. Specifying ODP computational objects in Z. In E. Najm and J.-B. Stefani, editors, *Formal Methods for Open Object-based Distributed Systems (FMOODS'96)*, pages 375–390. Chapman & Hall, 1996.

[ST97] R. O. Sinnott and K. J. Turner. Type checking in distributed systems: A complete model and its Z specification. In J. Rolia, editor, *International Conference on Open Distributed Processing (ICODP) and Distributed Platforms (ICDP)*, May 1997.

[TS97] K. J. Turner and G. Scollo, editors. *Special Issue on Specification Architecture*, volume 29 of *Computer Networks and ISDN Systems*. Elsevier Science Publishers, March 1997.

[Tur88] K. J. Turner. An architectural semantics for LOTOS. In H. Rudin and C. H. West, editors, *Protocol Specification, Testing and Verification VII*, pages 15–28. North-Holland, October 1988.

[Tur93] K. J. Turner. An engineering approach to formal methods. In A. A. S. Danthine, G. Leduc, and P. Wolper, editors, *Protocol Specification, Testing and Verification XIII*, pages 357–380. North-Holland, June 1993.

[Tur97a] K. J. Turner. Relating architecture and specification. *Computer Networks and ISDN Systems*, 29(4):437–456, March 1997.

[Tur97b] K. J. Turner. Specification architecture illustrated in a communications context. *Computer Networks and ISDN Systems*, 29(4):397–411, March 1997.

[Tur98] K. J. Turner. An architectural description of intelligent network features and their interactions. *Computer Networks and ISDN Systems*, 30(15):1389–1419, September 1998.

[Vog93a] A. Vogel. *Entwurf, Realisierung und Test von ODP-Systemen auf der Grundlage formaler Beschreibungstechniken*. PhD thesis, Humboldt-Universität zu Berlin, 1993. In German.

[Vog93b] A. Vogel. On ODP's architectural semantics using LOTOS. In J. de Meer, B. Mahr, and O. Spaniol, editors, *International Conference on Open Distributed Processing*, pages 340–345, Berlin, Germany, 1993. Gesellschaft für Mathematik und Datenverarbeitung.

[VSv91] C. A. Vissers, G. Scollo, and M. van Sinderen. Architecture and specification style in formal descriptions of distributed systems. *Theoretical Computer Science*, 89:179–206, 1991.

[WC89] J. P. Wu and S. Chanson. Translation from LOTOS and ESTELLE specifications to extended transition system and its verification. In S. T. Vuong, editor, *Formal Description Techniques II*. North-Holland, 1989.

20

Viewpoints Modelling

Howard Bowman   John Derrick

University of Kent, UK

20.1 Introduction

In this final chapter of this part, we continue with the theme of architecture by looking at an ODP viewpoints modelling case study. The purpose of the case study is to illustrate viewpoints and show how formal methods can be used in modelling and analysing them. In doing so we illustrate how different languages can be used in different viewpoints and introduce cross-viewpoint consistency and its checking.

In looking at ODP viewpoints we draw heavily on the material introduce in Chapters 1 and 2 of this book, and in focussing on a case study we show how some of the languages introduced in Part Two can be used for viewpoints modelling.

The particular case study that we are looking at is an IT system designed to keep track of a library collection and its borrowing process. We describe the enterprise viewpoint in Section 20.4 using UML (see Chapter 7) together with a policy specification language that has a mapping into Object-Z (see Chapter 6). Section 20.5 extends this Object-Z description to an information viewpoint specification, and the computational and engineering viewpoints are modelled using E-LOTOS, which was introduced in Chapter 5. The consistency of viewpoints written in different languages is clearly an issue, and we begin this chapter with a discussion of the problem of consistency in general terms. Section 20.6.2 then looks at a specific example of inconsistency in our case study.

20.2 Viewpoints and Consistency in General Terms

Viewpoints As discussed earlier in the book, ODP uses five predefined viewpoints – *the enterprise viewpoint, the information viewpoint, the computational viewpoint, the engineering viewpoint* and *the technology viewpoint,* and the use of viewpoints in ODP mirrors their increasing importance throughout software engineering, for example, in requirements engineering [FGH+94], object-oriented design methodologies [Boo94], formal system development [ZJ93] and software engineering in general [Som89]. In all of these approaches, rather than having a single thread of system development, in the style of the classic waterfall approach, multiple partial specifications (i.e., viewpoints) of a system are considered. Each particular specification represents a different perspective on the system under development and, in fact, may well be written by a different specifier.

One of the consequences of adopting a multiple viewpoints approach to development is that descriptions of the same or related entities can appear in different viewpoints and must co-exist. Thus, different viewpoints can impose contradictory requirements on the system under development and *consistency* of specifications across viewpoints becomes a central issue. The problem is complicated by the fact that viewpoint specifications may well be written in different languages (viz. languages particularly suited for the viewpoint at hand, for example, Z for the information viewpoint and LOTOS for the engineering viewpoint [BDLS95]).

Thus, providing techniques to check viewpoint consistency is one of the major research topics surrounding ODP viewpoints modelling, and a number of workers have responded to this challenge [BDLS96, BDF+97, FL93]. In the remainder of this subsection we will outline the approach to consistency that we will use in this chapter. This approach has arisen out of research into ODP consistency at the University of Kent at Canterbury and has been reported in a number of papers, for example, [BDBS99, DBBS99, BBD+00].

In order to be able to check the consistency of multiple viewpoint specifications we first need to define what is meant by consistency – at one time the ODP reference model alluded to three different definitions. However, this definitional uncertainty can be resolved by adopting the formal framework described in [BBDS96, BSBD01]. This provides a definition of consistency between viewpoints general enough to encompass all three ODP definitions.

Correspondences Because viewpoints overlap in the parts of the envisaged system that they specify, we need to describe the relationship between the viewpoints. In simple examples, these parts will be linked implicitly by having the same name and type in both viewpoints – in general, however, we may need more complicated descriptions for relating common aspects of the viewpoints. Such descriptions are called *correspondences* in ODP.

There are really two varieties of correspondence: those that are prescribed by the reference model and those that are specification-dependent. The former of these generally have a structural character. For example, the reference model prescribes that each computational object (which is not a binding object) corresponds to a nonempty set of basic engineering objects (with their associated communication channels). In contrast, specification-dependent correspondences are less general in nature; they are tied to the particular set of viewpoint specifications under consideration, and they define which items of these specifications should be viewed as corresponding.

In this chapter the correspondences between viewpoints will generally be very straightforward and will be discernible from the naming in the different viewpoints.

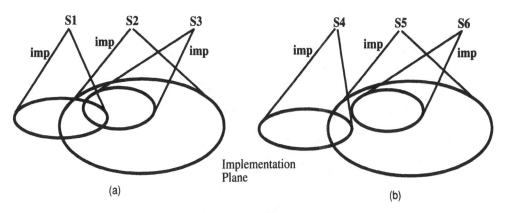

Fig. 20.1. Common implementation models.

However, for the interested reader, the paper [BBD$^+$00] presents a consistency check where determining the correspondences is more involved.

Consistency Intuitively we view a set of specifications as consistent if and only if there exists a physical implementation that is a realisation of all of the specifications, that is, they can be implemented in a single system. This interpretation of consistency has similarities to satisfaction in a logical setting. A conjunction of propositions $\phi_1 \wedge \phi_2 \wedge .... \wedge \phi_n$ is satisfiable if there exists a single model that individually satisfies all of the propositions.

Figures 20.1(a) and 20.1(b) illustrate our intuition of consistency; in both depictions descriptions are related to their set of possible realisations by an implementation relation (denoted **imp**). Thus, the Venn diagrams in the implementation plane depict the set of possible realisations of each description. It should be clear that the three descriptions in Figure 20.1(a) are consistent because their set of possible implementations intersect, that is, they have at least one common implementation. In contrast, the three descriptions in Figure 20.1(b) are not consistent, although the pairs S4 and S5 and S5 and S6 are mutually consistent.

However, rather than talk explicitly about implementation, as this interpretation does, we would like to work completely in the formal setting and define consistency purely in terms of descriptions and relations between descriptions. Thus, we define consistency in terms of development relations.

Development Relations These relate specifications during the development process. There are many different development relations, each with different fundamental properties, for example, *conformance relations*, *refinement relations*, *equivalence relations* and *translations*. The latter of these is perhaps the least familiar; it enables one to move between different languages, by translating from the syntax of one to the syntax of the other in such a way that the semantics are preserved.

Using the concept of a development relation, we can define consistency:

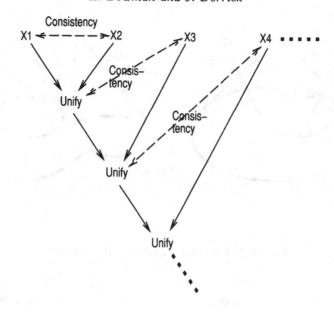

Fig. 20.2. Binary consistency algorithm.

A set of viewpoint specifications are consistent if there exists a specification that is a development of each of the viewpoint specifications with respect to the identified development relations and the correspondences between viewpoints. This *common development* is called a *unification*.

As just indicated, different viewpoint specifications may be related to the unification by different development relations. For example, the LOTOS computational viewpoint might be related by a conformance relation, while the Z information viewpoint might be related by the Z refinement relation. Thus, we obtain the following distinction:

A consistency check is referred to as *balanced* if all viewpoint specifications are related by the same development relation. A consistency check is *unbalanced* if distinct development relations are used.

Least Developed Unification Besides a definition of consistency, methods for constructively establishing consistency have also been investigated [BBDS99]. This involves defining algorithms that build unifications from pairs of viewpoint specifications. An important notion in this context is that of a *least developed unification*. This is a unification that all other unifications are developments of. Thus it is the *least developed* of the set of possible unifications according to the development relations of the different viewpoints.

Using least developed unifications as intermediate stages, global consistency of a set of viewpoints can be established by a series of binary consistency checks, as illustrated in Figure 20.2.

Unfortunately, it is not the case that least developed unifications can always be derived. However, we will not consider this issue further here. The interested reader is referred to [BBDS99], which considers the properties that development relations must possess for such least unifications to exist.

We now move on to discussing our case study. However, we will return to consistency issues in Section 20.6.2.

20.3 An Informal Description of the Case Study

The library that we consider in our case study contains a collection of books, periodicals, music scores and other reference material that may be borrowed by its members. In subsequent sections we look at the different ODP viewpoints and show how we might support their specification by using appropriate formal methods.

To motivate our specifications we begin by stating some of the library regulations that concern the borrowing process (extracted from the actual regulations of the University of Leeds central library).

(i) *Borrowing rights are given to all academic staff, all students (postgraduate and undergraduate) of the University and to honoury members.*

   Other persons may be given borrowing rights at the discretion of the Librarian.

(ii) *There are prescribed periods of loan and limits on the numbers of items allowed on loan to a borrower at any one time. These limits are detailed below.*

   (a) *Academic staff may borrow 25 books or periodicals. Periodicals may be borrowed for one week. Books may be borrowed for up to 6 months.*

   (b) *Postgraduates may borrow 10 books or periodicals. Periodicals may be borrowed for one week. Books may be borrowed for 3 months.*

   (c) *Undergraduates may borrow 4 books. They may not borrow periodicals. Books may be borrowed for 2 weeks. Students in the Department of Music may borrow, in addition, up to two music scores.*

   (d) *Other borrowers may borrow 4 books or periodicals. Periodicals may be borrowed for one week. Books may be borrowed for 4 weeks.*

(iii) *Items borrowed must be returned by the due day and time.*

(iv) *Fines are levied for the late return of items.*

(v) *No person shall borrow a book from the Library if any fine incurred has not been paid.*

These regulations will be used as our starting point for the viewpoint specifications below. Clearly the use of different formal methods raises the issue of consistency checking between the viewpoints, and in Section 20.6 we illustrate one approach by looking at a fragment of the library example. We begin first though with the enterprise viewpoint.

20.4 The Enterprise Viewpoint

A specification of the enterprise viewpoint must describe certain aspects: the community and its objective; the differing roles that objects play in the community and the policies that constrain the behaviour of the objects that fulfill roles in the community.

Such a specification contains many differing aspects, and we use UML to describe the community structure and the roles but choose a more formal language to specify the enterprise policies. When defining the community and the roles within it UML works well; however, the language is still evolving and does not as yet have a precise meaning. Therefore for the description of policies, where a precise meaning is necessary, it is useful to use a more formal notation.

To this end we use the policy specification language described in [SD99, SD00], which has a semantics given in terms of Object-Z, thus providing a link with other viewpoints specified in that language (e.g., the information viewpoint).

Returning to our library, our enterprise specification will contain a library community together with an objective, which we define as *to share its collection of books and other items fairly and efficiently amongst its members*. We will represent this as a UML package where the objective is written in a description field (see Figure 20.3). Of more interest are the roles in the community and the relationships between them. The roles in this example are fairly obvious, and we can identify the following: Borrower, Item, Librarian and Library Assistants.

These roles are fulfilled by one or more objects; for example, in our library the borrower role may be fulfilled by honoury staff, academic staff, postgraduates, undergraduates or external members. Items, on the other hand, are fulfilled by the physical items to be lent out, for example, books.

Figure 20.3 represents the library community in UML. Here we depict the roles that we identified together with objects fulfilling them. We can also represent relationships between roles; for example, a loan is a relationship between a borrower and an item. When a borrower borrows a book an instance of this relationship is established, which is dissolved when the book is returned. The relationship of delegation (where the librarian delegates her powers to an assistant) is also shown. Differing types of borrowers can borrow differing numbers of items, and we record this information at this level of abstraction because the enterprise policies describe constraints in terms of these attributes.

Using these roles we can now identify the behaviour of the enterprise objects in our library community, and actions will be associated with one or more roles. In our example we can identify (amongst others) the following:

- A **Borrow** action, when Borrower requests to borrow an Item. This action will involve a Library Assistant, who either issues the Item or denys the request, depending on the status of the Borrower and the Item.

- A **Return** action, where a Borrower returns a borrowed Item. A Library Assistant

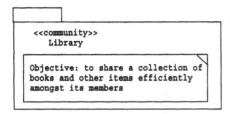

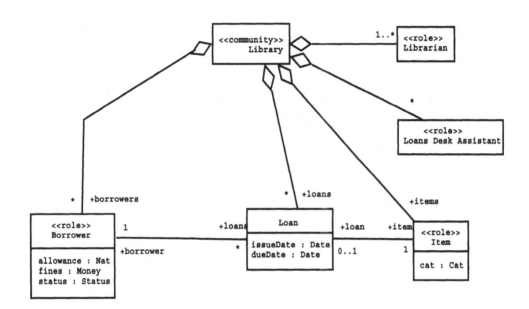

Fig. 20.3. The library objective and community structure.

will again be involved to check that the Item has been returned in time and, if necessary, collect a fine.

- A **Reserve** action, where a Borrower places a reservation for an Item already on loan to another Borrower.
- A **Renew** action, where a Borrower requests to extend the loan period for an Item already on loan to him or her.
- A **PayFine** action, where a Borrower pays off a certain amount of their fines.

These actions give rise to a description of the enterprise behaviour, which we could specify using a number of the UML behaviour diagrams. For example, a use case diagram could be used to identify enterprise actions, and this could then be refined further into activity or interaction diagrams (see [SD00] for a brief discussion of this aspect). We do not pursue the description of enterprise behaviour here; our discussion of behaviour in this viewpoint is confined to the specification of policies in Section 20.4.1.

We can also use UML to describe the relationship between a number of communities. For example, a library does not exist in isolation but relates to a wider community in which it serves its function. Thus our library serves a university community, and the roles in the university community are related to those in the library. For example, in a university we can identify roles of academic, academic-related (e.g., the library staff themselves), students and ancillary staff. Then the relationship between the university and library roles can be recorded as in Figure 20.4.

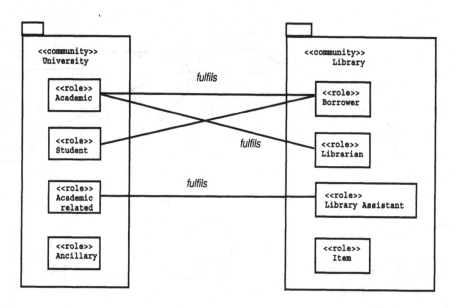

Fig. 20.4. Relating the university and library roles.

This shows that the role of a Librarian is fulfilled by an academic, whereas Library Assistants are considered as academic-related staff. A Librarian and a Library Assistant will therefore have differing borrowing rights. Ancillary staff cannot borrow from the library. This description can be seen to specify the first regulation given above, which is an instantiation rule relating roles in different communities.

20.4.1 Specifying Policies

We are at a point where we can specify the enterprise policies for the library, the purpose of which is to try to ensure that the library meets its objectives. The policies describe the permissions, obligations and prohibitions for the differing roles within the community, and we derive these from the informal regulations given above. For example, regulation 3 denotes an obligation to return items by a certain point in time, whereas regulation 2(a) denotes a permission to borrow books.

To formalise these [SD00] develops a simple logic-based policy language, with a formal semantics provided by defining a mapping of it into Object-Z. In addition to the usual benefits provided by formalization, this approach helps support consistency checking between different viewpoints since Object-Z has been suggested as a notation for the information viewpoint.

Policy statements often directly reference enterprise actions, expressing that they are required or allowed. Alternatively, they may specify that certain states of affairs are allowed or not, and then any behaviour leading to a forbidden state is considered prohibited. Therefore, to specify the policies we need to describe the allowable states and actions. These can in part be identified from the UML description given in Figure 20.3. For example, we will use the status and allowance of each borrower to determine which actions are allowed.

Each policy will consist of a number of statements, and each statement applies to a role, the subject, and represents either a permission, an obligation or a prohibition for that role. The general format of a policy statement is: 'A <role> is <modality> to ...', where the modality is one of 'permitted', 'forbidden', or 'obliged'. Policy statements conform to a grammar given in [SD00]. We illustrate the approach here with some examples.

The permission for borrowers to borrow items, but only as long as they have no fines, for example, is expressed as follows:

[R1] A Borrower is permitted to do Borrow(item:Item), if (fines = 0).

The action consists of a name (here Borrow) followed by optional parameter specifications (here Item) in brackets. The condition states that borrowers are allowed to perform a borrow action whenever fines is zero. There are, of course, other rules that prevent this, for example, in the case where the borrower already has reached the maximum number of loans allowed.

Permissions and prohibitions may involve a condition instead of an action. The permission for borrowers to borrow up to their allowance is an example of this. This condition should hold in all states that the borrower will be in. Thus it means that any behaviour that changes this condition from being true to being false is forbidden. We write this as follows:

[R2] A Borrower is permitted to satisfy (loan.size $\leq$ allowance).

Prohibitions are written in a similar manner; for example, the prohibition for undergraduate students to borrow periodicals can be written as:

[R3] A Borrower is forbidden to do Borrow(item:Item), if status(Borrower) = UG, where item : Periodical.

Here we have used a where-clause to constrain the parameter of the Borrow action to be a periodical, and an if-clause to constrain this prohibition to a certain set of states.

Obligations are more complicated because they prescribe some required behaviour, and thus often contain a deadline for this behaviour to occur. To describe this a before-clause is used, which contains a condition upon which the obligation should have been fulfilled. So to describe the obligation for borrowers to return items by the due date we write:

[R4] A Borrower is obliged to do Return(item:Item) before (today > dueDate),
            if $\exists\, loan \bullet loan.item =$ item $\wedge$ dueDate $= loan.item.dueDate$
            otherwise see R6.

Notice that here we can reference other rules that should be invoked if the conditions for this particular rule are not met.

A meta-rule is used to explain how the policies are combined; for example, in simple cases their combined effect may be the conjunction of the individual policy statements. Thus a borrower may borrow an item only when they have no outstanding fines *and* they have not reached their allowance.

The meaning and semantics of these policies are given by a translation into Object-Z (discussed in more detail in [SD00]). The translation defines an Object-Z specification of both the community structure and the policies. In the case of the former, the rules translate a role into an Object-Z class, and then the translations of the policy statements are added to the Object-Z class representing the role in the policy statement. The following rules are used:

(i) A permission to do an action translates to a precondition for the corresponding operation in Object-Z. If the permission is conditional, the constraint becomes the precondition (otherwise the precondition is true).

(ii) A permission to satisfy a certain predicate translates to an invariant (a predicate in the state schema) of the class corresponding to the role definition.

(iii) Prohibitions are translated in the same way as permissions, except that the associated predicates are negated.

(iv) Translation of obligations can only be partially automated, and sometimes they have to be refined first to a strategy for enforcing them (e.g., the borrower's obligation to return their books is enforced through a fining policy).

Thus the translation of the library enterprise specification will derive Object-Z classes for borrowers, items, librarians, and so on. A role relationship, such as a loan, will also be represented as a class. The policies will determine the state invariants and the operation definitions in these Object-Z classes. For example, policy R1 is a conditional permission, and this is translated to a precondition on the Borrow operation. Policy R5 specifies a permitted condition, and translates into a state invariant. Combined policies R1, 3 and 5 produce the following Object-Z fragment:

```
┌─ Borrower ──────────────────────────────────────────────────────┐
│  ┌──────────────────────────────────────────────────────────┐   │
│  │ allowance : ℕ                                             │   │
│  │ fines : Money                                             │   │
│  │ loans : ℙ Loan                                            │   │
│  │ status : Status                                           │   │
│  ├──────────────────────────────────────────────────────────┤   │
│  │ #loans ⩽ allowance                                        │   │
│  └──────────────────────────────────────────────────────────┘   │
│                                                                  │
│  ┌─ Borrow ───────────────────────────────────────────────┐     │
│  │ item? : Item                                            │     │
│  ├─────────────────────────────────────────────────────────┤    │
│  │ fines = 0                                               │     │
│  │ status = UG ⇒ ¬(item?.cat = Periodical)                 │     │
│  └─────────────────────────────────────────────────────────┘    │
│   ⋮                                                              │
└──────────────────────────────────────────────────────────────────┘
```

The translation of obligations is less straightforward. In general, one can only partly capture the concept of obligation in Object-Z. There are two issues here: one is that obligations usually involve timing constraints, for example, in the form of a deadline before which the obligated behaviour must have occurred. Of course, more complicated permissions may also refer to time. The second is that within these constraints policy may be implicit, whereas in an Object-Z specification all behaviour has to be explicit. Therefore the translation of an obligation produces an Object-Z template in which further explicit modelling may be required for certain actions.

One solution to this issue is to explicitly permit the obliged action but introduce some penalty for the object that violates the obligation (as an incentive to comply with the required behaviour). In the library case, the penalty for not returning items on time is that the borrower becomes liable to a fine, and no further items can be borrowed. Notice that the borrower can avoid paying fines by never visiting the library again. This is in accordance with the informal regulations given above: all those policies require that borrowing facilities were suspended in this situation. If further enforcement of paying debts is required, then this needs to be stated explicitly as a policy.

20.5 The Information Viewpoint

In this section we build on the Object-Z specification produced from the enterprise viewpoint description to specify the information viewpoint of our library system. It is feasible to adopt such an approach here because the difference in level of granularity between the two viewpoints is not large in this particular example. That is, the policies described in the enterprise dealt largely with dynamic aspects that are of direct concern in this viewpoint. In other examples this might not be the case and an independent information viewpoint would have to be built with checks for consistency undertaken between the two descriptions.

Our information viewpoint describes the information involved in the system, specifying neither the computational process nor the nature of the distributed architecture to be used. Although our description will be object-based (since we are using an object-oriented specification language) the information viewpoint does not identify computational objects or the potential distribution of objects to nodes: these concerns are dealt with by the computational viewpoint. The objects that we use here are used solely to help structure the specification in an appropriate manner.

Instead of describing the potential computational objects, the information viewpoint specifies a number of schemas:

Invariant schema - a set of predicates on one or more information objects that must always be true.

Static schema - the state of one or more information objects at some particular time.

Dynamic schema - a specification of the allowable state changes of one or more information objects ... subject to the constraints of any invariant schemata.

Although the use of the term schema is coincidental in some respects, these aspects can be realised in Z or Object-Z in an obvious way, as follows: invariant schema as state schemas, static schema as, for example, initialisations in a specification or call, and dynamic schema as operation definitions.

By using the partial Object-Z specification produced from the enterprise viewpoint we can describe the information viewpoint of our library. The enterprise specification has in effect described certain correspondences between the two viewpoints and has naturally partitioned the specification into a number of objects, such as *Borrowers*, *Items*, and so on. We will use these templates by adding to the constraints already imposed by the enterprise policies. We thus extend the *Borrow* operation of a borrower by describing the process of taking out an item, whilst keeping in place the constraints that are policies (e.g., that there are no fines outstanding). There are clear advantages in such an approach, however; it does imply that the viewpoints are developed sequentially to a certain extent.

We begin our specification by describing a number of types (HM = Honoury member, AC = Academic staff, etc.):

$[Date, Money, Time, User]$
$Cat ::= Book \mid Periodical \mid Music\_score \mid Other$
$Status ::= HM \mid AC \mid UG \mid PG \mid Other$
$Dept ::= Music \mid Other$

We use an *Item* object that records whether it is on loan and what sort of item it is:

```
  ┌─ Item ──────────────────────────────────────────────────────
  │  ┌─────────────────────────────────────────────────────────
  │  │  onloan : 𝔹
  │  │  cat : Cat
  │  ├─────────────────────────────────────────────────────────
  │  │  ┌─ CheckOut ──────────────────────────────────────────
  │  │  │  Δ(onloan)
  │  │  ├──────────────────────────────────────────────────────
  │  │  │  ¬ onloan ∧ onloan'
  │  │  ├─ CheckIn ──────────────────────────────────────────
  │  │  │  Δ(onloan)
  │  │  ├──────────────────────────────────────────────────────
  │  │  │  onloan ∧ ¬ onloan'
  └──┴──┴──────────────────────────────────────────────────────
```

Loans are associations between borrowers and items. A loan has an issue date and a due date, but no operations. The predicate states it is due back after it has been issued (definition of *after* elided):

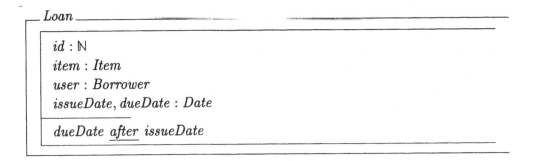

```
  ┌─ Loan ──────────────────────────────────────────────────────
  │  ┌─────────────────────────────────────────────────────────
  │  │  id : ℕ
  │  │  item : Item
  │  │  user : Borrower
  │  │  issueDate, dueDate : Date
  │  ├──────────────────────────────────────────────────────────
  │  │  dueDate after issueDate
  └──┴──────────────────────────────────────────────────────────
```

A *Borrower* has a status, a book allowance, a collection of outstanding fines and a certain number of loans. A *Borrower* can perform operations including *Borrow*, and so on, and if the *Borrower* is a student in the music department, they can borrow up to two scores in addition to the normal quota of books.

The *Library* is the main class through which the behaviour of the description is viewed. It consists of borrowers, items and a librarian. The operations cover both the issuing and returning of items, the collection of fines as well as operations to add new members, and so on, and update the stock of items held in the library. Since users can have more than one status, *borrowers* is a relation from *User* to *Borrower*, not a function. In fact this has consequences for the consistency of the viewpoints; see Section 20.6.2 below.

Borrower

$allowance : \mathbb{N}$
$dept : Dept$
$mscores : \{0, 1, 2\}$
$fines : Money$
$loans : \mathbb{P}\ Loan$
$status : Status$

$status = HM \Rightarrow allowance = 4$
$status = AC \Rightarrow allowance = 25$
$status = PG \Rightarrow allowance = 10$
$status = UG \Rightarrow allowance = 4$
$status = Other \Rightarrow allowance = 4$
$\#loans \leqslant allowance$
$mscores > 0 \Leftrightarrow dept = Music$

INIT

$loans = \varnothing \wedge fines = 0$

Borrow

$\Delta(loans, mscores)$
$item? : Item$

$fines = 0$
$status = UG \Rightarrow \neg\ (item?.cat = Periodical)$
$item?.cat = Music\_score \Rightarrow$
$\quad (status \in \{PG, UG\} \wedge mscores' = mscores + 1 \wedge loans' = loans)$
$item?.cat \neq Music\_score \Rightarrow$
$\quad (mscores' = mscores\ \wedge$
$\quad\quad \exists\ loan : Loan \bullet loan \notin loans \wedge loan.item = item? \wedge loans' = loans \cup \{loan\})$

$Return \mathrel{\widehat{=}} \ldots$

PayFine

$\Delta(fines)$
$amount? : Money$

$fines > 0$
$fines' = fines - amount?$

___ *Library* _____

    | *items* : $\mathbb{P}$ *Item*
    | *librarian* : *Librarian*
    | *loans* : $\mathbb{P}$ *Loan*
    | *borrowers* : *User* $\leftrightarrow$ *Borrower*
    |_____
    | $\forall$ *loan* : *loans* • *loan.item* $\in$ *items*
    | $\wedge$ *loan.user* $\in$ ran *borrowers*
    | $\wedge$ *loan* $\in$ *loan.user.loans*

    ___ *INIT* _____
    | *items* = $\varnothing$ $\wedge$ *loans* = $\varnothing$ $\wedge$ *borrowers* = $\varnothing$

Membership operations

    ___ *AddUser* _____
    | Δ(*borrowers*)
    | *new_user?* : *User*
    | *status?* : *Status*
    |_____
    | $\exists$ *borrower* : *Borrower* • *borrower* $\notin$ ran *borrowers*
    | *borrowers'* = *borrowers* $\cup$ {(*new_user?*, *borrower*)}
    | *borrowers.fines* = 0
    | *borrowers.loans* = $\varnothing$
    | *borrowers.status* = *status?*

RemoveUser $\hat{=}$ ...

ChangeStatus $\hat{=}$ ...

Stock control operations

    ___ *AddItem* _____
    | Δ(*items*)
    | *item?* : *Item*
    |_____
    | *item?* $\notin$ *items* $\wedge$ *items'* = *items* $\cup$ {*item?*}
    | $\neg$*item?.onloan*

RemoveItem $\hat{=}$ ...

Loan control operations

Borrow $\hat{=}$ [Δ(*loans*); *user?* : *User*; *item?* : *items* |
        $\exists$ *b* : *Borrower* • *b* $\in$ *borrowers*(*user?*)] •
     (*b.Borrow* $\parallel$
     item?.CheckOut $\parallel$
     [$\exists$ *loan* : *Loan* • *loan* $\notin$ *loans*
        loans' = *loans* $\cup$ {*loan*}
        loan.user = *b* $\wedge$ *loan.item* = *item?*])

$Return \;\hat{=}\; \ldots$

Fine operations

$PayFine \;\hat{=}\; [\, user? : User \mid \exists\, b : Borrower \bullet b \in borrowers(user?)\,] \bullet b.PayFine$

$UpdateFines \;\hat{=}\; \ldots$

20.6 The Computational Viewpoint

In relation to the previously considered viewpoints, that is, the enterprise and information viewpoints, the computational viewpoint decomposes the system into computationally distinct components, which are candidates for distribution. Thus, this viewpoint provides a description of the system in terms of communicating computational objects. This will become clear when we present our computational interpretation of the library example.

The basic concepts of the computational viewpoint were introduced in Chapter 2, and in Chapter 3 we discussed the possible notations that could be used to specify aspects of the computational viewpoint. All of the following techniques offer relevant specification capabilities – LOTOS, E-LOTOS, SDL, SDL 2000, UML (in particular, UML-Statecharts) and Object-Z. A notation such as Z is less likely to be suitable because it lacks the necessary object-based decomposition structures†. We choose E-LOTOS because its capacity to describe reactive behaviour is relevant to the case study and consistency checking techniques have been developed for LOTOS, which could also be used for E-LOTOS.

20.6.1 The Computation Viewpoint Specification

At the computational level, we can view the central library system as a single computational object that provides services to a number of different types of users. In fact, the top-level structure of the computational viewpoint is as shown in Figure 20.5. This provides a different service to different clients, for example, library staff (who access the system through the loans desk server) and borrowers (who access the system either inside the library via the in-library access server or outside the library via the outside library access server). In fact, there will typically be a subtyping relationship between the different services offered. For example, the loans desk should offer a superset of the operations of each of the other services, for example, the loans desk staff can perform the operation AddUser, to add a borrower, while this operation is not offered to the other two client types.

In addition, the central library system can be decomposed into a number of subobjects, as shown in Figure 20.6, for example, objects that provide access to the

---

† Notice that although many of the other techniques do not have explicit object structuring facilities, their process structures offer corresponding facilities, although claiming object orientation is frequently not appropriate as they typically lack inheritance capabilities.

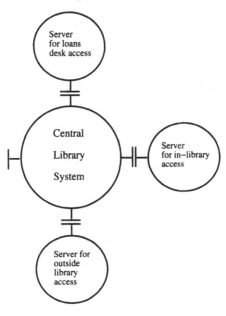

Fig. 20.5. Computational viewpoint of the central library system.

local and nonlocal catalogues (e.g., searching operations) and an object to allow access and update of the database of current loans.

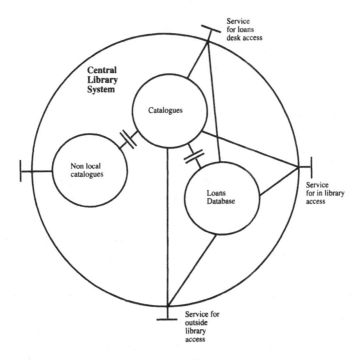

Fig. 20.6. Computational viewpoint, internal view of central library service.

Each computational object will be described by a process. For example, the top-level behaviour of the system as depicted in Figure 20.5 will use the following objects:

```
process CLS [Borrow,Return,AddUser,Reserve,,.....] is
....
endproc

process LDserver [Borrow,Return,AddUser,Reserve,...] is
....
endproc

process inLserver [Borrow,Return,Reserve,...] is
....
endproc

process outLserver [Borrow,Return,Reserve,...] is
....
endproc
```

Here the gate set of a particular process reflects the operations that the computational object can perform. Also, notice that, as suggested earlier, `inLserver` and `outLserver` do not offer the operation `AddUser`†.

These processes/objects would be composed in parallel with the appropriate interprocess interaction to give the top-level behaviour of the system. We use the convention here that if an invocation does not rename any of the observable actions, then the gate list is denoted [...].

```
CLS[...]
|[Borrow,Return,AddUser,Reserve,.....]|
(LDserver[...] ||| inLserver[...] ||| outLserver[...])
```

Thus, the `LDserver`, `inLserver` and `outLserver` evolve independently of one another (i.e., they do not interact). However, the central library system interacts individually with these three servers through the operations `Borrow`, `Return`, `AddUser`, `Reserve`, and so on. Due to space limitations, it is not possible to give a complete presentation of the behaviour of all of these objects. However, we can present a certain critical aspect of the behaviour that we will use to illustrate consistency checking.

Consider the central library system, the full behaviour for which could be:

```
process CLS [Borrow,Return,AddUser,Reserve,...] is
```

---

† It is also worth observing that action instances here do not exactly correspond to complete operations. This is because process algebra actions are atomic, while operations are not. Thus, strictly speaking, an action here represents the 'atomic' invocation of an operation and we abstract away from the actions required to model returning the result of an operation execution. However, these could be easily added.

```
Catalogues[...]
|[......]|
(NonLocalCat[...] ||| LoansDbase[...])
endproc
```

Now the idea is that the loans database and hence the central library system (which 'inherits' its behaviour) will control the number of loans that are allowed by a particular borrower via a behaviour of the following form:

```
loop forever
  Borrow?x:User [current(x)<max(x)];
     ?current:=update(current,x,current(x)+1)
  []
  Return?x:User [current(x)<>0];
     ?current:=update(current,x,current(x)-1)
  []
  .....
endloop
```

which would be embedded inside the behaviour of the loans desk. In this behaviour we have assumed that the following data types and operations have been defined in the obvious way:

- **current** - is a function that returns the current number of books on loan, for example, current(x) is the number of books on loan to user x;
- **max** - is a function that returns the maximum number of books that users can borrow at any one time, for example, max(x) is the maximum for user x;
- **update(c,x,n)** - returns a function from users to numbers that is the same as c apart from that c(x)=n;

Thus, the system will allow a user x to borrow a new book if she currently has less than her maximum number of books out and she can return a book if she has a book on loan (of course in reality more sophisticated checks would have to be performed, like whether the book being returned was indeed currently on loan to the borrower). Then in both cases, **current** is updated accordingly.

In addition, for a particular user, x say, the initialization of the **max** variables is performed as follows:

```
?max:=update(max,x,temp)
```

where,

```
?temp := if status(x,UG) or status(x,OTHER) then 4
         else if status(x,PG) then 10
              else 25
              endif
         endif
```

This definition uses the function **status**, which, given a user and a status indicator (i.e., **AC**, **PG**, **UG** or **OTHER**), will return **true** or **false** according to whether or not the user has the indicated status.

20.6.2 Checking Consistency of the Viewpoints

The specifications that we have looked at are not consistent. The problem has arisen because of ambiguities in the regulations and informal description, and is due to the uncertainty of borrowing rights when a member of the academic staff is also registered as a postgraduate.

Indeed at the University of Kent some of our colleagues (i.e., teaching staff) are also registered as postgraduates on a teacher training course. They have just one library card – how many books can they borrow? The policies given above are ambiguous, and only through experimentation did we find that the actual implementation of the current software in that particular library allows 40 books to be taken out in these circumstances. It is not clear that this was what was intended!

The regulations in Section 20.3 are ambiguous on this point, and the design decisions taken in the enterprise and information specification produced a scenario that allowed the total allowance to be the sum of the staff allowance and the postgrad allowance. (This is a consequence of the definition of the *Borrow* operation in the *Library* class in Section 20.5.)

However, in the implementation of the computational viewpoint users with multiple status cannot combine their allowances. Thus, for example, a member of staff who is registered for a PhD (i.e., is also a postgraduate) will have an allowance of just 10. Thus, according to this computational specification, a user with dual status would inherit the least generous of the two borrowing allowances.

In terms of the consistency checking techniques that we introduced in Section 20.2, this inconsistency between computational and information specifications arises because the information viewpoint allows (execution) traces in which the difference between the number of occurrences of the **Borrow** action and the number of occurrences of the **Return** action is greater than 10. Then, if the information viewpoint is being interpreted relative to refinement in Object-Z and the computational viewpoint is being interpreted relative to reduction in LOTOS, an inconsistency would arise. Of course this inconsistency could be easily corrected at the computational level by changing the logic of initializing **max**. For example, the following would be consistent with the current enterprise and information specifications:

```
?max:=update(max,x,temp)
```

where,

```
?temp := ACmax(status(x,AC)) +
         PGmax(status(x,PG)) +
         UGmax(status(x,UG)) +
```

```
OTHERmax(status(x,OTHER))
```

The `ACmax` function is defined as follows, and the functions `ACmax`, `PGmax`, `UGmax` and `OTHERmax` all follow a similar pattern:

```
function ACmax (is_an_AC:Bool):Nat is
  if is_an_AC then 25 else 0
endfunc
```

Alternatively, if the enterprise and information specifications were changed to allow users with dual status to inherit the most generous allowance (which in some respects is the most intuitive outcome), then the assignment to `temp` should change to:

```
?temp := if status(x,AC) then 25
         else if status(x,PG) then 10
             else 4
             endif
         endif
```

20.7 The Engineering Viewpoint

The computational viewpoint presents a decomposition of the system. However, it does not prescribe how this decomposition should be realised in terms of the physical distribution of components. Thus, the computational viewpoint identifies objects that are candidates for distribution, but it allows these components to be physically distributed in many different ways. The engineering viewpoint makes this distribution definite – it prescribes it – and through this process of prescription it also specifies the mechanisms by which objects interact.

It is beyond the scope of this section to give a detailed exposition of the engineering viewpoint, however, we can give an indication of the nature of the engineering viewpoint description by considering how our library would be specified in this viewpoint. To this end let us focus on the engineering description of the central library system, which is shown in Figure 20.7. Each computational object becomes a Basic Engineering Object (BEO) in the engineering viewpoint. Thus there will be a BEO for each constituent computational object in the central library system, that is, one corresponding to the *catalogues*, one corresponding to the *nonlocal catalogues* and one corresponding to the *loans database*.

In addition, the engineering viewpoint specifies how these basic engineering objects are distributed. For example, the two catalogue objects might be co-located within the same *capsule*, while the loans database may be located elsewhere (in a different capsule), on dedicated hardware, as shown in Figure 20.7. One consequence of this configuration is that interaction between the two catalogue systems can be optimized.

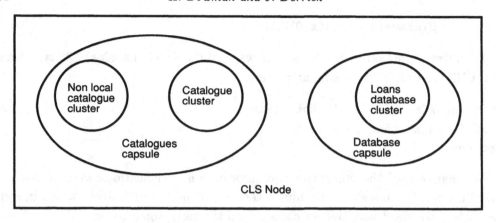

Fig. 20.7. Engineering viewpoint of the central library system.

In addition, the engineering viewpoint would specify the necessary channels between these BEOs in order to support inter-BEO interaction. Thus, suitable *stubs*, *binders*, *protocol objects* and *inteceptors* would be allocated.

This format for the engineering viewpoint would be reflected in our LOTOS description of the viewpoint, which, considering say the catalogues capsule, would have clusters defined by the following processes:

```
process NLCAT_cluster [......] is
.......
endproc
```

```
process CAT_cluster [......] is
.......
endproc
```

and the catalogues capsule would be modelled by a process:

```
process CAT_capsule [......] is
.......
endproc
```

which amongst other things would instantiate `NLCAT_cluster` and `CAT_cluster` with a suitable (communication) `Channel` between them, for example,

```
process CAT_capsule [......] is
.......
  (NLCAT_cluster[...] ||| CAT_cluster[...])
  |[.....]|
  Channel[.....]
.......
endproc
```

20.8 The Technology Viewpoint

The technology viewpoint links the set of viewpoint specifications to the actual implementation. It does this by listing how components of the system can be implemented by existing technologies, for example, which standards can be used to provide particular viewpoint operations.

For our library example the technology viewpoint might for example prescribe particular operating systems that can be employed at particular nodes of the system. In addition, it could state that many of the facilities of the CORBA de facto standard will be used in realizing the system, for example, that the necessary stubs and binders would be generated from the tool.

20.9 Conclusions

In any viewpoint-based approach the viewpoints described are not completely independent, and therefore viewpoint consistency has to be addressed at some level (although some researchers circumvent the issues of consistency by assuming an ordering between the ODP viewpoints, and they subsequently define transformations from the former to the latter [FL93, BDF⁺97]). In the consistency checking strategy discussed in [BDBS99, BBD⁺00] the key aspect is to build a common refinement of the multiple viewpoints with respect to the correspondences between the viewpoints. The difficulty in this approach is thus how to document the correspondences and how to cope with changes in the level of abstraction between the viewpoints.

General models of partial specification without predetermined viewpoints cannot in general use correspondences and have to resort to similarity checking [FST96] or low-level common models [ZJ93]. However, the fixed nature of viewpoints in ODP means that the reference model can prescribe a number of correspondences between the viewpoints (e.g., between computational objects and basic engineering objects). Often the common terms in a correspondence are identified by name alone [GLitV95], and the challenge is to relate single actions and objects to complete behaviours when dealing with viewpoints at different levels of granularity. Furthermore it is clear that the viewpoint correspondences must be considered at the same time as the viewpoint specifications, as opposed to attempting to describe the correspondences later.

Work on structuring complex specifications is relevant here, for example, the use of templates for ODP [FPV93] and in particular the idea of specification architectures as discussed in Chapter 19. Using these ideas, the open question is how best to exploit the facilities provided by specific languages in order to combine and relate viewpoints, for example, by using appropriate structuring mechanisms. In particular, specifications at different levels of abstraction need to be related.

The nature of ODP viewpoints can be exploited here by providing techniques that reflect their relationships. For example, the engineering viewpoint may provide standard communication components that are assumed when describing a computational viewpoint specification. This needs to be enhanced with mechanisms to relate portions of behaviour between viewpoints, for example, by using notions of action refinement [vG90, DB99].

Acknowledgements

This work has been funded by the UK EPSRC under the *Cross Viewpoint Consistency in ODP* and *ODP Viewpoints in a Development Framework* projects, and represents joint work by the authors together with Eerke Boiten, Peter Linington and Maarten Steen.

Bibliography

[BBD+00] E. A. Boiten, H. Bowman, J. Derrick, P. F. Linington, and M. W. A. Steen. Viewpoint consistency in ODP. *Computer Networks*, 34(3):503–537, August 2000.

[BBDS96] H. Bowman, E. A. Boiten, J. Derrick, and M. W. A. Steen. Viewpoint consistency in ODP, a general interpretation. In E. Najm and J.-B. Stefani, editors, *Formal Methods for Open Object-based Distributed Systems (FMOODS'96)*, pages 189–204. Chapman & Hall, 1996.

[BBDS99] H. Bowman, E. A. Boiten, J. Derrick, and M. W. A. Steen. Strategies for consistency checking based on unification. *Science of Computer Programming*, 33:261–298, April 1999.

[BDBS99] E. A. Boiten, J. Derrick, H. Bowman, and M. W. A. Steen. Constructive consistency checking for partial specification in Z. *Science of Computer Programming*, 35(1):29–75, September 1999.

[BDF+97] C. Bernardeschi, J. Dustzadeh, A. Fantechi, E. Najm, A. Nimour, and F. Olsen. Transformations and consistent semantics for ODP viewpoints. In H. Bowman and J. Derrick, editors, *Formal Methods for Open Object Based Distributed Systems (FMOODS'97)*, pages 371–386. Chapman & Hall, 1997.

[BDLS95] H. Bowman, J. Derrick, P. F. Linington, and M. W. A. Steen. FDTs for ODP. *Computer Standards and Interfaces*, 17:457–479, September 1995.

[BDLS96] H. Bowman, J. Derrick, P. F. Linington, and M. W. A. Steen. Cross viewpoint consistency in Open Distributed Processing. *IEE Proceedings Software*, 11(1):44–57, January 1996.

[Boo94] G. Booch. *Object-oriented Analysis and Design.* Benjamin/Cummings, 1994.

[BSBD01] H. Bowman, M. W. A. Steen, E. A. Boiten, and J. Derrick. A formal framework for viewpoint consistency. *Formal Methods in System Design*, 2001.

[DB99] J. Derrick and E. A. Boiten. Non-atomic refinement in Z. In J. M. Wing, J. C. P. Woodcock, and J. Davies, editors, *FM'99 World Congress on Formal Methods in the Development of Computing Systems*, volume 1708 of *Lecture Notes in Computer Science*, pages 1477–1496, Berlin, 1999. Springer-Verlag.

[DBBS99] J. Derrick, E. A. Boiten, H. Bowman, and M. W. A. Steen. Viewpoints and consistency – translating LOTOS to Object-Z. *Computer Standards and Interfaces*, pages 251–272, December 1999.

[FGH+94] A. C. W. Finkelstein, D. Gabbay, A. Hunter, J. Kramer, and B. Nuseibeh. Inconsistency handling in multiperspective specifications. *IEEE Transactions on Software Engineering*, 20(8):569–578, August 1994.

[FL93] K. Farooqui and L. Logrippo. Viewpoint transformations. In J. de Meer, B. Mahr, and O. Spaniol, editors, *2nd International IFIP TC6 Conference on Open Distributed Processing*, pages 352–362, Berlin, Germany, September 1993.

[FPV93]   J. Fischer, A. Prinz, and A. Vogel. Different FDT's confronted with different ODP-viewpoints of the trader. In J. C. P. Woodcock and P. G. Larsen, editors, *FME'93: Industrial Strength Formal Methods*, volume 670 of *Lecture Notes in Computer Science*, pages 332–350. Springer-Verlag, 1993.

[FST96]   A. Finkelstein, G. Spanoudakis, and D. Till. Managing interference. In A. Finkelstein and G. Spanoudakis, editors, *SIGSOFT '96 International Workshop on Multiple Perspectives in Software Development (Viewpoints '96)*, pages 172–174, 1996.

[GLitV95]   V. Gay, P. Leydekkers, and R. Huis in 't Veld. Specification of multiparty audio and video interaction based on the reference model of open distributed processing. *Computer Networks and ISDN Systems*, January 1995.

[SD99]   M. W. A. Steen and J. Derrick. Formalising ODP Enterprise Policies. In *3rd International Enterprise Distributed Object Computing Conference (EDOC '99)*, pages 84–93. IEEE Publishing, 1999.

[SD00]   M. W. A. Steen and J. Derrick. ODP enterprise viewpoint specification. *Computer Standards and Interfaces*, 22:165–189, 2000.

[Som89]   I. Sommerville. *Software Engineering*. Addison-Wesley, 1989.

[vG90]   R. J. van Glabbeek. The refinement theorem for ST-bisimulation semantics. In *Programming Concepts and Methods*. Elsevier Science Publishers, 1990.

[ZJ93]   P. Zave and M. Jackson. Conjunction as composition. *ACM Transactions on Software Engineering and Methodology*, 2(4):379–411, October 1993.

Author Index

Subject Index

Printed in the United States
By Bookmasters